Artaud's Metamorphosis

Pavement Books
London, UK
www.pavementbooks.com

Cover Image *N-82*, Oil on Canvas, 5' x 5'. Stephen Dicillo, 2013.
With permission from the artist.

British Library Cataloguing in Publication Data.
A catalogue record for this book is available from the British Library.

ISBN: 978-0-9571470-9-6

Artaud's Metamorphosis: From Hieroglyphs to Bodies without Organs

by
Jay Murphy

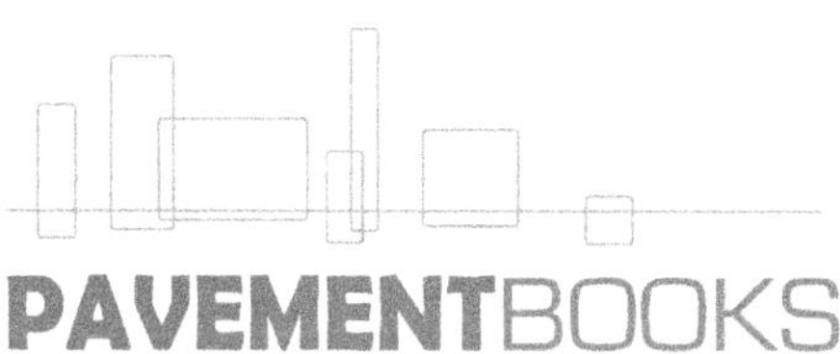

CONTENTS

ACKNOWLEDGMENTS

The first lines I believe I read from Antonin Artaud claimed no one was born by oneself, and no one died by oneself. This is all the more true of collective creations such as books.

Artaud's shift, or reversal as it has been called, is truly seismic but not easier to see for all that, and I was very slow in some instances in coming to the conclusions presented in this book. So I have to thank the various guides and providers of intelligent feedback through the various phases: this trajectory is only possible first of all due to the reclamation of Artaud undertaken by poet and translator Clayton Eshleman, in another way by Stephen Barber in his books, and in still another with the often stillborn, sometimes profoundly mistaken but nevertheless indispensable experiments of the 'anti-psychiatry' and critical psychiatry movements. With the manuscript itself it benefited from the gracious dialogue on various levels with especially Nikolaj Lübecker, as well as with Kriss Ravetto-Biagioli, Finn Brunton, Christopher Fynsk, and later with Martine Beugnet and Adrienne Janus. I owe much to Cécile Thiry, Christina Bojanic, and Gabrielle Decamous for navigating especially tricky translation issues, as well as encouragement from the burgeoning 'Artaud crazy' group of Artaud scholars and researchers in the UK. *Artaud's Metamorphosis* came into being through a period of research funded by a 6th century fellowship at the Centre for Modern Thought/University of Aberdeen. Grateful for the transdisciplinary academic site within which it first developed, I am also extremely fortunate to have the commitment and support of John Hutnyk and Sophie Fuggle at Pavement Books, who I feel share my urgent concern that the 'untimely' insights sometimes generated within the academy be multiplied in as many other terrains as possible.

Jay Murphy
March 2016
New Orleans, USA

LIST OF IMAGES

INTRODUCTION: METABOLISM AND IMMORTALITY

To title this endeavor *Artaud's Metamorphosis: From Hieroglyphs to Bodies without Organs* is already to make bold and defined what often remains evanescent in the work of Antonin Artaud. This is the first risk in a project that seeks to establish a more complete understanding and coherence for Antonin Artaud (1896-1948) one of the most seminal and visionary mid-20th century artists, whose mental and neurological disturbance, hard drug-addiction, and confinement for nine years in French asylums have made him a bona fide candidate for the *poète maudit* myth. Despite this difficulty in functioning – the sympathetic Dr. Achille Delmas told Artaud at the end of his life at Ivry-sur-Seine 'You need a gramme of heroin every day'[1] – it is the sheer profusion and complexity of Artaud's work that often makes it a challenge to decipher. This can make some judgments on Artaud seem odd, such as Michel Foucault's well-known conclusion in *Madness and Civilization* that Artaud's 'madness is precisely the *absence of the work of art*, the reiterated presence of that absence.'[2] One of the threads of remarkable consistency in Artaud is his hostility to the notion of and institution of 'art,' to be sure, yet his works were prodigious, in innovation not just quantity.

This venture is based on such consistency, while arguing that there is a transformation in Artaud, from his early works (from 1923-4 the time of his published 'Correspondence with Jacques Rivière' to his visit to the Tarahumara Indians in Mexico in 1936) to the Artaud of 1946-8 who emerged from the asylums to return to Paris. My argument regarding this transformation is based

[1] Quoted from a conversation with Artaud in Jacques Prevel, *En Compagnie d'Antonin Artaud*, Paris: Flammarion, 1974, p.139. Biographer Stephen Barber has estimated that by the mid-1930's Artaud was taking forty grammes of opium once every sixty hours (generally in the form of laudanum), with a maximum dose of seventy grammes. See Stephen Barber, *Antonin Artaud: Blows and Bombs*, London: Faber & Faber, 1993, p.78. For a brief comparison of Artaud's drug-taking with the opium use of Samuel Taylor Coleridge, Thomas de Quincey, and Jean Cocteau, see Clayton Eshleman, 'Introduction,' *Watchfiends and Rack Screams: Works from the Final Period by Antonin Artaud*, ed. and trans. Clayton Eshleman with Bernard Bador, Boston, MA: Exact Change, 1995, n.11, pp.45-6.

[2] Michel Foucault, *Madness and Civilization*, trans. Richard Howard, London & New York, NY: Routledge, [1961] 2001, p.272. Italics in original.

on the key idea in Artaud's early works of the 'hieroglyph' and the central role it plays in his famous theatre manifestoes, and how it shifts and disappears, exploding in the drawings, writings, and sound works of the 'later' Artaud. Artaud evokes the importance of hieroglyphics most memorably in his essay on the Balinese dancers he saw in the L'Exposition coloniale de Paris in 1931, one of the primary inspirations for his concept of the Theater of cruelty[3]: the Balinese dancers create an atmosphere of 'fear and hallucination' through a 'pure theater' based on 'gestures – diagrams.'[4] The actors move as 'animated hieroglyphs' that produce a sense of '*matter as revelation*.'[5] This world of moving matter is outlined by all the intersections of their lines, with all the intersections of their perspectives in the air.'[6] So many themes that for Artaud are wrapped up in this hieroglyphic constellation are strongly adumbrated here – the eclipse of identity and words and discursive logic, the evocation of a vast tonality or music (emphasised from first to last in the Balinese essay). Artaud here writes of 'ritual gestures' that impel a 'primary Physics,' for this superior dance that draws all before it has also a 'mathematical meticulousness.'[7] Foreshadowing how in his later writing Artaud would combine multiple literary and polemic forms in a single letter, in this essay Artaud elaborates all the different senses of a hieroglyph, in its original Greek sense of holy (hieros)/carving (glyph) as a kind of esoteric or original language, as pictograph or ideogram (Artaud's preference for languages like Chinese or Japanese ideogrammic script), or as phonogram (the emphasis on sound and voice and tonality that runs throughout Artaud's writings). If one thinks of the sense of the hieroglyph as an ideogram where the thing, the notion or idea of the thing, and the term for it are 'a whole wedded by the mark of the "character,"'[8] Artaud plumbs this mark also as the gesture that cannot be encapsulated by discursive logic, that poses another more primal logic of its own. A hieroglyph, as Gilles Deleuze defines it, is the situation where 'the essences are at once the thing to be translated and the translation itself, the sign and the meaning.' Echoing Artaud, Deleuze continues, maintaining that 'the hieroglyph

[3] I use the phrase 'Theater of cruelty' throughout, mainly since it follows more closely the French. Although 'Theatre of Cruelty' is quite common coinage for Artaud's notion in English, it tends to hypostasise and put in stone what is far from a definitive set of goals or occasions.

[4] Antonin Artaud, 'Sur Le Théatre Balinais,' *Œuvres complètes*, Vol. IV, Paris: Gallimard, 1964, p.64. Selections from Artaud's complete works hereafter cited simply by volume, year, and page number. All translations from Artaud and other authors in French, unless indicated otherwise, are my own.

[5] Ibid., pp.65; 72. Italics in original.

[6] Ibid., p.65.

[7] Ibid., pp.72; 69.

[8] Julia Kristeva, *Language, the Unknown*, trans. Anne M. Menke, Hertfordshire: Harvester Wheatsheaf, [1981]1989, p.93.

is everywhere; its double symbol is the accident of the encounter and the necessity of thought: "fortuitous and inevitable.'"[9]

While it may be more digestible analytically to isolate features of Artaud's hieroglyphic conception – the double, the virtual, the cruelty of action and so on, and deal with them one section or chapter at a time – this would involve considerable violence to its source. Instead, this project winds around the different problematics of the movement of Artaud's hieroglyphics, moving from one element such as his glossolalia or the place of the graphic sign, and then returning to it later in another context or another light. This is an attempt to be more faithful to Artaud, who has his own extremely fluid coherence but is far from ever systematising his development and metamorphoses. And while I often link and rely on a dialogue of a distinct earlier and later Artaud to illuminate each other, there is a rough chronological focus to the chapters that first focus on the Tarahumara experience and its ramifications, and then to the transformation of Artaud in the asylums and final works in Paris. In fact, the Artaud of a certain point in Rodez and later 1945-8, raises another set of terms that come to the fore in my last three chapters – the prevalence of magic, the battle with evil, the 'search for fecality,' the totem, and infinity, the form taken by the 'body without organs.' These concerns that can be lifted from Artaud demonstrate that his invention of the 'body without organs' has supplanted his earlier fascination with a hieroglyphically formed reality. Artaud's Mexican lectures in 1936 for instance, are eloquent in his description of a cosmos moved by ever-active sacred lines; with the construction of the 'body without organs' at the end of his life, this apocalyptic creation has freed itself from even those tangible lineaments.

In the quintessential 'early' Artaud of 'On the Balinese Theater,' the Balinese dancers evoke nothing less than the riddle of the universe, making of dance a primordial language that bypasses words. These notions had been building in Artaud for a time, who had already provided striking formulations of this hieroglyphic skein of signs or primordial reality in his writings on the paintings of André Masson, Pablo Picasso, and others in the 1920's.[10] It had fuelled his search for a Theater of cruelty that could re-ignite primitive ritual sources, and he had discovered in his research in 1933-4 for his biography of the mad 3rd century Roman sun king Heliogabalus various mystical and mythological foundations for it.[11] These obsessions crystallise with a desperation and clarity that are all Artaud's own in his journey to Mexico in 1936 where his various addresses in Mexico City best evoke this ultimate reality. Looking forward all the while to what he calls his own crucifixion, Artaud's participation in Tarahumara Indian peyote rites in September 1936 is such a crucial event in his life, that I will ar-

[9] Gilles Deleuze, *Proust and Signs*, trans. Richard Howard, Minneapolis, MN: University of Minnesota Press, [1964] 2000, p.102.

[10] See the section 'Explaining "occult geometry": Artaud's art criticism' in Chapter II.

[11] Artaud VII, 1967, pp.7-113.

gue there is a pre- and post-Tarahumara Artaud. With the Tarahumaras Artaud finds a living Theater of cruelty whose rites are based on strange signs the peyote priests draw on the ground and in the air. A confirmation of some of his deepest intuitions, the rites (or at least Artaud's interpretation and experience of them) also initiate Artaud in a world of sorcery and apocalypse that reach a fever pitch during his trip to Ireland the following year. Returning to France in a straitjacket in September 1937, Artaud undergoes numerous changes and mutations in identity and subjectivization, but this universe of bewitchment, central to his famous essay on painter Vincent Van Gogh written in 1947,[12] remains a constant.

It is in the dynamics of this universe that Artaud's conceptions of the hieroglyph changes. In Artaud's art writings, theatre manifestoes, and Mexican lectures (ranging from the mid-20's to 1936) his call for a ritual theatre is one of rites oriented around specific spatialisations, a subordination of time to space typical, as I will show, of most tribal rituals.[13] A current shorthand example of this typical subordination is found in contemporary Aboriginal art, or 'Western desert art.'[14] In the works of Geoffrey Bardon, Kathleen Petyarre, and Clifford Possum Tjapaltjarri, to take three examples, there are very complex senses of time, certainly, but what is overwhelming and what fill the painting is the different senses and becomings of space. The spiky lizard creature or 'mountain-devil,' the *arnkerrth* that inhabits most of the Western desert, is 'not represented figuratively but conceptualised spatially. In Anmatyerr art all living creatures, including human beings, are depicted as predominantly spatial rather than psychological beings, interacting in natural and cultural landscapes that occupy space over time.'[15] These paintings' predominant emphasis on spatialisation of phenomena place them within the millennial tradition of ritual art that Artaud seems to espouse in the 1930's only to overthrow later. The 'later' Artaud of the Rodez writings and afterwards, poses a choice, what he described in *To have done with the judgment of god* (1947-8) between the 'infinite outside, [or] that of the infinitesimal inside.'[16] Artaud's work never ceases to be located on this borderline, but his invention of the 'body without organs'(a body that has no

[12] Artaud XIII, 1974, pp.9-64.

[13] See the discussion of these anthropological and shamanic contexts in Chapters II and III, which draws on accounts of the Tarahumara rites as well as works by Marcel Mauss, Victor Turner, Claude Lévi-Strauss, Edmund Leach, Carlos Castaneda, José Gil, and others. This is extended into chapter IV that begins with a consideration of Artaud's spells, looks at the traditional notion of art as action, and then presents different aspects of Artaud's severe and creative manipulation of the figure of the cross in its contrast to perspectives offered by Carl Jung, Maya Deren, and René Guénon.

[14] See Elizabeth Grosz' arguments concerning this art in her *Chaos, Territory, Art: Deleuze and the Framing of the Earth*, New York, NY: Columbia University Press, 2008, pp.89-101.

[15] Christine Nicholls and Ian North, eds, *Kathleen Petyarre: Genius of Place*, Adelaide: Wakefield, 2001, p.10.

[16] Artaud XIII, 1974, p.85.

'interior') proposes to link to the infinite outside. A series of considerations on time as a means of overcoming the hypostasisation of 'being' is the overwhelming concern of mainstream European philosophy, especially since the latter part of the 19th century, and I have seen no need to rehearse that history here.[17] Contemporary complexity theory and sciences only reinforce this, with their discovery of the irreversibility of time.[18] Yet Artaud's loosing of the element of time so prominent in his 1946-8 works has far more shamanistic overtones, an example of what I slowly delineate in Chapters II, III, and IV as the opposition of sorcery (and its release of elements in a conflict of power) to religious rituals (where time is stuffed into space in the interest of tribal and cosmic harmony). It is part of Artaud's contemporaneity that already in 1927 he is writing how we can no longer believe in the image, his release of the element of time in his cinema theories forming one of the major fulcrums of Gilles Deleuze's later philosophy of film.[19] Artaud typically presents these problems in such a manner that it is difficult to discuss their credibility (such as Artaud's particular notion of eternity), without crossing over with him, to participate in the double or triple worlds he planned to discover among the Tarahumaras.[20]

It is by broaching the transformation of the 'hieroglyph' as my subject that I can show the true radicality, the extremity, the singularity of the final Artaud. Up to 1936 and Artaud's travel to the Tarahumaras as original (and in terms of the theatre manifestoes, quite lasting in effects) as Artaud's artistic contribution is, it is also comparable to many other early and mid-20th century artistic projects. The search for or prizing of a sometimes hidden, always-in-motion cosmological hieroglyphic matrix that can be created or triggered is central to Aby Warburg's founding of a new art history (one not based on texts), the films of Sergei Eisenstein, the use of the Chinese ideogram by Ernest Fenollosa and Ezra Pound to create a new art of poetry; it also informed much of the visual art of cubism and surrealism, and the projects of Wassily Kandinsky and Paul Klee. Even in this storied context Artaud stands out, since these projects are strictly aesthetic ones (with the possible exception of Warburg), and Artaud's proclamations cannot be reduced to simply renovating European theatre. In marked contrast, finding a complement to the 'final' Artaud who is released from Rodez asylum in May 1946 and returns to Paris, is extremely difficult, if not impossible.

---

[17] For a collection of texts, see Charles M. Sherover, ed., *The Human Experience of Time: the Development of its Philosophic Meaning*, Evanston, IL: Northwestern University Press, 1975. For a sharp consideration of the issue of time in the 20th century era of modernism and the avant-garde, see Peter Osborne, *The Politics of Time: Modernity and Avant-Garde*, London & New York, NY: Verso, 1995.

[18] See in particular Ilya Prigogine and Isabelle Stengers, *Order Out of Chaos*, New York, NY: Bantam, 1984.

[19] See the section 'The revelation of how the "hieroglyph" works in Artaud's film scenarios' in Chapter I.

[20] As Artaud wrote to Jean Paulhan 23 April, 1936, in Artaud V, 1964, p.276.

Artaud's 'late' work is so uncompromising and extreme that it no longer finds such commonality with multiple other avant-garde and modernist movements. This Artaud is one who so scorns any 'representation' and even the ghost of representation in the idea of 'virtuality'[21] that the notion of any hieroglyph at the centre of moving matter is also rejected. 'I abject all signs,' Artaud writes in 1947, 'I create only machines of instant utility.'[22] Whereas Artaud's 1930's Theater of cruelty could be reconciled with primitive ritual and even Aristotelian catharsis or purging, what Artaud advocates after his release is still a Theater of cruelty or theatre of blood,[23] but one in which time is released into its own autonomy; his concern now is with infinity. Artaud's creations, such as the drawings, or his daily laboratory that is his voluminous *cahiers*, a group of 406 school exercise notebooks, are also animated beings that serve to carry on his cosmic combat. They, as much as Artaud, are now a 'body without organs'– a war unto eternity. This 'body without organs' is a creation of Artaud's in the cauldron of a horrific psychiatric confinement,[24] simultaneously a defense of a shattered body and psyche and an offense against its torturers, at once a 'virtual' body[25] and a violent infinite gesture that does away with any signs. It is a double body, predicated on the actual one but not touching it at any point. Through it Artaud intends to abolish interiority once and for all and forgo the limitations of the physical flesh. This is a process that one cannot ever be completely 'done with,' and is part of Artaud's wager with infinity. The 'body without organs' is both a product of the Artaud who saw double and triple worlds in the Tarahumara rites, and his refutation of all mystical systems at the end of his life.

This later Artaud rejects the 'hieroglyphics and secret keyboard,'[26] and denounces all priests as flim-flam operators and conjurers, including the Tibetans and the Ciguri peyote priests among the Tarahumaras.[27] He is his own creation.

---

[21] Artaud XIII, 1974, p.258.

[22] Ibid. p.273.

[23] For a typical statement of this theatre in which 'something/will be won/*physically*,' written within a month of his death, see ibid., pp.146-7.

[24] See Chapter V 'Hieroglyphics as Passage.'

[25] Deleuze defined the virtual as 'real without being actual, ideal without being abstract,' a definition he borrowed from Proust. See Deleuze, *Difference and Repetition*, trans. Paul Patton, London & New York, NY: Continuum [1968] 2002, p.208. The virtual is far from the merely possible, but is fully real insofar as it is virtual, part of immanent active forms rather than a possibility based on or reliant upon a transcendent reality. There is a dialogue with Deleuze and Guattari, both together and singly, throughout the manuscript. For their interpretation of the 'body without organs' as a 'virtual' body see especially the discussion in sections of chapters V ('Artaud's "cure"') and VI ('The spherical body').

[26] Artaud XIV:1, 1978, p.151.

[27] Here Artaud's denunciation of religion and the occult in a 1 March 1947 letter to André Breton is representative, see 'Cinq Lettres à André Breton,' in Antonin Artaud, *Œuvres*, ed. Évelyne Grossman, Paris: Gallimard/Quarto, 2004, pp.1207-18.

The Artaud of the 1930's was immersed in various forms of mysticism. The Artaud of 1946-8 ferociously denounces all these forms as an avoidance of pain and individuation. The 'body without organs,' that will efface all traces of the hieroglyph, is typical of Artaud in its thinnest of borders between a kind of genius and marked disturbance: born of a defense against the various demonic forces he saw as erotically experimenting with his body, the 'body without organs' is a kind of recognition born from dementia or disturbance that also undeniably possesses an extraordinary poetry and insight into desire.[28] Its exploration of the potential infinity of the gesture has been but rarely followed up upon.[29] What is important for my own study is showing how it is the result of a transformation in ritual space and time – the infinity of the gesture with its rage to evoke the 'true body' in the late Artaud eclipses subordination to any spatial or social or metaphysical configuration, and that already marks it as different from the vast majority of traditional or tribal rituals. This eclipse is most clear in Artaud's sound works, his 1946-8 radio broadcasts,[30] with his *To have done with the judgment of god* (1947-8), an invitation to step beyond the patternings of reality into an unconditioned one. Even Jacques Derrida, who argued in his early essays on Artaud that he was trapped by the forms of representation he railed against, concluded in his final interview before his death in October 2004 of Artaud's voice that 'once you've heard it, you can no longer silence it. And so you have to read him with his voice, the phantom of his voice that you have to keep inside your ear…Those few recordings of the voice of Artaud are an essential part of what remains to us of his body, of his body's work.'[31] Artaud's late work is a wild thrust at immortality, with image, words, and screams impacted and posed for maximum effect. It is not a call for a 'work' to continue to live, in the sense of art Foucault was invoking, or as in the case of an author who wants his books' reputations to go on long after his or her death – with Artaud this is something more corporeal and more primal. It is also more difficult to fathom. What I present here, in Artaud's transformation of ritual space/time into the projection of the 'body without organs' where any hieroglyphic patterning is jettisoned, is a pro-

[28] This project walks the difficult tightrope, as it must, of crediting Artaud's immense lucidity while attempting to take into account his equally immense suffering born from possibly congenital neurological difficulties and ensuing drug addiction at the hands of doctors (like many, Artaud first became an addict on the prescriptions given him by his doctor). The word 'dementia' here is no confirmation of the usual psychiatric or psychological terminology towards Artaud, but is more along the lines of the insight found in thinkers as different as Deleuze, Lacan and Jung, that the path of human individuation is not necessarily neurotic, as Freud argued, but at every critical point runs the risk of psychosis.

[29] A salient exception is the Butoh experiments of Tatsumi Hijikata and Kazuo Ohno. See the brief outline concerning Butoh in Chapter I.

[30] See the section 'The voice at the end of the world' in Chapter VI.

[31] Jacques Derrida, 'Les voix d'Artaud (la force, la forme, la forge),' *Magazine Littéraire* 434 (September 2004), p.36.

posal at limning his ultimate achievement that alters our understanding of this artist, especially in a present where overwhelming processes of digitalisation make his assaults on representation take on a whole new, perhaps unexpected, relevance. Artaud's voice still resounds and yet is inadequately deciphered even now, in the early decades of the 21st Century.

I.
A PROJECT FOR UNDERSTANDING ARTAUD

In February 1948, when Artaud introduced *Suppôts et suppliciations*, what was not his last writing, but his last finished book, honed, and edited, considered a kind of last will and testament, he wrote that it had all begun with the 'search for an anti-cultural life.'[1] Artaud never tired of insisting on the 'nervous and physical labour of creation'[2] that is linked to dance and perpetual movement and not to any fixed form of book, statute, painting, or codified dance. Artaud's wager was on the utter fluidity of the nerves. As a complete book – of some seventy-three dictations, ten essays, and thirty-five letters – it is linked with Artaud's publications decades before in the mid-1920's before his confinement – *l'Ombilic des limbes*, *Pèse-nerfs*, or the *Fragments d'un journal d'enfer*. Yet, of these books it is perhaps with this last work, the *Suppôts et suppliciations*, that Artaud, and his project, is 'most totally exposed.'[3] Artaud suggested that it would be an impossibly annoying 'hassle'[4] for anyone to read in its entirety. This was because the book didn't really exist, but was 'the fruit of a consortium of incubi and succubi, fixed, stabbed, planted from all parts...turned and turned again from every side like a turkey on the grill.'[5] *Suppôts et suppliciations* is among the remarkable range of Artaud's late work – 'Artaud le mômo,' 'Here Lies' and the three radio broadcasts, including the banned and resonant *To have done with the judgment of god*, among numerous other letters, essays, and the extraordinary drawings and visual work, that have already prompted a major reevaluation.

In sheer output and quantity, the four volumes of notebooks of Artaud's return to Paris (1946-8), or the over 2000 pages of his *Cahiers de Rodez*, the prodigious drawings and *gris gris*, dwarf the earlier period in Artaud's career, for which he has been so well-known: the period from 1923 to 1937, when Artaud penned numerous poems and prose poems, was intimately involved with the

[1] 'Ce Livre se compose...,' Artaud XIV:1, 1978, p.165.

[2] Artaud XX, 1984, p.340.

[3] See editor Paule Thévenin's comments in Artaud XIV:1, 1978, p.229.

[4] Artaud uses the phrase '*emmerdant absolument impossible à lire;*' *emmerdant* conveys 'annoying' or 'hassling;' in its reflexive form, it means 'bored stiff.'

[5] Artaud XIV:2, 1978, p.234.

surrealists, overseeing incendiary poison pen letters to the Pope and the Rectors of European universities while editing the third number of *La Révolution surréaliste* and directing the Bureau of Surrealist Research; starred as an actor in numerous films including Carl Dreyer's *The Passion of Joan of Arc* (1928), René Clair's *Entr'acte* (1924), Abel Gance's *Napoléon* (1926), G.W. Pabst's *Three-penny Opera* (1930), Fritz Lang's *Liliom* (1934); wrote film scenarios and manifestoes concerning the potentials of 'occult cinema;' trekked to Mexico (1936) to participate in peyote rites; attempted to initiate his Theater of cruelty with his play *The Cenci* (1932) on the stages of Paris; and adumbrated avant-garde theories of theatre in essays and manifestoes whose influence has been matched perhaps only by those of Bertolt Brecht. Artaud's search for hieroglyphic keys to another, underlying reality links him to other seminal 20th century artistic projects, ranging from Aby Warburg's foundations for a new art history, to Sergei Eisenstein's cinema, Ernest Fenollosa and Ezra Pound's research into Chinese ideograms as a basis for poetry in their 'revolution of the word,'[6] and Charles Olson's extension of Pound's modernist revolution into a postmodern poetics.

In contrast to all this work in the years 1923-37, in a far shorter period, from 1945 to 1948, Artaud created a series of multifaceted elaborations of his lifetime obsessions which 'conveys a magnificent lucidity and lust for life…immensely versatile in terms of its imagery of the body, and in its linguistic experiments.'[7] This is after nine tortuous years in five different insane asylums, including sessions of electroshock treatments applied against his will, 51 applied in a single eighteen-month period in which one of his dorsal vertebrae was fractured and his remaining teeth fell out. The later work of the Artaud released from the Rodez asylum explicitly rejects the 'hieroglyphics' that grows out of the earlier formative activity for which he was best-known, based on a hieroglyphics of moving matter, inspired in turn from myriad sources including Balinese dancers, the Marx Brothers, and a Lucas van der Leyden painting. This recognition of the integrity of Artaud's entire artistic span has already been the premise of two 21st century museum retrospectives. With the centralisation of most of Artaud's archives at long last in the Bibliothèque nationale de France, it was possible for a 2006-7 exhibition to show Artaud's enormous output – films, drawings, writ-

[6] As in the title of poet Jerome Rothenberg's collection of mid-20th century experimental writing: See Rothenberg, ed., *Revolution of the Word: New Gathering of American Avant-Garde Poetry 1914-45*, Boston, MA: Exact Change [1974], 1999.

[7] Stephen Barber, 'Cruel Journey,' *Art in America*, February 1995, pp.70-5. Barber's biographies have been crucial to this revision of Artaud, see Stephen Barber, *Antonin Artaud: Blows and Bombs*, London & Boston, MA: Faber & Faber, 1993; *Artaud: The Screaming Body*, New ed., London: Creation Books, 2004; and *Artaud: Terminal Curses*, London: Creation Books, 2008. The appearance of Ros Murray's study *Antonin Artaud: The Scum of the Soul*, Basingstoke & New York, NY: Palgrave Macmillan, 2014, which examines the dynamics of matter and medium in relation to Artaud's different artistic or anti-artistic activity (in cinema and in his notebooks for example) also signals another phase in the ongoing appreciation of Artaud.

ings, in their 'surprising coherence' and 'in their globality.'[8] Likewise, in 2005 the Museum Kunst Palast in Düsseldorf, held its exhibition *ARTAUD, A Staged Life*, to show that the 'memory of Artaud in Germany will be redefined in the future, and that he will no longer be perceived as merely the theoretician of an avant-garde theatre, but as an important modern artist in his own right.'[9]

Freed from a kind of captivity at the Rodez asylum by a band of young literary artists outraged by his fate, the Artaud who returned to Paris in May 1946 was a 'cratered psyche...affirmatively ghastly in its power to at once protect and organise its loathed and beloved cores.'[10] As 'comebacks' go, Artaud's was staggering, volcanic, effectively perhaps unprecedented. And Artaud's use of the hieroglyph is remarkably at the centre of it. Here it is not a matter of employing some general 'theory' to 'understand' Artaud, but his full context entails reopening the discussion of what Michel de Certeau once referred to as 'the ethnography of communication.'[11] And it does imply a method that, as philosopher José Gil has described, is involved in 'taking indigenous languages seriously'[12] – not only in terms of the predominantly non-signifying languages such as Artaud's invented glossolalia or syllable-language, but also 'indigenous language' in the sense of understanding how Artaud participates in, seeks to reinvent, and ultimately overthrows the gestures of ritual of traditional societies. In the 'later' Artaud especially this 'indigenous language' also takes the form of turning the French language inside out, since it is increasingly the French tongue itself Artaud sees as responsible for his plight. Since I argue Artaud's recourse to the Tarahumara Indian peyote rites and their effects are a central, well-nigh irreversible event in his life, this is the minimum Artaud demands of us. Given this, the interrogations of tribal ritual and affect, from Marcel Mauss to Lévi-Strauss, Victor Turner, Maya Deren, and Michael Taussig, are given lengthy treatments in Chapters II, III, and IV. Artaud's effort to find resolution and inspiration for

---

8 Jean-Noel Jeanneney 'Preface,' *Antonin Artaud*, Paris: Bibliothèque nationale de France/Gallimard, 2006. The exhibition was held November 7, 2006 – February 4, 2007.

9 Jean-Hubert Martin, 'Artaud - A Staged Life', *e-flux*. Available: http://www.e-flux.com/announcements/artaud---a-staged-life/. Accessed March 11, 2016.
ARTAUD, A Staged Life was held July 16 – October 10, 2005. Other major 21st century reevaluations of Artaud have included the first retrospective of Artaud's work in Spain (curated by Marta Gonzâlez Obregozo at La Casa Encendida, Madrid, April 3 – June 7, 2009); Artaud's influence on artists and writers of the '50s, 'Specters of Artaud: Language and Art in the 1950s' curated by Kaira Cabañas and Frédéric Acquaviva at Museo Reina Sofia, Madrid (September 19 – December 17, 2012); 'Antonin Artaud,' curated by Jean-Jacques Lebel, Padiglione d'Arte Contemporanea, Milan (December 6, 2005 – February 12, 2006); and most recently, a juxtaposition of Artaud drawings and texts with Van Gogh paintings – 'Van Gogh/Artaud: The Man Suicided by Society' curated by Isabelle Cahn, Musée d'Orsay, Paris, March 11 – July 6, 2014.

10 Eshleman, *Watchfiends & Rack Screams*, p.29.

11 Michel de Certeau, *La Prise de parole*, Paris: Éditions du Seuil, 1994, p.186.

12 José Gil, *Metamorphoses of the Body*, trans. Stephen Muecke, Minneapolis, MN: University of Minnesota Press, 1998, p.xii.

his Theater of cruelty with the Tarahumara Indians is not only the catalytic event that inducts Artaud into a world of sorcery and apocalypse, but it fuels his later artistic projects as well down to his last radio recording *To have done with the judgment of the god* (1947-8) and collection of drawings *50 Drawings to murder magic* (1948), both of which draw directly on his Tarahumara experiences. How Artaud can be comprehended by anthropological and ethnographic observations and studies, and how he escapes them, becomes key to gauging the transformations he undergoes. The reconciliations of individual and tribe, self and world characteristic of successful tribal ritual are completely absent. Artaud's extraordinary re-formation and creation of a 'true body' at the end of his life cannot be separated from his cosmology of desperate conflict, demonic possession, universal war.

The matter of theory: updating 'cosmos=chaos'

Whether it is because of this evocation of a universe of sorcery and strife,[13] or largely despite of it, Artaud has inspired a rich field of theoretical inquiry and speculation. This has ranged from the post-1968 editors of *Tel Quel* searching for a more adequate and adventurous theory of materialism,[14] to Gilles Deleuze and Félix Guattari's borrowing of the term 'body without organs' to found their 'Capitalism and Schizophrenia' project,[15] which indicated another model of the body and drives was possible other than the thermodynamic model of Freud's death instinct.[16] Artaud has inspired often remarkable essays by Julia Kristeva, Philippe Sollers, Jacques Derrida, Roland Barthes, Jean Baudrillard, among oth-

[13] For a rich discussion of the universe as combat, inspired from Artaud, but also Nietzsche, Kafka, and D.H. Lawrence, see Gilles Deleuze's 'To Have Done with Judgment,' in his *Essays Critical and Clinical*, trans. Daniel W. Smith and Michael A. Greco, Minneapolis, MN: University of Minnesota Press, [1993] 1997.

[14] To this end they organised the 1972 conference 'Artaud/Bataille: vers une révolution culturelle.' For the collection of papers devoted to Artaud in this colloquium see Philippe Sollers, ed., *Artaud*, Paris: Union générale d'éditions, 1973. For histories of *Tel Quel*, see Patrick ffrench, *The time of theory: History of 'Tel Quel' 1960-83*, New York, NY: Clarendon Press, 1995; Danielle Marx-Scouras, *The Cultural Politics of Tel Quel*, Philadelphia, PA: Pennslyvania State University Press, 2004; and Patrick ffrench and Roland-Francois Lack, eds, *The Tel Quel Reader*, New York, NY: Routledge, 1998.

[15] Gilles Deleuze and Félix Guattari, *Anti-Oedipus*, trans. Robert Hurley, Mark Seem, and Helen R.Lane, New York, NY: Viking Penguin, [1972] 1977; *A Thousand Plateaus*, trans. Brian Massumi, Minneapolis, MN: University of Minnesota Press, [1977] 1987.

[16] Guattari gives the following glossary-type definition for the 'body without organs': 'Gilles Deleuze borrowed this idea from Antonin Artaud to describe the zero degree of intensity. The idea of the body without organs, unlike that of the death drive, does not implicate thermodynamic reference.' In Félix Guattari, *The Anti-Oedipus Papers*, ed. Stéphane Nadaud, trans. Kélina Gotman, New York, NY & Los Angeles, CA: Semiotext(e), 2006, p.416.

ers. My own project does not rest on any hubris of creating a *new* understanding of Artaud and his extraordinary, terrible journey, but it will insist on an altered understanding. This altered understanding, it will become evident, despite my own frequent recourse to the work of Deleuze and Guattari who are so indebted to Artaud, and in *A Thousand Plateaus* left what Christian Kerslake characterised as a 'late modern occult treatise,'[17] has to be created around the blind spots and aporias of many of the most well-known expositions of Artaud. Beginning from an admittedly somewhat primitive starting point strongly rooted in the history of the 'anti-psychiatry' movement,[18] *Artaud's Metamorphosis* is predicated on taking Artaud's positions and projects however at first apparently bizarre completely seriously, giving credit to their own context or *raison d'être*. Where this differs from many other treatments of Artaud is that this 'taking indigenous languages seriously' implies several things: a different consideration and valorisation of sorcery (the universe Artaud enters with his visit to the Tarahumaras in 1936) that opposes it to the universe of primitive ritual that would reorient individuals and society toward an original unity,[19] and it gives Artaud more than the benefit of a doubt in his battle with psychiatry and in the conflict over its characterisation of the content of his 'psychosis.' Artaud's glossolalia or his creation of a 'body without organs' are elaborated in terms of Artaud's immense creativity, not from psychoanalytic or psychiatric diagnosis. This implies coming to terms in a different manner to other authors with the double-bind Artaud presents from his first writings in the early 1920's to his last cries and exclamations in *To have done with the judgment of god* – Artaud demands to be read yet insists that he cannot be read; Artaud requires that others share his experience, all the while maintaining that this is impossible. Perhaps only the crucified Jesus Christ realises Artaud's predicament, and in the extraordinary texts for his 13 January 1947 appearance at the Vieux-Colombier[20] Artaud denounces that as a possibility as well – since he is the 'true Christ' who was crucified at Golgotha, and Jesus Christ the impostor. The experience of the cross and the crucifixion is another motif that runs from Artaud's writings in the 1920's to the last year of his life. It is one of the threads of consistency in a trajectory that takes extraordinary turns and ends in triumphant piercing final work that denounces many of the sources of the earlier. I will show how Artaud's astonishing transformation and subversion of the cross, itself a hieroglyphic figure, is not only a key to the metamorphosis of Artaud's complex of notions centered around the hieroglyph,

[17] Christian Kerslake, *Deleuze and the Unconscious*, New York, NY & London: Continuum, 2007, p.169.

[18] For a discussion of Artaud's relation to the historical movement of 'anti-psychiatry' in the 1960's and '70s, see the section 'Artaud's "cure"' at end of Chapter V.

[19] This opposition between sorcery that must challenge the social order and religious ritual that reinforces it is the main thrust of the discussion in section 'The Cross and the crossroads, redux,' in Chapter IV.

[20] The texts 'Histoire vécue d'Artaud-Mômo' are collected in Artaud XXVI (1994).

but is the primary pivot or means for Artaud's survival and re-formation of his psyche in the inferno of a nine-year asylum confinement. Although Artaud ultimately rejects the once all-important category of 'hieroglyph,' the elaboration of it in his very life is one of the reasons his treatment of it becomes one of the most original of any 20th century artist.

This can be illuminated on a theoretical level, but not without the possibility of 'crossing over' to the other side, or to one of the double or triple worlds Artaud insisted composed the world. There is an example of this in the controversial field studies of Jeanne Favret-Saada, who in studying witchcraft in the Bocage area of western France in 1968-71, became part of a sorcerers' network herself, partaking in spells and ceremonies, so that she could map the dynamics from the 'inside' so to speak.[21] What Favret-Saada found is that any process of 'unbewitching' must enter the symbolic system of witchcraft, since it possesses a 'performative efficacy,' it has real social and psychological effects.[22] This outlines what has long been the practice of 'ethnopsychiatry' in France, when in working with mental illnesses among the immigrant African population in France often surrounds the individual with a community that shares the person's belief system.[23] This entails viewing the symbolic system that must be entered as coherent and as having certain effects, not rejecting the movements of the gods in advance. Similar to the phenomenological 'bracketing' of beliefs so essential to the existential psychiatry of R.D. Laing, Aaron Esterson, David Cooper, and others in the 1960's, this is a move continued down to the present day, as advocated in current ethnopsychiatry practiced by Tobie Nathan.[24] As Nathan and Isabelle Stengers emphasise in their work *Médecins et sorciers* (2004), often structures of 'belief' must be jettisoned altogether.[25] This is a crucial step in 'understanding' Artaud, whose relation to the 'outside' is constantly in peril and in question, first from his neurological illness, the family problems and drug addiction,[26]

21 See Jeanne Favret-Saad, *Deadly Words: Witchcraft in the Bocage*, Cambridge: Cambridge University Press, 1980; and *Les Mots, la mort, les sorts*, Paris: Gallimard, 1985.

22 Jeanne Favret-Saada, *Désorceler*, Paris: Editions de l'Olivier, 2009. See also Favret-Saada, 'Unbewitching as therapy,' *American Ethnologist* 16:1, February 1989, pp.40-59.

23 The father of French 'ethnopsychiatry' is Georges Devereux, see his *Essais d'ethnopsychiatrie générale*, Paris: Gallimard, 1970.

24 See Tobie Nathan, *Principes d'ethnopsychiatrie*, Grenoble: La pensée sauvage, 1993; *L'influence qui guérit*, Paris: Odile Jacob, 1994; *Nous ne sommes pas seuls dans le monde*, Paris: Seuil/Les Empêcheurs de penser du rond, 2001; and *La Nouvelle interprétation des rêves*, Paris: Odile Jacob, 2011. Some of the ramifications of ethnopsychiatry are suggested and unpacked in Book VII of Isabelle Stengers, *Cosmopolitics*, II, trans. Robert Bononno, Minneapolis, MN: University of Minnesota Press, 2011.

25 See Tobie Nathan and Isabelle Stengers, *Médicins et sorciers*, Paris: Seuil, 2004, pp.49-53.

26 That Artaud's adolescent sanatorium stays were due to his rebellion and conflicts with his family especially his authoritarian father, was a conclusion reached by writer

then compounded by his psychiatric internment in which he was diagnosed as an 'incurable', 'paranoid-schizophrenic' by none other than Dr. Jacques Lacan himself.[27] Artaud is a person whose serious breakdowns, whether at age 19 in 1915, or at age 41 in 1937, partook of profound religious deliriums or conversions, who believed quite literally in doubles, that death was inevitably an affair of malevolence and black magic, and after a certain point that he was constantly subject to demonic assault and attack. These beliefs are as common to tribal societies as they are extremely rare in 20th century France or Western Europe. Yet to speak of 'outside' or 'inside' in this manner is to already betray Artaud, whose work seems to reside precisely on an ineluctable border or lining between the two. Artaud's ultimate achievement, his 'body without organs' exactly effaces such distinctions of surface and depth, of interiority and exteriority. This 'body without organs' is on one level the most esoteric creation of an imagination which once saw evanescent, moving hieroglyphs of matter as an ultimate reality disguised by 'normal' perception and realities, yet it leaves even this conception of form behind, as Artaud explicitly recognised.

Following Artaud's itinerary – the transformation of the 'hieroglyph' and its eventual rejection by the 'final' Artaud consumed in his creation of the 'body without organs' – demonstrates there is considerable 'sense' in Artaud's metamorphoses. To show the real efficacy of Artaud's 'body without organs' would require an extensive detour into the field of contemporary media, art, and performance,[28] especially via the early and original trajectory of Butoh dance, arguably the only artistic movement to viably advance Artaud's ideas.[29] And while

Pierre Guyotat among others. See Barber, *Antonin Artaud*, p.15.

[27] Lacan's prognosis that Artaud would never write another line for the rest of his life turned out to be as false as false can be. Artaud wrote six books among numerous other texts after this judgment was made. For a discussion of Artaud and Lacan, see the section 'The emergence of the full "body without organs"' in Chapter V.

[28] For a discussion of Artaud's influence in new media art, see Steve Dixon, *Digital Performance*, Cambridge, MA & London: MIT Press, 2007, pp.70; 256; 266; 341-3. For an introduction to the wide inspiration Artaud has exercised in film, new media, visual arts, performance, and current media theory, see Jay Murphy, 'The Artaud Effect,' http://ctheoryarchive.net/the-artaud-effect/, 15 September 2015. Accessed 17 September 2015.

[29] There is still all too little in English on Butoh, notwithstanding its great importance in Japan and internationally as well. Bruce Baird's study may begin to rectify this – Bruce Baird, *Hijikata Tatsumi and Butoh: Dancing in Grey Grits*, Basingstoke & New York, NY: Palgrave Macmillan, 2012. Other studies include Sondra Fraleigh and Tamah Nakamura, *Hijikata Tatsumi and Ohno Kazuo*, New York, NY & London: Routledge, 2006; and Sondra Fraleigh, *Butoh: Metamorphic Dance and Global Alchemy*, Champaign, IL: University of Illinois Press, 2010, and *Dancing into Darkness; Butoh, Zen, and Japan*, Pittsburgh, PA: University of Pittsburgh Press, 1999. For the surrealist influence on Butoh see Miryam Sas, *Fault Lines: Cultural Memory and Japanese Surrealism*, Stanford, CA: Stanford University Press, 1999. There is also Stephen Barber's *Hijikata: Revolt of the Body*, London: Creation Books, 2007, that is particularly emphatic in outlining Artaud's influence on Hijikata's dance. It is Barber's judgment that only Butoh carried

any relation to Artaud must remain singular in Jean Baudrillard's sense that there cannot be any mass or public admiration of Artaud,[30] there are still some theoretical fruits and wider ramifications or lessons in looking again at his 'case' or example. There are openings in the sciences that promote another look at Artaud, and a re-examination of Artaud's creativity and predicament in turn fuels these developments. One such starting point, that follows from these preliminary comments about sorcery and 'ethnopsychiatry' is a corollary to the wisdom of bracketing belief systems, and that is refraining from establishing universals but rather following 'cartography' of movement. As Félix Guattari advised, in cautioning against 'universals,'

> One can theorize a production of subjectivity, within a particular group or with respect to a neurosis or psychosis, without having to resort to the authority of science in the matter and refer instead to something that would imply a formalization of a sense of the universal in order to affirm itself as a universal truth... since theorization, in all the matters it may encompass, cannot amount to more than what I call a descriptive or functional cartography.[31]

With Artaud it is ever a question of not so much models and modelisation, which already imply forms of stasis or false abstraction, but of provoking the maps or cartography that have functionality. For Deleuze and Guattari this entails resorting to a 'magical chain' that 'brings together plant life, pieces of organs, a shred of clothing, an image of daddy, formulas and words: we shall not ask what it means, but what kind of machine is assembled in this manner – what kind of flows and breaks in the flows, in relation to other breaks and flows.'[32] This approach poses enormous advantages in regard to Artaud given his virulent rejection of metaphor and campaign against what Guattari would later call the 'despotism' of the signifier, especially as represented in Lacanian theory.[33] Artaud's advocacy of sorcery forms no obstacle here, since as Guattari specified at the beginning of his *Cartographies Schizoanalytiques*, 'I have no hostility whatsoever against magic, I would even say that in many cases it constitutes an

forward the vision of the late Artaud. As Butoh dancer Sumako Koseki claimed, 'Butoh is Artaud's voice at the end of his life'. See Barber, *Antonin Artaud*, p.5.

30 Jean Baudrillard, 'Baudrillard on Artaud,' 16 November 1996, New York, NY: The Drawing Center, New York.

31 Félix Guattari, 'Psychoanalysis Should Get a Grip on Life,' *The Guattari Reader*, ed. Gary Genosko, New York, NY & London: Routledge, 1996, p.72. Guattari makes this remark in the context of recognising 'the necessity of...mythic reference,' an issue to which I return in the section 'The opening to animism' in the final chapter.

32 Deleuze and Guattari, *Anti-Oedipus*, p.181.

33 For characteristic criticisms of Lacan see Félix Guattari, *Chaosmosis*, trans. Paul Bains and Julian Pefanis, Bloomington, IN & London: Indiana University Press, 1995, pp.37; 45; 48-9; 72-4. The 'despotism' of the signifier is an issue first raised in *Anti-Oedipus*, without the anti-Lacanian ire.

extremely interesting cartography of Psychic assemblages.'[34] Guattari's warning against 'universals' is in part derived from physicist Ilya Prigogine's proclamation, based on the achievements of complexity theory, of an 'end of universality' in science,[35] but it stems more immediately from the contingencies of any linguistics. As Guattari writes, 'There is no universality of language nor is there a universality of speech acts...Every signifying statement crystallises a mute dance of intensities that is simultaneously played out on the social body and the individuated body. From language to glossolalia, all the transitions are possible.'[36] Here much of the immense research in emergent properties and self-organising systems provide heuristic parallels to Artaud's journey and a fertile theoretical basis for the expansion of a contemporary critical or 'anti'-psychiatry; it is not a matter of postulating some external standard or 'optimal fit' of normality or sanity as much as it is accounting for a kind of bricolage, the putting together of parts and pieces in complex configurations that provide enough consistency, or 'sufficient integrity to persist...not because they fulfill some ideal design but simply because they are possible.'[37]

Much as Deleuze and Guattari argue at the beginning of *Anti-Oedipus* that in the cosmic mappings of Daniel Paul Schreber 'something is produced: machinic effects not mere metaphors,'[38] in seeking to understand Artaud we would do well in accepting a certain viability of his journey. Artaud postulates another way of thinking, another vocabulary, that 'works.' Artaud exhibited an extraordinary 'integrity to persist' in pursuing what was possible, what was deemed impossible. From invention of new terms like 'bodies without organs' to his subversion of the symbol of the cross and upending of various schisms and signs from archaic thought, Artaud preludes Bruno Latour's 'we have never been modern.'[39] Latour's 'we have never been modern' is not merely an artistic category in relation to Artaud but one that makes it possible to take Artaud's discourses on sorcery and bewitchment with a new kind of seriousness, since for Artaud, 'we are all bewitched,' and those who do not wish to believe this form 'part of the clan of bewitchers.'[40] To Artaud, 'it is bewitchment that exists

[34] Félix Guattari, *Cartographies Schizoanalytiques*, Paris: Éditions Galilée, 1989, p.47.

[35] Prigogine and Stengers, *Order Out of Chaos*, pp.217-8. A similar position is taken in Jack Cohen and Ian Stewart, *The Collapse of Chaos*, New York, NY: Penguin Books, 1994, pp.33-4. Also see the exposition of the consequences of this in Ilya Prigogine, *The End of Certainty*, New York, NY: Free Press, 1997.

[36] Félix Guattari, *The Machinic Unconscious*, trans. Taylor Adkins, Los Angeles, CA: Semiotext(e), [1979] 2011, p.32.

[37] Francisco J. Varela, Evan Thompson, and Eleanor Rosch, *The Embodied Mind*, Cambridge, MA: MIT Press, 1991, p.196.

[38] Deleuze and Guattari, *Anti-Oedipus*, p.2.

[39] Bruno Latour, *We Have Never Been Modern*, trans. Catherine Porter, Cambridge, MA: Harvard University Press, 1993.

[40] Artaud XXVI, 1994, p.49.

more than reality.'[41] It is due to the centrality of this notion in Artaud that it will be necessary to examine his journey, especially after his trip to the Tarahumara Indians in 1936, in the light of a certain ethnography, keeping in mind Latour's position that 'we have never really left the old anthropological matrix behind,'[42] even as I show Artaud ultimately challenges this matrix of interpretation as well.

Deleuze and Guattari are among the most frequently cited thinkers in this account not because they hold to a similar chronological argument about Artaud, (they do not) but because their insistence that 'Metamorphosis is the contrary of metaphor'[43] is so central to Artaud. They are writing about Kafka but they could have been writing about Artaud when they claim:

> Kafka deliberately kills all metaphor, all symbolism all signification, no less than all designation…There is no longer any proper sense or figurative sense but only a distribution of states that is part of the range of the word. The thing and other things are no longer anything but intensities overrun by deterritorialized sound or words that are following their line of escape.[44]

There are differences with Artaud – Deleuze and Guattari's analysis of 'faciality' for instance is quite different to what Artaud evokes in his writings on the face,[45] but their elucidation of the 'body without organs' is remarkably close to its source in Artaud. Its occult resonance and its radical challenge to the basis of science, art and medicine (all beholden for Artaud, and for Deleuze and Guattari, to the organism) are echoed throughout *A Thousand Plateaus*, for instance. In the hands of Deleuze and Guattari the 'body without organs' becomes a kind of strange attractor or processual paradigm for the age of multinational capitalism. Given the targets of the new militarised world order of the Cold War Artaud denounces in *To have done with the judgment of god* this can be reconciled as part of Artaud's vision as well.[46] In Deleuze and Guattari's *Capitalism and Schizophrenia* project Artaud's double body that has no 'inside…no localization of internal conscience,'[47] is a kind of body=degree zero intensity found throughout the social field. It is produced, Deleuze and Guattari argue in *Anti-Oedipus*,

[41] Ibid., p.147.

[42] Latour, *We Have Never Been Modern*, p.47. For a continuation of Latour's argument see his *On the Modern Cult of the Factish Gods*, first chapter, trans. Catherine Porter and Heather MacLean, Durham, NC & London: Duke University Press, [1996] 2010.

[43] Gilles Deleuze and Félix Guattari, *Kafka. Toward a Minor Literature*, trans. Dana Polan, Minneapolis, MN: University of Minnesota Press, [1975]1986, p.22.

[44] Ibid.

[45] See the discussion of this in 'Artaud's "graphic cruelties": the face of the void' in Chapter VI.

[46] This is the starting point of Frédéric Neyrat's works on Artaud, see the discussion of Neyrat's work in my 'Conclusion: Erasing the Line'.

[47] Artaud XXIII, 1987, pp.202-3.

when the usual operation of 'desiring-machines' breaks down, or is suspended,[48] and as will be shown, various processes of suspension are central to both the early and the later Artaud. The 'body without organs' provides a powerful alternative to Freud's equilibrium thermodynamic model of the 'death drive'[49] while following it ever so closely. For Deleuze and Guattari the 'body without organs' is 'the unproductive, the sterile, the unengendered, the unconsumable. Antonin Artaud discovered this one day, finding himself with no shape or form whatsoever, right there where he was at the moment,' since desire is also desire for death, and 'the full body of death is its motor.'[50] The attractions and repulsions of the (complex and capitalistic) social field create intensities, which are not in opposition to each other or tend towards a 'natural' state of equilibrium, as in the model of the later Freud. Rather they are positive and potentially unlimited in relation to the body without organs, and fill it up. It is these bands of intensity, Deleuze and Guattari write, that are lived and not representative, that Artaud describes in his *Nerve Scales* (1925) – 'one's entire soul flows into this emotion that makes the mind aware of the terribly disturbing sound of matter, and passes through its white-hot flame.'[51] Here Deleuze and Guattari project the 'body without organs' – a late invention of Artaud's – backwards in time.

In such an interpretation Artaud is the mind touching matter, illuminating the body without organs and its intensities, which 'are not metaphors, but matter itself.'[52] Despite the break from hieroglyphic conceptions at the end of his life, this hostility towards metaphor and the probing of matter, is a feature that remains consistent (as is his desire to create a new theatre). Artaud regularly breaches what Pierre Lévy called the 'ontological Iron Curtain'[53] between mind and matter. In this reading, Artaud in his writings in the mid-20's, at the end of his life, and even frequently in the asylum, is in relation to the outside, to the volcanic and active properties of creative matter. One must contrast this with the prevalence of psychoanalytic readings of Artaud that stress the isolated wretch in the asylum, whose persecutory delusions are suffering caused by split-off portions of his personality. In fact Artaud never left the social field, even in the midst of terrible suffering in his asylum confinement, where Artaud draws on no fewer than four Virgin Marys as fluidly as he draws in the figures of Hitler, Churchill, Stalin and de Gaulle into his delirium that is also the world's. Sylvère Lotringer has even accounted for Artaud's anti-semitic remarks in this

48 Deleuze and Guattari, *Anti-Oedipus*, pp.7-10.

49 Sigmund Freud, 'Beyond the Pleasure Principle,' in Vol. XVIII of *Complete Psychological Works of Sigmund Freud*, trans. and ed. James Strachey, New York, NY: Vintage, [1922] 2001.

50 Deleuze and Guattari, *Anti-Oedipus*, p.8.

51 Artaud I:1, 1956, p.112. Cited in ibid., p.19.

52 Deleuze and Guattari, *Anti-Oedipus*, p.283.

53 Lévy cited in Guattari, *Chaosmosis*, p.108.

way – not that Artaud was an 'anti-semite' but that he was using another code or resource in the social that he could put into play.[54]

The 'personological' interpretations typical of psychoanalysis[55] inevitably fall prey to the splittings Artaud was so opposed to. Despite the acuteness of her detailed readings and deep scholarship in the matter of Artaud, this is the case with Évelyne Grossman who writes that it is fragments and projections detached from the body of Artaud that return to him in persecutory phenomena that eventually include electroshock treatments, the 'radiophonic machine,' 'the war machine of the Americans,' and the 'social machine' all wrapped up in 'his ensemble.'[56] This provides not a bad example of what Guattari criticised as the 'personological theater' of psychoanalysis that creates a 'system of representations cut off from the real desiring production.'[57] Guattari's perspective that insists on keeping Artaud in the social field – as Deleuze and Guattari write in Anti-Oedipus '*there is only desire and the social, and nothing else*'[58] – is certainly closer to Artaud's own point of view. Artaud saw the severance of theatre and art from life as invariably a kind of repression, a con from the European 'Holy Family' that extended from the reproductive order and the nuclear family to the state and the art museum and gallery system, all implicated in a theology of God the Father. Artaud in the last twenty-two months of his life has not so much 'internalised' his Theater of cruelty in any common psychological sense but set it off in a fiercely interactive and dynamic field. This included startlingly experimental and perverse use of mass media including prime-time radio and mass newspapers like *Combat* where through his published letters Artaud inserted his invented syllable-language. Artaud in his theatre manifestoes had written of latent 'hieroglyphic' realities that are 'eternal laws which are those of all poetry and all viable language.'[59] The post-Rodez Artaud is not concerned with evoking eternal laws but rather with a rage to affirm the void and its disfiguration, the violent conflict of one element with another. After the failure of Artaud to actualise a Theater of cruelty on the stages of Paris in the 1930's or to create in an adequate cinema medium, and after nine years of often brutal asylum confinement, at the end of his life Artaud was however still obsessed with creating

---

[54] See his remarks in 'Sick, Evil, and Violent: Interview with Sylvère Lotringer, Edward Scheer, and Jane Goodall,' in *100 Years of Cruelty: Essays on Artaud*, ed. Edward Scheer, Sydney: Power Publications, 2002, pp.311; 322; 324.

[55] Félix Guattari used the term 'personological' to characterise the primary role given persons, identities, and identifications in psychoanalytic theory, cutting off analysis from the flux of actual desiring machines. See Félix Guattari, *Molecular Revolution: Psychiatry and Politics*, trans. Rosemary Sheed, New York, NY: Penguin Books, 1984, p.290.

[56] Évelyne Grossman, *Artaud, 'l'aliené authentique,'* Paris: Leo Scheer/Farago, 2003, pp.32-3.

[57] Guattari, *Molecular Revolution*, p.290.

[58] Deleuze and Guattari, *Anti-Oedipus*, p.29. Italics in original.

[59] Artaud IV, 1964, p.133.

a Theater of cruelty. Even if a more fully operating one was not at his disposal he created works that he realised closely approximated it. For Artaud, against the literature of failure that often continues to surround him, had glimpses of a living Theater of cruelty, not only among the Tarahumaras, but also in his own work. In a letter to Fernand Pouey, who had commissioned Artaud's scheduled February 1948 broadcast, Artaud wrote of his enthusiasm that *To have done with the judgment of god* 'could furnish a miniature model of what I want to do in the *Theater of cruelty*.'[60]

Artaud's difference: sense and signification

Already in early 1964 Michel Foucault predicted a point in the not too distant future when 'Artaud will belong to the ground of our language, not its rupture.'[61] Key to this aspect of reappraisal of Artaud is a nearly unavoidable attention to if not reliance on the qualities of his writing, since there is indeed so much of it. Here it is important to keep utmost in mind the distinction, crucial in the work of both Félix Guattari and Jean-François Lyotard, between sense and signification. Without it, a defense of Artaud could be well-nigh impossible. Quite consonant with the bracketing of belief and belief-systems in 'anti-psychiatry' and 'ethnopsychiatry' practices, Guattari for example developed a brand of polysemiosis, elaborating the dynamic, connective effects of asignifying or postsignifying semiotics which established links and valences and efficacities between and among various material fluxes regardless of whether they signify or fail to signify something for someone.[62] For Guattari language is not axiomatic or autonomous but always open to other levels of semiotisation. He makes a recourse to Louis Hjemslev, who argued that content and expression 'are defined only by their mutual solidarity, and neither of them can be identified otherwise...[being] mutually opposed functives of one and the same function.'[63] This 'solidarity' for Guattari 'radically relativizes the classic opposition signifier/signified,'[64] and provides a means to avoid the fetishism of the signifier, which for Guattari (as very much so for Artaud) is the expression of the dominant powers, the

60 Artaud XIII, 1974, p.127. Artaud's italics.

61 Michel Foucault, *History of Madness*, 2nd rev. ed., trans. Jean Khalpa and Jonathan Murphy, New York, NY & London: Routledge, 2005, p.541. These remarks were first published in 'La Folie, l'absence d'œuvre,' *La Table Ronde* 196, May 1964, pp.11-21.

62 Guattari's first foray into defining his brand of semiotics, which rehearses much of the terminology, such as 'faciality' for instance, that would play such a defining role later in *A Thousand Plateaus*, is his *The Machinic Unconscious* (1979). For a brief specification of his recourse to Hjemslev, for example, see *The Machinic Unconscious*, pp.41-3.

63 Louis Hjemslev, *Prolegomena to a Theory of Language*, trans. Francis J. Whitfield, Madison, WI: University of Wisconsin Press, 1961, p.60.

64 Guattari, *The Machinic Unconscious*, p.42.

expression of authority through signs. Overcoming this binary split is the key for Guattari that opens up to the semiotic fluxes or 'substances' that produce the forms hierarchised and reified by structuralism generally. He writes 'It is only by starting from non-linguistic – or non-signifying linguistic – semiotic assemblages, that these substances may be produced: in other words, "before" the constitution of significative redundancies and without that which would confer to them a status of priority or hierarchal superiority vis-à-vis other semiotic productions.'[65] Guattari transposes Hjemslev's categories of form (which Guattari identifies with his 'abstract machine' independent of particular substance); substance (a mode of actualisation of abstract machinism with the stratifying double articulation of expression/content); and of matter, sometimes termed by Hjemslev's translators 'matter-meaning' or 'purport' (in Guattari's sense of the 'machinic' rather than of signification). Guattari admits that Hjemslev's use of terms 'still belongs to the particular mode of formularization proper to signifying semiotic.'[66] Yet for Guattari his notion of 'abstract machinism'[67] is necessary for the nonsemiotically formed matter and semiotically formed substances to have a common basis – this 'abstract machinism must surely be able to subsume both and enable us to pass from one to the other.'[68] As I will show in different discussions, for instance focusing on the issue of rhythm in Artaud in Chapters III, IV, and V, this passing from one level of semiosis to another, from multiple levels of meaning, that parallels the movement back and forth from an often abject and desperate physicality to extreme spiritualism that constitute a remarkable kind of resurgent 20th century Gnosticism, is a kind of double or multiple-play and metamorphosis often in operation in Artaud; the 'late' Artaud is characterised by an insistence on matter that must be doubled, a smashing of the false voids of notions not emitted physically, not directly rooted in the 'true body'. An understanding such as Guattari's enables one to follow the *sens*, the fungible in Artaud's poetics.

---

[65] Ibid.

[66] Guattari, *Molecular Revolution*, p.99.

[67] 'Abstract machine' is an elemental concept in Guattari and Deleuze that enables planes of consistency through 'double articulation' to actualise into identifiable forms and functions. The 'abstract machine' can be seen as this double articulation or double bind, inseparable from the formation of a determinate entity and the unpredictable or dynamic processes from which it derives and into which it can further evolve. In *A Thousand Plateaus*, Deleuze and Guattari conclude, 'Every abstract machine is linked to other abstract machines…because their various types are as intertwined as their operations are convergent.' *A Thousand Plateaus*, p.514. For useful expositions on the notion of 'abstract machine' see Jeffrey Bell, *Philosophy at the Edge of Chaos*, Toronto: University of Toronto Press, 2006, pp.4-9; 211-2; 218-26; and Brian Massumi, *A user's guide to* Capitalism and Schizophrenia, Cambridge, MA & London: MIT Press/Swerve, 1992, pp.22; 27; 47.

[68] Guattari, *Molecular Revolution*, p.96.

Guattari's notions allow him to construct a radical semiotics not beholden to the signifier/signified split, thereby carrying out a parallel operation to Artaud's vehement lifelong rejection of the distancing actions of metaphor. In contrast, the way this signifier/signified binary division usually operates according to Guattari is that 'the totality of fluxes is held in the "snapshot" of signification which places an object facing a subject; the movement of desire is sterilized by a relationship of representation; the image becomes the memory of a reality made impotent, and its immobilization establishes the world of dominant significations and received ideas.'[69] This creative avoidance if not destruction of what M.C. Dillon characterised as 'semiological reductionism'[70] means Guattari's particular method can investigate in a political manner the various semiological functions, revealing the planes of power which underly the various formularisations of content and expression, 'for all contents, before being structured by language, or "like a language," are structured at a multitude of micro-political levels.'[71]

Artaud's glossolalia: a user's guide

These ideas are relevant to understanding Artaud's later invented language, or 'syllable-words,' that gain more and more power in Artaud's work at Rodez and afterwards, and are a phenomenon returned to in this project more than once, in different contexts and for different reasons. Here Artaud's description of his *Suppôts et suppliciations* – that of a text turned over and over from side to side – also bears some significance with his use of the 'syllable-words,' which run as kind of alternate line, roar, sound or 'rant block,' not so much interrupting Artaud's fluidity of thought as re-emphasising its immediacy, its urgency, its accessible physicality. Artaud advised that he inserted them for the reader to find his or her own rhythm and tempo and thought through the work.[72] Judging from Artaud's first description of them, they are also a means of protection against demons and various vampirish forces and an act of aggression against them; in this sense a continuation of his *sorts* and 'spells' of the late-30s. Organised in regular stanzas, usually in lines of one to three words, so integral are they to his work it is difficult to find any later text of Artaud that does not contain them. Artaud used them regularly at least from 1945 while at the Rodez asylum and they appear in a 29 March 1943 letter to his psychiatrist Dr. Gaston Ferdière

[69] Ibid., pp.87-8.

[70] M.C. Dillon, *Semiological Reductionism*, Albany, NY: State University of New York Press, 1995.

[71] Guattari, *Molecular Revolution*, p.83.

[72] Artaud, *Œuvres*, p.1015.

where Artaud calls them part of a 'transcendental initiation'[73] and of a lost holy book he had written sometimes referred to simply as *Letura d'Eprahi*; but one of his later texts, 'Ten years that the language is gone,'[74] refers to one of these combinatory writing-drawing-incantations as early as October 1939, during his first confinement in the asylum at Ville-Évrard. It is difficult to separate them from the hummings, chanting, sneezing, spitting, hex-making and other forms of 'abnormal' behaviour that were a feature of Artaud at Ville Évrard and when he was first brought to Rodez. As Bettina Knapp has related:

> He would begin telescoping his syllables, indulge in verbal gyrations, make strange noises, change his intonation and the vocal range of which he was a master: speak first in a sonorous, then monotonous, and finally in an insipid register; whereupon, he would break out in mellow and full tones. At meal time, Artaud frequently stopped eating, quite suddenly, and for a few seconds or minutes would go through a whole series of rituals such as spitting, getting down on his hands and knees and psalmodizing, drawing magic circles, indulge in auditive hallucinations, gustatory antics, belch in rhythmic patterns, etc...At other times hours were spent articulating words forcefully, injecting each syllable with a kind of metallic ringing sound; treating words as something concrete, actual beings possessing potential magic forces. For the non-initiated, or those unable to understand Artaud, those syllable-words seemed to blossom forth helter-skelter; for Artaud, however, they created a tapestry of verbal images and rhythms... emanations of a superior will which hovered around mankind eternally.[75]

When integrated into his letters, proclamations and other texts, these blocks are both visual, centered on the page and invariably set off, and often have a certain 'sense' in terms of referring to actual words: they not only play with Greek and Latin endings of words and Latin declensions, or Greek and Latin variations of words, but often words for parts of the body or processes of exorcism, actual historical incantations that we know Artaud borrowed from an 1902 book of Assyrian magical incantations, *La magie assyrienne: Étude suivi de textes magiques*, which Charles Fossey had translated into French.[76] As one scholar writes:

> Many of the magic syllables found in these incantations crop up in Artaud's poetry. Some of them denote parts of the body and were used in rituals designed

[73] Ibid., p.882.

[74] Artaud wrote 'And after a certain day of October 1939 I have no longer written without also drawing,' in Artaud, *Œuvres*, p.1513. At the end of his life Artaud in several notes maintained that his writing-drawings and *gris gris* began as early as his internment at Ville-Évrard. See ibid., pp.1421; 1467. The text of 'Ten Years Have Gone' is also available in *Antonin Artaud, dessins et portraits*, Paris: Gallimard, 1986.

[75] Bettina Knapp, *Antonin Artaud: Man of Vision*, New York, NY: David Lewis, 1969, pp.160-1. Knapp draws heavily here on descriptions found in H.J. Armand-Laroche, *Antonin Artaud et son double*, Périgueux: Pierre-Franlac, 1964. Armand-Laroche, who provides a sort of psychiatric portrait of Artaud, is one of the few Artaud biographers who had access to Artaud's medical records while at Rodez.

[76] Naomi Greene, *Antonin Artaud: Poet Without Words*, New York, NY: Simon & Schuster, 1970, p.214.

to cure sickness and disease: ka (mouth), eme (tongue), ma (womb). Still others refer to the process of exorcism itself: enim-enim-ma (exorcism), ta-mat (to be exorcised), tu-tu (incantation).[77]

Many of them cite Artaud's reoccurring concerns and obsessions – papa, mama, *peste* or plague, kurbura for *courbature* or ache, kana for cane. They are enriched by the polygot of languages Artaud must have heard around him as a child growing up in the Mediterranean melting pot of Marseille; and Artaud's mother was a Levantine Greek. Artaud had enormous linguistic resources on which to draw. These 'syllable words' are essential in creating and completing the striking all-important rhythmic quality in Artaud but they also call out to be vocalised. If there is one matter Artaud insists upon at Rodez and after, it is that his words must be sounded, must be vocalised, to be activated, to have effects. The passages of 'syllable words' ensure that Artaud's own texts must be sounded in this way. There were moments when Artaud explained this quite clearly. In a 22 September 1945 letter to Henri Parisot, Artaud refers to the lost book in glossolalia, and offers the reader a large sample. Artaud writes 'one can only read them in cadence, based on a rhythm which the reader himself must find in order to comprehend and to think:

ratara ratara ratara
atara tatara rana

otara otara katara
otara ratara kana

ortura ortura konara
kokona kokona koma

kurbura kurbura kurbura
kurbata kurbata Kenya

pesti anti pestantum putara
pest anti pestantum putra

But this is only valid when uttered in an urgent flow; picked out syllable by syllable it becomes worthless.'[78] Similarly, in Artaud's essay 'Coleridge, the Traitor'(1946), he explains 'For *after*, say "poematic," after comes the time of the blood. Since *ema*, in Greek, means blood, and since po-ema must mean

afterwards,
        the blood,
the blood afterwards.'[79]

---

[77] Ibid.

[78] Artaud, *Œuvres*, pp.1015-6.

[79] Artaud XXIV, 1988, p.309.

The so-called 'syllable words' certainly appear to have a very specific and critical role in Artaud's work. How they are related to Artaud's other experiments in sound and gesture is illustrated in one of his earliest and most primitive attempts in plumbing 'levels of sound,' in the early play *The Spurt of Blood* (1925). Here a girl and boy exchange declarations of love, but in highly inflected repetitions, bordering on declamations, that wrench new tonalities and rhythms from the ordinary, banal lines of dialogue.[80]

As Eric Sellin has pointed out,[81] these experiments quickly become more sophisticated, as in the detailed specifications for the speech of the Harlequin in *The Philosopher's Stone* (1931). The words of the Harlequin's introduction are juxtaposed to the instructions for delivery:

JE VIENS POUR FAIRE TIRER DE MOI LA PIERRE PHILOSOPHALE	Increasing silences after each bit of sentence, in a bleating, cadenced voice. A brief pause after: *je viens* – long pause after: *de moi* – still longer pause reinforced by the stopping of gestures on: *phale*. The tone of a hoarse voice deep in the throat and at the same time high-pitched: the voice of a hoarse eunuch.[82]

Later Artaud's attention to discordant sound is reflected in his directions for *The Cenci* (1935), where Cenci's name is first pronounced on one long, prolonged, sharp note and then in two-beats, like the pendulum of a clock – Cenci, Cenci, Cenci, Cenci.[83] These effects reached their most complex relation in the cacophony of synchronised cries, animal roars, scatting and glossolalia so prevalent in the *To have done with the judgment of god* (1947-8) radio broadcast. In Artaud's later texts the glossolalic texts are often facing each other, juxtaposed on the page, the fruits of wild dialogues Artaud would stage with actor Roger Blin, in which both would scream and declaim face-to-face in Artaud's invented language; Artaud called these sessions going into 'the monkeys' cage.'[84]

Released from confinement at Rodez on 7 May, 1946, the stage or films were a world closed to him; once merely a huge investment risk, Artaud was now untouchable. In the spirit of Nietzsche's 'we ourselves want to be our experiments and guinea pigs,'[85] Artaud's laboratory for a 'projection of the true body' was no

80 Artaud I:1, 1956, pp.74-5.

81 In his concise and immensely valuable study, *The Dramatic Concepts of Antonin Artaud*, Chicago, IL & London: University of Chicago Press, 1968, p.118.

82 Artaud II, 1961, p.86.

83 Artaud IV, 1964, p.244.

84 Barber, *Antonin Artaud*, p.152.

85 Friedrich Nietzsche, 'The Gay Science,' *The Portable Nietzsche*, ed. and trans. Walter

longer any theatre company but what resources his own singularity, his own particular body and spirit, could mobilise; Artaud may have been reduced to the body, but at this point it was the sole resource in which he continued to believe. The 'syllable words' were an essential part of this churning activity, what would become the 'grinding over' of the Theater of cruelty in the last work. They are full of 'sense' even when they most lack 'signification.'

The yoga of the scream

This is also the case with Artaud and his 'affective athleticism' or yoga of the scream – that is first prescribed as part of the program with the manifestoes of *The Theater and Its Double* (1938), and then comes into its own with the 1946-8 radio recordings, especially in the *bruitage*, or noise effects, of Artaud's last masterwork *To have done with the judgment of god*. This is part of Artaud's consistency: his pounding away with his various hammers and fire pokers at Ivry-sur-Seine after his release from Rodez, with such force that he eventually broke one into pieces (as he wrote in 'Pounding and Gism' – 'I do not use words and not even letters' but 'in fact I do nothing other than keep quiet and pound'[86]) and vocal exercises with his 'screambox,' are a direct continuation of his earlier pre-war Theater of cruelty. In terms of the scream, in a letter to Jean Paulhan from Mexico, 5 April, 1936, Artaud had described how his work as an actor was linked with this primal roar – of 'bringing up my fear in the noise of rage, in a solemn roar…I scream in dream/ but I know that I dream/ and over the TWO SIDES OF THE DREAM/I make reign my will.'[87] This cry or scream, '*is* a dream./But a dream which eats the dream.'[88] It is with this 'hieroglyph of a breath' that Artaud discovers again the 'idea of a sacred theatre.'[89] This text, 'Seraphim's Theater,' was supposed to be included with the other essays of *The Theater and Its Double*, but for some reason was not. It is a text all the more remarkable in terms of the 'late' Artaud, although it expands many of the themes found in his essay 'An Affective Athleticism,'[90] a work which was included in *The Theater and Its Double*, and probably was originally intended as a conjoint, second part to it, as his overall instructions and suggestions for the actors of the Theater of cruelty. These instructions already elaborated six principal combinations of the breath, based on the Kabbalah, and referenced the alternation of convex and concave, male and feminine, and the 380 pressure points of Chinese

Kaufman, New York, NY: Viking Penguin, 1954, p.101.

[86] Artaud XIV:2, 1978, p.26.

[87] Artaud IV, 1964, p.178.

[88] Ibid., p.179.

[89] Ibid., p.184.

[90] Ibid., pp.154-64.

acupuncture, in order to explore the 'localisations' of the body in the expression of the soul. These instructions had already concluded with the need 'to exacerbate these [pressure] points as a musculature being flayed. The rest is achieved through screams.'[91] Having forgotten their bodies, Artaud complains, actors had also forgotten the use of their throats, now 'no longer an organ but a monstrous abstraction which speaks.'[92] In 'Seraphim's Theater' Artaud describes his screams as an attempt at a 'terrible feminine,' a cry as if it came from the bottom of the abyss itself.[93] Alternating between the masculine, active and located in the stomach, whose willpower must ultimately be suppressed, and the neuter, which 'harbours slaughter,' in evoking this feminine descent, Artaud must make a terrifying fall, into an 'underground' from which he cannot emerge, 'nevermore *in the Masculine*.'[94] His cry has evoked a 'walled cavern' and he is a 'dumbfounded warrior, whose cry is struck by fear.'[95] Yet his scream creates a sound of cataracts, an impression of rushing water, a 'double' that is 'more than an echo' in the cavernous walls; it is 'the memory of a language of which theatre has lost the secret.'[96] Through this language 'the whole magic of existence will have passed through a single chest when the Measures have closed themselves up.'[97] This not only introduces the intensity of the physicality that rarely ceases to be at work in Artaud, the primacy of the voice that is emphasised, but also the problematic gendering of reality that is central to his 1937 prophecy *The New Revelations of Being*,[98] a reflection of psychic splits arguably central to Artaud's shattering and return to France in a straitjacket that very year.

What is crucial here is the role of the neuter in holding the force, the capacity for the scream, which eventually surges up in a 'terrible warlike sound.'[99] In his balance of the masculine and the neuter, Artaud is able to fill his lungs with an awesome 'sound of waterfalls' the irruption of which would destroy his lungs, if the scream he had wanted to push out was not also a state of dream.[100] The neuter is like an empty placeholder, and indeed sometimes is a 'spatial Neuter;' Artaud describes it as the force of will lying in wait, ready to rattle, to shake out the war, the war Artaud wants to wage against the war waged against him.[101] Between the two breaths, the neuter extends itself, stretches itself, as if it is the

---

91 Ibid., p.163.

92 Ibid.

93 Ibid., pp.175-6.

94 Ibid., p.179.

95 Ibid.

96 Ibid., p.180.

97 Ibid.

98 See the discussion of this work in Chapter V.

99 Artaud IV, 1964, p.180.

100 Ibid., p178.

101 Ibid., p.176.

space itself that extends. It is a kind of 'asphyxiated void,' or 'choked void' in the throat. This, for Artaud, is how the breath can then descend to the pit of the stomach, creating a profound and bottomless void there and then launch itself back up powerfully to the very top of the lungs.[102] The feminine here, in Artaud is described as solid and vast as the vaults of the cavern, walled-in on all sides; a 'warrior who no longer has an army' alone on its floor uttering an extraordinary and awful cry, Artaud attests to a profoundly splintering identification with, and dissociation from, this element. Typical of the other manifestoes of the Theater of cruelty, these dynamics revolve around spatialisation, even if this is distending space so as to touch the void; it is due to Artaud's eventual transformation in his understanding of this hieroglyphic matrix that in his later written and sound works and drawings that time is no longer subordinated to space in this way – all his activity becomes an opening onto infinity, as in his phrase from *To have done with the judgment of god,* 'the *opening*/of our consciousness/towards possibility/ unlimited/insatiable and immeasurable.'[103] This idea of infinity looks backward, to the Baudelaire who wrote of 'An infinite that I have loved in vain,'[104] and forward, to Félix Guattari's characterisation, following Marcel Duchamp, of the 'event' as that which 'comes as a rupture with the coordinates of time and space...behind relations of temporal discursivity, there is always a possible index into the point of crystallisation of the event outside time, which crosses time, transversal to all the measures of time.'[105] This is infinity as a pure becoming.[106]

This fearsome, hideous cry Artaud describes has the function of what Catherine Clément has called a 'syncope,' a suspension or delay that also functions as an *enjambement.* This can be the delay in the syncopation of a beat, a suspension of the breath; it is an ecstatic moment that is profoundly desubjectifying yet opens the space for another movement, another insight, and so becomes a function of rhythm, yet is itself a weakness, an orgiastic blackout of consciousness.[107] This encompasses and takes a wide variety of forms: from the rapture before

[102] Ibid., p.177.

[103] Artaud XIII, 1974, pp.91-2.

[104] Charles Baudelaire, 'Hymn to Beauty,' *Flowers of Evil*, ed. by Marthiel and Jackson Matthews, New York, NY: New Directions, 1955, p.51.

[105] Félix Guattari, 'On Contemporary Art,' *The Guattari Effect*, ed. by Éric Alliez and Andrew Goffey, London and New York, NY: Continuum, 2011, p.52.

[106] This also has an analogue in Henri Bergson's notion of world as immanent creativity and motion, for which no unmoved mover is necessary. 'The Absolute endures', wrote Bergson, 'being creativity itself'. See Bergson, *Creative Evolution*, trans. Arthur Mitchell, Mineola,NY: Dover Publications, [1911] 1998, pp. 262; 315. For more development of Artaud's version of infinity, see the section 'Artaud's 1947-8 notebooks' in Chapter VI.

[107] Catherine Clément, *Syncope: The Philosophy of Rapture*, trans. Sally O'Driscoll and Deirdre M.Mahoney, Minneapolis, MN: University of Minnesota Press, 1994.

epileptic fits of Dostoyevsky's Prince Myshkin in *The Idiot*,[108] a deep paradoxical pleasure Dostoyevsky himself knew all too well, to the human scream. This latter phenomenon Clément is reticent about, other than citing Louis Aragon's *Elsa's Madman* [*Le Fou d'Elsa*]:

> However, there must be some singing
> I can't be only a scream
> This violent thing in me
> Seeks a lack, a crack there
> Where mutiny can pass.[109]

For Clément the scream 'does violence to the throat, which is suddenly turned into a hole, as if there were no other way out but to break through a wall.'[110] Despite all of the relevance of this comment to Artaud, both it and Aragon's poem, are written at such a lower charge or intensity of energy, and Clément's syncope is an idea, or intellectual construct, rather than any relating of direct encounter or experience, that limits its application to the subject at hand. Here the seminal American poet Robert Duncan's words are apropos – 'Artaud's "charge" is higher, in an entirely other category, than the charge at which I work. Yet I am concerned. His art – in which we have intimations of what we call "insanity" – makes articulate what without this communication we would not be prepared to feel.'[111] Artaud focused on the scream as the most elemental and first human expression, or more simply, as he wrote in a letter 13 November 1926, 'If I were only capable of being faithful to myself, I could only formulate, translate by the raw working of my temperament what I feel, what I think of myself, I would be nothing but a long scream.'[112]

The virtue of a notion like Clément's, despite her scant, hurried attention to the human cry, is to link Artaud's scream to a much larger range of ecstatic practices based on suspension. Clément points out that these were studiously contained or negated in the mainstream of Western thinking, yet incorporated with broad religious and popular bases in India in the East; in Western philosophy the syncope reached philosophical expression in the elegiac fragments and aphorisms of Friedrich Hölderlin, Søren Kierkegaard and Friedrich Nietzsche, just as its more direct expressions were being medicalized as 'madness.'[113] Clément resorts to the term 'short circuit' to describe the 'unworking' of the synco-

---

108 Fyodor Dostoyevsky, *The Idiot*, trans. David Magarshack, New York, NY: Penguin, [1887] 1955.

109 Louis Aragon, *Le Fou d'Elsa*, Paris: Gallimard, 1983, p.309.

110 Clément, *Syncope*, p.9.

111 Robert Duncan, *Derivations: Selected Poems 1950-6*, London: Fulcrum Press, 1968, p.90.

112 Artaud VII, 1967, p.326.

113 Clément, *Syncope*, p.21.

pe, especially as it threatens to disrupt the order of the faculties in Kant, or the logic of history in Hegel. It is significant that she cites at some length, to define these 'short circuits,' the persuasive description of inspiration given by André Breton in the 'Second Manifesto of Surrealism' (1930), where Breton uses this term. Breton wrote:

> We can easily recognize it by that total possession of our mind which, at rare intervals, prevents our being, for every problem posed, the plaything of one rational solution rather than some other equally rational solution, by that sort of short circuit it creates between a given idea and a respondent idea...In poetry and in painting, Surrealism has done everything it can and more to increase these short circuits. It believes, and it will never believe in anything more wholeheartedly, in reproducing artificially this ideal moment when man, in the grip of a particular emotion, is suddenly seized by this something 'stronger than himself' which projects him, in self-defense, into immortality.[114]

Using such suspensions to project himself into immortality was precisely the operation of the 'later' Artaud, what he characterised as *The projection of the 'true body'* (1946-8) in the drawing of that name.

In Clément's description the syncope is related above all to music, to song, as in Artaud's insistence all worthwhile poetry had to be declaimed, freed from the written or printed page; Artaud even dictated prose works like his *Heliogabalus: The Anarchist Crowned* (1933-4),[115] so that it would have added rhythmic fluency and punch.[116] Artaud's form of enchantment likewise cancels the normally speaking 'subject' self and continually risks falling into *infans*, yet with the pulsion and drive and lucidity of much of his work at Rodez and after rarely does.[117] Artaud's scream is not simply a falling into or evocation of the animal, or a pre-linguistic experiential ground, but was part of his 'progressive exercises' to evoke a primordial, pre-Tower of Babel language, and for the later Artaud to create the envelope of the 'body without organs.' For Artaud language had to be *scandé*, the sound and gesture fused. As Paule Thévenin described his way

[114] André Breton, *Manifestoes of Surrealism*, trans. Richard Seaver and Helen R. Lane, Ann Arbor, MI: University of Michigan Press, 1969, p.39.

[115] Artaud VII, 1967, pp.9-143.

[116] Barber, *Antonin Artaud*, p.60.

[117] In my discussion of the different levels of meaning usually at play in Artaud, it would be misleading to go down the route of a discussion on voice or speech based on *infans* significantly begun in Jean-Francois Lyotard, *Lectures d'enfance*, Paris: Galilée, 1991; and continued by Christopher Fynsk, *Infant Figures*, Stanford, CA: Stanford University Press, 2000 and Giorgio Agamben, *Infancy and History*, trans. Liz Heron, London & New York, NY: Verso, 1993. Just as Artaud's 'speech' is profoundly differentiated from *infans*, his writing will be just as strongly distinguished from 'schizo talk' and the interpretation offered in Gilles Deleuze, *Logic of Sense*, trans. Mark Lester and Charles Stivale, ed. Constantin V. Boundas, New York, NY: Columbia University Press, [1969] 1990. See the discussion in 'The emergence of the full "body without organs"' in Chapter V.

of working at Ivry-sur-Seine, where 'he would strike a block of wood with an enormous hammer or knife,' while he 'accompanied his work with rhythmic humming, in a language all his own.'[118] This means of creating, allied with ecstatic suspensions, screams, that are paradoxically *enjambements* if you will, were the crucial resource of the later Artaud pursuing his project of 'perpetual metamorphosis' or perpetual rebirth, this 'crucible' of 'fire and real meat,' that entailed this continual remaking of the human constitution. Otherwise, 'the body is keeping its breaths in irons.'[119]

Paule Thévenin, who would study the poems of Charles Baudelaire and Gérard de Nerval with Artaud at Ivry-sur-Seine, gives us an idea of what was entailed working with the post-Rodez Artaud:

> I had to invent a melody and sing the verse. I could, in this way, understand the importance of the words in general and also sense the relationship between one word and another. I tried to read a poem after having practised this technique for a while. I did not always succeed in satisfying Artaud. I had to begin all over again and work until he was satisfied...I had to learn to scream, to let this scream die out only when it had reached the point of annihilation, to go from the over-shrill to the deep tones, to prolong a syllable until my breath was exhausted. I believe I understood during the course of those sessions what the 'theatre of cruel purgation' really was.[120]

Artaud's suspended scream is strikingly similar to the gesture of *mié* in Japanese Kabuki theatre, where an expression is frozen at the moment of its greatest intensity. This device developed from the circumstance that the actors in the early plays performed almost completely in the dark, followed by stage-hands who would illuminate the actors and action with candles on little dishes attached to long poles. In this way the actor's face, arms and torso would be visible to the spectators but not the stage assistants. Given that spectators were often also eating, drinking tea, talking, it was necessary to hold the light and expression on crucial moments, as if in a freeze frame. *Mié* means literally 'to show.' The practice of *mié* also meant simply 'stopping,' or 'cutting,' – 'Why cut? The actor's pose could be described as stopping the film in that particular frame where the actor is showing a special tension: hence the meaning of cutting the action and of blocking a living immobility.'[121] The Kabuki actor went from one moment of paused or caught intensity to the next. Later this would be even further elaborated in a dynamics of the voice in Noh and then Butoh theatre, the latter

[118] Paule Thévenin, 'A Letter on Artaud,' *Tulane Drama Review* 9:3, Spring 1965, p.106.

[119] Artaud, *Œuvres*, pp.1544-48.

[120] Paule Thévenin, 'A Letter on Artaud,' p.107.

[121] Nicola Saverese, 'Theatre in the Showroom,' cited in Eugenio Barba and Nicola Saverese, *A Dictionary of Theatre Anthropology: The Secret Art of the Performer*, trans. Richard Fowler, New York, NY: Routledge, 1991, p.110. I was directed to this source from Philippe Alain-Michaud's brilliant study *Aby Warburg and the Image in Motion*, trans. Sophie Hawkins, New York, NY: Zone Books, 2004, p.271.

inspired to a great extent from the Artaud experiment. Kazuo Ohno, with Tatsumi Hijikata the most noted and pioneering Butoh dancer, in his long career rarely performed uttering any intelligible words, aside from at times exclaiming 'Father!' or 'Mother!' Ohno developed exercises for tautening the back, so that no audible utterance could emerge, precisely at the moment of manifestation of the most heightened emotion. Nearly choking himself with these blocked vocal chords – as Artaud discussed the 'choked scream' – this 'muted' voice means the body must act as its own voice and means of expressive language.[122] The Kabuki and Noh historian and performance critic Tamotsu Watanabe distinguished between dances in which the body embodied a voice, and those that remained 'dead silent, like stone.'[123] Here the body becomes its own moving sign, beyond any quotidian language or ordinary communication. The body moves thus in the void Artaud advocated, often full of sense, if often empty of more normative signification.

The 'figural' and the language of the body

This disentangling of sense and signification is a crucial task, itself a political as much as linguistic or philosophical act that is necessary to give Artaud the credibility he requires. Guattari's anarchic linguistics restores the vast polyvocity on a theoretical plane that is necessary for such an undertaking. A further justification of this is provided, oddly enough perhaps given his critique of Deleuze and Guattari,[124] by Jean-François Lyotard in his notion of the 'figural' in his definition of the 'unconscious' and 'discourse':

> To make the unconscious a discourse is to omit the energetic. To do so is to remain complicit with a Western ratio that kills art at the same time as the dream. One does not at all break with metaphysics by finding language everywhere, rather, one accomplishes it; one accomplishes the repression of the sensible and jouissance. The opposition is not between form and force, or rather that one confuses form and structure! Force is nothing other than the energy that folds, which wrinkles the text and makes of it a work, a difference, that is to say, a form.[125]

[122] See the discussion in Kazuo Ohno and Yoshito Ohno, *Kazuo Ohno's World*, trans. John Barrett, Middletown, CT: Wesleyan University Press, 2004, p.21.

[123] Ibid. Tamotsu Watanabe was the author of a score of books on those subjects, including: *Kabuki gekihiyo*, Tokyo: Asahi Shinbunsha, 1994; *Butai to iu shina*, Tokyo: Shinchosha, 1994. Watanabe tended to assimilate Butoh into Noh and other traditional Japanese theatrical arts, an assimilation Kazuo Ohno was not as interested in, and Hijikata fiercely if paradoxically rejected.

[124] See Jean-François Lyotard, *Libidinal Economy*, trans. Iain Hamilton Grant, Bloomington, IN: Indiana University Press, [1974] 1993.

[125] Jean-François Lyotard, *Discours, figure*, Paris: Klincksieck, 1974, p.14.

Lyotard can only act here as a supplement, for various reasons: his version of force is beholden to Freud and the death drive, the precise target of Deleuze and Guattari in *Anti-Oedipus* who substitute Artaud's 'body without organs' as a nonequilibrium thermodynamic model against the equilibrium thermodynamics of the death instinct however close the two notions might at times appear; philosophically Lyotard is a son of Freud rather than Nietzsche as is the case with Artaud, Deleuze and Guattari and Foucault; and Lyotard often seems to carry forward, in David Rodowick's terms, a hermeneutic model of 'linguistic surface and libidinal depth,'[126] as opposed to the body without organs that disregards metaphors of surface/depth.[127] Despite all these differences, Lyotard's model is still worth invoking here since it proffers a non-dialectical schema of the unconscious.[128] And it is a notion of language and signification based in the body, not on chains of structuralist signifiers. This lends it some use in Artaud's struggle, which, as later paraphrased by 'anti-psychiatrist' David Cooper, is based on the reality that the unconscious is not structured like a language, but rather that language must be structured like the unconscious.[129] This also follows from Lyotard's model, in that there is a spatialization, an exteriority that discourse cannot 'interiorize as *signification*.'[130] Any discourse or *énoncé* for Lyotard is 'plunged into a gestural space that surrounds it…riddled from within by deictic holes whose function is to indicate positionality in space (here/there) and in time (now/then).'[131] This relation of body and space draws on language but is incommensurable with it, all returns to the 'primary intimacy of the body, its space (and time).'[132] The radical heterogeneity suggested here between any linguistic system and visual space Artaud extends into a radical disjunction between all sensory modalities – the eye, the ear, the voice – which do not rest on any common ground. Whereas in Lyotard arguably there is no transcendence or hierarchy of one modality or faculty over the other, or canceling out of one by the other, in the later Artaud there is indeed a Nietzschean battle for supremacy in which the modality with the greater force wins out. This is but one of Artaud's legacies from his experience with the Tarahumaras in 1936, but it is one of the most significant and lasting ones.[133]

---

126 David N. Rodowick, *Reading the Figural, Or, Philosophy After the New Media*, Durham, NC & London: Duke University Press, 2001, p.10.

127 For further discussion of this aspect of the 'body without organs' see the section 'A spherical body' in Chapter VI.

128 Lyotard, *Discours, figure*, p.52.

129 David Cooper, *The Language of Madness*, Harmondsworth & New York, NY: Penguin Books, 1978, p.22.

130 Lyotard, *Discours, figure*, p.13.

131 David N. Rodowick, *Reading the Figural*, p.6. Rodowick presents a cogent description of Lyotard's contribution, especially in pp.1-18.

132 Lyotard, *Discours, figure*, p.39.

133 For the discussion of this conflict among the faculties in Artaud, see the last section

The form this conflict takes for Lyotard is one of negative spaces or negativities that inhabit both language and sight. For Lyotard there is a form of negativity that is at the 'foundation of our spatial existence, mobility constituting depth.'[134] But there is another order that crosses both that of language and spatiality, that of the 'figure' or 'figural' that is strictly unrepresentable. It can only be indicated in a 'lateral fashion,' it is the 'proper space of desire, the stakes in the struggle that painters and poets have ceaselessly launched against the return of the Ego and the text.'[135] When Lyotard writes of two terms that are not placed on the same plane or in reversible positions, but rather of heterogeneous states that are juxtaposed in an 'irreversible anachrony,'[136] he sounds quite close to Artaud's practices. In fact, the 'figural' as Lyotard describes it functions remarkably like the 'hieroglyph' as it is illuminated in Artaud's art criticism of the 1920's and addresses in Mexico City in 1936 published as *Messages révolutionaires*,[137] places where this evanescent notion is perhaps clearest in Artaud's *œuvre*.[138] Yet this overwhelming positivity of desire that is the unrepresentable 'figural' ultimately derives from the repetition of the death drive, a force that will undermine or disarticulate any structure.[139] Lyotard's innovation lies not in this recourse to Freud's death instinct but is in the consequences of this for his theory of the unconscious and desire – force in the form of desire does not signify, yet it has sense; in Lyotard not only is the unconscious not structured 'like a language,' it is a highly mobile and unstable form that is not a structure at all.[140] Constructing sense, Lyotard argues, entails deconstructing signification, and 'there is no model for this evasive figuration.'[141]

A strong virtue of Lyotard's work here, and a link to Guattari's creative use of linguistics, is his stressing of the non-linguistic aspects of Freud's *Traumarbeit*, or dream-work – the workings of the *Traumarbeit* all involve the creation of a visible figure/s or space (the figures of condensation, displacement, conditions of representability, secondary revision for example) that draws on the spatial dimensions left out of linguistics, it privileges seeing and undoes saying. In this

in Chapter II, the section by that name in Chapter III, and various sections, for example on Artaud's 1947-8 notebooks and the radio broadcasts, in Chapter VI.

134 Lyotard, *Discours, figure*, p.56.

135 Ibid., p.135.

136 Ibid., p.137.

137 Collected in volume VIII of Artaud's *Œuvres complètes*.

138 See the discussion of these essays in Chapter II.

139 In Deleuze this role is assumed by the disarticulation of the perpetually or eternally recurring movement of time, of being as Nietzchean becoming. See the development of this in David N. Rodowick, *Gilles Deleuze's Time Machine*, Durham, NC: Duke University Press, 1997.

140 Rodowick, *Reading the Figural*, p.9. In this, as Rodowick notes, Lyotard is in broad agreement with Deleuze and Guattari.

141 Lyotard, *Discours, figure*, p.19.

process of destabilisation, what Freud in *Interpreting Dreams* (1899) termed word and thing-presentations are rearranged for their potential in bringing out the figural. The early Freud was still open to the idea that the case of hysteria, for example, 'does not take linguistic usage as its model at all.'[142] In Lyotard's version, the dream-work only pretends to have linguistic signification, but in its replacing of texts by figures it is not recuperable by visual language or semiosis either. Lyotard emphasises (sounding much like Artaud) how 'the dream-work is not a language...[it is] discourse and figure at the same time, the work lost in hallucinatory scenography, originary violence.'[143] The figural, emerging from primal fantasy or desire, can only de-form or violently distort what it comes into contact with. In Lyotard's view, then, the figural is not merely a gap or chiasmus between sight and sound, but a radically unconscious, incommensurable realm. It is inherently transgressive, an 'other space,' that 'takes words for things' and that carries an 'energetics indifferent to the unity of the whole.'[144] This 'other space' is a 'matrix' which is not an origin but an 'initial nonplace.'[145] This 'nonplace,' that generates forms and images and verbalisations, yet is not captured by any linguistic or plastic representation or order, 'is difference itself.'[146] Acting thus, the form as recognisable figure is disrupted as much as linguistic discourse.[147] This powerful disfiguration, or variously 'unbinding' in Lyotard's words, or 'principle of figurality,' is none other than the death drive revealed.[148]

In further limning this incommensurable realm of the figural, Lyotard locates it as the *entremonde* or 'between world,' the *Zwischenwelt* of which artist Paul Klee writes. Klee termed these not always visible worlds 'between' worlds, since 'I sense it present between the worlds that our senses can perceive externally, and because internally I can assimilate it well enough to be able to project it outside myself in symbolic form. It is in this direction that children, the mad, and the primitives have conserved – or rediscovered – the faculty of seeing.'[149] As Lyotard notes, this discussion takes place as a fairly anguished one concerning the role of imagination, Klee so strongly emphasising that such visions must be 'sufficiently assimilated (the between world) in order to project it *outside of*

[142] Sigmund Freud and Josef Breuer, *Studies on Hysteria*, trans. James and Alix Strachey, Harmondsworth: Penguin, 1986, pp.254-5.

[143] Lyotard, *Discours, figure*, p.270.

[144] Ibid., pp.275; 277.

[145] Ibid., p.271.

[146] Ibid., p.278.

[147] As Lyotard writes, 'the images the matrix generates are both sharply defined and blurred at the same time. The effect is as if multiple scenes, having certain segments or areas, some plastic element only, in common, were superimposed on the same film, but at the right exposure.' Ibid., pp.327-8.

[148] Ibid., p.354.

[149] Klee cited ibid., n.32. p.224. This quote is taken from Felix Klee, *P. Klee par lui-même et son fils Felix Klee*, Paris: Les libraires associés, 1963.

the self.'[150] It is emphatically not a matter of the subjective imagination for Klee, which inspires Lyotard's description of *entremonde* as 'an other possible nature,' that is without model, and that does not fall into the subjective.[151] Lyotard uses Klee as his example since Klee's paintings do not 'write' with geometries like the cubist painters, but are concerned rather with nonspatial perception, the unrepresentable province of the virtual and the figural. They do not outline signifiers or draw a contour of a silhouette, Lyotard argues, rather they present a 'trace of energy.'[152] Whereas Lyotard sees the figural occupying a nonspatial place in the primary processes of the unconscious, drawn on by Klee but not the cubists, in Artaud's art criticism of the 1920's these artists' virtues are often merged. Klee is a 'mental painter' who presents 'cosmic syntheses where all secret objectivity in things is rendered sensible.'[153] Although Artaud's Theater of cruelty can be seen as evoking the figural in its own light, for Artaud there is a process of outlining, of *cerner*, of a 'culture in space'[154] that cubism also explores in its skein of lines. The 'later' Artaud does not herald this outlining as showing the actual hieroglyphic lineaments of reality but rather congratulates it, as in his 16 January 1946 letter to painter Georges Braque, on the 'putting into question of the linear occult world.'[155]

Yet for all the radicality and disruptiveness of Lyotard's figural, and its apparent kinship with the primal forces Artaud also wants to erupt, it remains an aesthetic concept. The figural may distort and disrupt any recognisable form, but 'it works' as a 'trace of energy' that is a 'plastic possibility.'[156] The unplaceable 'space' of primary processes of the unconscious also preserves the figural as a space of aesthetic or artistic possibility. Hence we have the crucial reliance on the aesthetic that characterises Lyotard's writings throughout the 1970's and '80s. As David Rodowick points out, in contrast Deleuze resorts to the older category of *aesthesis*, or sensation, and the aesthetic dimension does not even remotely hold the same pride of place as it does with Lyotard.[157] In regard to Artaud, whether during his engagement with the Paris surrealists 1926-9, or after his release from Rodez in May 1946, art and the 'aesthetic' is an intimate part of the matrix of vicious repression of family, church, and state – it has to be

---

150 Ibid.

151 Ibid., pp.224-5.

152 Ibid., p.238.

153 Artaud I:1, 1956, p.196.

154 Artaud, *Œuvres*, p.702.

155 Artaud XIV:1, 1978, p.157. See the beginning of Chapter II for a discussion of Artaud's art criticism and its elaboration of his idea of hieroglyphic space and 'occult geometry.'

156 Lyotard, *Discours, figure*, p.238.

157 Rodowick, *Reading the Figural*, pp.17-8.

refused at all costs.[158] So while the figural as a resource for art is paradoxically a limitation in looking at Artaud, it retains a strong relevance in other ways. This is because in the figural there is a compact hieroglyph, an intermixing and penetration of word and image that is common to our electronic media environment today and finds its theoretical complement in some ways in the liberation of 'writing' from discourse in thinkers like Derrida and Foucault, who open up the discussion of writing onto the manifold dimensions of spacing and the visible. Despite its use in Lyotard, there is in the figural many prime components that only with much discomfort or violence can be reconciled with strictly aesthetic categories or regimes.[159] It is important to spend some time with this notion in a project on Artaud because the figural broaches so many of the important issues of the hieroglyph, that hybrid of image and text and sound, that suggest its force, virtuality and fluidity; Lyotard discovers it in the 'primary processes' of the Freudian unconscious, the early Artaud in the sinews of the dream, in the inhuman movements of Balinese dancers, in virtual planes of his various internal states – in short, he finds it as a kind of matrix of the universe. It may have 'logic,' but it is a profoundly disfiguring, threatening one. Artaud combines all the various senses of a 'hieroglyph' in his theoretical writing on the theatre, and in his work, which is innovative whether in 1935 or in 1947 in terms of sound, and seeks to produce an unassimilable shock or image. The forceful original way that Artaud uses this resource brings out all the immense power a thinker like Lyotard grants to the figural, while stripping these notions of any psychoanalytic context they might have. While Freud compared the language of the dream 'rebus' to hieroglyphs and Chinese ideograms, he did so to formulate an internally coherent methodology for dream interpretation;[160] Artaud, on the other hand, as a good surrealist, exploited the dream as a resource to find the 'absolute image' that would overwhelm the spectator/viewer, producing an absolute fissure, in the case of his film scenarios a 'collision enacted on the eyes.'[161]

---

158 The most eloquent statement of this may be Artaud's last communication with André Breton in a letter of 1 March 1947, where he refuses participation in a new surrealist exhibition and denounces in no uncertain terms the Parisian art world. See Artaud, *Œuvres*, pp.1207-18.

159 Rodowick, *Reading the Figural*, p.33.

160 Typical characterisations of the 'hieroglyphic' and 'archaic' qualities of dreams, emphasising how ambiguous and reversible their contents and meanings can be, are found in Sigmund Freud, *Introductory Lectures to Psychoanalysis*, trans. and ed. James Strachey, New York, NY & London: W.W.Norton, 1966, pp.178-81; 228-32.

161 Artaud V, 1964, p.19.

The revelation of how the 'hieroglyph' works in Artaud's film scenarios

Lyotard's notion of the 'figural,' its 'hieroglyphic' configuration of the 'unconscious' is a valuable entrée into how the hieroglyph appears in so many different forms in Artaud. The 'hieroglyph' becomes a key category in Artaud's theatre manifestoes published in 1938, and while the Theater of cruelty had many sources and inspirations, it is difficult to overestimate the admiration Artaud felt for the Balinese theatre troupe he saw in Paris in 1931.[162] Its panoply of effects was one of the strongest models for Artaud's projected theatre. With pride of comparison, Artaud wrote of the 'striking similarity' of a terrifying devil of the Balinese, which he thought was of Tibetan origin, to a puppet with leafy green nails, hands extended with white gelatine, in one of the first plays of his Alfred Jarry theatre (1926-30). Watching the Balinese, Artaud sensed that they had worked from a 'state before language and were able to choose their language: music, gestures, movements, words.'[163] They were for Artaud indeed a 'new language,' signs set alive and in motion, with real effects. It was nothing less than a 'revealing of matter,' through 'gestures made to endure.'[164] It was a 'Speech before words.'[165] The Balinese theatre, its actors in their costumes, 'composed veritable hieroglyphs which live and move,' hieroglyphs in three-dimensions, radiating obscure and 'mysterious signs' repressed by the West.[166] It was strongly inspired from the Balinese that Artaud, in his second manifesto of the Theater of cruelty gives perhaps his fullest description of the proposed theatre, a theatre whose combination of sounds, cries, objects, rhythms, is the creation of a 'true physical language based on signs and no longer words.'[167] Artaud makes clear that this is a theatre where in the use of words, it is their 'incantatory sense' that is 'truly magic' that takes precedence, through their forms, the 'sensible emanations,' and not only through their logical meaning, or *sens*. What will preside over this 'pure theatrical language' is the 'spirit of the most ancient hieroglyphs.'[168] When Artaud in the Theater of cruelty manifestoes speaks of hieroglyphs, loosing primal forces on the stage, or raising the human body 'to the dignity of signs,'[169] forms depicted in 'their encounters with Becoming,'[170] he is harking back to what he saw at the time as the sacred origins of drama. This is the

[162] Artaud IV, 1964, pp.64-81.
[163] Ibid., p.74.
[164] Ibid., p.72.
[165] Ibid.
[166] Ibid., p.73.
[167] Ibid., p.149.
[168] Ibid.
[169] Ibid., p.112.
[170] Ibid., p.84.

original drama, which according to Hinduism issued forth from the breath of Brahma, in Indian mythology. Likewise Noh theatre was said to originate in a dance of the gods. Artaud after Rodez will relentlessly strip out any religious or mystical connotations to his work, and to his prior work, but in the manifestoes of the early 1930's there is still a sacred element, albeit one in Artaud's unsettling and macabre version. Even in this period Artaud uses words like 'metaphysical,' 'religious,' 'mystical' or 'alchemical' solely for their power of evoking another indescribable world, another inexpressible reality, and so their use has more to do with shock of preconceived expectations than any conventional wisdom of religion. At the end of his essay 'Metaphysics and the Mise-en-scéne' Artaud says as much, making light of words linked to his title – 'it suffices elsewhere to pronounce the words *religious* or *mystic* to be confounded with a priest, or a profoundly illiterate monk outside a Buddhist temple, good for no more than physically turning the prayer wheels.'[171]

In terms of how this 'hieroglyph' is supposed to act on the spectator or viewer there are intriguing glimpses provided by one of Artaud's most fragmentary if brilliant contributions, that of his film scripts and manifestoes. Artaud's engagement with the cinema was intense if short-lived, primarily in the years 1927-30, and by 1933 Artaud is already denouncing the cinema's 'idiotic world of images' and 'closed world of vibrations.'[172] Yet it gave birth to the very first surrealist film, *The Seashell and the Clergyman* (1928), directed by Germaine Dulac[173] from a scenario by Artaud and Artaud's ideas about montage reappear and structure his accounts of the Indian Tarahumara ceremonies. His account of the dream and critique of the dream reverberate throughout his later work but are found in a pristine state in his film writings. In his theatre writings Artaud sought to bring out the virtual plane he associated with the 'double,' a notion of the virtual pioneered in several of his 1925-7 writings on his own mental, physical, 'inner' states, what he called his inner 'culture of the void.'[174] It was this 'double' that must be activated for theatre to ignite its sacred roots. This is also at the heart of why initially Artaud had such high hopes for the new art form of cinema. As film scholar Jacques Aumont has argued, film especially draws on these relations, since to 'montage is to manipulate the images…in such as way as to draw out the virtual in them.'[175] For Artaud this meant that film could produce a 'kind of physical exhilaration that communicates directly to the brain the rotation of

[171] Ibid., pp.55-6. For more on Artaud's consideration of the 'dead language' of words like 'religious,' 'mystic' and 'metaphysical' see the discussion in Chapter II.

[172] Artaud III, 1961, p.99.

[173] For the significance of Dulac's work in film, see Tami Williams, *Germaine Dulac: A Cinema of Sensations*, Champaign, IL: University of Illinois Press, 2014.

[174] Artaud VIII, 1971, p.20.

[175] Jacques Aumont, *Amnésies: Fictions du cinéma d'après Jean-Luc Godard*, Paris: P.O.L., 1999, p.18.

images' where 'the spirit riots and revels in itself outside of all representation. This sort of virtual power of the images probes at the foundation of spirit for possibilities unutilised today. The cinema essentially reveals an entire occult life with which it puts us directly in relation.'[176] Artaud saw his scenario *The Seashell and the Clergyman*, the only scenario of Artaud's that was produced, as an attempt to 'participate in this research of a subtle order, of a hidden life that I wanted to render plausible, plausible and as real as the other.'[177] Cinema had arrived at just the point where human thought had lost any power of symbol and was exhausted in a play of representations. This was an epoch where 'insensible substance takes body, seeks to attain the light. Cinema takes us closer to this substance.'[178] Cinema has a unique ability to unite thought and life, that life which would become more and more inseparable from the primordial powers of the mind. It was not enough, in Artaud's vision, to illustrate by way of dream-states, or representations of dream-states, as in the early surrealist films of Luis Buñuel and Jean Cocteau, but to show the birth and movement of thought itself, not the dream but to reveal the sinewy structure of dreams. That is why the scenario of *The Seashell and the Clergyman* sought to show the '*mechanics of a dream*, without truly being a dream itself. This is to say that it restores the pure work of thought.'[179] Surpassing the usual preoccupations of the cinema of his time, Artaud's ambition was to decisively 'pose the problem of *expression*.'[180] These hopes gave way to a deep disillusionment, barely six years later Artaud is attacking this 'idiotic world of images':

> All fantasies based on a slow or accelerated motion apply only to a closed world of vibrations which does not have the talent of enriching and nourishing itself on its own; the idiotic world of images that sticks like glue to the myriads of retinas, will never perfect the image we are able to make of it. So the poetry that cannot break away from all that is only a tentative poetry, the poetry of what might have been, and we cannot expect the cinema to restore the Myths of man and of life today.[181]

Some of this animus would stem from Artaud's personal disappointment that he was asked neither to act in or help direct *The Seashell and the Clergyman*, and what Artaud saw as Germaine Dulac's imposition of a 'logic' upon the picture, even if it were the logic of a dream. According to one account, but widely considered apocryphal by others, this led Artaud, the poet Robert Desnos, and other friends of Artaud's to disrupt its showing, when it was first screened by

[176] Artaud III, 1961, p.80.

[177] Ibid., p.82.

[178] Ibid., p.81.

[179] Ibid., pp.77-8. Italics in original.

[180] Ibid., p.78. Italics in original.

[181] Ibid., p.99.

Studio des Ursulines in Montmartre 8 February 1928, shouting that Dulac was a 'cow' and smashing the mirrors in the lobby as they were shown the door. The next year the film would be decisively overshadowed by Salvador Dalí and Luis Buñuel's far more successful surrealist provocation *Un Chien andalou* and then by *L'Âge d'or* the year after that. Another aspect of Artaud's disillusionment would derive from just how advanced and premonitory Artaud's conception of the cinema would prove to be. Artaud in his brief engagement produced some real innovation.

For Artaud in his film writings sound and image were opposed: sound, for instance, 'bursts into the room,' and acts with far more intensity and power than the image, which he describes as 'only a kind of illusion of sound,' limited by its nature as a direct translation or 'transposition' of the real; so between the two, 'there is no possible identification.'[182] Against any notion of film naturalism or realism Artaud's filmic strategy called for these incompatible elements to jar and grate against each other with as much extremity as possible, as part of his search for a film form, that, in one instance, would have 'purely visual sensations in which the force would come from a collision exacted on the eyes,'[183] a resonant and fruitful coincidence of phrasing given that *Un Chien andalou* was in production at the time. Another part of Artaud's innovation is the use and depiction of time. In the scenario *18 Seconds* Artaud juxtaposed the 'real' or 'conscious' clock-time of eighteen seconds of thoughts going through the head of a young man, that constitutes the actual duration of the scenario, 'seconds passing with infinite slowness across the screen,' with the extraordinary drama depicted of the events and imagination of his 'inner' world, where time is boundless.[184] In *The Butcher's Revolt* an obsessive, even banal snippet of dialogue from the butcher, 'I've had enough of cutting the meat without eating it'[185] is set off alone in blocks of white type across a background of black void, with all images of the scenario interrupted, halted. This disjunction of sound and image, of words treated as spatial, plastic objects, of sound as shock, the use of intertitles emphasised as separate elements disclocated from any other narrative aspects, would largely lie fallow until Jean-Luc Godard's more and more decisive departures from commercial movie-making in the mid-1960's. It is why Deleuze discusses Artaud as perhaps the prime progenitor of the 'unlinked' or 'time-image' based on differentiation and disjunction, not association, in his *Cinema 2*.[186]

These ideas of disjunction profoundly colour Artaud's experience and interpretation of the Tarahumara rites shortly afterward in 1936. When Artaud goes

---

[182] Ibid., p.377.

[183] Artaud V, 1964, p.19.

[184] Artaud III, 1961, pp.11-15.

[185] Ibid., p.51.

[186] Gilles Deleuze, *Cinema 2: The Time-Image*, trans. by Hugh Tomlinson and Robert Galeta, Minneapolis, MN: University of Minnesota Press, 1989.

up into the Sierra Tarahumaras to do peyote rites with the Tarahumara Indians Artaud's experience of the rites is eminently hieroglyphic. He describes 'things that emerged from my spleen or my liver were shaped like the letters of a very ancient and mysterious alphabet chewed by an enormous mouth…these signs were swept in every direction in space.'[187] Artaud's account is nothing if not dramatic. The peyote rites are credited with producing an immense 'reversal,' 'I said *reversed* to the other side of things, as if a terrible force had been given that you be *restored* to that which exists on the other side.'[188] With the peyote priest spelling out large letters in the earth and tracing figure 8's in the sky with his large sword Artaud could understandably believe he was witnessing the movement of the 'sacred hieroglyphs' whose awakening he had called for in his *The Theater and Its Double* manifestoes, written but not yet published at the time. In the Tarahumara ceremonies Artaud to a great extent found, through his encounter with Ciguri the 'master of the universe' revealed by peyote, what he had abandoned finding through the cinema. The Tarahumara experience was so profound and traumatic a rupture for Artaud that one can well postulate a pre and post-Mexico Artaud, so shattering were its implications. It fulfilled many of Artaud's artistic hopes, since he saw the Rites of the Tutuguri as a living Theater of cruelty and even writes that the three days on peyote were the 'most happy of my existence.'[189] It was also largely anticipated in Artaud's abortive cinema – the cacophony, the splitting of sound and image, the 'absolute' images written in the air, the moving from one incommensurable element to another. With the Tarahumara Indians Artaud has seen the dream laid bare.

Artaud's investigation bears analogy with that of Aby Warburg and Sergei Eisenstein, also seminal figures of mid-20th century art, who followed in different ways the 'anthropological turn' of Nietzsche in his *The Birth of Tragedy* (1872); all three had their course irrevocably marked by their encounter with the 'primitive,' with extant rites, although they cannot be entirely encapsulated in these encounters. In the case of Artaud, he thought he had found a veritable Theater of cruelty, leading to *To have done with the judgment of god*, filled with *bruitage* and effects that simulated the Tarahumara ceremonies. All this talk of 'primitive' or tribal ritual inevitably raises the question of Artaud's relation to this ritual, whose theater manifestoes call for a return to ritual or 'alchemical' theater. Although Artaud is at one point in the 1930's immersed in mysticism and studies of magick[190] and ritual, his transformation of ritual is central to the

---

187 Artaud IX, 1971, pp.32-3.

188 Ibid., p.32.

189 Ibid., p.117.

190 I use the Early Modern spelling for magick instead of the more common and general magic precisely to indicate it as a practice, a means for altering and transforming the world according to one's intentions, that has little in common with other senses of magic such as stage magic or magic as a sense of wonder. This was the sense of its use

movement and change in the notion of the hieroglyph that occurs by the end of his life. That is why so much space in this project, in Chapters II, III, and IV especially, is devoted to analyses of ritual and Artaud's relation to it. At the end of his life Artaud is far from advocating any ritual that produces social reconciliation and unity, in fact looking at the example of Artaud shows how distinct the idea of sorcery and its project of magical defense and transformation is from religious ritual. Inspired from the Tarahumaras, Artaud's own Theater of cruelty becomes an apocalyptic one that requires the end of the known world. As head of the Bureau of Surrealist Research in 1925 Artaud directed one of the only two positive letters in a battery of poison pen attacks to the Dalai Lama in Tibet. At the end of his life after his release from Rodez in 1946 priests of all stripes are condemned, and the suggestion of any mysticism in his own work is relentlessly denied. This is not merely a semantic or ideological or theological tic, it is central to the redefinition of Artaud's practices. It is an essential component of Artaud's world view where hieroglyphic reality is no longer operating for him; it is no longer a sacred one whose glimpses were called for in *The Theater and Its Double* and Artaud searched for in Mexico. Artaud's assault on mysticism paradoxically makes sense as he replaces the subordination of time to space characteristic of the vast majority of tribal ritual (and to which his theatre manifestoes can be reconciled) with the liberation of the 'true body' from time and space, as the ferocity of its gestures propel it into infinity.

The persistence of myth: Artaud the mystic without mysticism, the shaman without community

When Artaud emerges from nine years of insane asylums, he is unremitting in his assault on mystical systems of all kinds. A text from October 1946 is typical, which starts with one of his incantations in bold:

trita yoga
dvipura yoga
dretta yuga
kali yuga soutra

---

and introduction in Heinrich Cornelius Agrippa's *De Occulta Philosophia* (1533), the 1651 translation of which was *Three Works Concerning Occult Philosophy, Or Magick*. This use of the word magick continued and was popularised by 20th century occultists like Aleister Crowley and writers in his tradition such as Kenneth Grant. For Artaud's conception of art as action or means of altering the world, see the section 'Casting Spells' in Chapter IV. A detailed exposition of different forms of the occult and their difference from spiritualism, from an author very close to the Paris surrealists is Sarane Alexandrian's *Histoire de la philosophie occulte*, Paris: Éditions Seghers, 1983.

I manipulate men and the beings
But also and above all the institution of ages
I manipulate the ages of a great inexistent clock.
This is the same order of things I remake night and day since 1 year and 6 months through the rupture of every movement and every axis and the institution of an astral city.

. . .

These instructors are criminals who before the current human state established things following an order which asphyxiates us.
man is no longer free
because nature thinks before him,
how?
Following a fixed measure established by these instructors.[191]

As an autochthonic creation, Artaud challenges all 'manipulators,' 'priests,' and 'instructors' of the cosmic order. Here, the 'Measures,' or '*les Temps*' that previously passes the 'magic of existence' through a single chest of an actor of the Theater of cruelty in 'A Seraphin's Theater,' is ontologically self-created, much as in 15th century Asha'rite Islamic theology the world is created anew each instant, willed into existence by a joyful Allah, except that here Artaud has usurped the post of God. He displaces mystical concerns and arrangements by his autoreference to the 'body without organs,' his self-creation.

For the later Artaud, 'the occult is born out of laziness.'[192] 'The extreme point of mysticism,' Artaud writes, 'I hold it now in the real and in my body, like a toilet broom.'[193] Considering one of the origins of poetry, in the West as in numerous traditional cultures, in lists and list-making,[194] it is perhaps significant that we see Artaud making numerous lists of these 'manipulators' and in what he no longer believes. In one of his first texts upon his return to Paris, his 'Toward a Xylophone of the Obscene from a Conscience in Agony,' Artaud begins by listing twenty-five facets in which he no longer believes, beginning with 'words,' and ending with both 'heroism' and 'cowardice.'[195] To call this apophatic or negative theology is to short shrift Artaud on his originality and defuses his hatred of religious orders.

The early Artaud is insistent that through his declamations and special breathing techniques he is evoking latent and transformative hieroglyphic qualities. But in the late Artaud they are purged and shredded of any 'religious' con-

---

191 Artaud XXIV, 1988, p.27.

192 Artaud, *Œuvres*, p.1211.

193 Artaud XIV:2, 1978, p.68.

194 See Jerome Rothenberg, *Technicians of the Sacred*, Berkeley, CA: University of California Press, 1985; *Shaking the Pumpkin*, New York, NY: Doubleday, 1972. Also Larry Fagin, *The List Poem*, New York, NY: Teachers and Writers Collaborative, 1991.

195 Artaud XXIV, 1988, p.9.

tent, including any influence from his previously beloved Kabbalah or numerology. So what are they? Although the Renaissance alchemist Mylius could say 'For those who have the symbol the passage is easy,'[196] for Artaud it is no question of symbol or myth or even image to hold onto. He makes this most clear perhaps in his thoughts on Gérard de Nerval, a *poète maudit* to whose example Artaud often returned. In 'On the Chimeras,'[197] Artaud, on 7 March 1946, still at Rodez, in an essay-length unsent letter, writes that:

> the proof of the meaning of lines of the Chimeras cannot be reached through Mythology, alchemy, tarots, mysticism, dialectics or the semantics of psychurgy, but uniquely through diction. All the lines have been written, first of all, to be heard, concretized by loud, full voices and it's not even that their music sheds light on them and that they can then speak by simple modulations of sound, and sound by sound, for it is only outside the printed or written page that an authentic line of poetry can take on meaning and there it requires the space of breath between the flight of all the words. The words fly from the page and soar. They fly from the heart of the poet who drives home their force of untranslatable assault.[198]

Nerval's 'les Chimères'[199] poems have to be, upon '*each* reading, *expectorated*' – 'For it is in this way that their hieroglyphs become clear.' Then, Artaud argues, 'all the keys of their so-called occultism die out in the finally useless and ominous convolutions of brain matter.'[200] These resorts to occultism and mysticism are a denial, an avoidance of pain:

> in fear of entering it too close, of likewise suffering it too close, I mean for fear of knowing the soul of Gérard de Nerval as one knows plague boboes, or the frightening black marks on a suicide's throat...like priests in the liturgies of the mass flee the spasms of a crucified man.[201]

The chimeras of Nerval are 'unusual and marvelous machines of consciousness,' with a life that 'seems to *precede* Mythology and history, and not, as in Shakespeare and other poets, *issue* from them.' Only a few 'rare great poets in history have wielded the power of being, and the creative emission of objects;'[202] the

---

[196] Quoted in C.G. Jung, *Psychology and Alchemy*, Volume XII of *Collected Works*, trans. R.F.C. Hull, Princeton, NJ: Princeton University Press, 1968, p.225.

[197] Artaud XI, 1974, pp.184-201.

[198] Here I am using directly the translation by Clayton Eshleman and Bernard Bador in Artaud, *Watchfiends & Rack Screams*, p.53.

[199] English translation found in Robert Duncan, *Bending the Bow*, New York, NY: New Directions, 1968. Reprinted later in Gérard de Nerval, *Aurèlia and other writings*, Boston, MA: Exact Change, 1995. Duncan was the author of an early homage to Artaud in the 1950's, see 'Distant Counsels of Artaud,' in Duncan, *Derivations*, p.97.

[200] Artaud, *Watchfiends & Rack Screams*, p.54.

[201] Ibid.

[202] Ibid.

products of history, mythology, the tarot and alchemy, have come from this 'internal animistic current,' and not the other way around.

It is difficult to imagine a stronger repudiation, in this aspect, of the earlier Artaud, the 'old Artaud assassinated/in the other life/and who will not enter any longer this one,'[203] the Artaud of the '20s and '30s who often immersed himself in the occult and occultist literature and mythology. In the '20s Artaud had written 'it is necessary to relearn how to be a mystic, at least in a certain fashion.'[204] In 1946, Artaud calls 'contemplative states…the states of a lubricious buzzard, of astrayers of deeply grounded energy, of those with their *anomaly* circumcised. The *anomaly* being the evidence.'[205] Artaud now 'reborn' sees alchemy, for instance, as a 'determined number of scientific abortions…the now outdated cooking of the semantics of a ritual.'[206] It is a negative work, in contrast to the explosions of being in a Nerval work, work that is '*animated*, the Great Work of a metamorphosis of the very principle of action, an expansion outside the unknown of innocent consciousness foundation of the most incredible explosions of language that a human being has ever reckoned.'[207] Such works, like those of Artaud's elective affinities with Baudelaire, Edgar Poe, Hölderlin, the Comte de Lautréamont, François Villon and Rimbaud, are the exact opposite of what Artaud calls mystical science's 'historical symbolism of affective fabulations, to an already existent semantics of feelings and their forms.'[208]

Artaud is insistent that this explosion of being is 'untranslatable.' It is all of a piece with the gauntlet he throws down in the middle of 'Here Lies':

All true language
is incomprehensible
like the clap
of clapperdudgeons;
or the claptrap (cat house)
of the toothed thighbone (bloodied).[209]

Artaud here typically ensnared in the coils of material life – Artaud's *la claque/ du claque-dents* translated as 'clapperdudgeon' meaning a wretch, a brothel, or 'a beggar born;' 'claptrap' here meaning not false applause so much as a brothel where one gets the 'clap.'[210] Here Artaud both affirms the commonplace that

[203] Artaud XII, 1974, p.52.

[204] Artaud I:1, 1956, p.215.

[205] In 'Letter to Peter Watson,' written 27 July 1946, in *Watchfiends & Rack Screams*, p.88; Artaud XII, 1974, p.238.

[206] Artaud, *Watchfiends & Rack Screams*, p.56.

[207] Ibid., p.58.

[208] Ibid.

[209] Artaud in *Watchfiends & Rack Screams*, p.229; Artaud XII, 1974, p.95.

[210] See Eshleman's note on this translation in *Watchfiends & Rack Screams*, p.340.

once one participates in any ritual activity, one's conscious beliefs about the rightness or wrongness of it, or philosophical niceties, get swept away and Artaud certainly intends to bring off a new contemporary ritual, while he also affirms or advocates a more potent theatre of affect. Within weeks of his death, Artaud is still seeking to create this new theatre.

Artaud's work with breathing, variously described in the Theater of cruelty manifestoes, had become an enormously honed system by the end of his life, when he could maintain that:

> in the human breath sudden shifts and breaks of tone and, from one scream to another, abrupt transferences by which the openings and soarings of the entire body of things can be suddenly evoked, which can support or liquefy an organ like a tree you might prop up against the massy mountain of its forest.[211]

Through the projection of a breath and scream of sufficient intensity, the body could catapult itself 'up to those brilliantly lighted planes where the Superior Body is already waiting for it.'[212] So the *entremonde* or in-between world for the 'late' Artaud, as with the manifesto-writer of the '30s, is that disjunction or interval which, in the suspension of the scream, enables a fierce launching pad for his 'projection of the true body,' a crucible for his 'anatomies-in-action.' As Artaud had announced in one of his first and most effective poetic statements, with the Rimbaldian title, the *Fragments from a Journal in Hell* – 'I work in the unique duration.'[213] This duration Artaud suggests seems to come from the gap between modalities, much as he maintained in his essay 'Oriental and Occidental Theater' (1935) that 'all true feeling is in reality untranslatable. To express it is to betray it. But to translate it, this is to *dissimulate* it.'[214] For Artaud, 'true expression hides what it makes manifest,'[215] so he must continue to activate these limits of possible experience, of any possible language, in effect moving from one aspect of the hieroglyphic sign – its graphic inscription, for example – to another, its sounding for instance, creating 'meaning' through the very movement. Artaud helped inspire Gilles Deleuze's thinking about these matters, who in his book on Foucault describes how thinking can only appear in the 'interstices' or 'disjunction' (Artaud's 'duration') between speaking and seeing, in 'the space between the two…creating a flash of light in the midst of words, or unleashing a cry in the midst of visible things.'[216] The early Artaud is obsessed with capturing

---

[211] Artaud, 'Theatre and science,' *Artaud Anthology*, trans. Daniel Moore, pp.171-2; Artaud, *Œuvres*, pp.1546-7.

[212] Ibid., p.172; ibid., p.1547.

[213] Artaud I:1, 1964, p.113.

[214] Artaud IV, 1964, p.86. Italics in original.

[215] Ibid.

[216] Gilles Deleuze, *Foucault*, trans. and ed. Séan Hand, Minneapolis, MN: University of Minnesota Press, 1988, p.116.

the pure movement of thought. For Deleuze, thought makes both 'seeing and speaking attain their individual limits, such that the two are the common limit that both separates and links them.'[217] Artaud continues to battle against these barriers and attempt to breach them. He will write of his drawings 'not one properly speaking is a work,' but rather 'soundings and staggering blows in all directions of chance, possibility, luck, or destiny.'[218] As Artaud moved between modalities, he moved between mediums of writing, sound, performance and image. Similarly, in Artaud's view Vincent Van Gogh is both a devotee of 'pure painting' and a 'tremendous musician.'[219]

Artaud in his later phase no longer tried to possess or trap elusive pure thought but rather is intensively preoccupied with leaping the gaps and intervals of the void, affirming it even as his rhythm moves beyond and through it.[220] Artaud at Rodez and after is an extraordinary exemplar of what Deleuze will later call 'powers of the leap, the interval, the intensive and the instant; powers which only cover difference with more difference.'[221] Artaud's adamant insistence that these 'demons' or 'sign-bearers' (in Deleuze's terms)[222] are rooted in the vagaries of the body not the 'spirit' is a primary reason the later Artaud, however still at struggle with them, rejects God and mysticism. The figures of Jesus Christ and the cross are transformed in the tumult. In filling out his theory of cinema, where again Artaud plays a major role, Deleuze discovers that what is important is no longer any transcendent reality, or even belief in a transformed world – 'it is only, simply believing in the body.'[223] The cinema, in Deleuze's view, as if with eyes in the back of its head, takes up the position of a seer, 'giving discourse to the body, and, for this purpose, reaching the body before discourses, before words, before things are named: the 'first name,' and even before the first name.'[224] This kind of film writing that goes beyond all codes to the beginning of codes, to the body, is so discourse can begin again, in what Deleuze, discussing the films of Stan Brakhage, called 'the dawn of ourselves.'[225] Nearly a half-century before

---

217 Ibid., pp.116-7.

218 Artaud, 'Le Visage Humain,' *Œuvres*, p.1535.

219 Artaud XIII, 1974, p.47. See the section on Artaud's essay on Van Gogh in Chapter VI.

220 Here there is an echo of Guattari's finding that subjectivity always moves away from or counters the void, since it is its opposite. *See The Anti-Oedipus Papers*, p.55. For discussion of this issue of rhythm in Artaud see 'The case of Artaud's "Tutuguri" (1948)' in Chapter III.

221 Deleuze, *Difference and Repetition*, p.182. For development of this point see the section 'The conflict of the faculties' in Chapter III.

222 Ibid.

223 Deleuze, *Cinema 2*, p.172.

224 Ibid., pp.172-3.

225 Gilles Deleuze, *Cinema 1: The Movement-Image*, trans. Hugh Tomlinson and Barbara Habberjam, Minneapolis, MN: University of Minnesota Press, 1986, p.84.

these remarks, this is territory Artaud had already laid out, in much anguish and in blistering specifics. While never failing to rail against the 'Initiates,' the 'manipulators' or 'instructors,' the 'priests,' all 'the false monsters of the schism of spirituality and sensibility,'[226] Artaud articulates a landscape of the body, and of a new, or 'Superior Body,' that to date had only been conjured by such. Whether the Original Adam of Judaism, the Perfect Man of Islam, the reborn Christ of Christianity, the 'rainbow body'[227] of Tibetan Buddhism and various Tantric practices, the arena of Artaud's 'body without organs' had been a profoundly religious conception, dominated, in Artaud's parlance, by 'the judgment of god.' Yet by the end of his life, even the Tibetans, heralded in Artaud's 1925 'Address to the Dalai Lama,' are 'filthy Europeans after all;'[228] and the Balinese fare no better. What we have at the end of his life is an Artaud who has inexorably shredded, as in a series of moltings, 'religious' or mystical trappings; he is a startling image of singularity. Or, in poet Clayton Eshleman's words, 'a writhing piece of star gristle.'[229] That's why the movements of a Butoh dancer: the excruciating slow emergence of an insect from larvae, an ant dance, the blasted solitude of an now elderly and unwanted geisha, humans as if still entrapped in birth entrails, stricken gestures establishing what is inside and what is outside, remain sort of fitting dramatic images to Artaud. As dancer Tatsumi Hijikata, emulating the deathbed of Artaud found with shoe in hand, reads the shoe as a fish clenched in the teeth, as Artaud crossed over to the other side.

There are a number of shamanic coincidences in Artaud's terrible journey, so prominent they reoccur frequently in my account. Artaud after all is doing nothing other than probing different levels of realities. One of his many parallels with Nietzsche is that the latter continually exhorts the 'overman' to 'perish,' and

---

[226] Artaud, *Œuvres*, p.1547.

[227] The 'rainbow body' (*ja lü*) is the reputed dissolution of the physical body, the melting away of gross matter into a state of pure energy or light, each element of the body returning to the energy or type of light from which it arose. See Reginald Ray, *Secret of the Vajra World: The Tantric Buddhism of Tibet*, Volume II of *The World of Tibetan Buddhism*, Boston, MA & London: Shambhala Publications, 2002, pp.302; 323-5.

[228] See Artaud's 'Adresse au Dalaï-Lama,' *Œuvres*, p.138. The original, positive tribute to the Dalaï Lama is found in Artaud I:2, 1964, pp.262-3. At the time of the 'Address to the Dalai Lama' (1925) Artaud's close friend the poet and surrealist colleague Robert Desnos had referred to Eastern philosophy as 'the citadel of all hope,' see the discussion of the relationship of Surrealism and Buddhism in Maurice Nadeau, *Histoire du Surréalisme*, Paris: Seuil, 1945, pp.740-6. The writer René Daumal also espoused the East as a model, whose views were quite close to Artaud's; and the surrealists at one point considered an alliance with the 'orientalist' René Guénon. Nothing came of this, but Guénon was another favorite of Artaud's, see Florence de Mèredieu, *C'était Antonin Artaud*, Paris: Fayard, 2006, pp. 291; 302; 624. This turn toward the mystical is even more predominant in André Breton's writings after World War II. In his 'On Surrealism and Its Living Works' (1953) Breton concludes that surrealism is the 'road to Gnosis,' citing Guénon. See Breton, *Manifestoes of Surrealism*, p.304.

[229] Eshleman, *Watchfiends & Rack Screams*, p.43.

find joy in the extreme necessity of this perishing, much as the 'early' Artaud frequently writes of his impending crucifixion and the 'later' one writes of experiencing it. Writing 'You all do not suffer from what I have suffered,' Nietzsche tells his collection of 'higher men' that 'ever more, ever better ones of your kind shall perish – for it shall be ever worse and harder for you. Thus alone – thus alone, man grows to the height where lightning strikes and breaks him: lofty enough for lightning.' This lightning he did not wish 'to conduct it away: it shall learn to work for me.'[230] It is pertinent here that in the lore of shamanism, the adept is frequently initiated by a crisis, an induced state of death over which the initiated has no control – a spasm of insanity, epilepsy, but also often an actual bolt of lightning that strikes the initiate. In an ordeal that involves extraordinary suffering, the initiate is bodily dismembered, with entrails replaced with a 'new body' of quartz crystals, that are associated with lightning; indeed a shaman is often defined as one with a 'new body' that is 'stuffed with "solidified light."'[231] This new shaman, with a sacrificed but now re-membered body, is endowed with a new language to summon allies and banish foes, and often also takes on a new name. It is the shaman's duty to keep a sort of ecological balance and communication of the *axis mundi*, between the axes of the earth, sky and underworld via the 'World Tree' located at the 'Center of the World' (also referred to as the Bridge, Stair or Pillar). Journeys to the sky or underworld (in Native American culture as in many other shamanic-based cultures, the 'underworld' is ascended to through a ladder, or some other sort of bridge, it is reached through a hole or opening in the sky, no 'descent' is involved) are usually accompanied by rhythmic drumming; his healing ceremonies often include spitting, speaking in tongues and in an androgynous, falsetto voice.[232] These were all behaviors char-

230 Nietzsche, 'Thus Spoke Zarathustra,' pt. 4, *The Portable Nietzsche*, pp.400-1.

231 Mircea Eliade, *Shamanism: Archaic Techniques of Ecstasy*, trans. Willard R. Trask, Princeton, NJ: Princeton University Press, [1951] 1974, p.138.

232 All of these details are culled from Eliade's *Shamanism: Archaic Techniques of Ecstasy*. They are cited to show how much of Artaud's journey fits the itinerary of a typical shaman, as classically described. However, it is important to note the controversy of Eliade's conclusions: the ideas that shamanism all revolves around the originary belief in a celestial Supreme Being or Supreme God, and that it is primarily characterised by the ascents referenced here, have been profoundly disputed. See for instance Johan Reinhard, 'Shamanism and Spirit Possession' in *Spirit Possession in the Nepali Himalayas*, ed. John Hitchcock and Rex Jones, Westminster: Aris & Phillips, 1976. In Jane Monnig Atkinson's study of the prime shamanic ritual (the *mabolong*) of the Wana of Sulawesi, Indonesia, she finds the visionary travels Eliade describes are linked to relatively recent political changes in the composition of the tribe, not from some ur-form of shamanic experience; the Wana journey to the sky, for example, rather than being the most important act in the shaman's toolkit, is found by Atkinson to be not an essential element of the *mabolong* performance at all. See Jean Monnig Atkinson, *The Art and Politics of Wana Shamanship*, Berkeley, CA: University of California, 1989, pp.17; 159; 196-7. On a different level, for a critique of the consequences of the messianic theory of history and the 'spiritual nationalism' of Eliade's far right-wing career, see the sections devoted to Eliade in Steven M. Wasserstrom, *Religion After Religion*, Princeton, NJ: Princeton

acteristic of Artaud, and why Dr. Gaston Ferdière pronounced him 'incurable' at Rodez. The 'World Tree' itself is far from merely an exotic reference here, since it radiates out through most religions – synonymous with the 'navel of the world,' the omphalos, the Cosmic Mountain, it is the land untouched by Noah's Flood; similarly Golgotha, the site of the Cross/World Tree, was located at the 'Center of the World,' the tip of the Mountain where Adam was created and buried, so that 'thus the Savior's blood falls on Adam's skull, buried exactly at the foot of the Cross, and redeems him.'[233] This is the religious and mythological background to Artaud's extraordinary texts on the cross and the crucifixion, since the cross as World Tree is the source and site of 'absolute reality and immortality.'[234]

Having proclaimed the immortality of the 'body without organs,' Artaud saw his impending death (he realised his illness was fatal) as a defeat on multiple levels:

> And they have pushed me over
> into death;
> there where I ceaselessly eat
> cock
> anus
> and caca
> at all my meals,
> all those of THE CROSS.[235]

Indeed, for Artaud, who according to Paule Thévenin died when and probably how he wanted, death was a 'finally lost combat…a social, religious and sexual swallowing.'[236] It is not too much to envision Artaud as a burnt-out tree trunk, scoured by lightning; much as one shaman-initiate in the Nuba Mountains, who did not have the usual propitious or animal-spirit dreams, but whose hut was struck by lightning, and 'as he put it, "he was dead for two days."'[237] Artaud was struck by what one observer has called 'a particularly pernicious kind of twentieth century lightning, electroshock,'[238] during which at one point Artaud, in a remarkable account, related how he felt he had died and witnessed his body ravaged and dismembered by hungry ghosts. Later the marks, *coups*, or blows

---

University Press, 1999. For Eliade's lifelong espousal of a fascist version of the 'New Man' see ibid., pp.131-2.

233 Eliade, *Shamanism*, p.268.

234 Ibid., p.271. A contemporaneous plea against the destruction of the World Tree is found in poet Charles Olson's 'Hotel Steinplatz, Berlin, December 25 (1966),' in his *The Maximus Poems*, ed. Charles Butterick, Berkeley, CA: University of California Press, 1983, pp.569-72.

235 Artaud, *Antonin Artaud, dessins et portraits*, p.16.

236 Barber, *Antonin Artaud*, p.161.

237 Eliade, *Shamanism*, p.55.

238 Eshleman, 'Introduction,' *Watchfiends & Rack Screams*, p.39.

of Artaud's drawings he called 'lightning passages' are proposed in turn 'to electrocute God.'[239]

None of this is to yet resolve Artaud's 'resemblance,'[240] or lack of it, with actual shamanistic practices, or to demonstrate how his dynamism of hieroglyphics and subversion of the cross may have been at the heart of his immense psychic re-organisation during confinement at Rodez.[241] So this is only to suggest the beginnings of the conceptual quakings that accompany Artaud's existence, its challenges and survivals. Personifying a sweeping 'event horizon' or catastrophe theory, Artaud, returning to his Tarahumara experience, wrote that 'In chaos I undertook a first designation of all the larval possibilities that one day formed culture.'[242] Aside from Deleuze and Guattari's judgment 'Even if Artaud didn't succeed for himself, it is certain that through him something succeeded for us all,'[243] this project can help illuminate how Artaud, to a greater extent than usually realised, succeeded for himself as well.

239 Jacques Derrida, Talk at MOMA, 1996. Yet Derrida also has publicly linked and credited the effects of electroshock treatments to Artaud's 'comeback' or re-emergence at Rodez. Jacques Derrida, 'Artaud: Writing/Drawing,' Panel discussion, 11 October, 1996, The Drawing Center, New York, NY.

240 Eshleman, *Watchfiends & Rack Screams*, p.37.

241 This is the subject matter of Chapter V, 'Hieroglyphics as Passage.'

242 Artaud XII, 1974, p.245.

243 Deleuze and Guattari, *A Thousand Plateaus*, p.164.

II.
IN THE LAND OF THE TARAHUMARAS

Artaud was at the heart of the search, running from the early through the late 20th Century that sought in the resources of the hieroglyph-pictogram a way out of dead and stultifying culture, what Artaud called 'European barbarism.'[1] For Artaud this was exemplified not only by the theatre as it was presently constituted, but literature and design, the cultural complex of Europe in its entirety. Artaud's revolt against this degeneration led to his invention of the 'true body' or 'body without organs,' a process that ultimately effaces his concern with hieroglyphic reality. On the way to this transformation, a most decisive event is Artaud's visit to the Tarahumaras Indians in 1936: this both crystallises Artaud's search for a living Theater of cruelty, where potent hieroglyphic imagery and ritual is exploited to cataclysmic effect, and inducts Artaud into a world of sorcery where eventually he discards these fascinations based around the moving hieroglyphs. To discover more precisely the lineaments of what the constitutive elements of the hieroglyph are for Artaud, there is no better primer than his lectures in Mexico before he goes up into the mountains to attend the peyote ceremonies, although there are tantalising glimpses already present not only in Artaud's famed theatre manifestoes but in his far less known art criticism of the 1920's. This chapter will present Artaud's hopes for what he sought in Mexico, show the shape of the different parts of what he called an 'occult geometry,'[2] and look at the constituents of the Tarahumara rites themselves, whose impact on Artaud cannot be overestimated. Artaud was often full of stupendous hopes for the results of his projects. His broadcast *To have done with the judgment of god* was going to awaken the 'corporeal glory'[3] of the oppressed French people. His project for the Theater of cruelty sought to erase hundreds of years of what was given as performance arts in Europe. In his preface to his *Theater and Its Double* collection, Artaud had written that in Mexico, 'there is no art, things serve. And the world is in perpetual exaltation.'[4]

---

1 Artaud, *Œuvres*, p.733.

2 Ibid., p.703.

3 Artaud XIII, 1974, p.131.

4 Artaud IV, 1964, p.16.

Artaud on ancient Mayan hieroglyphs: the 'Space where Life dies'

Artaud went to Mexico to find that exaltation through cultures still participating in a realm that recognised cruelty. In Mexico, Artaud wrote at the beginning of *The Theater and Its Double*, they 'capture the *Manas*, the forces asleep in every form, which are not able to leave through a contemplation of the forms for themselves, but which emerge from a magic identification with these forms. And the old Totems are there to hasten this communication.'[5] It is uncertain when Artaud wrote this preface, it could well have been after his return from Mexico.[6] It is all of a piece with his dramatic expectations expressed before leaving, his search for a 'living culture,' and an actual Theater of cruelty. In articles published before he left France, and then in three lectures at the National Autonomous University of Mexico in Mexico City, and numerous journal or newspaper articles, collected as *Messages révolutionnaires*, Artaud is extremely eloquent in describing his search. He refers specifically to two Mayan hieroglyphs, the Codex Borgia, and the cross of Palenque,[7] but these aesthetics of the ancient Mayan hieroglyphs can hardly be unwound from their context, as Artaud spins it, of the 'persistence of ancient magic,' Mexican paganism and totemism, the descent of the all too living gods to which Indian culture, unlike rootless Europe, still had access. Artaud wrote, 'In Mexico as elsewhere it is the White who has perverted the race. The revolutions in Mexico are a revolt against this state of things. Insomuch as the government will not belong to the true Indian race, Mexico will be in revolution.'[8] This revolution for Artaud is manifestly not the Marxist or socialist one popular at the time but one of the indigenous peoples who raise the spectre of 'collective totemism.'[9] In Mexico, Artaud will search for 'the bases of a magic culture which is still able to emerge from the forces of the Indian soil.'[10] For all this talk of blood and revolution and primordial forces, Artaud also expects life modelled on the kind of cosmic microcosm Paracelsus had been the first to 'formulate in clarity its tenacious reality,' a culture based on mass action that activates tremendous forces much as the 348 points of Chinese acupuncture acts on specific organs of the body.[11] Artaud often reiterates in these Mexican addresses Paracelsus' *tria prima* of mercury, sulfur and salt, elements the 16th century alchemist claimed were the three principles of the universe: mercury being the agent of transformation, sulfur the binder of differ-

[5] Ibid.

[6] See editor Paule Thévenin's notes in ibid., pp.343-4.

[7] Artaud, *Œuvres*, pp.703; 720.

[8] Ibid., p.672.

[9] Ibid., p.673. Artaud refers to this frequently in his Mexican writings.

[10] Ibid., p.692.

[11] Ibid., pp.679; 691.

ent substances and salt the agent of fixity and solidification.[12] Artaud's use and reiteration of these categories is all the more prominent in his Mexican lectures given his later castigation of them.

Artaud had advocated a theatre based on certain arrangements of space, and it is to spatialisation that Artaud calls special attention when he discusses these two Mayan hieroglyphs. It is central to what he terms reviving an 'organic culture,' where 'a culture based on spirit in relation to its organs, where spirit swims in all the organs, while they respond simultaneously.'[13] For Artaud, this culture is above all 'an idea of space,' and true culture for him could only be understood through space, through 'an oriented culture, like the theatre is oriented.'[14] In the essay 'Theater and the gods' that Artaud published in the Mexico City newspaper *El Nacional* in 1936, he continued:

> Culture in space means culture of a spirit that does not cease to breathe and feel life in space, and that calls to it the bodies of space like the same objects of its thought, but insomuch as spirit situates itself in the middle of space, that is to say at its point of death.
>
> This is perhaps a metaphysical idea this idea of the death point of space through which the spirit must pass.
>
> But without metaphysics there is no culture. And this means this notion of space hurls suddenly in culture, according to the affirmation that culture is inseparable from life.[15]

Culture is this movement through the void, going through it toward form, and reentering, into 'the void as in death.' These forms must be burned in order to gain life, in an incessant movement of successive destruction. The ancient peoples in Mexico, Artaud argued, 'knew no other attitude than this going and coming of death in life.'[16] What Artaud called 'this terrible interior station,' this movement of respiration and breath, this was culture, 'that moves at once in nature and in spirit.'[17] All of the 'pure races' Artaud claimed, feel and sense at once, both death and life. Artaud is exploring his theme of 'Speech before words' here, since in this scheme of things, writing cannot but be a contributor to false culture, to idolatry, since 'to write is to prevent spirit from moving in the milieu of forms like a vast respiration. Because writing fixes spirit and crystallises it in a form, and in the form, is born idolatry.'[18] So, for Artaud, the theatre, like true

[12] Artaud's friend Dr. René Allendy had a strong interest in Paracelsus and published a study of him just a year after Artaud's trip to Mexico: René Allendy, *Paracelse, le médecin maudit*, Paris: Gallimard, 1937.

[13] Artaud, *Œuvres*, p.702.

[14] Ibid.

[15] Ibid.

[16] Ibid.

[17] Ibid.

[18] Ibid., p.703.

culture, can never be based on written language, but as he articulated in his theatre manifestoes and reiterated in his Mexican addresses, the theatre is based on a movement in space that is at once gesture and sound. Such a process of occupying space can 'hound life, and force it from its dens.'[19]

Artaud sees this at work in the 'occult geometry' of the crosses with six branches in ancient Mexican temples; the outlines of the crosses, always at the center of the murals, correspond to 'a magic idea,' since this implies it is placed at the centre of a kind of void, and pushes out around it. They are there, 'to reveal how life enters the space, and how outside of the space is rediscovered the foundation of life. Always the void, always the point, around which matter thickens itself.'[20] Whoever wants to sense the gods, must search for the place of the gods, this is the significance of the ancient murals and codexes. In one essay Artaud claims that if man is the catalyst of the universe, then one must conclude that man's moral forces are in accordance with the forces of the universe, 'these forces which, according to the teachings of high monist philosophy, are neither physical or moral, but assume an aspect moral or physical depending on the sense in which one desires to use them'; this is the 'double action' which for Artaud is 'contained precisely' in the cross of Palenque.[21] The cross, inscribed in stone, shows a 'unique energy' traversing the cross of the space, 'passing through the four cardinal points, going from man to animal and to plants.'[22] Artaud will find a similar dynamic in the crosses that mark the territory of the Tarahumaras, crosses which bear no relation to Christ or Catholicism, but of man 'quartered in space, Man with open arms, invisible, nailed to the four cardinal points,' illustrating that the Tarahumaras are 'manifesting an active geometric idea of the world, to which even the form of Man is linked.'[23] Indian culture is still able to vibrate these forces and unique energies of the gods, calling out through their 'musics of forces; and the theatre through its musical distribution of forces call to it the power of Gods. Each has its place in the vibrant space of images.'[24] The gods appear through a cry or a face, and the 'colour of the face has its cry,' just as the cry carries a palpable weight of images each element relying on the other for its perception, in the 'Space where Life dies.'[25]

---

19 Ibid.

20 Ibid.

21 Ibid., pp.719-20.

22 Ibid., p.720.

23 Ibid., p.755.

24 Ibid., pp.703-4.

25 Ibid., p.704.

Explaining 'occult geometry': Artaud's art criticism

It is not surprising given Artaud's attention to 'outlining' and 'lines' in early essays on painters ranging from Paolo Uccello to his contemporaries Pierre Bonnard, Paul Klee, Pablo Picasso, Balthus, Jean Dubuffet and André Masson that these gods' existence is bound up in a similar process of *cerner*, of definition, of this 'active geometric idea of the world.' It is the same as the '*filaments*' and '*lanières*' Artaud sees in the paintings of Jean de Bosschère, 'where the irritating force of fire lacerates the interior firmament.'[26] Artaud claims that the gods of Mexico, by means of a figure regain forces in the void, a void that has lost reality. These gods according to Artaud are prey to a loss of force, and vertigo of thought, and it is 'lines which show overtop their heads giving a melodious and rhythmic means of showing thought through thought.'[27] It is this figuration, that enables the gods not to petrify within themselves, but rather to work, to move:

> 'I advance in war,' seems to say the God which makes in its fist an arm of war, and which it carries before it; 'And over through this advance I think,' says a sort of line in clarity which zigzags above its head – And this line in some point of space, multiplies itself anew.[28]

Artaud insists that there is harmony in these lines, 'a kind of essential geometry that corresponds to the image of a sound. For the theater a line is a sound, a movement is a music, and the gesture which emerges from a sound is like a clear word in a phrase.'[29] In other words, the theatre is a fully functioning, powerful hieroglyph. The gods of Mexico, Artaud claims, are these 'open lines' indicating all that has left the premises, and at the same time are a means of re-entry and re-emergence. These are 'open forces,' Artaud writes, and it doesn't take much time in Mexico, Artaud maintains, to sense these realities, this 'open Mythology.' This is the 'sole way of the land,' Artaud concludes, 'that proposes to us an occult life, and *proposes it at the surface of life*.'[30] Where Ernest Fenollosa or later Charles Olson found in hieroglyphic languages a kind of primordial or 'ideal language' that could be activated again in its original poetry – in the instance of Chinese characters what François Cheng called the 'traits' or strokes that captured the movement of powerful natural or cosmic forces[31] – Artaud sees these

[26] Artaud I:1, 1956, p.149.

[27] Artaud, *Œuvres*, p.704.

[28] Ibid.

[29] Ibid.

[30] Ibid.

[31] See François Cheng, *Chinese Poetic Writing*, trans. Donald A. Riggs and Jerome P. Seaton, Bloomington, IN: Indiana University Press, 1982.

signs as plentiful and abundant in Mexico. This surface is the pattern of lines-in-motion, the point of access for humanity, point of re-entry for the gods.

What Artaud is preparing himself to see, and what he claims to find in Tarahumara culture, was already envisaged for instance in his texts about the paintings of his friend André Masson. In the Tarahumara ceremonies Artaud describes a male and female confronting each other, then dancing, their entwined hands with the angle of their arms forming two triangles, as in the common geometric symbol of two triangles joined by a base, oblong line, symbolising the 'World Tree.' In a text for *La Révolution surréaliste* in January 1925, Artaud writes of Masson paintings, their revolutions and convolutions, mirroring Artaud's own: 'The cold agitation of the columns split my spirit in two, and I touch my sex to me the sex at the base of my soul, which rises in an inflamed triangle.'[32] Shortly after, Artaud would expand on these themes, in a text on Masson's oil-on-canvas *Homme* (1924), included in his collection *Umbilicus of Limbo*. 'The canvas is deep and stratified,' Artaud wrote, 'The painting is well-enclosed in the canvas. It is like a closed circle, a sort of abyss that turns, and splits apart in the middle. It is like a spirit that sees and deepens itself, it is remixed and worked without ceasing by the clenched hands of spirit. Or, spirit sows its phosporus.'[33] Masson's canvas is described as if it is remaking, tossing up nature, full of afflicted elements, but through an architecture that is 'indifferent,' that does not speak. Artaud describes depictions of an organic, gestating, exploding world with 'grooves from a magic nail,' but turned inside out, as it were, inhuman, its stratifications are those of an 'arrested universe,' filled with its transformative shapes, the egg, mountain, tongue of fire, the circular stomach, and its spire that has the 'importance of the most pressing thought.'[34] Masson, flush in the energies of the newly dubbed 'Unconscious,' paints a translucid, constantly receding 'mountain,' that acts as a 'sensation of the eternal horizon.'[35] To Artaud, the painting is nothing less than an introduction to reality, 'an ideal space, absolute.'[36] In another essay on Masson, Artaud writes of his 'applying the method of cubism to the restitution of natural objects,' with its goal of a 'rethought nature.'[37] So already in Artaud's earliest published writings he is questioning the makeup of 'nature,' questioning any permanent order or hierarchy within it even as he is about to be completely immersed in mystical and mythological systems of thought that often proclaim to present just that.

Artaud echoes and rejoins this line of thinking about 'nature' toward the end of his life, when on 16 January 1947 he writes to cubist painter Georges Braque

[32] Artaud, *Œuvres*, p.123.

[33] Artaud I:1, 1956, pp.62-3.

[34] Ibid., p.63.

[35] Ibid., p.64.

[36] Ibid.

[37] Artaud II, 1961, p.213.

to thank him for his contribution of paintings to the extremely successful auction put on for Artaud's benefit and asylum release. Artaud writes that 'cubism is a putting into question of the linear occult world, and is even more a matter of the tear of internal tissue,' since a task of painting is to surprise or confound the internal mechanics of an already made cosmos.[38] Artaud tells Braque that before his canvases he had always been impressed with 'the will of total genesis, without drama elsewhere the pure element sought following its intrinsic necessity, as in calm and without passion.'[39] He suggests 'if the world resumes so that its genesis was criminal…and this is not read at once,' then 'by looking attentively [at] certain freed forms, recomposed by you one would have to say that you know it.'[40] Braque's paintings remind Artaud of Etruscan mysteries, 'a sensibility that guards itself through unctions of a moistened heart.'[41] The remainder of Artaud's letter is an invective against the forces of black magic that interned him for nine years, and continued to plague and harass him after his release. This view of cubism was foreshadowed in Artaud's writing about it some twenty-four years earlier. Artaud wrote about Picasso's work, having met him in 1922 when he played Tirésias in Jean Cocteau's adaptation of Sophocles' *Antigone*; Picasso had done the set design. Picasso also seems to participate in what Artaud in Mexico will call the profound geometric principle of the world – he is not only a great painter conjuring worlds, he is a 'seer' activating an 'authentic magic.' Artaud wrote in the essay 'Theater after the war in Paris' (published in Mexico in 1936) of a Picasso painting that:

> The lines show through a rose splotch. Picasso throws out to pull back, to reflect, to orient, and the lines, around it are placed emerging through a living geometry…The lines emerge one could say fatally. And these lines compose a geometry that go to support one knows not what, something which, in the middle of the wall, goes rapidly to set ablaze something one does not know...His hand goes and comes – seeming the hand of a seer – and at one stroke, opposite us, as attracting through an authentic magic, we are able to contemplate a brilliant column.[42]

Artaud had also criticised Picasso's post-cubist work in 1924, as 'striving to think in classifiable, determinable forms.'[43] In contrast, the cubist work showed a 'prodigious life force' that 'crackled through the dense lines, an unknown and profound reality in which the whole soul finds itself again.'[44]

[38] Artaud XIV:1, 1978, p.157.

[39] Ibid., pp.157-8.

[40] Ibid., p.158.

[41] Ibid.

[42] Artaud VIII, 1971, p.218.

[43] Artaud II, 1961, p.219; *Œuvres*, p.34.

[44] Ibid.

The splintering and cosmic fragmentation of cubism, its separation of the perceived world into planes-in-motion, appealed to Artaud, and so did the art of Paul Klee, whom Artaud characterised in similar terms in 1923 as a 'mental painter,' who put his 'nightmares, these mental syntheses conceived as architectures…cosmic syntheses where all secret objectivity in things is rendered sensible.'[45] So Klee, too, makes visible a hidden order. The paintings of Artaud's close friend Balthus, whom he once rescued from a suicide attempt, however oneiric and eccentric, were invariably figurative and still based in a naturalist vein, and therefore quite different from those of Klee and either the cubists or surrealists, but even in this instance, Artaud singled out in Balthus' work the virtue of metamorphoses occurring before the viewer's eyes. Of Balthus' painting *La Toilette de Cathy* (1933) Artaud wrote in a text published in *La Nouvelle Revue Française* in 1934:

> Concerning poetry, it enters in the painting of Balthus…where the young and amorous body of a woman imposes itself like a dream in a painting which has the realism of *l'Atelier* by Courbet. Imagine in life a painter's model transformed at once into a sphinx and you are a little close to the impression that this canvas is able to make.[46]

The outline of the canvas, or tableau, was itself a 'Space where Life dies.' It was at once a mise-en-scène of birth (an introduction into reality) and a unity of discrete bits, fragments that doubled as a tomb, or funereal landscape, a 'measurable and synthesized landscape.'[47] As in the Masson painting Artaud so admired and identified with, it was a space both organic or, in this instance, biomorphic, and structured through the abstractions of geometry. In Lucas van den Leyden's painting that inspired his Theater of cruelty, Artaud found that the painter seemed 'to have knowledge of certain secrets concerning linear harmony, and of means of making it act directly on the brain, like a physical reaction.'[48] So van den Leyden's early Renaissance painting succeeded in doing what Artaud came to believe was impossible for the cinema to do. It was simultaneously representational (although representational in the way a hallucination is representational, and inevitably a combustion) and like 'ideas in Plato's cave.'[49] As Artaud's commentary on Masson's *Homme* shows quite well, and as his essay on Van Gogh would much later, Artaud's view of painting was one where normative 'objectivity' and boundaries of 'inner' and 'outer' had no place; Artaud is at one with the convulsions and cataclysms in this *other* space of the painting. As he wrote in one of his earliest reviews in 1921, 'The value of a painting has

45 Artaud I:1, 1956, p.196.

46 Artaud II, 1961, p.242.

47 Artaud I:1, 1956, p.205.

48 Artaud IV, 1964, p.43.

49 Ibid.

become for us above all a question of metaphysics;'[50] as such, it was a site of the Theater of cruelty. It is notable that in a 'fourth letter on language' Artaud writes to Jean Paulhan on 28 May 1933, he places the Theater of cruelty in a lineage of painting: van den Leyden's *Daughters of Lot*, certain of Goya's *Sabbaths*, El Greco's *Resurrections* and *Transfigurations*, Hieronymous Bosch's *Temptation of St. Anthony*, and Brueghel the Elder's *Dulle Griet*. These paintings are all characterised by the 'lines of force' that Artaud called for in his Theater of cruelty play on the fall of Montézuma.[51] Artaud would later advocate such an extreme mobility in his own visual work, paintings, drawings and *gris gris* that began to pour forth with volcanic intensity starting from his years at Rodez and then after his release, in a process he wrote required 'the unsticking of the retina.'[52] In Brueghel the Elder's *Dulle Griet*, Artaud describes the effect of the painting such as to 'freeze from a metre [away] of the canvas the medusa'd eye of the spectator.'[53] The painting is suffused with a 'torrential red light' that seems to 'surge from all sides;' this is a theatre where every part of it 'swarms.'[54] It is a 'mute theatre,' but one which 'speaks more than if it had received a language in order to express itself.' 'True life,' Artaud writes, articulating the 'double sense' of the paintings he uses as examples, 'is moving and white; the hidden life is livid and fixed, it possesses all the possible attitudes of an incalculable immobility.'[55] All of the paintings, as with the projected Theater of cruelty, 'reveal mysterious or terrible aspects of nature and of spirit.'[56]

As these pointers indicate, the static visual arts such as painting remained a crucial privileged space for Artaud, a transitional or intermediary space that was not one of self-abolition, far from it, but one rather where the *filaments* of the body and its expression, in this *other* space, this 'Space where Life dies,' one could touch infinity, where interlaced, drawn signs could be lived and deciphered for an undetermined amount of time.[57] As with Artaud's experimentation in the cinema, where the screen is a skin or membrane, at once near and far, its projection a materiality that of necessity goes beyond its fixed surface, revealing the presence of the occult, as he later characterised it in Mexico in 'The Theater and the Gods'(1936) – 'at the surface of life.' Much as he described the cinema as a 'space virtual and absolute,'[58] he characterises the paintings of Masson and others; at this intersection of painted signs and written lines, far

[50] Artaud II, 1961, p.186; Artaud, *Œuvres*, p.33.

[51] Artaud IV, 1964, p.153.

[52] Artaud XXI, 1985, p.233.

[53] Artaud IV, 1964, p.145.

[54] Ibid., pp.144-5.

[55] Ibid., p.145.

[56] Ibid.

[57] Évelyne Grossman, 'L'art crève les yeux,' *Antonin Artaud*, p.163.

[58] Artaud III, 1961, p.151.

from contemplative passion Artaud envisages his 'culture in action' of dance, of the viewer-participant in motion. What Artaud reveals in his art criticism is not merely colourful rhetoric but an elaboration of this space of culture that is a corporealised space, a place of potential transformation and convulsion. As he announced in his introduction to *The Theater and Its Double*, the lack of 'constant magic' in the lives of Europeans was due to their losing themselves in contemplation of 'imagined form,' whose ability to think in 'forms, signs, representations' with the 'faculty of deriving thoughts from acts, instead of identifying acts with thoughts' have made them monstrosities.[59] It is not difficult to see Artaud's *œuvre*, with all its changes and gyrations, as a plea against death and the stasis of death, as this is played out in the stasis of the image. He advocated 'to have done with masterpieces' but could easily have called 'to have done with the stasis of the image.'

Commentator Évelyne Grossman has argued that although the 'transitory' or 'virtual' intermediary space posed by Artaud is well-known to psychology and psychoanalysis it is not always so well encapsulated or explained by these.[60] Donald W. Winnicott, for example, theorised a 'transitional' psychic space that through means of play and 'transitional objects' infants and young children successfully, or not, linked their interior and exterior realities, creating the basis for future human and cultural development.[61] This is at once applicable to Artaud, Grossman has observed, and far from sufficient, since Artaud's work cannot be consigned to primary or regressive stages of development, or even as a matter of resurrecting the archaic.[62] Rather Artaud, in posing his dilemmas of expression, is about an invention simultaneously corporeal and psychic. If he returns to sources of inspiration that are 'primitive' and archaic, it is in order to redouble his energies of projection in the present. Rather than 'regression,' Grossman has theorised that Artaud's movement between writing, theatre/performance, and drawing is another type of space she has called *discorps*.[63] This is a place of 'harmonious discord,' much as Artaud suggested in 'Theater and Culture'(1935) when he wrote that 'the multiple twists of the Serpent Quetzalcoatal, they are harmonious, it is they that express the equilibrium and the bends of a dormant force; and the intensity of forms is there only to seduce and capture a

---

[59] Artaud IV, 1964, p.13.

[60] See Évelyne Grossman, *Artaud/Joyce, le corps et le texte*, Paris: Nathan, 1996. Another extrapolation of this would be the work of psychoanalyst and artist Bracha Ettinger, whose 'matrixial space' is also a shared collective, 'transitional' space, one of emergence beyond the masculine/feminine theorised by Lacan. See Bracha Ettinger, *The Matrixial Borderspace*, ed. Brian Massumi, Minneapolis, MN: University of Minnesota Press, 2006.

[61] Donald W. Winnicott, *Playing and Reality*, London: Tavistock, 1971.

[62] Grossman, *Antonin Artaud*, p.164.

[63] Grossman, *Artaud/Joyce, le corps et le texte*, pp.52-61.

force which, in music, would arouse agonizing keys.'[64] This *discorps*, according to Grossman, is a potentially infinite opening between text and reader, image and viewer, the scene or stage and the hall, all of which bridge the void or gap or chiasmus between body and discourse. This is a sort of tracing of lines in the air, evoking another reality, as Artaud described the Balinese dancers of 1931. It is a process that not so much promises a finished work, as creates as its work this fluidity in space and perception that one follows as it goes along, as in Artaud's suggested gyrations of Quetzalcoatal.[65] Here the notebook page (in the later Artaud), the stage, the canvas are platforms, launching grounds, themselves materialisations enabled by interval, what Artaud often termed *la grille*.[66] Eminently applicable to Artaud, where it entails being caught up in a terrible flux of creation, a notion like Grossman's *discorps* truly comes into its own in virtual reality-based and interactive cinema[67] like that of Toni Dove. Dove has described the blurring of boundaries necessary to navigate her work *Artificial Changelings* (1998), for example: '[Your] body is stuck to the movie, a part of it, lost in space and time. This effects the way a viewer moves, and perhaps how we might think about what a body is – the boundaries and edges go soft.'[68] Artaud's way of moving between diverse media, in practice and in theory, anticipates the 'trance-like state'[69] Dove later writes about.

Even in these early considerations of painting, Artaud sites the canvas as a possible 'true space,' a ground for the link of magic, that energy acting at a distance that unites words and things. As Artaud wrote in one of his very last texts in 1948, arguing that his drawings were not figuration or representation of any kind, but rather:

> The reproduction on
> The paper
> Of a magical action
> That I have performed

[64] Artaud IV, 1964, p.15.

[65] In regard to Artaud and the question of the 'work,' see Jean-Michel Rey, *Les Promesses de l'Œuvre: Artaud, Nietzsche, Simone Weil*, Paris: Desclée de Brouwer, 2003, but also especially, the essays of Maurice Blanchot in *Le Livre à venir*, Paris: Gallimard, 1959 and *L'Entretien infini*, Paris: Gallimard, 1969.

[66] For a discussion of the blank, white page as launching ground, see Maurice Blanchot, *The Space of Literature*, trans. Ann Smock, Lincoln, NE & London: University of Nebraska Press, 1983. For Artaud's reference to '*la grille*' as 'the most terrible moment for the sensibility, for matter,' see Artaud I:1, 1956, p.104.

[67] See for instance Stephen Schrum's argument that Artaud needs rereading and reconsideration given new technologies in his 'Introduction' to *Theatre in Cyberspace*, ed. Stephen Schrum, New York, NY: Peter Lang, 1999.

[68] Toni Dove, 'Haunting the Movie: Embodied Interface/Sensory Cinema,' *New Visions in Performance*, eds Gavin Carter and Colin Beardon, Lisse: Swets and Zietlinger, 2004, p.110.

[69] Ibid.

In true space
With the breath of my
Lungs
With my hands
With my head
And my 2 feet
With my torso and my
Arteries, etc. —[70]

His insistence on 'magical action' here echoes his earlier self, who wrote in *Nerve Scales* (1925) 'there is a phosphorescent point where all reality is recovered, but changed, metamorphosised – and by what? – a point of magic utilization of things.'[71] His thought, Artaud writes, 'searches in the ether of a new space.'[72] As I will go on to examine, the later Artaud even more explicitly opposes magic to the image, force to stasis. Magic, as Artaud defined it in 'Le Mexique et la civilisation' (1935), is precisely this intermediary or 'true' space – 'a constant communication from interior to exterior, from act to thought, from thing to word, from matter to spirit.'[73]

How this site of painting is fiercely implicated, indissolubly, with Artaud's own intense 'internal' struggles and dilemmas, and how through his immense force of projection or creation of energetic link, he attempts to resolve them, can be seen in the 'mental drama' he penned personifying Renaissance artists Paolo Uccello, Brunelleschi, and Donatello, titled 'Paul the Birds, or the Place of Love' (1924).[74] I am discussing it here in league with Artaud's view of painting since its concerns are so very consonant. 'Paul the Birds,' as well as his already discussed film scenario *18 Seconds*, magnify and translate into an objectified form, convey his anguish, and are closely inspired by his relationship at the time with Romanian-born actress Génica Athanasiou; a slightly later essay on Uccello, 'Uccello, Le Poil,'[75] was dedicated to her. It can argued that these works show Artaud looking at his issues from a more distant or detached standpoint than his early, symbolist-influenced poetry, and by objectifying his conflicts, they are projected into theatre where they have an independent, collective existence apart from his tortured solitude.[76] It is typical of an Artaud work in its combina-

70 Antonin Artaud, *50 drawings to murder magic*, ed. Évelyne Grossman, trans. Donald Nicholson-Smith, London, New York, NY & Calcutta: Seagull Books, 2008. p.16.

71 Artaud I:1, 1956, p.90.

72 Ibid., p.112.

73 Artaud, *Œuvres*, p.680. This text was not published in Artaud's lifetime but was one of the very first addressing these issues he made in Paris before he left for Mexico.

74 Artaud I:1, 1956, pp.205-12; Artaud, *Œuvres*, pp.85-9. A quite different version was published a little less than a year later in *Umbilicus of Limbo*. See ibid., pp.55-9; ibid., p.107.

75 Ibid., pp.138-40; ibid., pp.198-9.

76 Knapp, *Antonin Artaud*, p.45.

tion of both bloody violence and high consideration of ideas or metaphysics, its extreme chaos of events coupled with precise intellectual modelling. Although one could view all three historic personas as split off segments of Artaud's personality, Uccello, with the nascent abstraction of his paintings, is clearly close to Artaud. As if he is suffering from the same affliction Artaud had detailed in his 'Correspondence with Jacques Rivière' the drama opens with Uccello's reflection that he is lost in a 'vast mental tissue where he has lost all the roads to his soul and even the form and suspension of his reality.'[77] Responding to a harassing voice or 'Spirit,' a language of fire that wants his tongue, Uccello tears it out, while Brunelleschi and Donatello maul each other. Although according to many mythologies and religions, the mouth and speech are often organs linked to Spirit, coupled with the element of fire, as in the Holy Spirit in the New Testament, where the Holy Ghost appears to the Apostles in flames,[78] in Artaud's case the Spirit and language of fire demand his silence.

In the version modified for *Umbilicus of Limbo* (1925) Artaud appears to insert himself, representing a strenuous effort to think beyond the confines of what is described as a separating mental lens or glass, as if Artaud is trying to think or experience these other aspects yet remains cut off from them. Trapped on one side of the glass, Artaud can only watch the drama unfold, even though, while Brunelleschi protests, Uccello's wife Selvagia is dying of hunger. Uccello is characterised as a fly stuck in a painting, *his* painting, an after-effect of 'stratification.'[79] The action takes place in a dimensionless void, beyond space and time, as if suspended in one of Uccello's paintings. Artaud asks in this script, in this 'mental poem' that takes place 'purely in the Spirit' – 'Does one die of hunger in the Spirit?'– and answers in the affirmative. Interestingly, Uccello is represented as a disembodied figure with a barely perceptible voice, his 'physique stratified like an insect or an idiot'[80] (Artaud the actor was ridiculed as the 'barbed wire man'). A decade later Artaud will describe a dance among the Tarahumaras as mimicking a mass of 'planetary ants at the compass of a celestial music,' and another dancer imitating the 'step of a tiny ant which was tottering.'[81] Donatello is compared to St. Francis before the stigmatas, a thorough man of Spirit although still of the earth; Brunelleschi resembles Dante, a fully sexual and fleshly being, who lusts after Selvagia and thinks of little else. Uccello on the other hand, does not ignore sexuality, Artaud writes, but sees it as if in a vitrine, 'mercurial, and

---

[77] Artaud I:1, 1956, p.55.

[78] C.G. Jung, *Symbols of Transformation*, Vol. V of *Collected Works*, trans. R.F.C. Hull, Princeton, NJ: Princeton University Press, 1956, p.99.

[79] Artaud I:1, 1956, p.56.

[80] Ibid., pp.55-6.

[81] In 'The Rites of the Kings of Atlantis,' in Artaud IX, 1971, p.91.

cold like the ether.'[82] In the course of the drama Brunelleschi and Donatello attack and tear into each other while the author Artaud watches on the 'other side of all mental glasses,' both observer and observed of his 'mental poem.' Despite the bloody conflict of the action, this void is also a space of transformation and metamorphosis, 'the fire where those glasses macerate is translated into a beautiful fabric.'[83] In its surreal conclusion, Brunelleschi is inflated into an enormous white bird, like a sperm cell, twirling around in the air. Thus what can seem like fragments of inner drama change into a skein of universal signs. As Artaud wrote in 'Uccello le poil' – 'Two or three signs in the air, where is the man who pretends to be more than these three signs and from whom, throughout the hours that cover him, one would think of asking more than the silence that precedes or follows them?...You, Uccello, are learning to be only a line and the heightened level of a secret.'[84]

The magical geometry Artaud extols in Paolo Uccello, and later in Masson and Picasso, is firmly rooted in Western traditions of painting. What leads Artaud to Mexico is paradoxically, the wisdom of the 'Essential' fully known to the pre-Renaissance and High Renaissance painters of Italy. In one of his writings in Mexico before he went up to the Sierra Tarahumaras 'The Land of the Magi Kings' (1936) Artaud opens by musing that the blue skies of Fra Angelico and other painters, and the 'vast perspectives of their backgrounds' in their Nativities, derived not from the Mediterranean but from Mexico, since Mexico is pre-eminently this land of 'first effects.'[85] Artaud goes so far to say that it was no 'religious spirit' that led Piero della Francesca, Lucas van Leyden, Fra Angelico, Piero di Cosimo, and Andreas Mantegna to paint their Nativities, rather an exploration of 'first principles and first explosions of Nature' that finds expression through Europe's absurd designation of 'UNIVERSAL ESOTERISM.'[86] This supposed 'esoterism' is nothing less than a 'secret science which modern science has not yet completely rediscovered,' expressed in the 'astronomical science of nature.'[87] The path of the three magi, in the pagan myth of Christmas, Artaud claims, was along the geographic line of the great Solar tradition, what he stresses was the '*Scientific* Worship of the Sun.'[88] This astronomical worship of the sun is expressed for Artaud in signs – the Double Cross as in the Cross of Palenque; the 'universal' fertility symbol of the Swastika; the anserated Cross;

[82] Artaud I:1, 1956, p.57.

[83] Ibid., p.56.

[84] Ibid., p.140.

[85] Artaud IX, 1971, p.77.

[86] Ibid., pp.78-9. Artaud makes fun of this term as I have shown he earlier made light of words like 'religious,' 'mystical,' and 'metaphysical.'

[87] Ibid., pp.77; 80.

[88] Ibid., p.79.

the large circle with a dot in the middle; four triangles pointing at four cardinal points surrounding a dot that Artaud claimed to have seen hundreds of times in the Sierra Tarahumara, which is also the cross of Rosicrucian tradition;[89] three dots; the two linked opposing triangles Artaud saw in a peyote dance in the Tarahumaras; the twelve signs of the Zodiac. These geometrical figures, Artaud wrote in a 4 February, 1937 letter to Jean Paulhan, are nothing less than the 'constituted Signs of a language based on the very form of the breath when it is released in sounds.'[90] Artaud saw all these signs in the Tarahumaras, as well as an 'infinity of others.'[91] These painters of the pre-, Early and High Renaissance can be read 'with the affective fibers of the soul,' but as well with the 'high rational Science of the mind.' 'A colour,' Artaud continues, 'if it enchants the heart, corresponds to an exact and scientific vibration in which the Primal Numbers can be found.'[92] Yet in the Sierra Tarahumaras, Artaud is in a land 'literally haunted by these signs,' where they pour forth from Nature itself. This 'awesome vibration of Nature' is recoiling with the 'same signs, the same forms, the same lights, the same secrets' of the painters from Florence, Assisi, and Como.[93] Artaud dubs them 'Primitives,' given they have the same apprehension of reality and access to 'secret objectivity of things' as traditional peoples.

It is tempting here to broach the question whether Artaud prefigures contemporary studies such as those by Georges Didi-Huberman on Fra Angelico, which focus on how the 15th century Renaissance painter utilised techniques of increased verisimilitude only to heighten opposite qualities of 'spiritual' or 'divine' abstraction – through colour that announces approaching divinity, paint drippings that simulate anointments, or the dynamic use of empty or negative space.[94] Or how Artaud, in his idiosyncratic manner, is pointing to 'mystical science' of the Italian Renaissance painting much the way other, later art historians would discuss various artists, from Brueghel the Elder to J.M.W. Turner to Jackson Pollock, as painters of the networked cosmos, of the patterns of a largely chaotic nature.[95] In this light, it is intriguing that the alternative destination Artaud closely considered for his flight from Europe was Tibet. Artaud would have found perhaps an even more direct phenomenology of spirit in visual representations, as well as traditional conceptions of Heaven, Purgatory and Hell

[89] Ibid., pp.123-4.

[90] Ibid., p.124.

[91] Ibid., p.137.

[92] Ibid., p.80.

[93] Ibid., pp.79-81.

[94] Georges Didi-Huberman, *Fra Angelico: Dissemblance and Figuration*, trans. Jane Marie Todd, Chicago, IL: University of Chicago Press, 1995.

[95] Pierre Sterckx, 'Andreas Gursky, réseaux et particules,' *artpress* 277, March 2002: 25-29. Sterckx compares these artists to contemporary photographer Andreas Gursky, whose work is similarly based on the 'becoming of the universe.'

not so alien from Christianity as Artaud's earlier surrealist broadside in 1925 would have led one to believe.[96] Yet the visual culture of Tibet and the East does confirm some of Artaud's intuitions on the 'virtual' nature of the cosmos, much as the Balinese theatre inspired his essays on doubling and 'virtuality.' Ancient and classical Asian art has typically depicted figures and events that *exist* only in the mind and heart of the viewer. So the painted or carved icons are not idealisations or 'ideals' in any mundane, empirical sense but only in a mathematical one. Their coherence relies on a presumed archetypal structure of the mind, where intelligibility, not resemblance or likeness, is what is supposed to shine through. *Yantras*, for instance, are pictograms of a deity, not related except by coincidence to more worldly known and common entities; likewise *mantras* are aural representations of divine sound. As Ananda Coomaraswamy has written:

> The parts of an icon are not organically related, for it is not contemplated that they should function biologically, but ideally related, being the required component parts of a given type of activity stated in terms of the visible and tangible medium. This does not mean that the various parts are not related, or that the whole is not a unity, but that the relation is mental rather than functional.[97]

In the *Upanishads*, objects in space are referred to as coloured areas, since space is recognised as a conventionalised, mental category.[98] At its best, this is an art of manifestation, what Coomaraswamy refers to as a 'continuous condition,' for the dance of Shiva takes place not merely at Cibambaram or Taraka Forest, but in the heart of the worshipper. The goal is that the finally presented, externalised art-object be as indistinguishable from the inner visualisation as possible. The highest artistic practitioners will create items so that the viewer sees not just recognisable versions, mirrors of his or her own projections, but sees realities without distinction of inner and outer, without dualism. This recognition of being implies, in the *Upanishads* as in Christian Scholasticism or Islamic philosophy, that ultimately art disappears in this merging; in the Indian Vedanta the seer, seen and the process of seeing dissolve, into an undivided and ecstatic One. Eastern religious art to a great extent modelled itself on Alighieri Dante's maxim that 'Who paints a figure, if he cannot be it, cannot draw it.'[99]

---

[96] This is borne out in the collection of some 200 *thangka* paintings of the Rubin Museum of Art, New York, that spans eight centuries and includes each different visual artistic tradition. See Marylin A. Rhie, Robert A.F. Thurman, and David Jackson, *Worlds of Transformation: Tibetan Art of Wisdom and Compassion*, New York, NY: Harry Abrams, 1999. Other major collections are documented in Valrae Reynolds, *From the Sacred Realm: Treasures of Tibetan Art from the Newark Museum*, New York, NY: Prestel, 2000; and Barbara Lipton and Nima Dorjee Raqnubs, *Treasures of Tibetan Art: Collections of the Jacques Marchais Museum of Tibetan Art*, Oxford: Oxford University Press, 1996.

[97] Ananda K. Coomaraswamy, *The Transformation of Nature in Art*, New York, NY: Dover, 1956, p.29.

[98] Ibid., p.56.

[99] Quoted in ibid., p.7.

Yet in the ferocity of the later Artaud's rejection of any representation and opposition of magic to magic, image to image, it is doubtful whether this hierarchic and static art of visual depiction would have remained standing. As Artaud claims in the *Retour à Paris* notebooks, 'This that is, is such that I am not an arrested organism, but moving…Do not forget the science of the photomaton, which is that internal perceptions are false, do not ever respond to any world and are not there in the exterior world.'[100] Whereas many of Artaud's earlier creations relate to Klee's *Zwischenwelt*, a 'transitory' or 'transitional' space, an *entremonde*, at the end of his life the 'body without organs' has changed many of these relations – Artaud is staking his legacy on an infinite gesture that is no longer subordinated to spatialisation. The body without organs is not an in-between space as much as it is a completely exterior body that has no inside. The possibility of this is already present in Artaud's experience with the Tarahumaras, an extraordinary event to which I now turn.

The visit to the Tarahumaras

One must not forget the personal urgency of this trip for Artaud, who withdrew from his addiction to opiates to visit the Tarahumaras and participate in their rituals, and already had behind him a long series of distinctly unsuccessful detoxifications from drugs in Paris. So for Artaud, the stakes expressed in these theoretical positions or mystic polemics in his addresses in Mexico City before the rites could not have been higher. As he titled one essay, he was in Mexico 'fleeing European civilization;'[101] in an extremely fragile state – according to Artaud he was so weak on his horse going up the Sierras that his *mestizo* guides had to close his hands around the reins – Artaud looked forward to '*my crucifixion*.'[102] This was the price for the 'grinding' of the ritual, which 'reduces dawn to darkness – that this thing be pulled out, and that it *serve*.' In calling the experience a 'crucifixion,' perhaps Artaud had some awareness that he was 'going under,' in Nietzsche's phrase. Other commentators have noted the urgency of Artaud's writings on the Tarahumaras, as if the ritual news could be lost, and he could be condemned to be one of those lost being 'burnt at the stake, signaling through the flames.'[103] The series of writings Artaud publishes on the rituals when back in Paris, no longer appear under his own name. At the conclusion of his article 'Peyote Dance,' Artaud writes, 'Through this I knew that my physical

---

[100] Artaud XXIII, 1974, p.336.

[101] Artaud, *Œuvres*, p.733.

[102] Ibid., p.775.

[103] Artaud IV, 1964, p.18.

destiny was irreparably attached. I was ready for all burnings, and I awaited the fruits of the burning, in view of a soon generalized conflagration.'[104]

Artaud's journey to the Tarahumaras has been compared to Rimbaud setting off for Abyssinia, since they both entailed a certain renunciation of literature; in one of the last letters Artaud wrote to Jean Paulhan before his trek into the mountains, Artaud conveyed his relief 'to be finally rid of passé literariness.'[105] These voyages of 1936 and to Ireland in 1937 have been described as 'a headlong rush towards breakdown and silence,' although 'a profusion of strange images and signs in his work may be traced back to these profoundly exploratory journeys.'[106] In Artaud's Mexican writings, he not only reads the signs of Nature literally inscribed in the landscape, all sorts of metaphysical augurs are increasingly described as located in specific parts of the body. In 'The Peyote Rite of the Tarahumaras' (1947), one of his later edited versions of his experiences, for example, the liver is named as the 'organic filter of the *Unconscious*.'[107] This has been too much for many commentators, one of whom compares these speculations to 'the level of the most maligned practices of the alchemists and the discarded theories of medieval medicine.'[108] Artaud writes:

> There is one thing that the Peyote priests of Mexico helped me to observe and that the little bit of Peyote that I had taken opened in my conscience. This is that it is in the human liver that produces this secret alchemy and this work through the self (*moi*) of each individual chooses that which is convenient to it, adapts

---

[104] Artaud IX, 1971, p.62. Here I am translating Artaud's *combustion* as 'conflagration,' as does Helen Weaver in Antonin Artaud, *The Peyote Dance*, trans. Helen Weaver, New York, NY: Farrar, Straus, & Giroux, 1976, p.58.

[105] Évelyne Grossman, *Antonin Artaud, un insurgé du corps*, Paris: Gallimard, 2006, p.50. For Rimbaud's journey to Abyssinia, see Alain Borer, *Rimbaud in Abyssinia*, trans. Rosemarie Waldrop, New York, NY: William Morrow, 1991; and Enid Starke, *Arthur Rimbaud in Abyssinia*, Oxford: Oxford University Press, 1937.

[106] Barber, *Antonin Artaud*, p.73.

[107] Artaud IX, 1971, p.37.

[108] Sellin, *The Dramatic Concepts of Antonin Artaud*, p. 28. Yet, as anyone with even the most casual acquaintance with Eastern practices such as various forms of meditative visualisation, acupuncture, reiki, herbal medicine, or yoga, knows, these are all based on specific localisations of energy in the body, and are inconceivable without such. In a much broader sense, the liver as the seat of the soul, or karmic center of the body, is also an extremely widespread belief in folk wisdom and cultures, as well as being a mainstay of holistic medicine. Artaud knew this firsthand, since he resorted to acupuncture, this system of Chinese therapy based on 'sympathies' of organs with other organs in the body, several times in his drug detoxification attempts. Artaud was treated by Dr. George Soulié de Morant, who had been impressed by the success of acupuncture in treating cholera cases in China. What is remarkable about Artaud and his acupuncture treatments is that at one point he felt he had been cured physically of his drug addiction, the only time this ever occurred; what remained, however, was the metaphysical anguish, for which acupuncture was not a remedy, and so drug use again ensued. For Artaud and acupuncture, see Florence de Méredieu, *La Chine d'Antonin Artaud*, Paris: Blusson, 2006, pp.41-4.

> or rejects, among the sensations, the emotions, the desires, that the unconscious itself forms and which composes its appetites, its conceptions, its true beliefs, and its *ideas*. It is there that the I becomes conscious and that its power of appreciation, of extreme organic discrimination is employed. Because it is there that *Ciguri* works to separate that which exists from that which doesn't. The liver appears therefore to be the organic filter of the *Unconscious*.[109]

In justice to Artaud, there is an extraordinary payback and richness here, for Artaud, in vividly tracing the gestures and bodily movement/symbology of the peyote priests, finds they are tracing letters in the earth, and following a hieratic numerology straight out of the 'animated hieroglyphs' he had called for in his theatre manifestos.

In describing the ritual, Artaud writes that he believes in 'seeing in this Dance the point where the universal unconscious is ill. And that this is outside of God.' Artaud observes that

> The priest first touched his spleen and then his liver with his right hand while with the left he struck the earth with a staff. Each of these touches was echoed by a distant attitude of the man and the woman, at one moment, of desperate, haughty affirmation, at the next moment, of enraged renunciation. But after several hurried blows struck by the priest, who now held his cane with both hands, they advanced rhythmically toward each other, their elbows wide, and their hands joined in two animate triangles. And at the same time their feet sketched circles on the earth and something resembling the parts of letters, an S, a U, a J, a V.[110]

The ritual dance between the man and women continues for eight distinct movements, and on the eighth the priest places himself to the north for the climax of the rite Artaud describes:

> And with his staff he traced a large 8 in the air. But the scream he uttered at that moment had what it takes to revolutionize the work of the death throes of the dead man black with his ancient sin, as stated in the old buried poem of the Mayas of Yucatan...The scream of the priest was as though to reinforce the outline made in the air. While crying out in this manner the Priest made a sudden movement and represented in the air with his whole body and on the earth with his feet the same figure of eight, until he closed this eight on the South side.[111]

This scream of the peyote priest indicates a peak of seriousness and consequence in this veritable Theater of cruelty, whose 'terrible splendour' has been compared to that of the *shite*, or hero, in the Noh drama.[112]

What is the significance of this rite? In Raymonde Carasco's film *Ciguri 99 – Le Dernier chaman* (1999), one can see, so many decades later, the hieroglyphic

109 Artaud IX, 1971, pp.36-7.

110 Ibid., p.28.

111 Ibid., p.29.

112 Sellin, *The Dramatic Concepts of Antonin Artaud*, p.30.

signs Artaud described, written with fire and water in the earth, written with the elements, in a special grotto. The filmmaker herself, who entered into an initiation with the latter-day Tarahumara priests, seeks to elucidate the series of rites by evoking a contrast between *rêve* and *Sueño*, the dream and the all-encompassing Dream, for which no comparable word exists in French, neither *rêve* nor *songe*. In oral Tarahumara dialect, the distinction is between *gochî-mera* (*rêve*) and *ri-muka* (*Sueño*). This *Sueño*, according to 'the last shaman' of the Tarahumaras, in the Spanish language that was the intermediary between Carasco and the Tarahumaras, is *un trabajo del pensamiento*, a work of or in thought. Carasco seeks to characterise this as a 'trembling, a determination-indetermination' which for the most part escapes European categorisation; it is emphatically another way of seeing and of thinking, 'a relationship (or not) between the question of the body and the question of thought.'[113] Carasco claims this *Sueño* has little to do with the dream of sleep, and even less the power of the imagination, but is rather an untranslatable 'Awakening,' an *éclair*, or strike of lightning. Artaud reports he had a vision of Ciguri that was judged 'authentic' by the Tarahumara priest. Artaud describes this realm of Ciguri, 'who is God,' as an extraordinary, dramatic *reversal*. 'One arrives at such a vision,' Artaud writes, 'only having undergone a tearing and anguish, after which one feels turned around and *reversed* from the other side of things and one no longer understands the world that one has just left.'[114] Artaud does justice to this immense physical tearing and uprooting during his peyote-vision:

> I said *reversed* to the other side of things, as if a terrible force had been given that you be *restored* to that which exists on the other side. One no longer feels the body which one has left and which secured one within its limits, but one feels much happier to belong to the limitless than to oneself, for one understands that what one was has come from the head of this limitless, the Infinite, and that one is going to see it. One feels as if in an effervescent wave which gives off an incessant crackling in all directions. Things which seem to have emerged from what was your spleen, your liver, your heart, or your lungs keep breaking away and bursting in this atmosphere which hesitates between gas and water, but which seems to call to it things and command them to reassemble.[115]

Artaud's peyote experience has the 'ineluctable necessity,' he judges, of a true Theater of cruelty, and it is here, in his incessantly worked and reworked descriptions and evocations of the peyote rites, from Paris in 1937 to Rodez in 1943 to the month before his death in 1948, that we find the origin of the 'body without organs,' although its definitive formation took place in the extreme later circumstances of Artaud's asylum confinement. This 'body without organs' revealed in Mexico at least in part has itself its origin in an hieroglyphic language:

---

113 Raymonde Carasco, 'Approche de la pensée tarahumara,' *Antonin Artaud*, p.134.

114 Artaud IX, 1971, p.32.

115 Ibid.

The things that emerged from my spleen or my liver were shaped like the letters of a very ancient and mysterious alphabet chewed by an enormous mouth... these signs were swept in every direction in space while I seemed to ascend, but not alone. Aided by a strange force. But much more free than when I was on earth alone.[116]

A bewildering experience even for the author of *Nerves Scales* and *Fragments from a Journey in Hell*, Artaud is aided in that he believes he has seen complements to this vision, for the vision of Ciguri corresponds to the 'transcendental representation *painted* of the ultimate and most high realities; and the Mystics have passed through these states and such images before attaining the formula of supreme burnings and rendings.'[117] Because it is one of the most crucial encounters in Artaud's existence, it makes sense to recount some more of this vision, which, like the rite of the Tutuguri performed by the priests, is similarly beholden to signs. Artaud writes:

At a moment something like a wind rose and space shrank back. On the side where my spleen was, an immense void was hollowed out which was painted grey and pink like the shore of the sea. And at the bottom of this void there appeared the form of a stranded root, a kind of J that had at its summit three branches surmounted by an E that was as sad and luminous as an eye. Flames came out of the left ear of the J and, passing behind it, seemed to push all things to the right, to the side where my liver was, but far beyond it. I saw no more and everything vanished or it was I who vanished as I returned to ordinary reality. In any case, it seems that I had seen the very Spirit of Ciguri.[118]

For Artaud, giving another sense of what he called this 'reversal,' peyote unveils 'MAN not born, but INBORN, and that with it the atavistic and personal consciousness is summoned and supported,' since peyote gives consciousness the sense of how it can go, and how far it can go without sinking into the unreal, or the 'unprepared;' peyote, Artaud claims, leads one to see clearly and distinguish perceptions sometimes issuing from the depths but not yet even the hallucinatory products of one's unconscious, and the 'images and emotions of the real.'[119] There is in consciousness, Artaud argues, a '*Marvellous* with which one can go beyond things. And peyote tells us where it is.' It is a 'Fantastic' that is of 'noble quality, its disorder only apparent, it really obeys an order that is fashioned mysteriously and on a level which normal consciousness does not reach but which *Ciguri* allows us to reach, and which is the same mystery of all poetry.'[120] Ciguri is Artaud's double, the 'Master of All Things' whose energetic realm of 'reversal'

116 Ibid., pp.32-3.

117 Ibid., p.33.

118 Ibid., p.33.

119 Ibid., p.34.

120 Ibid., p.35.

is nonetheless inscribed in signs. After the experience, Artaud could be exuberant in what he had found. He had predicted this when he wrote to Jean Paulhan on 23 April 1936 that he would have 'many stunning things' to tell when back in Paris, 'which will show to all the world that the world in effect is double and triple.'[121]

Interpreting the Tarahumara rites

So many utterances Artaud relates in his writings on the Tarahumaras can sound like pure projection, not an uncommon occurrence with psychotropic drugs. One priest tells Artaud that 'With Him [Ciguri] I no longer know the lie and I no longer confuse *that which wills* truly in every man with that which does not will but mimics being with ill will…And soon that is all there will be, this obscene mask of someone sniggering between the sperm and the dung.'[122] Although this, and other statements, may sound like vintage Artaud, Artaud takes special care to vouch for their absolute authenticity, that the priest's 'lucidity' was far too important to change his words in any way. What tends to lend credence to Artaud's extremely vivid and articulate account, is the similar description of the rites many decades later from Carasco, who also managed to capture some of the rituals on film. Artaud opens his essay 'The Peyote Rite of the Tarahumaras' describing being pricked by a double-edged sword between his heart and spleen by the Tarahumara priest, who then quickly withdraws several steps and traces a wide circle in the air with his sword, before lunging at him with full force, yet without harming him in any way. Carasco, like Artaud, describes the rite of the Tutuguri as a preparatory rite linked into the following ritual of Ciguri. The Tutuguri, or Yumari rites are a pre-Colombian danced ritual of request and thanks to the deities, practiced by virtually all the Tarahumaras. The Ciguri, or Jíkuri, are the far more rare, secret shamanic peyote rituals. So under wraps are some aspects of the ceremony that Carasco filmed the Tarahumaras from 1977 to 1985 before ever witnessing the 'rite of the knife,' the extremely important bridge between the Tutuguri and Ciguri ceremonies. Carasco reports the same knife or sword that slays a bull used to begin the rituals, as seen in her films *Ciguri 96* and *Ciguri 98*, is waved in the air by the peyote priest tracing ritual signs. Carasco finds herself, as was Artaud, impressed by the extreme rigor of the mise-en-scène of the collective rite.[123] Following Eric Sellin's characterisation of solar and lunar theatres,[124] Carasco describes the rite of the Tutuguri as the solar rite preparatory to the all-night lunar ritual of the

[121] Artaud V, 1964, p.278.

[122] Artaud IX, 1971, p.31.

[123] Carasco, *Antonin Artaud*, p.137.

[124] Sellin, *The Dramatic Concepts of Antonin Artaud*, pp.11-15.

Ciguri. But it is not merely the remarkably intact rituals that so follow the schema laid out by Artaud in 1936-7 that Carasco confirms, but in many respects their meaning as well.

During Carasco's own initiation, it becomes clear that Ciguri in one sense is the double of the priest, often accessed through the deity called Gloria. Gloria does not speak or teach, but seems to lead or guide an initiate into a certain mode of investigation or development nonetheless. A relation of language is involved, Carasco makes clear, but it is an extremely unstable one, one with the potential to turn usual meanings and usages inside out (as in Artaud's suggestion of an immense 'reversal'). According to her, what was essential to her dialogues with whom she dubs 'the last shaman' was the trembling *intranquilité* in a conversation that neither belonged to one nor the other, to him or her, neither as subjects nor common persons in the accepted sense of the terms. In this nonetheless shared thinking, Carasco characterises speech as acting as 'some sort of infant,' undergoing the same experience of the dawn of thinking, undergoing a search for words, the right words to allow the thought to carry possible meaning and move, without ever ceasing to restart and renew itself. This poverty of language, as she characterises it, leads to an extreme precariousness of equilibrium between herself and the 'last shaman.' This placing in question of what each word said or meant, was part of what Carasco accounts for the unprecedented charm of her encounter. Her play of meaning with the shaman is replicated in his long years of apprenticeship with the silent deity Gloria, who offers no stable linguistic meaning or teaching, but only the 'power of the other, the assistant, to test his power of seeing the invisible.'[125] Carasco strongly emphasises that initiation is not a teaching, but a rigorous research open to anyone who has the patience for the work of seeing.

The ritual of Ciguri enacts this seeing. The white powder of peyote that the Indian priest poured into Artaud's hand, the size of a ripe almond, he was told was sufficient to see God/Ciguri two or three times.[126] Carasco documents the choreography of this enaction: the priest of the rite, she writes, 'operated through strange signs,' slicing semi-circles in the air before the altar of offerings, while other *cantadores* come and go in the axis of the altar, between one cross-dressed in white, the other in red, symbolising male and female polarities, connected by a strap holding the horns of the sacrificed bull.[127] Later towards the end of the nocturnal ceremony, just as the sun begins to rise, another man, a *ayudante* from the now also thoroughly drunk participants, traces rays of the sun starting from the cross in the centre passing through the soil by each participant. One part of the drawing is traced for men (to the left), the other for women (to the right), both enclosed in the circle, creating a type of hermaphroditic sun. By

[125] Carasco, *Antonin Artaud*, p.135.

[126] Artaud IX, 1971, p.31.

[127] Carasco, *Antonin Artaud*, p.136.

this time, after the days of peyote imbibing and a night of drunkenness before the dance of the dawn, an inebriated, enervated dance-trance exists among the participants. Carasco sees the earth-drawing as 'this hieroglyphic birth of a New Sun, of a new dawn.'[128] Artaud recollected a similar moment of revelation of Sun worship in his 1948 poem 'Tutuguri,' – 'its interior full of stars, of incandescent corpuscles; as if the sun while coming took with it a celestial system. It is here that the sun took rank. It took form of a milieu of a celestial system. It is placed all at once at the center of a formidable explosion.'[129]

As Carasco explains, Gloria is also the *Raspador* that it makes its assistant, head of the shamanic line, named such due to the grater, or *râpe*, that he plays during the nighttime ceremony. The 'rite of the knife' that the shaman conducts, when the participants are in the height of a panic and drug-induced trance, is the opening to practices of sorcery. Two mirrors are carefully placed on each axis of the line of vision of the *Raspador*. As the 'last shaman' interpreted to Carasco, the mirrors are 'necessary to see if someone has done evil to someone.'[130] If the mirrors are clear, then the work is good, there is no evidence that one is bound by another, or has been bewitched by another. The 'rite of the knife' both manifests and treats by slicing and cutting through the nightmares due to bewitching. It is an ancient custom of revealing spells. Perhaps one of the reasons Artaud successfully had himself admitted to these rites despite his foreignness was that he powerfully felt himself undergo a spell on his way up the mountains. Referring to himself as a 'dislocated assemblage, this piece of damaged geology,' Artaud claims barriers had been raised against his entering the steep mountains. 'And since I've been up there, the supernatural no longer seems to me something so extraordinary that I cannot say that I was, in the literal sense of the word, *bewitched*.'[131] This claim was first posted in these lines from 'Peyote Dance,' written when Artaud returned to Paris in 1937, but it was one he returned to time and again in his life, and never ceased to believe. Carasco suggests that Artaud's bewitchment reverses itself on his return to Paris in 1946 and after, when he speaks of great global delirium or bewitchment – then it is the world that is bewitched. Artaud will then write 'One bewitches, the mass bewitches, individuals bewitch. All the world knows it. Nobody says a word.'[132] Yet Artaud's rage against the *envoûtement* of especially the Western world, as truly global and far reaching as it was, was also an invective that continued to be directed to the black magic sent against *him* in particular, so it is hardly as simple a matter as a mere reversal. In Artaud's sorcery against sorcery what is outside and what is inside is a line that never ceases to be challenged. Artaud, who was

[128] Ibid., p.138.

[129] Artaud IX, 1971, p.72.

[130] Carasco, *Antonin Artaud*, p.138.

[131] Artaud IX, 1971, p.49.

[132] Artaud XXVI, 1994, p.9.

constantly making signs and hexes, spitting, sneezing and waving off energies, cut a strange figure at the end of his life on the Paris metro; Artaud by this time was deeply immersed in the 'generalized conflagration.' Any audience, he wrote André Breton in 1947, could only be reached through 'barricades and bombs.'[133]

It is not too much to say there was an Artaud before his journey to the Tarahumaras, and an Artaud after, so great a rupture or break is implied.[134] So what was his vision of Ciguri, to which he continually returns? At first sight, Ciguri seems a multiple, a multiplicitous reality or realm. The *Sueño*, Carasco reports, in a sense is really Ciguri, who is not only a being or double of oneself or the Tarahumara people, but also the 'most great of the world-Jíkuri.'[135] These ceremonies of healing, for Carasco demonstrate that in terms of relation to the body, it is not a question of an ideal, transcendental society, a perfect body that the Tarahumaras must emulate, but rather that the Tarahumaras are themselves a world-principle, an immanence, based on the notion, dear and elemental to them, of *reversion*, what Artaud termed 'reversal.' The ceremonies of healing allow this perception of Ciguri. The 'last shaman' tells Carasco that they believe men have three *santés*, or bases of health, women four. If someone is afflicted and still has two there is a possibility of reducing the level of evil or illness; if only one, it may no longer be possible. Carasco calls the *Sueño* this power of seeing the 'other body.' The adepts get a sample or 'taste,' of this other body through the possession of Ciguri. Although Ciguri may not often speak, Ciguri *sounds* through the practice of *Raspador*, the rattling of the grater. This quality of being in-between, in two worlds, which are reversible, is why Carasco argues the Tarahumaras are an 'experimentation…a creation in act, and not a submission to the law of Jíkuri.'[136] As the 'last shaman' describes to her:

> Jíkuri is able to be young or old, like the plant itself. Very fresh and green when one collects it. Then it's old and withered. Jíkuri is like the people: it is there in the old, the young, the beautiful and the ugly, of the little shriveled, of all the young, of boys and also of young girls.[137]

Jíkuri is at once the landscape, the bodies in the landscape, *Jíkuri mayor*, the most great of Jíkuri, and the *Gobernador*, or Governor. Described as both the field of immanence and as the Supreme Authority, this creator-god is such that 'Jíkuri has the power to heal the illnesses of Jíkuri…There is, at the same time,

133 Artaud, *Œuvres*, p.1207.

134 Mèredieu, *C'etait Antonin Artaud*, p.540. This is the case even if one sees the rupture in a largely negative light, as Mèredieu appears to, as an experience that permanently 'destabilised' an already fraught and drug-addicted personality.

135 Carasco, *Antonin Artaud*, p.139.

136 Ibid.

137 Ibid.

absolute singularity and total multiplicity.'[138] And this god of multiplicity (also 'terribly jealous'), never stops being the peyote plant itself as well. As the shaman continues:

> This Jíkuri, this superb peyote, this is my Friend...He is like the *Gobernador*, the *Síriame* in tarahumara, that which commands. He commands from the second of going to collect the food [in the offering]. It is He who directs me when I walk, it is with Him that I go. He is my companion. For me, it is like I walk at the side of my Friend. Yes, I know Him and He speaks to me. He speaks to me in tarahumara. I speak with Him in the *Sueño*.[139]

For Carasco, this description of the Sueño constitutes a '*personnage conceptuel*' necessary to enter into the thought of Jíkuri, 'this being which reassembles us, as well as we reassemble him, without any transcendence on his part.'[140] There is no contempt for the present physical body, Carasco maintains, but rather this Jíkuri thought, this thinking of the Tarahumaras, revolves around 'another body,' what Artaud came to speak about in his last works as the 'body without organs.' Referring to Chinese ideograms and Egyptian hieroglyphs in particular, and claiming through his abandonment of written texts he was multiplying the possibilities of theatre, Artaud had argued in a 28 September 1932 letter to Jean Paulhan that the Theater of cruelty participated in 'eternal laws which are those of all poetry and of all viable language.'[141] Later Artaud will characterise the order of Ciguri/Jíkuri in exactly the same words, 'that is fashioned mysteriously and on a level which normal consciousness does not reach but which *Ciguri* allows us to reach,' this order he maintains, 'is the same mystery of all poetry.'[142] Ciguri would appear for Artaud to be of the same realm and energy as of the 'ancient hieroglyphs,' fused at the base of the Theater of cruelty.

Artaud, who at the end of his life was dedicated to resurrecting a Theater of cruelty, a 'theatre of blood,/a theatre where each representation will have been won/*physically*,'[143] saw this task as inseparable from creating the 'body without organs.' The 'body without organs' was necessary because 'every organ is a parasite...Reality has still not been constructed because the true organs of the human body have still not been composed and placed.'[144] To what is Artaud referring? For Carasco, the 'body without organs' is the body making and remaking itself, into a full, joyous body, a becoming-intense bringing it closer to eternity

[138] Ibid., pp.139-40.

[139] Ibid., p.140.

[140] Ibid.

[141] Artaud IV, 1964, p.133.

[142] Artaud IX, 1971, p.33.

[143] Artaud XIII, 1974, p.146.

[144] Ibid., p.287.

and various forms of ecstasy.[145] She finds 'body without organs' a contemporary phrasing of Ciguri thought, though her description of it appears to owe much to Deleuze and Guattari's influential gloss on Artaud in their two-volume work *Capitalism and Schizophrenia*. Her recommendation of how to attain the 'body without organs' – she emphasises an 'experimentation' at once prudent, patient, that is simultaneously an experience of limits – could be straight from plateau six of *A Thousand Plateaus*.[146] Following Carasco's suggestion, one can see the seeds of Artaud's 'body without organs' within the Tarahumara rites themselves, years before he re-constructs his psyche in the asylums and invents a new language for doing so. Artaud signaled his commencement of the 'body without organs' at the conclusion to *To have done with the judgment of god*:

> I say, for him [Man] to remake his anatomy,
> Man is ill because he is badly constructed.
> It is necessary to strip him bare in order to scrape
>   this animalcule which itches him to death,
>
>   god,
>   and with god,
>   his organs.
> Because tie me down if you like,
> but there is nothing more useless than an organ.
>
> When you will have made him a body without organs,
> then you will have delivered him from all his automatisms
>   returned him to his true liberty.
>
> Then you will teach him again to dance from the inside out
> As in the delirium of the music halls,
> And this inside will be his true side out.[147]

By continuing to look at aspects of the Tarahumara experience through the lens of other shamanistic initiation literature in the next section, it will be possible to begin a comprehension of this process, begun later in earnest and in the most utterly dire conditions during Artaud's asylum confinement. Artaud's 'body without organs' is his ultimate self-generation that comes into its own at the same time Artaud makes clear in several different manners that the notion of secret evanescing hieroglyphics no longer has the same significance for him. It is the site of multiple reversals: the reversal of his ordinary body and identity, of

---

[145] Carasco, *Antonin Artaud*, p.140.

[146] In this section, 'How Do You Make Yourself a Body Without Organs?' Deleuze and Guattari often sound the note of caution. For instance, they write, 'Staying stratified – organized, signified, subjected – is not the worst that can happen; the worst that can happen is if you throw the strata into demented or suicidal collapse, which brings them back down on us heavier than ever.' Deleuze and Guattari, *A Thousand Plateaus*, p.161.

[147] Artaud XIII, 1974, p.104.

space and time, of mortality into immortality. It seems the final fruit of Artaud's Tarahumara initiation into what he called 'reversed to the other side of things.'

'Stopping the world': Artaud's double, triple worlds

The Tarahumaras provided Artaud with what was a peak experience of hieroglyphics, as quickly as it seemed to shatter Artaud. It is as if these powerful hieroglyphics in what Artaud saw as a living Theater of cruelty had in turn effaced themselves and their traces, or reversed themselves, a process seen enacted many years later in his drawings where signs coalesce and emerge and are meticulously sometimes ferociously rubbed out. The drawings are haunted by doubles that are incised and then negated; in them any remaining hieroglyph is a palimpsest that is scarred, or used as platform for the totemisation of Artaud's body double.[148] This 'new body' Artaud seeks to create at the end of his life also, as Carasco suggests, seems to be a legacy of this 'reversal' over 'to the other side of things' Artaud experienced in the rites. So paradoxically the height of the appearance of sacred hieroglyphics in Artaud's life self-destruct and lay the seeds for Artaud's distinctly non-hieroglyphic creation of his 'body without organs.'

While Artaud at the end of his life will rail against any mystical interpretation of his life or predicament some of the few parallels to this esoteric process can be found in shamanic initiation literature. This is perhaps especially exemplary in Carlos Castaneda's accounts of his practices with the northwestern Mexican shaman Don Juan, who Castaneda is introduced to in Arizona.[149] Like Artaud, using peyote (*lophophora williamasii*), but also jimson weed (*datura inoxia*) and a species of psilocybin mushroom as devices, Don Juan taught that the main perceptual results of such psychotropic drugs involved the 'ally,' who

[148] For this analysis of Artaud's drawings, see the sections 'Artaud's 1947-8 notebooks: the combustion of hieroglyphics' and 'Artaud's "graphic cruelties": the face of the void' in Chapter VI.

[149] That Castaneda was so severely challenged as legitimate initiation literature or fieldwork (characterising Yaqui shamanism in a manner that more reflected Huichol practices, creating misleading composites among other errors, etc.) only makes him a more apropos parallel to Artaud. As Hans-Peter Duerr observed, 'there is no neutral way of testing what reality is, there is no such thing as an epistemological Switzerland.' Hans-Peter Duerr, *Dreamtime: Concerning the Boundary Between Wilderness and Civilization*, new ed., Oxford: Blackwell, 1987, p.93. Profoundly Artaudian in their exploration of 'direct creation,' as Deleuze and Guattari write, 'so much the better if the [Castaneda] books are a syncretism rather than an ethnographic study, and the protocol of an experiment rather than an account of an initiation.' Deleuze and Guattari, *A Thousand Plateaus*, p.162. Couched in the language of an ethnographic study, Castaneda explores experimental methodologies for touching the 'outside.' One valuable recent elucidation of this aspect of Castaneda's work is found in Caspar Bruun Jensen, 'Two forms of outside: Castaneda, Blanchot, ontology,' *Hau: Journal of Ethnographic Theory* 3:3, 2013, pp.309-35.

so contacted aided in 'removing one's body,' the goal being 'to remove the body of the practitioner.'[150] This was a necessary precondition for the activity of *seeing*. A young anthropology student at the time, Castaneda compared the millennia old practices of Native American sorcery to a kind of science, obscure since it had radically different 'units of meaning.'[151] This Castaneda sought to provide through his descriptions that suspended judgment. An 'ally,' for instance, was a 'power' that allowed one to move beyond the limits of ordinary reality.[152] Each 'ally' revealed by the plant was manipulable, promulgated a 'rule,' and operated in a realm that could be verified by what Castaneda came to term 'special consensus.'[153] Important for my discussion here, and all the apparent ambiguity of communication with Ciguri, the 'ally' is described as elementally 'formless;' that is, it could be perceived through its sensory and other effects on the sorcerer, and existed as a fully independent entity, but for all that was not visible. Although Castaneda describes the different, sometimes anthropomorphic forms the 'ally' takes, these are all 'qualities of the senses,' the 'ally' is 'not visible at any time.'[154] So these practices of sorcery that Castaneda takes pains to elaborate as a full-blown conceptual system in its own right, are fully compatible with Artaud's opposition of the image and magic and his calls for a 'new science.' This he foreshadowed in his early text, 'Position of the Flesh' (1925), where Artaud writes 'it is necessary to step slowly along the route of dead stones, especially when one has lost the *consciousness of words*. This is an indescribable science and one that explodes in slow pressures.'[155] For Artaud, the 'Sense, and the Science, of all thought is hidden in the nervous vitality of the marrow.'[156]

Castaneda's work is vital in providing a rare contemporary account of what Artaud in *The Theater and Its Double* called 'totemism,' the term 'shamanism' not always being widely used in Paris in the 1920s and '30s. Mircea Eliade's study *Shamanism*, for example, did not appear until 1951. Yet one of the founding texts of the 1937 Collège de Sociologie, a grouping around Georges Bataille, Roger Callois, Michel Leiris, Alexandre Kojève, Artaud's editor Jean Paulhan and others, would be Bataille's essay *L'Apprenti sorcier*,[157] and a seminar on Siberian shamanism supervised by Marcel Mauss as one of its first events. It is not too much to speak of a 'shamanic scene' in Paris at the time, as does Scottish

---

[150] Carlos Castaneda, *A Separate Reality*, London: The Bodley Head, 1971, pp. 15; 18.

[151] Ibid., p.19.

[152] Carlos Castaneda, *The Teachings of Don Juan*, London: Penguin Books, [1968] 2004, p.199.

[153] Ibid., pp.214-27.

[154] Ibid., p.200.

[155] Artaud I:1, 1956, p.236.

[156] Ibid., pp.235-6.

[157] See Denis Hollier, ed., *College of Sociology: 1937-39*, Minneapolis, MN: University of Minnesota Press, 1988.

poet and theorist Kenneth White in his study on Artaud.[158] While Artaud called for a theatre performed by 'specialists in its objective and animated sorcery,' and compares theatre to 'musics of healing by certain tribes that we admire on records but that we are incapable of making appear among ourselves,'[159] the Collège de Sociologie participants also saw themselves as 'medicine men' of a society in its death throes.[160] 'Nagualism' is yet another term, widely used especially in Mexico and Guatemala and often embedded with many concepts directly applicable to Artaud's sojourn with the Tarahumaras. It is a term with a long and colourful history, first surfacing in early Spanish and ecclesiastical writings in the 'New World' of Middle America. In 1894 D.G. Brinton defined it, with not a little paranoia, as:

> Not merely the belief in a guardian spirit, as some have asserted; not merely a survival of fragments of the ancient heathenism, more or less diluted by Christian teachings, as others have maintained; but that above and beyond these, it was a powerful secret organization, extending over a wide area, including members of different languages and varying culture, bound together by mystic rites, by necromantic powers and occult doctrines; but, more than all, by one intense emotion – hatred of the whites – and by one unalterable purpose – that of their destruction, and with them the annihilation of the government and religion which they had introduced.[161]

Later anthropologist George Foster would concur that 'nagualism' was a term used as a catchall by Central American tribal peoples, for such a wild variety of magical beliefs and practices, that as a coherent 'complex,' it did not exist at all.[162] Foster could still conclude that 'nagual' originally meant 'transforming witch,' a term applied to any person capable of shape-shifting or metamorphosis. Both words being of Aztec origin, 'tonal' and 'nagual,' the former word conveyed fate or fortune, the latter any individual capable of changing shape.[163] This was also the sense of 'nagual' in accounts such as Oscar Lewis' *Life in a Mexican Village* (1951), where it refers to a person capable of changing into an animal.[164] Perhaps due to this original meaning, 'nagual' was also often used as a term for companion or guardian animals or spirits, becoming interchangeable with this Amerindian concept. Seeking to debunk the coherence of 'nagual' as a term, anthropologist Benson Saler has indicated the wide range of phenomena 'nagual' has been

158 Kenneth White, *Le Monde d'Antonin Artaud*, Paris: Éditions Complexe, 1989, p.69.

159 Artaud IV, 1964, pp.88; 99.

160 White, *Le Monde d'Antonin Artaud*, p.71.

161 Quoted in Benson Saler, 'Nagual, Witch, and Sorcerer in a Quiché Village,' *Magic, Witchcraft, & Curing*, ed. John Middleton, Austin, TX: University of Texas Press, 1967, p.69.

162 Quoted in ibid, p.70.

163 Ibid.

164 Oscar Lewis, *Life in a Mexican Village*, Urbana, IL: University of Illnois Press, 1951, p.279.

applied to, ranging from the New World syncretism of one Guatemala peasant who referred to St. James as 'the *nagual* of El Palmar,' to its identification with the prospects of day of birth or zodiac sign, the attributes and links to a companion animal (although all of these examples appear to reference the notion of 'soul' or 'double' as well).[165] All these different uses of 'nagual,' among others, in Saler's account are confined to a single village in southwestern Guatemala.

This mutability of meaning was not such an obstacle to Marcel Mauss, who in his *A General Theory of Magic* (1902), noted the closeness of 'nagual' to 'mana,' so widespread a term, Mauss writes, that it has been applied to the entirety of religion and magic. 'Naual,' Mauss writes, is a totem, but so is the sorcerer a *naual*; he is a *nauali*, having the ability to transform himself; while 'naual' also refers to the power enabling him to do so. In keeping with what Saler found much later in rural Guatemala, Mauss writes that the 'naual' or 'nagual' is an individual totem, or an animal species associated with one from birth, but also far more than that. For Mauss it is no contradiction that 'naual/nagual' refers to shamanic powers at large and, etymologically speaking, from the earliest Nahuatal texts, meaning 'secret science,' linked to the earliest notions of 'thought' and 'spirit' in that language, conveying the idea of being mysterious, hidden, disguised. The term therefore seems to Mauss to be excellent shorthand for the idea of a separate spiritual power or 'magic.'[166] Artaud must have found tremendous confirmation in Mauss' conjunction of these ideas, which he read as one of his sources for *Heliogabalus* (1934).[167]

Despite his denigration and general explaining away of the coherence of the term, Saler provides an example of 'nagual' and 'nagualism' that cuts to the heart of Mauss' analysis, as well as illustrating the sense of accounts such as those by Artaud, Carasco, and Castaneda. Saler writes of an Indian medium who is possessed by the 'Earth Essence,' or '*El Mundo*,' '*Santo Mundo*.' He is known as *aj-nagaul mesa*, which quite literally if clumsily means 'one who pertains (*aj*) to the spiritual essence (*nagual*) of the Table (*mesa*).'[168] In this instance, the medium becomes possessed while sitting at an especially consecrated wooden table. In the same area, Saler finds that for the 'calendar shaman' (who works with the powers or *nagual* of the birth date), this sacred *mesa* is not a wooden table, but rather the '*mesa* of the World' is any place where people burn copal to *El Mundo*, or 'Master of the World,' who is the 'spiritual essence' of the 'material world.'[169] The *mesa* of the shaman in this example is a small wooden cross, which distin-

[165] Saler, 'Nagual, Witch, and Sorcerer in a Quiché Village,' pp.75-9.

[166] Marcel Mauss, *A General Theory of Magic*, trans. Robert Brain, London & New York, NY: Routledge, [1902] 2002, p.142.

[167] The crucial importance of Mauss' description of *mana* for Artaud will be continued in the next chapter of this work.

[168] Saler, 'Nagual, Sorcerer, and Witch in a Quiché Village,' p.77.

[169] Ibid.

guishes the shamans who have received such a *mesa* from those who have not. The altars that surround the village Saler studied are the 'tables' or 'burning places' of *El Mundo*, each altar being being a manifestation of this 'Earth Essence.' Saler recognises what the two different shamans share is the notion of *El Mundo* as the spiritual essence or ruler of the material Earth, signified by 'certain consecrated landmarks.'[170] In this sort of 'primitive' earth religion, as Don Juan at one point tells Castaneda, 'the earth is a sentient being.'[171] The earth is 'the very being that allows warrior-travelers to leave on their definitive journey.'[172] As gradually becomes clearer in Castaneda's accounts, any powers that accrue to the apprentice, that are developed through contact with the 'ally,' are ultimately a gift from the body of the earth.[173] As such, Castaneda's formulation does not contradict the role of the earth's bodies in Deleuze and Guattari's account of modern and contemporary capitalism's 'vast privatization of the organs, which corresponds to the decoding of flows that have become abstract.'[174] The marking, tattooing and scarification of bodies in 'traditional' societies, shows they are invested as 'the earth's products,' and functioning as signs they are 'attracted, repelled, miraculated, following the requirements of a socius' as a 'full body, an earth.'[175]

The words that convey these experiences, beliefs, or realities of the earth's bodies, these 'infants' in Carasco's parlance, are as mutable as those in dreams. This fluid change of meaning depending on context was a challenge Mauss was eager to meet. How foreign these realities can appear to ordinary language in ordinary states of mind is one of the virtues of the dialogues shared by Castaneda with Don Juan. This is not entirely due to secrecy, although at one point Don Juan tells his student that his chants and songs, for example, are those granted to him by his protector, they are not to be shared with anyone else. The name of the protector, likewise, is only to be used to call the protector in certain instances, and is a code between the initiate and the protector not applicable to any other person. As Don Juan tells Castaneda, 'If some day he accepts you, he will tell you his name. That name will be for you alone to use, either to call him loudly or to say quietly to yourself. Perhaps he will tell you his name is José. Who knows?'[176] When Castaneda presses Don Juan for information after his first use of peyote, Don Juan confirms that the spirit or 'protector' in the peyote, Mescalito, speaks,

---

170 Ibid.

171 Carlos Castaneda, *The Fire From Within*, New York, NY: Washington Square Press, 1991, p.205.

172 Carlos Castaneda, *The Active Side of Infinity*, New York, NY: Harper Collins, 1998, p.260.

173 Carlos Castaneda, *Tales of Power*, New York, NY: Simon & Schuster, 1974, p.292.

174 Deleuze and Guattari, *Anti-Oedipus*, pp.142-3.

175 Ibid., p.144.

176 Castaneda, *The Teachings of Don Juan*, p.103.

'But not in words...He talks differently to every man.'[177] There were ultimately no exact steps therefore for encountering and proceeding along the path of knowledge with Mescalito, whose uniqueness meant 'he was not the same for every man.'[178] It is more accurate to say Mescalito 'showed' knowledge, or how to live – on his hand, among the rocks, on the trees, or immediately in front of the initiate. Don Juan calls it a 'teaching' rather than a 'picture.'[179]

Although Castaneda's accounts confirm the *intranquilité* and ambiguity of language involved, they also serve to functionally explain terms like 'nagual' and its counterpart, or opposite, the 'tonal,' in the shamanic context. What anthropologist George Foster had tried to define in 1944 as 'fate or fortune,'[180] the tonal 'makes up the rules by which it apprehends the world. So, in a manner of speaking, it creates the world.'[181] Much is made of this distinction between 'nagual' and 'tonal' in the fourth book in Castaneda's series, part and parcel of his initiation into living as 'warrior,' 'man of knowledge,' and thereby passing into an existence beyond 'interpretation.' Deleuze and Guattari's gloss on these passages is especially acute. They write:

> The tonal seems to cover many disparate things: It is the organism, and also all that is organised and organising; but it is also signifiance, and all that is signifying or signified, all that is susceptible to interpretation, explanation, all that is memorizable in the form of something recalling something else; finally it is the Self (*Moi*), the subject, the historical, social, or individual person, and the corresponding feelings. In short, the tonal is everything, including God...Yet the tonal is only an island. For the *nagual* is also everything. And it is the same everything, but under such conditions that the body without organs has replaced the organism and experimentation has replaced all interpretation, for which it no longer has any use.[182]

The *nagual* is 'also everything,' hence Artaud's '*reversed* to the other side of things.' In Castaneda's terms, it demands an effacement of 'personal history;' in Deleuze and Guattari's language it is 'becomings-molecular' that have 'replaced history, individual or general.'[183] For Artaud it is the double or virtual body. Rather than interpretations, memories and projections of subjectification, there are colours, intensities, sounds, movements of becoming without a 'Self.' The first task Don Juan sets Castaneda is to find his 'place,' his place of strength or power, on Don Juan's porch. Castaneda eventually finds it, in a process that takes all night, through noticing a distinct change in hue in his peripheral vi-

---

177 Ibid., p.53.

178 Ibid.

179 Ibid.

180 Foster quoted in Saler, 'Nagual, Sorcerer, and Witch in a Quiché Village,' p.70.

181 Castaneda, *Tales of Power*, p.125.

182 Deleuze and Guattari, *A Thousand Plateaus*, p.162.

183 Ibid.

sion, as well as involuntary and profoundly disturbing changes in posture when he reaches an opposite, or 'weak,' spot. He finds he has to ward off the interpretations of his usual 'tonal' self on the absurdity of his rolling around and marking territory on a wooden porch for most of a night. The corralling, shrinking, or effacement of the tonal is necessary, Don Juan later tells him, in this process that he calls 'stopping the world.' Castaneda judges this an apt term, since:

> "Stopping the world" was indeed an appropriate rendition of certain states of awareness in which the reality of everyday life is altered because the flow of interpretation, which ordinarily runs uninterruptedly, has been stopped by a set of circumstances alien to the flow. In my case the set of circumstances alien to my normal flow of interpretations was the sorcery description of the world.[184]

Castaneda is able to find these spots of ally and enemy, due to the technique of becoming 'cross-eyed,' even if he was unaware of what he was doing. Becoming 'cross-eyed' is the technique of seeing double-images, holding the image of an object separate in each eye without the usual image conversion into single plane of vision.[185] The cultivation of such double perception or double vision is what enables one to perceive minute changes and feelings in the landscape that ordinary vision will not register. Don Juan tells him that all of the teachings he has given him from the very beginning, such as double perception, have been techniques for 'stopping the world.'[186] 'Stopping the world' is precisely the phrase Artaud uses in *To have done with the judgment of god* and similar descriptions of what it entails punctuate much of the material in his *Cahiers du retour à Paris* (1946-8). It is essential to Artaud's statements about punching holes in, or otherwise altering, time – 'I manipulate the ages of a great inexistent clock.'[187] Artaud could have come across this term in his conversations with the peyote priests, or through his reading in Aztec and Toltec mythologies, which he made part of his energy maps and diagramming in his studies on non-western cultures, in preparation for his Mexican journey, diagrams which illustrated a 'state of things we lack in industrial civilization.'[188]

Castaneda comes to learn that psychotropic plants are merely an 'aid', to jolt those with dogmatic certainties, what is more elemental and essential is that all of the lessons of sorcery Don Juan imparts are means of 'stopping the world.' At the conclusion to *Journey to Ixtlan*, Castaneda presents this as an actual experience or occurrence. Preceded by sitting for a time in a 'power spot' on a moun-

---

184 Castaneda, *Journey to Ixtlan*, New York, NY: Washington Square Press, 1972. p.xiii-iv. Also see the chapter by that name, pp. 246-56.

185 Ibid., p.49.

186 Ibid., p.xii.

187 Artaud XXIV, 1988, p.27.

188 Artaud VIII, 1971, pp.129-158, p.158. See the discussion of these diagrams at the beginning of the section 'Casting spells' in Chapter V.

tain and having a conversation with a coyote, who speaks in what resemble sentences, with nouns and verbs, the animal metamorphoses into a 'luminous being' who touches Castaneda in 'some undefined part of myself and my body experienced such an exquisite indescribable warmth and well-being that it was as if the touch had made me explode.'[189] The ordinary world disappears for Castaneda, who becomes 'transfixed' in this 'peak experience' where he loses for an undetermined period of time all bodily perceptions.[190] Then he becomes 'struck,'

> The sun was almost over the horizon. I was looking directly into it and then I saw the 'lines of the world.' I actually perceived the most extraordinary profusion of fluorescent white lines which crisscrossed everything around me. For a moment I thought that I was perhaps experiencing sunlight as it was being refracted by my eyelashes. I blinked and looked again. The lines were constant and were superimposed on or were coming through everything in the surroundings. I turned around and examined an extraordinarily new world. The lines were visible and steady even if I looked away from the sun.[191]

As Don Juan explains to him, this was an authentic experience of 'stopping the world,' meaning that Castaneda was now prepared for *seeing*, for the activity of moving between two worlds. The communication with the coyote was only possible, Don Juan points out, and his body capable of recognising it, 'because the world had collapsed.'[192] To believe coyotes 'talk' is to belong to the sorcerer's realm; to believe there is no way coyotes can 'talk' is to remain stuck in ordinary reality. Likewise, it is in the sorcerer's realm that one can see the 'lines of the world.' However peculiar, or however particular to a certain line of indigenous New World shamanism Castaneda's account may seem to be, it accords with all of the criteria pragmatist psychologist William James elaborated in his definition of 'religious experience.' Arguing there were as many mystical experiences as there were people who experienced them, James still described the attributes of such experience as ineffability, having a noetic quality, transiency, and passivity – all characteristics of Castaneda's journey.[193] They are also the characteristics of Artaud's Tarahumara rites. It is in trying to account for and integrate them that to a great extent Artaud will spend the rest of his life. One could remain here and cast Artaud's experience within the terms of classical mysticism,[194] but

[189] Castaneda, *Journey to Ixtlan*, p.252.

[190] Psychologist Abraham Maslow referred to various 'religious' and ecstatic states as 'peak experiences,' see Abraham H. Maslow, *Religions, Values, and Peak-Experiences*, New York, NY: Penguin, 1970; also Maslow, *The Further Reaches of Human Nature*, New ed., New York, NY: Arkana, 1994.

[191] Castaneda, *Journey to Ixtlan*, p.252.

[192] Ibid., p.253.

[193] William James, *The Varieties of Religious Experience*, New York, NY & London: Macmillan Publishing, [1902] 1961, pp.299-300.

[194] For a comprehensive definition and overview see Evelyn Underhill, *Mysticism*, 2nd rev. ed., London: One World Publications, 1999.

Artaud at the end of his life condemns the peyote priests as well as the 'filthy' Buddhists as manipulators and conjurers; his own breach into infinity does not allow any priestly guides and the 'body without organs' as a kind of absolute self-reference sets its own terms.

Touching the outside

Artaud insisted in one of his earlier texts 'like the world has its geography, the interior of man has its geography which is a material thing.'[195] He had long given primacy to the movement of an 'essential geometry,' as in his preface to a book of watercolours by artist Jean de Bosschère which appeared in 1929, where he had written of a 'mucous life which is in process between the lines or in the body of the same lines and carries the suggestions of a world that has absolutely nothing to do with thought.'[196] In one of his letters to Janine Kahn, on 15 August 1926, Artaud relates his visit to the seer Madame Sacco, the fortune-teller immortalised in André Breton's novel *Nadja* (1928), and tells of her prediction that in order to deliver himself, to continue to write, he must leave France and Europe, that journeying is what will enable him to recover what he calls the 'life plane' [*vie plane*].[197] This 'life plane' has no localisable consistency except in those enigmatic lines. The later Artaud, as he made clear enough in Paris after his return from Rodez in 1946, insisted he created space – 'I am not forced into a made space, I create it without cease, without possible halt, forever.'[198] This is an insistence on absolute self-creation, not an adherence to an ultimate hieroglyphic of lines. To define Artaud in a particular state or condition, the final Artaud claimed, is to destroy him.[199] Artaud's 'foundation' is a 'perpetual variable,'[200] which is not ever a world of meter and measurement.[201] What can only be suggested here for the moment, is that in the complex relation of interiority and exteriority in Artaud, the 'later' Artaud of the 'body without organs' will give preference to the 'outside,'[202] the movement of breath and gesture, in defiance of any system of measure and static imagery, among which he will include most mystical complexions of beliefs. This is true even if one thinks, following Deleuze, that this interiority to which we refer is one we 'must conjure up' as an 'illusory interiority in order to restore words and things to their constitu-

195 Artaud VIII, 1971, p.150.

196 Artaud II, 1961, pp.223-227.

197 Artaud, *Œuvres*. p.212.

198 Artaud XXII, 1986, p.436.

199 Ibid., p.39.

200 Artaud XX, 1984, p.66.

201 Artaud XXII, 1986, p.436.

202 White, *Le Monde d'Antonin Artaud*, p.131.

tive exteriority.'[203] For Artaud will never stop participating in the 'occult,' but for him there will increasingly be two occults: one, that he will denounce, involves the 'bewitchment' that submits the visible to the invisible. To this, Artaud will oppose the 'true occult,' that 'extension of the visible and the sensible into the world least penetrated.'[204] This is the extension that will battle the demons and spirits and all the other false conjurations. This will correspond for him as well to two modes of hallucination, the ones of false vision stigmatised by psychiatric incarceration, and the active operation of magical principles that Artaud enacts through his writing (in the widest sense), in his drawings, his syllable language and spells. This activity, for Artaud, challenges the distinction between interior and exterior.[205] Hence his frequent recourse to figuration in the drawings, since 'I'm still not sure of the limits at which the body of the human self can stop.'[206] That Artaud's 'sacred hieroglyphs' adumbrated in the theatre manifestoes eventually disappear will become clearer through a close look at his drawings, their double-movement of projection and return in the flesh, and what is at stake in their reliance on 'the spontaneity of line.'[207]

For now I must reiterate the extraordinary resonance and importance of this life-long interrogation and fascination with 'lines' or 'zigzags,' as part of what can be said to be Artaud's engagement with the 'outside,' and pursue the possibility of what Artaud thinks in common with Foucault's sense of a thought:

> as though setting its limits from without…making its dispersion shine forth… not in order to grasp its foundation or justification but in order to regain the space of its unfolding, the void serving as its site, the distance in which it is constituted and into which its immediate certainties slip the moment they are glimpsed.[208]

What I am examining here is not necessarily the identity of the 'lines' Castaneda describes in his experience of 'stopping the world' with those described by Foucault and Deleuze, but precisely their coincidence in the relations described by Artaud. This coincidence is far from fortuitous, given Deleuze's characterisation of these lines as a 'double, with all our double's otherness.'[209] Deleuze's description here, as elsewhere, relies much on his reading of Artaud. This function of lines in Deleuze, and in Deleuze and Guattari's collaborative work, is

203 Deleuze, *Foucault*, p.43.

204 Artaud XXVI, 1994, p.173.

205 Jean-François Chevrier, 'Le vérité de l'hallucination contre "le mensonge de l'Être,"' *Antonin Artaud*, p.206.

206 Artaud, *Œuvres*, p.1535; *Watchfiends & Rack Screams*, p.278.

207 Ibid.; ibid., p.279. For this discussion of Artaud's drawings see Chapter VI.

208 Michel Foucault, 'Maurice Blanchot: The Thought from Outside,' *Foucault/Blanchot*, trans. Brian Massumi, New York, NY: Zone Books, 1990, pp.15-16.

209 Gilles Deleuze, *Negotiations: Interviews 1972-1990*, trans. Martin Joughlin, New York, NY: Columbia University Press, 1995, p.110.

quite central since it is lines that compose any cartography, their alternative to methodologies that rely on the dominance of the signifier.[210] Deleuze and Guattari's use of 'lines' is therefore extremely complex, since these lines define any kind of positionality in relation to any type of body or system, as they write in *A Thousand Plateaus*, 'we are composed of...bundles of lines, for each kind is multiple.'[211] In *A Thousand Plateaus* Deleuze and Guattari distinguish between three kinds of lines: the molar or rigid line of any segmentarity, a line that absolutely must be followed (the line from life to death, for example, or home to work); molecular or supple lines that resist or escape molar coding or overcoding (and that significantly for our discussion here, originate in presignifying regimes); and finally, lines of flights that indicate deterritorialisation, a 'vector of escape' or 'move between milieus,' in complexity theory a move that triggers bifurcations.[212] Lines of flight can be read as the 'primary constituents' of any assemblage, body or space, but are never pure for all that, since they must still cover or pass numerous borders, boundaries, segmentations of various sorts.[213]

Artaud's 'lines,' what he termed 'occult geometry,' also broach an 'outside,' though in a different language and a different vocabulary. Here I should note once more how Artaud objected to the language in which he was forced to describe his Theater of cruelty, as he also referred to it as an alchemical or metaphysical theatre. In his address on the theatre on 8 December 1931 in Paris, Artaud, as if in self-criticism, seemed to assimilate such words to 'dead language, impermeable to spirit, the handling of which is reserved to Erudite souls.'[214] What remains today the fastest indicator of a concern with 'transcendence,' the word 'metaphysic' for Artaud indeed conveys this, but in the 'transcendent' sense of opposing psychological theatre, the symptom of the world that exists, a fatally decayed Western culture, for which he has unremitting hostility, and in opposition to has to take recourse to such *other*, dubiously abstract terminology, for what is a comprehensive action of cruelty. In an article published in *Paris-Soir,* 14 July 1932, Artaud makes clearer his use of terms like 'metaphysical' or 'religious' in the context of his theatre: he had written of a 'religious and metaphysical idea of the theatre' certainly, 'but in the sense of magical, real, absolutely efficacious action.' 'And it is necessary to understand,' Artaud continued, 'that I take words like "religious" and "metaphysical" in a sense which has nothing to

[210] For the importance of this 'functional cartography' for an understanding of Artaud, see 'The matter of theory' section in Chapter I.

[211] Deleuze and Guattari, *A Thousand Plateaus*, p.202.

[212] These last definitions are taken from Mark Bonta and John Protevi, *Deleuze and Geophilosophy, A Guide and Glossary*, Edinburgh: Edinburgh University Press, 2004, p.106.

[213] Ibid., p.107.

[214] Artaud V, 1964, p.12.

do with religion, nor with metaphysics as one habitually understands them.'[215] This is true even though Artaud compares the construction of the physical space of this theatre to the principles of sacred architecture in both the churches of the West and in the temples of Tibet. 'Metaphysical' for Artaud is above all a term of the most extreme possible contrast, which for Artaud in the 1930's is indeed a contrast of West and East. 'Metaphysics' is a word which in its ordinary or conventional use may be 'one ineffectual and dead idea which conveys little enough even to the mind,' but Artaud uses it to evoke the 'whole complex of gestures, signs, postures, and sonorities which constitute the language of stage performance, this language which develops all its physical and poetic effects on every level of consciousness and in all the senses.'[216] This activation of elemental forces that Artaud wanted to evoke in his theatre of the East has not ceased to touch. As noted in the previous chapter in the 1920s the East for Artaud, as for many of the surrealists, is a real pole of hope and possibility beyond the critical stagnation of Europe. Later in life, Artaud moves beyond the duality of this West/East dichotomy as well, writing 'I am without East nor West,/I move through the lacunae without foundation.'[217] Or, more dramatically, 'My self rejected from the East in the West,/I wanted to centre a stone in my body/to show that I was outside East and West.'[218]

If Artaud's journey to the Tarahumaras was manifestly a 'line of flight' in Deleuze and Guattari's terms, Artaud's utilisation of the Theater of cruelty he found extant with the Tarahumara Indians was arguably a mode of crossing the 'line' altogether – Artaud challenges 'molar' lines that for Deleuze and Guattari are impregnable, such as the line of life/death. In Deleuze and Guattari's terms an absolute 'line of flight' is not possible; vanishing lines, as in Western perspective painting that took hold in the Early Renaissance in landscape painting and so on, are not lines of flight at all but rather are fixed vectors, flows that have been reterritorialised.[219] This radicality of Artaud's 'solution' in that he holds out the possibility of crossing the line, including 'molar' lines – and he is often trying to replicate the insight and ritual he found among the Tarahumaras in different ways at the end of his life – can be approached closely by Deleuze and Guattari but it is difficult to conclude that their elaborations on the line, that must remain within a plane of immanence, that is a conceptual space, fully encapsulates Artaud's project. These dilemmas of 'crossing the line' was addressed by Deleuze in one of his late interviews as the question – 'how far can we unfold

---

215 Ibid., pp.35-6.

216 Artaud IV, 1964, pp.53-4.

217 Artaud XIX, 1984, p.184.

218 Artaud XXII, 1986, p.177. Yet Chinese theater remained an important pole and 'atmosphere' for Artaud's work at Rodez and after, see for example Mèredieu, *La Chine d'Antonin Artaud*, pp. 62-4.

219 Bonta and Protevi, *Deleuze and Geophilosophy*, p.107.

the line without falling into a breathless void, into death, and how can we fold it, but without losing touch with it, to produce an inside copresent with the outside, corresponding to the outside?'[220] For Deleuze it is a matter of 'practices,' to 'make it [the line] endurable, workable, thinkable.'[221] In the case of Foucault's version of the line that is quite close to Deleuze, crossing the line is bound up with the question of what is beyond knowledge and power, with the 'inability,' for instance, adumbrated in his essay 'Lives of Infamous Men,' 'to cross the line, to get to the other side…always the same choice, on the side of power, of what it says or what people say…'[222] This 'line' or relation that is no longer a power relation Deleuze found 'difficult to talk about.'[223] Its location is 'everywhere thought confronts some thing like madness, and life some thing like death'– liminal locations in other words in which Artaud spent an extraordinary amount of time. The best approximations for this relation or 'line' Deleuze finds only in literature or visual art:

> Miller used to say you find it in any molecule, in nerve fibers, in the threads of a spider's web. It's the fearsome whaling line, which Melville says (in *Moby Dick*) can carry us off to strangle us as it flies out. For Michaux it's the line of drugs, 'headlong acceleration,' the 'whiplash of a frenzied coachman.' It may be a painter's line, like Kandinsky's, or the one leading to Van Gogh's death. I think we ride such lines whenever we think bewilderingly enough or live forcefully enough. They're lines that go beyond knowledge (how could they be 'known'?), and it's our relations to these lines that go beyond power relations (as Nietzsche says, who could call it 'a will to control'?)…it's the line Outside.[224]

This 'line outside' is 'our double, with all our double's otherness.' This 'return' from the Outside is also a confrontation with it. The sort of shock that produces all thinking, has the capacity as well in that it 'destroys all thinking, like the drugs Michaux had to stop using.'[225] What is crucial is 'bending the line so we manage to live upon it, with it: a matter of life and death.'[226] What precisely is this 'outside,' that elsewhere Deleuze describes as simultaneously an interiority more 'inside' than any internal world, and an exterior or 'outside' further away than an external world? Deleuze writes that this 'outside' is 'not a fixed limit but a moving matter animated by peristaltic movements, folds and foldings that together make up an inside: they are not something other than the outside, but precisely

[220] Deleuze, *Negotiations*, p.113.

[221] Ibid., p.111.

[222] Michel Foucault, 'The Lives of Infamous Men,' in *Power, Truth, Strategy*, ed. Meaghan Morris and Paul Patton, Sydney: Feral Publications, 1979, pp.76-91.

[223] Deleuze, *Negotiations*, p.110.

[224] Ibid.

[225] Ibid., pp.110-1.

[226] Ibid., p.111.

the inside *of* the outside.'[227] Interpreting Foucault, Deleuze argues that the classical age already maintained 'an inside of thought, the unthought,' when it spoke of the finite, of the different orders or folds of infinity; from the 19th century on it is the different dimensions of finitude itself that constitute a depth.[228] Foucault wrote of the 'unthought' as 'the Other that is not only a brother but a twin, born, not of man, nor in man, but beside him and at the same time, in an identical newness, in an unavoidable duality...both exterior to him and indispensable to him.'[229] The unthought was thus an 'insistent double.' As an 'inside' which is manifestly a fold of the 'outside,' Deleuze thought the best example Foucault's Renaissance madman who is put out to sea in a boat; Deleuze writes 'Thought has no other being than this madman himself.'[230] Of this madman, Foucault observes:

> It is for the other world that the madman sets sail in his fools' boat; it is from the other world that he comes when he disembarks. The madman's voyage is at once a rigorous division and an absolute Passage. In one sense, it simply develops, across a half-real, half-imaginary geography, the madman's *liminal* position on the horizon of medieval concern – a position symbolized and made real at the same time by the madman's privilege of being *confined* within the city *gates*: his exclusion must enclose him; if he cannot and must not have another *prison* than the *threshold* itself, he is kept at the point of passage. He is put in the interior of the exterior, and inversely.[231]

So the mentally ill, or 'mentally alienated' in the old parlance, personify this border – much as figures such as Artaud, Nietzsche or Van Gogh all mark a chiasmus in Western perception – although Foucault also distinguished between the conditions of 'mental illness' and madness.[232]

As Foucault explored in his book with the deceptively simple title *This Is Not a Pipe*,[233] his study of René Magritte, any kind of knowledge is irreducibly double, since it involves speaking and seeing, but we do not see what we speak about, or speak about what we see. Foucault writes that the 'slender, colorless, neutral strip' that separates text and figure in Magritte's painting *Ceci n'est pas*

---

227 Deleuze, *Foucault*, p.96-7.

228 Ibid., p.97.

229 Michel Foucault, *The Order of Things*, trans. Alan Sheridan, New York, NY: Vintage, [1966] 1973, p.326.

230 Deleuze, *Foucault*, p.97.

231 Foucault, *Madness and Civilization*, pp.8-9.

232 Foucault's position was quite similar to R.D. Laing's 'Let no one suppose that we meet "true" madness any more than that we are truly sane. The madness that we encounter in "patients" is a gross travesty, a mockery, a grotesque caricature of what the natural healing of that estranged integration we call sanity might be.' R.D. Laing, *The Politics of Experience*, London: Penguin Books, 1967, pp.118-9.

233 Michel Foucault, *This Is Not A Pipe*, trans. James Harkness, Berkeley, CA: University of California Press, [1973] 1981.

une pipe (1926), functions as a 'crevasse – an uncertain, foggy region now dividing the pipe floating in its imagistic heaven from the mundane tramp of words marching in their successive line.' A radical disjunction, in other words, operates between the representation or drawing of the pipe, from the statement 'this is a pipe.'[234] What this disjunction creates is not so much a gap, as an 'absence of space,' that space that would fill in the common understanding of the signs of words with the image's lines. Instead of a 'common place' what emerges is a 'non-place,' where all the links are broken, where no one is present any longer.[235] In these wildly dispersing exteriorities of word and image, neither the representation, the phrase, or the 'this' are the 'pipe,' these relations no longer have a 'place where they can meet,' either on the black canvas or above it.[236] In his critique of phenomenology, Foucault argued that a true phenomenological 'bracketing' would necessarily involve going beyond words and phrases to 'statements,' and beyond the thing or 'thing-itself' to 'visibilities.' But 'statements' only testify 'language is,' not to any subject or thing. And 'visibilities' only demonstrate their 'light-being' in forms and proportions that likewise exist immanently, free of phenomenology's intentional gaze.[237] Intentionality for Foucault therefore becomes dysfunctional, an invalid category, unable to sustain its capacity between 'visibilities' and 'light-being.' Any kind of intentionality must fall and fail within this void, of the non-relation between speaking and seeing. This negotiation of irreducible forms – of 'visibilities' and 'light-being' neither of which can be defined in terms of the other – can only be subject to what Deleuze calls a 'double capture' through an 'audiovisual battle,' a matter of 'a pure relation between forces that emerges in the irreducible separation of forms.'[238] Since knowledge is created from the two forms in 'non relation,' it must ascribe a relation between them. Here is not, according to Deleuze, the 'fold of Being, but rather the interlacing of its two forms.'[239] This incompatibility of forms is the 'source of battle.' What sets up relations between the two forms are thus of necessity power relations. Both of these forms, having become knowledge, or knowledge-being, for Deleuze become forms of exteriority, jockeyed into position by 'power-Being.' These relations of power are an 'unformable and unformed Outside which gives rise to forces and their changing combinations;' this 'figure of Being' is characterised as a 'floating line with no contours which is the only element that makes

---

[234] Ibid., p.28.

[235] Ibid., pp.31; 41.

[236] Ibid., p.28.

[237] For the formation of 'statements,' see Foucault, *The Archaeology of Knowledge*, trans. Alan Sheridan, London: Tavistock, [1969] 1972, pp.89-98; 146.; for 'light-being' see Foucault, *Death and the Labyrinth*, trans. Charles Ruas, London: Athlone Press, 1987, pp.105-8.

[238] Deleuze, *Foucault*, p.112.

[239] Ibid.

the two forms in battle communicate.'[240] Power-relations, Foucault would come to argue in his later *History of Sexuality*, have a 'directly productive role, wherever they come into play.'[241]

This non-relation between modalities is Artaud's issue from the beginning, in an especially dramatic form as his 1923-4 letters to Jacques Rivière attest, but his relationship to this problematic changes. It is crucial to the significant shift between the 'early' and 'late' Artaud. Whereas the early Artaud is in anguish due to this disjunction, this lack of ability to capture even for an instant his thought and capacity, the later Artaud (at Rodez and after, 1945-8) continues in anguish, no doubt, but affirms the void and non-relation of image and word and sound. Rather than lament his lack of connection to body and world, Artaud proclaims a 'new body' and a new world, predicated on the destruction of the existing one. In his drawings and even more spectacularly in a work like *To have done with the judgment of god* (1947-8) this chasm between image and word and sound and movement and meaning is a cosmic and cosmological one for Artaud, one whose repercussions are irreparable. In marked contrast to Artaud, and to the theoretical sources of Foucault and Deleuze, one could look to Maurice Merleau-Ponty's version of these dynamics in his notion of the 'chiasm' as he outlines it in his last work *The Visible and the Invisible* (1964). Merleau-Ponty describes a perceptual realm first grasped not as things, but as 'a perception of *elements* (water, air...) of *rays of the world*, of things which are dimensions, which are worlds.'[242] This description of a world of rays or dimensions at first glance resembles the world that disappears into the 'essential geometry' that Artaud limns in his art writings or Mexico City addresses. In trying to push the discoveries of phenomenology past philosophies of reflection and intuition as well as psychoanalysis (specifically in the works of Sartre, Bergson and Freud), Merleau-Ponty sought to explore the '*flesh* of things,'[243] pushing the implications of embodiment much further than these other thinkers. What Foucault examined as the abyss between the sayable and the visible is replayed in Merleau-Ponty as the separation or *écart* between the sentient and the sensible. But for the latter this separation enables the transitivity of communication in a field of being. In the case of the visible, there has to be a 'prepossession' of it, so that 'he *is of it*.'[244] There is a 'cross-situating' of the modalities of the visible in the tangible (which

240 Ibid., p.113.

241 Michel Foucault, *A History of Sexuality: Vol. 1, An Introduction*, trans. Robert Hurley. New York, NY: Pantheon, 1978, p.94.

242 Maurice Merleau-Ponty, *The Visible and the Invisible*, ed. Claude Lefort, trans. Alphonso Lingis, Evanston, IL: Northwestern University Press, [1964] 1968, p.218. Italics in original.

243 Ibid., p.133.

244 Ibid., pp.133; 135. Italics in original.

carries visual evidence) and the tangible in the visible.[245] Their implication in each other indicate a common world, an 'order of being' so that 'one who looks must not himself be foreign to the world that he looks at.'[246] The 'thickness of flesh' between viewer and thing seen is no 'obstacle' but rather their 'means of communication.'[247] The body according to Artaud offered a choice between the 'infinitesimal inside' and an 'infinite outside.'[248] For Merleau-Ponty it is the body that melds and combines through its ontogenesis its different dimensions and aspects, the inside and outside. There is a preobjective and prereflective unity of the body, Merleau-Ponty maintains, that is already also intersubjective and intercorporeal, part of a shared world. It is therefore a 'Sentient in general before a Sensible in general.'[249] The body, in other words, participates in the 'order of being. This participation is not ensured through belonging to the same order of "consciousness," but rather of a "carnal adherence" of the visible returning to itself, the sentient to the sensible, by means of the very gap or fission between them.'[250] This is a patient process with the other which consists of being making itself the inside of its outside and the outside of its inside.

One could look at the late career of Artaud especially as precisely this transitive movement. Yet for Merleau-Ponty the flesh is not at all chaos and sheer contingency as it is for Artaud (and by extension as theorised by Foucault and Deleuze). It is a 'texture that returns to itself and conforms to itself.'[251] The body, in contradiction to the later Artaud, and to the reading of the 'body without organs' by Deleuze and Guattari, for Merleau-Ponty is not synonymous with matter. Neither is it some conjunction of body and spirit, those contraries that once so dominated the thought and life of Artaud. The body as the flesh of the world is 'the concrete emblem of a general manner of being.'[252] These qualities of visibility and tactility for Merleau-Ponty are reversible but this is a reversibility that is never actually realised. They are experiences, Merleau-Ponty recognises, that never overlap exactly. Yet there is an unshakeable, unbreakable hinge between them: 'spanned' by the totality of the body and the being of the world, they do not reveal an ontological void. The flesh for him revolves around clear zones that rely on the more opaque ones, a primary visibility reliant on the lines

[245] Ibid., p.134.

[246] Ibid.

[247] Ibid., p.135.

[248] Artaud XIII, 1974, p.85.

[249] Merleau-Ponty, *The Visible and the Invisible*, p.142. The distinction between sentient and sensible corresponds to that of the phenomenal and objective body in the phenomenological tradition.

[250] Ibid.

[251] Ibid., p.146.

[252] Ibid., p.147.

and dimensions of a 'second visibility.'[253] What for Merleau-Ponty is a 'hiatus' or location of a 'hinge' of 'the general manner of being' is indeed for Artaud an 'ontological void,'[254] one he must leap across by means of rhythm, or impact by means of the scream.[255] This could indeed be encompassed by what Merleau-Ponty means by 'paradox of expression,' but it does not imply a 'general manner' or unity of being, it defies the void by doubling it. This is extremely paradoxical, since in contrast to the 'early' Artaud who agonises over his inability to retain his powers of thought, or capture a moment of expression (in the letters to Jacques Rivière, in *Umbilicus of Limbo* or *Nerve Scales*), there is an affirmation of the void in the 'later' Artaud, even as he assumes demonic forms to leap through it.[256]

There is no doubt Merleau-Ponty forms the basis of a powerful alternative interpretation of Artaud, most especially as it was extended in the work of Francisco J. Varela with his exploration of the 'virtual self'[257] and the developments of neurophenomenology.[258] His contribution has to remain one of contrast here, for manifest reasons of space and time.[259] Since my object to see what happens to the notion of the 'hieroglyph' and the changes in what it means to him, the interpretive modes that I am emphasising are those closest to Artaud. Artaud's elaboration of the interval, what Merleau-Ponty termed the 'hiatus' or 'hinge,' was most singular. To highlight these issues, in conclusion, I am going to look at an analysis of contemporary *yagé* rites that makes extremely Artaudian points. I am entering a tricky realm of circularity here, since Michael Taussig's protean theoretical framework includes large doses of Artaud.[260] In Taussig's researches,

---

253 Ibid., p.148.

254 Merleau-Ponty's terms in ibid.

255 Compare Merleau-Ponty's comments on 'sonorous being' and the human cry in ibid., pp.144-5. For him phonation like seeing and touching is also a reflexive movement.

256 On this situation of 'leaping demons,' using Deleuze's terms, see the section 'The conflict of the faculties' in Chapter III.

257 One of Varela's most succinct and clearest expositions of his encounter between neuroscience, Merleau-Ponty's phenomenology, Buddhism and psychoanalysis is his *Ethical Know-How: Action, Wisdom and Cognition*, Stanford, CA: Stanford University Press, 1999. Given his early death in 2001 at age 55, Varela had in some ways only begun this heady journey.

258 Here the works of Varela, Hubert Dreyfus, Walter Freeman, Evan Thompson and Antoino Damasio are particularly important. See Jean Petitot, Francisco J. Varela, Bernard Pachoud and Jean-Michel Roy, eds, *Naturalizing Phenomenology: Contemporary Issues in Phenomenology and Cognitive Science*, Stanford, CA: Stanford University Press, 1999.

259 Likewise one can contrast Merleau-Ponty's treatment of Proust in *The Visible and the Invisible* (pp.148-53) with Deleuze's *Proust and Signs* (1964), or his analysis of the 'touch' with the dynamics of Deleuze's *The Fold* (1988).

260 See the powerful, determinant citations from Artaud in Michael Taussig, *Shamanism, Colonialism, and the Wild Man*, Chicago, IL: University of Chicago Press, 1987,

the power or effectiveness of shamanic ceremonies lies precisely in the exploitation of these gaps or *écarts* I have been discussing. They are particularly prevalent, Taussig shows, in the relation of the shaman with the client, 'between the figure who sees but will not talk of what he sees, and the one who talks, often beautifully, but cannot see.'[261] This relation in Taussig's accounts is no matter of cosmological harmony, but one of montage, of experimentation in discontinuity, in montage's ability 'to provoke sudden and infinite connections between dissimilars in an endless or almost endless process of connection-making and connection-breaking.'[262] The *yagé* ceremony as an example is one filled with interruptions, uncertainty, and displacements, 'with little or any room for either the sensationalistic or the mysterious.'[263] The *yagé* ceremony, instead of vesting power in the figure of the shaman, produces such back and forth, such disjunction, that the participant is led to see where the power or *mana* creates itself, in these very discontinuities between seeing and speaking. According to Taussig, 'it is this that has to be worked through if one is to become a healer.'[264] Taussig rages against the designation of the shaman as some unitary being, or repository of wisdom. For Taussig the place of the healer is rather a becoming or carrying forth as relation, a relation of movement among the profound disorientation and discontinuity of the activated interval. Perhaps as in Aby Warburg's *Atlas* project (1929–) one has to rely on the 'virtual self' to navigate such territory where normal consciousness has been disabled or is at a loss. Whatever 'theatre' is projected is one Artaud-style, created and enacted out of the death of the self.

In the next chapter I will examine several of the most powerful interpretations of primitive rituals, ranging from Marcel Mauss and Victor Turner to Claude Lévi-Strauss and José Gil, with a view toward gauging more fully what is at stake in the Tarahumara ceremonies, Artaud's experience of them, and how he ultimately turns the entire world into a ritual theatre, transformed according to his dictates.

---

pp.5; 442.

261 Ibid., p.446.

262 Ibid., p.441.

263 Ibid.

264 Ibid., p.446.

III.
RITUAL ACTS

It is at least generally true that Artaud, from the very beginning, never chose to write about any phenomenon that he had not experienced firsthand. An exception are the travel articles for magazines he wrote in financial desperation in the early '30s, about the Galapagos Islands and Shanghai, places he had never been.[1] This has been enough for some commentators to doubt Artaud's exceptionally vivid accounts of the Tarahumaras,[2] complicated by the different states of mind in which Artaud wrote them.[3] Several, including the central 'The Peyote Rite Among the Tarahumara,' were written during Artaud's self-described phase of 'religious mania' at the Rodez asylum, so that the later Artaud would fiercely annotate them and correct their mystical and even Christian leanings. In 'Supplement to Voyage to the Land of the Tarahumara'[4] Artaud portrays his peyote experience as 'the true story of Jesus Christ.'[5] Although I will take up a closer examination with Artaud's obsessive and mutational positioning of Jesus Christ,

---

1 See 'Deux textes écrits pour "Voila"', Artaud VIII, 1971, pp.31-58.

2 One representative of this would be J.M.G. Le Clézio's essay 'Antonin Artaud, Le rêve mexicain,' in *Europe*, November-December 1984, pp.110-20, where he maintains the physical visit to the Sierra Tarahumaras is of little import, since the resonance of the event reverberates most fundamentally in Artaud's imagination, and has the status of a dream.

3 Artaud's Tarahumara writings span a dozen years; beginning with 'La Montagne des signes' written while in Mexico and just returned from his peyote initiation, in October, 1936, to 'Tutuguri', written weeks before his death in 1948. 'D'un Voyage au pays des Tarahumaras' and 'La Danse du peyotl' were written in Paris in 1937 before Artaud left for Ireland; the three essays 'Le Pays des Rois-Mages,' 'Un Race principe,' 'Le Rite des Rois de L'Atlantide,' along with 'La Montagne des signes', were written before Artaud left Mexico and were published in *El Nacional* in 1936; his 'La Race des hommes perdu' was published in *Voilà* in Paris in 1937. 'Le Rite du peyotl chez les Tarahumaras' was written at Rodez in 1943, but didn't appear in print until 1947. Likewise, his 'Une Note sur le peyotl' was written for a Tarahumara collection published by Marc Barbezat in 1947. One of his more evocative renderings, 'Tutuguri, le rite de soleil noir,' was written October 1947 as section of the banned *To have done with the judgment of god* radio broadcast.

4 Artaud IX, 1971, pp.103-14.

5 Ibid., p.105.

and its relation to his reinvention of the body in later sections, at this moment I will pause to consider the body's role in the rites, which goes to the heart of Artaud's 'sense' in these matters, a sense that he increasingly revolves and rails around in his last writings: his flesh as the site of constant return.

Artaud called for a theatre that performed 'particular exorcisms,'[6] and that was as cataclysmic as any ancient rites. How do they operate? With perspicacity, Artaud notes in 'The Peyote Rite Among the Tarahumaras' that the peyote priests themselves do not understand all of the gestures and ritual movements they make. They are, rather, obeying on the one hand 'a kind of physical tradition,' and on the other 'secret commands issued to them by the Peyote whose essence they absorb before they start dancing.'[7] In the trance of the peyote ceremony, their bodies 'repeat it like a type of lesson,' doing what the peyote leads them to do, but like their fathers or grandfathers before them, they no longer consciously understand the rites.[8] At least in terms of Artaud's search, he had been right to zero in on this particular group. Jane Harrison, in her classic study *Themis: A Study of the Social Origins of Greek Religion* (1912), gave two continental American examples of surviving practices of primitive Greek dance; the Yumari and Rutubari dances of the Tarahumaras were one, the Grizzly Bear dance of the North American Indians was the other.[9] Harrison singled out the Tarahumaras due to their animal dances, the bird headdresses their shamans wore, indicating bird-*mana* – 'Like Teiresias, like Mopsos, like Melampos, like Kassandra, these shamans understand the speech of birds.'[10] According to Harrison, with the Tarahumaras it is the animals who teach the dances who do the real 'work;' in shades of Artaud, the word for dancing in Tarahumara Harrison reports as *noláova*, literally to 'work.'[11] Harrison's classifications anticipate those of contemporary art and architectural historian Vincent Scully, who found that to continue his investigation of ancient Greek rites entailed studying and spending time with the Pueblo Indians of Arizona and New Mexico, whose intricate dances were their modern embodiment.[12] Yet the Tarahumara dances were also the result of a profound amalgamation, having been converted by the Jesuits in the 15th Century before they expelled the Jesuits in the 19th; the Tarahumaras continued to use dances adapted by the Jesuits for the Tarahumaras, imported from Venice.[13] The Tarahumaras transformed these dances for their own pur-

---

6 Artaud IV, 1964, p.108.

7 Artaud IX, 1971, pp.14-15.

8 Ibid., p.15.

9 Jane Harrison, *Themis: A Study of the Social Origins of Greek Religion*, 2nd rev. ed., Cambridge: Cambridge University Press, [1912] 1927, pp.111-12.

10 Ibid., p.111.

11 Ibid., p.112.

12 Vincent Scully, *Pueblo*, 2nd rev. ed., Chicago, IL: University of Chicago Press, 1989.

13 Lotringer, *100 Years of Cruelty*, pp.315-6.

poses, as they did the Christian cross. The syncretism at work with the Tarahumaras was so similar to Artaud's own, and was likewise not based on following to the letter an ancient rite so much as putting similar forces in motion.

Maps of the 'unconscious'

When Artaud maintains that even the peyote priests no longer consciously understand the rites they perform, he has hit on the notion, perhaps awkwardly coined, by philosopher José Gil, of the 'unconsciously conscious' operating in these kinds of primordial rituals.[14] In his commentary on the anthropological accounts of African rituals by Victor Turner,[15] Gil distinguishes between the total structure of organisation of signs in the rituals of the Ndembu Turner describes, that the ethnologist or anthropologist perceives or constructs, and the more concrete coherence of the ritual actions themselves. For Gil there is a 'double coherence' occurring here, neither aspect of which the Ndembu, who are 'living' their polysemy, according to Turner, fully comprehend or could articulate. Turner describes this arena of symbols constructed by the outside observer, that may explain a structure, but has nothing to do with indigenous thought, this way:

> If one is looking holistically at each of these symbols, in isolation from one another and from the other symbols in the symbolic field (in terms of indigenous exegesis or symbol context), its multivocality is its most striking feature. If, on the other hand, one is looking at them holistically in terms of the classifications that structure the semantics of the whole rite in which they occur, then each of the senses allocated to them appears as the exemplification of a single principle. In binary opposition on each plane each symbol becomes univocal.[16]

What reinforces Turner's characterisation here is his map, or diagram, of the *Isoma* ritual in his work *The Ritual Process*.[17] Eschewing a discussion starting with mythological or cosmological cycles, rare in any case with the Ndembu, and bypassing the debate regarding differentiation between symbol, sign and signal, Turner honed in instead on *usage* in the Ndembu ritual context. Doing so, he finds that each ritual element, or *chijikijilu* (that literally means 'landmark' or 'trail,' as in 'to blaze a trail'), acts as a metaphor, a link between known and unknown territory, that juxtaposes the structured against the chaotic – in the

[14] Gil, *Metamorphoses of the Body*, p.79.

[15] Victor Turner, *The Drums of Affliction: A Study of Religious Processes among the Ndembu of Zambia*, Oxford: Clarendon Press, 1968; *The Ritual Process: Structure and Anti-Structure*, New York, NY: Aldine Publishing Co., 1969; *The Forest of Symbols*, Ithaca, NY: Cornell University Press, 1967.

[16] Turner, *The Ritual Process*, p.42.

[17] Ibid., p.30.

instance of the *Isoma* ceremony, this is the realm of the sensorially perceptible against that of the invisible ancestral 'shades' that are responsible for the disturbance.[18] So the *chijikijilu* are composed of parts known and unknown, and their roles are to make the mysterious and dangerous intelligible.[19] These particular 'rites of separation,' designed to placate and reconcile the matrilineal 'shades' that have awakened a fertility curse, allied here with *Mvweng'i*, a powerful spirit that personifies mature masculine power, have a 'strong overtone of witchcraft,' for 'what has been undone by the curse has to be done all over again, although not in precisely the same way, for life crises are irreversible.'[20] It is the village diviner who decrees that the rite must begin at the burrow or hole of a giant rat, or an ant-bear, since both of these creatures stop up their burrows after digging them. Such active metaphors typify Turner's approach to finding meaning in the rituals through the 'molecules,' the small, accreting details, proceeding 'atomistically and piecemeal from "blaze" to "blaze"' as Turner writes, rather than through any immediate access to a great myth or deep 'structure' in Lévi-Strauss' sense.[21]

It is not too difficult to imagine the ritual's unravelling through pursuing these metaphorical or metonymic fragments as if they were part of Deleuze and Guattari's 'magical chain'[22] discussed in chapter I. In that way the ceremonies would open up onto energetic linkages ad infinitum. This is precisely what the later Artaud seeks to accomplish with his 'new body' that cannot be bounded. That these rites do not open up into such cartography has a lot to do with the precise and exact spatialisations of the rites. In this instance the rites are located near the river stream where divination has found the curse originated, but the spatial direction and orientation of the rituals are based around the animal's burrow path. The animal stands in for all the afflicting entities (the aroused 'shades,' the witch who cast the afflicting curse, the *Mvweng'i*). In an exact spatial configuration, knots of grass are first placed atop a filled-in entrance to the burrow, with another knot four feet away. Holes are dug at both these points, and then fires placed at ten feet from each. One fire is considered to be on the right-side (the perspective from the animal's burrow), and is occupied by the male adepts of the tribe; the other, left-side, is reserved for the women. Next to the first burrow senior assistants or adepts to the tribal doctor set down a broken calabash, part of a panoply of ritual medicines; the female adepts put in edible roots from their gardens; these different potions and materials represent the 'body' of the patient. The two holes are further excavated until they are four to six feet deep – one, the animal's hole, is called the 'witch,' and is 'hot,' the other

[18] Ibid., p.15.

[19] Ibid.

[20] Ibid., p.19; 21.

[21] Ibid., p.20.

[22] Deleuze and Guattari, *Anti-Oedipus*, p.181.

is called 'the new hole' and signifies coolness, or 'domesticating.' The holes are dug until they meet halfway, making a tunnel large enough so that a person can pass through. A large ring is created around these two burrows using branches of trees, that cordons it off from the surrounding bush, called *chipang'u*, the same term that designates the fence around a chief's dwelling and his medicine hut.[23] As with the other complex metaphorical links among the Ndembu 'there is in the semantics of this symbol a union of ecology and intellect that results in the materialization of an idea.'[24]

The diverse medicines that are collected complete the arrangements that give visibility to the ritual, consecrated space.[25] One mixture is heated and placed by the ant-eater's hole, the other is cool and placed by the 'new hole;' the cool medicines representing life, the hot ones death – respectively womb and tomb. The afflicted woman, who must enter the tunnel of life and emerge through the tunnel of death, will be dowsed with both cold and hot medicines. In the rites all the hot/cold, left/right, male/female differentiations are expressed spatially, so that each symbol has a spatial orientation and cannot be separated from its material encumbrance or object. Yet this spatial symbolism goes far beyond Lévi-Strauss' 'binary discriminations,' as Turner seeks to show. The procession of movement from cool to hot, amid many splashings of medicines, occurs many times. In the ceremonies Turner witnessed, the couple were poured with medicines twenty times, thirteen times in the cool burrow, seven times in the hot, a ratio of nearly two to one.[26] During these splashings, both the group of men on the right and women on the left sing songs of various Ndembu initiatory rites and life crises. Turner finds the rites dominated by three sets of triadic relations – first, the witch, the shade, and *Mvweng'i*; the doctor, wife-patient, and her husband; and finally the 2:1 ration of hot and cold ablutions, that for Turner contains 'a dialectic that passes from life through death to renewed life.'[27] All of these criss-crossing pairs of binary oppositions found in the *Isoma* ritual lie along different planes in ritual space, that Turner characterises as longitudinal, latitudinal and altitudinal; those oppositions, such as animal-made burrow/man-made hole, left/right, above/below, relate to the paired values of death/life, female/male, candidates/adepts, although Turner emphasises they cannot be regarded as equivalent merely since they transect each other.[28] Some single symbols intersect on each plane of classification. In the *Isoma* ritual, the red cock/white

---

23 Ibid., p.23.

24 Ibid., p.26. The use of the *wuvumbu* tree reinforces this notion – a tree whose roots are exposed. The tree is used, one tribesman tells Turner, to 'bring everything to the surface. In just the same way everything in *Isoma* must be clear.' Ibid., p. 27.

25 Ibid., p.28.

26 Ibid., p.35.

27 Ibid., p.38.

28 Ibid., p.39.

pullet (one given to the husband, the other to the wife) operates symbolically on all planes – the longitudinal, latitudinal and altitudinal – leading Turner to his consideration of the polysemy or multivocality of ritual symbols, 'that they possess many significations simultaneously.'[29] It is only by looking at the symbols in terms of the planes of classification that structure the semantics of the whole that they can appear as this 'exemplification of a single principle.'[30] Wrapped as they are in 'a material integument shaped by their life experience,' Turner stresses the role of the ritual scene and ritual symbols as powerful activators of force and feeling, against Lévi-Strauss' stronger emphasis on cognition.[31]

This level of holistic 'univocality' Turner describes existing on one level or plane of classification is 'unconscious' in the structural, Lévi-Straussian sense, José Gil argues, and the carrying out of the ritual is thus both conscious and unconscious. This is since the tribe sees the rites as profoundly meaningful even though many of them could not explain why or how the stable linkages between the rite's different aspects are made. Gil asks a similar question as Lévi-Strauss in his essay 'The Effectiveness of Symbols'[32] – who or what negotiates this passage from the 'unconscious' order to the 'unconsciously conscious' or conscious one? From the 'unconscious' structure to the more accessible one of the *vécu-pensé* of indigenous thought? Given the wealth of means, discourses and modes of representation – songs, dances, techniques of mind and body – employed in just about any ritual, the complex question is 'who' is 'thinking of all that at the same time? "Who" brings together these different registers, many of which are of the order of nonverbal communication?'[33] Any sort of ritual, Gil argues, following Edmund Leach's paraphrase of Lévi-Strauss, participate as 'machines for the suppression of time.'[34] The irreversibility of time is wrapped, as it were, captured and turned back. 'Traditional' societies therefore have a history, or 'stories,' but not historicity. Perhaps here Gil should have distinguished between the 'folding' of time as it occurs in rituals and the more ordinary sense of time that continues in normal society, since conscious change and even a sense of 'history' appears in most tribal societies.[35] It is not so much that these tendencies do not exist,

---

[29] Ibid., p.42.

[30] Ibid.

[31] See the comments in Turner, *The Forest of Symbols*, pp.28-30; 54-5.

[32] Claude Lévi-Strauss, 'The Effectiveness of Symbols,' *Structural Anthropology*, trans. Claire Jacobson and Brooke Grundfest Schoepf, New York, NY: Anchor/Doubleday, 1967.

[33] Gil, *Metamorphoses of the Body*, p.79.

[34] Edmund Leach, *Culture and Communication*, Cambridge: Cambridge University Press, 1976, p.44.

[35] For a treatment of this question, see in particular James Clifford, *The Predicament of Culture*, Cambridge, MA: Harvard University Press, 1988. For Clifford 'non-Western historical experiences' all too often 'are hemmed in by concepts of continuous tradition and the unified self...identity, considered ethnographically, must always be mixed,

but that they are controlled. As Deleuze and Guattari write, 'The primitive machine is not ignorant of exchange, commerce, and industry; it exorcises them, localizes them, cordons them off, encastes them...so that the flows of exchange and the flows of production do not manage to break the codes in favor of their abstract or fictional qualities.'[36] Yet for Gil the key to this lack of a fully 'progressive' sense of history, the incorporation of lacunae or nothingness into society and society's sense of time as a kind of motor of movement, in 'traditional' or 'primitive' societies, lies in the notion of a 'manipulable death.'[37] That is, death is a 'mode of being.'[38] The extraordinary constructions of symbolic thinking in primitive societies around ancestors and the dead ensure that time, far from being something that cannot be thought, organised or controlled, becomes subject to the 'tissue of relations among being' and a 'series of relations to things in space.'[39] Instead of future-oriented, 'progressive' senses of time, time and the present looks backward towards the dead and society is organised in a time of 'recurrent flux.'[40] In this way, the forces of the dead and death are organised to guarantee life; in such societies life and death are mixed powers, they cannot act unilaterally or independent of one another and are subject to modes of negotiation; the living act in such negotiation with them and retain a certain measure of control. This patterning of time as recurrent makes possible the emergence of powers that are the same and yet another, constantly changing with each cycle of time yet remaining self-identical (according to the mythic origin of their beginnings).[41] It is 'in this perspective,' Gil writes, that 'time comes back because things come back, because power comes back.'[42] Time cannot be seen as infinite or as irreversible when it is contained and organised (completely, with no leakages) in a specific temporal arrangement of beings; likewise death is not taken as a power (in its own right) when it is donated to the powers of the dead. These arrangements call for a certain definite relation to, and organisation of, space, hence the extraordinary importance of the choreography of traditional rituals. These rites of the earth's bodies are filled with powers, but powers both finite and untranscendable – that are born, die, and yet remain. What this accomplishes is that time must be full and empty simultaneously.

Space is also limited, Gil maintains, but in a similarly absolute sense – that power draws its source from space and 'there is no space outside the space of power' but this is a delimited, finite space that is created from the earth, where

---

relational, and inventive.' Ibid., p.10.

36 Deleuze and Guattari, *Anti-Oedipus*, p.153.

37 Gil, *Metamorphoses of the Body*, p.53.

38 Ibid.

39 Ibid.

40 Ibid.

41 Ibid., p.61.

42 Ibid.

all efficacy derives. These spaces and powers are turned back and closed in on themselves, finite yet absolute, since the 'outside' or 'other' inhabits the heart of any of these territories.[43] This is seen in the panoply of tribal beliefs in the inside and the outside, the ally and the stranger, in their ceaseless marking of territoriality. The notion of territory must remain extremely ambiguous here, since primitive societies can be seen as a 'territorial machine' that is the 'first form of socius, the machine of primitive inscription,' or 'megamachine,' following Deleuze and Guattari, but this does not mean that they are territorial in the sense of marking by any separate political sovereignty or authority, such as a state or state-form.[44] This 'territorial machine' may subdivide people, but it does so on the basis of an 'indivisible earth.'[45]

Putting 'time back on track'

These rituals, as recounted by Turner, have Artaud's sense of the 'symbolic' in that they are more real, conjure forces more terrible, emotions more powerful, than experience in daily life ever could.[46] In the early Artaud this power of the symbolic is expressed through his belief that a murder or crime could have far more impact 'in the requisite theatrical conditions' than the 'same crime, realized';[47] this is transformed in the later Artaud who espouses with Van Gogh that 'myth should be deduced from the most earthy things in life...Because reality is terribly superior to all history, to all fable, to all divinity, to all surreality.'[48] Concerns with marking and remaking time stud his *Cahiers du retour à Paris* (1946-8). In Gil's interpretation of ritual ceremonies, their effectiveness has everything to do with the manipulability of time. The controlled yet extreme and wild oscillation between the functioning binary poles Turner sets up in his account, each time also corresponding to a particular organisation of space,[49] has the effect of undermining irreversibility. While Artaud's theatre writings of the 1930s call for a new kind of ritual, the later Artaud's transformation of any kind of ritual sense is clearly indicated in his obsession with the freeing of time, in marked contradiction to the compression and trapping of time characteristic of traditional ritual. In traditional ritual, in moving between two symbolically opposite poles (as Turner so minutely described and is related here), at the climactic moment an 'about-face' or 'radical mutation' occurs; where irreversibility

43 Ibid., pp.61-2.

44 Deleuze and Guattari, *Anti-Oedipus*, pp.141; 145.

45 Ibid., p.145. For the earth as the ground of any production, see ibid., pp.140-1.

46 Turner, *The Ritual Process*, pp.42-3.

47 Artaud IV, 1964, p.103.

48 Artaud XIII, 1974, p.29.

49 Turner, *The Ritual Process*, p.39.

would begin, the event switches and arrests its meaning in a way that goes back to previous events, or establishes new meanings through analogies (Turner's woman in *Nkula* is likened to a pubescent girl in an initiation ritual, others as in the *Isoma* ritual represent a child being born or born again), and irreversibility is thus wrapped in a reversible occurrence. In the passages Turner describes this includes a maximum negative moment – the client or patient for instance is covered in feathers and drenched in blood, accentuating the symptoms of the patient to point of 'total sickness' or death; this sign of negative possession (by the 'shade' or the ancestor) is allowed to completely consume or take over the person. The sheer excess of this kind of homeopathic process is taken to such an extreme extent that it effects a reversal, where instead symptoms of health begin to appear, and correspondingly the signs of the cosmos/ritual create a total, successful reorganisation of the person. For this success in putting 'time back on track,' in Gil's terms, the therapeutic rituals must have extraordinary multivalence in meaning, power and applicability to various areas and 'domains' of life.[50] Each 'sickness' impacts on the collectivity and 'implies a whole set of signifying networks.'[51] So ritual cures simultaneously act on the individual body or soma, the symptom, the supernatural cause, while healing the social rift or disorder the 'sickness' potentially represents.[52] What they effect is a veritable 'transformation of forces.'[53] The final Artaud poses a transformation of forces, but one which does not owe any of its complexion to ritual order, however much his earlier activity may have pointed to it; his autochthonous evolution is based on the irreversible conflict between body and society and supernatural entities that may be assaulting it.

In traditional societies the cure effected is reflected in the specific organisation of 'sacred,' as opposed to 'secular,' space in tribal ceremonies where what the Ndembu, for example, call the 'revelation' occurs. This space of polysemy and epiphany is veritably overloaded with signs. As Gil takes pains to point out, it is not a matter here of symbols acting from afar, rather through gestures and precise actions they set forces in motion and 'designate realities' very much in the present.[54] This is in league with Artaud's notions regarding the extraordinary power of gesture, 'whereby every gesture is counterbalanced by a gesture and every action by its reaction,' in a conflict of chaotic forces that must emerge through theatre.[55] The powerful forces unleashed by the ritual that 'cure' the

---

[50] Gil, *Metamorphoses of the Body*, pp.77-8.

[51] Ibid., p.78.

[52] For Turner's description of the righting of social relations involved in the Isoma ritual, see *The Ritual Process*, pp.18-20.

[53] Gil, *Metamorphoses of the Body*, p.81.

[54] Ibid.

[55] Artaud IV, 1964, p.38.

patient, usually through the intervention of the dead or ancestors, is at once a 'cycle of transformation' and a 'way of decoding and recoding the patient's forces.' So, one way of putting this is that the sick person in the tribe is manifesting a problem that shows a 'surplus energy in relation to known signs.'[56] The ritual invests this body with forces that are even stronger, through various trances and dances and rites of 'possession,' thereby establishing a new balance of forces and signs. But, Gil writes, if these powers from other realms are profoundly overdetermined symbolically, which would emphatically seem to be the case, then those that show up in the body of the patient are also in response to the 'ordinary codings' of the symbolic systems that establish and regulate equilibrium in the life of the tribe. There is a translation at work. The rituals are thus carried out as if these supernatural powers are recoded and 'reordered according to the regular logic of the symbolic system' and can be distributed eventually corresponding to the 'regular, everyday circulation of this energy.'[57] This is necessary for a cure to 'work.' I am spending some time on these ritual descriptions since one of Artaud's resonant calls in his addresses in Mexico was for a 'unitary culture' that would make it possible to 'feel life in its totality.'[58] When Artaud in Mexico proclaims, 'we are all awaiting a revolution of consciousness that will allow us to heal life,' he is relying on the initiatic promise of such rites, which 'reconciles man with nature and with life.'[59] This is a basis that will no longer hold for the later Artaud, but stark insights, reflected in his various Tarahumara accounts, hold the key to how Artaud shifts and transforms these ritual bases; it delineates how the forces tapped or aroused in the most powerful and hieroglyphic ritual for Artaud ultimately leads to the reversal of his hieroglyphic concerns. In all the mutations Artaud achieves after his experience with the Tarahumaras, one can read the pivot of the body as transductor, translator, operator of the various powers and entities and forces that traverse it; in Artaud's doubling of his body in the 'body without organs' this is the key insight.

The body is the operator

Although none of these descriptions of ritual space and time at this point may appear especially controversial, they bear many implications especially crucial for this project of understanding Artaud. If the different energetic powers or fluxes can be separated and then organised again effectively into signs, or conversely, if different raw powers or fluxes can be fused together or condensed (e.g. the 'sickness' and symptom as the manifestation of previously uncoded modes

[56] Gil, *Metamophoses of the Body*, p.81.

[57] Ibid, p.82.

[58] Antonin Artaud, *Messages révolutionnaires*, Paris: Gallimard, 1998, p.121.

[59] Ibid.

and fluxes of energy), an operator or translator is involved.[60] This process of translation (in terms of both condensation and displacement) allows all of the codes to come into play simultaneously in the ritual, acting directly and with immediacy on the body. This operator is none other than the body itself – that in the case of Turner's Ndembu marks with different codes through scarification, that drinks herbal medicines, is applied with leaves and other implements that carry magic powers, or through various procedures is opened to the presence of the dead. This is why, Gil concludes, the tribes have no need to interpret the 'unconscious' meaning of all the various signs, symbolic powers and acts they employ, since 'they carry them in their bodies.'[61] Gil makes many extrapolations from this, including that it is at the moment the body ceases being able to put space and time in relation to each other in such a 'symbolic tissue' that 'thinking about power antinomically emerges,' so that 'an imbalance between political power and social power (and the appearance of nonegalitarian state societies) would have as their source certain events for which the body would be the seat.'[62] In these rituals of magical-religious therapy, as it were, the gods do what the people left to their own devices cannot do – make energy circulate freely.[63] The rites, successfully carried out, ensure that the tribe can harness the powers of the gods to make its group continue. Hence the extraordinary power in the position of the shaman, who makes, in the instance of the rites, humans coincide with the gods.

One way of looking at rituals, therefore, would be that they raise the question of channelling, if not capturing, the different powers or forces that make up or traverse the body.[64] The power to control such forces, inevitably enters into economic, social and political relations – it is these sort of causalities that in the rituals 'can be included and overcome.'[65] In Gil's view, the (extremely variable) relations between signs and forces in tribal ceremonies usually serve to prevent the assumption of despotic meanings, or despotic overcoding. Thus, primitive societies ward off the privatisation and abstraction that become typical of the 'abstract, despotic Urstaat,' the decoding involved in creating the despotic socius

---

[60] Gil, *Metamorphoses of the Body*, p.82.

[61] Ibid., p.83.

[62] Ibid., pp.83-4. Gil expands on this analysis in part III of *Metamorphoses of the Body*. See also Pierre Clastres, *Society Against the State*, trans. Robert Hurley, New York, NY: Zone Books, 1977. A continuation and updating of Clastre's concerns can be seen in David Graeber, *Possibilities*, Oakland, CA & Edinburgh: AK Press, 2007. For a contemporary example of unorthodox resistance to state power and tribal practices preventing the exercise of state power, see Graeber's account of Madagascar, in Graeber, *Lost People: Magic and the Legacy of Slavery in Madagascar*, Bloomington, IN: Indiana University Press, 2007.

[63] Gil, *Metamorphoses of the Body*, p.84.

[64] Ibid., p.85.

[65] Ibid.

or machine, followed by the capitalist one, that are all haunted by the primordial emergence of the state-form, as Deleuze and Guattari write, 'there has never been but one State.'[66] This Urstaat demands what under capitalist conditions becomes an ever more extreme and 'vast privatization of the organs, which corresponds to the decoding of flows that have become abstract.'[67] So, despite what Nietzsche so memorably and grimly described as a mnemotechnics of cruelty in traditional societies,[68] where bodies are marked, scarified, incised, sewn up into the meaning of the earth and the collectivity, as it were, in the primitive socius it is still the case that 'desire is not yet trapped, not yet introduced into a set of impasses, the flows have lost none of their polyvocity, and the simple represented in representation has not yet taken the place of the representative.'[69] It is for these series of reasons that Deleuze and Guattari maintain that traditional societies, even while binding desire through a veritable '*system of cruelty*, maintain an infinitely greater affinity with desiring-machines than does the capitalist axiomatic.'[70]

This reinforces Gil's point that the key to establishing this variability in tribal ceremonies is the primacy of the body, usually consigned to border zones, the gap-filling of symbolic codes, or otherwise ignored. This function of the body in tribal rites was signalled for Lévi-Strauss in the term 'floating signifier.' In discussing Mauss' treatment of the notion of *mana*, Lévi-Strauss likened such ideas to 'algebraic symbols' that stood in for an 'indeterminate value of signification, in itself devoid of meaning and thus susceptible of receiving any meaning at all.'[71] The function of a concept like *mana* was to 'fill a gap between the signifier and the signified, or, more exactly, to signal the fact that...a relationship of non-equivalence becomes established between signifier and signified, to the detriment of the prior complementary relationship.'[72] There is an all-at-once quality to the dawn of human language for Lévi-Strauss, that moment of emergence when the world becomes susceptible to signification. When 'the entire universe...became *significant*, it was none the better *known* for being so.'[73] Yet, especially from this beginning, and continuing in other modes in later societies,

[66] Deleuze and Guattari, *Anti-Oedipus*, pp.252; 220. This primordial State becomes a 'supraterrestial' and 'metaphysical system' – it emerges, according to Deleuze and Guattari, 'all at once...the model of everything the State wants to be and desires.' Ibid., pp.222; 217.

[67] Ibid., pp.142-3.

[68] Friedrich Nietzsche, *On the Genealogy of Morals*, trans. Walter Kaufman and R.J. Hollingdale, New York, NY: Vintage Books, [1887] 1989, II, pp.1-7.

[69] Deleuze and Guattari, *Anti-Oedipus*, pp.184-5.

[70] Ibid., p.184.

[71] Claude Lévi-Strauss, *Introduction to the Work of Marcel Mauss*, trans. Felicity Baker, London: Routledge, Kegan & Paul, [1950] 1987, p.55.

[72] Ibid., p.56.

[73] Ibid., p.60.

there are meanings, there is something signified, but it is not possible to assign a particular meaning to the signified; so some signs remain, floating, without anchor. This 'floating signifier' Lévi-Stauss calls simultaneously the 'disability of all finite thought' as well as 'the surety of all art, all poetry, every mythic and aesthetic invention,' which the investigations of science can only partially control.[74] An idea like *mana* therefore enables symbolic thinking to function, despite, or because, of all the contradictions inherent in it, since *mana* is 'force and action; quality and state; substantive, adjective, and verb all at once; abstract and concrete; omnipresent and localized.'[75] *Mana* is a '*zero symbolic value*,' a sign that marks the necessity of a 'supplementary symbolic content over and above that which the signified already contains.'[76] This can be any value at all, Lévi-Strauss argues, as long as it is part of the available reserve, and not already a term in an existing set.[77]

This 'floating signifier' or 'zero symbolic value' emerges in an extraordinary situation, full of danger. Without it the symbolic order or the symbolic codes could find it impossible to continue to pass over the inadequate relation between signifier and signified, and lose the ability to function or distinguish altogether. This is the situation that occurs in certain states of pathology, where the limits or boundaries between the known and unknown are completely confused, as shown for instance in scrambled linguistic expression.[78] This is precisely the danger evaded by drawing on the 'floating signifier', what Lévi-Strauss calls the 'supplementary ration,' that can rebalance the 'non-fit and overspill which divine understanding alone can soak up,' and thus restore the complementary relation of signifier and signified.[79] The area of 'overspill' the floating signifier takes up, by definition is the space in-between, separating, or in excess of existing codes. These 'semantically disordered zones' can consist of two classes of objects, or 'two worlds.'[80] It should not be surprising therefore that the floating signifier is found on the borders or boundary zones of tribal life – occupied by practices of sorcery and magic, divination, curing, shamanic rites and pretty much any field that has escaped symbolic coding.[81] In short, floating signifiers find a 'non-place' in the liminality Artaud occupied for much of his life. The challenge of deciphering much of Artaud's writing, not only the output during his asylum years

[74] Ibid., p.63.

[75] Ibid., p.64.

[76] Ibid. Italics in original.

[77] He cites here the work in linguistics on the 'zero-phoneme,' of Roman Jakobson. See Roman Jakobson and John Lotz, 'Notes on the French phonemic pattern,' in Roman Jakobson, *Selected Writings*, I, The Hague: Mouton & Co., [1949] 1962.

[78] Gil, *Metamorphoses of the Body*, pp. 93-4.

[79] Lévi-Strauss, *Introduction to the Work of Marcel Mauss*, pp.62-3.

[80] Gil, *Metamorphoses of the Body*, p.94.

[81] Ibid., pp.94-5.

but many of his final texts as well, lie in this aspect of their manifest energetics that cannot be recuperated or symbolically overcoded. Often full of the most heavily laden or archaic symbols possible – Satan or Jesus, various demonic powers or the Virgin Mary – Artaud refuses in his presentation of such conflict any definitive overcoding. What Artaud does present is force, and rival forces, as being the source for each affect and each movement.

Although I have already elaborated on the immense flexibility and dexterity of *mana* as a concept, it is also described by Mauss as 'power, *par excellence*, the genuine effectiveness of things which corroborates their practical actions without annihilating them' – such as fertility in agriculture, health in medicine, strong supports in architecture.[82] *Mana* denotes force or energy no longer explained or represented in the usual symbolic codes but on the edge of or beyond them – Gil gives as examples attacks of sorcery, or a person in an episode of madness. This is relevant to Artaud not only due to the fact that he saw himself as a sorcerer and was diagnosed as mad, but as an operator of the will to power, a will to force. Artaud's proposed Theater of cruelty can already be seen as a kind of will to power,[83] yet there is a transformation to come with that when the 'final' Artaud creates the 'body without organs' through a prodigious exercise of will or 'walking will.'[84] *Mana* is a kind of *lingua franca* for Artaud. *Mana*, like all its relatives *hau*, *orenda*, or *wakau*, (Lévi-Strauss also gives the example of American slang, like saying a woman has 'oomph'!), are energy impossible to be defined completely in a code, since it relates not to objects and their relations, but to what makes them possible.[85] Gil's argument that passages from one state to another put in motion energies that rituals (take for instance those around such events as birth, puberty, marriage, as well as more unconventional shamanistic ceremonies) free or liberate may seem unexceptional, only that it leads directly to what is mistaken in Lévi-Strauss' assertions in regard to *mana* and Mauss. The floating signifier not only corrects the 'overspill' between signifiers and signifieds in the given semantic structure but it crucially *acts* in what is certainly an even more decisive manner as the mediator and exchanger of codes, in an 'enigmatic movement' that is also due to the pulsion of a certain force.[86] This is key to any understanding of Artaud. As a good structuralist, for whom it is the codes that are ultimately real, Lévi-Strauss maintains that 'the notion of *mana* does not belong to the order of the real, but to the order of thinking,

[82] Mauss, *A General Theory of Magic*, p.137.

[83] Lotringer, *100 Years of Cruelty*, p.318.

[84] See the discussion in 'Artaud's 1947-8 notebooks: the combusion of hieroglyphics' in Chapter VI; in Artaud's late notebooks this emphasis is quite frequent. As Artaud writes in one of them 'I am a magician,/nothing makes itself through nature, entirely through the will.' Artaud XXIV, 1988, p.213.

[85] Gil, *Metamorphoses of the Body*, p.95.

[86] Ibid., p.96.

which, even when it thinks itself, only ever thinks an object.' So *mana* exists to restore a unity, 'not a lost unity (for nothing is ever lost) but an unconscious one, or one which is less completely conscious than those operations themselves.'[87] For Lévi-Strauss *mana* does indeed present a 'mysterious force' or 'secret power,' but only insofar as that is the place-holder it takes up in the thought of Mauss, and later, following Mauss' lead, in Emile Durkheim, 'for such is the role it plays in their own system.'[88]

Yet, these energies, whether called *mana* or *hau* or *orenda*, are real enough. They are what Artaud traces, and what he produces. They exist due to the body's place as the 'empty' site of flow and recurrence, not an empty set but an ever-potent switchboard. In other words, this could have been the sense of, in the late Artaud's shorthand, 'the flesh has always transcended the spirit;'[89] or, 'the self is not the body, it is the body that is the self.'[90] Or, in Deleuze and Guattari's terms, the 'intensity=0' that distinguishes Artaud's body without organs.[91] This may be the most elemental testament of Artaud, who has provided, if nothing else, an extraordinary recording of the body as site of coding and recoding, of invasion, propulsion and ejection of entities, who, on another plane of consistency, to be sure, largely coincides with Gil's argument.[92] The tremendous forces corralled under the mantle of *mana* exist in a sense, Gil writes, 'even more than the fixed signifieds of the symbolic codes,'[93] since they make them possible in the first case. What makes Mauss' description of *mana* truer or more resilient than Lévi-Strauss' later emendation, is exactly this recognition, or at least presentiment, of the language of magic or sorcery being a passage from one code to another, a potent interchange of codes, due to the pulsion of a certain force. But not able to think the level of codes and the level of forces on different registers or levels, Mauss ends up collapsing them together.[94] In tribal societies, it is the role of the variously named shaman, sorcerer, *brujo*, medicine man or magician, to enable these transitions from one code to another, to allow, provoke and mix the operating of numerous codes at once, that traverse simultaneously the body of the client or 'sick' person, and the collectivity (Mauss never fails to stress magic as a collective activity, a 'social fact'). It is due to this activity of translation, Gil points out, that the extraordinary relationships in tribal societies are

[87] Lévi-Strauss, *An Introduction to the Work of Marcel Mauss*, p.59.

[88] Ibid., p.57.

[89] Artaud XXIV, 1988, p.330.

[90] Artaud XIV:2, 1978, p.53.

[91] Deleuze and Guattari, *Anti-Oedipus*, p.21.

[92] As Gil writes, 'In effect, if it is not the spirit it must be the body,' in *Metamorphoses of the Body*, p.99.

[93] Ibid., p.95.

[94] Ibid., p.96.

established, between animals and humans and food and the planets.[95] Keeping in mind one of Artaud's last reflections, that perhaps more than artist or poet, he was a magician, what is involved here?[96] An examination of the metamorphoses and efficacies of codes in shamanistic rites, whether in Artaud's account of the Tarahumaras, or in anthropological or sociological accounts via Mauss, Lévi-Strauss, and Gil, will lead back to the role of the body as floating signifier, since 'it is because the energy that goes from one object to another is also the energy of the body that it has a meaning.'[97] What is at issue is nothing less than the mysteries of emergence and individuation – as in Artaud's obsessions with birth, especially central in key texts of the later work, such as 'Le Retour d'Artaud, le mômo'[98] – which delivers us, as Gil argues, right into the 'very source' of any signifying function, 'the problem of translation at the heart of linguistics.'[99] Rather than mere fragmentation or disorder, Artaud is at the heart of any possible language, asserting the body as the ultimate operator.

The conflict of the faculties

With Artaud the central role played by metaphor in Lévi-Strauss is replaced by the action, the gesture, the enaction, much as in any shamanistic rite, where the thing and symbol coincide. Yet Artaud's Tarahumara experience is hardly one where 'all the protagonists have resumed their places and returned to an order which is no longer threatened.'[100] In discovering Ciguri as the 'root of all poetry' there is no such reassuring stability. It is often a prejudice of anthropological accounts to privilege a restored 'wholeness' through tribal ceremony. Elsewhere Victor Turner has written that what is sought in tribal ceremonies is an 'indivisible unity.'[101] But Artaud's intuition, for him confirmed in the Tarahmara rituals, that the 'world is double and triple' is difficult to qualify as 'pure' unity. What is more to the point is to look at Artaud's experiences in the Sierra Tarahumaras as what Deleuze termed 'a fundamental *encounter*.'[102] This encounter may refer to

[95] Ibid.

[96] For Artaud practicing magick in the asylums and after, see Artaud XIV: 2, 1978, pp.144-5; Artaud, *Watchfiends & Rack Screams*, pp.271-2.

[97] Gil, *Metamorphoses of the Body*, p.101.

[98] Artaud XII, 1974, pp.13-20.

[99] Gil, *Metamorphoses of the Body*, p.96. For translation as most basic issue of linguistics see the correspondence between Roman Jakobson and N.S. Trubetzkov in N.S. Trubetzkoy, *Studies in General Linguistics and Language Structure*, ed. Anatoly Liberman, trans. Anatoly Liberman and Marvin H. Taylor, Durham, NC: Duke University Press, 1999.

[100] Lévi-Strauss, *Structural Anthropology*, p.197.

[101] Victor Turner and Edith Turner, *Image and Pilgrimage in Christian Culture: Anthropological Perspectives*, New York, NY: Columbia University Press, 1978. pp.254-5.

[102] Deleuze, *Difference and Repetition*, p.176. Italics in original.

recognisable objects and can be experienced by other senses and faculties, but its most basic characteristic is that it 'gives rise to sensibility in a given sense…It is not a sensible being but a being *of* the sensible. It is not the given but that by which the given is given. It is therefore in a certain sense the imperceptible [*insensible*].'[103] This encounter, therefore, relies on the emergence of the sign, rather than mere quality. That which can be sensed, and yet at the same time cannot be encapsulated by recognition or linked to the network of common sense through the usual coordination of the faculties, 'finds itself before its own limit…and raises itself to the level of a transcendental exercise.' For this sensibility to join the conditions of a 'joint labor' among the faculties, it enlists common sense, thereby making it enter into a 'discordant play, its organs become metaphysical.'[104] Deleuze's conception is profoundly indebted to Artaud, even more so when he is not being directed cited.[105] As Deleuze maintained elsewhere, there is no Logos but only hieroglyphs.[106] Each faculty, Deleuze argues, 'must be borne to the extreme point of its dissolution,' to its 'threshold point' where it is subject to a 'triple violence' – 'that which forces it to be exercised, of that which it is forced to grasp and which it alone is able to grasp, yet also that of the ungraspable (from the point of view of its empirical exercise).'[107] Reaching this limit is both the 'final power' and the 'unique passion' of each faculty, the triggering of its 'differential and repeating element' along with the 'eternal replay of its object, its manner of coming into the world already repeating.'[108] For Deleuze the hieroglyphs speak the 'transcendent language' of a faculty, whereas even its 'point of departure,' sensibility encountering 'that which forces sensation,' is a matter of contingency that 'presupposes neither affinity nor predestination.'[109] In this situation, even the gods are forms of recognition, Deleuze writes. What are encountered, rather, are the demons or 'sign-bearers' – 'powers of the leap, the interval, the intensive and the instant; powers which only cover difference with more difference.'[110]

Deleuze would lead us to emphasise the liminality of Artaud's experience, where each faculty and sensory modality finds its limit before the void, in con-

---

[103] Ibid. Italics in original.

[104] Ibid.

[105] See for instance his definition of 'Univocal being' as 'one and at the same time nomadic distribution and crowned anarchy,' taken from Artaud's *Heliogabalus* and the discussion of 'doubles' in Chapter IV. Ibid., p.47 and pp.273-4.

[106] Deleuze, *Proust and Signs*, p.101.

[107] Deleuze, *Difference and Repetition*, p.180.

[108] Ibid. For a full treatment by Deleuze of the Kantian doctrine of the faculties, see Deleuze, *Kant's Critical Philosophy*, trans. Hugh Tomlinson and Barbara Habberjam, Minneapolis, MN: University of Minnesota Press, [1963] 1985. Deleuze's modifications of Kant are among the central lines of thought in *Difference and Repetition*.

[109] Deleuze, *Difference and Repetition*, p.182.

[110] Ibid.

trast, for example, to Edmund Leach's positing of an abstract logic of translation:

> Thus we can visualize what we hear in words; we can convert written texts into speech; a musician can transform the visual patterns of a musical score into movements of the arms, mouth and fingers...at some deeply abstract level, all our different senses are coded in the same way. There must be some kind of logical mechanism which allows us to transform sight messages into sound messages, and vice-versa.[111]

Such translation occurs, the question is how, and what it implies. As Gil points out, already in Merleau-Ponty[112] there is the statement that there is no 'high' for a pure spirit.[113] No 'spirit' can translate the eminently sensual, empirical, and differential codes and concepts such as 'high' and 'low,' 'left' and 'right,' 'hard' and 'soft.'[114] Even in Lévi-Strauss' structural logic that must lead the mind to think in symbolic relations, it is the body that must organise sensation and all the different sensory stimuli into an immanent flow, it is the body that must carry all the symbolic exchanges and codes that are in play. This is not surprising, Gil writes, since 'on its own the body signifies nothing, says nothing. It always speaks only the language of the other (codes) that come and inscribe themselves on it.'[115] The body in all its relays allows signification to exist. So in tribal ceremonies, according to Gil, there is a 'double scene' occurring – the decoding of the body that is ill and the 'revival' or recoding of this same body as healthy and cured.[116] The first is achieved through pushing the body through codes, social conventions and languages so hard that they shatter – through musical trance, drugs, possession experiences that herald the emergence of the open or 'virgin' or uncoded body, where meanings can begin anew. These experiences for Lévi-Strauss were where the shaman performs as a 'professional abreactor,' in that he relives his own prior 'call' as shaman by effectively bringing up his own initiatory experience in all its 'vividness, originality, and violence,' since 'normal thought cannot fathom the problem of illness, and so the group calls upon the neurotic to furnish a wealth of emotion heretofore lacking a focus.'[117] This is a 'universe of symbolic effusions' where the ill person and the sorcerer, who is of aid precisely because he is neurotic, perform a rite that is collectively participated in by the rest of the

---

[111] Leach, *Culture and Communication*, p.11.

[112] For such terms to have sense, Merleau-Ponty argues, they must already be part of a 'spatiality of situation,' not a pre-existing and objective 'spatiality of position,' See Merleau-Ponty, *Phenomenology of Perception*, trans. Colin Smith, 2nd rev. ed, New York, NY & London: Routledge, [1945] 2002, pp.100-1. Italics in original.

[113] Gil, *Metamorphoses of the Body*, p.99.

[114] A treatment of the complexity of such differentials is found in chapter five of Claude Lévi-Strauss, *The Savage Mind*, London: Weidenfeld and Nicholson, 1966.

[115] Gil, *Metamorphoses of the Body*, p.99.

[116] Ibid., pp.99-100.

[117] Lévi-Strauss, *Structural Anthropology*, pp.180-1.

tribe that watches the 'fireworks' from a safe distance.[118] While Artaud's Tarahumara experience was full of 'fireworks,' it only slides with extreme unease into classification as Lévi-Strauss' end goal of a re-integration 'within a whole where everything is meaningful.'[119] Artaud's releasing and doubling of the energies of the body at the end of his life cannot be contained within any ritual framework such as that discussed by Turner or Lévi-Strauss; Artaud aims at multiplying powers not at reconciliation of self and tribe, tribe and cosmos.

The case of Artaud's 'Tutuguri' (1948)

The various states of mind and situations in which Artaud treated the Tarahumara rites is extremely complicating to any understanding of their significance for him. These periods include his 'religious mania' at Rodez in 1943 and 1944 when Artaud would often go into town to pray at the Rodez cathedral, imbibing an extraordinary number of hosts at Eucharist and communions. As he wrote to Jean Paulhan at the time, 'If from Dublin to here at Rodez I have not practiced religion, it is because there was no church at Sotteville-lès-Rouen, Sainte-Anne, or Ville-Évrard.'[120] His impressions of the Tarahumaras were also heavily influenced by the bouts of electroshock coma he experienced during three periods of extremely traumatic application in 1944.[121] As an initiatic journey the Tarahumara experience was foreshadowed in earlier experiences and texts and merged with others later. Art historian and Artaud biographer Mèredieu argues that certain of the sensory modifications of peyote, notably the loss of usual coordinates of space and time, are reproduced in Artaud's asylum experience, especially magnified during the episodes of electro-shock coma, so he merges and combines the perceptions. As she notes, the most inspired, and most flamboyant, of Artaud's Tarahumara accounts are those written at Rodez.[122] Yet the most 'black' accounts, if one accepts journalist Maurice Saillet's shorthand of an Artaud 'white' period followed by crossing over the threshold into a 'black' period,[123] are surely those of the late Artaud, who was writing again of his peyote rites within a fortnight of his death.[124] At the very end of his lifespan, Artaud is reformulating once more his Theater of cruelty, and realises he is dying of

[118] Ibid., p.182.

[119] Ibid., p.197.

[120] Artaud X, 1967, p.105.

[121] Barber, *Antonin Artaud*, p.112.

[122] Mèredieu, *C'était Antonin Artaud*, pp.574-5.

[123] Maurice Saillet, 'In Memoriam: Antonin Artaud,' in Artaud, *The Theater and Its Double*, trans. Richard Howard, p.155.

[124] The text 'Tutuguri,' was written 16 February 1948. See Artaud, *Œuvres*, pp.1694-7; Artaud IX, 1974, pp.69-74.

cancer, indeed, he writes to publisher Marc Barbezat that he finished this last Tarahumara text swimming in a sea of his own blood,[125] he returns again to the Tarahumaras. As he wrote in *To have done with the judgment of god*, 'I prefer the people who eat right out of the earth the delirium that gave birth to them,/I am speaking of the Tarahumaras.'[126] It is here that Artaud's descriptions most closely approximate Deleuze's formula, of 'chaos=cosmos.'[127]

In Artaud's Tarahumara experiences, one can trace the explosion of his adherence to systems of mysticism such as numerology, astrology, alchemy, the Tarot, even while so deeply immersed in them. The patterning Artaud attributes to the rites at the end of his life owes little to any of these, although the immediate aftermath of Artaud's Mexican journey was a profound and shattering religious delirium. For Artaud the dance of the Tutuguri has the purpose 'to kill the sun in order to establish the kingdom of black night' and 'to split the cross so that the spaces of space will never again meet or cross.'[128] The Tarahumaras had thus produced what Artaud had anticipated in his Mexican addresses as that void, that 'Space where Life dies.'[129] The rite, as Artaud describes it in this segment from *To have done with the judgment of god*, is resplendent and harrowing. The rite is that of a 'new sun' that 'passes through seven points before exploding at the earth's orifice.'[130] The six suns are represented by six men, and a seventh man, dressed in black and red, leading a horse who 'is the sun completely.'[131] Artaud describes the condensation and imploded power of the ritual:

> On the rending of a drum and of a long, peculiar
> trumpet,
> the six men
> who were lying down,
> *rolled up* flush with the ground,
> spring up successively like sunflowers,
> not suns at all
> but turning soils,
> lotuses of water,
> and to each upspring
> corresponds the increasingly gloomy and repressed
>   gong
>   of the drum
> and suddenly we see coming in full gallop, at vertiginous speed,
> the last sun,
> the first man,

125 Artaud, *Œuvres*, p.1694. Given Artaud's rapidly deteriorating physical condition, the 'sea of blood' was no mere metaphor.

126 Artaud XIII, 1974, p.74; Artaud, *Watchfiends & Rack Screams*, p.286.

127 Deleuze, *Difference and Repetition*, p.150.

128 Artaud XIII, 1974, p.74; Artaud, *Watchfiends & Rack Screams*, p.287.

129 Artaud, *Œuvres*, p.704.

130 Artaud XIII, 1974, p.77; Artaud, *Watchfiends & Rack Screams*, p.288.

131 Ibid.; ibid.

the black horse with a
man naked,
absolutely naked
and *virgin*,
on it.[132]

Artaud argues the primary aim or 'tone' of the rite is 'precisely THE ABOLITION OF THE CROSS.'[133] He describes the men circling the six crosses, while the 'horse of bloody meat panics' and 'caracoles without stopping.' At the climax,

Having finished turning
They uproot
The earthen crosses
And the man naked
On the horse
Raises high
An immense horseshoe
Which he has tempered in a cut of his blood.[134]

As difficult as it may be to answer what this means, it may be even more challenging to follow the methodology suggested at the beginning of Chapter I and ask how this functions. As Deleuze and Guattari sought to describe their particular cartography in terms of a 'magical chain' that 'brings together plant life, pieces of organs, a shred of clothing, an image of daddy, formulas and words: we shall not ask what it means, but what kind of machine is assembled in this manner – what kind of flows and breaks in the flows, in relation to other breaks and other flows.'[135] This may be more faithful to Artaud's own itinerary, for whom the 'abolition of the cross' ultimately involved his attempt to jettison any received patterning from spiritual systems.

Such a path would lead one far from many of the interpretations surrounding Artaud, which despite everything, often still link him to a Christian pathos and mysticism,[136] or encases him despite what Derrida called his 'multiple aggressions' against them, in psychoanalytic or even alchemical-psychoanalytic frameworks,[137] as well as pointing to Artaud's use of representation (in this case,

132 Ibid., p.78; ibid., pp.289-90.

133 Ibid., p.79; ibid., p.290.

134 Ibid.; ibid.

135 Deleuze and Guattari, *Anti-Oedipus*, p.181.

136 Ludovic Cortade, *Antonin Artaud, la virtualité incarnée*, Paris: L'Harmattan, 2000.

137 This is the case despite the manifest virtues of Bettina Knapp's profoundly Jungian *Antonin Artaud, Man of Vision* (1969). For other, more typically Freudian accounts, see Leo Bersani, 'Artaud, Defecation, and Birth,' in *A Future for Astyanax: Character and Desire in Literature*, Boston, MA: Little, Brown, & Co., 1969; and Carlo Pasi's treatment of Artaud's oedipal scene in *Artaud Attore*, Firenze: La Casa Usher, 1989. Although it would probably require a dissertation in its own right to discuss the contributions of Kristeva's various treatments of Artaud, whatever the limitations of the Freudian and

the much-maligned art of writing) as a combative field, or launching pad, necessary to his imprecations and assaults, and so a key to his fluidity and movement. This is not the Artaud diagnosed as trapped in representation in Derrida's deconstruction.[138] Artaud often wrote and spoke as if there were ontological planes largely independent of any social or historical insistence, and so he invites such treatments. In 'Tutuguri' he writes of the great '*reversal*' discussed in the previous chapter – the cross is a black, abject sign that must be burned, burned in the Tarahumaras' Theater of cruelty that introduces the '*eternal* death of the sun.'[139] The ceremony Artaud so vividly describes is a veritable cosmological 'grinding over.' Lifting up over what Artaud calls the 'atrocious insistence' of the monotonous beat of the drumming and cacophony of effects, is a kind of obscene wind, a breath from the night that flagellates one. It bears a visage, what Artaud describes as a 'painted face,/a figure sniggering and without mercy.'[140] It is without mercy because 'the justice that it brings is not of this world.'[141] It emanates from a ceremony described as a forest struck by lightning, a volcanic crater at the moment of its eruption. This emergence of the sun, where it takes rank in the celestial system, is accompanied by immense and unprecedented noise and panic, a noise that seems to call all nothingness before it, since this emergence is also an eclipse. The qualities of exhaustion and exasperation Artaud describes in the Tutuguri rite could well have been his own. It is symptomatic that in the very first letters Artaud sends from Mexico City upon his return from the mountains, the ceremonies are not mentioned at all. There is a period of recovery from what on many levels must have been a gruelling journey, before Artaud makes his series of grand claims regarding the Tarahumara rituals. In the late text 'Tutuguri' it is the chanted rhythm of 'an army *en marche* or gallop of a panicked charge' that is emphasised throughout.[142] The steadily beating tympanum is 'always an introduction of nothingness,/always this introduction of nothingness.'[143] It was Gilbert Rouget's conclusion in his study *Music and Trance* (1985), that trance

---

Lacanian tradition of psychoanalysis from which she emerges, her precise attention to the material qualities of Artaud's writing and other works, give it a very different salutary effect. For Kristeva's various treatments of Artaud see Julia Kristeva, *Powers of Horror*, New York, NY: Columbia University Press, 1984; *Desire in Language*, New York, NY: Columbia University Press, 1982; *Revolution in Poetic Language*, New York, NY: Columbia University Press, 1984; and *The Sense and Non-sense of Revolt*, New York, NY: Columbia University Press, 2000. Her most valuable single contribution on Artaud remains 'Le sujet en procés,' in *Artaud*, ed. Philippe Sollers, Paris: Union générale d'éditions, 1973.

138 This is elaborated in the context of Artaud's drawings, in part VI.

139 Artaud IX, 1971, p.69. Italics in original.

140 Ibid., p.71.

141 Ibid.

142 Ibid., p.73.

143 Ibid.

or possession experience was essential to any ritual in terms of the uncoding or recoding body, although music was often strangely optional. In 'Tutuguri' the steady beating of the rhythm is the key to unraveling the significance of the text. The attraction of the Tarahumaras for Artaud, and his interpretation of their rites, also emphasises that for Artaud these are apocalyptic strivings. This pulsion toward apocalypse is dramatised in 'Tutuguri' like few other texts. Although this fervor is found in much of Artaud's work, it is with his later work that such a cataclysm becomes an overriding obsession. One can view his last notebooks, for example, as 'instruments for the incitement of apocalypse... [that] must confront that apocalypse-eluding world.'[144]

'Tutuguri,' on the face of it a blatant contradiction to other Artaud writings on the Tarahumaras, such as his Rodez-era 'Supplement to Voyage to the Land of the Tarahumaras,'[145] where Ciguri is identified with Jesus Christ, acts rather as a palimpsest, where this version is contained within others. Read in this way, as a kind of *turning*, one could read the wild paradoxes of 'Tutuguri' – that seems to announce the birth of the sun through its abolition – as a figure for the Artaud who has emerged after the six years of silence in asylums.[146] 'Tutuguri' is open to perhaps the most classical reading possible, that it is a metaphor for itself, the poem creating itself. Yet even this most conservative approach yields enormous results, if one sees Artaud's text, as does Jacob Rogozinski in his perceptive essay on Artaud, as revolving primarily around its rhythm, as a 'hymn...to the solar advent of rhythm.'[147] In this reading, the seventh Tutuguri, with his 'chanted rhythm' and his 'music from another time' that interrupts the cross and the circle of repetition of the six suns, the Tutuguri with the 'gash of blood' leading a triumphant horse, is Artaud. This is not a persona, but rather a *contretemps*, a counter-rhythm that is a 'memorial of a resurrection.'[148] The poem is riven with strife, of conflict between the sun and the cross, between the ritual and rhythm, with the seventh Tutuguri crossing the mise-en-scène. The mise-en-scène as the poem also summons up the 'informal outside,' as a 'battle, a turbulent, stormy zone where particular points and the relations of forces between these points are tossed about,' dominated above all by the 'sonic echo of the battle raging above them.'[149] Yet this outside, haunted by death – Artaud writes of this strange music as a 'breath issued from the caves of a humanity abolished'[150] – is also haunted,

[144] Barber, *Artaud: Terminal Curses*, p.60.

[145] Artaud IX, 1971, pp.103-14.

[146] Jacob Rogozinski, 'Tutuguri, ou le rythme d'Artaud,' *Lignes* nouvelle série, October 2000, pp.71-86. Rogozinski later expanded these reflections on Artaud, see Rogozinski, *Guérir la vie: La passion d'Antonin Artaud*, Paris: Éditions du Cerf/Passages, 2011.

[147] Ibid., p.72.

[148] Ibid., p.81.

[149] Deleuze, *Foucault*, p.121.

[150] Artaud IX, 1971, p.71.

and constituted by, the peculiarities of Artaud's particular, staccato rhythm. So many of Artaud's terms here – breath, wind, the jump or leap [*saut*] – are curiously reversible. They could refer or be inscribed in the order of the cross (the row or repetition of six that obstruct the solar power) or that of the sun, so that the oppositions in the poem seem to operate or move within each other.[151] They seem to attest, as Rogozinski has suggested, 'to a most radical ambivalence, that of rhythm itself.'[152] This ambivalence, and this rhythm, is at once that of the life of Artaud's body, and of the cosmos itself, which swings or oscillates from a measure of order to disorder.

Similarly, Artaud's poem may also be read in radical ambiguity as to whether its music is a testament to Artaud's rebirth, or witness to his years in the hell of confinement, since it combines elements of both. Artaud's concern with rhythm is connected with his insistence on creation by will at the end of his life. As he wrote to Fernand Pouey on 11 December, 1947 about *To have done with the judgment of god*:

> To have done with the judgment of our acts
> by fate
> and through a force
> dominating
> is to signify
> one's will
> in a way
> that is new
> in order to indicate that the rhythmic order of things and of
> fate has changed its course...[153]

In this regard, 'Tutuguri' worked as part of the 'mini-model' of *To have done with the judgment of god* as well.

One of the striking aspects of 'Tutuguri' is how it revisits and attempts to transform Artaud's earliest preoccupations and so indicates the metamorphosis of the late Artaud. In *Nerve Scales* (1925) detailing his suffering the different types of 'constant loss of normal level of reality,' Artaud was already characterising this as a 'crossroads of separations.'[154] This was a 'Crossroads of separation of sensation from my flesh,/Abandoned by my body, /Abandoned by all sen-

[151] One is tempted here to compare how these gyres work with Henri Bergson's modification of the notions of microcosm and macrocosm, where they are opened up and linked, not as closed circles inscribed one within the other, but as processes of becoming linked to an irreducible and irreversible temporal dimension, found in chapter one of Bergson, *Creative Evolution*. For more on this comparison, see the discussion of 'Artaud's becoming versus being' in Chapter V.

[152] Rogozinski, '*Tutuguri*, ou le rythme d'Artaud,' p.75.

[153] Artaud XIII, 1974, p.125.

[154] Artaud I:1, 1956, pp.89; 108.

timent possible to man.'[155] In this early, stricken writing Artaud complains of lacking words that are in accord, which could be linked with each minute of his changing states of mind.[156] More precisely, at each point in his thinking there were 'gaps, stops' – 'I do not mean, understand me well,' Artaud writes, 'in time, I mean in a certain sort of space.'[157] Writing that he is the one who knows the inmost recesses of loss, this is not the loss of a sequence of thoughts, only one, an 'INNER thought,' and not a thought of Pascal's or a philosopher's thought, rather that of a 'contorted fixation, a sclerosis of a certain state.'[158] In this agony of a 'suspended sensibility,' what was necessary was the reassembly of 'all these sort of mental gems around a point that is justifiable to find…a phosphorescent point where all reality is recovered, but changed, metamorphosised…'[159] In his 'Correspondence with Jacques Rivière' (1923-4) Artaud had characterised his malady as a series of 'stops and starts' in his poems, resulting from his inability to concentrate on an object.[160] This concern with the 'stops and starts' continues in the late writing, usually in reference to 'spasms.'[161] Yet in the later writing Artaud is affirming the void, and not lamenting a lost presence. In his 'Supplement to a Voyage' Artaud writes that in his peyote experience he had 'gone beyond the cross of the spasm in which my heart by bursting was made new,' and 'reemerged on earth as if struck by lightning in my mind.'[162] This link of the cross that he has surpassed and gone beyond, with the rhythm of the spasm is one of the key motifs of 'Tutuguri.' When Artaud first arrives in the Sierra Tarahumaras, he notes all the crosses, but these crosses he sees in each village are not the cross of Christ or the Catholic church, but of 'Man quartered in space… nailed to the four cardinal points.'[163] The cross in 'Tutuguri' similarly does not link, in Heideggerian fashion, the earth and the sky, or any other entities or divinities, rather, the six crosses are there to block the path of the sun.[164] This is why the cross is an 'abject sign that matter must burn.'[165] In light of the later writings, it is tempting to assimilate the notion of 'spasm' and 'jerks' to a *con-*

[155] Ibid., p.108.

[156] Ibid., p.93.

[157] Ibid., p.94.

[158] Ibid.

[159] Ibid., p.90.

[160] Ibid., p.39. Although Artaud acknowledges that this lack of attachment to an object is characteristic of his age as a whole, as witnessed in the writings of Tristan Tzara, André Breton, and Pierre Reverdy, for example, their lack does not spring from physiological or neurological ailment, as it does with Artaud.

[161] Artaud XIV:2, 1978, pp.116-7; Artaud XXVI, 1994, p.233.

[162] Artaud IX, 1971, p.112.

[163] Ibid. pp.85-6.

[164] Ibid. p.69.

[165] Ibid.

tre-rythme of death, as Artaud writes in *Suppôts et suppliciations* of the 'obscene spasms of the copulation of death.'[166] And, at numerous points in the late work, death for Artaud is not inevitability but rather a late historical invention, the handiwork of black magic. This spasm is the death-in-life that Artaud despairs of, from his earliest published works, to his last rants: that fracture that makes for an impossibility of any living present, of having to respond to an affect or a power that is already absent, of not feeling alive, or of being dead before any natural death (here, Artaud's electroshock comas, as the most extreme version of this Artaud suffered, are relevant). The significance of the cross here reiterates the notion that for Artaud this fracture or *arrêt* or delay, is a contrivance of space, not temporal. Part of the impetus of the body without organs is the overcoming of this blocking of the cross, jumping, moving through the spasm of enforced death, subjecting the spasm to an infinite temporality. The 'body without organs' substitutes for the body of flesh that, rather than the site of an interlacing of affects and sense-impressions, or reflection of a primordial sensibility, can only form a 'crossroads of separations' – a cross of bloody tearing of organs, not a place where the different axes meet. Artaud, in *Histoire vécue d'Antonin Artaud* (1947), will write an extraordinary account of his dying on the cross at Golgotha, this limit-site, or non-meeting of the different faculties and sensibilities, a bloody crucifixion already prefigured in *Fragments of a Journal from Hell* (1925) where Artaud describes as above all human activity, 'this monotonous crucifixion, this crucifixion where the soul never ends with losing itself.'[167]

So the cross comes to stand in for the spasms of death, for that intersection where the axes do not meet, that Artaud writes of as 'death multiplied from myself,' an 'intersection of phenomena...But all this flesh is only beginnings and then absences, and then absences and absences.'[168] The cross becomes one with the 'affliction of death.'[169] In Rogozinski's persuasive reading of 'Tutuguri,' it is these *affres*, these stops and delays of death-in-life, that Artaud, the seventh Tutuguri, the stranger riding the horse to the closed circle, intends to write through and over, instantiating a rhythm of life, since 'one will never stop life.'[170] As will become increasingly clear in the writing and works of post-Rodez Artaud, this lifelong malady of stops and gaps, of extraordinary *impouvoir*, of affect and thought swallowed up by the void, what Artaud describes as the correspondingly icy and glacial flesh, is opposed to the singularity (or in Artaud's parlance, the *cruelty*) of the event, the *souffle*, the gesture, life. These holes and gaps are opposed by the rhythm of life, because 'life is that which never repeats, which does not ever pass through the same point, which only returns beating

166 Artaud XIV:2, 1978, p.117.

167 Artaud I:1, 1956, p.111.

168 Ibid., pp.241-2.

169 Artaud XII, 1974, p.58.

170 Ibid., p.236.

its source in the beating of the same heart.'[171] In a text like 'Tutuguri,' then, Artaud attempts to perform this rhythm, without repetition, punctuating it with beats that cannot be repeated, in the rhythm and breath of life that is always new, always other, in its coming again.[172] One can read the poem as a massive renunciation and repudiation of the chiasm the cross represents for Artaud. The rhythm of the poem wildly exceeds this disjunction of the cross, as the Tutuguri rite is itself designed to destroy its breaking and arresting action.[173]

If I paused or terminated my look at 'Tutuguri' at this point, with merely the suggestion of Artaud's life against death, I would surely be forking on a mistaken and all-too simplistic if well-trod path, the same path that Christianises Artaud's journey of remaking the body, depicts Artaud as a benign vitalist, or seeks a dialectical process in his movement. 'Tutuguri' advocates not so much 'life' as what Deleuze called in his work on artist Francis Bacon an 'almost unlivable Power.'[174] According to Deleuze this is a 'rhythmic unity' that 'can be discovered only by going beyond the organism,' into where rhythm 'plunges into chaos, into the night, at the point where differences of level are perpetually and violently mixed.'[175] Deleuze argues that it is also a 'spasm' that is operative in Francis Bacon's paintings, '*the action of invisible forces on the body*.'[176] What Bacon's paintings offer is a 'translation' between spasms. Deleuze frequently invokes Artaud in describing how Bacon serves up not intelligible dialectical structures, or a 'pathic' moment of 'existential communication' as in phenomenological accounts,[177] but rather a 'body without organs' that is composed of vibration, this 'wave that traces levels or thresholds in the body according to the variations of its amplitude. Thus, the body does not have organs, but thresholds or levels.'[178] This 'vital power' that 'exceeds every domain and traverses them all,' or, in the language of *Difference and Repetition*, that scands the limitations of each faculty, is none other than rhythm. 'What is ultimate,' Deleuze writes, 'is thus the relation between sensation and rhythm, which places in each sensation the levels and domains through which it passes.'[179] This 'Power' that runs throughout life is not life itself but the nonhuman movement of rhythm, that which links the most elementary and 'primitive' structures, as Elizabeth Grosz describes it in her gloss on Deleuze, 'of even the most simple organisms to the implacable

171 Ibid., p.219.

172 Rogozinski, '*Tutuguri*, ou le rythme d'Artaud,' p.78.

173 Artaud XIII, 1974, p.251.

174 Gilles Deleuze, *Francis Bacon: the Logic of Sensation*, trans. Daniel W. Smith. Minneapolis, MN: University of Minnesota Press, [1981] 2003, p.44.

175 Ibid.

176 Ibid., p.41. Italics in original.

177 Ibid., p.42.

178 Ibid., pp.44-5.

179 Ibid., p.42.

movements of the universe itself: art, as music, sculpture, painting, architecture, dance, resonates or transmits force through every structure.'[180] It is this rhythm that links life to all 'nonorganic forces and qualities of materiality itself.'[181] It is through this rhythm that Artaud articulates his relation, his cries to the 'outside,' that clangy battle, what he called 'this carnage,'

> ...this skirmish of extinguished fires, of dried-up cries
> and slaughter,
> one does nothing, one says nothing, but one suffers, one despairs,
> and one fights, yes, I believe that one really does fight. __ Will the struggle
> be evaluated, will it be judged, will it be justified?
> No,
> Will it be denominated?
> No again,
> naming the battle is to kill nothingness, perhaps.
> But above all to stop life...'[182]

Artaud writes this in the course of his letter 'To Peter Watson' where he remarks that 'life makes a leap, but that is never written in history and I have never written except to fix and perpetuate the memory of these cuts, these scissions, these ruptures, these abrupt and bottomless falls...'[183] Writing through this scansion, through a 'differential in repetition,'[184] in recording these 'terrible leaps,' through his breath of life and rites of suspension, is how the final Artaud touches upon and projects immortality, if not what Rogozinski terms his 'trajectory of a rebirth, of a recovery.'[185]

The space of Artaud's apocalypse

This notion of rhythm cannot be thought apart from Artaud's peculiar construction of space, and re-construction of the body, in the version of the late Artaud this advocacy of the breath being at once an affirmation of immortality of the 'body without organs,' and the apocalypse that it must bring to current civilization. The apocalyptic fervor that animates 'Tutuguri' is in continuity with that of the Surrealist Research Bureau broadsides of 1925 (that Breton so quickly felt he had to corral), or the prophecy of the coming destruction of the world in *The New Revelations of Being* (1937). This is a thread of consistency in Artaud between the earlier and later incarnations; only that the fury for destruction

---

[180] Grosz, *Chaos, Territory, Art*, p.19.

[181] Ibid.

[182] Artaud XII, 1974, p.236; Artaud, *Watchfiends & Rack Screams*, p.86.

[183] Ibid., p.235; ibid., p.85.

[184] Rogozinski, '*Tutuguri*, ou le rythme d'Artaud,' p.86.

[185] Ibid., p.82. The issue of Artaud and 'cure' or 'recovery' is taken up in Chapter V.

in the final Artaud is far more volcanic and overwhelming and complete. That Artaud's work is consistently obsessed with provoking the end of the world – as the post-Rodez Artaud would walk the streets of Paris and fantasise about the elimination of different buildings and institutions, predicting the immediate erasure from the city of the Cathedral de Notre Dame for example[186] – has rarely been sufficiently emphasised.[187] Here perhaps Artaud appears not 'untimely' in Nietzsche's sense that any worthy thinker must think 'counter to our time,'[188] but simply out-of-time given that Hitler, Stalin and the Allied bombing campaigns in Germany and Japan had all accomplished mass destruction of cities just years earlier. Artaud's 'certain black line'[189] running through the geography seems to presage similar destruction.[190] Artaud's projection of the 'true body' is an immense, unprecedented work of creation; it also entails enormous destruction. As Artaud asks in 'Interjections,'

> And now, I ask men to tell me how many deaths I have caused, among men,
>
> since a certain day in the month of April, 1945,
> How many houses and cities I have leveled,
> How many unexplained fires I have illuminated,
> How many epidemics I have made to burst out,
> How many bizarre illnesses I have provoked,
> How many human torsos I have slashed and shredded,
> How many human sexual organs I have scarred and cut through.[191]

At the time of the *To have done with the judgment of god* broadcast, Artaud declared 'The general historic apocalypse has begun.'[192] This apocalypse is linked with the emergence of the 'body without organs,' as Artaud writes to gallerist Pierre Loeb on 23 April 1947, that 'The time when man was a tree without organs or functions,/but of intention,/a tree of intention which walked/will re-

---

186 Prevel, *En Compagnie d'Antonin Artaud*, p.114.

187 A salient exception is Stephen Barber's lucid exposition concerning the last notebooks, *Artaud: Terminal Curses* (2008), as well as the works on Artaud by Sylvère Lotringer, *Antonin Artaud*, New York, NY: Scribner's, 1990; *Fous d'Artaud*, Paris: Sens et Tonka, 2003; and, with Jean Baudrillard, *Oublier Artaud*, Paris: Sens et Tonka, 2005. Lotringer classes Artaud with Louis Ferdinand Celine, Georges Bataille and Simone Weil as 'crazed modernists' who in their very different ways were all harbingers of the coming Holocaust. See *Fous d'Artaud*, pp.13-38. Julia Kristeva has also written of Artaud's passion for 'complete destruction.'

188 Friedrich Nietzsche, *Untimely Meditations*, trans. R. J. Hollingdale, Cambridge: Cambridge University Press, 1983, p.60.

189 Antonin Artaud, XIV:2, 1978, p.154.

190 See for instance Stephen Barber's comments in Barber, *Artaud: Terminal Curses*, p.74.

191 Artaud XIV:2, 1978, p.153.

192 Artaud XIII, 1974, p.278.

turn./It once was, and it will be again.'[193] At the end of his life, as during his arduous 1936 journey to the Tarahumaras, for Artaud 'if the body is not incessantly reimagined, reconfigured, and set into gestural mutation, the alternative is immediate death…time, space, all objects all perceptions and all sensations, must also join that process of impossible mutation.'[194] This is the sense of the drawings, that

> will meet their apocalypse
> for they have said too much
> to be born
> and too much in being born
> not to be reborn
> and take on a now
> authentic form.[195]

These drawings take place in, and rearrange, space. As the intimate attention to choreography in 'Tutuguri' would also indicate, the reinvention of space is of cardinal importance. One of his earliest preoccupations, he outlined why in the remarkable beginning to *Nerve Scales* (1925):

> I really felt you were breaking up the atmosphere around me, that you were clearing the way to allow me to advance, to provide room for an impossible space for that in me which was as yet only potential, for a whole virtual germination which must be sucked into life by the space that offered itself.
>
> I often put myself into this state of impossible absurdity in order to try to generate thought in myself. There are a few of us in this era who have tried to get hold of things, to create within ourselves spaces for life, spaces which did not exist and which did not seem to belong to actual space.
>
> I have always been struck by that obstinacy of the mind in wanting to think in terms of dimensions and spaces, and in fixing on arbitrary states of things in order to think, in thinking in segments, in crystalloids, so that each mode of being remains fixed at a starting point, so that thought is not in immediate and uninterrupted communication with things – this fixation and this immobilization, this tendency of the soul to construct monuments occurring, as it were, BEFORE THOUGHT…
>
> …
>
> But I know not what nameless, unknown lucidity gives me the tone and the cry of these contacts and makes me experience them myself. I experience them with a certain insoluble totality, I mean a totality about whose emotional impact I have not the slightest doubt. And I, in relation to these disturbing contacts, am in a state of minimal tremor, I would have you imagine an arrested void, a mass of mind buried somewhere, become virtuality.[196]

---

[193] Artaud. *Œuvres*, pp.1602-3.

[194] Barber, *Artaud: Terminal Curses*, p.49.

[195] Artaud, *50 drawings to murder magic*, p.11.

[196] Artaud I:1, 1956, pp.85-6.

Here this new space that must be created is characterised as a 'virtual' one, described in his text on Masson's painting *Homme* as an 'ideal, absolute space, but a space that would have a form introducible into reality.'[197]

At the end of his life, this concern with new space is still present, but it is typically a transformed one, emphatically connected to and acting with the 'new anatomies' of the 'body without organs.' Artaud is no longer interested in enacting gestures born from primal hieroglyphic patterning but in an entirely new creation. In the late Artaud space forms itself with corporeality and his project of corporeal transformation:

> Whoever has pain in his teeth like me, pain in all of his absent teeth
> like me,
> he will not see himself, all of a sudden, at my side,
> but it's space which will feel far from him, and also
> from me,
> and which will feel shame at its existence and at its being,
> to be space, when we are there!
> So, what pudenda will make that space?[198]

Artaud will rail in 1947 that 'there is nothing that I abominate and that I shit upon more than this idea of spectacle, of representation,/therefore of virtuality, of non-reality./attached to all that is produced and shown.'[199] His rage against representation is against all that makes 'the possibilities of explosive deflagration which are too dangerous for life pass instead by the channel of the stage, the cinema, or the microphone, and so turn them away from life.'[200] Yet this passion for activation of the 'true body,' the world that is 'not yet,' since 'the reason for being has not yet been found,' is also what Artaud carries from his kindred apocalyptic participation with the Tarahumaras. I can suggest what the Tarahumara rituals *meant* through Artaud's various depictions of the experience, how they *function* for Artaud can be seen in their immediate aftermath: Artaud makes pictograms and spells to enact metamorphoses, often harmful or death threats, but sometimes protective, to certain individuals; these spells enable the coming world conflagration; and he plans further travels, this time to the Aran Islands off the coast of Ireland, to imbibe the still-present putative geomagnetic powers of the pre-Christian Druids, a prime location, Artaud thought, to witness the coming apocalypse. Artaud goes to Ireland, he explains, searching for the 'last true descendent of the Druids' who know that 'humanity must disappear by water and by fire.'[201] After the Tarahumara rites Artaud is driven to visualise and

[197] Ibid., p.64.

[198] Artaud XIII, 1974, p.248.

[199] Ibid., p.258.

[200] Ibid., p.259.

[201] Artaud VII, 1967, p.202.

spatialise his 'hieroglyphic' flux, much as a peyote priest moves in a carefully choreographed path with his staff. (And indeed, at this juncture Artaud carried his own staff, a cane he believed had once belonged to Saint Patrick.) Yet this hieroglyphic ground is already irredeemably shifting in aspect. In 1937 this flux had colliding aspects – an intensely and increasingly hallucinated 'inner' sphere, coming to a silent if violent combustion, and the stunning and barren 'external' landscape around Inishmore.[202] It may have been Artaud's ambition, as Saillet wrote of his pilgrimage to the Tarahumaras, 'at last he might become the equivalent of a natural phenomenon.'[203] He might have hoped, as Kenneth White writes, not only to work in a 'geo-cultural' vein like D.H. Lawrence, but to become, more than a poet, a landscape-in-himself, or an entire world, thus constituting 'cosmopoetic culture' cutting across known lines of geography.[204] Yet Artaud's world now served as a platform for the abolition of the world.

[202] The author and playwright J.M. Synge had been attracted to the Aran Islands, and in 1931 Robert Flaherty made the film *Man of Aran* there. For a cinematic exploration of Artaud's pilgrimage there, see Mathias Sanderson, *Une Histoire de fantôme: le voyage irlandais d'Antonin Artaud*, iO Productions, 1999.

[203] Saillet, 'In Memoriam: Antonin Artaud,' p.155.

[204] White, *Le Monde d'Antonin Artaud*, pp.108; 131.

IV.
TRANSFORMING RITUAL ACTS

Artaud's spells, first sent from Ireland in 1937, have formed a significant part of Artaud's visual *œuvre*, when displayed in international museum retrospectives, from 1980 to 2014. They can be read as indicative of the near-intolerable psychic pressures and tensions Artaud was living, which grew and violently imploded during his stay in Ireland. But rather than exploring them as fascinating relics of psychopathology, they will be examined here more on their own terms, in that they participate in a universe where there is a concept of art as *action*, as a practice of magick or betwitchment, for Artaud an extreme and aggressive means of self-defence. To gain some understanding of their dynamics in this way is to see that Artaud's *sorts* were far from a short-lived method of attack that preceded his 'crack up' and his psychiatric commitment in Le Havre on 29 September 1937. After his journey to Mexico in 1936 and prediction of global meltdown in Paris that immediately followed, Artaud has entered a world in which these acts of sorcery have an efficacy and effect. All of the means Artaud will later develop – of chants and syllable-language, his drawings and sound works – are extrapolated from this same complex where art operates and cannot be disentangled from its effects in the world. Artaud's understanding of this complex at first draws on the kind of cosmic hieroglyphics he saw demonstrated among the Tarahumaras; later Artaud discards this, but he still sees the world as a conflict among forces in which he must survive through making counter-spells and counter-sorcery. In these first versions of spells sent from Ireland in 1937, they remain the most immediate concrete versions of a matrix that for Artaud leapt and moved through matter. To look at their dynamics is to see Artaud's movements in their most elemental form.

Casting spells

These apocalyptic spells or curses, as pictograms, are prefigured in Artaud's diagrams of energy he drafted in 1936 before his journey to the Tarahumaras. Like the travels he would immediately embark upon, these lines for Artaud are linked to world cultures, ancient, rarely still extant, yet still capable of sparking the discoveries or renewal in cruelty Artaud is searching for. In this Deleuze and Guattari linked his pilgrimage to the migrations of Rimbaud or Nietzsche, that 'crossing of thresholds' that entail a confrontation of races and cultures – 'In the aggregate of departure there is the social formation, or rather the social formations: the races, the classes, the continents, the peoples, the kingdoms, the sovereignties; Joan of Arc and the Great Mongol, Luther and the Aztec Serpent.'[1] Artaud characteristically draws the 'zigzags' or maps of these 'lines of flight' in his 'Notes on the Oriental, Greek, Indian Cultures,'[2] a collection of notes that date from 1933 to 1937, much of which provides the raw material for the series of Artaud's lectures in Mexico City in 1936 before he goes up into the Sierra Tarahumaras. Packed full of Artaud's delineations from Hinduism, Buddhism, Taoism, Sufism, the ancient Greeks, the Kabbalah, the Toltecs and ancient cultures of Mexico, what is notable here is Artaud's building blocks, his breaking down into elemental fluxes culled from each distinctive philosophical or spiritual tradition. For Artaud these are characteristically gendered – the Yan, or action being positive and male, the In or re-action, being negative and female; at least this provides Artaud's starting point until he quickly delves into how each transforms into the other in different systems. Whether Artaud is listing the seven energies or principles of Hermeticism, or the assigned locations or geographic directions of four Mexican deities, he is in brevity designating different base elements, often picturing their relations as intersecting squares, circles and diamonds.[3] In his diagramming of the Vedas, the Brahamanic rituals form the centre of a half-diamond shooting out vertically in diagonal and central directions.[4]

It is with this sort of sacred geometry, crudely transformed to be sure, that Artaud picks up for use in his spells, begins sending from Ireland in September 1937, and then continues in the asylums at Ville-Évrard and Rodez. Once confined in the asylums, Artaud maintains that 'after a certain day in October, 1939 I no longer wrote without also drawing.'[5] One could look at these spells of Artaud's as evidence of the direct impact the Tarahumara ceremonies, lodged in the 'mountains of signs,' had on him – his attempt to continue the revelations as the living, 'efficacious' action and physicalised language he had called for in the theatre manifestoes, shortly to be finally published as a collection. The spells – curses at first, but also later words of protection, such as to Jacqueline Lamba, André Breton's daughter, who was sent a spell in the form of a double

[1] Deleuze and Guattari, *Anti-Oedipus*, p.101. For the comparison of Artaud with Rimbaud and Nietzsche, see ibid., pp.86-7.

[2] Artaud VIII, 1971, pp.129-58.

[3] Ibid., pp.142; 143.

[4] Ibid., p.139.

[5] Artaud, *Œuvres*, p.1513.

cross – were written on small pieces of paper, surrounded by sacred diagrams and drawings in brightly coloured inks; then the paper would be torn and burnt by cigarettes perforating the paper. Scarred, burned, rubbed, blotted, sometimes blood-spattered as in the spell delivered to Roger Blin, these letters that are also acts of magick and threats were mailed to close friends; doctors; women of a new, invented family Artaud will later call 'daughters of the heart, to be born;' and Adolf Hitler (to whom Artaud will dedicate his book *The New Revelations of Being* in the asylum); the spells are meant to wreak havoc and harm on whatever Artaud deemed to lack purity at the time. With the cigarette burns, Artaud violated the drawing paper that was the surrogate for the target's body. A spell given to one of the doctors at Ville-Évrard, a warning to an occultist that Artaud believed was practicing black magic against him, announced its own power:

> Its efficacy of action
> is immediate and
> *eternal*
> And it *breaks* every
> *bewitchment.*[6]

Amongst the first spells were those sent, via Breton, to socialite Lise Deharme, who had angered Artaud before he left Paris due to her left-wing sympathies (Artaud had given a reading of his play *The Torture of Tantalus* at her home in November 1935); Deharme had called Artaud a 'ham actor' and said he should be burned as a sorcerer for his polytheism.[7] Artaud sent her death threats from Galway, Ireland. The spell is symptomatic of the ferocity that engulfed Artaud in Ireland, as well as the desperation as he felt his prophecies about the coming apocalypse (England, for instance, would sink into the ocean) drain away into inaction. This first spell is extremely violent. Smudged with coins on four sides and marked with kabbalistic signs, Artaud writes that 'I will push in/a cross of fire/red as fire in its tone/sex stinking of jew/and ham it up then/over your corpse to/prove to you that there are/STILL GODS!'[8] Whether missives of hate, such as the spell directed to Deharme, or the letter of protection addressed to Breton's daughter, these early spells are still primarily written, so that one could conclude the violence of their language (whether the threat against Deharme or the warning of the Antichrist in the latter spell) overshadows the kabbalis-

6 Text of spell in *Antonin Artaud, dessins et portraits*, pp.138-9.

7 Barber, *Antonin Artaud*, p.93.

8 Text of spell in (ill. 18) *Antonin Artaud*, p. 37. This is far from the only instance of anti-semitism in Artaud's notebooks. That Jews are attacked as virulently as the human race as a whole, and less frequently than Artaud's assaults on Christianity and priesthoods of all kinds, hardly makes it more excusable. There is also extraordinary ambivalence here. According to Jacques Prevel, Artaud bought a rare copy of the Kabbalah at the end of his life, since he felt it was in danger. This is at the same period of his text, 'Shit to the Kabbalah.' See Mèredieu, *C'était Antonin Artaud*, p.905.

tic signs and jottings that surround it.[9] Yet here, and in various letters of 1937 that are also dotted with myriad hieroglyphic or pictogramic signs[10] Artaud is returning to drawing and making visual signs, in a manner he had not since his drawings for the theatre a decade previously. Writing of some of these works, Artaud in February 1947, called his drawing a 'counter-figure that would be an ongoing protest against the laws of the created object.' He continued,

> The goal of all these drawn and colored figures was to exorcize the curse, to vituperate bodily against the obligations of spatial form, of perspective, of measure, of equilibrium, of dimension and, via this vituperative act of protest, to condemn the psychic world which, like a crab louse, digs its way into the physical, and like an incubus or succubus, claims to have given it shape.
>
> ...
>
> And the figures I made thereby were spells – that I burned with a match after having so meticulously drawn them.
>
> After this I changed my manner. And I have changed it while understanding that I was like a magician that was interned, poisoned, and bewitched.[11]

The spell to Jacqueline Breton announces that 'there is one too ugly/voice/this is the Anti-Christ.'[12] This spell, the 'First that dares/to touch you,' is criss-crossed by an upside down cross, topped by a kabbalistic 'reduction' of the date, and anchored at the bottom by a number of horizontal lines that emphasise Artaud's warning of the lurking Antichrist, forming a kind of mise-en-scéne for the message or text, as it were.[13] Even in these early spells, where the written message is perhaps dominant, the receiver of the message still gets the point of the missive in a manner that is *immediate*. In the later spells from 1939 the visuals tend to take precedence, or rather, the visual and the textual are mutually entangled and fragmented, playing off of each other and cancelling each other in a centrifugally charged, exploding space, that will be characteristic of many of Artaud's late drawings.[14] In the spell to Roger Blin, for example, images and words are burnt to a fine filament of their legibility, or erased through fire completely. Given different coloured inks and crayons by the asylum doctors, Artaud in his spells to Sonia Mossé and Dr. Léon Fouks uses a purple marker for his words as well

[9] Agnès de la Beaumelle, 'Spells and Gris-Gris, Introduction,' in *Antonin Artaud: Works on Paper*, ed. Margit Rowell, New York, NY: Museum of Modern Art, 1996, pp. 39-40.

[10] This begins with the letter of 4 February 1937 to Jean Paulhan, where Artaud draws in some of the signs he claims he witnessed in the Sierra Tarahumaras, and includes strange signs in his letters of the same year to André Breton, Jacqueline Breton, Anne Manson and Marie Dubac. Odd hieroglyphic drawings, marks and signs also accompany several of Artaud's letters from Ville-Évrard later in 1941. For examples of these see Artaud, *Œuvres*, pp.760-4; 803; 810; 813; 817; 828; 832; 838; 866; 867.

[11] Artaud, *Œuvres*, p.1467.

[12] Text of spell in (ill. 19) *Antonin Artaud*, p.38.

[13] Ibid.

[14] For acute descriptions of these spells and their significance, see Stephen Barber, 'A Foundry of the Figure: Antonin Artaud,' *Artforum* 26:1, September 1987, pp.88-95.

as for the leaping, spiralling snakes, the row of crosses (an image from the Sierra Tarahumaras Artaud will use often), stars of David. The text and images here are inextricable; they now truly 'form one body.'[15] The edges of the paper are also burnt, perforated, otherwise torn, as if refusing the boundaries of any given platform or spatial plane. (This too, anticipates Artaud's last notebooks, where the finite form of the school rule-books paradoxically serve the promptings of an infinite process in an infinite space).

Artaud is practicing here a form of talismanic art, often operative in the West before the 10th Century, that combined esoteric writing, cosmic geometry, and the use of an image of evil against evil – a sort of homeopathic or gaze of Medusa strategy introduced as long ago as Moses' brazen serpent in the Book of Numbers in the Bible that cured Hebrews bitten by 'fiery serpents.'[16] Therapeutic images in Western art have almost invariably been linked with faith: in 1657 as a devotion Cristofano di Filippo fixed an image of the Madonna of the Oaks in the branches of a tree near Perugia; passing by several months later he would pray with more or less success to this Madonna to cure his ill wife.[17] Matthias Grünewald's *Isenheim Altarpiece* (16th c.) was similarly homeopathically designed for victims of St. Elmo's Fire, syphilis, and other plagues.[18] Even given the enormous differences between weeping Byzantine icons and Congo fetish figures and Artaud's spells, they do all participate in a notion of art as efficacious action, composed of objects that are items of psychic safety or harm. The Baule people of the Ivory Coast, for example, make no distinction between visible and invisible powers, nor do they distinguish between spirits, the quotidian physical objects that may house them, or more aestheticised sculptures in which they may dwell as well. 'For the Baule,' art historian Susan Vogel writes, 'the very meaning of most art objects, and the strong emotional resonances those objects have, derive precisely from their ability to act…Like all religious art objects, the exhilarating hope or physical terror that the object inspires in the believer by its ability to *act* is part of its significance and content.'[19] Vogel goes on to note 'a similar attitude toward art, spiritual forces, and religious objects underlies most non-Western and many European art traditions except for the modern European one – a conspicuous exception in the history of world art.'[20] This comparison

[15] Beaumelle, 'Spells and Gris-Gris, Introduction,' p.40.

[16] Jacques Mercier, *Art That Heals: The Image as Medicine in Ethiopia*, New York, NY: Prestel/Museum of African Art, 1997, p.19.

[17] David Freedberg, *The Power of Images*, Princeton, NJ: Princeton University Press, 1989, pp.138-9.

[18] Andrée Hayum, *The Isenheim Altarpiece: God's Medicine and the Artist's Vision*, Princeton, NJ: Princeton University Press, 1989.

[19] Susan M. Vogel, *Baule: African Art, Western Eyes*, New Haven, CT & London: Yale University Press, 1997, p.85. Italics in original.

[20] Ibid. One of the very few complements to Artaud's spells in modern and avant-garde art would be the 'cut-ups' of William S. Burroughs and Brion Gysin. See Robert So-

of Artaud's pictograms with the practices of African art is not fortuitous – it is one he made himself. At the bottom of a drawing made in January 1945, Artaud wrote 'Never real and always true/not art but/the rat-tle of Sudan and the Dahomey.'[21] Artaud compared his chanting and beating out rhythms in the asylums to African drumming and his affinity to African spiritualities, especially those derived from the Yoruba religion (which include the New World syncretisms of *santería*, *vodun* and *candomblé*) is particularly striking in three charcoal drawings of staffs, crosses, irons, and swords from February 1944;[22] in some societies such works could easily be read as tributes to Ogún, the blacksmith warrior-god of protection. One of Artaud's most highly prized objects was a stiletto he received from a sorcerer in Cuba in 1936 on the way to Mexico.

Historians of this tradition of 'curative ritual' stress that the efficacy of such acts is creative and activating, yet not objective and predictive; in other words, there is no guarantee. Hence Artaud's precision in reality-testing, counting what disasters come from his spells, and which ones do not. Even the fetishism of such objects resist their customary attributions. As Jacques Mercier has noted, the Portuguese pilgrims who have received miraculous cures and leave wax limbs at the altars of local saints, are not so much simply leaving substitutes of the sick limbs themselves, but rather what one author has called 'a returned component of the pilgrim's own person, simultaneously spiritual and material.'[23] Yet, while Artaud went to the Tarahumaras for the *guérison*, the healing or recovery, he had often noted as part of the Theater of cruelty in his manifestoes,[24]

---

bieszk, *Ports of Entry: William S. Burroughs and the Arts*, Los Angeles, CA & New York, NY: LACMA/Thames & Hudson, 1996; also William S. Burroughs and Brion Gysin, *The Third Mind*, New York, NY: Viking Press, 1978. On the other hand, in terms of contemporary art evoking healing, alchemical processes, or the 'salvational image' the roster is much larger, and would include Joseph Beuys, James Lee Byars, Marina Abramovic, Wolfgang Laib, Sigmar Polke, Mel Chin, Ann McCoy, Carolee Schneemann, Michael Tracy, Ana Mendieta, Mary Beth Edelson, among others. See the discussion in David Levi-Strauss, *Between Dog & Wolf: Essays on Art & Politics*, Brooklyn, NY: Autonomedia, 1999. For the relation to sorcery of William Burroughs' photography, specifically, see Jay Murphy, '"The Target Moves": Reflections on William Burroughs' Photography', *MAP*, June 2014. Available: http://mapmagazine.co.uk/9732/jay-murphy/. Accessed 5 April 2016.

21 Drawing (ill. 50) in catalogue *Antonin Artaud*, p.64. The term Artaud uses here that I translate as 'rattle' is *ra-tée*, also, given Artaud's fondness for anagrams, a possible play on the words for 'art' and 'rat,' as well as referring to the gourd or rattle used in tribal ceremonies.

22 See drawings (ill. 8,9, 10) in *Antonin Artaud: Works on Paper*, pp.52-3.

23 Mercier, *Art That Heals*, p.18. He quotes from an article by Giordana Charuty, 'Le Vœu de vivre,' *Terrains* 18, 1992, pp.46-60.

24 In 'Theater and cruelty' Artaud calls for a 'therapeutic of the soul,' and in 'No More Masterpieces' for theatre as a 'purification,' like that of the 'healing music' of 'certain peoples that we admire on records but are incapable of making ourselves.' Artaud IV, 1964, pp.102; 99. For Artaud his theatre was to put the violence of blood at the service of the violence of thought, a far stronger reality, so that he defied the spectator, once

and underwent a painful detoxification in the mountains on his way to meet them, the Artaud impacted or transformed by that experience is hardly one 'cured' of his obsessions. Artaud moves on different registrations of being or energy at the end of his life, different planes of immanence in Deleuze's term, in a manner that is difficult to reconcile with Freud's description that 'What we take for a morbid production, a form created in delirium, is in reality an attempt at a cure, a reconstruction.'[25] As if in reply, Artaud would claim of his drawings that not one was 'the reintegration of a sensitivity misled.'[26] Rather, these drawings were made

> Through a blow
> anti-logical
> anti-philosophical
> anti-intellectual
> anti-dialectical
> of a language
> through my black pencil pressed
> and this is all.[27]

So while Artaud's spells participate in a tradition of talismanic or magical art that was never completely lost even in the West, they rely more on effects of sheer sorcery, not of the 'salvational image' or 'curative ritual.' They act in a sorcerer's universe – Artaud had written in his wildly evocative essay 'On the Balinese Theater' of the 'Double' or automaton who, 'roused by the repercussion of the noisy turmoil, moves unconscious in the milieux of spells of which he has understood nothing'[28] – but not with any goal of restoring an order 'wherein all the protagonists have resumed their places.' Yet, in cultures where sorcery is practiced, the lines between white and black magic are often hopelessly blurred. As Melville Herskovits wrote in relation to religious belief and practice in the Kingdom of Dahomey in West Africa:

> Good and bad magic are merely reflections of two aspects of the same principle…The character of the *gbo* is such that while one of these charms helps its

exposed to the Theater of cruelty, to continue to live, outside the theatre, the 'ideas of war, riot, and outright murder.' Ibid., p.99.

25 Sigmund Freud, 'Psychoanalytic Notes Upon a Autobiographical Account of a Case of Paranoia (Dementia Paranoides) (1911),' in *Three Case Studies*, ed. Philip Rieff, New York, NY: Touchstone Books, 1996.

26 Artaud, *Œuvres*, p.1513.

27 Ibid. This contrasts with the early Artaud, who on occasion would point to the 'dialectical' character of the human errors and aberrations involved in the alchemical 'Great Work' as reflected in the Balinese dancers (in 1932), and in reference to German cinema, even had good words to say about the influence of Hegelian dialectics (also in 1932). See Artaud IV, 1964, p.59; and Artaud III, 1961, pp.112-3.

28 Artaud IV, 1964, p.81.

owner, giving its aid to protect him from evil intentions or deeds of enemies, it also possesses the power to do harm to the one who would do such evil to its possessor…The Dahomean is relating what is, to him, an obvious fact when he says that good magic and bad magic are basically the same.[29]

This is consistent with what one of Herskovits' sources tells him – that before a child is born, 'Mawu [God] tells him [/her] "It is true that I have sent disease into the world, but I have also sent cures."'[30] Some of this seemingly unfathomable ambivalence and ambiguity in Artaud's spells, is typical of Artaud's spell for Hitler, to be sent in September 1939 with the onset of the Second World War, but withheld by the asylum authorities. In the middle of the missive, Artaud is clear enough – '*I raise today, Hitler, the barricades that I have placed!/ The Parisians have need of gas/ I am yours*.'[31] Yet Artaud alternates between genial advice and threat, ending with

> P.S. Of course, dear Sir
> this is hardly an in-
> vitation! It is above all a
> warning.[32]

As with other references to Hitler in the notebooks, it is as if Artaud was undecided what he thought of Hitler, or how to place him.[33] Hitler is referred to as one of the Initiated, those with power, perhaps one who could intervene for Artaud with the asylum doctors, or on the other hand, was another source of menace and ill-will. As became evident in Ireland, Artaud lives now in a universe of ritual and counter-ritual, one of allies and enemies, one of imminent prophecy, a stark and somber world that Artaud still often refers to as a game, or play, *un jeu*.[34] The spells begin with Artaud's particular delirium or apocalypse, that is marked from his preparations for his voyage to Ireland, his *New Revelations of Being*, and that will remain with him until his last days.[35] In fact, just as the asylum itself increasingly becomes a site for Artaud's Theater of cruelty and his vocal and visual experimentation, upon his release and return to Paris in May 1946 it is as if there is little difference between the asylum and the world

[29] Melville J. Herskovits, *Dahomey: An Ancient West African Kingdom*, Vol. 2, Evanston, IL: Northwestern University Press, [1938] 1967, pp.285; 287. A *gbo*, or *bo*, is any object that can be activated. This can have as many purposes and uses as practitioners.

[30] Ibid., p.256.

[31] Text of spell (ill. 7) in *Antonin Artaud: Works on Paper*, p.50.

[32] Ibid., p.51.

[33] Mèredieu, *C'était Antonin Artaud*, p.706.

[34] For instance in the letter to journalist Anne Manson with whom Artaud had a relationship, of 8 September 1937. Artaud writes to Manson 'I constitute for you a beautiful spectacle, but you do not enter into the game.' Artaud VII, 1967, p.274.

[35] Mèredieu, *C'était Antonin Artaud*, p.694.

'outside;' they are both full of epicenters, flash points of bewitchment Artaud must constantly combat.

In his spell to Dr. Léon Fouks, a young doctor-intern at Ville-Évrard, dated 8 May 1939, Artaud wrote, 'Here is the spell that I have promised you. /It constitutes for you a force of invisible attraction/ toward the most difficult grandeur./ It is repulsive for all your enemies. And you have them terribly.'[36] Some of the letters addressed to Dr. Fouks sought to protect him from his own double, since in Artaud's eyes there was a Dr. Fouks who hated him as well as a Dr. Fouks who supported him in his struggle against the Initiates.[37] In the spell of May 8, Artaud lauds Fouks as one who assisted in the 'transfiguration of God,' and who was 'the preferred disciple of God.'[38] Artaud hails Fouks as a great poet who will write a perfect, revealed work, and as one who already has, 'because you are John of the Apocalypse,/and it is you who wrote more than 20/centuries ago this book that I am not able to read again without crying.'[39] Yet the Initiates want to steal this coming poetic work. The Initiates' harm and evil never stop, Artaud warns, and to write great poems, one must live them – 'And to live it is necessary first of all to free oneself from the Initiates.'[40] Hence Artaud's constant working of sorcery; the Initiates' attempted assassinations and poisonings of Artaud had failed, but their bewitchments remain a total and consistent menace. The Initiates are implicated in the fire ravaging them and their sects, and ravaging the world; the city of Paris, Artaud predicts, no longer has many weeks. On its last page, at the bottom of the fulgurating ideogram, burned through in the middle, Artaud instructs in how to use the spell: 'Guard this spell with your heart. And in case of danger touch your heart with the Index and the Middle of the Right Hand AND THE SPELL WILL LIGHT UP.'[41]

Artaud's apocalypse as initiation, or 'complete voyage'

In testing the approach suggested in Chapter I, at least in its anti-psychiatric aspects, it is necessary to continue emphasising the possible intelligibility of Artaud's acts, despite their manifest liability to the clinical diagnoses of paranoid delirium they incurred. Artaud's spells, for one who advocated a theatre of sorcery and exorcisms, are hardly 'out of character.' Their activation of the space of the letter, in his spells the beginnings of the experimentation in *cahiers*

[36] Text of spell, (ill. 21) in *Antonin Artaud*, p.40. This spell to Fouks comprised four pages – two double notebook pages.

[37] Mèredieu, *C'était Antonin Artaud*, p.702.

[38] Text of spell (ill. 21, 22) in *Antonin Artaud*, pp.40-1.

[39] Ibid.

[40] Ibid.

[41] Ibid.

de brouillon of Artaud at Rodez and after, are also remarkably consistent with the theatre manifestoes that so emphasised the theatre as '*expression in space* (the only real expression, in fact),' that had 'existence only in proportion to its degree of objectification *on the stage*.'[42] The 'magic' of the Theater of cruelty, Artaud wrote in his 'On the Balinese Theater,' came from the 'primitive junctions of Nature that a double Spirit has created. What it puts into motion is the MANIFESTED. This is a sort of primary Physics, from which the Spirit has never detached itself.'[43] Artaud may have become his own Theater of cruelty, his convolutions one of those 'veritable hieroglyphs that live and move.'[44] Yet, with the onset of the Second World War, the medical doctors Artaud had counted as friends in some sense, who knew him and his 'case' well – Dr. Édouard Toulouse who had treated Artaud in 1920, or Dr. René Allendy – were disconnected from Artaud by events.[45] The absence of these doctors, add to the poignancy and isolation of Artaud's condition in the various rapidly deteriorating asylums soon to come under occupation by the Nazi army. Even this forced seclusion did not prevent Artaud from a prodigious participation in the playing of social codes, from complete imaginary engulfment in the world trauma. If however Artaud's journey can be regarded in any sense as R.D. Laing's 'complete voyage' leading, past breakdown, possibly forward into an 'existential rebirth,'[46] then the lack of any functioning or therapeutic community is all the more stark. As David Cooper, the South African existentialist who coined the controversial term 'anti-psychiatry,' writes, Artaud during his years in the asylums, like Friedrich Hölderlin before him, 'had no one to "be with."'[47] Laing outlined such a journey, often stigmatised as schizophrenia, in this way:

> 1) A voyage from outer to inner,
> 2) from life to a kind of death,
> 3) from going forward to a going back,
> 4) from temporal movement to temporal standstill,
> 5) from mundane time to aeonic time,
> 6) from ego to the self,
> 7) from being outside (post-birth) back into the womb of all things (pre-birth),
>
> and then subsequently a return voyage from
>
> 1) inner to outer,
> 2) from death to life,
> 3) from the movement back to a movement once more forward,
> 4) from immortality back to mortality,
> 5) from eternity back to time,

---

[42] Artaud IV, 1964, pp.106; 65.

[43] Ibid., p.72.

[44] Ibid., p.73.

[45] Mèredieu, *C'était Antonin Artaud*, pp.668-9.

[46] Laing, *The Politics of Experience*, p.106.

[47] David Cooper, *A Grammar of Living*, New York, NY: Pantheon Books, 1974, p.63.

6) from self to a new ego,
7) from a cosmic foetalization to an existential rebirth.[48]

What Laing envisaged was nothing less than an 'initiation ceremonial, through which the person will be guided with full social encouragement and sanction into inner space and time, by people who have been there and back again. Psychiatrically, this would appear as ex-patients helping future patients to go mad,' since 'Madness need not be all breakdown. It may also be break-through.'[49] On the other hand existing psychiatric interventions often served, Laing argued, to produce what Herbert Marcuse had called 'one-dimensional man,'[50] in short, to adapt one to a shrunken and repressive social order. 'True sanity,' Laing wrote, 'entails in one way or another the dissolution of the normal ego, that false self competently adjusted to our alienated social reality: the emergence of "inner" archetypal mediators of divine power, and through this death a rebirth, and the eventual re-establishment of a new kind of ego-functioning, the ego now being the servant of the divine, no longer its betrayer.'[51] For Cooper it was a matter of emphasising the 'omega point' that (just barely) separated true sanity from madness or psychotic breakdown, with both of these states, diagrammatically related, at opposite poles from an unconscious, unthinking yet successfully socialised state of 'normality.'[52]

The lack of a functioning community that can relate in any capacity to Artaud's predicament is a huge factor in his travail. Yet Artaud's journey is not one of the self realigning to a higher, divine Self as in Laing's (or Carl Jung's) spiritual hermeneutics. The 'inner' dimension of his peregrination however is emphasised in Artaud's Rodez notebooks. It was not a matter, Artaud wrote:

> of a voyage to the Land of the Tarahumaras or to Ireland, but of a voyage more chaotic and dramatic and that is not in order to espouse geographic convulsions of the terrestial sphere at the centre north or of the West but rather of translating better the genetic spasms of a thought in full formation, in full essence, to the crucial point of mental explosion where the words of the Verb are not still issued, nor already born, but where the soul burns like a country that dislocates in every sense [like] the invasions of Barbarians, and these Barbarians are the desires-passions, the internal psychic states, the effluvia and aromas of self at the moment where unconscious being takes form in that which will be the drama force and the thought in the Manifested.[53]

48 Laing, *The Politics of Experience*, p.106.

49 Ibid, pp.106; 110. Italics in original.

50 Laing refers to the mass conformism described by Herbert Marcuse in *One-Dimensional Man*, New York, NY: Beacon Press, 1964.

51 Laing, *The Politics of Experience*, p.119.

52 David Cooper, *Psychiatry and Anti-Psychiatry*, London: Tavistock, 1967, p.16.

53 Artaud XV, 1981, p.11.

So here, in the midst of confinement, Artaud still writes in the terms of his manifestoes, which urged creating this 'language in space' that must be 'carried to the point of becoming signs,' a theatre that evoked 'a spasm where life is constantly lacerated.'[54] It implies a writing of 'terrible leaps,' that risks interruption, which converts the spasms of interruption, of death, into a rhythm that never repeats. This helps to account for the wide and wild variety of Artaud's texts, who can write an elegant work like 'Revolt Against Poetry'[55] in 1944 at Rodez, in midst of his experiments in sound language, glossolalia and the growing graphic momentum of his notebooks, where word and image grew inextricably entwined, as well as Artaud's taste for ellipsis, parataxis, asyndeton as literary tactics.[56] Artaud's broad variations in intensity and accent serve to cross this chiasm, introducing such irregularity and transgression that it becomes an 'other element.'[57] The reader must make this *saut*, or leap through repetition, each time, weaving the flux anew.

Yet Artaud's project is not just one of writing that *vivre vivant*; in the later Artaud it becomes impossible to disentangle from his 'impossible mutation' of immortality and the 'body without organs.' As I will examine in the following chapters, there is the possibility that Artaud's notebooks – that Jean Genet told Paule Thévenin were a 'poisoned gift' – were supposed to take on his presence and immortality, to continue his combat in the wake of his coming death. This is linked to the sense of Artaud's exclamation to Breton in 1947 that he could only communicate with his audience at Vieux-Colombier if he killed one or some of them – 'to get them to listen one has need of barricades and bombs…there is no longer a language other than that of bombs, machine guns, barricades and all that follows.'[58] In the same letter Artaud maintains he would have waded into the crowd with Breton, attacking them, 'to be massacred or mutilated with him.'[59] Similarly, Artaud told Jacques Prevel after his 1947 reading at Galérie Pierre with an exhibition of his drawings, his last public appearance, 'I believe that with all those people, in order to really make them understand something, you would have to kill them.'[60] The idle or numb spectator is sacrificed or must disappear in order for Artaud, the originator of the apocalypses, to continue. Artaud thus in his way remains a surrealist of the 'Second Manifesto of Surrealism' (1930), for whom 'the simplest Surrealist act consists of dashing down into

---

54 Artaud IV, 1964, pp.107; 110.

55 Artaud IX, 1971, pp.121-3; *Œuvres*, p. 937-8. There is an excellent translation of this text in Eshleman, ed. and trans., *Conductors of the Pit*, New York, NY: Soft Skull Press, 2005, pp.181-3.

56 Rogozinski, '*Tutuguri*, ou le rythme d'Artaud,' p.84.

57 Artaud IX, 1971, p.172.

58 Artaud, *Œuvres*, pp.1207-8.

59 Ibid., p.1216.

60 Prevel, *En Compagnie d'Antonin Artaud*, p.178.

the street, pistol in hand, and firing blindly, as fast as you can pull the trigger, into the crowd.'[61] Artaud claims that for him revolution cannot 'impose itself except through bombs and machetes, through iron and through blood.'[62] Artaud, who insists 'No one will initiate me into anything,' castigates at this point any form of 'hidden science' or mysticism, but maintains that although:

> There is no occultism, no occult magic, there are spells, obscene ritual spellbinding maneuvers periodically set up against certain consciousnesses in which all of society participates not just with its unconsciousness in complete abandon, but indeed and in all consciousness, and then makes use of certain other maneuvers, first obscene, then mathematical, to hide it, and to hide it from itself by forgetting it.[63]

Artaud claims to Breton in this same letter that he has been in 'open struggle every night and day with all the sorcerers and initiates of the earth' for exactly ten years, ever since his visit to the Tarahumaras.[64]

It is here where Laing's approach from existential psychiatry, while allowing us an access and understanding of Artaud and his intentionality we might not otherwise have had, may reach one of its limit-cases, and the practices of 'ethnopsychiatry' first developed by Georges Devereux must be taken into account as a necessary supplement. The demarcations between these two forms of critical psychiatry were already blurring, in any case, in the 1960's, despite their political differences. 'Anti-psychiatry' also incorporated some 'ethnopsychiatric' practices – gathering around the 'mentally ill' the resources of their community, those with fluency in the spirits and demons the patients claimed were plaguing them – particularly in work undertaken in 'Third World' situations where there were strong indigenous cultures such as Cuba, Mexico, Brazil and Tanzania.[65] In the case of Artaud, there is no such community – unless we count the small band of supporters that were with him after his release from Rodez in May 1946, and it would be an extraordinary stretch to claim any of them shared Artaud's view of 'reality' (belief in doubles and so on), rather than a shared appreciation of his value.

---

61 Breton, *Manifestoes of Surrealism*, p.125.

62 Artaud, *Œuvres*, p.1210.

63 Ibid., p.1211.

64 Ibid.

65 For one such experiment see Cooper, *The Language of Madness*, pp.87-8. Cooper discusses others in his books *The Death of the Family* (1971) and *A Grammar of Living* (1974); these include the introduction of pilot 'anti-psychiatric' methods through use of the local Committees of Defense of the Revolution in Cuba in 1968.

The world of sorcery as 'permanent liminality'

Artaud's increasingly literal belief in doubles, his prediction and advocacy for world apocalypse, the notions of his 'body without organs,' all have their roots in Artaud's experience of the Tarahumaras. But whereas the early Artaud clearly and forcefully prioritised space over time, in the sense that any ritual worthy of the name would, the later Artaud becomes obsessed with projecting immortality, so corporeal transformation also becomes bound up with issues of temporality. This metamorphosis of relation to space and time is key to how Artaud's notion of the 'hieroglyph' transforms – from the ghostly yet sharp moving geometric 'hieroglyph' of the Balinese dancers in 1931 into the later 'body without organs' announced in 1947 that replaces Artaud's concern with 'animated hieroglyphs.' Keeping in mind Mauss' insistence on sorcery and magic as collective realities, as social facts, the Tarahumara rites form the most primary collective experience for the adult Artaud, outside of the short-lived and ill-fated collaboration with the surrealist group. It introduces Artaud into a kind of constant liminality that was characteristic to a great extent of the Tarahumaras themselves. This liminal position of the Tarahumaras and the peyote rites, that Artaud often remarks upon, will further complicate the discussion of Artaud's Tarahumara journey as a kind of limit-experience. They are possessed of what Turner describes as a kind of 'permanent liminality,' otherwise they could fit more easily into what Arnold van Gennep wrote of as a more delimited 'liminal phase' of *rites de passage*.[66] These passages of 'transition' for van Gennep consisted of three stages – separation, margin and aggregation, or re-aggregation (corresponding to preliminal, liminal, and postliminal stages that are all applied in a spatial sense, that is, as Turner elucidates, 'units of space and time in which behavior and symbolism are momentarily enfranchised from the norms and values that govern the public lives of incumbents of structural positions').[67] The first term denotes the radical detachment of a person or group from their previous social station or situation; during the second period of this *limen* or threshold, any social standing is ambiguous, and there is no sign of previous or future status. In the third phase the individual or group is indeed re-integrated into a stable state once more and has newly defined social position and obligations.

In applying any of this to Artaud, one could conclude that he remained suspended in a liminal position, with his collapse of social identity and utter loss of civil status in the asylums, which Artaud nonetheless pivots into a germinative

[66] Turner, *The Ritual Process*, p.145; Arnold van Gennep, *The Rites of Passage*, trans. Monika B. Vizedom and Gabrielle L. Caffee, London: Routledge and Kegan Paul, 1909.

[67] Turner, *The Ritual Process*, p.166. As Turner remarks, in the 'liminal' stage of rituals one finds a profound diminution of 'structure' in the mainstream sense of British social anthropology (i.e. institutionalised arrangement of social position), and marked increase in 'structure' in Lévi-Strauss' sense of primordial, pre-structuring mythologies. Ibid., p.167.

position, as he seems to comment on in the inflected black humour of his late text 'Civil State' – 'I let the merinos piss, while kicking beings about, so they'll/ get away from my fire.'[68] This perhaps becomes even more resonant given that Victor Turner discusses as the best example of this possibility of permanent liminality Jesus Christ, especially in how he was interpreted by the Franciscan Order.[69] In the most profound sense this link is made by Artaud, who returns to the figure of Jesus Christ with all the ferocity he musters in the last year-and-a-half of his life. In Turner's commentary on van Gennep, he recognises the difficulty of assigning attributes to either groups or the 'threshold people' who by definition are in-between codes or beyond any patchwork of classification. However their indeterminate status produced a rich well of imagery in ritual societies concerning liminality – as being close to death, to being in the womb, to invisibility, darkness, bisexuality, wilderness, the eclipse of the sun or moon.[70] Persons who have become 'liminal entities' may be represented as possessing nothing, be dressed as a monster, or even go naked as sign they have no status. This enforced sort of submission or poverty during puberty or other initiation rites does not simply consolidate social hierarchy, but rather for Turner illustrates a 'sacred' condition of the possibility of *any* human society. 'Liminality implies,' Turner writes, 'that the high could not be high unless the low existed, and the high must experience what it is like to be low.'[71]

In the case of Artaud, there is recognition of not just the profound marginality of the Tarahumaras. He describes them such that they 'live as though they are already dead...They do not see reality, and draw magical powers from the contempt which they hold towards civilization.'[72] So Artaud is not only undergoing an extreme rite in the series of Tarahumara peyote rituals, he is doing so in a group conditioned by a kind of permanent liminality, in its status on the far outskirts of Mexican civilization, bordering on extinction. Perhaps to find some complement of this extremity in Western culture, Artaud will fasten on the figure of Jesus Christ and insist that it was he, '*Moi, Antonin Artaud*,' who was the one crucified at Golgotha.[73] Artaud brings these fixations with him to the Tarahumara ceremonies and, during his short-lived Christian phase at Rodez,

---

[68] Artaud XIV:2, 1978, pp.32-3; trans. Clayton Eshleman in *Conductors of the Pit*, pp.190-1.

[69] Turner, *The Ritual Process*, pp.145-7.

[70] Ibid., p.95. For a compendium of just such liminal lore, from dreams, fairy tales and various mythologies, see Hans Peter Duerr, *Dreamtime: Concerning the Boundary between Wilderness and Civilization.*

[71] Turner, *The Ritual Process*, p.97. For his table of properties contrasting liminality with the social status system, see pp.106-7.

[72] Artaud IX, 1971, p.79.

[73] This forms the basis and the thematic continuity of the text Artaud prepared for his performance at Vieux-Colombier in Paris, on 13 January 1947, texts he largely discarded during the event (contained in Artaud XXVI, 1994).

will describe the Tarahumaras' supreme deity Ciguri as Christ, and the peyote bud with its configuration or appearance resembling both male and female elements and sexual organs, as Christ's embodiment. In doing so, Artaud is close to the syncretism of many North American Indian tribes, who also took the prescribed, militarily imposed religious doctrine of Christianity and used its terms to describe the often banned peyote rites that conflicted with the tribal religions as well as the white authorities.[74] For Artaud, Christ often cannot be separated from these dramas of the cross in all their different permutations in his life – composing the most elemental hieroglyphic matrix for Artaud in his writings in the 1920s and 1930s, performing a similar function during a brief period of Christian return at Rodez, and after Easter 1945 when he vehemently rejects Christ and the cross, the primary symbol of what blocks entry into becoming. Even in his refusal of it, the cross remains a central focus of his obsessions and it is the abolition of the cross that is called for in his *To have done with the judgment of god*, celebrated as accomplished fact in 'Tutuguri.'

Artaud and Jesus Christ

Despite the dramatic transformation in the Artaud who emerges from the asylums in 1946, he continues to revolve around Jesus Christ as a figure for his own sufferings. This is one of the threads of consistency in Artaud, from the *Fragments of a Journey from Hell* in 1925, to Artaud's Tarahumara experience in 1936, to his last proclamations in the year before his death. It is Jesus Christ who instructs Artaud to go to Ireland the year after his Tarahumara journey to witness the coming 'destruction of the world by fire.' Christ is intimately bound up with Artaud's spatial elucidations and choreography – this is true during the 1930s when Artaud looked favourably upon mysticism and it is true of his later notebooks that are aimed against all priesthoods and all mysticisms. Christ as the centre of the world, prime mover of the universe as well as 'king' was also strongly predominant in various esoteric lore, which Artaud would know well.[75] Understanding the traditional esoteric and mystical significance of Jesus Christ is important for understanding Artaud's transmutations, since Christ has often symbolised various key positions within cosmic pictograms, mappings of energetics that greatly fascinated Artaud, that he mobilised for his own use, that he would increasingly upend and subvert, until he had attained what was, at least

[74] See for example the account by Anonymous, 'The Autobiography of a Winnebago Indian,' in *The Portable North American Indian Reader*, ed. Frederick Turner, New York, NY: Viking Press, 1978.

[75] Poet-translator David Rattray ruminates on the esoteric and mystical literature Artaud checked out from the Bibliothéque nationale de France during his research for *Heliogabalus* (1933-4) in his essay 'Artaud's Cane' collected in his *How I Became One of the Invisible*, Brooklyn, NY: Semiotext(e), 1992, pp.143-172.

to his mind, a militantly anti-mystical and anti-religious position with his 'body without organs.' The most significant of these subversions would be his transformation of the cross itself and its attendant powers. Because it is so central to Artaud's last metamorphosis it is extremely useful outlining some of these pictogrammic roles of Christ. The first to be examined is the psychoanalysis of Carl Jung whose mix of early Christian theology, Gnosticism, and medieval/ Early Renaissance alchemical sources would all have been well-known to Artaud. Jung explicates the figure of Christ as 'our nearest analogy of the self and its meaning.'[76]

In Jung's theory of archetypes Christ is only one-half and must be completed by the Antichrist, 'just as much a manifestation of the self, except that he consists of his dark aspect.'[77] For Jung, '[B]oth are Christian symbols, and they have the same meaning as the image of the Saviour crucified between two thieves.' The symbol communicates that the progressive differentiation of consciousness involves ever more conflict and awareness of conflict, involving 'nothing less than a crucifixion of the ego, its agonising suspension between irreconcilable opposites.'[78] Jung's viewpoint is based on a kind of sacred geometry or cosmic matrix that remains influential in some circles, if only as a sign of the coherence of the universe. Its basic postulates would likely be as accepted by the Artaud of the 1930s as it would violently attacked by Artaud after a certain point in his confinement at Rodez in 1945.

The nature of Christ as figure for the self in Jung leads directly to its representation in a quaternion of opposites: in terms of individuation the self is unique and occurs once, but the self is also a 'transcendent concept' in Jung's words, composed of both conscious and unconscious elements, 'that can only be expressed in antinomial terms' – attributes must be complemented by their opposites.[79] The cross, or crossroads, is thus a quadrilateral of opposite poles – unique/universal, unitemporal/eternal; like Christ the self is unique and historical, formed of a symbol or God-image that is universal and eternal.[80] The transcendent and the earthly aspects of Christ have their complement in the differing good/evil, spiritual/chthonic aspects of the self, forming a sort of totality or four-sided *quaternio*. Hence Jung's picture of individuation as a '*mysterium coniunctionis*' – the growing awareness of the self having to incorporate

[76] Jung, *Aion: Researches in the Phenomenology of the Self*, Volume IX: 2 of *Collected Works*, trans. R.F. C. Hull, 2nd ed., London: Routledge, Kegan & Paul, 1968, p.44.

[77] Ibid.

[78] Ibid.

[79] Ibid., p.63.

[80] Also see C.G. Jung, 'The Relations between the Ego and the Unconscious,' in *Two Essays on Analytical Psychology*, Vol. VII of *Collected Works*, 2nd ed., London: Routledge, Kegan & Paul, 1966.

opposite halves in a 'nuptial union.'[81] This *quaternio* of light and dark, male and female aspects that constitutes the 'psychological self' has often been symbolised by the marriage *quaternio*.[82] Christ signifies this paradox of the 'self' most dramatically, a striving for perfection that must suffer from the opposite of his intentions for the sake of his wholeness; as Jung writes, 'The Christ-image fully corresponds to this situation: Christ is the perfect man who is crucified.'[83]

Pace Artaud, to Jung this conjunction of opposites represents a paradox, 'since a union of opposites can be thought of only as their annihilation.'[84] In fact, Artaud's 'body without organs' will inspire Gilles Deleuze's explicit advocacy of the Antichrist as the 'power of affirmation' against divine order.[85] Writing in commentary on Pierre Klossowski's novel *Le Baphomet* (1965), Deleuze writes in the terms of Artaud after Easter 1945 at Rodez – 'God is essentially the Traitor: he commits treason against spirits, treason against breath itself, and, in order to thwart their riposte, doubles the treason by incarnating himself.'[86] Deleuze argued this since divine 'judgment prevents the emergence of any new mode of existence.'[87] But for Jung this image of Christ as wholeness connects with an entire range of geometric signs of divine order based around the circle and quadernity and their corresponding numerology; especially in quadratic figures divided into four and the symbol of the cross.[88] It is from the circle and quadernity that the symbol of the crystal is derived, as well as the *lapis philosoporum* that was closely related to Christ in the workshops of the medieval and Early Renaissance alchemists, so much so they can often not be recognised apart. Different *quadernios* can be linked together in different ways, as different accounts of Jesus and his dark brother the Antichrist would suggest, or indeed the Zodiac or the 'Wheel of Life.' The squaring of the circle represented in these alchemical accounts, according to one anonymous alchemist author, involves reducing the *lapis* or stone to four elements, and then combining them into one – 'This One, to which the elements must be reduced, is that little circle in the centre of this squared figure. It is the mediator, making peace between the enemies or elements.'[89] In this 'vessel' Jung recognises the mandala in the dreams

81 C.G. Jung, *Mysterium Coniunctionis*, Vol. XIV of *Collected Works*, 2nd ed., London: Routledge, Kegan & Paul, 1970.

82 C.G. Jung, 'The Psychology of the Transference,' in *The Practice of Psychotherapy*, Vol. XVI of *Collected Works*, 2nd ed., London: Routledge, Kegan & Paul, 1966.

83 Jung, *Aion*, p.69.

84 Ibid., p.70.

85 Deleuze, *The Logic of Sense*, pp.292; 296. This is developed in his discussion of the work of Pierre Klossowski, ibid., pp.280-301.

86 Ibid., p.292.

87 Deleuze, *Essays Clinical and Critical*, pp.134-5.

88 Jung, *Aion*, p.224.

89 Quoted in ibid., p.239.

and 'active imagination' drawings of his patients, the mandala standing in as image of totality, the reconciliation of opposites, the divine self, or God.[90] When Artaud calls for a 'unitary culture'[91] in various addresses in Mexico, he does so on the basis that may reference many world esotericisms, but his primary referent is the energetic polarities outlined in Western alchemy.

Especially in the figure of the *uroboros*, these alchemical and pictographic diagrams are depictions of energy. Jung credits early theories of aggregation in alchemy as being the beginnings of a scientific theory of energy; its nonscientific precursor being the far more ancient notion of *mana*.[92] The factor common to antagonistic elements, Jung writes, 'is *molecular movement*, and that the states of aggregation correspond to different degrees of this movement,' which in turn corresponds to a different quantum of energy.[93] Energy is 'that abstract concept which is indispensable for exact description of the behavior of bodies in motion,' bodies that can only be defined by space-time coordinates. In alchemical position, these coordinates are taken up by a space-time quaternion that replaces the four elements; here the element that takes up the time-coordinate, or the fourth in the alchemical series of elements, is an element that has an exceptional position, as in the case of fire or earth.[94] The space-time *quaternio* follows the ratio of the four elements (3+1, or 3:4), for example, with its coordinates of height, width, depth and time. This space-time *quarternio*, Jung writes, 'is the archetypal *sine qua non* for any apprehension of the physical world – indeed, the very possibility of apprehending it.'[95] The space-time *quarternio*, viewed from the standpoint of the three-dimensionality of space, yields time as the fourth dimension. Yet, if the three aspects of the *quarternio* are viewed in terms of attributes of time instead of space – past, present, future – then static space, in which all changes of state must occur, is what must be added as the fourth term. In each instance, the fourth factor stands in for 'an incommensurable Other that is needed for their mutual determination.'[96] This has the consequence, Jung concludes, that space is measured by time and time by space, in a sort of mutual arising. Any of the alchemical states of aggregation are ultimately based on the space-time *quarternio*. This *quarternio*, Jung argues in thoroughly Kantian

[90] See C.G. Jung, *Mandala Symbolism*, trans. R.F.C. Hull, extracted from *The Archetypes and the Collective Unconscious*, Vol. IX:1 of *Collected Works*, Princeton, NJ: Princeton University Press, 1992.

[91] Artaud, *Messages révolutionnaires*, p.121.

[92] One could argue that Jung's definition of the 'unconscious' functions precisely like *mana*, that we have a relation to only through some 'fluid entity' that 'stands in for the unknown.' See Kerslake, *Deleuze and the Unconscious*, n.22. pp.206-7.

[93] Jung, *Aion*, pp.250-1.

[94] Ibid., p.251.

[95] Ibid., p.253.

[96] Ibid., p.252.

fashion, forms a 'psychological apriori,' that is 'altogether indispensable for acquiring knowledge of physical processes.'[97]

In this scheme of things what Artaud does at the end of his life is cast his lot with the disjunction of the Antichrist, with a theory of movement that owes nothing to these cosmic symmetries. In doing so he turns his back on what he had most valued in the mystical systems and lore in which he had become so erudite by the mid-1930s. With his creation of the 'body without organs' Artaud broaches a fourth dimension that has nothing to do with divine creation but rather is in direct conflict with it.

The cross and the crossroads, redux

For the final Artaud, Jung's quadernities are sheer fantasies, bulwarks against the fluxes that make up reality. Yet this quadernity, or equilateral crossroads of Jung's, has talismanic aspects frequently foregrounded in indigenous ritual. Artaud at the end of his life still celebrates the Tarahumaras if not the closed dictates of their priests. To take an example from African currents, to which Artaud sometimes referred, and whose New World syncretisms he came into contact with on his way to the Tarahumaras in the form of a *vodun* ceremony in Havana, Cuba,[98] is the revelatory role of Legba/Ghede in *vodun*. Here is an alternative version of the cross that helps explicate Artaud's convolutions concerning it. Its play with doubles and undecidability and extreme multivalence are realms Artaud enters during his crises at Rodez recounted in my next chapter. For *vodun* in Haiti, Maya Deren wrote, the cross was nothing less than a plunge into the 'cosmic mirror,' the gate to 'les Invisibles,' it was 'the most important of all ritual figures;'[99] in other words a substitute for the Christ for which Artaud at various moments will substitute himself. As the 'cosmic mirror,' the sign of the cross 'appears everywhere, whenever communication or traffic between the worlds is to be indicated.'[100] Every *vodun* ceremony opens with an appeal and homage to the guardian of the crossroads, the *loa* of crossing, yet, as Deren points out, this figure is different depending upon what perspective, from which world, one is addressing it. When permission is sought for access to the life source, to the keeper of the gate between worlds, he is addressed as Legba, whose colour is white. When one aims to approach the cosmic cemetery of all the souls of the dead, he is Ghede, whose colour is black. All rituals begin with an invitation to

---

97 Ibid., p.257.

98 Barber, *Antonin Artaud*, p.79.

99 Maya Deren, *The Voodoo Gods*, St. Albans: Paladin, [1953] 1975, p.42. (*The Voodoo Gods* a UK edition of Deren's *Divine Horsemen*, New Paltz, NY: McPherson & Co., [1953] 1985.)

100 Ibid.

Legba, and end with a salutation to Ghede.[101] Ghede, Deren emphasises, is the wisest of all the gods, and 'the greatest of the divine healers.' He is the Lord of Life as well as the Lord of Death. As Deren writes, 'And if the souls of the dead enter the depths by the passage of which Ghede is guardian, the *loa* and the life forces emerge from that same depth by the same road.'[102] As the axis of both the physical cycle of generation and the metaphysical one of resurrection, as Deren characterises it, the cross is pre-eminently his symbol – for 'He is the beginning and the end.'[103]

It is Legba through whom any appeal to any *loa* must be addressed, who seems at the point of both sides of the mirror world, and whose knowledge is supposed to encompass the entire universe. Legba is often represented as an elderly, crippled peasant, 'as the sun, setting into dark waters, might there appear as a new darkly rising moon.'[104] This guardian of the crossroads, located at its centre, in this tangled web of gods is twinned with his opposite, Carrefour (or Kalfu). It is Carrefour who can loose demons of misfortune and injustice. In Deren's telling, 'If Legba is the divinity of the cardinal points; Carrefour is the master of the points between.'[105] Legba rules the divinities of the day, Carrefour the demons of the night. In keeping with this undecidability of tribal gods, Carrefour can also offer protection against the same demons he can unleash. He therefore operates as a mirror opposite of Legba, on the other side of the glass, as it were, but is not a malefic or evil double. In contrast to Legba, who can be portrayed as an elderly, broken peasant, Carrefour is always vigorous and in the prime of life. He raises his arms in the form of a cross. In such solemnity, there is no murmur, no smiles, in his presence.[106]

What is remarkable in these configurations in regards to Artaud, is that these indigenous intuitions of *vodun* reverberate with Artaud's 1948 description of the 'Tutuguri' rites where the sun is also a black sun and where the appearance of the sun implies its abolition and eclipse. Legba is the sun, at first full of sexual prowess, then growing old and crippled; Ghede is 'the master of that abyss into which the sun descends.'[107] As Deren notes, in Joseph Campbell's studies the sun is often linked to the Tree of Life, the Sun Door to the Navel of the Universe, that constitutes the universal crossroads 'through which man ascends and God descends.'[108] This purported transcendence of opposites at the crossroads, as the

[101] Ibid., p.43.

[102] Ibid., p.44.

[103] Ibid.

[104] Ibid., p.99.

[105] Ibid., p.100.

[106] Ibid., p.101.

[107] Ibid.

[108] Joseph Campbell, *The Hero with a Thousand Faces*, Oxford: Princeton University Press, [1949] 2004, pp.41-6; 260.

fate of the solar order, is preserved only through vestiges in Haitian *vodun*. 'The Sun motif,' Deren writes, 'has almost vanished.'[109] The extraordinary figure of Ghede communicates that even the sun must arrive at this timeless crossroads; yet the sun that in each year is reborn. Deren writes, 'If Carrefour is the night death which attends each day, then Ghede is the night sun, the life which is eternally present, even in darkness.'[110] Legba is the Lord of Life; Ghede the Lord of Resurrection; the difference between them, is death itself. These strange images of 'night sun,' where the solar order disappears and dies only to reappear with the dawn, are central to Artaud's Tarahumaras experience, yet what Artaud will make of it will have little in common with any ideology of *mystica coincidentia*, where the conflicts of the universe are mysteriously harmonised.

What may be more crucial here, rather than any qualities of belief, is the issue of spatiality, the often beautiful *vevers*, the ceremonial drawings on the ground, made in the form of crosses for Legba, for Ghede, and for Simbi, the 'river snake,' as well, the choreography of power that sucks down the spirits required. Deren may want to report her findings in accordance with thinkers like Jung and Campbell, but what she shows is that a great variety of these cosmic complexes can be realised, even in contradiction to Jung's painstaking schemas of quaternaries. In fact what Deren shows of *vodun* ceremonies is that there is profound difference or antagonism between the active forces of sorcery that she describes and any resolution of ritual order that Jung would make a kind of eternal patterning of the universe. This is what makes these *vevers* useful in limning the transition Artaud ultimately makes from mystical hieroglyphics to the rage of the self-created 'body without organs.' Made of wheat, maize flour or ashes, the *vever* consecrates the area to the *loa* it wishes to reach, and is characterised by both fragility and as if it were an 'emblazoned shield.'[111] The elaborate design, that Deren remarks 'requires real technical skill,' is ultimately effaced and destroyed in the course of the ritual, where the *vever* is eaten on, danced on, smeared with the organs of sacrificed animals – 'destroyed bit by bit…finally its remnants are swept away.'[112]

The *vever* for Marassa, the Divine Twins, may also illuminate these issues in regard to Artaud's intense problematic in the appearance of the double.[113] In true *vodun*-style, the Divine Twins are the first humans, and also the first, or original dead, as well; half-human, and half-divine. The Marassa, and the Dead, are celebrated in Haiti on the same night, All Souls' Night. Given homage in ceremonies before any *loa*, the twins are in many senses the origin of all *loa*, and

[109] Deren, *The Voodoo Gods*, note, p.100.

[110] Ibid., p.102.

[111] Ibid., p.194.

[112] Ibid., pp.193; 194.

[113] For an acute commentary on doubles in traditional societies, see Marc Augé, *Pouvoirs de vie, pouvoirs de mort*, Paris: Flammarion, 1977.

more powerful. The Marassa represent the cosmic totality segmented into two horizontal planes, and two vertical planes – in one sense a sexing of the original androgynous unity. What is intriguing here is that the ceremony for the Marassa is composed of the *vever* for the figure three, a number Deren explains illustrates all possible metaphysical variations, and affirms cosmic unity – the sense that any bifurcation still does not escape the large totality.[114] Yet while from this view the three resists any effort at total separation such segmentation may offer, it also implies that male, female and issue is 'an affirmation of multiplicity…the statement that generation is the result of the relationship of the segments.'[115] Here the Marassa offer an alternative to Jung's fourfold totality that represents consciousness of parts; instead of 3:4 or 3+1, Haitian *vodun* offers a segmented triangle – the apex the androgynous whole and each leg male and female, legs that are segmented into the physical body and the metaphysical world. As Deren explicates the Divine Twins, 'it is the relationship of segments which is important.' For *vodun*, therefore, one + one equals three; two + two equals five; it is the third or fifth parts which make the segments coherent.[116] In contrast to Jung's four, in Deren's reading it is the figure of five that is decisive, that 'contains man's entire nature.' This five is the crossroads 'plus the swinging of the door which is the point itself of crossing, the moment of arrival and departure.'[117]

It is not too much to suggest that this opening onto multiplicity, or 'swinging of the door,' is more faithful to what is opened through Artaud's interval, what Artaud often called *la grille*, or passage from sensation to sensation, from thought to thought. Deren's focus on the five challenges her own contrast of magic and religion,[118] the former being 'always…an individualistic triumph, whether for good or for evil,' loosed from the collective context, ritual and constraints of religion.[119] Although it risks taking us too far from the subject at hand to discuss it at length here, Deren's questionable contrast of 'individualistic' magic (in contrast to Marcel Mauss, for example, who insisted on its collective character) to religious mythic structures that hold a homogeneous morality, ducks the possibility of what Deleuze and Guattari termed the 'pragmatics…by sorcery'[120] that must necessarily unravel such structures, a 'pragmatics' at the heart of indigenous magical and sorcery practices. Artaud's own *cruelty*, as the next chapter will show, in the midst of much dementia and disorder, nevertheless manifests its own pragmatics, in a re-formation if not ever a re-integration

114 Deren, *The Voodoo Gods*, p.46.

115 Ibid., p. 47.

116 Ibid.

117 Ibid.

118 See ibid., pp.78-9 and 190-1.

119 Ibid., p.190.

120 Deleuze and Guattari, *A Thousand Plateaus*, p.506.

of his faculties as Artaud maintained, and would seem to have much to do with indigenous rites, rites that must challenge any collective order.[121]

The 'universal' cross: enter Guénon

Artaud moved from universal religious or 'spiritual' symbolism of the cross as crossroads to an extraordinary personal experience of it as sign of rendering and tearing, his crucifixion as ultimate symbol of the Void that is both unrepresentable and irredeemable. Having glimpsed some of the wild multiplicity the figure of the cross is put in Caribbean *vodun*, to explain this further it is wise to look at how some of the more traditional polarities of the cross are indicated, and how Artaud situates himself within them. René Guénon, the 'metaphysician' and apostle of 'traditional science' whose writings were very highly admired at one point by both Artaud and André Breton, had elaborated some of these dilemmas of the cross in his 1931 book *Le Symbolisme de la croix*. Guénon, who warned against Western syncretisms of the great mystical traditions as partial and even harmful, had converted to Islam in 1912 and moved to Cairo in 1930.[122] Guénon's ideas were a continuation, in one sense, of the notions of 'microcosm' and 'macrocosm' found in early Renaissance Hermeticism, which had their origin, Guénon wrote, in ancient Greece and had Arabic equivalents.[123] For Guénon the horizontal line of the cross represented the 'amplitude,' the 'integral extension of the individuality taken as basis for realization;' the vertical dimension draws the hierarchy of all the multiple states possible, all that could be considered in the 'total synthesis of "Universal Man."'[124] The horizontal line is the given starting point for any being's realisation of Unity or 'Universal Man,' a concept that indicates 'the sum total of the states of manifestation.'[125]

What is crucial in the case of Artaud, is that Guénon also included 'states of non-manifestation' in his definition of 'total being,' since for Guénon 'being,' especially when referring to higher states, could only have an analogical sense. Guénon sought to illustrate this by reference to the mathematical sphere, where the 'geometrical point' is 'quantitatively nil and occupies no space although … it is the principle by which the whole of space is produced, the latter being no

[121] Hence the eminently political role of the shaman and the 'Trickster' figures, who play off their social indecidability.

[122] Mircea Eliade credits Guénon in part for the decline in influence of the occult in France. See Eliade, *Occultism, Witchcraft, and Cultural Fashions*, Chicago, IL: University of Chicago Press, 1976, p.66.

[123] René Guénon, *The Symbolism of the Cross*, trans. Angus Macnab, Hillsdale, NY: Sophia Perennis, [1931] 2004, p.12.

[124] Ibid., pp.16-17.

[125] Ibid., p.13.

more than the development or expansion of its virtualities.'[126] In Guénon the cross contains a synthetic realisation of the geometrical representation of being and all its multiple states, one that is quite complex given its permutations contain all ultimate realities. In shades of Artaud's essay 'Mountain of signs' (1936), for Guénon the cross is typical of any true symbol, in that, far from having been invented by man, is found in nature, given that 'the whole of nature amounts to no more than a symbol of the transcendent realities.'[127] Guénon maintained that the plane of the equator and the axis joining both poles and perpendicular to it, represent a vertical cross; the two lines joining the pair of solstitial points and the pair of equinoctial points, constitute the horizontal cross. The vertical cross represents the totality of being; the horizontal cross is the 'integration of the human state'[128] that forms a mirror to the other. Both crosses combined, which thus have the same centre, yield the three-dimensional cross, whose branches are oriented in the six directions of space (such as outlined in the Mayan temples discussed by Artaud in 1936); these six directions correspond to the six cardinal points, that with the centre, form the septernary. The cross thus forms the centre of the world. Guénon cites Clement of Alexandria, saying something similar, that it is from God, the 'Heart of the Universe,' that 'issue all the directions of space.'[129] And the Jewish Kabbalah shares the same symbolism, in that the 'Holy Palace' or 'Inward Palace' is located at this centre of the six directions of space. The name Jehovah likewise, with its three letters with its sextuple permutation in six directions, indicates the presence of God in the centre of the world, the Logos residing in the primordial point.[130] This centre is the centre of space as well as time, the primordial point where the Word is uttered. This interpretation is itself limited and perceived in space and time since it is a specifically human interpretation, Guénon acknowledges, given this is the universe whose conditions of existence can be expressed in language; but it also holds an analogical truth in relation to all the worlds. It is the primordial point that radiates lines in all directions, as in the 'hair of Shiva' of Hinduism.[131] The point at the centre of the cross and hence the centre of all worlds is the ultimate symbol of unity, that exists only through this radiation in all directions (otherwise it would be pure virtuality), yet it can only be comprehended when one locates oneself in space. Given any location in space, that point then becomes the centre.

The tradition of the Kabbalah is one in which letters emerge to express hieroglyphically these latent states. The hidden, primordial point, for instance,

---

[126] Ibid.

[127] Ibid., p.22. For similar conception in Islamic mysticism, see Annemarie Schimmel, *Deciphering the Signs of God*, Albany, NY: State University of New York Press, 1994.

[128] Guénon, *The Symbolism of the Cross*, pp.37-8.

[129] Ibid. Also see pp.28-9.

[130] Ibid., p.23.

[131] Ibid., n.14, p.24.

is expressed by the letter *yod.* It is from this letter that all the other letters of the Hebrew alphabet are formed, which itself symbolises the manifested world. From this same hieroglyphic principle, the primordial cross forms a '"system of coordinates," to which the whole of space can be referred.'[132] So from this central point all the actualities and virtualities of the world radiate out. This principal point is also the focus of the 'inner ruler,' or 'king of the world,' frequently another euphemism for Christ, who directs all from its primordial interiority.[133] It is at this centre where all oppositions are reconciled and overcome, being the illusion of 'particular points of view of knowledge in distinctive mode.'[134] In the Eastern tradition, this is the perfect equilibrium of the cosmic wheel, what the *Tao Te Ching* describes as 'The Principle is always actionless, yet everything is done by it.'[135] This central point is the 'Pivot of the Law' (the 'invariable middle' of Confucianism or the 'Way' of Taoism), the motionless centre of a circumference, 'the fixed point around which all the revolutions of the world are accomplished and which is itself the direct emanation of the center.'[136] In alchemical terms, this primordial point is the ether, into which all dissolves. In this view of cosmic, 'principal unity,' there can be no 'irreducible opposition,' since any such difference or opposition will always be resolved or integrated at a higher level of synthesis.[137] To argue otherwise would introduce a notion of disequilibrium into the cosmic order itself. The sage stands at the centre of this motionless motion, as Guénon at one point refers to in the qualities of alchemy:

> Fire and water, types of contraries in the 'elemental world,' cannot harm him, for in truth they no longer exist for him *qua* contraries, since by balancing and neutralizing each other by a union of their apparently opposed but really complementary qualities, they have re-entered the indifferentiation of the primordial ether.[138]

Yet using this cosmic or primordial point as a hinge for disequilibrium is precisely what Artaud does. Elements such as fire and water can only neutralise each other through a relation of one overpowering the other. Identifying with

---

[132] Ibid., p.28.

[133] Ibid., n.6, p.32. On this matter see also Guénon, *The King of the World*, ed. Samuel D. Fohr, trans. Henry D. Fohr, Hillsdale, NY: Sophia Perennis, [1927] 2001.

[134] Guénon, *The Symbolism of the Cross*, p.41.

[135] Chapter 37 of Lao Tse, *Tao Te Ching*, trans. Stephen Aldiss and Stanley Lombardo, New York, NY: Hackett Publishing, 1993; see also chapter 19 of Chuang Tzu, *The Book of Chuang Tzu*, trans. Martin Palmer, New York, NY & London: Penguin, 2006, for description of how the sage occupies the 'neutral point where there are no conflicts.'

[136] Guénon, *The Symbolism of the Cross*, p.48. This is also found in mainstream Western philosophy, at the very beginning, such as Aristotle's 'unmoved mover' at the heart of the universe. See Aristotle, *The New Aristotle Reader*, ed. J.L. Akrill, Oxford: Clarendon Press, 1986.

[137] Guénon, *The Symbolism of the Cross*, p.39.

[138] Ibid., p.47.

Jesus Christ who through Artaud's varying interpretations is often a Great Destroyer, Artaud's ultimate introjection of the cross in the asylums re-forms his level of becoming onto another level while it restores the state of the world to its originary chaos. This is the complex development of Artaud in the asylums described in the next chapter. To set the stage for this account, this chapter concludes with a reading of Artaud's prophecy *The New Revelations of Being* (1937),[139] that is both a symptom of Artaud's impending breakdown and a philosophical disquisition that stakes out in some clarity how just the sort of universe Guénon describes is constituted for Artaud not by a hinge point of unity but rather by one of violent disjunction ruled indeed by forces of 'irreducible opposition.'

Artaud's The New Revelations of Being *(1937)*

Even when Artaud was most immersed in philosophies of mysticism, in the 1930s, he introduced stark qualities of conflict, force and becoming quite incompatible with its sources. Indebted as he is to these mystical, alchemical and occult sources, even in this period he is far from being completely determined by them. Few texts demonstrate this more dramatically than his *The New Revelations of Being*. Far from a tract that merely confirms Artaud's looming psychosis, *The New Revelations of Being* introduces the themes of world-destruction and apocalypse to which Artaud remains faithful to the end of his days; perhaps to oversimplify this point – in shorthand, it is the theory or reflection, for which his later works that meld and cancel each other in a cacophony of image versus text, of sounds pulling in and destroying other sounds, continue as the practice. What are the components of *The New Revelations of Being*? Its astrologically influenced Tarot castings (as form of occult geometry), its frenzied warnings, its extremely polarised gendering of the imminent conflagration, and Artaud's own pivotal if still highly ambiguous role in this apocalypse, all parallel the spells he was making during this same time. That it is signed simply, *Le Révélé*, at the end, is merely one symptom of what the anonymous author relates as his vastly increased level of alienation and 'withdrawal' from the world. What Guénon describes as the 'Great Peace,' or '"Divine Presence" (*as-Sakinah*), the immanence of Divinity at that point which is the "Centre of the World"...in the absolute simultaneity of the Eternal Present,'[140] for Artaud is an Eternal Now characterised by the collapse of the usual significations of the phenomenal world, engulfed in the Void of warring entities.

[139] Artaud VII, pp.115-44; Artaud, *Œuvres*, pp.787-99.

[140] Guénon, *The Symbolism of the Cross*, pp.52-3.

Artaud introduces this 34-page pamphlet, with the irreconcilable conflict of earth and sea and air and fire. Far indeed from the harmonies of the *mystica coincidentia*, Artaud presents a parable of his war universe:

> The fire in the water,
> the air in the earth,
> the water in the air,
> and the earth in the sea.
> They are not yet insane enough, they are not enough at each other's throats, and the more furious, the more enraged, the nearer and dearer they are.
>
> Here where the Mother eats her sons,
> Power eats Power:
> Short of war, no stability.[141]

Artaud writes this just prior to his journey to the Aran Islands and Ireland, an extraordinarily turbulent and shattering period that immediately precedes his psychiatric confinement. The missives Artaud will send from Ireland speak of increased dementia and the invasion of hallucinated malefic beings that, among other torments, steal his semen. Yet, in the maelstrom Artaud enters he is still able to give names to invading entities and invent forms to combat their activity – acts of remarkable lucidity given the depths of his psychic desperation. *The New Revelations of Being* give a glimpse into this yawning chasm – a 'psychosis' in which Artaud often remains extraordinarily detached and actively reflective. This is the sense in which later in the asylums Artaud 'undermines and unscreens notions of psychosis,' in the process of which he 'blatantly *uses* madness, puts madness to use, to take apart its social structure [and] to produce a transmissible language from that process of disassembly.'[142] In *The New Revelations* Artaud presents himself as someone who is absenting the world, although Artaud suggests that only the Void is real and existent, 'my sufferings until now consisted in refusing the Void.'[143] For Artaud it is the Void that makes the world and its illusions, and he has 'left reality behind.' As Artaud writes, 'This is a real Madman talking to you, one who never knew the happiness of being in the world until now that he has left it and become absolutely separated from it…I am not dead, but I am separated.'[144] But though Artaud has left the world, it is this very condition that allows him to utter the prophecy – 'no longer existing, I see that which is.'[145] This herald of 'the destruction of the world by fire' is a 'superior transmutation' performed by 'A MADMAN WHO IS ALSO A

141 Artaud, *Œuvres*, p.787.

142 Barber, *Antonin Artaud*, pp.7-8.

143 Artaud, *Œuvres*, p.788.

144 Ibid., p.788.

145 Ibid.

SAGE AND WHO HIMSELF SEES HE IS A SAGE AND A MADMAN.'[146] The world will be separated into its elements by a 'MOUNTEBANK OF A LOUT,' and reassembled by the 'TORTURED MAN,' who likewise 'APPEARED AS A MADMAN BEFORE THE WHOLE WORLD,' who dispenses justice, 'on all levels simultaneously in motion,' but a justice that consists of 'taking it away.'[147] This total destruction according to Artaud was also a '*Conscious and Rebellious* Destruction…that we must consent to burning…*every thing that represents things for us*, in order not to expose ourselves to being burnt up whole.'[148] It is the Tortured Man who comes to stand as the revealed, with the illumination of the destruction, and the flash of lightning.[149] So while Artaud has exited the world, he nevertheless stands in the centre of this conflagration, his engulfment that now spreads throughout the known world.

Years later, to add to and heighten the ambiguity of the personifications of the Madman and the Tortured Man, Artaud on 3 December 1943, then in his sixth year of asylum incarceration, would dedicate a copy of *The New Revelations* to Adolf Hitler. Artaud could have seen Hitler as the 'MADMAN' who fulfilled his predictions of the division and destruction of the world, although in Artaud's proclamations from Ireland, it is Artaud himself who is front and centre producing these cataclysms. *The New Revelations* feature a shifting subject – the Madman, the Tortured Man – the moving focus or form of a dictator who is remaking the world along cosmic lines that makes the violence of Artaud's 1925 surrealist broadsides look pallid in contrast. Although Artaud may later draw a parallel to Hitler, in this 1937 text, through his cane and sword, it is Artaud who has wrought this apocalypse.[150] In Artaud's dedication he refers to meeting Hitler at the Romanisches café in Berlin in May 1932, a meeting that was just possible.[151] Although Artaud's 1943 dedication to Hitler can be seen in a critical political light – as a most backhanded 'tribute' to the man who dominated Europe while Artaud was confined in asylums,[152] this neglects the truly fascist trajectory that is also a current that runs through Artaud.[153] According

[146] Ibid., p.792.

[147] Ibid., pp.792; 796-7.

[148] Ibid., p.798. Italics are Artaud's.

[149] Ibid., p.799.

[150] Ibid., p.793.

[151] Barber, *Antonin Artaud*, pp.50-1. In addition to being a literary hangout, the Romanisches had a political clientele, including Hitler. Artaud visited Berlin frequently in the early '30s for film work.

[152] This was the interpretation, for instance, of poet-translator Jack Hirschman in his *Artaud Anthology*. See p.105.

[153] This is not the subject of this project, but if it were, the author would have to deal with how far this trajectory went – from the notions of 'blood' and 'soil' in Artaud's *Messages révolutionnaires* to his attempted collaboration with F.T. Marinetti in 1930, then the state poet of Mussolini's regime. When in the asylums, Artaud appealed to

to writer and sometime surrealist Georges Bataille in his diary *Le Surréalisme au jour de jour*, one day he meets Artaud in passing on the street in Paris, and Artaud 'gripped my hand energetically' insisting to Bataille that '"Believe me, we need to create a Mexican fascism!"'[154] In other letters written shortly before his release from Rodez, Artaud would acknowledge that news of the famines and concentration camps of World War II reached the asylum, developments he claimed *The Theater and Its Double* not only predicted but welcomed.[155]

Part of the world Artaud will leave behind will be astrology and numerology, but not the elements, 'Like the Lightning of fiery Ether/Of which Heraclitus has already spoken.'[156] And *The New Revelations* operates in an eminently hieroglyphic manner, relying as it does on the diagrams and the 'occult geometry' of its astrological castings that form the armature of the prophecy. The pamphlet was first published without the diagrams and Artaud added them to a copy owned by Manuel Cano de Castro, who published them as a key to *The New Revelations* in the magazine *K* in 1947.[157] Their diamond shapes recall Artaud's 'zigzags' and diagrams in his 1933-7 'Notes on the Oriental, Greek, Indian Cultures,' now transferred to the base of his own existence, the 'Man' that 'has been re-installed in the Absolute.[158] In the instance of Artaud this 'Man' is:

> Dead to the world; dead to that which is for everyone else the world,
> fallen at last, fallen, uplifted in this void that I once refused, I have a body
> that submits to the world, and disgorges reality...
> And I know why the dead have been hovering around their corpses for

Pierre Laval, who he counted as a friend, to secure his release. Laval was then French President of Nazi-occupied France. Laval was executed as a traitor after the war. (See Barber, *Antonin Artaud*, pp.40-1; 111.) To situate this problematic, however, in a one-sided manner that ignores the extraordinary multivalence of Artaud's work is the flaw of Kimberly Jannorone's *Artaud and His Doubles*, Ann Arbor, MI: University of Michigan Press, 2010. The accusation that Artaud, in theory and practice was a dictatorial director, and his prescription for theatre little better than a Nazi rally is an old one, after all. For example, John Peter in *Vladimir's Carrot*, London: Methuen, 1987, to cite only one text, has already rehearsed this. These authors have been unable to answer the simple question why if Artaud, who was frequently in Germany in the 1930s for film work, felt Nazi rallies were the fulfillment of his ideas, he never once said so.

[154] Georges Bataille, *The Absence of Myth*, trans. and ed. Michael Richardson, London & New York, NY: Verso, 1994, p.43. Bataille continues, 'The incident gave me a disagreeable feeling, but only partly: he frightened me, but not without giving me a strange feeling of sympathy.' Bataille's portrait of Artaud, like Anaïs Nin's, is somewhat pitiable. It has to be contrasted to many of the photos of the young Artaud, such as those by Man Ray, where he appears as a handsome dandy, indeed one of the most dandified of the surrealists, and the description of Jean-Louis Barrault, who, in characterising Artaud's aristocratic bearing, wrote 'Artaud was a prince.'

[155] Barber, *Antonin Artaud*, p.120.

[156] Artaud, *Œuvres*, p.795.

[157] David Rattray in *Artaud Anthology*, p.84.

[158] Artaud, *Œuvres*, p.787.

> exactly the same thirty-three Centuries that my Double has been incessantly turning.[159]

Not only do these phrases sound the themes and imagery of his last writings – the beings trapped in the bardo levels he witnessed during the bouts of electro-shock, for instance – they also signal Artaud's immense desire to disappear into a pure fused corporeal intensity that no longer requires his proper name. It is at about this time that Artaud in numerous letters cites his recognition of doubles, in a quite literal sense, that he will carry through the rest of this life. That the world is double and triple, as Artaud wrote to Jean Paulhan regarding his discoveries in the Sierra Tarahumaras, is a perceived truth that Artaud lives. This corporeal entity perpetually launches itself, 'For I am an unpardonable Brute, and so I shall be until Time is no longer Time.'[160] What is crucial here is that Artaud's doubling requires the visual signs or spatialisations of its manifestations, much as Deleuze would later theorise that differences in quality would always be subtended by spatial differences.[161] Part of Artaud's influence in Deleuze's *Difference and Repetition* lies in the treatment of doubling. Just as any actualisation requires the series of space, time and consciousness, this elementary consciousness not only 'itself trace directions,' it 'doubles movements and migrations.' Contrary to Husserl's consciousness that must be consciousness of something, Deleuze maintained that consciousness is 'the double of this something, and everything is consciousness because it possesses a double, even if it is far off and very foreign.'[162] Artaud's double is much like a shamanistic 'ally' in its treachery, that it is the agency that steals his thought, that produces his illness, that threatens to end his life; it is nevertheless even in the early Artaud the origin of theatre, and in the later work it is also a means of revival of the 'true body.' One of Artaud's most vivid depictions of this is one of his very last drawings, made in December 1947-January 1948, *The projection of the true body*. In it Artaud in a recognisable visage, hands shackled, is being executed by a firing squad, his knees riddled with bullets, while opposite and bound to him stands his double a black skeleton, exploding from its bones and breaking free in all directions.

159 Ibid., pp.788-9.

160 Ibid., p.788.

161 Deleuze, *Difference and Repetition*, p.261. This is true since 'There is in general no quality which does not refer to a space defined by the singularities corresponding to the differential relations incarnated in that quality.'

162 Ibid., p.273.

The cross as a test of rhythm

As his continuing preoccupation with the cross and crucifixion attests, this early spatialisation of these questions is increasingly subject to such flexibility that it is difficult to localise, in the sense Artaud uses this term in *Nerve Scales* (1925) where he complains of being 'completely paralysed by my terms, by a chain of terminations.'[163] The points of the cross for Artaud can only be a form of multiplicity, and in their intense pressure as part of a complex Artaud will come to perceive as the end of the world must not merely in its form as unity be resisted, but transformed through the acts and gestures of rhythm. His late or final works are the product of this ferocious rhythmic play. Artaud in the most dire straits still retains the extraordinary creativity to pursue and move in these voids and situations of permanent flux, much as in the possibility Bergson limns when he writes of 'instinct that has become disinterested, self-conscious, capable of reflecting upon its object.'[164] At the borders of liveable experience, Artaud indeed exhibits a kind of 'unliveable Power' in his response to being subject of pure forms of space and time. Pure forms such as those described by Deleuze in his example in *Difference and Repetition* of the extraordinary movements of the embryo in the womb, 'intensive' movements no adult organism could survive. For most people these spatio-temporal forms are subjected and overwhelmed by needs and constraints of a profoundly practical nature, the trappings of 'normal' existence. Deleuze emphasises that 'a pure spatio-temporal dynamism, with its necessary participation in the forced movement, can be experienced only at the borders of the liveable, under conditions beyond which it would entail the death of any well-constituted subject endowed with independence and activity.'[165] Deleuze describes this as a 'dynamism external to concepts, and, as such, a schema – it is internal to Ideas – and, as such, a drama or a dream.'[166] Artaud emphasises his project is that of 'a dream which eats the dream,'[167] that subjects the dream to further lucidity. The instance of the cross is the dream as order that must be transformed at all costs, changed back into its resident flux.

The mutual arising of space-time complexes Jung and Guénon describe as constitutive of the cross, for Artaud is very much tied up with the counter-propagation of rhythm. In Deleuze and Guattari's analysis, rhythm cannot be separated from the issue of territorialisation, the marking of a spot, or putting up of

[163] Artaud I:1, 1956, p.92.

[164] Bergson, *Creative Evolution*, p.176.

[165] Deleuze, *Difference and Repetition*, p.118.

[166] Ibid. For further discussion of different mental disorders as 'dramatizations' of spatio-temporal dynamisms, such as obsessional neurosis, see Gilles Deleuze, 'The Method of Dramatisation,' in *Desert Islands*, New York, NY & Los Angeles, CA: Semiotext(e), 2004.

[167] Artaud IV, 1964, p.179.

a placard, even if this is fixing 'a fragile point as a center' in a surrounding black hole.[168] As they write, 'From chaos, *Milieus* and *Rhythms* are born.'[169] What is of pertinence here is rhythm's role as go-between and in-between, as moving interval and response from milieus to encroaching chaos; central to this notion is that rhythm 'ties together critical moments, or ties itself together in passing from one milieu to another.'[170] They second Gaston Bachelard's idea that rhythm invariably operates on a different plane from the one upon which action is carried out (actions are in milieus, rhythms in-between milieus).[171] This serves to underline their characterisation of milieus as 'not unitary,' as 'essentially communicating' and perpetually undergoing operations of transduction and transcoding that serve as the basis for its constitution, its establishment or sliding atop one milieu or indeed its dissipation into yet another. It is the presence of transcoding that indicates the creation of a new plane, which rhythm's modality as a passage or bridge leads to. Milieus or portions of milieus form territories for Deleuze and Guattari precisely when they become dimensional instead of directional, no longer functional but expressive.[172] Their immediate example is colour in birds or fish, a membrane state reflecting interior hormonal status that is functional when linked to actions of sexuality or flight, but becomes expressive when it acquires its 'signature' – a marking of temporal constancy and spatial range that indicates its 'territory.' In their analysis, it is the mark that makes the territory.[173] Functions in any territory rather presuppose the qualities of expression that create and demarcate any given territory. In this definition, 'territorialization is an act of rhythm that has become expressive, or of milieu components that have become qualitative…it is a rhythm.'[174] As Deleuze and Guattari emphasise, this marking and demarking becomes a matter of style, 'In effect, *expressive qualities or matters of expression enter shifting relations with one another that 'express' the relation of the territory they draw to the interior milieu of impulses and the exterior milieu of circumstances.*'[175] Although this sort of marking and signing, delimiting and then surpassing certain territorialisations, is characteristic of Artaud's writing,[176] there is also the larger issue of Artaud's boundary-formations

[168] Deleuze and Guattari, *A Thousand Plateaus*, p.312. A discussion they borrow from the writings of painter Paul Klee, see Klee, *On Modern Art*, trans. Paul Findlay, London: Faber & Faber, 1966.

[169] Ibid., p.313.

[170] Ibid.

[171] Ibid., Gaston Bachelard, *La dialectique de la durée*, Paris: Bovin, 1936, pp.128-9.

[172] Deleuze and Guattari, *A Thousand Plateaus*, p.315.

[173] Ibid.

[174] Ibid.

[175] Ibid., p.317. Italics in original.

[176] In this light see two studies of Artaud's writing: Adrian Morfee, *Artaud's Writing Bodies*, Oxford: Clarendon Press, 2005; and John Cameron Stout, *Artaud's Alternate Genealogies*, Waterloo, ON: Wilfrid Laurier University Press, 1995.

and reformations, these movements of his psychic/somatic boundaries continuous with and as fluid as his writing practice became, as a critical embodiment of what Deleuze elsewhere characterises as 'naturing Nature.'[177] This provokes a truer challenge and test to the coherence and intelligibility of Artaud's journey, since Artaud's elaboration of hieroglyphics can hardly ever be confined to any aesthetic method, not even as a program for renewal of the theatre in the vastly expanded sense in which he thought and wrote about it. Artaud speaks to the power of evoking 'hieroglyphs' in his theatre since they are the deepest movements of reality itself. Artaud warned of their disorder and their cruelty, and it is to this in his own experience I will now turn, with a view towards showing how Artaud's manipulation of the hieroglyphic of the cross is absolutely central to Artaud's survival and reconstitution in the long nine years of asylum confinement. Paradoxically it is by the means of this severe subversion of the cross that Artaud is able to create a new or 'double' body, the 'body without organs' he proclaims to the world in *To have done with the judgment of god*.

177 Gilles Deleuze, *Bergsonism*, trans. Hugh Tomlinson and Barbara Habberjam, New York, NY: Zone Books, [1966] 1988, p.106.

V.
HIEROGLYPHICS AS PASSAGE

Artaud at the end of his life left texts like 'Tutuguri,' that seem to illustrate spheres moving within spheres, that take his own moves of extreme boundary-change as their 'subject,' and constitute their rhythm, belying the shift from his earlier work to the later as only an exponential increase in fury. Artaud's agonised assertion of breath and movement from its inception brings a case against being, a term that is difficult to employ without envoking models from God. Artaud will end up asserting, 'I was there before God.'[1] This makes Artaud's 'hieroglyph' not a theory exactly, but more than simply an anti-theology, or even a map, cartography of extremely mobile boundaries, it becomes a remarkable means of survival and re-structuring in the asylums. First named as a principle of theatre in the Artaud of the 1930s, in the late ever more embattled Artaud, the hieroglyph becomes enmeshed and then annihilated in the 'body without organs' projecting itself despite the imprecations of demonic assault and treachery in Artaud's universe of war. It is in this universe and in the cacophony Artaud wants to produce that the 'hieroglyph' is ultimately replaced and jettisoned. Artaud of the theatre manifestoes urged the creation of ritual spaces that could trap or reverse time and purge crime, even produce healing, much as in many tribal rites; Artaud released from the foundry of Rodez in May 1946 bets on an immortality of the 'body without organs' that remains visceral in its infinite gesture. In his transformational use of the cross, especially, during his nine years of asylum confinement, embroiled in a complex and torturous re-formation, Artaud uses a hieroglyphic means to not merely survive an extraordinary assault on multiple levels, but to emerge on another registration of becoming and creativity – one that becomes the most continuous and enormous in terms of work in his life. In the process he challenges the notion of psychoanalytic or medical 'cure' but posits an undeniable, changed reality nonetheless. This is his 'body without organs,' another 'plane of immanence' in Deleuze and Guattari's term, which unlike his earlier theatre manifestoes cannot be reconciled so easily with Aristotelian ideas of catharsis, that no longer seeks to 'heal' the void but affirm it.[2]

---

[1] Artaud XIX, 1984, p.189.

[2] Yet even this generalisation must be qualified. In Artaud's late notebooks the word *guérison* does appear time to time as in the theatre manifestoes, and in the 1947 text

This chapter will focus these themes in the following way: first, by revisiting the issue, so often stressed in this project, of how Artaud's singular notion and movement of becoming broaches its own model, and cannot be encapsulated in the holisms or microcosm/macrocosm distinction of most mystical discourse (alchemy being a prime example); then I will show how the hieroglyphic figure of the cross becomes the primary trigger or organising point for Artaud's strenuous, if not unprecedented re-structuring in the cauldron of the asylum, and flash point for his re-making of the body that for Artaud has been in fact tortured to death; this is followed by a description of the construction of Artaud's 'body without organs' as a 'double' body. This crowning achievement, that constitutes itself in the late radio works and drawings and forms the moving substrate of Artaud's *cahiers* examined in the last chapter, is also Artaud's ultimate challenge to psychiatry and psychoanalysis, and serious consideration of it is hardly possible without engaging in the perspectives of 'critical,' 'ethno; or 'anti'-psychiatry, themselves sometimes directly inspired from Artaud. In the very last section here, I will present how Artaud's meta-commentary anticipates and provides fodder for a number of approaches that have likewise widely challenged many of the ideologies of psychiatry in a thorough-going fashion; these, in turn become crucial for understanding Artaud. The 'body without organs' thus becomes both Artaud's 'cure' and his defiant rejection of any normalising psychiatric solution.

Artaud's becoming versus being

Artaud asks in the *Cahiers de Rodez*, 'Not having ever begun but finishing each day by being a being/where and in what is this abyss without beginning?'[3] In one of Artaud's earliest texts, in 1923, he is already writing that to understand thought, it is necessary at first to exist, to be, 'It is necessary to have the beginning of thought.'[4] Thought exists, thought has a beginning in Artaud, yet, as in his anguished insistence in his correspondence with Jacques Rivière in 1923-24, such thought is robbed, is stillborn, so Artaud, paralysed by this treachery, sinks back into the gaps and intervals, the ever-present void. Artaud's efforts to span these intervals relies on a number of devices, but primarily through them an activation of rhythm, a dance Artaud creates that in its 'essence,' is profoundly 'fusional,' Évelyne Grossman has argued.[5] The reader is forced into the same rhythmic movement as Artaud, losing any comfortable self-identity

'Alienate the Actor' Artaud writes that theatre is the place or point where 'the human anatomy can be seized/and used to heal and direct life.' Artaud, *Œuvres*, p.1520.

3 Artaud XVIII, 1983, p.176.

4 Artaud I:1, 1956, p.211.

5 Grossman, *Artaud/Joyce*, p.25.

in the process; like the 'author,' the participant-reader moves on an unstable and extraordinarily supple boundary line, neither inside nor outside of it. As Grossman articulates so well in her comparison of Artaud and James Joyce, the reader who would refuse this fluctuation indeed makes the texts unreadable.[6] Here Grossman's conception of 'intersubjective' space relies on Henri Meschonnic's studies on the poetic language of rhythm, especially operative in prophetic writing, where rhythm, as the body-element in the writing or literature, is 'transindividual' by definition, and rhythm is precisely that force that organises the passage of a subject to another subject, and thus 'constitutes them as subjects through this same passage.'[7] Meschonnic's use of the term 'subject' is problematic in the case of Artaud, although his delineating the role of rhythm as the prime transducer or transcoder, as the agent that opens up the liminality of passage from one mode to another, is more to the point. This passage is a passage of the body, of this thought which is lived as Artaud's 'immediate and direct crystallization of myself,' so its interruption is one felt as devastating pain and loss in the body, as 'corporeal uprootings,' since it is precisely in Artaud's body that often he does not belong, that he will exit in order to fashion another body from the outside.[8] Insofar as the body takes form, makes links in words, these are the connections that Artaud complains fails him, as each possible formation aborts.[9] This remains confusing, since Artaud writes in a 1931 letter that there is no reason to catch a thought here or there, or here rather than there, since '*there is no reason to begin to think*.'[10] Whereas the early Artaud of the Rivière correspondence struggles with capturing the fruits of the birth of thought, or puts himself into what he calls an 'impossible position' to think and create, the Artaud of Rodez and later will affirm that language and thought is a perpetual abortion. He writes, '[S]yllables are only the scrape, the race, the trace, of a fundamental flaying...Things do not come through engenderment and conception but through scraping, one body on another body and emerges then freed in an other body than that from which it was torn/this is all history...'[11]

These uprootings of body from body, the intense ruptures of what he had described to Rivière as the struggle to maintain the 'consistence of its own proper substance,' these doublings and redoublings of his spirit, are located in what he calls at one point the 'infinite musicality of nerve waves,' characteristically emphasising creation direct from the nervous system, but in some of his early dramas is already displayed as an identity diffracted to infinity through a play of

6 Ibid., pp.24-5.

7 Ibid., p.24; Henri Meschonnic, *Les Etats de la poétique*, Paris: PUF, 1985, p.137.

8 Artaud I:1, 1956, pp.53;117; Artaud XXIV, 1988, p.173.

9 Artaud I:1, 1956, p.185.

10 Artaud II, 1961, p.270. Italics in original.

11 Artaud XXIII, 1987, p.48.

mirrors.[12] Each identity becomes or is contained in the others, in a dizzying play of *dédoublements*. A 'mental drama' like Artaud's 'Paul the Birds, or the Place of Love' (1924), as it is discussed in Chapter II, can well be viewed as a prism of Artaud's conflicts. Here in this immediate context it is more valuable to examine how each character transforms into the other, since the play, like the canvas of a painting or the later notebook page, for Artaud never fails to be a site of metamorphosis. The different personae of this play – the painters Uccello, Donatello, Brunelleschi, and Selvaggia; these are all emanations from Paul the Birds, who is simultaneously himself and all the others. The painter Paolo Uccello here is himself split. Each persona, Artaud writes, is sometimes the container, sometimes the contained. As he writes of Uccello, 'He is ACTUAL, I mean actual to us, men of 1924, and he is himself. He is Paolo Uccello, and he is his myth, and he becomes PAUL THE BIRDS.'[13] Paolo Uccello is his historic 'real name,' and Paul the Birds is the name through which he is understood for us who are beyond his time. So the characters are a fluid congregation composed of Uccello-Donatello-Brunelleschi-Selvaggia-Paul the birds-Artaud-and any reader. Truly, as Artaud writes in one version, 'Two, three, ten problems are crisscrossed all at once with the zigzags of their spiritual tongues and all the planetary displacements of their plans.'[14] As Artaud describes it, 'little by little he builds his history, and little by little he detaches from himself. The responses intersect in him outside of time.'[15] Placed outside of time and so encased in the ideas of spirit and love that he has renounced his human being, Selvaggia's death does not disturb him, although he can see she is now death itself, and Artaud writes, reverting to the first person, 'I touch the impalpable line.'[16] Much as Artaud begins this drama with Uccello in a strange type of absent space, 'without any kind of space where to mark the place of his spirit,' as the drama progresses the author notes *l'évanouissement* or vanishing of form, 'not the line that encloses all the others but the same one that begins no longer is.'[17] The demarcations between characters, their spatial and temporal delineation, however provisional or temporary, seem to consist of this line, passing from interior to exterior, as if the thought of Uccello in its movement constituted a supreme reality. Artaud's second version, in 1925, is radically simplified, but has the same characteristics. Its relation to the late Artaud is not only this abolition of limits and simultaneity of events and personages, but also what Grossman characterises as its systole and diastole, its movements of expansion and contraction, in which being includes the other,

[12] Artaud I:1, 1956, pp.29; 127. Grossman, *Artaud/Joyce*, p.36.

[13] Artaud I:1, 1956, p.206.

[14] Ibid., p.56.

[15] Ibid., p.206.

[16] Ibid., p.207.

[17] Ibid., p.206.

then separates from it, becoming other, in a strange dance of individuation.[18] This 'mental poem' ends as it begins, in an estranged suspension of reality.

A similar dynamic is underway in a text Artaud wrote shortly before his trip to the Tarahumaras, 'Vie et Mort de Satan le Feu' (1935),[19] part of a projected book *Satan* Artaud was to write for Gallimard but never finished. What would be termed 'microcosm' and 'macrocosm' in Hermetic or mystical philosophy is uprooted in Artaud's analysis of Satan as fire. While he could carry out an 'alchemical reduction,' he writes, Satan shows the crack in the all-too anthropomorphic notion of being, and his identification with fire is problematic as well: it is only through an image of Satan that is reduced, calcified, in fact, that he begins to die to itself, and that can be then linked to an image of fire, 'through an effect of extreme tension/that resembles all that is.'[20] It is through an abstraction, Artaud writes, that Satan belongs to this fire, although it is nature itself that comes into being through abstraction, this abstraction that 'causes me to invent nature, in a sort of infernal movement.'[21] So even Satan, this '*unique* image of rebellion,' that separates and separates from itself, that burns and punishes itself, is solidified into a notion of being.[22] Yet in Artaud's strange conclusion to this short text, he affirms the importance to him of dedicating this text to Satan, the 'inexpressible respiration' or breath that separates itself from itself, that castrates its own movement, and that 'conforms to the spirit of Satan.'[23] In notes in the margin, Artaud had written of 'the eternal movement of Nothingness.'[24] In the projected book, Artaud planned to explain that everything that 'prevents us from living is only a refraction of satanic thought…'[25] Artaud seems to constitute a unity, albeit a negative one, a notion of being that owes more to negation than affirmation, but one susceptible to a dialectic, even a Hegelian one. As he wrote in the following 'Notes on Oriental, Greek, Indian Cultures' (1933-7) in reference to Heraclitus, 'All is exchanged against fire, and fire against the rest.'[26] Similarly in *Heliogabalus* (1934) Artaud will refer to a hermaphroditic monism or dialectical unity yet the 'crowned anarchy' of the Roman boy-king paradox-

---

18 Grossman, *Artaud/Joyce*, p.37. Although the term conveys more or less different senses in Deleuze, Lacan, Jung and Bergson, 'individuation' still commonly designates this change or coming into form, the differentiation that occurs through integration or interaction with other elements. As Isabelle Stengers writes the 'problem of individuation' is one 'through which an individual characterised by discreet relationships with its milieu is produced.' Stengers, *Cosmopolitics*, II, p.291.

19 Artaud VIII, 1971, pp.119-25.

20 Ibid., p.122.

21 Ibid.

22 Ibid., p.121.

23 Ibid., p.122.

24 Ibid., n.13., p.401.

25 Ibid., p.123.

26 Ibid., p.150.

ically rests on the irremediable severing of the points of dialectical unity, and from its inception Heliogabalus' solar monotheism is no unitary signifier that can annul the blunt negations of all possible multiplicities; differences are cancelled while contraries are fused.[27]

As if to confirm this reading, Artaud wrote a second part or an addendum to *Satan*, entitled 'The Respiration that Returns to God…', which opposes the element of ice to fire, presenting the 'superior face of celestial bounty that evil has contaminated.'[28] In this 'translucid' realm the breath still fuels events and Artaud writes of the 'shifting frame of a dazzling spirit that seeks the great way,/ resembling from one side an angel and from the other the face of Satan' – as if again they form a unity.[29] In a style that harks back to his early poems, 'La Respiration…' speaks of the power of these flecks of ice to rebirth the region, that 'sifts and situates in the dancing mass of atoms recognised and counted up until infinity,' in a rain of 'crucified mirrors,' which concludes with the compressed sound of a 'system, frozen,' as if there is a cosmic arcade with a single point that links up two immensities.[30] Resting in a kind of symbolist poetry, Artaud has two absolutes as elements linked yet completely differing, playing images of perpetual movement and total immobility off against each other.

In his exploration of these elements that can be somehow linked together yet not contained one within the other, Artaud appears to be groping toward the revisions of the notion of 'microcosm' and 'macrocosm' Henri Bergson discusses in his beginning to *Creative Evolution* (1910), where, without ever using those terms, he suggests a model of becoming incompatible with such categories. Not wishing to repeat Bergson's entire complex argument here, it suffices for my purposes to say that for Bergson 'Anything that is irreducible and irreversible in the successive moments of a history eludes science.'[31] In arguing that by necessity we must have partial views of a possible continuity or whole and can only perceive successive states, we therefore artificially isolate, Bergson writes:

> A very small element of a curve is very near being a straight line. And the smaller it is, the nearer. In the limit it may be termed a part of the curve or a part of the straight line, as you please, for in each of its points a curve coincides with its tangent. So likewise 'vitality' is tangent, at any and every point, to physical and chemical forces; but such points are, as a fact, only views taken by a mind which imagines stops at various moments of the movement that generates the curve. In reality, life is no more made of physico-chemical elements than a curve is composed of straight lines.[32]

---

[27] See the commentary on *Heliogabalus* in Deleuze and Guattari, *A Thousand Plateaus*, p.158.

[28] Artaud VIII, 1971, p.124.

[29] Ibid.

[30] Ibid., p.125.

[31] Bergson, *Creative Evolution*, pp.29-30.

[32] Ibid., p.31.

Bergson here could be taken for presenting a quasi-scientific refutation of representational thinking and this is a key contribution of Bergson to Deleuze's later project in *Difference and Repetition* (1968). There is little evidence of any direct influence of Bergson on Artaud,[33] but through the perilous necessity and experimentation of his own life Artaud presents a similar line of thought. Although in texts like *Heliogabalus* and *Satan* a unity or monism is presented, it is in the form of a fusion that can barely be sustained, being based as it is on a movement that is indeed without such 'stops.' In the later Artaud it is this flux and the rhythm of this flux that he asserts above all, but already in *Satan* 'nature' is questioned as a false representation or abstraction and the symbology of alchemy can only be a 'reduction.'[34] As usual, these assertions cannot be wrenched from the fluctuations of Artaud's subjectivity and they only become all the more relevant in Artaud's asylum experience, where personifications of these fusions and contraries battle for Artaud's soul. In the asylum, Artaud's ability to name invading entities and shift boundary-states enables him to recreate himself, on the ashes of what he describes as the old, assassinated Artaud.

The fulcrum of the Cross: Artaud's 'Gnostic' delirium

One of the reasons Artaud's itinerary is so remarkable, is not merely his lucidity in mapping his changes and transformations – President Daniel Paul Schreber and Louis Wolfson were also highly articulate 'schizophrenics'[35] – but how

[33] Artaud does refer to Bergson in one of his Mexican addresses, precisely in the context of Bergson's 'pure duration' that Artaud cites as evidence that thought does not ever stop. See 'L'Homme contre le destin' in *Œuvres*, p.693.

[34] The most thoroughgoing examination of Artaud's often contradictory relation to alchemical motifs is found in Florence de Mèredieu, *Antonin Artaud, les couilles de l'ange*, Paris: Blusson, 1992.

[35] Louis Wolfson, *Le Schizo et les langues*, Paris: Navarin, [1970] 1984; Daniel Paul Schreber, *Memoirs of My Nervous Illness*, new ed., trans. and ed. Ida Macalpine and Richard A. Hunter, New York, NY: NYRB Classics, [1903] 2000. Wolfson, who called himself 'the student of demented idioms,' concocted an extraordinary linguistic/language system. For Deleuze's introduction to Wolfson, see 'Louis Wolfson; or, The Procedure,' in *Essays Critical and Clinical* (1997). Schreber's case was the basis of Freud's famous 1911 commentary on paranoia, 'Psychoanalytic Notes upon an Autobiographical Case of Paranoia (Dementia Paranoides)' in *Three Case Studies* (1996). Lacan commented on Schreber in his 'On a question preliminary to any possible treatment of psychosis,' in *Écrits*, trans. Bruce Fink, New York, NY & London: W.W. Norton, [1966] 2007; but his most extensive remarks on Schreber are found throughout the discussion in *The Seminar of Jacques Lacan, Book III: The Psychoses, 1955-6*, ed. Jacques Alain-Miller, trans. Russell Grigg, New York, NY & London: W.W. Norton, [1981] 1997. Schreber was a German judge who began psychiatric treatment at age 42, and was in and out of mental institutions for the next twenty-seven years. Schreber is also central to Deleuze and Guattari's *Anti-Oedipus* (1972) in a far more positive light as one of the principal mapmakers of the 'body without organs.' A highly influential text for 'an-

Artaud's notions of 'zigzag lines,' of permeable and ever-moving membranes that challenge relations of the container and contained, the fluid 'hieroglyph' in short, are keys to his re-construction and re-formation of spirit and body, in the horrific conditions of the wartime asylums. This awesome metamorphosis, what Julia Kristeva characterised as Artaud's self-analysis, had elements that were, in the judgment of psychoanalyst and author Serge André 'absolutely unique.'[36] Evidence of this is that some of Artaud's richest writing on the cross, that ultimate 'hieroglyph' for Artaud, that becomes a scaffolding and scansion placed directly in the body situated between the complementary expelling activities of the mouth (in vocalisations) and the anus (excrement), is found in the first two volumes of his *Cahiers de Rodez.*[37] There Artaud writes 'I am the vertebral cross.'[38] Despite the extraordinary complexity and confusion of Artaud's experiences during his long, enforced stay in the French asylum system, one can delineate different chronological periods, due not only to medical records and many accounts from his doctors, but from the 'patient' himself – Artaud was often extremely precise regarding dates. First of all, quite roughly, there was the period of what Artaud himself sometimes referred to as his 'silence,' from his internment in October 1937, to January 1943, when he began writing and communicating again. From January 1943, at Rodez, to his death in March, 1948, Artaud will prodigiously produce, in the form of notebooks, correspondence, essays, books and honed, performative texts, more than twice as much writing as in the years 1923-37. This is still an extremely rough demarcation since during the period of Artaud's 'silence' there were sometimes daily letters to his psychiatrists, pleas for food, missives demanding drugs and relief, or detailing the cosmic battles over his fate, even the beginnings of an autobiography requested by one of his psychiatrists; many of these letters remain in medical collections and in private hands, although several of Artaud's letters to Dr. Léon Fouks were published in Thomas Maeder's 1978 biography *Antonin Artaud.* Deciphering the notebooks from Rodez can be especially challenging, given its onslaught of symbolics – the detaching of the Antichrist from Satan, or the assertion of a Jesus Christ at war against God – that sometimes borders on the unintelligible. Artaud's lived conflicts erupted with extreme vehemence and volatility during his sojourn in Ireland, leading to his expulsion to France in October 1937. Artaud had written in *The New Revelations of Being* 'I am truly identified with this

ti-psychiatry' was Morton Schatzman's treatment of the Schreber case in *Soul Murder*, new ed., London & New York, NY: Pelican, 1976, which emphasised the ghoulish and oppressive regimens of Schreber's father and their influence on his son.

[36] Serge André, *L'Épreuve d'Antonin Artaud et l'expérience de la psychanalyse*, Brussels: Èditions Luc Pire, 2007, p.112. My account of Artaud's transformations at Rodez is heavily indebted to André's detailed and empathetic overview.

[37] Volumes XV and XVI in his *Œuvres Complètes*, that contains writings spanning February-June 1945.

[38] Artaud XV, 1981, p.326.

Being, this Being that has ceased to exist.' It is out of such obscurity, and of such extreme conflict and psychic extremity, that the cross – as one remembers the key form Artaud sighted on his journey up the Sierra Tarahumaras, along with the H that Artaud saw as the sign of conjoined, warring dualities – becomes a kind of armature, a pivot, exactly at the point when Artaud begins to construct his new body, the 'body without organs.'[39] In letters that June and July of 1937 to Jean Paulhan and André Breton Artaud again predicts his impending death.[40] This is inseparable, paradoxically, from Artaud's hopes of a striking and definitive resolution. As he writes to Anne Manson on 8 August 1937, it is that year of '37 'where a decisive Truth will appear.'[41] In his long September 5 letter to André Breton, Artaud outlines many of the themes that appear throughout his Rodez-era writings and that have already been rehearsed in *The New Revelations of Being* and the drafts for *Satan* – the elaboration against this 'criminal force of Being which does not allow us any repose.'[42] For Artaud there is a law superior to that of nature, itself 'unconscious and criminal,' that expels beings into an infinity. This is the role of Christ, to restore the 'Pagan Truth,' whereby 'from Man to the primordial Non-Being we are this Non-Being and these Gods, undergoing a formidable hierarchy of gods.'[43] It is ourselves who make Life, Artaud writes to Breton, in order '*to punish in ourselves* this criminal force of Being that does not allow us repose.'[44] This 'Pagan Truth' is the realisation that 'it is necessary to destroy the law. Because the sole secret is to learn to destroy the law in order to fall again into the Non-Being *even beyond that of Eternity*. AND THIS ALSO IS THE LAW…the Law is to return to repose, beyond the possible and the impossible, beyond Eternities.'[45] This Being in its various forms, which seems positively inescapable, perverts Man and god itself. It is these writings especially that locate Artaud in the realm of Gnostic speculation, that for all its febrile variety was often focused around the hostile or evil demiurge that created nature and the universe.[46] Artaud writes that 'The principle contradiction is in nature as in being, and it is necessary to go so far as to kill being in order to escape from this contradiction.'[47] This being that needs to be eradicated one will see later in Artaud's Rodez writings as manifested primarily in *jouissance*

[39] Artaud, *Œuvres*, p.788.

[40] Artaud VII, 1967, pp.226-7; 235-7.

[41] Ibid., p.246.

[42] Ibid., p.267.

[43] Ibid., pp.265; 267.

[44] Ibid., p.267. It is characteristic of Artaud's writing from this period, and through to Rodez, of contrasting God and gods, Being and beings.

[45] Ibid.

[46] One of the best accounts of Gnosticism remains Hans Jonas, *The Gnostic Religion*, 3rd rev. ed., Boston, MA: [1963] 2001.

[47] Artaud VII, 1967, p.269.

and the sexual torture carried out on Artaud in his violent and vivid hallucinations. It is through one's existence as a sexual being that these contradictions and depredations of 'the LAW' hold sway; and it is this sensual existence that Artaud ultimately seeks to extinguish. This early insistence on the necessity 'to kill being' is also refracted in the later Artaud as the necessity to 'have done' with God. Although Artaud signs this particular letter, he announces that 'after this there will be another name.'[48]

Much as there has been the splitting of the elements of earth, air, water and fire in Artaud's *New Revelations of Being*, in letters immediately preceding his breakdown and afterwards through the delirium at Rodez, there is a similar process centralised in the Holy Trinity, which becomes a field of combat between its different components. As Artaud elaborates in a long 14 September 1937 letter to André Breton, Christ is an *Enragé*, one of the Initiated, same as the 'son-Shiva,' who aids those bringing destruction to Life, such as Artaud himself. Artaud's Christ is 'the Prince of Destruction...the Negative of Creation.'[49] In the scheme of this theological war that will continue to be played out and articulated at Rodez, Artaud writes that it was 'while searching INEXISTENCE that I rediscovered that this was God. So if I speak therefore of God this is not in order to live but in order to die.'[50] God in Artaud's eyes becomes a sort of placeholder or field, created by humanity itself, in which these conflicts are wrought, between the 'law,' and those that struggle against it. In his 14 September letter to Breton he makes clear that the 'Son-Shiva' is against creation, nature and the 'law of things' manifested by the Father, and maintained by the Holy Spirit, so the Holy Trinity is irredeemably split.[51] This 'Son-Shiva' is the 'Force of Transformation,' of destruction of forms, and so is the force identical in Artaud's eyes to non-manifestation, the 'Absolute.'[52] As this battle unfolds, the Father will employ the Antichrist, against the Christ who becomes the *Enragé*, and Artaud himself is allied with or directly becoming the 'true Christ,' a theme that in different versions continues until his death. More immediately it produces, in the years 1938-43, Artaud's fervent turn to an often profoundly heretic form of Christianity.

What is crucial in this material is not so much the importance of tracking these symbolic permutations in themselves, as Susan Sontag characterised

[48] Ibid., p.269. There are numerous commentaries on Artaud's various changes in name and their psychic and symbolic dynamics, which for reasons of space are not adequately delved into here, see Allen S. Weiss, 'Psychopompomania,' in *The Aesthetics of Excess*, Albany, NY: State University of New York, 1989; also Serge Marcel, *Aliénation: Antonin Artaud – les généalogies hybrides*, Paris: Editions Galilée, 2008; and John Cameron Stout's *Antonin Artaud's Alternate Genealogies* (1995), already cited.

[49] Artaud VII, 1967, p.278-9.

[50] Ibid., p.286.

[51] Ibid., p.287. For Artaud the Christian Father, Son and Holy Spirit are equivalent to the Hindu Brahma, Shiva, and Vishnu.

[52] Ibid.

Artaud's writings as the most comprehensive and complete self-recording of Gnostic beliefs and symbolism in existence,[53] but that these conflicts require, as Artaud maintains again and again, his death – the replacement of his self by another. For Artaud this death occurs – at Ville-Évrard in August 1939.[54] It is at this point of absolute destruction that the work of restoration could begin – Artaud writes, 'it is at this moment that God began to return there with the aid of his Angels.'[55] This death for Artaud is preceded – in the months of May, June and July 1939 – by a series of name changes and renunciation of his name, as well as the enumeration of a number of historical personages (Alexander, Rameses II, Anaximander) he claimed to be the reincarnation of. It is a full two years after this death that Artaud takes on the identity with the name Antonin Nalpas, that he maintains carries in his body the memory of the entire life of the now deceased Antonin Artaud, as his continuation on earth.[56] This is indeed a 'Miracle,' Artaud claims. His old self was not able to resist the vampirish assaults and thefts of the various entities and beings that plagued it. Yet it is through this death that Artaud's problematic shifts dramatically from the soul to the body ('the spirit of a body is only the sweat of this body' Artaud will write in March 1945),[57] from complaining of the loss of thought (as in the early writings) to affirming it and jumping past it through this rhythm of the 'projection of the true body.' This is a complex transformation, one will see, where the cross takes on a central role. Artaud's new name comes with a mythic family, a father Joseph, mother Mary, and siblings Gaspar and Balthazar (a family that by no accident includes the two *prénoms* of the parents of Jesus Christ and of two of the Magi Kings).[58] When Artaud does return to his proper patronymic, at first in a 17 September 1943 letter to his supervising psychiatrist at Rodez Dr. Gaston Ferdière, it is under the extraordinary pressure of the series of 51 electroshock treatments that were begun in June of that year.[59] The servile, uncharacteristically tame nature

---

53 Susan Sontag in 'Artaud,' *Antonin Artaud: Selected Writings*, ed. and trans. Helen Weaver, New York, NY: Farrar, Straus & Giroux, 1976, pp.xlv-liii. For Artaud's relation with Gnosticism see also Jane Goodall, *Artaud and the Gnostic Drama*, Oxford: Clarendon Press, 1994.

54 Artaud writes of this several times in 1943, for example, the letter to Jean-Louis Barrault of 15 April 1943 in Artaud X, 1974, p.40.

55 Ibid.

56 Ibid., p.71.

57 Artaud XV, 1981, p.36.

58 André, *L'Épreuve d'Antonin Artaud et l'expérience de la psychanalyse*, p.97.

59 Antonin Artaud, *Nouveaux écrits de Rodez*, Paris: Gallimard, 1977, pp.59-62. On the subject of Artaud and electroshock treatment, see Florence de Mèredieu, *Sur l'électrochoc. Le cas d'Antonin Artaud*, Paris: Blusson, 1996; and Emmanuel Venet, *Ferdière, psychiatrie d'Artaud*, Lagrasse: Verdier, 2006. The most notorious blast against Artaud's psychiatric treatment remains Isidore Isou's *Antonin Artaud torturé par les psychiatries*, Paris: Lettrism, 1970. We also have the testimony of two men who worked in the asylums that housed Artaud: see Laurent Danchin and André Roumieux, *Artaud*

of this letter (Artaud will continue, in subsequent letters, with eminent reason, to demand an end to the use of electroshock)[60] has evoked some properly aghast commentary.[61] The return to 'Antonin Artaud' can be read as primarily a ploy against psychiatry, against which he was powerless. Yet thinkers from Georges Bataille to Jacques Derrida have attributed Artaud's later productivity to the beneficial effects of electroshock.[62] Rather, when Artaud 'returns to reality' then in Autumn 1943, it is really the 'reality of the psychiatrist' he returns to.[63]

Artaud's return to his given patronymic, under the intense pressure of his psychiatrist and experimental electroshock treatments, is also linked to another growing change in orientation. If the Christian period of Artaud's Rodez internment can be divided into 'evangelical' and 'theosophical' phases,[64] the 'evangelical' taking place in most of 1943 and 1944 when Artaud swore he would go into the priesthood after the asylum, full of prayers and sermons and vows to make God known to man, followed by the 'theosophical' phase, it is in this latter phase where Artaud returns to earlier characteristic themes and invectives launched against God himself. For this incarnation of Artaud, 'it is christ who makes God,'[65] not the other way around. By Easter 1945, Artaud will reject his earlier 'Christianity,' in both forms, as a demonic insinuation that had possessed

---

et l'asile, 2 vols, Paris: Séguier, 1996. The dire condition of wartime asylums under Nazi occupation was not widely known in France, but became available in the case of Artaud with the 1978 publication of Thomas Maeder's biography and the efforts to publicise this of Philippe Sollers. See Philippe Sollers, *Watteau in Venice*, trans. Alberto Manquel, New York, NY: Simon & Schuster, 1995; and 'Sur Artaud,' *L'infini* 56, 1996, pp.93-106. Sollers' most sustained treatment of Artaud remains his writing in the *Tel Quel* period, see Sollers, *L'Ecriture et 'L'Expérience des limites,'* Paris: Seuil, 1971.

60 Artaud's letter of 15 June 1943, pled with Dr. Ferdière to stop the electroshocks 'which my body obviously cannot stand' and complained of 'this unbearable sensation of shattering in the back.' Artaud, *Nouveaux écrits de Rodez*, pp.40-1. The treatment had in fact fractured one of Artaud's dorsal vertebrae. Yet when Artaud's back healed, the electroshocks resumed.

61 See for example in André, *L'Épreuve d'Antonin Artaud et l'expérience de la psychanalyse*, pp.97-8.

62 For the extraordinary remarks of Derrida and others concerning Artaud's electroshock treatments on a Drawing Center (New York) panel in 1996, see Jay Murphy, 'Magic Act: The Late Drawings of Antonin Artaud,' *New Art Examiner*, May 1997, p.21. It is as if in contexts like the New York art world, more than fifty years after the fact, what Artaud suffered in the asylums had still not registered. For Bataille's remarks on Artaud's psychiatric treatment see Bataille, *The Absence of Myth*, pp.44-5. Bataille saw the savage criticism of Dr. Ferdière, so prevalent in the Parisian post-war art community at the time, as profoundly unfair.

63 André, *L'Épreuve d'Antonin Artaud et l'expérience de la psychanalyse*, p.99. Artaud in this letter discusses the different patronymics as a matter of point of view, as if this 'civil status' of the name bordered on the banal. Artaud, *Nouveaux écrits de Rodez*, p.60.

64 The suggestion of Françoise Bonardel in her *Artaud*, Paris: Balland, 1987.

65 Artaud XV, 1981, p.70. Significantly, Artaud usually capitalised Christ only in his letters to his psychiatrists.

him, but in the first years at Rodez, this Christianity forms a bulwark against the 'filthy erotic maneuvers' of the demons that hound him day and night.[66] It is clear in Artaud's many letters to his psychiatrists that in this earlier version or period Christianity is against human sexuality and against sexual reproduction. Many times Artaud will claim it is this act of sexual reproduction that renders humanity prey to the 'villainy of things,' and 'slaves of the Antichrist and of Satan.'[67]

Artaud begins his re-formation: the cross and the sexuality of the 'true body'

It is crucial to attempt to identify why sexuality is so repugnant to Artaud, who nonetheless had a series of serious amorous relationships before his internment, not because Artaud's extremely problematic gendering of reality is my subject, but since these reasons are at the founding of Artaud's new body and effort to create a new sexuality, and new family, freed from human organicism. The cross and Artaud's profound rejection of human sensuality and sexual reproduction are at the root of his reinvention of the body. There are two bases of Artaud's objection to sexuality that also change and transform themselves in time. The first, that characterises his early years at Rodez, is the loss of being associated with sexuality for Artaud, with sperm standing in, interchangeably, for excrement, saliva and urine. This is the Artaud for whom at that time the 'spirit' takes precedence from the body before this relationship revolves and becomes the converse. The second, following Serge André's analysis, is that it is through sexuality that Artaud becomes subject to the '*jouissance* of the Other;'[68] it is this objection that carries through into Artaud's later work. Artaud's confinement in the asylums is a bewitchment so that Satan and the Antichrist can use his sperm and excrement for ritual masturbation; his body becomes a laboratory for the *Initiatés*, and it is through sexual desire that they are able to do their work. The body emptied out and deserted with his 'death' in August 1939, becomes home not only for these obscene *Initiatés*, but for Antonin Nalpas as well and spirits from his mother's lineage, that wage combat over his soul.[69] Although shortly I will present the sharp limitations of such a Lacanian analysis of Artaud's predicament, commentators like André are not wrong in pointing to the parallel

66 Artaud X, 1974, pp.18-9. That these demons have a strong sexual aspect, robbing their victim, Artaud, of sperm and so on, has been a constant since Artaud's visions/hallucinations in Ireland.

67 Ibid., p.314.

68 André, *L'Épreuve d'Antonin Artaud et l'expérience de la psychanalyse*, p.103.

69 Artaud for example names four Holy Marys of the Sea active in his maternal lineage, in Artaud, *Nouveaux écrits de Rodez*, p.60.

function of religious belief, on one level, and drugs like opium and heroin, on another, as what Artaud calls 'the antidote to the eroticism and the occult bewitchments of the demon,' that is, as barriers to regulate *jouissance* and pleasure, his helpless subjection to the wild desire of the other.[70] Sexuality and desire offer an intolerable invitation to these others (in Lacanian terms, whether the small 'other' of female desire, or the teeming demonic populace that stands in for the big 'Other').

Artaud, in a letter to one of his psychiatrists, suggests that this death in August 1939, was not sufficient. Artaud writes, 'the virulence of Evil is so great that sex is still not able to be removed, and it is necessary that the body expiate through horrible sufferings this sexuality which for him is like the tunic of Nessus.'[71] It may aid in understanding the roots of Artaud's 'body without organs,' that he writes at Rodez 'The law of Christ is the law of the Virgin, incarnated in the Virgin Mary.'[72] Jesus Christ is not only a force against the various demonic possessions, he is a force-field within the Virgin Mary, and so responds, one could say, to the law of the Mother, not the Father.[73] Artaud's invocation of his mother's family name, the various Virgins, and paradoxically Christ, will create a kind of becoming-female, one in which Artaud in his self-generation seeks to found an alternative to human sexual reproduction.[74] Artaud more than once at Rodez will envoke a pre-Adamic state where generation occurs as with the angels 'through pure fluidic transmission of breaths come from the heart with the aid and the magnetic sanction of the Holy Spirit of God.'[75] Psychoanalyst Serge André maintains that this form of generation, however eternal and pure, still demands a physical substitute for the sexual organs, which Artaud provides with the heart; towards the end of 1945 at Rodez Artaud will create his *filles du coeur, naître*. It is significant, and should be emphasised, that this is months after Artaud's Easter 1945 renunciation of God, and so implies extraordinary new powers of self-generation on Artaud's part; and his 'daughters of the heart' have the same power of self-generation as Artaud; both together form a kind of polysexual army against God and the Devil, incubi and succubi and threats of all sorts. Artaud describes their creation in a letter, after Rodez, to Gilbert Lély, a biographer of Marquis de Sade:

---

70 Artaud X, 1974, p. 15; André, *L'Épreuve d'Antonin Artaud et l'expérience de la psychanalyse*, p.104.

71 Artaud X, 1974, p.37.

72 Ibid., p.67.

73 André, *L'Épreuve d'Antonin Artaud et l'expérience de la psychanalyse*, p.106.

74 One can quite validly argue that here Artaud incorporates the feminine only in order to eliminate it all the more, as theorist Kelly Oliver maintained in regard to Nietzsche and Derrida in her *Womanizing Nietzsche*, New York, NY & London: Routledge, 1994. But this far from exhausts, as I will show, what is going on in Artaud's 'body without organs,' or Artaud's becoming-female within it.

75 Artaud X, 1974, p.34.

> I thought a lot about love at the asylum of Rodez, and it was there that I dreamed about some daughters of my soul, who loved me like daughters, and not as lovers – me, their pre-pubescent, lustful, salacious, erotic and incestuous father;
>
> And chaste also, so chaste it makes him dangerous.[76]

Artaud may have written of himself as an incestuous father, but his meticulous re-generation of his body in the asylums also made him female, a mother capable of birthing and thus able to create the daughters. Artaud will write, 'It is myself who is the Virgin.'[77] For Artaud the centre of self-creation was the heart, and 'the heart [is] a stick,

> the stick the stomach the stomach of Satan
> underfoot a diaphragm,
> the diaphragm the spirit of femurs against the kneecap,
> the kneecap the spleen of infinity,
> infinity the navel of the erect phallus that carries the spasmodic stone of the heart
> ...
> and the churner this stick which will be body when the soul will have returned after death'[78]

As Artaud writes in September 1945, 'The real vagina of my thighs is realised in the bodies of my daughters with a little phallus of the heart. This is a little body active between the thighs which always wants to go back to the interior of the vagina in order to make itself and to be a child.'[79] Two months later Artaud writes, 'the uterus, this is me.'[80] In terms of what has been called 'womb envy,' Artaud participates here in an almost typical obsession in especially Western culture in its 'hero' myths and their themes of separation from the mother and self-generation, as well as the sexual confusion arguably at the base of much 'schizophrenic' disorder.[81] Yet, in Artaud's usual fashion, he does not stop there. Part of his re-thinking of the question of love at Rodez, as he wrote to Lély, the dynamics of Artaud's daughters fills hundreds upon hundreds of pages of his Rodez notebooks; they are absolutely central to his re-organisation. It is not too

---

[76] Artaud XIV: 1, 1978, p.148.

[77] Artaud XV, 1981, p.107.

[78] Artaud XVII, 1982, p.242.

[79] Artaud XVIII, 1983, pp.20-1.

[80] Ibid., p.262.

[81] See for instance the critique of Joseph Campbell's account of mythology in Mary Daly, *Gyn/ecology*, Boston, MA: Beacon Press, 1978; for a survey on the literature of the links between profound dysfunction in gender identification and the etiology of schizophrenia, see E.H. Nassar, Natalie Walders, and Janis H. Jenkins, 'The Experience of Schizophrenia: What's Gender Got to Do With It,' *Schizophrenia Bulletin* 28:2, 2002, pp.351-362. This issue was also primary in Carl Jung's concept of the genesis of schizophrenia, see C.G. Jung, *The Psychogenesis of Mental Disease*, Volume III of *Collected Works*, trans. R.F.C. Hull, Princeton, NJ: Princeton University Press, 1960.

much to suggest that their dynamics are what enable Artaud to begin speaking of a new body, of a 'body without organs' upon his release from Rodez. Elsewhere in the *Cahiers de Rodez*, Artaud maintains that the

> love of the daughter contains the Father in his heart…there are 2 daughters that are flames turning at the base of the abyss of being and where the father comes remaking himself in body, then they die and he resuscitates their soul in order to give them body while they penetrate [him] after which they have contained him.[82]

In this passage Artaud describes how the daughters, born from the Father or incestuous Father-Mother, remake the Father's body, thus giving Artaud a new form, in new relations of container and contained. It is clear that it is these daughters who paradoxically restore Artaud to the Father/male position, from his identification with the uterus just noted. It will be remembered, in Artaud's first writings after his correspondence with Rivière, that he speaks of the 'self to come,' of 'remaking oneself.'[83] Here in the unlikely circumstances of Rodez Artaud with 'the churner this stick' is accomplishing such a mutation. Not only is the aggressive and paratactic literary style of the 'late' Artaud emerging here, but also his insistence on indomitable will – 'And there is not periods of action or of repose but my caprice and my will.'[84] Increasingly in the late Artaud the rhythm of this action, the excruciating effort of material shedding, will hinge on this will. In looking at Artaud's drawings in the next chapter, it will be difficult to disengage the gesture of this marking from the notion of will, that creates the works, and Artaud's ultimate 'body without organs.'

The daughters were usually six, but sometimes greater in number and included both his grandmothers as well as past girlfriends such as Cécile Schramme and women such Anie Besnard, whom Artaud had an enormous, if Platonic, attraction for. Artaud imagined them suffering enormous torments and tortures in their efforts to free him from the asylum. As an imaginative resource, it is difficult to overestimate their value to Artaud in his struggle to survive his remaining time in the asylum. Artaud believed his survival could be assured with the aid of these 'immortal young girls,'[85] he wrote to one of the *filles*, Colette Thomas. The subject of many of his later drawings, in texts like *Fragmentations* Artaud portrays these 'daughters of the heart' in fierce counterattack against his enemies.[86]

These 'daughters of the heart, to be born' are crucial not just as the succor they undoubtedly were, but because they begin to illustrate the power and ex-

[82] Artaud XVII, 1982, p.189.

[83] Artaud I:1,1956, pp.49; 97.

[84] Artaud XVII, 1982, p.195.

[85] Ibid., p.84.

[86] Ibid., p.21.

tent of Artaud's self-generation. This grows out of the peril that Artaud specifies at the beginning of his time at Rodez, of the *impouvoir* of God himself, who has not been able to prevent the French people in their entirety from passing over to the rule of the Antichrist and Satan, and who are responsible for Artaud's tortures in the asylum.[87] This is one of the reasons, André argues, why an appeal to the Father, or law of the Father, is completely futile with Artaud.[88] The Father has been proved hopelessly weak and corrupt. At Rodez Artaud will pass through measures of extreme defence against this divine *impouvoir*, such as his complete reconstruction (which entails construction of another body), that leads ultimately to his equally complete repudiation of God by Easter 1945. God is represented elsewhere in the Rodez notebooks as having its own being stolen.[89] God in its Being, with capital B, is 'the eternal Cross...Refusal of all of this that wants exit in order to be and to exteriorise itself [into being].'[90] Yet Artaud's potent identification with the cross allows him to miraculously alter the situation, precisely to make an exit into another kind of becoming (if not being) with another body. Whereas the failure or loss of the Trinity to being demands the sacrifice of not only the Son but the Father as well (with its stolen being), and Jesus Christ through his incarnation can only be a betrayal of God, christ with a small c remains 'this one which has always existed and which in order to live has never had need of being.'[91] The suppression or cancellation of being, Artaud writes more than once, entails the suppression of masculine-feminine, and the disappearance of the biologic couplet father-mother.[92] This imperative for self-generation is in the urgency and creativity of Artaud's very language that is embodying and rhythmically embedding these movements and conflicts. And although Artaud typically gives a precise date, that from October, 1939, he no longer had written without drawing, it is particularly starting from 1943, and then more predominantly in 1945-8, that the driving force of Artaud's increasingly unique language is at one with this self-reconstruction. Language has to have the force of vital expulsion, whether of the voice from the mouth exclaiming the tongue of syllable-words as in the glossolalia that increasingly punctuate each of his texts, or of feces expelled from the anus, hence Artaud's 'search for fecality.'[93]

---

87 Artaud X, 1974, p.19.

88 André, *L'Épreuve d'Antonin Artaud et l'expérience de la psychanalyse*, p.113.

89 Artaud XV, 1981, p.28.

90 Ibid., p.29.

91 Ibid., p.27.

92 Ibid., p.130.

93 Thus Artaud titled one of the key sections of *To have done with the judgment of god* (1947-8), though fecality is a strong theme of Artaud's that takes prevalence from 1943 onwards at Rodez. In *To have done with the judgment of god* we have, as much as we can, Artaud's bizarrely definitive statement concerning it. See Artaud XIII, 1974, pp.81-7.

The 'search for fecality' in the creation of the new body

Artaud had been given excerpts from Lewis Carroll to translate by Dr. Ferdière as part of the psychiatrist's notion of art therapy. Illustrating his idea of 'fecality,' Artaud later wrote what he thought of Lewis Carroll to one of his publishers Henri Parisot:

> When one probes the shit of being and of language, it is necessary that the poem feel sick, and *Jabberwocky* is a poem that its author is very careful to stand by in the uterine being of suffering where all great poetry is tempered and where, birthing itself, feels sick. There is in *Jabberwocky* passages of fecality, but this is the fecality of an English snob, who curls in himself the obscene like curlers in a hot fire, like a kind of taster of the obscene which guards itself well from obscene being, himself, like Baudelaire in his terminal aphasia or like Edgar Poe through his sewer mouth the morning he discovers death from an apoplexy of Prussic acid or of cynanide of potassium. *Jabberwocky* is the work of a coward who does not want to suffer his work before he writes it, and this one sees.[94]

Language had to be emitted as a physical force and ineluctability. Artaud makes known that the writers he loves – he names François Villon, Baudelaire, Edgar Allan Poe and Gérard de Nerval – are the poisoned, whose 'poems are torturers of language which are in ruin in their writings, and not of those who affect losses in order to better flaunt their conscience and their science and of the ruin and of the writing.'[95]

It is Artaud's theory of 'fecality' that demonstrates this new reversibility of the soul/body, where now the body takes priority. It will lead him to write, for example, about 'the fecal destiny of the soul, in the uterus of its own foyer…*caca* is the material of the soul…The breath of remains has a centre and this centre is the chasm *Kah-Kah, Kah* the corporeal breath of shit, which is the opium of eternal survival.'[96] Using the Egyptian term for the soul, the double of the body 'Kah,' that Artaud as a reader of *The Egyptian Book of the Dead* was well familiar with, Artaud's extreme reversal will have the soul=shit. One can well argue that the voice, the 'corporeal breath' has a priority in Artaud over the anus,[97] but as

---

[94] Artaud IX, 1971, pp.185-6.

[95] Ibid., p.186. Artaud more than once lists his particular peer group, or genealogy, that often also included Nietzsche, Lautréamont, Rimbaud and Hölderlin, as in Artaud XIV: 1, 1978, pp.187-8. There is a more expansive list, that also begins with his 'great passions' Baudelaire, Poe and Nerval, that occurs in another section of Artaud's *Cahiers du retour à Paris*, where he includes a number of other largely Romantic writers whose worth in some cases 'are not decided,' that he 'bordered on.' See Artaud XXIV, 1988, p.165.

[96] Ibid., p.191-2.

[97] Barber, *Artaud: The Screaming Body*, p.199; André, *L'Épreuve d'Antonin Artaud et l'expérience de la psychanalyse*, p.124. One of the more detailed explorations of Artaud's 'search for fecality' is Julia Kristeva's 'Le sujet en procès' in *Artaud*, ed. Philippe Sollers, Paris: Union générale d'éditions, 1973.

this passage illustrates, for Artaud they are united in the pulsional activity of the body, from which any *sujet* cannot be separated.

As extreme as Artaud's discourse may be at this point, it follows from his strident rejection of metaphor in his *Theater and Its Double* manifestoes. In the ancient hieroglyphic Egyptian the name, soul and body were all inextricably linked, so when the *Kah* fled so did the soul, to destroy the name was to destroy the entity and therefore also lose the body. In a similar process at Rodez, Artaud has carefully and at the cost of much torment de-linked the name, soul and body, only to re-constitute them, in an entirely different manner, and on a different basis. In a Freudian or Lacanian reading, this can be seen as the result of the failure of the 'paternal metaphor' with Artaud, the dysfunction of the process Freud elaborated in his 1925 text 'Negation,' where through a complex mechanism of negation and affirmation the subject comes to differentiate between objects and the symbolic, the imaginary is constituted and a significant repression allows this mechanism to produce a discourse substituting for the repressed.[98] In the case of Artaud this would result in what Lacan would call the 'lack of a primordial signifier,'[99] the default of the symbolic signifier that separates subject and object and makes the human ego possible – a failure that makes up the basic structure of psychosis.[100] As André argues in the context of Artaud's glossolalia, what is lacking is precisely the *sujet*. As applicable as this model is to Artaud, it banks on the validity of the tripartite model of symbolic/imaginary/real and the dominance of the signifier to one who has rejected it and explicitly proposed another model entirely. In terms of his invented syllable-language, Artaud might respond to André in the manner of the 'anti-psychiatry' he helped inspire decades later – it is not the unconscious that is structured like a language, but language that must be structured like the unconscious.[101]

Opposed to the 'failure' and 'psychosis' postulated by the Freudian or Lacanian reading, Artaud's 'search for fecality' has an eminently constructive role as an intimately allied part of the construction of his 'body without organs' which has been constituted, or at least begun, through the eminently hieroglyphic pivot that is the cross. It is in large part through Artaud's example that later thinkers like Deleuze and Guattari will envision the organless body as characterised not by dislocation and lack caused by the loss of the establishment of a primal signifier (the name of the father Lacan argues is coextensive with access to language

[98] André, *L'Épreuve d'Antonin Artaud et l'expérience de la psychanalyse*, pp.124-7; Sigmund Freud, 'Negation [1925],' in *The Ego and the Id and Other Works*, Vol. XIX of *Standard Edition of the Complete Psychological Works of Sigmund Freud*, ed. James Strachey, London: Hogarth Press, 1971, pp.233-40.

[99] See the discussion of 'primordial signifiers and the lack of one' in Lacan, *The Psychoses*, pp.196-205.

[100] André, *L'Épreuve d'Antonin Artaud et l'expérience de la psychanalyse*, p.188.

[101] As David Cooper argues in *The Language of Madness*, p.22.

itself) but rather by 'the realm of physics' since 'the body without organs and its intensities are not metaphors, but matter itself.'[102] Such a point of view reinforces the cosmological or cosmopolitical process that is at stake in the 'schizophrenia' of Artaud. Deleuze at one point, using Artaud as an example, maintains that it is a 'mistake when we define schizophrenia in negative terms or in terms of a lack (dissociation, loss of reality, autism, foreclosure) and when we model schizophrenia on a familial structure in which this lack can be located.'[103] Deleuze will advocate that we simply stop talking about the symbolic, the imaginary, and the real, since this psychoanalytic grid does not in fact exist, hence 'a cartography and never a symbolics.'[104] It is cartography that is more operative and applicable since it is the machinic elements or partial objects that are primary, that are crucial in creating the difference between desiring-production, and the derivative 'structural whole' of the imaginary and the symbolic, 'which merely forms a myth and its variants.'[105]

Artaud's project to metamorphosise bodily wastes and extracts into new beings freed from the signifier and usual signifying chains in Freudian and Lacanian terms, when further explored is also quite beyond an extreme instance of auto-eroticism, although this is what psychoanalytic theory would tend to consign him to. Artaud will see his drawings as beings that have a kind of immortality and battle for protection for him. Their process of creation entailed piercing screams and Artaud's yoga of the breath. In his radio works done after release from Rodez it is especially through the voice of the body, that the infinity of the body is hurled, projected, continued.[106] These are the fruits of the 'true body.' For Artaud it is clear that just about all levels of creation exclude him, from the biological order of procreation to that of language – 'the principle of creation desires for the beings and the worlds, it does not desire for me'[107] – so as an absolute matter of survival the project of self-creation falls to him. Although Artaud goes through a series of re-organisations of the body at Rodez that cannot be fully recounted here, it can be argued that at first Artaud's attempt to reach the material body – that died in August 1939 – is by engaging with the most symbolic and abstract one, hence his concerns circling around the mysteries of the Incarnation. Artaud explains 'I incorporate myself into my detachment by rejection of infinity not in order to have a body like God who is only a pig but in

[102] Deleuze and Guattari, *Anti-Oedipus*, p.283.

[103] Gilles Deleuze, *Two Regimes of Madness*, ed. David Lapoujade, trans. Ames Hodges and Mike Taormina, New York, NY & Los Angeles, CA: Semiotext(e), 2006, pp.25-6.

[104] Gilles Deleuze and Claire Parnet, *Dialogues II*, trans. Hugh Tomlinson, Barbara Habberjam and Eliot Ross Albert, New York, NY & London: Continuum, 2006, p.83.

[105] Deleuze and Guattari, *Anti-Oedipus*, p.83.

[106] Barber, *Artaud: The Screaming Body*, p.104.

[107] Artaud XV, 1981, p.336.

order to burn up until this idea of the body disappears.'[108] This project entails becoming other, Artaud writes elsewhere in the same notebooks, 'but not the other.'[109] What is foundational to this process is Artaud's manipulation of the cross.

The cross is the pivot in this creation of the 'true body'

Artaud in the Rodez notebooks continually and centrally envoked the cross, and Artaud's cross is not placed through simply introjecting the Christian cross – he makes clear at one point he is placing the cross inside his body as an armature[110] – Artaud's cross he explains can only represent a total refusal of any representation of being. Artaud's cross acts, as André points out, therefore, both as an extraordinary symbolic specification and purification of the Christian cross, and as its opposite, given that the Christian symbol of the cross is precisely a cross without the crucified body. Artaud writes:

> The Cross of the One which is beyond the eternities does not represent and it is not able to represent but it represents its refusal of holding itself to being and to a being through the crucifying division of the eternal of possibilities and their rejection.[111]

This cross is absolutely elemental to Artaud's refection. As he writes, 'the body of my spirit represents itself in being through the block starting from a cross.'[112] The cross in these notebooks seems to link parts of Artaud's body, while it is also a tool and object of ever-present war:

> The cross of the smelly soul from the heart to the nose, formed while
> dripping red or nitrous boy Virgin.
> God is a spirit, so pure that he is this nothing
> inexistence,
> he has always struggled, struggled,
> but against himself,
> through the cross, …[113]

The cross at one point represents the dominance of Being or God, its warning of no exit from being and the 'law.' The cross is both a representation and a sign irrevocably pulled beyond any representation, a distillation or condensation of all the warring polarities within and without Artaud that have their site there.

[108] Ibid., p.47.
[109] Ibid., p.239.
[110] Ibid., p.53.
[111] Ibid., p.27.
[112] Ibid., p.137.
[113] Ibid., p.323.

Amid this journal of unmistakable 'religious' delirium and what he calls in one place the 'dental turbulence of the cross,'[114] the cross acts to orient the different polarities involved in Artaud's reconstitution. Artaud writes at one point of his complete merging into the cross, so that:

> I am not Christ, I am only a man who does not want to sin neither consciously nor unconsciously, I am not the man that I am currently, I am not the being where the worlds pass before myself and which contains them, I am the vertebral cross.[115]

Artaud continues:

> I am not the one who did not want to be a being and who had been taken by the beings. This production has been reversed and the fluidic work where it was able to be born annihilated. I am the one at the base of the spine and who against the conscience of being is shown today through 3 affirmations of will in the long echelons of the spine and who has taken these three affirmations for suppression, it containing through the cross of fire these affirmations emerging today from the nose. One person. One other person emerged from the diaphragm in globes of fire: Jesus-christ. – Tomorrow the spine will resume and burn because of this scale of body. There is an other and an other measure.
>
> The 3 points where burns the fluidic body of myself only values through relation to a dimension of being that myself imposes and an one dimension, a diapason, a placement of the spine which is not the true.[116]

Much like his early writings in *Umbilicus of Limbo* and *Nerve Scales* in 1925, Artaud is meticulous here about minute positionings of states, while it remains difficult to grasp directly the movements of which he speaks. This 'carnage' can be read as desire itself, as Deleuze follows Artaud in describing its movement as 'not internal to a subject, any more than it tends towards an object: it is strictly immanent to a plane which it does not pre-exist, to a plane which must be constructed, where particles are emitted and fluxes combine.'[117] The voids and deserts of such a 'plane of immanence' are part of desire itself. So although Artaud's chain of signifiers can themselves be deciphered, the value of Artaud's extraordinary journals at Rodez is that they provide a cartography of what Deleuze and Guattari termed the 'magical chain' typical of his painstaking re-assembly.[118] The heretical semantics of Artaud's rethinking of the Trinity and the Antichrist, or advocacy of the Cathars matters less on their face as symbolics than how they act as a means or reflect energetics, as the pathway Artaud uses in this cauldron to reorganise himself into the generator of the later work. Artaud at Rodez finds himself in a situation where for a year-and-a-half he is

[114] Ibid.

[115] Ibid., pp.325-6.

[116] Ibid., p.326.

[117] Deleuze and Parnet, *Dialogues II*, p.66.

[118] Deleuze and Guattari, *Anti-Oedipus*, p.181.

subjected to electroshocks precisely for his humming, spitting and chanting, the preparatory activities for his art, his daily counter-sorcery, where his drawings are considered of 'no interest whatsoever.'[119] It is in these circumstances Artaud doubles his body, making a new one that has no interior.

Artaud writes, 'the beings fight at the moment of the formation of my body from death because if I have no other being than the one which wants corporeal resistance of the cross the being of Antonin Artaud and his body are not mine.'[120] As mobile as this cross is, it is the pivot around which Artaud organises his 'resistance.' He places this cross in his body at first to protect the soul, at the point he is allying himself with the Holy Virgin, and it is the cross 'which the beings do not want, they want to make evil with my force of soul when this is in the principle that was of the Holy Virgin.'[121] It is as if Artaud's cherished prophetic cane, that he used to carry with him on his walks through the streets of Paris, with its steel tip striking sparks on the pavement as he went along, or his prized stiletto given to him by a black sorcerer in Havana, both of which he lost in different circumstances of his breakdown, were now transposed into the figure of the cross, that he places inside himself. In the journals for February-April 1945, for example, Artaud explicitly connects his cane and the cross:

> The internal Cane which walks with the imprinted cross or the arms deployed? To be like His Cross is to have the epaulets because the secret of the cross is never having been said before the hour, being that which has merited itself all time. There is not an eternal secret. With a baton nothing touches me but all is dragged and rolled along. It is necessary of the arms to push and prevent being. This is the cross for that which is and there it is for this that is not: sleep. And there is the cross of internal Principle and it is myself that am this internal Principle, the Holy Spirit, and it is only thus that I am remade today, 31 March, Saturday, at 2:26 in the afternoon.[122]

All the formidable power Artaud associated with the cane given to him by St. Patrick (an incarnation of Christ) – prophetic and cosmological as well as phallic and sexual – is now in the form of the cross and the struggles surrounding it. The cross has a similar phallic and generative property; it is often allied with the activities of Artaud's 'daughters' once they have been activated. In passages from June 1945, Artaud writes that he 'was having to avenge myself completely from the heart.

> It is a matter of having humus of virulent and acrid shit
> and not of soft manure.
> Elsewhere I had not a soul until here then 3 women
> who are horror of *au-deurs*, of perfumes, of songs,

[119] Dr. Ferdière quoted in Barber, *Antonin Artaud*, p.112.

[120] Artaud XV, 1981, p.331.

[121] Ibid., p.53.

[122] Artaud XV, 1981, p.162.

of song,
of speech,
and who cry or rage while *scraping* the soul always.
Myself, I SHAKE the cross.[123]

Artaud's relation to the cross is nothing if not generative – he moves from a kind of identification, to battling and then challenging it. In the process he has incorporated the cane/phallus into his autochthonic scheme that has its vital axis along the spine from the mouth to the anus that shortly will also give birth to his protective progeny, the various 'daughters of the heart.' From a state of merging and immersion, Artaud becomes more and more active and aggressive in regard to this all-powerful sign, until in one of his final works, *To have done with the judgment of god* (1947-8), created almost two years after his release from Rodez, he can imagine an army descending from the rite abolishing the Christian cross to enforce the new 'body without organs,' and Artaud can then write that 'I *shit* on the cross/I abject any cross.'[124] Artaud has used the cross as a critical means of passage at Rodez that he later rejects.

The full 'body without organs' emerges

As I have indicated, in Lacanian terms Artaud has a failure in establishing the paternal metaphor. To extend that analysis a bit will help illuminate Artaud's originality as well as highlight the role his new language plays in the full emergence of the 'body without organs.' For Lacan, Artaud's rejection of the symbolic must throw him into a 'psychotic' process of compensation; not recognising the law or the arbitrary 'no' of the paternal/symbolic, Artaud's 'psychosis' must become the law itself. Having rejected God, he must become God. As Lacan describes it, the 'psychotic' for all his or her elucidations and flood of imagery, remains stillborn somehow in the preverbal limbo of the preconscious. In one of Lacan's seminars on psychoses, he could have been referring to Artaud when he characterises a 'barbaric poetry.' 'Everything of the order of this preverbal,' Lacan claims, 'thus partakes of what we can call an intraworldy *Gestalt*, within which the subject is the infantile doll that he once was, he is an excremental object, a sewer, a leech.'[125] Here Lacan could have cited Artaud's frequent recourse to the mummy, the child, feces, or of his characterisation of the human being as a 'sewer with teeth.'[126] Lacan continues, 'Analysis has called upon us to explore this imaginary world, which partakes of a sort of barbaric poetry – though it is

[123] Artaud XVI, 1981, p.199.

[124] Artaud XIII, 1974, p.274.

[125] Lacan, *The Psychoses 1955-6*, pp.164-5.

[126] Artaud XII, 1974, p.100.

in no way the first to make it felt, certain poetic works have been.'[127] Lacan limns this realm as the 'world of the child' dominated by a sort of 'universal equivalence' where high equals low, back is front.[128] One could imagine a substantial basis of discussion between Artaud and Lacan on the subjects of the divided self, being trapped in the preconscious, the fragmented body (Lacan's *corps morcelé*), even on performance and the combination of didactic and creative elements in a single essay and so forth, though in real-life their relations were of another sort: intense enmity on Artaud's part and detachment if not complete dismissal from Lacan.

The head psychiatrist when Artaud was interned at St. Anne's in 1938, Lacan professed little interest in Artaud's case, telling his visitor Roger Blin at the time that Artaud was 'fixed,' that he would live another forty-eight years but not write a single line.[129] As it turned out, Lacan was profoundly mistaken on both counts: it was Artaud's body that wore out just a decade later, having contracted cancer, while his later writings greatly dwarfed in number and arguably in value the output of his surrealist years (Artaud wrote six books and hundreds of notebooks after this diagnosis). According to friends, even at the end of his life, Artaud continued to revile Lacan, and the 'erotomaniac' psychiatrist 'Dr. L.' of the Van Gogh essay, is none other than Lacan.[130] There is only one occasion in all of Lacan's voluminous seminars and writings when he mentions Artaud. In a lecture in Rome in 1967 Lacan warns his followers against becoming 'inflamed' like Artaud, warning that if they did, they should be 'calmed down' – an ominous statement given the treatment Artaud actually received.[131] Whether viewed as part of the real-life political and power-relations between the two, or on another separable level, Artaud posits an entirely different approach to Lacan. Part of Artaud's loathing of human sexuality and reproduction lies precisely in its symbolic division, its necessary differentiation of male and female, inside and outside. For Artaud the body is a '*maison de chair close*,'[132] the flesh as literally 'closed house' or brothel. It is precisely this closed body that lends itself to the generalised hysteria of compulsive 'erotomania' against which Artaud

---

[127] Lacan, *The Psychoses 1955-6*, p.165.

[128] Ibid.

[129] Blin, *Souvenirs et propos*, p.31.

[130] Artaud XIII, 1974, pp.15-6. On the attribution of 'Dr. L.' to Lacan see Guy Scarpetta, 'Artaud écrit ou la canne de Saint Patrick,' *Tel Quel* 81, August 1979, p. 67.

[131] Jacques Lacan, *Autres écrits*, Paris: Éditions du Seuil, 2001, p. 349. Much of Artaud's bitterness from his experience at Saint Anne's appears reasonable – it was due to the lack of any precise diagnosis of his case at Saint Anne's, other than that he was paranoid, obsessive and incurable, that he was sent to the large general asylum at Ville-Évrard, where he was shunted from one ward to another – housed with epileptics, maniacs, cripples, undesirables and others also diagnosed as incurable. See Barber, *Antonin Artaud*, p.9; Mèredieu, *C'était Antonin Artaud*, pp.671-3.

[132] Artaud XII, 1974, p.214.

warns. The manufactured lack in this symbolic condition (and in the creation of the symbolic, in Lacan's terms), is exactly what Artaud so centrally challenges.[133] But while Artaud loathed Lacan, he saw Freud's theory of the libido as an ally, a support for his view that all human pain and illness was somehow rooted in sexual differentiation and desire. This is how Artaud in an 11 February 1944 letter to Dr. Ferdière can argue the case for sexual abstinence:

> because it is the practice of sexuality that summons the demons to us, and that creates maniacs, neuropaths, perverts, and criminals. All demons are obscene lubricious ideas which in the course of time have deranged the human brain, and I believe that it is this idea that Freud had at the bottom of his mind when he created the scientific term 'libido,' which incriminates sexuality as the cause of all pain and all evil.[134]

Artaud's denunciation of sexuality only grows more intense, his vituperation at 'sexual hyperaesthesia...unveiled criminal fornication.'[135]

At each point Artaud's complex symbolic and visceral turning is also enacted in the tourniquet of language. Artaud writes in December 1945 that 'I am the mother father and not the father mother because it is through mother the land of my body that I make my being in myself and not by the sole spirit of will.'[136] As Serge André notes, Artaud's creation from ex-pulsion of voice and excrement is not simply a regression to a primitive auto-erotic stage, a conclusion his own Lacanian perspective might lead him to believe, it also always implies a profound self-regeneration and invention on the level of language.[137] Although Artaud only uses the term 'body without organs' once he has been released from Rodez in May 1946, his mature themes are already evident in the *Cahiers du Rodez* from July to December 1945,[138] and so are their tone:

> The body at base is inexhaustible, but its manner of forming in being is an expulsion from all that which then has always refused to be, that is to say man and body, and has wanted to remain spirit when there is only the body that exists and it's the spirit that is the illusion of the cowardice of certain bodies which do not want to suffer in order to be.[139]

---

133 See the valuable discussion of Artaud and 'erotomania' in the context of his relation to Lacan in Lorenzo Chiesa, 'Lacan with Artaud: *j'ouïs-sens, jouis-sens, jouis-sans*,' in Lacan, *The Silent Partners*, ed. Slavoj Žižek, London & New York, NY: Verso, 2006, pp.336-43.

134 Artaud, *Nouveaux écrits de Rodez*, pp.84-5.

135 Artaud XXV, 1990, p.205.

136 Artaud XIX, 1984, p.46.

137 André, *L'Épreuve d'Antonin Artaud et l'expérience de la psychanalyse*, p.161.

138 In volumes XVII and XVIII of his *Œuvres complètes*.

139 Artaud XVIII, 1983, p.35.

But where André persists in seeing phallic metaphors is a ferocious insistence from Artaud on materiality. To merit the phallus, Artaud writes, it is necessary 'to play with the diarrhea of blood in order to suppress a being of damning its infinity through the real of a body finally inexpugnable from infinity.'[140] Here André remains correct in that Artaud's link to any phallic value is through the object of material expulsion only;[141] in Artaud's eyes this has the tremendous value of continuing to deny metaphor and the power of metaphor (and thus the symbolic) in this combustible politics of the flesh. Part of Artaud's rites becomes the expulsion of the enormous burden of religious symbology. Artaud writes that 'I will shit for eternity the soul of christ Jesus-christ and his antichrist: *his body*.'[142] Along with the extraordinary dynamics of the *filles du cœur*, sometimes born from or identified from specific parts of his anatomy,[143] and the graphic funnel or machinic forms that begin to punctuate the text, Artaud's syllable-language also gains an ever-increasing importance, itself self-generated and not beholden to the normal logics of grammar or signification.

Since Artaud, never more than at this momentous point at Rodez, is living language in the body, it pays to look again at his invented language to elucidate the 'body without organs.' More is involved than a purgatory within the preconscious, as Lacan would have us believe. But also more than what Deleuze leads us to in his *Logic of Sense* discussion of Artaud and Lewis Carroll. There he compares Artaud with Lewis Carroll as 'primary order and secondary organization,'[144] with Artaud's language of bodily affect the primary organisation, and Carroll's glancing, rolling plays on words the secondary one. Artaud is credited as a 'genius' in his exploration of the 'infra-sense' but for all that is still lost in the 'depths of bodies.'[145] This is because with the 'collapse of the surface' that is the condition of schizophrenia, 'the entire world loses its meaning.'[146] Words as incorporeal effects distinct from the body, or as ideational contents divorced from the present moment, do not exist; all language becomes, as Artaud had advocated, intensely physicalised, full of passion- and action-words, but really bare of articulation. A language that has become an action of breaths, howls, fragment-

[140] Ibid., p.169.

[141] André, *L'Épreuve d'Antonin Artaud et l'expérience de la psychanalyse*, p.162.

[142] Artaud XVIII, 1983, p.57.

[143] See for example ibid., pp.77-9.

[144] Deleuze, *The Logic of Sense*, p.91.

[145] Ibid., pp. 93; 88. Deleuze's analysis on 'infra sense' and the theory of signs in schizophrenia is heavily indebted here to Gisela Pankow's studies. For Pankow's work, especially on use of signs and body-image in schizophrenia see Pankow, *Structuration dynamique dans la schizophrenia*, Bern: Verlag Hans Huber, 1956; as well as her later *L'Être-là du schizophrène*, Paris: Aubier-Montaigne, 1973; 1981. Yet Deleuze writes that her analysis does not adequately address the functioning of the body without organs. See *Logic of Sense*, n.10, pp.342-3.

[146] Deleuze, *The Logic of Sense*, p.87.

ing alimentary and excremental bits, indicates the goings on of the 'infra sense' of the body at the cost of replacing, at its limit, not only grammar and syntax but even syllabic or literal values. In *Logic of Sense* Deleuze claims, 'with Artaud… there is no longer a problem of sense properly speaking.'[147] Even though Deleuze recognises there are words in Artaud's translation of Carroll's *Jabberwocky* that are at least roughly equivalent to portmanteau words, this characterisation profoundly underestimates the lucidity in Artaud's project. Given Artaud's central role as the key paradigm in Deleuze and Guattari's *Capitalism and Schizophrenia* project it appears that Deleuze considerably revised these judgments. Almost immediately upon the publication of *Logic of Sense* in 1969, Paule Thévenin wrote a rebuttal published in two parts in *Tel Quel* to Deleuze's notion that Artaud's writing was 'the language of schizophrenia,'[148] citing Artaud's sophisticated use of associative and sound blocks in different examples from different periods, including his Lewis Carroll translation.[149] Thévenin's meticulous and painstaking essay remains a very powerful argument that in Artaud's use of language 'the word is far from losing its sense, it is even often charged with senses profound, remote, forgotten.'[150] Thévenin's reconstructions make clear the word-play where Artaud's French makes such full use of the languages that surrounded him in his Marseilles childhood – Greek, Turkish, Arabic – as well as of his use of strong guttural sounds more common in German or Spanish than French. This would demonstrate less Artaud's 'schizophrenia' than a truly extraordinary linguistic inventiveness.[151] Yet Thévenin's presentation of the multiple senses at work in Artaud's flow of poetry begs the question to what degree, with so much hidden or portmanteau signification, Artaud is creating a new language, one that would escape the binding chains of signification. According to Artaud, the reader, through a rhythm he or she finds, is able to understand and 'think' even the glossolalic passages – implying that the language is accessible to anyone regardless of what national languages they know or do not know. Yet this is accessibility to a flow of language, that 'emerges from a blow,'[152] that

[147] Ibid., n.11, p.343.

[148] Ibid., p.84.

[149] Thévenin's essay 'Entendre/Voir/Lire' is collected in Thévenin, *Antonin Artaud, ce désespéré qui vous parle*, Paris: Éditions du Seuil, 1993. For a distinctive treatment of the poetic sense and transformations of Artaud's writings at Rodez, see also Jean-Michel Rey, *La Naissance de la poésie, Antonin Artaud*, Paris: Métaillé, 1991; and Pierre Bruno, *Antonin Artaud: realité et poesie*, Paris: L'Harmattan, 1999.

[150] Thévenin, *Antonin Artaud, ce désespéré qui vous parle*, p.203.

[151] Ibid., p.205. Jacques Derrida has pointed out the importance of the polygot of Mediterranean tongues in deciphering Artaud's exclamations, especially Greek. Artaud would have picked up many of these languages during his childhood, and his mother was a Levantine Greek. Derrida Talk at 'Artaud: Writing/Drawing,' The Drawing Center, New York, NY, 11 October 1996.

[152] Artaud IX, 1971, p.188.

does not necessarily signify anything at all. In this, Artaud presents a radically different experience than either Lewis Carroll or the later James Joyce, where there is signification, however veiled or allusive.[153]

Even in the midst of the profound transformations and disorder of his Rodez internment Artaud used writing on multiple levels – his letters to his psychiatrists, his letters to friends, to publishers, what gains force as his own proper even 'literary' language that would be available for publication, his spells and fully articulate and honed essays – are all notably different.[154] So, for one who in the words of his chief psychiatrist Dr. Gaston Ferdière was supposedly in danger of 'becoming a vegetable,'[155] Artaud was well aware of his different publics and their different roles. As several observers have noted, the first art therapy assignment given to Artaud by Dr. Ferdière, on the 16th century poet Pierre de Ronsard, was a model of intelligence and scholarship, of an order perhaps his psychiatrists did not grasp.[156] Similarly, when Artaud vigorously advocated and identified with the Cathar heresy at Rodez, they did not seem to realise that the Cathars, a Manichean cult suppressed during the Crusades, originated from the Languedoc, the region of Rodez itself. There is often an element of play, of gaming in Artaud, who perhaps never ceased in some sense to be an actor, even, or especially, when the stakes were as high as they were at Rodez. This seemed lost on his doctors, although one of them, Dr. Jacques Latrémolière, also ended his life highly disturbed and full of 'mystical' ideas.[157] In terms of the visual art, inseparable from the writing Artaud was beginning to make at Rodez and that would further explode upon his release, painter and *art brut* founder Jean Dubuffet, a prominent collector of art of the insane and self-taught 'outsider' art in France, considered Artaud's works in a wholly other category than either of these. But it is Artaud's language that most clearly refutes the notion he is completely lost in affect of the body with no level of detachment, as if it has any relation to the typical word salad of 'schizo talk.'[158] For example, in the notebooks for September 1945, Artaud often plays with the Greek TAU in the

[153] André, *L'Épreuve d'Antonin Artaud et l'expérience de la psychanalyse*, p.169.

[154] Artaud's essay 'Surrealism and the End of the Christian Era' written at Rodez, rivals in clarity any of his theatre essays in the 1930s or the earlier surrealist broadsides. See Artaud, *Nouveaux écrits de Rodez*, pp.157-60; and Paule Thévenin's commentary *Antonin Artaud: fin de l'ère chrétienne*, Paris: Éditions Léo Scheer, 2006.

[155] Ferdière quoted by Sylvère Lotringer in *100 Years of Cruelty*, pp.309-10.

[156] See the remarks by Jane Goodall and Sylvère Lotringer in ibid.

[157] See the account of Artaud and Dr. Latrémolière in Lotringer, *Fous d'Artaud*, pp.91-157.

[158] As has been noted, it is Artaud's detachment/lucidity, his aspect of 'control' that is perhaps his most 'mad' quality. See Sylvère Lotringer in *100 Years of Cruelty*, p.319. For comparison of Artaud's language with another diagnosed 'schizophrenic,' one can look at the documentation of Kingsley Hall resident David Bell, in films by Glasgow artist Luke Fowler, *The Nine Monads of David Bell* (2006) and *What you see is where you're at* (2003).

middle of his name. This play – I-TAU or ITAU, AR-TAU, KRISTAU, TAU – is also wound up in the imagery of re-formation of the body, Christ, the T having all the overtones of the tiny sword of Toledo Artaud was given in Havana, or of his St. Patrick's cane. As he writes in the middle of these experiments with parts of his name and recounting the travails of the *filles du cœur*, 'I do not take on christ, I do not make him to be, I only see his assassination,…christ is a word of killings of the spirit and not of corporealisation of this spirit. Malediction of christ the spirit by christ of the malediction.'[159] This TAU, drawn, also represents the cross of St. Antoine, and bears relation to the hieroglyphic sign for the Egyptian *Ka*, that contains two emanating lines like protective arms from a central perpendicular one. So the play with TAU is intimately allied with Artaud's metamorphoses around the cross, being perhaps an exact point where an (new) image of the body emerges from the letter.[160] Artaud refers to the 'Tau' as a 'double-movement' linked to his 'fecality' – 'Me I suspend a Tau of my tail in my humps and I take again the Tau and the humps in the hole of my ass where I shit it' – illustrating this with a drawing of right-side up and reverse T's.[161] Even this most scatological or excremental example that may not have the signification his psychiatrists desire or understand, is still hardly without 'sense.'

The 'sense' of this is precisely the creation of the 'body without organs,' that cannot be separated from Artaud's language in a veritable 'double movement.' As Artaud writes, 'The Mystery of the Verb and the Mystery of the body are the same, they come from an incoercibility that wrings itself from itself from base to base.'[162] Here Artaud's doubling bears comparison with the doubles and the repetition machines that populate the work of his countrymen Alfred Jarry, Raymond Roussel and the celibate-machines of Marcel Duchamp,[163] except that in Artaud it contributes to a full-fledged glossolalia. Artaud is driven to this other language since it is the French language itself at fault – 'it is french which is the cause of the carnage and of the universal madness.'[164] Although Paule Thévenin

[159] Artaud XVIII, 1983, p.21.

[160] André, *L'Épreuve d'Antonin Artaud et l'expérience de la psychanalyse*, p.137. In André's terms, it is the hinge for a new relation for the body between the symbolic, the imaginary and the real.

[161] Artaud XVIII, 1983, p.83. However primitive the thrust of this fragment, the complexity of it is difficult to render in English. Artaud uses the word *bugne*, translated here as 'hump,' as in the Old French *buigne* Artaud must have been drawing on, while the contemporary meaning of *bugne* is a fried dough or doughnut from the South of France. Similarly, the verb for 'to shit' Artaud uses is *emmerder*, which has the sense of hassle, or 'to have done with.'

[162] Ibid., p.183.

[163] The term 'bachelor machines' dates from Michel Carrouges, *Les Machines célibataires*, Paris: Arcanes, 1954. In it he describes the miraculous machines in Kafka, Alfred Jarry, Edgar Allan Poe, Roussel and Duchamp. For a discussion of Roussel with Artaud, see Laurent Jenny, *La Terreur et les signes*, Paris: Gallimard, 1982.

[164] Artaud XVIII, 1983, p.291.

often stresses the parts of Greek or Turkish words that can found in Artaud's constructions, and others have been traced back to Assyrian spells, it also often relies on the reader's invention. As Artaud counsels, 'one is only able to read them chanting, through a rhythm that the reader/himself has to find through understanding and through thinking,' adding, after a burst of such language, that it can only emerge from a blow or *coup*, from a gesture.[165] The glossolalic passages in Artaud's texts or letters function much the way he prescribed text in his film scenarios – they exist on their own, without any reference to what has gone before or what comes later – a blast that has to be taken on its own terms; words treated more as objects than signs.[166] Many of them appear to exist by turning French inside-out; hence the use of letters rare in French, such as the letters 'h' or 'k,' repeating consonant pairs (for example *rt* or *nt*), and a wildly disproportionate use of vowels.[167] In relation to what Artaud would later call 'the unsticking of the retina'[168] in reference to his drawings, a radical stimulation of the motility of the eye, that is part of the unravelling process of the vulnerability of the body where the entirety of its responses is called up confronting the work, here one must move to the ear for the words to work. What these glossolalic phrases have in common with Artaud's other writing is that, after a certain point, they were often dictated. Rather than chastising his secretary, whether Minouche Pastier or Paule Thévenin, for mistakes, Artaud would riff on the errors and thereby make a new creation, not so dissimilar from jazz improvisation that was all the rage in the post-war Paris into which Artaud was released.[169] The powerful rhythm such vocables evoked were allied with the semantics of the 'message' and the often invading visuals of the later notebook pages in that they overwhelmed the listener or participant's usual empathies and responses. This was a process that reached its most successful crescendo in Artaud's 1946-8 sound works for *radiodiffusion*.

Artaud's 'cure'

Artaud's humming and chanting, his churning up of his syllable-language in the process of his refection, was the ground for threats of electroshocks at Rodez. It is not the place of this project to belabour the behaviour of his psychiatrists that have come off so very poorly in retrospect, but the continuing use

[165] Artaud IX, 1971, p.188.

[166] They are 'objects…that speak of their own fact.' Artaud XX, 1984, p.370.

[167] André, *L'Épreuve d'Antonin Artaud et l'expérience de la psychanalyse*, pp.170-1.

[168] Artaud XXI, 1985, p.233.

[169] This atmosphere and the discussion of Artaud's dictation are among the many virtues of the double film on Artaud by Gérard Mordillat and Jérôme Prieur, *En Compagnie d'Antonin Artaud/La Véritable histoire d'Artaud le mômo*, La Sept, 1993.

of psychiatric terminology and stigmatisation in regard to Artaud, from Gilles Deleuze in 1969 to the curator of Artaud's 1996-97 exhibition in New York's Museum of Modern Art Margit Rowell, must indeed be challenged in any effort to take Artaud seriously. Artaud's own approach in denouncing psychiatry is well articulated by Stephen Barber when he writes that it was 'manipulative in the extreme...

> Artaud's total refusal of psychiatrically formulated madness is also an intense questioning of its constitution. With self-probing intricacy, Artaud's refusal undermines and unscreens notions of psychosis. It blatantly *uses* madness, puts madness to work, to take apart its social structure and to produce a transmissible language from that process of disassembly. In Artaud's final recording, this refusal of psychiatry probes and also screams.[170]

As Barber notes, Artaud's withering critique of psychiatry, of those Artaud characterised 'who have, to palliate the most appalling states of anguish and human suffocation, only a ridiculous terminology,'[171] is of such precision and 'destructive delight' that it elides what Doctors Paul Seriéux and Joseph Capgras in the early 20th Century called *délire d'interprétation*, that is, the coherent systems in their own terms of the highly obsessive world views and paranoiac patterns of 'psychotic' or 'schizophrenic' patients.[172] It was upon such a delirium, that of Judge Daniel Paul Schreber, that Freud and Lacan erected much of their theories. In contrast, Artaud speaks of his ambition to be *l'aliéné authentique*, or 'true madman.'[173] This is mentioned many times, but it is in his essay on Van Gogh that it is described in unmistakable clarity. The 'true madman' is one who 'prefers to become mad, in the social sense one understands, in order not to forfeit a certain superior idea of human honor...Because the madman is also a man that society does not want to understand and that it wants to prevent uttering intolerable truths.'[174] Here Artaud anticipates the profound cleavage drawn between 'true madness' and mental illness by Foucault and R.D. Laing in the early 1960s. Laing claimed, 'Our sanity is not "true" sanity. Their madness is not "true" madness...The madness that we encounter in "patients" is a gross travesty, a mockery, a grotesque caricature of what the natural healing of that estranged integration we call sanity might be.'[175] Foucault wrote of how 'madness releases itself from its kinship ties (ancient or recent, according to the scale we chose)

[170] Barber, *Antonin Artaud*, pp.7-8.

[171] Artaud XIII, 1974, p.15.

[172] Barber, *Antonin Artaud*, p.8; Paul Seriéux and Joseph Capgras, *Les Folies raisonnantes: le délire d'interprétation*, Marseille: Laffitte, [1909] 1982.

[173] See the elaboration of this in Évelyne Grossman, *Artaud, l'aliéné authentique*, Tours/Paris: Farrago/Léo Scheer, 2003. Grossman writes that among other things, it is a means for Artaud of exploring the non-human.

[174] Artaud XIII, 1974, p.17.

[175] Laing, *The Politics of Experience*, pp.118-19.

with mental illness...madness and mental illness are undoing their belonging to the same anthropological entity.'[176] Later David Cooper would complain of the dearth of real madmen in the English asylums.

But for Deleuze and Guattari, '*Artaud makes a shambles of psychiatry, precisely because he is schizophrenic and not because he is not*' (their italics).[177] Despite the overwhelming affirmation of 'madness' and radical schizophrenia in their *Capitalism and Schizophrenia* project as a revolutionary force of deterritorialisation against the controls and canalisation of desire in the oedipalised family of contemporary capitalist societies, Deleuze and Guattari insisted on retaining the psychiatric terms, however their valuation turned such terminology inside-out, and even if, as they acknowledge at the beginning of *Anti-Oedipus*, 'there is no specifically schizophrenic phenomenon or entity.'[178] In a later book, *The three ecologies* (1989), Félix Guattari takes a swipe at Artaud, writing that Guattari could not imagine a society that 'has done' with psychiatric clinics and prisons.[179] This is in stark contrast to the 'anti-psychiatry' movement Deleuze and Guattari's analyses in many respects grow out of, that (at least one prominent wing of) called for immediate abolition of psychiatry and practices of compulsory detention. Just as the 'anti-psychiatry' movement could imagine a post-capitalist/bureaucratic socialist society without class exploitation, it could imagine one without psychiatry and psychiatric institutions. As the January 1975 statement from the International Network Brussels urged, 'We must also abolish the relations between those administering treatment, the attendants, and those receiving it which reproduce class domination.'[180] In many of the writings of David Cooper, in particular, Artaud's syllogisms have new life, and approach Artaud's logic proclaimed in his first radio work, *The Patients and the Doctors* (1946), that without the psychiatrists there would be no patients, turning psychiatric justification on its head. Although at first in the work of

176 Foucault, *History of Madness*, p.549.

177 Deleuze and Guattari, *Anti-Oedipus*, p.135.

178 Ibid., p.5. On the frequent incoherence and difficulty of 'schizophrenic' symptomology, see Gilles Deleuze, 'Schizophrenia and Society,' in *Two Regimes of Madness*, pp.22-8.

179 Félix Guattari, *The three ecologies*, trans. Ian Pindar and Paul Sutton, London & New Brunswick, NJ: Athlone Press, [1989] 1992, p.59.

180 See Appendix II, 'Statement of the International Network,' in David Cooper, *The Language of Madness*, p.171. One can also look to a contemporary group like Critical Resistance, that is dedicated to creating alternatives to incarceration and monitors police behaviour in the US. See www.criticalresistance.org. 'Anti-psychiatry' also continues in the activism of groups like Mind Freedom International, National Association for Rights Protection and Advocacy (NARPA), and 'therapeutic communities' such as Arbours Association, founded by Laing's associate Joseph Berke in 1970 in north London. (www.mindfreedom.org, www.arboursassociation.org). The most significant recent developments in critical or counter-psychiatry both theoretically and practically remains the work of Tobie Nathan's 'ethnopsychiatry' with African immigrants in and around Paris.

R.D. Laing and his collaborators the etiology of schizophrenia was explored as an individual 'symptom' that implied a family/communicational disorder, and then slowly widened out from 'schizophrenic' families to larger social patterns and groupings, in this process often the term 'schizophrenic' was eventually overhauled and then, in the work of the most political practitioners, dropped altogether.[181] Cooper, who broke with Laing in the early '70s over the latter's emphasis on spiritualism over political struggle, came to define 'schizophrenia' as a strictly political label. His definition of the role of the 'mad' is a paraphrase of Artaud's in his Van Gogh essay: 'Schizophrenia has no existence but that of an exploitable fiction. *Madness exists as the delusion that consists in really uttering an unsayable truth in an unspeakable situation*.'[182] 'Madness' was to be recovered and reintegrated into social life, with the understanding that this required turbulent revolutionary transformations in economic and political structures.

The widening acceptance of the efficacy of bio-chemical treatments for 'schizophrenia,' often without much attention to the social contexts of the patient; the extension of community care facilities (as opposed to hospitalisation) at least for a time, with assorted results; and the fading away of the force of the militant New Left in the early 1970s, resulted in a mixed sort of consequences for the legacy of 'anti-psychiatry' today, though one recent critique still urges the issue of mental health be given priority in efforts for radical social change.[183] For better or for worse, the debates around different forms of 'anti-psychiatry' are still vitally at stake with Artaud. For Artaud posed his own solution against psychiatry in the form of his 'body without organs.' As Artaud had called for evoking 'doubles' in his theatre manifestoes and found with the Tarahumaras that the world was double and triple, in painful construction at Rodez and the earlier asylums, Artaud created a 'double' body, itself a double-creation of re-organisation and creative language. In doing so, Artaud performed no psychoan-

[181] For Laing's development see: R.D. Laing, *The Divided Self*, Harmondsworth: Penguin, 1960; *Self and Others*, London: Tavistock, 1961; with Aaron Esterson, *Sanity, Madness, and the Family*, London: Penguin, 1964; *The Politics of the Family and Other Essays*, London: Tavistock, 1971. For critiques of Laing see Peter Sedgwick, *Psycho Politics*, London: Pluto Press, 1992, as well as the harshly critical and fictionalised romp of Clancy Sigal's novel *Zone of the Interior*, New York, NY: Pomona Press, [1976] 2005. Sigal was a patient for a time at Kingsley Hall.

[182] Cooper, *The Language of Madness*, p.149. Italics in original.

[183] See Mark Fisher, *Capitalist Realism*, London: Zero Books, 2009, pp.34-8. For Fisher it is not so much a question of drawing on the resources of a radicalised or deterritorialising 'schizophrenia' as it is of challenging the preponderance of psychopharmacology and drugs to treat populations, in the UK and the US at least, with remarkably high levels of bi-polar disorder, depression and clinical depression. Both the massive use of drugs and the manic-depression cycles seem requirements for the neo-liberal corporate system to function. A primer on the vibrancy of current 'anti-psychiatry' struggles, largely in Canada and the UK, is Bonnie Burstow, Brenda A. Lefrançois, and Shaindl Diamond, eds., *Psychiatry Disrupted: Theorizing Resistance and Crafting the (R)evolution*, Montréal and Kingston: McGill-Queen's University Press, 2014.

alytic 'cure' on himself, a cure questioned in any case in the late Freud and then Lacan,[184] but he succeeded, out of the near catatonia and rampant splitting of his earlier, shattered condition, to re-form onto another quite immense level of creativity and becoming, that he characterised as his 'true body.' The nature of it is key to how Artaud refutes psychiatric claims, though, in a typically reversible Artaudian fashion, it may take as much power away from Artaud to claim he was not 'psychotic,' as to maintain that he was.[185] Artaud wrote that his language became a 'mass of flesh moving in and through the general anatomy.'[186] It comes to constitute another outside, another boundary that Artaud creates through a process of expelling himself from himself: 'I am not inside,' Artaud writes;[187] the 'body without organs' forms an 'exterior body.'[188] Artaud realises 'the problem is that I am the organ and the body and that the question is always posed for me to impose myself through relation to my body which is that of the sacrosanct universe.'[189] Just as Artaud does not dispute ordinary, chronological time but seeks nonetheless to exist in another, multiple and eternal sense of time, Artaud recognises the organed body while posing distance from it as an entity that can only be defined by being, God, or the Other of Lacanian theory. So while Artaud writes 'My body is mine from the head to the feet' there is 'no one inside…I have absolutely no internal function, no localization of internal conscience.'[190] The 'body without organs' is the result of the constitution of a new 'outside.' Artaud has carried out a *dédoublement* of the body; the body with organs is the body captured and defined and in principle divided by the others, successfully subjected to hierarchal order, whereas the body of the void is the 'true body' existing alongside or outside, as it were, of the organed body. One can see this notion in the later reflection by Deleuze and Guattari where the 'body without organs' has 'nothing to do with the body itself, or an image of the body.'[191]

This newly erected border between the two bodies, for a commentator such

---

[184] See Sigmund Freud, 'Analysis Terminable and Interminable [1937]' in Vol. XXIII of *Standard Psychological Works of Sigmund Freud*, ed. James Strachey, London & New York, NY: Hogarth Press/Macmillan, 1964; and Jacques Lacan, 'The direction of the treatment and the principles of its power,' in *Écrits*.

[185] One reasonable view is the position of novelist Henri Thomas, then secretary to André Gide, part of the band of literati that succeeded in releasing Artaud from Rodez, that despite the seriousness of Artaud's illness or sickness, he was a bit in love with it, and exaggerated it. So while Artaud was profoundly disturbed and supremely self-conscious concerning his gyrations, he also fell well short of being 'insane.' See Thomas' comments in the film *La Véritable histoire d'Artaud le mômo*.

[186] Artaud XXII, 1986, p.133.

[187] Artaud XXIII, 1987, pp.202-3.

[188] Artaud XIII, 1974, p.63.

[189] Artaud XXIII, 1987, p.203.

[190] Ibid., pp.202-3.

[191] Deleuze and Guattari, *Anti-Oedipus*, p.8.

as André, serves against heteroeroticism, the desire of the Other, but in doing so, he asks, doesn't death come to occupy the place of sexual pulsion since the latter lacks the necessary phallic support? Artaud, in this argument, has not only excluded sex, but life itself, Artaud has become a necropolis.[192] In this view, Artaud's self-creation does not continue past the *filles du cœur*, finding itself blocked at the level of anal eroticism (from whence they came).[193] André finds support in this with all the walls and boxes and bottles and coffins that populate Artaud's later drawings – all monads that illustrate Artaud's closing off of any *jouissance*. Yet for Artaud, the 'body without organs' implies a strongly 'affirmative matter.'[194] And the drawings – each a 'machine that breathes'[195] – are themselves filled with machinic forms, animated bodies. Artaud writes:

> I seek a body consistent, *irréel*, animated, corporeal, as that one anchored in my brain…and I seek it not in infinite idea but finite, not in infinity but in space, not in deepening inexistence but in affirmative matter,
>
> the body remote, impossible, imperceptible, unobstructed by any descriptive, discriminating conscience, and which nevertheless will be more and more there, weighing down and arresting the conscience which wants to traverse it.[196]

Artaud has posed another perspective, and another language, against both psychoanalytic and psychiatric characterisations. With the increasing importance and prevalence of his drawings, especially, Artaud will argue that what appears to be his universe of rampant animism and fetishism have to be taken on their own terms, terms (as I will show in a section in the next chapter) that often differ profoundly from the standard descriptions of animism and fetishism.

The rhythms and graphic work that have been gaining force at Rodez prodigiously explode upon Artaud's return to Paris in May 1946 – and the 'body without organs' is the notional substrate upon which all this work is founded. As Artaud maintains in 'The Theater of cruelty' (1947):

> It is the affirmation
> of a terrible
> and moreover inescapable necessity.[197]

It is these 'anatomies in action'[198] that best show Artaud's rebuttal, if not ruthless exploitation of 'madness.' The drawings are increasingly seen as animated bod-

---

192 André, *L'Épreuve d'Antonin Artaud et l'expérience de la psychanalyse*, p.185.

193 Ibid., pp.186-7.

194 Artaud XVIII, 1983, p.186.

195 Artaud, *Œuvres*, p.1513.

196 Artaud XVIII, 1983, p.286.

197 Artaud XIII, 1974, p.110.

198 An 21 August 1947 letter collected in Artaud, *L'Arve et l'aume suivi de 24 lettres à Marc Barbezat*, Décines: L'Arbalète, 1989, p.82.

ies that protect him, that carry on the battle in his body, and will serve to continue to do so – Artaud works all the more ferociously as he realises he is dying. The drawings, Artaud makes clear in his text for *50 drawings to murder magic* (1948), exceed any and all anatomical definition, thereby evading the 'cuts' or 'breaks' of the discretely organed organism/body.[199] In terms of the discussion here, it has to be stressed that Artaud's drawings are also creations from his strange uterine-anal matrix; they are also a 'mass of flesh' from his expulsive dynamics. So his dynamics had fruitfulness beyond the birthing of the *filles du cœur*.

In terms of the 'pathology' or 'cure' of Artaud's 'search for fecality,' his case brings to mind the most well-publicised and spectacular instance of controversial 'healing' at Kingsley Hall, the experience of Mary Barnes. Barnes was a nurse who had suffered several breakdowns and institutionalisations when she entered Kingsley Hall in 1965, under the care of Dr. Joseph Berke, where she was allowed the most frightening and complete regressions in the faith that she would emerge from the other side. Barnes' behaviour was far more 'anti-social' than any act of Artaud's, who aside from violent rhetoric, never reportedly attacked anyone, other than the scuffles with police in Ireland of which we know little of the circumstances. Barnes went into violent rages, assaulted others, and at least once appeared in the common rooms completely naked, covered in her own excrement. Barnes also saw her excrement as her children, which led her to painting her room first in her feces, then in oil paints. Having excavated a buried path of emotional and psychic development, Barnes went on to a noted career as an artist and lecturer on mental health issues in the US and Europe.[200] As Florence de Mèredieu notes, artist Hans Bellmer also dealt openly with themes of coprophagy and coprophilia, though this time those themes were cloaked in a 'reassuring aestheticism.'[201] In the example of Artaud, there is no larger psychic whole or aesthetic grouping to which such concerns are subordinated, and so no such reassurance. Artaud is also strictly different – again singular, irreducible – from Mary Barnes, who had to 'go down' to come back up as a larger, more broadly functioning human being in a recognisably cyclical, sacred pattern. Artaud's graphic work on the other hand, served to 'renounce the umbilical cord'[202] and create the 'true body,' while serving as platform for world-renouncing sorcery. There was nothing cyclical about his journey.

Just as Artaud cannot be assimilated to a sacred return of healing, nor aes-

[199] Artaud XXII, 1986, p.131.

[200] Barnes' story is told in Mary Barnes and Joseph Berke, *Mary Barnes: Two Accounts of a Journey Through Madness*, new ed., London & New York, NY: Penguin Books, 1973. For her later art career, see Barnes' *Something Sacred: Conversations, Writings, Paintings*, London: Free Association, 1989.

[201] Florence de Mèredieu, *L'Affaire Artaud*, Paris: Fayard, 2009, p.646.

[202] Florence de Mèredieu, *Antonin Artaud, Portraits et gris gris*, Paris: Blusson, 1984, p.61.

thetic recuperation of some accursed share, he is not an apostle of expenditure, or energetics of spending without reserve in Georges Bataille's sense, either.[203] Spurred from an analysis of the wealth dissipating mass gifting ceremony of primitive societies' *potlatch*, Bataille explored economy as a process of loss, not accumulation. In his 1933 essay 'The Notion of Expenditure' Bataille wrote that human societies could have 'an *interest* in considerable losses, in catastrophes that, *while conforming to well-defined needs*, provoke tumultuous depressions, crises of dread, and, in the final analysis, a certain orgiastic state.'[204] To push society towards this orgiastic state was Bataille's aim, and one of the sources of his politics. It is linked to his theory of general economy in which life was seen as experience that must open up to its limit, to its excess no system can entirely corral or control, but which 'must necessarily be lost without profit; it must be spent, willingly or not, gloriously or catastrophically.'[205] This excess was transindividual and as cosmological as it was social. In contrast limited economy was a situation of closure that refused, rerouted or cancelled excess. Not unlike Artaud's relationship with Lacan, that one could have imagined quite differently, Artaud's dialogue with Bataille was also stunted and short-circuited; as recounted in the discussion of Artaud's *New Revelations of Being* in Chapter IV Bataille was largely frightened and repelled by Artaud. They were two authors one could imagine sharing a broad range of obsessions in common – Bataille was also seduced by the most macabre primitive rites, orgiastic losses of consciousness, a black eroticism and what he judged as the collapse of European civilization. But this lack of relation is telling: Bataille's project is unfailingly devoted to an interrogation of the limits of the Hegelian dialectic and the blackout or loss (in its very fulfillment) of Hegel's 'Absolute Consciousness;' this pursuit for Bataille most characteristically and frequently hinges around the phenomenon of sacrifice. This exploration of sacrifice – an overweening motif in Bataille – is largely absent in Artaud.[206] Discussion of Hegel is extremely rare in the 'early' Artaud and the 'later' Artaud is unremittingly hostile to any notion of dialectics or dialectical logic; his relentless mark-making is an assault on any such synthesising reason. Artaud's project is one of lucidity and a holding onto lucidity even amid the most astounding and disturbing states of mind; his 'body without organs' is, on one level, an extraordinary eruption of will, not a pursuit of transgression

[203] See Georges Bataille, 'The Notion of Expenditure,' in *Visions of Excess*, ed. Allan Stoekl, trans. Allan Stoekl with Carl R. Lovitt and Donald M. Leslie, Jr. Minneapolis, MN: University of Minnesota Press, 1985.

[204] Ibid., p.117. Italics in original.

[205] Georges Bataille, *The Accursed Share Volume One*, trans. Robert Hurley, New York, NY: Zone Books, 1991, p.21.

[206] Despite one important reference to sacrifice in Artaud's essay on Van Gogh (treated in a section in the next chapter), in contrast Bataille's essay on Van Gogh takes this as its primary theme. See Bataille's 'Sacrificial Mutilation, or the Severed Ear of Van Gogh,' in *Visions of Excess*.

or even loss of consciousness in a Bataillean sense. Despite this, Bataillean notions of local and general economy and expenditure of energy have formed a prevalent mode of looking at Artaud's journey;[207] key elements of which inform the critique of Artaud from Jacques Derrida and Allen Weiss, both of whom I address in the next chapter. Artaud does not revel in excess or explore transgression so much as practice an *askésis* that will escape thermodynamic models of desire altogether. Rather than a sacrifice, this 'new body' can be projected into immortality, although it may well require the sacrifice of others or its enemies.

Artaud's challenge is not so much the contradictions and aporias of local and general economy, or point of sacrificial consciousness but rather another operation that indeed aims to abolish consciousness in another modality in the form of a 'true body.' No circle or interlacing circles, only a violent flurry of conflicting and intersecting lines that often blacken each other out. In the next chapter, I will show how the all-important scaffolding that helped Artaud arrive at this point – in the hieroglyphic sign of the cross – is discarded along with any fascination with a hieroglyphic matrix of reality. As Artaud moves between media especially in the last year-and-a-half of his life, the relation of word to image to sound can at times still appear hieroglyphic, but more often the elements are so conflicting they produce a black engulfment, indicating that Artaud has shredded as a notion or sign even that last vestige of representation. As he goes into his final battles, Artaud spits on the 'innate christ' and proclaims himself the 'true christ,' even while he 'abjects any cross.'[208] In his impassioned essay on Van Gogh, any 'shadow' of reality has more force than any 'hieroglyph.' It has gone up into flames in the final conflagration.

---

[207] For excerpts from Bataille's economic writings and expositions of 'general economy' see *The Bataille Reader*, ed. Fred Botting and Scott Wilson, Oxford: Blackwell Publishers, 1997.

[208] Artaud, *Œuvres*, pp.1555-62; Artaud XIII, 1974, p.273.

VI.
THE FRACTURING OF THE VOID AND THE EXPLODING HIEROGYLPH

When Artaud's collaborator and friend, the actor Jean-Louis Barrault, put down his ideas on theatre, he came up with some eminently Artaudian reflections. In each art form, Barrault wrote, it was a question of one form or element confronting another, since 'a Human Being struggles in space. The theater is the art of the human being in space.' Each art is a kind of confrontation where

> a brush rubs a canvas
> a pen scrapes paper
> a hammer strikes a string.[1]

We find this is especially true of Artaud's 'late' work, that is, at Rodez and after his release. Just as Artaud did not so much lack a 'primordial signifier' as have all too many of them, at the end of his life, Artaud may be operating in a void, but it is far from a empty one, rather it is over-stuffed with forces. Not the plentitude of the shining Buddhist void *sunyata*, neither is it, Artaud writes, 'the symbol of an absent void,/of an appalling incapacity of people to realize themselves in life;' when he continues, 'It is the affirmation/of a terrible/and moreover inescapable necessity,'[2] he is affirming a consistency with the third of the 1932 'Letters on language' that limned cruelty as determinable action or 'blind rigor' in *The Theater and Its Double*.[3] Artaud's last works are above all, an *action*, a setting of forces into motion. In examining how he accomplishes this, largely from the springboard of the copious 406 lined school notebooks of which there are some more than 30,000 pages, at times there is the temptation to mimic his method by fracturing the field, separating out the elements that come into conflict, such as sound image text, or even their constituent bodily sources, and it is by such recourse that I isolate the treatment of the face and the voice at the end of this chapter; to see better how they interact, meld, hover, disintegrate or invade

1 Jean-Louis Barrault, *Reflections on Theater*, trans. Barbara Wall, London: Theatre Book Club, [1947] 1951, p.61.

2 Artaud XIII, 1974. p.110.

3 Artaud IV, 1964, p.137.

other elements in a choreography or cacophony that is as much a world-spell as any of the burnt missives Artaud sent from Galway.[4]

I begin this chapter with an introduction to the wider resonance of Artaud's construction of the 'body without organs,' that Deleuze describes as a 'spherical body' or 'scroll painting' in which 'everything happens' and Guattari limns as a fuller 'disequilibrium' of a virtual universe. These brief remarks are the setting for the ensuing discussion of Artaud's notebooks and drawings, which themselves illustrate the movement of the 'body without organs.' A section follows this on the dynamics of text, image and theme in the last year of Artaud's *cahiers*, which often reach a crescendo of conflict between their different elements. Here it will be shown that while Artaud's later graphic work and prodigious drawings may emerge from the hieroglyphic complex that concerned him earlier, the operation of the 'body without organs' tends toward an engulfment and an eradication of *jouissance* as well as a distinct form that bans even the notion of 'hieroglyph' as a kind of representation. Artaud's attitude to his own drawing, to sound, to words and tonality are no better illustrated than in his 1947 essay on Van Gogh. The section 'the opening to animism' examines and introduces how the universe of the 'late' Artaud, peopled with entities and demons, at struggle with God and Satan, often seems to reference an animistic world, yet typically this is on Artaud's terms, in which the usual anthropological and psychoanalytic definitions of the phenomenon of totemisation, for example, do not apply. Artaud in his late work creates rampant forms of totems (Artaud's double and doubling again), and in examining their significance I look more closely at what seem to be the occult soundings of Artaud's essay on Van Gogh, where the usual notions of the totem clearly implode in Artaud's heralding of 'direct creation.' This brings to the foreground the struggle over the figure and figuration in the late Artaud, specifically in the form of Jacques Derrida's 1986 essay on Artaud's reliance on the 'subjectile,'[5] an obscure term from the history of Italian Renaissance painting that refers to the *subjectum*, what lies below or beneath or in-between a form, that is a sort of surface or support for a painting or sculpture but is distinct from it, that strictly speaking is not part of its meaning or representation. The *subjectile* thus forms part of Artaud's battle with the inescapable support or platform or medium of any art form. This examination

[4] Three facsimiles of Artaud's late notebooks have been published, so that they are now available to the public in an entirety previously difficult to access. These include the already cited edition of *50 drawings to murder magic* (2004/08), and Artaud's *Cahier Ivry, janvier 1948*, ed. Évelyne Grossman, Paris: Gallimard, 2006, as well as the most complete edition yet of Artaud's notebooks and drawings, prepared through the work of his nephew Serge Malausséna, that were made available to the public at the Bibliothèque nationale de France as of summer 2010 and were published in October 2011. See Antonin Artaud, *Cahiers d'Ivry: Février 1947 – Mars 1948*, 2 vols, Paris: Gallimard/Hors Série Littérature, 2011.

[5] Derrida's essay was first published in Thévenin and Derrida, *Antonin Artaud, dessins et portraits*, Paris: Gallimard, 1987.

of figure and means of representation leads to discussion of the special significance of the face in Artaud, who became the author of so many portraits, of himself, of close friends and sometimes of writers who made a pilgrimage to see him. The face is the key to the abyss of the body for Artaud, its sole remaining authentic element. It also often doubles in his portraits and pictures of friends (so that they are recognisably self-portraits as well). This discussion of Artaud's drawings is followed by a précis of Artaud's 1946-8 radio works, the last, and notoriously banned one, *To have done with the judgment of god*, Artaud himself felt functioned as a real Theater of cruelty. The radio works are not only significant in their own right, they demonstrate how the releasing of different elements in their making, in particular Artaud's use of the scream and various extreme noise effects produced from the human body or the human cry abolish even the idea of 'hieroglyph' as form. Already in the development of Artaud's drawings a different set of concerns arise that have little to do with Artaud's hieroglyph but rather from the enactment of the 'body without organs' that is replacing it as the matrix of Artaud's world. Artaud's acknowledges in various places that the 'hieroglyph' is no longer such a central concept for him, and in the engulfment or void created by a work like *To have done with the judgment of god*, it no longer functions.

The spherical body

What becomes evident is that Artaud's later work has no concern with evoking depths (as in the 'collective unconscious' of the Jungian imagination), or play with sheer surfaces (what he condemned in Lewis Carroll), but rather with an unrolling and unravelling membrane of the organless body, what Deleuze called 'a sort of spherical body or scroll painting.'[6] It keeps to Deleuze's sense that 'in this book everything happens' on this 'body without organs' – any point or 'horizon of convergence lies in a chaos or is constantly displaced by that chaos'[7] – and Artaud, keeping to the flux of matter, stays with this rhythmic fluctuation at all costs, poised between an 'eternal return' of the flesh and chaosmodic foldings that disregard even this 'structure,' in the interests of an even more unpredictable emergence threatened and enveloped by catastrophe, accident, the abrupt finitude of death. What Artaud approaches in the later work is close to what Guattari described as the perpetual difference of a fuller autopoiesis, 'based on disequilibrium, the prospection of Virtual universes far from equilibrium.'[8] A state that however far from God or man, still constitutes a 'diagrammatism' that

[6] Deleuze, *Two Regimes of Madness*, p.66.

[7] Deleuze, *Difference and Repetition*, p.123.

[8] Guattari, *Chaosmosis*, p.37.

is a 'proto-subjective diagram,'[9] hence Foucault's remark that Artaud belongs to the foundation, not the rupture, of language.[10] As Artaud wrote to the director of the radio station who banned *To have done with the judgment of god*, the work concerned itself 'with voices, drum and xylophonics,' with 'alerting separate individualities so they may form a body.'[11] The broadcast, Artaud wrote in an earlier letter before the work was censored, was composed of 'enough elements' that are

> grating,
> throbbing,
> discordant,
> dissonant,
> so that they need only be *assembled* in a new order to prove that
> the desired end has been achieved,
> my function was to provide you with elements.[12]

It is these elements that are to provide the work's 'unusual values.'[13] In the 1930s Artaud urged that hieroglyphic languages worked more directly on the viewer or spectator's 'unconscious;' in the last year-and-a-half of his life Artaud has separated out or dissembled the elements of any moving, zig-zagging 'hieroglyph' of matter, that must still be 'read,' or in the instance of the radio broadcasts, 'heard,' yet Artaud has set up profound discordances between these elements, in his most violent and far-reaching challenge to any detachable representational process. Artaud activates this process to pierce through to infinity, his puncturing of spaces serving to open up not any ritual reconciliation between space and time (in the form of any hieroglyphic figure), but to release the gesture of the 'true body' into the infinite void.

Artaud's 1947-8 notebooks: the combustion of hieroglyphics

The foundry for these 'unusual values' increasingly emerged from and is inseparable from Artaud's notebooks, that he began in September 1945 at Rodez, and continued to work in daily until his death on 4 March 1948.[14] They do not function as a writer's notebook in any conventional sense of preparation for

9 Ibid.

10 Foucault, *A History of Madness*, p.541.

11 Artaud XIII, 1974, p.132.

12 Ibid., p.125.

13 Ibid.

14 Although many of my comments would apply in a more general way to many if not most of Artaud's notebooks, which began at Rodez, I am concentrating on the last year of them (April 1947 - March 1948) written at Ivry-sur-Seine, that exemplify the issues raised in this project the most.

a discrete work, or the fabled memories recollected in tranquility. Although drawings and texts separated themselves out from the ferment to stand on their own, the notebooks are their own process, their own working out, ultimately their own kind of processual paradigm. The 406 school exercise workbooks highlight this process above all. Artaud after his release from Rodez worked constantly on and through the children's exercise books carried folded up in his jacket – on the metro, during his walks in the city of Paris, in cafes and dictated from his bed. But when he still had the strength to, Artaud often invented and performed his texts standing up straight, facing his notebook sheets, while pounding on a block of wood provided for this purpose with an iron hammer. The hammer eventually broke into pieces from the force of Artaud's blows. So Artaud is still performing what he termed in *The Theater and Its Double* an 'affective athleticism.' Although André Breton chastised Artaud after his notorious 13 January 1947 appearance at Vieux-Colombier for still being a man of the theatre these performative rites are largely performed at his pavilion turned workshop at Ivry-sur-Seine, not in public, although Artaud declaimed his work and banged gongs at Galérie Pierre in Paris on 4 and 18 July 1947 – his only other public performances.[15] Artaud's 'affective athleticism' is therefore mostly performed in and evident from the notebook pages themselves, that are often scarred, interpenetrated one element from another, one notebook from another – Artaud worked on more than one notebook simultaneously – so that one cannot tell where one element or process began, or where it ends. This is a basic introduction into a kind of infinite temporality that Artaud inducts us into, in a process he tells us is 'first and foremost/magical.'[16] In some notebooks it is clear the words came first, in others it is the graphics or drawings, the words written into or over them. In others what would normally be the end of a sentence turns into part of a drawing, or begins a drawing, so again we are in a kind of Moebius strip, or endless uroboric strips. The shifting complexity of these notebooks is especially ill-served, despite the intense dedication and good intentions of Artaud's editor, Paule Thévenin, in his *Œuvres complètes*, where certain versions of texts are separated out (without their accompanying *gris gris* and drawings) and put in a linear, chronological order.[17] As useful as this is for Artaud scholars – precisely or paradoxically because of his immense fluidity Artaud is an artist for whom any understanding chronology is of utmost importance – it mars any viable representation of the notebooks' process, given Artaud worked on multiple

[15] In the first of these Artaud banged on gongs while hidden from view; in the second gathering he read and performed his work in person. See Prevel, *En Compagnie d'Antonin Artaud*, pp.151; 155.

[16] Artaud, *50 drawings to murder magic*, p.4.

[17] A chronological order is in any case often impossible to decipher. In a further point of controversy, scholar Florence de Mèredieu has challenged many of Thévenin's transcriptions of Artaud's notebooks, see Mèredieu, *L'Affaire Artaud*, pp.275-90.

notebooks at the same time and that the graphic elements are inseparable from what he was trying to achieve.

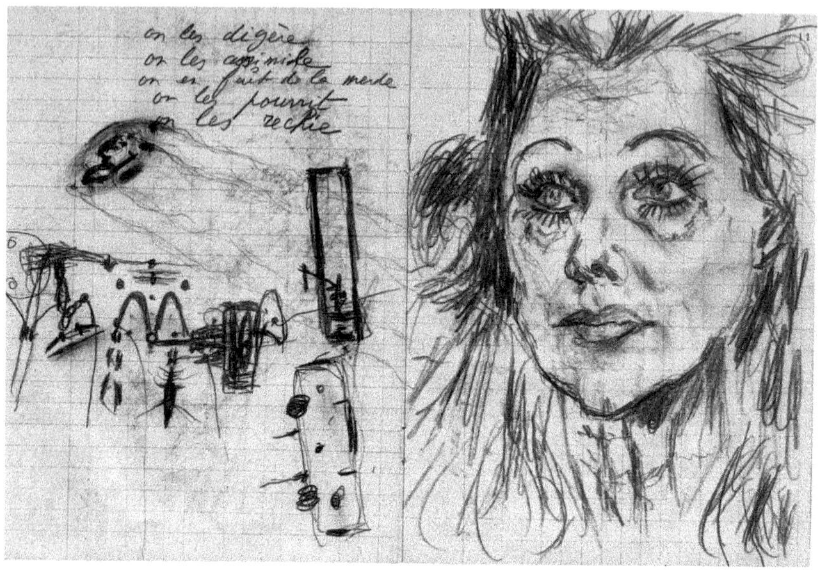

from Cahiers #310, June 1947. © 2016 Artists Rights Society (ARS), New York/ADAGP, Paris.

In this whirl of multiple and contradictory spaces the notebooks constitute, we see the movement of Artaud's constructed organless body. Much as Artaud is not 'inside' his physical body, but inhabits his 'body without organs,' it is between the pages and lines of the notebooks that what Artaud calls 'the corporeal and real materialisation of an integral being of poetry'[18] is actualised. Quite apart from the usual use of a writer's notebook where thoughts are recorded as an *aide-mémoire*, there is no such fixity here, but rather the invention of a means of support for phrases that at any moment can be reassembled or mobilised into movement in a different way.[19] This is Artaud's *subjectile*,[20] put to extraordinary plastic use, rather than, as Derrida has argued, an entrapment in processes of representation. Their force of expression is the fruit of Artaud's 'search for fecality' – which is why Artaud compares himself to the force of eruption of the Mexican volcano Popocatepl in his *Suppôts et suppliciations*.[21] The 'anus is always terror,'[22] Artaud will write to Henri Parisot, but there is an undeniable *jouissance*

[18] Artaud, *Œuvres*, p.1019.

[19] Évelyne Grossman, 'Quitter la lettre écrite,' her preface to *Cahier Ivry, janvier 1948*, p.14.

[20] For Derrida's commentary on this term in Artaud, see Derrida, *The Secret Art of Antonin Artaud*, trans. Mary Ann Caws, Cambridge, MA & London: MIT Press, 1998.

[21] Artaud XIV:1, 1978, pp.23-4.

[22] Artaud, *Œuvres*, p.1013.

and play and *volupté* in this constant movement of inside and outside, of oral and anal expulsions, not only horror.[23] As Grossman points out in her extremely perceptive commentary on one of Artaud's January 1948 notebooks, the *fécal* for Artaud is not the excremental; rather the 'fecal' is the movement and expulsive force of desire, of the 'body without organs,' and the excremental is the loss, and inevitable loss of soul, associated for Artaud with the physical body. To merely identify the fecal and the excremental, creation with defecation, would leave Artaud stuck in the regression of Freud's notion of infantile sexuality, or the 'father-mother' of the 'Holy Family' of theology and the reproductive order – fates he is pledged to avoid at all costs.[24] Rather, the fecal is the enormous pulsion that can constitute the organless body, which makes up a 'perpetual system,' that eternally puts the world of life back on track, traversing itself and remaking itself in this infinite proliferation that is the 'body without organs.'[25] It is this inverse, inside-out operation that Artaud describes in the conclusion of *To have done with the judgment of god* where 'true liberty' will entail a 'dance inside out /as in the delirium of the dance halls/ and that inside out will be his true side out.'[26]

It is this 'body without organs' that transforms what Artaud deplores as the uniformity of human time, that 'order which asphyxiates us'[27] in the excerpt from the *Cahiers du retour à Paris* discussed in the last section of chapter I. Not only is this the result of hoodwinking and diabolical manipulation from the religious castes of priests, it traps humanity in the oral-anal tract or canal, in the servitude of the physical body whose axis must be metamorphosed into the organless body. I have noted more than once that Artaud is often scrupulous about dates, so this is not a matter of abolishing human temporality, but of transforming it. As Évelyne Grossman points out, in one passage of the January 1948 notebooks Artaud in his incantatory spells uses virtually all conjugations and senses of the verb *passer* (or *traverser, dépasser*) so that it becomes impossible to distinguish what is before or after, in front or behind, above or below, enacting the dance Artaud calls for.[28] This is also 'to have done with the judgment of god,' since for Artaud it is not a matter of opposing the successive, human time of Chronos to the eternal time of God or the gods, Aion – this would be the spiritual eternity of Christianity and of the 'father-mother' Artaud explicitly denounces.[29] Rather

---

23 Grossman in *Cahier Ivry, janvier 1948*, p.15. This is also a point Kristeva frequently makes in regard to Artaud.

24 Here Grossman's interpretation diverges sharply from that of Stephen Barber, who at least in his earlier Artaud books, translates '*la recherche de fécalité*' from *To have done with the jugement of god* as 'the search for the excremental.' In his revised edition of *Artaud: The Screaming Body* he drops this for 'search for fecality.'

25 Grossman, *Cahier Ivry, janvier 1948*, pp.14; 16.

26 Artaud XIII, 1974, p.104.

27 Artaud XXIV, 1988, p.27.

28 Grossman, *Cahier Ivry, janvier 1948*, p.17.

29 This 1947 letter to Breton is typical, see Artaud, *Œuvres*, p.1216.

it is a matter of what Artaud calls 'the endless duration of the body,

of the same man
undergoing time
without stop,
and space,
eternally fathomed.[30]

The notebooks are the field wherein Artaud enacts and creates this 'semipiternal time' that is difficult if not impossible to separate from the task Artaud described as 'to reassemble a new human body'[31] – already the goal of some of his earliest Rodez drawings. Artaud writes:

There will always be in me
something
which will be in awakening
and stretched from the side
of infinity[32]

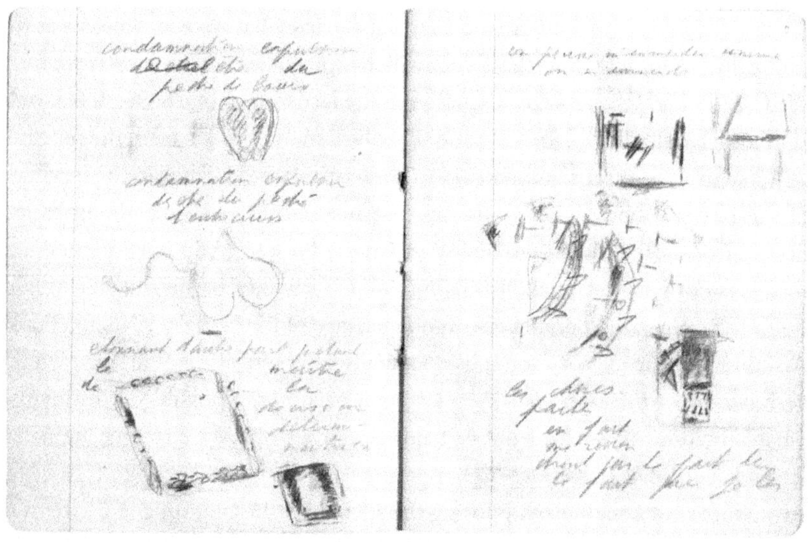

from Cahiers #386, May 1947.

In the notebooks, as in Artaud's drawings, at times all available space is filled and stuffed, so when it alternates with pages of blank space the shock of the void is all the more evident. What is clear in looking at the writing of Artaud's notebooks is that Artaud is acutely aware of these processes and combats, so his remarks are a running meta-commentary on the notebooks themselves. Not

30 Ibid., p.1702.

31 Artaud XVIII, 1983, p.73.

32 Artaud, *Cahier Ivry, janvier 1948*, p.28.

only does Artaud claim the human body is the site of all true and worthwhile transformation – the notebooks themselves demonstrate such a process. This is what entails such a brutal battle against representation, since 'the body is sound/ when it does not think.'[33] Although Artaud writes he would like to sleep, this would be sleep 'that no longer leaves reality/ but that makes it slowly advance to the point where physically' Artaud will make men 'worthy of this [new] reality.'[34] In the notebooks of January 1948, Artaud can be programmatic, and dogmatic – he does not want sexuality, nor the female, or any kind of corporeal rapprochement, but only the body that returns to the body, and repeats in the body, but this will be a body in which nothing is 'inside' since 'Elsewhere the world was never based/on sentiments or passions.' Striking a Nietzschean chord, not for the first time, Artaud continues that the base of the world has ever been the 'difficult accomplishment of the law of the just and the unjust…the greatest detachment/the greatest disinterestedness/the greatest remoteness' of corporeal affect.[35] It is Artaud's urgency that he

> …make there
> a body
> that holds
> and resists everything
> in the limited
> and the unlimited
> the real
> and the unreality
> that will go there.[36]

This body entails that transformation of time into a 'unique duration,' 'because I have made/things one/after the others/and not at the same time.'[37] Artaud attempts to describe this different sense of time as the function of events 'that are produced without filling it.'[38] It is necessary, Artaud writes, to free time from its task of uniformity – the time of a bus conductor is not that of a merchant or a writer at his desk – robbing each of its own time, which to Artaud is a gross project of abjection, a 'uniformisation of time' that keeps humanity trapped in its *canal d'abjection*, a 'uniformisation of the bodies.'[39] He has never met, Artaud writes, two men with the same body, yet this 'uniformisation of bodies' demands the quotidian servitude of eating, excreting, pissing, that are all the 'most odious

[33] Ibid.
[34] Ibid., p.33.
[35] Ibid., p.34.
[36] Ibid., p.35.
[37] Ibid.
[38] Ibid., p.36.
[39] Ibid., pp.36-7.

and derisory and of time.'[40] So the project of extending the body, or creating the 'body without organs,' is bound up with the rejection of ordinary time. It is not necessary to retain the body, Artaud argues, but rather it is necessary to 'allow it/to abdicate itself/and abject itself/to the limits of/the abdication/of the abjection/when all the body is abjected/then the true battle begins/because time begins where ends/the sensibility.'[41] Artaud's project is completely uncompromising: the true body can only commence where the knowledge and science which 'makes man' ends.[42]

Artaud's late notebooks are the laboratory for this process. In them he is acutely aware of the use and distribution of space, the voids in space, eruptions in space. The notebooks seem to stage an extraordinary confrontation between what is visible and what is invisible. In some pages, Artaud has placed six different texts in differing arrangements on the page; in others he has written across both double pages of the open notebook in an exaggerated emphasised scrawl. Other passages remarkably seem to outline or open up a void to their left or centre. This is writing as gesture to such an extent that the boundary between word and image becomes extremely blurred. Artaud is relentlessly exposing and showing the forces and the movement he is describing, and in such a conflict-ridden environment what is image and what is text are often in strident opposition as forces yet interchangeable as gesture. The drawings that emerge seem to have every conceivable relation to the texts – as illustration and exclamation, or as violently invading entity. The notebooks detail Artaud's struggle to recreate his self and body, all while pillorying the normal or 'uniformised' physical body. As Artaud writes in a passage in January 1948 'the human body/is a disgrace/fetal from one part/and fecal on the other.'[43] Paralleling the growing presence of the drawings, that gain their own dynamic and by the end of 1947 have a tremendous vitality as their own element, Artaud claims in December 1947 that 'I have made/a body.'[44] This entails wrenching himself away from the beings that have stolen his body, 'the beings in my body from bottom to top,' since 'the beings have made much evil.'[45] In Artaud's notebooks, the drawings often emerge at mention of the 'demons,' the 'spirits,' 'spectres' or other entities Artaud is in combat with. The centering of texts on the page punctuated or

[40] Ibid., p.38.

[41] Ibid., p.39.

[42] Ibid., p.41.

[43] Antonin Artaud, Cahier #393/January 1948. Courtesy: Bibliothèque nationale de France, Paris. Thanks to the permission and support of the director of the Bibliothèque Nationale, Guillaume Fau and the literary executor of the Artaud estate, Serge Malusséna, I was able to consult the Artaud archives in June 2010. I cite the notebooks here by number and date; very few of the notebooks have pagination, and none of the quotations cited here carry any. All translations from the notebooks are my own.

[44] Artaud, Cahier #389/December 1947.

[45] Artaud, Cahier #285, 284/April 1947.

ended with Artaud's syllable language, so often accompanied by signs or *gris gris* for emphasis, often look remarkably like his spells of the 1930s or *The New Revelations of Being*, and seem to have a similar function. The frequency of extremely densely drawn and characterised figures that are then smudged into near-oblivion, others that are splotches added for dramatic effect, add to the impression that one is witnessing another set of Artaud's spells. The notebooks are supremely self-conscious experiments for Artaud, who writes in one spot 'it is necessary to be Antonin Artaud himself,' or 'because this is me Antonin Artaud,'[46] and segments are often signed for emphasis or to signal a stop. The project of the notebooks even shares the tone of prophecy with the prior spells. In a passage of June 1947 Artaud writes 'I have prepared this which is to come' covered by a large drawing.[47]

Especially in the last year, the notebooks become a last will and testament. The pages communicate not only wildly different emphases in gesture, but at times extreme increases in velocity, resulting in writing that goes right off the page, that on the one hand is so extremely light as to be illegible or on the contrary so enforced and stark and emphasised that the graphite pencil seems to break off; likewise some passages are written over others. Artaud's attention to all sorts of line and spacing arrangements to the text make this a highly lucid exercise. And populating this landscape above all are the strange box and grill figures, that Artaud at one point calls 'these coffins.'[48] The images that fill the notebooks are as diverse as the types of writing – flying anvils or screws, propelled machinic forms (Artaud refers to 'the machines of my breath'),[49] all sorts of totemised figures and boxes, tombs and mounds, portraits of recognisable figures or one of Artaud's 'daughters of the heart' that miraculously and unexpectedly emerges from the inferno. On one page a standing figure seems linked by spiralling coils of vertebrae to stacks of a machinic figure on the next page. Although the prevalence of the boxes or coffins or bottles may lend credence to commentators like André who insist that Artaud's later universe is one of a blinded bottle, a shut-off 'necropolis,' this would ignore the numerous struck boxes, or figures emerging from them (rather than trapped within). As Artaud writes about himself, simply, 'Antonin Artaud…the non-coffin.'[50] For Artaud the field of the notebooks is evidence of a 'great reversal.'[51] They are a product of a 'movement that rocks the breath.'[52] This is a movement that perhaps cannot be completely 'done with,' so the motion of creating the new body is contingent upon the consistent and

46 Artaud, Cahier #314, 319/June 1947.

47 Artaud, Cahier #316/ June 1947.

48 Artaud, Cahier #293/May 1947.

49 Artaud, Cahier #287/April 1947.

50 Artaud XX, 1984, p.261.

51 Artaud, Cahier #287/April 1947.

52 Artaud XXI, 1985, p.267.

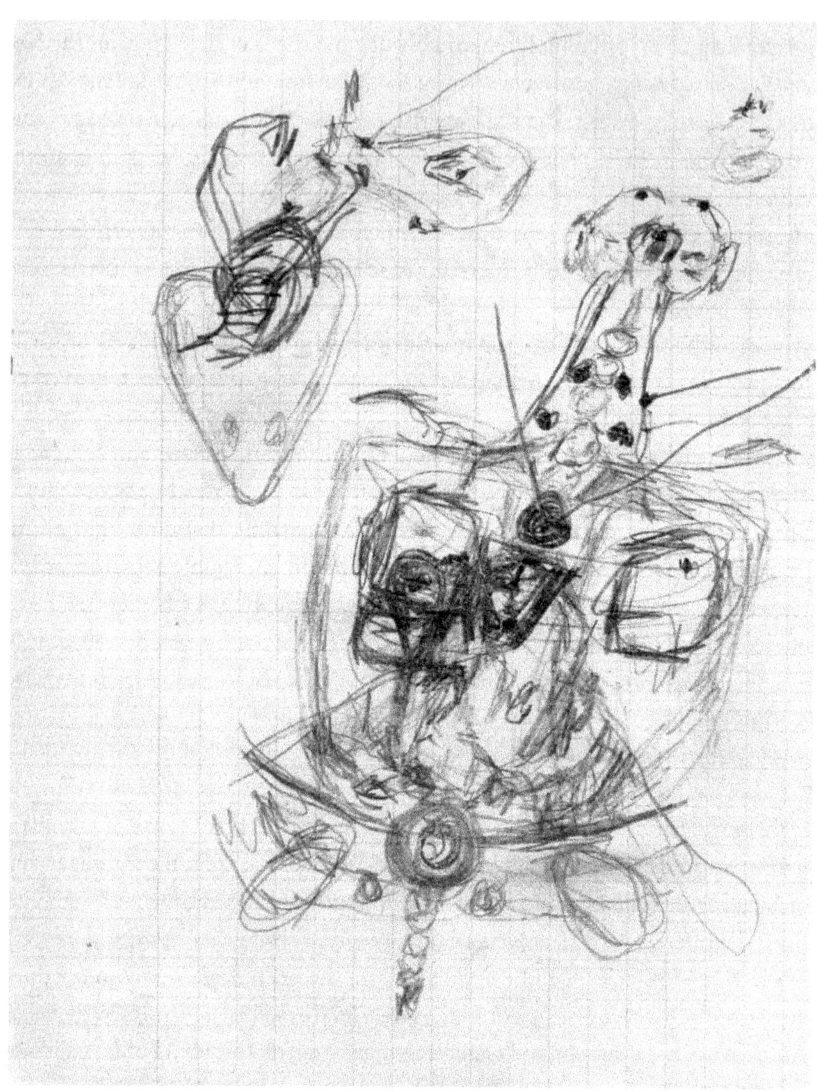

from Cahiers #351, August 1947. © 2016 Artists Rights Society (ARS), New York/ ADAGP, Paris.

constant dismantling of the old one. The early parts of Artaud's notebooks, like his earliest drawings, reflect this, the horror of his confinement and especially of his electroshock treatments,[53] and detailing of the process of dismemberment of the 'old Artaud.' Yet this process, as documented in Artaud's journals and the 'progression' of his visual work, is followed by the emergence of the 'true body,' the 'body without organs.' One process is not possible without the other. In the dismemberment of the older Artaud the hieroglyphic matrix also finds its grave.

It is a process that demands a closing down of *jouissance*, in Lacanian terms, since Artaud's sworn and frequently indicted enemy in the notebooks is sensuality and sexuality. At the same time there is a stubborn joy in his will to new creation. In the same notebook of December 1947 in which Artaud triumphantly affirms that he has indeed 'made/a body,' he writes, 'one burns all the graves of sensuality [in order for it] to disappear.'[54] On the same page Artaud has drawn the outlines of a human figure whose arms juggle or throw two three-sided beams or lines; next to this is a completely abstract form of swirling lines and a small circle. Underneath the drawing Artaud has penned the word *ouverture*, or 'opening.' This notebook, like many in the last four or five months of his life, feature a strong collision of image and text, while Artaud affirms yet again that he will no longer eat, shit, urinate, that he is of no country, no culture, no language. Artaud's 'true body' is based on a program of eradication. This is one reason why Artaud appears so often as a totem, draws so many totems, and refers to himself as the 'totem immutable: myself''[55] – the body is both himself and other; the totem is a double. Paradoxically, this site is still one of transformation, even given its basis in immense pain. In one of Artaud's early writings about his drawings at Rodez, the description of his body serves as a description of the drawing and vice versa, 'a nail of thick wood stuffed with pain.'[56] Much as Artaud will at one point catalogue his bodily organs as a rollcall or index of pain and dysfunction, he will open another notebook with the phrase 'all my flesh my torture.'[57]

The issue of totemisation is crucial to any 'success' or 'failure' of Artaud and his 'body without organs,' and perhaps to his coherence as well. Artaud writes that all he has ever been known to make are totems, walls, bars,[58] but in the later notebooks human figures are shown standing next to coffins or grills, and in one

[53] Artaud's first drawings at Rodez, encouraged as art therapy by Dr. Ferdière, were of dense agglomerations of weapons, constituting a field of protection perhaps. It was these drawings that Ferdière found of 'no interest whatsoever.' When Artaud began drawing on his own initiative in January 1945, his products were frightening displays of extreme bodily torture and dismemberment. Barber, *Artaud: The Screaming Body*, pp.52-3.

[54] Artaud, Cahier #389/December 1947.

[55] Artaud XVII, 1982, p.146.

[56] Artaud XXI, 1985, p.259.

[57] Artaud XVI, 1981, p.215; Artaud, Cahier #295/May 1947.

[58] Artaud XXIII, 1987, pp.484-5.

page from April 1947, there is a figure with large cans or piston-like feet floating or levitating above a bed. Underneath it Artaud has written, 'I am one and not many.'[59] So Artaud's graphics question whether Artaud's 'true body' is walling off all alterity, as commentators like André have insisted,[60] and imply Artaud is rather inventing an alterity more on his own terms. When Artaud depicts himself in the notebooks, the self-portraits are often startling in their emergence. In a notebook from July 1947 there is an elongated, thin, stick-like figure with round ball for pelvis and very large head with one eye, complete with Artaud's familiar shock of hair. Here Artaud portrays himself as a scarified totem. It is in the same notebook that Artaud depicts a figure reaching out of a box as if emerging from the dead, and a bizarre facing off of two forms that seem in equal parts magnetised and repelled from the other. These sort of doubling forms (including what seems to be an outline of a double brain in January 1948) crop up so frequently in the last year of Artaud's notebooks that the contrast is all the more striking that in Artaud's very last notebook, in a set of *cahiers* that are nothing if not a record of intense energetics and pulsions, on Thursday, 4 March, there are forms that seem to be coupling and travelling all in the same direction.

The linchpin of this process of totemisation and transformation is what Artaud calls 'the point of will.'[61] Typical of Artaud's affirmations, Artaud writes, 'I am a man/man/ *en marche*/and it is/while moving…that I/understand/this that I want/while moving/and/while declaiming.' Artaud concludes, 'I will remake the being of the body.'[62] As Artaud writes elsewhere, 'the body does not come from conception and its notion, from a sense or from a sentiment, but from a grievous will that does not ever suffer but exalts while carrying its contradiction.'[63] So this new body is a creation of indomitable will. The emphasis on this is frequent in Artaud's later writings and indeed practiced by him on a daily basis – deteriorating rapidly and dying of cancer yet boarding the metro each day to go into Paris to write and rehearse his radio broadcasts. While Artaud's emphasis on the will – 'I advance, walking'[64] – again recalls Nietzsche,[65] this process is far from being 'beyond good and evil.' On one page of his journals, Artaud asserts the powers of the 'daughters' followed by a drawing of Satan. And Artaud cries,

[59] Artaud, Cahier #285/April 1947.

[60] André, *L'Epreuve d'Antonin Artaud et l'éxperience de la psychanalyse*, p.202.

[61] Artaud, Cahier #312/June 1947.

[62] Artaud, Cahier #390/January 1948.

[63] Artaud XXII, 1986, p.119.

[64] Artaud, Cahier #391/January 1948.

[65] As Nietzsche emphasised in 'Thus Spake Zarathustra': '"It was" – that is the name of the will's gnashing of teeth and most secret melancholy…The will cannot will backwards; and that he cannot break time and time's covetousness, that is, the will's loneliest melancholy…All "it was" is a fragment, a riddle, a dreadful accident – until the creative will says to it, "But thus I willed it."' Nietzsche, *The Portable Nietzsche*, pp.251-3.

I will regenerate myself
from God
I say God
God himself
not the demiurge
...but God
the authentic God
It has only been with the agency of God that
me, Antonin Artaud
that all humanity
has emitted, asphyxiated,
polluted and with the
authentic help of God[66]

Artaud's self-creation and activation of the 'body without organs' is thus a direct challenge and affront to God, an abjection of God, Artaud will say. Artaud is now far from his earlier self – his emphatic rehearsal of totemisation, of the creation of his double or 'true body' through the stark means of will is no longer a plea for connection to the extraordinary hieroglyphs that create all poetry and all reality – Artaud rather poses himself as his own mythic reference and own creation.

The opening to animism: the 'body without organs' as mythic autoreference

It is at this point that I must ask if the 'cartography' that has been invoked from the beginning of this project, and referred to frequently thereafter, that operates without any appeal to 'universals' or necessarily to bound semantic chains of signifiers, is truly sufficient for an approach to Artaud. Deleuze may argue 'never symbolics,' but the late Artaud is arguably more embroiled with 'symbolics' than ever – with the different entities, God, Jesus, Satan and the various real, imaginary or invented 'daughters.' In one of his most crucial post-Rodez manuscripts, the text he prepared for his Vieux-Colombier reading, Artaud does not reject the experience of Jesus Christ and the crucifixion so much as assume it himself. Deleuze and Guattari's notion of 'cartography' can still be held to as a guide through this fearsome territory if we keep in mind Guattari's insistence in his later writings on the importance of passing through the archaic and modes of archaic thought for any renewal and renovation of subjectivisation. Archaic thought was certainly such a resource for Artaud. As Guattari maintained, 'Archaic societies are better armed than White, male, capitalist subjectivities in charting the multivalence and the heterogeneity of components and of semiot-

[66] Artaud, Cahier #296/May 1947.

ics that help bring about the process of subjectivization.'[67] And in the essay cited in Chapter I, when Guattari argues that the limits of theory are such that it can in no way lead to the 'formalization of a sense of the universal in order to affirm itself as a universal truth,' he does so while affirming 'the necessity of...mythic reference.'[68] It is what Guattari is getting at in *Chaosmosis* when he writes, 'Pure creative auto-reference is impossible in the apprehension of ordinary existence. Attempts to represent it can only succeed in masking it, travestying it, disfiguring it, making it pass through mythic and narrative myths of reference – what I call metamodelization.'[69] It is clear that Artaud's 'body without organs' serves as such a meta-model, not only due to the central role it plays in Deleuze and Guattari's *Capitalism and Schizophrenia* project, but also as the paradigm for the current stage of capitalism it plays in Guattari's own social and political writings. Updating the critique from *Anti-Oedipus* Guattari in his bold essay 'Regimes, Pathways, Subjects' (1989) argued that within the domination of 'integrated world capitalism' there is also the advent of the age of 'planetary computerization', which creates 'the possibility for creative and singularizing processuality to become the new fundamental point of reference.'[70] In this situation of potentially liberatory 'existential re-appropriation and self-valorization'[71] Artaud's 'body without organs' becomes the primary meta-model: 'With the figureless and foundationless Body without Organs of self-reference we see spreading before us an entirely different horizon, that of a new machinic processuality considered as the continual point of emergence of all forms of creativity.'[72]

Guattari's sense of 'mythic reference' is also bound up more generally and fundamentally with his notion of any kind of subjectivity as an assemblage (a collection of heterogeneous elements), and the analogy of this notion with archaic thought's animism. This type of conception is useful when looking at the kind of totemisation and animism involved in Artaud's late work, in his essay on Van Gogh, on the creation of his 'body without organs' reflected in his graphic work. Anthropologist Eduardo Viveiros de Castro clarified Guattari's writings on animism in this way –

> Guattari speaks of a subject/object in such a way that subjectivity is just an object among objects and not in a position of transcendence above the world of objects. The subject, on the contrary, is the most common thing in the world. That is animism: the core of the real is the soul, but is not an immaterial soul in

67 Guattari, *Chaosmosis*, p.45.

68 Guattari, *The Guattari Reader*, p.72.

69 Guattari, *The three ecologies*, p.57. Guattari contrasts 'metamodelisation' to 'modelisation' in that the former 'uses terms to develop possible openings onto the virtual and onto creative processuality.' See *Chaosmosis*, p.31.

70 Guattari, *The Guattari Reader*, p.98.

71 Ibid., p.107.

72 Ibid., p.98.

> opposition to or in contradiction with matter. On the contrary, it is matter itself that is infused with soul. Subjectivity is not an exclusively human property, but the basis of the real and not an exceptional form that once arose in the history of the Cosmos.[73]

Guattari used the notions of animism to indicate its greater dimensionality – avoiding pitfalls of both a reductionist modernity and the structuralist flattening out of profoundly rich alterity and communicative practices into solely symbolic interpretations. Citing the work of Marc Augé on the manifold registers of the Legba fetish object in the African societies of the Fon, Guattari emphasises how its heterogeneity is 'not simply of a relational order but of the order of being.'[74] The fetish's use and interpretative praxis is supple and ontological, and cannot be restricted to a symbolic basis. Legba, Guattari enumerates, is a dimension of destiny; a universe of vital principle; an ancestral filiation; a materialised god; a sign of appropriation; an individuated entity; a fetish of the entrance to a house, to the portal of the house, and after an initiation process, to the entrance to the bedroom. It is a handful of sand, a receptacle, and the expression of relation to others. It is eminently a transducer in that emits all sorts of messages, questions and answers; it relates to the dead and the ancestors – 'It is both an individual and a class of individuals; a name and a noun.'[75] Just as Artaud even in the 1930's is not searching for a lost 'origin,' Guattari doesn't advocate this dimensionality as any sort of 'return' to a lost unity, but as a way into understanding contemporary processes of subjectivisation. 'Contemporary machinic assemblages,' Guattari writes, 'have even less standard univocal referent than the subjectivity of archaic societies. But we are far less accustomed to the irreducible heterogeneity, or even the heterogenetic character, of their referential components.'[76] The nature of contemporary subjectivisations, like the Fon fetish object, cannot reasonably be subject to universal translatability. As opposed to structuralist theorising where there is no ontological standing or guarantee for the movement from symbol to symbol, or signifier to signifier, the 'heterogeneous machines' envisaged by Guattari, composed of such widely varied referents and 'partial enunciative components,' he argues, much like the salvo against the

[73] De Castro quoted in Angela Melitopoulos and Maurizio Lazzarato, 'Machinic Animism,' in *Animism*, Vol. I, ed. Anselm Franke, Berlin: Sternberg Press, 2010, p.98. *Animism* was published as the catalogue for the exhibition 'Animism,' at Extra City-Kunsthal Antwerpen and the Museum of Contemporary Art, Antwerp (M KHA), January 22 – May 2, and Kunsthalle Bern, May 15 – July 18, 2010. *Animism* Vol. II was published in conjunction with the iterations of the exhibition in Vienna in 2011 and Berlin in 2012. That a very similar notion of animism was present in Deleuze's philosophy before he met Guattari is maintained in Eric Alliez, *The Signature of the World*, trans. Elliot Ross Albert and Alberto Toscano, London & New York, NY: Continuum, 2004. Also see the discussion in Christian Kerslake's *Deleuze and the Unconscious* (2007).

[74] Augé quoted in Guattari, *Chaosmosis*, p.46.

[75] Guattari, ibid.

[76] Ibid.

'uniformisation of time' in Artaud's *50 drawings to murder magic*, 'do not produce a standard being at the mercy of a universal temporalisation.'[77]

Guattari embraced reviving archaic thought as part of a project of a new general cartography of notions of the 'unconscious' that consisted of nine widely varied 'inputs,' including the first Freudian model of the drives, Sartre's existential psychoanalysis, Pierre Janet's 'automatisms of repetition,' Jung's 'collective unconscious' and its 'imago,' the 'capitalistic unconscious' of MGM and Sony, among others.[78] For my purposes, the most plangent of these is the model of the unconscious Guattari dubbed 'analogical semiotics,' after Herbert Silberer whose analysis of symbolisation in dreams was cited in Freud's *Interpreting Dreams*. Silberer's 'functional interpretation' referred to the ability for symbolic generalisation, for convergence from 'material' symbolisations to more universal ones based on the structure of the psyche.[79] Both Freud and Ernest Jones criticised Silberer's work as having the flaws of Carl Jung's whose notion of symbol-formation belied the operation of the libido and Freud's deferral of desire in the present in the rush to find a meaning in dream-interpretation based on spiritualistic elevation.[80] Guattari resurrects Silberer (and Jung) in that he maintains their model 'should restore specificity to the semiotic productions of archaic societies and the mythological conceptions of subjective productions.'[81] In this archaic thought, 'there is a whole economy of souls, of spirits, a whole apprehension by affect that does not involve discourse on a signifying level, yielding a knowledge of the universe that precedes any discursive process.'[82] Although this model has the virtue of taking us into the occult, Artaud's native habitat, in Silberer and Jung's versions it has also has the profound deficit of bringing us back to the theology Artaud is struggling to free himself from. The original sense of 'analogical interpretation' is indeed the theological one of lifting mystical meanings from literal ones. Jung's version of symbolism was especially difficult to disentangle from his fondness for the idea of enantodromia, that any psychic state (and corresponding symbol), pushed to its extreme, turned into its opposite (Christ into the devil, and vice versa).[83] This point of view is indebted to a

77 Ibid., p.48.

78 Félix Guattari and Suely Rolnik, *Molecular Revolution in Brazil*, trans. Karel Clapshow and Brian Holmes, Los Angeles, CA: Semiotext(e), 2008, pp.308-11.

79 See Herbert Silberer, 'Report on a method of eliciting and observing certain symbolic hallucination-phenomena' [1909] in *Organization and Pathology of Thought*, ed. David Rapaport, New York, NY: Columbia University Press, 1951; and *Hidden Symbolism in Alchemy and the Occult Arts*, trans. Smith Ely Jelliffe, New York, NY: Dover, [1914] 1971.

80 Ernest Jones, 'The theory of symbolism,' *Papers on Psychoanalysis*, Boston, MA: Beacon Press, [1916] 1961.

81 Guattari and Rolnik, *Molecular Revolution in Brazil*, p.309.

82 Ibid., p.310.

83 See for example Jung, *Symbols of Transformation*, pp.375; 438.

classical physics where there is always a possibility of reversibility of processes. It is quite opposed to the principal ideas of Ilya Prigogine and Isabelle Stengers, for example, that Guattari made such use of, such as the 'irreversibility of time' (what Prigogine claimed was the principal discovery of the new physics) that allowed for processes of thermodynamics 'far from equilibrium.' As opposed to the models of classical physics, Prigogine (who was awarded the 1979 Nobel Prize for Chemistry) and Stengers proposed an 'order by fluctuations' whereby fluctuations can lead a system so far away from normal equilibrium that it undergoes an irreversible transformation. One can see how this idea can be directly applied to clinical situations such as Artaud's: instead of recommending that stability be restored by a 'calming down' such as Lacan advised in the case of Artaud, the process could be allowed and even pushed toward a transformation in nature, as in practices of anti-psychiatry, later proposed in a different manner by 'schizoanalysis,' or practiced by 'ethnopsychiatry.' So while analogical thinking as in archaic societies can help restore dimensionality, resonance and a measure of credibility to a discourse like Artaud's that is drenched in such thought, it is also profoundly limited given Artaud's ferocious demolition of representation. What remains relevant is Deleuze's definition of a symbol as an 'intensive compound.'[84] Echoing the definition of the poem in Ezra Pound's Vorticism, it is this notion of a symbol as a sign that is efficacious action, a construct of energy – Deleuze writes that it 'vibrates and expands' but 'has no meaning,'[85] that ultimately escapes the binds of representation, and that most links with the work of the later Artaud.[86]

Artaud on Van Gogh: the totem and the implosion of the hieroglyphic figure

It is Artaud's notion of his drawings as 'machines that breathe,' the totemisation of his 'double body,' the attempt to make a new nature, that make animism a necessary consideration. Artaud's later notebooks, in particular, aim to induct one into Artaud's universe. As he writes at one point of them, simply – 'my

84 Deleuze, *Essays Critical and Clinical*, p.134.

85 Ibid.

86 This still begs the question of Deleuze and Guattari' relationship to Jung's archetypes, which they treat so positively in *A Thousand Plateaus* as establishing extremely flexible series or cycles of conversion of nature into culture and culture into nature due to its prioritisation of the imagination into series of terms and analogies. Deleuze and Guattari, *A Thousand Plateaus*, pp.235-6. Whatever the necessities of a detour onto a 'mythic reference' may be, in Artaud's late work, his utilisation of the scream, especially, aims to escape any recuperation into representational thought or repeatable form of any type. See Jay Murphy, 'Artaud's Scream', *Deleuze Studies* 10.2, 2016, pp.140-161.

signs act.'[87] As I will examine shortly looking more closely at a few of Artaud's drawings, Artaud's totemisation is a necessity for this doubling or 'double body' of his 'body without organs,' and his series of self-portraits, begun with a few rare examples at Rodez in 1944, likewise have the aim of producing his double. This becomes quite explicit as well in his portraits of others, that often feature a violent scarification of the face, that feature Artaud will call an 'empty force, a field of death.'[88] That Artaud's drawings, and any visual work he deems of any value by anyone else, are indeed not *objets d'art* in any usual sense, but animated and living force fields, elements in their own right, is most forcefully expressed in his famous February 1947 essay on Van Gogh. In this essay, there is hardly any sentence about Van Gogh that does not also apply to the author – whether of the malice of psychiatry and family collusions, or the purported force of the works themselves – so Van Gogh is also a double in that sense, and there is yet another doubling operation that with his 'suicide' society puts itself in his place, replacing him. Artaud writes, 'it is the anatomical logic of modern man to never have been able to live nor think of living other than one possessed.'[89] Where Artaud most relates to Van Gogh is the elemental ferocity and transformation, the 'revolving force,'[90] of his painting, that is neither nature, nor Deleuze's 'nature naturing,' but an extraordinary power vision. One could say this is an occult vision, except for Artaud at this stage in his life Van Gogh's paintings ward off and attack the occult. It is '"the great work" of a semipiternal tempestuous transmutation.'[91] It has a tremendous force akin to that of nature – Artaud writes of Van Gogh's paintings as a hail of atoms – but of a different sort. Plucked from the heart, these immense powers are such that 'no one knows…what strange force is in process of being metamorphosed.'[92] For Artaud it is a brooding and sinister 'possible permanent reality.'[93] To get at this meaning, Artaud contrasts Van Gogh to his fractious comrade in painting Paul Gauguin. Gauguin according to Artaud is the lesser artist due to his greater belief in representational thought – he wanted to raise the things of the world to the status of myth and the symbol; Van Gogh, on the other hand, saw that any myth had to be deduced from the most ordinary or earthy things in life, 'because reality is terribly superior to all history, to all fable, to all divinity, to all surreality.'[94] But far more enigmatically, there is an important element of prophecy operating in Van Gogh,

---

87 Artaud, Cahier #364/October 1947.

88 Artaud, *Œuvres*, p.1534.

89 Artaud XIII, 1974, p.21.

90 Ibid., p.46.

91 Ibid., p.26. Typically Artaud uses a term taken from medieval/early Renaissance alchemy (whose definition was 'the Great Work') while indicating a different process.

92 Ibid., p.25.

93 Ibid., p.27.

94 Ibid., p.29.

for I believe that this time,
today,
now
in this month of February, 1947,
it is reality itself,
the myth of reality itself, mythical reality itself which is materializing.[95]

These are transmutations that go far beyond 'apparent reality,' and at the level of consciousness is a 'stage of illumination in which disorderly thought surged back through the invading discharges of matter,/and where thinking is no longer exhausting,/*and no longer exists*/and where the only thing is *to gather bodies*, I mean/TO PILE UP BODIES.'[96] This world that lies beyond consciousness and even the brain is not an astral world into which the discoveries of Nerval and even Van Gogh were sometimes forced, but is that of 'direct creation.'[97] This creation cannot be disentangled from an immense apocalyptic destruction, and this apocalyptic fervor is what Artaud claims continues to smolder in Van Gogh's canvases. This is why in Van Gogh's visage Artaud also sees 'the spellbinding face of a butcher.'[98] Although the emphasis on and calling for a destruction of the world is not new in Artaud, the references to sacrifice specifically in the Van Gogh essay are. Although Artaud was always enamored with the purported macabre roots of any culture, unlike Georges Bataille he was not seduced by the notion of sacrifice itself *per se*. Yet Van Gogh's paintings are an 'iron shadow… It is nature in naked and pure view, such as she reveals herself when one knows to approach it closely':

> Witness this landscape of melted gold, of bronze baked in Ancient Egypt, where an enormous sun leans heavily on rooftops so cowered under the light that they are as if in decomposition.
>
> And I know of no apocalyptic, hieroglyphic, ghost-like or pathetic painting that gives, to me, this sensation of the strangled occult, of a cadaver of a futile hermeticism, head split open, which has rendered on the block its secret.[99]

The 'hieroglyph,' so key and articulate a figure in Artaud's theatre manifestoes more than a decade earlier, is here another inadequate sign under the 'iron shadow' Van Gogh's work casts. The furnace of Van Gogh's work, and, by deep association, Artaud's, is such that no signs or thought can survive, even ones as malleable as the hieroglyphic. Artaud confirms this when he insists that if 'there was neither spirit, nor soul, nor conscience, nor thought,

95 Ibid., pp.29-30.

96 Ibid., p.34.

97 Ibid., p.35.

98 Ibid., p.33. I follow here the translation of Mary Beach and Lawrence Ferlinghetti in *The Artaud Anthology*, p.145.

99 Ibid., p.44.

there was the fulminate
of a ripe volcano,
of trance-stone,
of patience,
of tumors,
of cooked tumor,
and of the scars of the flayed.[100]

In Van Gogh's universe, as in Artaud's, there can be only 'first elements at times chained and unchained.'[101]

Artaud's universe is one of the circulation of souls and spirits, but unlike tribal animisms they are not necessarily found in nature, since nature is also in question. Instead of referring Van Gogh's creations to nature, Artaud argues for the reverse, 'to understand a sunflower in nature, it's necessary now to go back to Van Gogh; just as to understand a storm in nature,/a stormy sky,/a plain in nature,/it will be forever impossible not to return to Van Gogh.'[102] Artaud alternates describing the immense power of Van Gogh's canvases with the universe of sorcery that ultimately killed him. Subject to a 'collective spell' like Nerval or Coleridge or Edgar Allan Poe, Van Gogh died since 'nothing is ever due to chance, and [that] everything bad that happens is because of a conscious, intelligent, concerted ill-will./Which psychiatrists never believe./Which geniuses always believe.'[103] In the final post-script Artaud describes the nights in Paris when the collective spell was cast on Van Gogh in 'certain generalized dirty tricks…one of those mass unfurlings of hatred.'[104] Still Artaud ends his essay on an explosive and surreal note, comparing his own arrival in Paris to the volcanic eruption of Popocatepetl, writing of the mysterious enormous white stone that falls on the corner of Boulevard de la Madeleine and Rue des Mathurins, two streets in Paris that do not in fact intersect.[105]

Derrida's Artaud: the vicissitudes of the 'subjectile'

It is this relation or relationship of Artaud to Van Gogh that allows Derrida to plumb the meanings of the *subjectile* in Artaud, Artaud's operation that is one of maddening, inflaming, or 'unsensing' the *subjectile*.[106] What Derrida analy-

[100] Ibid., p.52.

[101] Ibid., p.53.

[102] Ibid., pp.47-8.

[103] Ibid., pp.35-6.

[104] Ibid., p.63.

[105] Ibid., p.64.

[106] For the history and rareness of this word, bound up with the history of painting, especially of the early Italian Renaissance, see Derrida, *The Secret Art of Antonin Artaud*,

ses as the *subjectile* has a double function, it is the (neutral) surface or support of a representation, but to the extent that it participates in the *jetée* or 'throw' of Artaud's thought it becomes a more dynamised trajectory, it is a membrane with the trajectory (or projectile in Derrida's phrase) passing through its skin as it were.[107] For this to occur, the *subjectile* must not resist so much that it can no longer be a medium, yet it also must be revealed, unveiled as what it is, as not merely a support for something else, a representation. If it resists too much it must be violently attacked so that it remains the medium for the projectile. Derrida stresses how the subjectile is a block, a fiend and a torture, as Artaud writes, 'after having exploded the wall of the problem'[108] – the *subjectile* as an interval that resists the interval. The *subjectile* is a matter of both throwing and being-thrown, Derrida argues, subjected in turn from another throwing, that of birth. The difference between the two (throwing and being-thrown) is typically of Artaud extremely precarious, critical, unstable, reversible. 'Thrown throwing,' Derrida writes, 'the subjectile is nothing...but a solidified interval *between* above and below, visible and invisible, before and behind, this side and that.'[109] It is in this double constraint of resistance but not so much resistance that it cannot overcome, in this interval of laying down and throwing, Derrida argues, the *subjectile* is neither subservient nor dominating, neither subject nor object, in fact it becomes unrepresentable.[110] In this difficult double role, the *subjectile* is a 'figure of the other toward which we should give up projecting anything at all.'[111]

This process of Artaud's is a sort of 're-routing of the process of birth' so that his becoming is not stolen but available to the 'true body' being constructed.[112] Since according to Artaud man has been 'badly constructed,' the present body must be re-arranged; perception itself and the vision of things is disturbed and mistaken, and 'this conjunctivitis is endemic to being.'[113] This entails that in order to be seen anew any (designed) work must be upended and destroyed. This process involves the play of words, surely, as Derrida notes, Artaud's passages in the Van Gogh essay through motif, motet, and so on constitute a play through the surface or formal attraction of the words, and although through this attraction 'you draw or sing rather than speaking, you write the unwritable,' and this is part of Artaud's aim, it also does something else and something more—it

---

pp.63-5.

107 Ibid., p.76.

108 Artaud XIV:1, 1978, p.135.

109 Derrida, *The Secret Art of Antonin Artaud*, p.78.

110 Ibid., p.77.

111 Ibid., p.78.

112 Edward Scheer, 'Sketches of the jet,' *100 Years of Cruelty*, p.62. Like Derrida, Scheer compares this process to an abortion, or re-abortion.

113 Ibid.

envokes the multiplicity of voices of a motet in Van Gogh's painting.[114] For although Artaud writes of Van Gogh as a 'tremendous musician' and puts him in the league of his favourite *poètes maudits*, so that Van Gogh is also in some sense a writer, emphasising the shifting modalities of perception characteristic of a Van Gogh work, Artaud also treats Van Gogh as 'pure painting,' and 'nothing else but a painter.'[115] The potentials Van Gogh ignites are those vibrations still to be utilised in painting for Artaud, returning to the site of his early art criticism in the 1920s on Masson, Picasso, Balthus and other figures. When Artaud writes 'It is nature in naked and pure view, such as she reveals herself when one knows to approach it closely,'[116] Derrida reads this as

> Music, nature, seeing: the same: seen. Such a proximity confines you to madness, but the one that snatches from you the other madness, the madness of stagnation, of stabilization in the inert when sense becomes a subjectivized theme, introjected or objectivized, and the *subjectile* a tomb. But you can force the tomb.[117]

Artaud is definitively 'forcing' the properties and supports of representation, to be sure, but for Derrida this entails a 'forcing' or 'unsensing' of the *subjectile* until 'unsensed from birth – it gives way to the innate which was assassinated there one day.'[118] Artaud indeed writes in the Van Gogh essay that 'the suffering of the prenatal is there,'[119] yet it seems a far reach to maintain, as Derrida does, that this is part and parcel of Artaud's wanting to restore some innate or original state. This would make the construction of the 'true body' less creative and unprecedented than in fact it is, less of a 'direct creation.' It makes Artaud a kind of naive ecologist or even, as Derrida has insisted, a 'man of the Enlightenment.'[120] This reading of Artaud can be reconciled with many of his pronouncements of the 1930s, though even this will be strained, however, it is far more difficult to describe the post-Rodez Artaud in this manner. Derrida sees no shift, change, or development from the early Artaud before the journey to the land of the Tarahumaras in 1936, and the Artaud in 1946-8 who has emerged from nine years of asylum confinement. This insistence by Derrida is all the more odd since he realises that in writing the essay on Van Gogh Artaud is giving himself over to a process, to the throw or jet which is a trajectory of cruelty, 'just at the moment when he is refusing to describe the stability of a painting.'[121] This process or experiment, Derrida realises, moves through and against different perceptual

[114] Derrida, *The Secret Art of Antonin Artaud*, p.73.

[115] Artaud XIII, 1974, p.48.

[116] Ibid., p.43.

[117] Derrida, *The Secret Art of Antonin Artaud*, p.74.

[118] Ibid.

[119] Artaud XIII, 1974, p.43.

[120] See Derrida, Lecture on Artaud at MOMA, 10 October 1996.

[121] Derrida, *The Secret Art of Antonin Artaud*, p.75.

modalities, it

> is *modalized* and disperses itself in the trajectories of the *objective*, the *subjective*, the *projectile*, *introjection*, *objection*, *dejection*, and *abjection*...The subjectile remains between these different *jetées*, whether it constitutes its underlying element, the place and context of birth, or interposes itself, like a canvas, a veil, a paper 'support,' the hymen between the inside and outside, the upper and the lower, the over here or over there, or whether it becomes in turn the *jetée*, not this time like the motion of something thrown but like the hard fall of a mass or inert stone in the port, the limit of an '*arrested* storm,' a dam.[122]

The essence of Derrida's criticism is not so removed from that of a Lacanian analyst like Serge André's, they both see a block or repression in the position of the sheet of paper, the canvas, a substrate Artaud can never completely overcome, sublate or sublimate. Yet Derrida identifies in Artaud the *jetée*, the throw, that precisely in its scattering and motion in-between objective and/or subjective qualities makes a flux of now confused psychoanalytic nomenclatures. Separating this throw from matter itself is not possible for Deleuze and Guattari in their description of the 'body without organs;' it is questionable whether it is possible for Artaud himself. For Artaud it is this rhythmic fluctuation that is supreme, and brings into play the power of 'direct creation' and any mutually arising space-time complexes. Characteristic of this in regard to the 'true body' is Artaud's drawing in October 1947 of a vertical column of three heads or faces stretched beyond recognition, almost inside-out, their faciality or facial features subjected to an immense overhaul, accompanied by passages that insist that it was 'uniquely/from evil/that [I] will succeed/in making my own body.'[123] It is in the same notebook that Artaud writes 'me, Antonin Artaud, does not think anything.' The throw, or the *jet*, is Artaud's thought itself, as long as we recognise these gestures as infinite. Artaud has recognised in Van Gogh another artist who lives for and in the infinite; it is the refusal of life in the infinite by society that mandates Van Gogh's death.[124]

In Derrida's interpretation this insistence on the infinite is one of 'Force before form...this is Antonin Artaud's thought itself'[125] – this 'thought' that is the throwing, the gesture of compulsion and expulsion. This has to be bound up with an impossible presence for Derrida, since as he wrote in an early essay on Freud, 'there is no life present at first which would then come to protect, postpone, or reserve itself in *différence*.'[126] What is at issue here is whether Artaud is involved in a reappropriation, although he claims quite explicitly his drawings

[122] Ibid.

[123] See Artaud, Cahier #368/October 1947.

[124] Artaud XIII, 1974, pp.60-1.

[125] Derrida, *The Secret Art of Antonin Artaud*, p.76.

[126] Derrida, 'Freud and the Scene of Writing,' *Writing and Difference*, p.203.

do not seek some 'truth and lost *mécanique* they rediscover.'[127] In lectures on Artaud, Derrida has maintained he 'resists everything in this work that in the name of a proper body, a reaffirmed body without organs, a reappropriation of self consistent with an ecological, naturalist protest' that would deny or protest the various protheses, parasites, specters, supports of reproductive representation; in short, Artaud's 'metaphysical rage for reappropriation.'[128] Yet Artaud is not reappropriating his body as much as creating a new one. As he writes in one of his last notebooks, 'within the body there is not anything.'[129] Artaud's advocacy of the gesture is so complete it is not possible to say that through it he is merely affirming a prior presence. Even given all the battles with God and Christ and evil in Artaud's notebooks – and the existence of evil never stops being very real for Artaud – in one of his last notebooks there are long passages questioning the existence of that ultimate presence, God.[130] Derrida emphasises Artaud's *coups* or *corps*, homonyms that Artaud used as doubles, his mark that is invariably a double-mark, a doubling that contains a purity and therefore resists any homeopathic function, that is more than evil against evil.[131] But rather than viewing Artaud's double-mark as a desperate holding onto through a gesture of purity, one can more easily see it as a 'double articulation' in Deleuze's sense.[132] This would make such mark-making a kind of eternal recurrence, in Deleuze and Guattari's sense that 'each stratum is double.'[133] The first articulation draws deterritorialised flows, or molecular becomings (of the virtual or the 'body without organs') into a plane of consistency (a 'statistical order of connections and successions').[134] The second articulation constructs functional, stable forms and structures, 'molar compounds in which these structures are simultaneously actualized.'[135] How to make the body an organism, Deleuze and Guattari write, is precisely a problem of such articulation. In a more Nietzschean sense, the first articulation (Dionysus, for example) is an affirmation that can only be recognised as an affirmation when it is repeated as a second reaffirmation or articulation (that of Ariadne).[136] It is in this way that any 'abstract machine' in Deleuze and Guattari is composed of such double articulations or double binds, and

[127] Artaud, *Œuvres*, p.1536.

[128] Derrida, Lecture on Artaud at MOMA, 10 October 1996.

[129] Artaud, Cahier #312/June 1947.

[130] Artaud, Cahier #385/December 1947.

[131] Derrida, Lecture on Artaud at MOMA, 10 October 1996.

[132] For a sample explanation of double articulation see Deleuze and Guattari, *A Thousand Plateaus*, pp.40-1.

[133] Ibid., p.40.

[134] Ibid.

[135] Ibid., p.41. This example is the passage or 'folding' from sediment to sedimentary rock, though its applications are almost infinitely variable.

[136] For the Nietzschean analogy see Bell, *Philosophy at the Edge of Chaos*, p.226.

which draws out from the chaos any identifiable immanence or plane of consistency. Artaud's gestural drawings are eminently such a double articulation putting into motion a machine of becoming, rather than affirming his entrapment in the codified, organic body, his marks are his construction of an organless one.

I will conclude this critique of Derrida's limitations in regard to Artaud by returning to the notion of the *subjectile* as a 'figure of the other.'[137] It is in attempting to answer whether the *subjectile* is truly and properly a figuration or figure of the other, and if it is possible for this figuration to accept any limits, that Derrida returns to the term pictogram. Rather than pictographic in the terms of the hieroglyphic that has been explored in this project, in terms of relation to a primary or original writing, the action of spells, language as the 'book of nature' or of the psyche as in medieval and early Renaissance alchemy, Derrida explores it in the sense that has also been broached here and from the beginning, in terms of movement between modalities of senses, between media, how one perception depends for its existence on a perception in an entirely different register. To Derrida this is the pictographic that crosses the border quite *literally* between painting and drawing, drawing and 'verbal writing,' but more generally, that which crosses the borders between space and time, in short that which ultimately 'assures the synergy of the visible and invisible.'[138] This 'rhythmic projection' and 'inscription of a projectile' is beyond the usual opposition of word/image, and is precisely what Artaud means when he calls his notebooks 'written drawings'[139] in a letter written at Rodez in 1945. What Artaud accomplishes on a notebook page is the erasure of this limitation or opposition of word and image. In Derrida's view, 'Everything is singular each time and each time analogical: a figuration of the other.'[140] Yet to attribute Artaud's border erasures of what is 'drawing' and what is 'writing' to a kind of infinitely refracted mirror play, a mise-en-abyme, is to reduce Artaud's prodigious doubling to the same, precisely where he is introducing difference. This pictogram according to Derrida operates as a device of destabilisation, but within a 'relationship of representation…destabilization made into work.'[141] With a meticulous respect to Artaud's process, Derrida nevertheless reinforces Artaud's productions as 'works' and a denial of what Artaud has entered into since his visit to the Tarahumaras.[142] In

137 Derrida, *The Secret Art of Antonin Artaud*, p.78.

138 Ibid., pp.78-9.

139 Artaud XI, 1974, p.20.

140 Derrida, *The Secret Art of Antonin Artaud*, p.79.

141 Ibid., p.80.

142 Compare the rousing rhetoric of André Breton's tribute in his 'Tribute to Antonin Artaud,' that is also an affirmation of Artaud's 'double and triple' worlds – 'I know that Antonin Artaud *saw*, the way Rimbaud, as well as Novalis and Arnim before him, had spoken of *seeing*. It is of little consequence, ever since the publication of *Aurèlia*, that what was *seen* this way does not coincide with what was *objectively visible*.' André Breton, *Free Rein*, trans. Michel Parmentier and Jacqueline d'Amboise, Lincoln, NE:

the context of Artaud's notebooks especially, the drawings trigger beings and writing of them activates visual signs as hexes to exorcise them. There is hardly a page where Artaud is not obsessed with the operation whereby 'I nail and abject there where they are.'[143] And the exclusive concern with the vagaries of the *subjectile*, a term that appears in Artaud only three times in all of his published work, risks slighting the real physical mutations Artaud tracks. With all of the limitations of the psychoanalytic tradition, ironically this is not the case with an acute reading such as Julia Kristeva's, that posits Artaud's dilemma in terms of drives:

> In a man, Artaud, the fundamental sign/body of enunciative truth can only be castration. In Artaud's texts, Abelard and Heliogabalus are perhaps not mere fantasies, but rather the necessary culmination of the process of "true" writing. This is so corroborated by the *jouissance* of the text describing these bodies, these moments of castration.[144]

With what Kristeva insists are 'corporeal fundamentals...biological limits,'[145] Artaud cannot be successful in his later rhythmic drive to double the body, to create a 'body without organs,' what Deleuze will characterise as a 'powerful, non-organic vitality' of desire.[146] The conflicts and successes, as well as missed dilemmas, of these interpretations are best played out, I will argue here in my conclusion to this chapter, in what Artaud himself regarded as his graphic legacies and 'mini-model' – the breathing, battling remains of his graphic work and the recordings of his screaming body.

Artaud's 'graphic cruelties': the face of the void

Instead of the immediate effect of the spells, Derrida put his faith, rather, in a postponed effect, or deferral, citing the banning of *To have done with the judgment of god* in Artaud's lifetime, but its ready availability today on compact

University of Nebraska Press, 1995, p.78-9.

143 Artaud, Cahier #390/January 1948.

144 Julia Kristeva, 'The True-Real,' in *The Kristeva Reader*, ed. Toril Moi, New York, NY: Columbia University Press, 1986, p.236. The relation of Artaud to any castration complex is a moot issue there is not sufficient room to explore in this project; his 'body without organs' would be a concerted attempt to surpass this psychoanalytic limit as well. For an introduction to how Artaud's doubling or absolute reversibility of the world is based on anti-sexuality or non-genitality see Rex Butler, 'Non-Genital Thought,' *100 Years of Cruelty*, pp.33-56.

145 Kristeva, 'Artaud: Madness and Revolution/Interview with Julia Kristeva,' *100 Years of Cruelty*, p.276.

146 Deleuze, *Essays Critical and Clinical*, p.131.

disc.[147] Uncannily, the issues Derrida raises here are the wedded ones of Artaud's efficacy and immortality. As the painter André Masson so strongly emphasised about Artaud to author Sylvère Lotringer, the issue of 'prestige' was always foremost on Artaud's agenda – playing for all and playing for keeps.[148] This is nowhere more true than in Artaud's drawings, what Derrida called Artaud's 'graphic cruelties,'[149] that in the notebooks themselves seem to gain greater and greater autonomy. There has been speculation that what Artaud wanted for his last will and testament was a wicked pact just the opposite of Kafka's with Max Brod – Kafka swore Brod to destroy his work in the expectation he would do just the opposite. Artaud left the bulk of his drawings for safe keeping with Paule Thévenin in the expectation that she would follow his secret wishes and destroy them in a final fury of immolation.[150] Given Artaud's vehement rejection of any participation in the Parisian art world in his final letter to André Breton, one would expect that hanging his drawings in museums would be the last thing he would want. Museums and art galleries are part of the matrix of repression of the 'Holy Family,' as malicious as the state or the family.[151] Leaving aside the theorist Gayatri Spivak's point that the emergence of an 'Artaud industry' demonstrates that Artaud has been snapped up by the latter day 'culture industry'[152] – what are Artaud's drawings doing? In his terms, how do they 'act'? Made independently, fused with his notebooks, or emerging full-blown out of them, in actuality, they provide an ongoing cartography of Artaud's 'body without organs.' Through the engulfment Artaud aims for any kind of hieroglyphic evocation appears a thing of the past and Artaud clearly seems to no longer have any use for this as a term. Artaud writes in the *Suppôts et suppliciations*, for instance, that '*papa-mama* itself will have ceded the place to man, without hieroglyphics and secret keyboard'[153] – that is, without signs and without mysticism, without any 'zig zags' of sacred geometry.

147 Derrida, 'Artaud: Writing/Drawing,' at Drawing Center, 11 October 1996; Antonin Artaud, *Pour en finir avec le jugement de dieu*, CD. Brussels: Sub Rosa, 1996 (a single disc of *To have done with the judgment of god*); there is also Artaud's *Pour en finir avec le jugement de dieu*, Marseilles: André Dimanche Éditeur, 1995 (a boxed set of all of Artaud's radio recordings).

148 Lotringer in 'Sick, Evil and Violent,' *100 Years of Cruelty*, p.306.

149 Derrida, Lecture on Artaud at MOMA, 10 October 1996.

150 See Barber, *Terminal Curses*, p.116-8. As Barber writes, 'Artaud's 406 notebooks did not necessarily have to survive...Thévenin always subsequently believed that by obeying Artaud, she had betrayed him.' Ibid., pp.117-8.

151 As Derrida points out, as early as 1923 Artaud is questioning the technical qualities that go into any work of art. This aesthetic quality of *principe du dessin*, as opposed to creation emitted by the nerves and the body remains a target of the late Artaud.

152 Spivak's statement was made during the group panel 'Artaud: Writing/Drawing' at The Drawing Center, 11 October 1996.

153 Artaud XIV:1, 1978, p.151.

The human visage is a primary force for Artaud in his drawings, and not only because he did so many portraits, in a few cases commissioned to do so.[154] When Artaud writes of the void, he uses the face as his name for it. For instance in *Suppôts et suppliciations*, Artaud writes of the 'unfathomable abyss of the face':

> for god in his true name is named Artaud, and it's the name of this kind of unnameable thing between the abyss and nothingness,/which has something of the abyss and nothingness,/and that is neither called or named;/and it appears that it is a body too,/and that Artaud is a body too,/not the idea, but the fact of the body,/and the fact that what is nothingness should be the body,/the unfathomable abyss of the face, of the inaccessible surface level through which the body of the abyss is revealed...the abyss body.[155]

As Derrida recognised in his explication of Artaud, Artaud's war against sublimation and artistic canonisation was often waged on behalf of the face, and the experience of the face, what Derrida termed the 'virtual prosthesis of the gaze.'[156] Artaud wrote in his powerful and poignant, short text 'The Human Face' that the human visage is all that remains of 'the old revolutionary demand of a form that was never in keeping with this body, which left to be something other than the body.'[157]

As already recounted, Artaud's earliest drawings at Rodez consisted of fields of weapons, and fearsome diagrams of a disintegrated body. A charcoal drawing of 1944 featuring swords and staffs strongly recall the implements of African spiritual rituals, included in shrines to Ogun, god of fire, for example.[158] Artaud was no stranger to drawing, portraits or graphic designs, since not only did Artaud execute many sketches for scene décor for his theatre projects, even earlier, from 1915-21 he had also completed portraits, self-portraits and expressionist-style watercolors. These would all be beholden to some extent to the *principe du dessin* he later castigates.[159] In the earliest drawings at Rodez, Artaud often seems concerned with filling the space completely, as in his *Being and its fetuses* (January 1945), or *Never Real but Always True* of the same month.[160] (It is in this latter drawing that Artaud writes it derives from the Sudan and the Daho-

---

[154] There were two commissioned portraits by Artaud, neither has been found. Thévenin, 'Search for a lost world,' *The Secret Art of Antonin Artaud*, n.74, p.52.

[155] Artaud XIV:1, 1978, pp.146-7.

[156] Derrida, Talk at MOMA, October 10 1996.

[157] Artaud, *Œuvres*, p.1534.

[158] As noted, Artaud often compared his work to African rituals. For a summary of the Yoruba African deities, that in various forms carried over to the New World in *santería* and *candomblé* rites, and remain strongly present in the Old World, see Daniel Lainé and Tobie Nathan, *African Gods: Contemporary Rituals and Beliefs*, Paris: Flammarion, 2007.

[159] For a detailed introduction to Artaud's history of engagement with visual art, see Paule Thévenin, 'Search for a lost world,' in *The Secret Art of Antonin Artaud*, pp.3-56.

[160] See ill. 11 and ill. 14 in *Antonin Artaud: Works on Paper*, pp.63; 66.

mey in Africa, not from 'art'). In these first drawings Artaud could have been moved above all by the horror of his electroshock treatments and his perceived disintegration of the body. Electroshock is associated with a horror of the void, the threat of complete annihilation. What shows up as an extremely active and acute use of the voids and emptiness of space in the various notebook pages is also in the drawings of teeming heads and faces. Whether or not one attributes this to Artaud's horror of the void, this is also characteristic of his last drawings at Ivry-sur-Seine shortly before his death: drawings that are fields of faces and heads written-over and drawn-over in barely recognisable (the faces are of self and friends) near-cacophony.[161] Much as Artaud in his notebooks would at times list bodily organs and their dysfunction, their pain, or their doubling,[162] his drawings at Rodez – *The Machine of Being* (January 1946) or *The Immaculate Conception* (January 1945) for instance – would show the imagery of this body or bodies in all their heterogeneous instability. This operation of separating elements out into their ultimate micro-fragmentation (as Artaud often refers to 'microbes' and 'microbes of being' in his notebooks), however provoked in Artaud's instance by the violence of psychiatric torture and isolation, has continuity with the notions of surrealist collage. As interestingly or ironically enough, Jacques Lacan in describing how drives would have to be pictured, invokes just this example of surrealist montage. It would not be a montage, Lacan argues, derived from any action with finality – he gives as an example a specific form such as a cardboard outline of a falcon that makes a hen head for cover. Rather,

> The *montage* of the drive is a *montage* which, at first, is presented as having neither head nor tail – in the sense in which one speaks of *montage* in a surrealist collage. If we bring together the paradoxes we just defined at the level of *Drang*, at that of the object, at that of the aim of the drive, I think that the resulting image would show the working of a dynamo connected to a gas-tap, a peacock's feather emerges, and tickles the belly of a pretty woman, who is just lying there looking beautiful. Indeed, the thing begins to become interesting from this very fact, that the drive defines, according to Freud, all the forms of which one may reverse such a mechanism. This does not mean that one turns the dynamo upside-down – one unrolls its wires, it is they that become the peacock's feather, the gas-tap goes into the lady's mouth, and the bird's rump emerges in the middle.[163]

What is to the point here is not a superficial analogous relation between images of the drives and some kinds of surrealist art, but is in the context Lacan makes this comparison, which follows Freud's assertion that the object is strictly indif-

[161] See ill.s 66, 67, and 68 that date January-February 1948, ibid., pp.130; 131; 133.

[162] For example in Artaud XXI, 1985, p.123.

[163] Jacques Lacan, *The Seminar of Jacques Lacan, Book XI, The Four Fundamental Concepts of Psychoanalysis*, ed. Jacques Alain-Miller, trans. Alan Sheridan, New York, NY & London: W. W. Norton, [1973] 1998, p.169. Italics in original.

ferent to the drive, indeed, is '*a matter of total indifference*.'[164] This leads Lacan to posit how pleasure is not 'located' in erogenous zones, but that 'Desire is concerned – thank God, we know only too well – with something quite different, and even with something quite different from the organism, while involving the organism at various levels.'[165] This is an opening to the exploration of the assemblage of desire that one finds throughout Artaud's drawings, that are also a plea against reduction either to drives or organismic functioning.

Artaud leads one to consider processes of the 'body without organs' as a doubling or totemisation in multiple ways. In one of his most eloquent later texts on his drawings, Artaud refers to them as 'the innate totem of man' -

> The amulet to come back to man
> All the breaths in the dugout curvature
> hollow
> pesti-ferous
> of my real teeth.
>
> Not one that isn't a
> breath launched
> with all the force
> of my lungs
> of all the skein
> of my respiration...[166]

In the first drawings at Rodez, having experienced death and a profound out-of-the-body occurrence during electroshock treatments, Artaud is grappling with discovering what form or 'innate totem' remains. This seems the point to a drawing in graphite and crayon of September 1945, the first one Artaud signs with his name. *Couti l'anatomie*, or *To price anatomy* is filled with micro collections and connections of bones and body parts, as if to assess and document an immense still active and breath-full fragmentation. The words strung across the top and bottom of the drawing refer to the scattering of bones. The phrase *os sema*, Évelyne Grossman elucidates, derives from a play on the Greek, and brings to mind the 'Pythagorean soma-sema,' the body-tomb into which the soul has fallen.[167] In a text Artaud wrote about this drawing at Rodez, he refers to an 'existence lost before birth,' but speaks of it as a resource for 'reassembling a new human body. This drawing represents the effort that I take in this moment to remake the body with the bone of the musics of the soul...'[168] Artaud's texts in his drawings as in his notebooks provide a meta-commentary on the proceedings; typical of this is the text for an October 1945 drawing that reads 'the

[164] Ibid., p.168. Italics in original.

[165] Ibid., p.172.

[166] Artaud, 'Dix ans que le langage es parti,' *Œuvres*, pp.1515-6.

[167] Grossman in Artaud, *Œuvres*, n.1, p.1037.

[168] Artaud, *Œuvres*, p.1037.

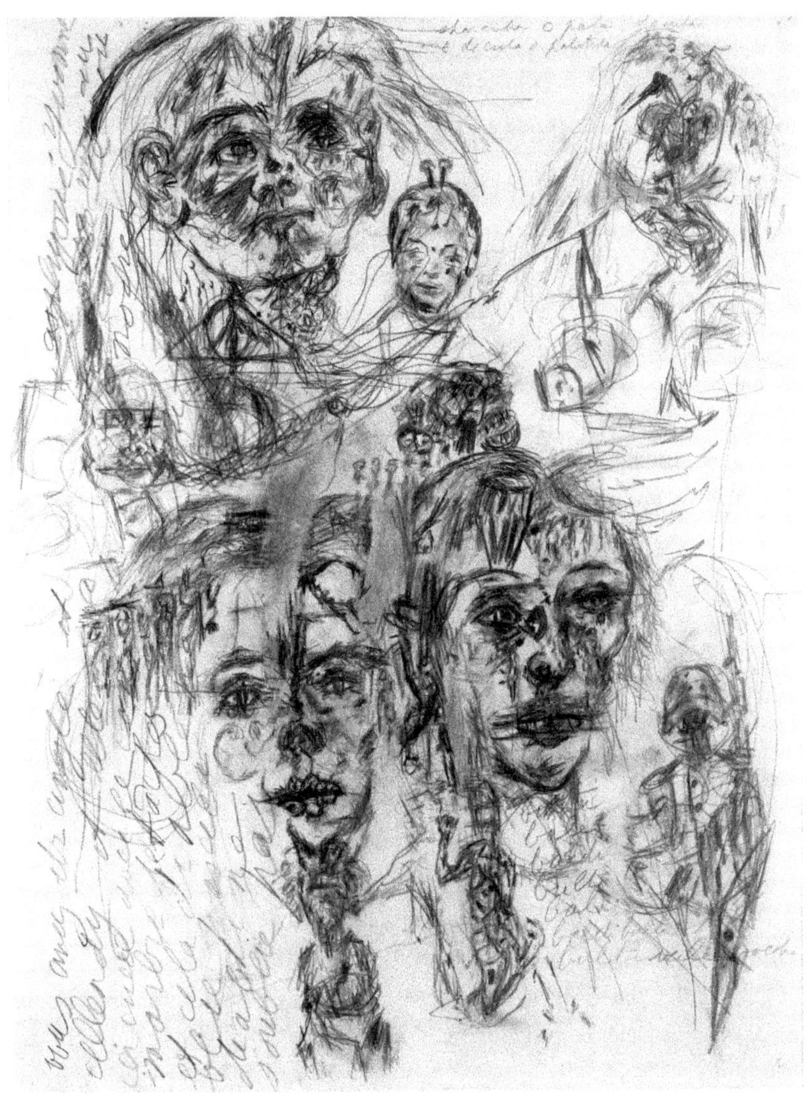

Untitled, January 1948 (crayon, 64 x 49 cm). © 2016 Artists Rights Society (ARS), New York/ADAGP, Paris

gallows of the chasm/ is being and not/its soul/and this is its body.'[169] Despite some of his writings about the drawings at Rodez during his 'religious' phases, this re-construction has little to do with bringing back any original form *before* it was stolen, in a 'search for a lost world'[170] in Paule Thévenin's words, rather than a re-creation.

Artaud's drawings would remain an unbearably stark record of human destruction, what Barber has called 'an imagery of the irreparable' comparable to the drawings of the same period by concentration camp inmates, except for the traces of new human figures in the wreckage.[171] This is symbolised in *Totem* (December 1945 – February 1946),[172] where a figure trailing boxes and sporting bleeding legs, one apparently a sawed off stump, is fitted with an animal or totemic head (most closely resembling a horse). The figure is nailed in the middle, as crucified as many of the figures or nailed, pinned, scarified totems that will crop up in Artaud's notebooks. Despite his torture, Artaud is tracking the morphing of a new form. Once again, the enduring importance of Artaud's Tarahumara experience is underlined. Artaud's enthusiasm for the totemism he expected to be alive and well in the Mexico of 1936 was expressed in his text 'The Reawakening of the Thunder-Bird' (1935), where he heralded the

> magical procedure that consists of linking the destiny of an individual, of a clan, of a country or of a sect with the life of a beast, the *durée* of an animal species… Through this identification, through this symbolism which is not imaginary but real, the Mexicans avow and proclaim living forces, the violent blood, the active and magnetic fluid that they have attracted and that they are able to attract still through their commerce with animals.[173]

His late notebooks contain passages discussing again the language or 'signs' of animals, animal-life, animal-beings.[174] In this time of crisis if not resurrection, Artaud in *Totem* shows a human totemising or metamorphosing, 'becoming-animal' in Deleuze and Guattari's parlance.[175] Although Artaud in his text

---

169 Ill. 16 in *Antonin Artaud: Works on Paper*, p.68.

170 The title of Paule Thévenin's essay in *Antonin Artaud, dessins et portraits* (1986).

171 Barber, *Artaud: The Screaming Body*, p.54. As Barber notes, the drawings by concentration camp inmates show fellow prisoners and the environment of wooden barracks and barbed wire, prison guards and dying friends, memories of sorely missed homes and families. In Artaud's remarkably internal and solitary record, there is no such 'human solidarity' to be found.

172 Ill. 18 in *Antonin Artaud: Works on Paper*, p.71.

173 Artaud, *Œuvres*, p.673.

174 See for example in Artaud Cahier #364/October 1947.

175 For their notion of 'becomings-animal' differentiated from the usual accounts of myth or totemism, see Deleuze and Guattari, *A Thousand Plateaus*, pp.242-3; 257-60. It is differentiated largely due to the animal predilection for the pack over the type of 'family' filiation totem often signifies, and totemism's reliance on symbolic correspondence. This is one of the reasons Lévi-Strauss wrote about totemism as the predecessor to

from *Messages révolutionnaires* just quoted is still using the old language of identification, it is in reference to Artaud's later drawings that Deleuze and Guattari's definition of the construction of an assemblage is most apt – 'an infinite undertaking…that is affect in itself, the drive in person, and represents nothing.'[176] Artaud's drawing-assemblages do not rely on any symbolic correspondence, but rather the destruction of it; this includes the notion of a hieroglyphic unifying or structuring of reality.

This process of doubling or totemisation, that in fact has little in common with psychoanalytic identification, is also if not most at work in Artaud's numerous portraits of self and others. This is most starkly present in his last drawing at Rodez in May 1946: he depicts what is titularly a self-portrait, but the main head or portrait-image seems composed of both heads that are also drawn smaller in size to its lower left and right.[177] Artaud appears to have drawn the visages of both himself and Dr. Ferdière, and then merged them in a ferocious struggle. An assistant psychiatrist to Ferdière Artaud was fond of, Dr. Jean Dequeker, witnessed the act of the drawing:

> On a large sheet of white paper, he had drawn the abstract corpus of a face, and within this barely sketched material – where he had planted the black marks of future apparitions – and without a reflecting mirror, I saw him create his double, as though in a crucible, at the cost of an unspeakable torture and cruelty. He worked with fury, shattering pencil after pencil, suffering the internal throes of his own exorcism…I saw him blindly dig out the eyes of the image.[178]

The 'double' here is much like a shamanic 'ally' that first seeks to kill one, whose force must be mastered, turned around and one's own power reasserted in a struggle for survival. Artaud battles with the force of his sitters not only in this portrait. In the combined portrait of Artaud/Ferdière Artaud attempts to draw out and excavate the neglected anatomy or destiny of an individual and manifest it. The face of Artaud with its particular bone-structure often crops up in his portraits of others.[179] What Dequeker described was Artaud's standard operating procedure. Paule Thévenin, who sat for three portraits, then in her early twenties, described the experience as 'being skinned alive.'[180] Artaud could often begin his portraits with an accurate, academic likeness and then ground in lines and marks and images of nails and weapons into the paper in an aggressive, of-

the State and State-forms.

176 Ibid., p.259.

177 Ill. 32 in *Antonin Artaud: Works on Paper*, p.86.

178 Jean Dequeker, 'Naissance de l'image' [1950], in *Artaud Vivant*, ed. O. Virmaux, Paris: Oswald Èditeur, 1980, pp.155-6.

179 Barber, *Artaud: The Screaming Body*, p.63.

180 Ibid.

ten frightening assault, until the visage had been utterly transformed.[181] Artaud told Paule Thévenin that in her portrait of 24 May 1947 'I have given you the face of an old empress from a barbaric era.' To Jany de Ruy, a young woman who also found the experience of sitting for Artaud a frightening experience, Artaud told her that her portrait was 'a head of weapons.'[182] After the subject had sat for several hours, Artaud would habitually work on the final product alone in his pavilion. It is in this final solitary process that Artaud unleashed an intense, gestural work of scarification – mutilating, charging, assaulting the image in the process of emanating another one – a process Artaud wanted no one else to witness. In the instance of the May '47 portrait of Paule Thévenin her face becomes magnetically surrounded by blocks of metal and shards of metal and nail seem to blast off from her face in a portrait that has now added some fifty years onto her actual age.[183] Typically, Artaud has written around the face on all sides, not just top and bottom, so that to read the writing, and to identify all the images, one must turn the paper in each possible direction. Here, Artaud has written in part, 'I place my daughter in sentinel…' putting Thévenin among the 'daughters of the heart' that were the subject of many drawings, and referenced in others.

It is not only that certain works were titled *Theater of cruelty* (March 1946) or *The projection of the true body* (1946-8) that Artaud's drawings can be seen as another realisation or 'mini-model' of the violent gestural combustion Artaud called for in his Theater of cruelty. They function in the manner Artaud wanted his largely unrealised theatre and film projects to. With the eyes of the portrayed sitter confronting the eyes of the viewer, what Artaud had called the process of provoking an 'unsticking of the retina,' an opening to experience the vulnerability of the body, to encounter its hidden layers or folds, is at first glance akin to Ethiopian medicinal scroll paintings in their attempt to induce trance through solely visual not aural or musical means. Made from the skin of sacrificed animals the scrolls are designed to double and seal off the patient's body in order to evoke a possessing spirit. These talismans are designed 'to operate by truly pictorial means, in a manner immanent in perception.'[184] For Deleuze and Guattari, Ethiopian scroll paintings were singled out as the 'purest case' of 'faciality,' of the multiplying despotic regime: 'This is the signifying despotic face and the multiplication proper to it, its proliferation, its redundancy or frequency.

---

[181] Compare the first and second portraits of Colette Thomas, ill. 49 and 57, in *Antonin Artaud: Works on Paper*, pp.113; 131. The first is a clear enough likeness of Thomas at her then current age, imbued with kindness, the second is a frightening, scarred disintegration.

[182] Barber, *Artaud: The Screaming Body*, p.64; Prevel, *En Compagnie d'Antonin Artaud*, p.171.

[183] See *Portrait of Paule Thévenin or Paule with Irons*, ill. 51 in *Antonin Artaud: Works on Paper*, p.115.

[184] Jacques Mercier, *Art That Heals: The Image as Medicine in Ethiopia*, New York, NY: Prestel/Museum of African Art, 1997, p.95.

A multiplication of eyes. The despot or his representative are everywhere. This is the face seen from the front, by a subject who does not so much see as gets snapped up by the black holes.'[185] One has to keep in mind here that 'faciality' in Deleuze and Guattari is the inverse of that in Artaud, or what the latter describes in a text like 'The Human Face.' For Deleuze and Guattari 'The face is not a universal. It is not even that of the WHITE MAN; it is the white man himself, with his broad white cheeks and the black hole of his eyes. The face is Christ. The face is the typical European...'[186] So 'faciality' functions as an abstracting, binarising grid, less a particular body part than a profoundly reactive 'diagram,' a sort of reduction of complex communicational and semiotic levels to the ordering of the patriarchal same.[187] This notion therefore has very little to do with Artaud's face as 'revolutionary demand of a form that was never in keeping with this body.' What it does share is the face, as Christ, put into question, into struggle, in the contest for a new body and new regime of signs.

While Artaud's treatments of the face are also 'performative,' as Jacques Mercier describes the scroll paintings, they have a quite opposite intent than restoring a sight 'immanent in perception.' Artaud addresses this in his drawing at Rodez, *The Machine of Being*, also sometimes titled *Drawing to be looked at askew*, after another bit of text found in it, in this instance drawn across the top.[188] Artaud described it as a 'serious attempt to give life and existence to that which, until today, had never been received in art, the spoiling of the subjectile, the pitiful awkwardness of forms that collapse around an idea after having toiled for how many eternities to rejoin it.'[189] Noting the drawing's crumpled, 'dirty and faulty' sheet of paper, Artaud characterises the figures as 'drawn by the conscience of a child.'[190] Artaud embraces the awkwardness of the construction, since it allows him to show the searching and torment of that consciousness that moves 'in the middle of and around their idea to make sense for once,...for in that work there is an idea.'[191] Having written elsewhere that he had despaired of 'pure drawing,'[192] Artaud describes this same process when he treats the drawing

185 Deleuze and Guattari, *A Thousand Plateaus*, p.224. One of Félix Guattari's most extended treatments of 'faciality,' discussing the photographs of Keiichi Tahara, is found in Guattari, *Cartographies schizoanalytiques*, pp.311-8. Also see chapter 4 of *The Machinic Unconscious*.

186 Deleuze and Guattari, *A Thousand Plateaus*, p.176.

187 See Brian Massumi's gloss on 'faciality' in his *A User's Guide to Capitalism and Schizophrenia*, Cambridge, MA & London: MIT Press/Swerve, 1992, n.54; 55, pp.172-3. Indeed, one way of uniting the terminologies of *Anti-Oedipus* and *A Thousand Plateaus*, he argues, is to see the phallus as the 'operator' of faciality.

188 Ill. 21 in *Antonin Artaud: Works on Paper*, p.75.

189 Artaud, *Œuvres*, p.1039.

190 Ibid.

191 Ibid.

192 Artaud XXI, 1985, p.226.

La Pendue (January 1945) as 'research' of the body battling its arbitrary extension, the fixed forms of its Creator blocking its access to infinity.[193] Artaud's aggression against these forms, including the support or subjectile of the paper itself as in the spells, is at one with his deliberate awkwardness in drawing, a turning askew of the received order of the world. The *principe du dessin* must be dismantled as part of the false and falsified perception perpetrated by society. Artaud is not so much abolishing the subjectile, since it is the subjectile (the place or spatialisation) where things take form, but forcing it, scarring it, 'maddening' it in Derrida's term, to act or perform where to date it has only acted falsely, or not been activated or acting at all. Artaud aims to restore it to its 'impossible truth.'[194] What Edward Scheer has called a 're-routing of the process of birth'[195] is Artaud's violent response to God's malformation that is also an ocular *maladresse* or awkwardness. Artaud addresses himself to this 'opaque spot on the eye,' an ocular deformation, suppression, oppression, 'reverted and suffocated by certain malversations on the principle of our cranial structure... from the coccyx at the bottom of the vertebrae, up to the assizes of the forceps of the sustaining jaws of the brain.'[196]

The battle is with these misappropriated and deformed forms that Artaud claims are 'stippled and chiseled [with] all the angers of my combat, in view of a certain number of totem beings, of which only these miserable little specimens remain, my drawings.'[197] So Artaud's drawings are themselves totems, products of this struggle, but they are totems-in-creation, in motion. As Artaud continues, these 'totem beings' are 'concretely signified through lines and points... these lines are what one might call *interstitial* lines. Interstitial they are, as if being held in suspense in the movement they accompany, movement which rocks the breath.'[198] Artaud's drawings inhabit this in-between space, Paul Klee's *Zwischenwelt*. They may seem suspended in space and time, images *frozen* like the haystacks or piers in Van Gogh's paintings, but unlike a ritual art that would subordinate time to space and thereby produce a reconciliation with the gods and society, Artaud's images demand, Artaud observes in his passage concerning the 'unsticking of the retina,' to be looked at more than once. If one does so, Artaud writes:

> I think it remains then not in space but in time, at that point of the space where a breath from behind the heart holds onto existence and suspends it, in viewing close up I would like it if one could find there that kind of unsticking of the retina,

[193] Artaud, *Œuvres*, p.1035.

[194] Edward Scheer, 'Sketches of the jet,' in *100 Years of Cruelty*, p.63.

[195] Ibid., p.62.

[196] Artaud XXI, 1985, p.266.

[197] Ibid., p.267.

[198] Ibid.

that quasi virtual sensation of a retina detaching itself which I had in unfixing the upper skeleton *in regard to its setting in my eye.*[199]

In the later Artaud generally, the concern is with restoring becoming to infinity, loosing the potentials of time no longer subaltern to space even ritual space; in this way the malformations of being are turned back or askew in the creation of the bodies without organs, a never-to-be-finished or entirely done with process of totemisation. Artaud is still discussing lines and interstitiality as in his earlier writings, but not in order to access an underlying sacred geometry, rather to combat an occult one, in a process where all phenomena are truly jointed and created anew. To the extent any hieroglyphic patterning is pre-existing and pre-ordering it is also false, and must be skewered, rendered anew, or destroyed.

The voice at the end of the world: the final sound works

Artaud was not at first interested in working in radio, his now notorious broadcasts were sollicited, and he was disappointed in the results of the first two recordings he made in 1946. But he came to see the *To have done with the judgment of god* recording as a 'mini-model' of the Theater of cruelty.[200] Experimentation in sound was crucial to *The Cenci* in 1933,[201] and the notion of tone and sound reverberates through Artaud's Mexican addresses, *The Theater and the Double*, and the essay on Van Gogh. In his film script *The Butcher's Revolt* (1929) Artaud emphasised the multiple spatial levels of any sound entering the cinematic space, where the 'voices are in space, like objects.'[202] The making of the drawings were often accompanied by hideous cries and screams, the propulsive qualities of the sonic. In the lecture Artaud gave at the Sorbonne in 1931, 'Mise-en-scène and Metaphysics,' Artaud elaborated that

> Words have their own potential as sound, they have various ways of being projected into space, which are called intonations. And there is a great deal that could be said about the concrete value of intonation in the theater, about this quality that words have – apart from their concrete meaning – of creating their own music according to the way in which they are uttered, which can even go

199 Ibid. p.182.

200 Artaud XIII, 1974, p.127.

201 For *The Cenci* Roger Désormière not only introduced stereophonic sound in the theatre for the first time, in order to produce the extremely loud volume Artaud desired, he used jarring 'peak production' factory noises for the scene in which Beatrice Cenci is tortured, shades of Godard's use of factory noise in his 1970 *British Sounds* (released in the US as *See You at Mao!*). Désormière also used a recently invented electronic keyboard that produced oscillating Martenot waves that moved from nearly inaudible sounds to roars louder than any existing symphonic orchestra. See Sellin, *The Dramatic Concepts of Antonin Artaud*, p.122.

202 Artaud III, 1961, p.54.

against that meaning – of creating beneath language an undercurrent of impressions, correspondences, analogies...[203]

For the Artaud after Rodez, creating an 'undercurrent of impressions, correspondences, analogies' would not be nearly ambitious enough, since 'the act I'm talking about aims for the true organic and physical transformation of the human body.'[204] Artaud's last sound works provide an extremely focused expression of all his late themes – the reinvention of the human body, the collision of imagery, language and compulsion, the will that arises from this combustion 'to walk,' that is, through intensity of gesture touches and pierces through to infinity.

Despite the literature of failure that surrounds Artaud and Artaud's radio works especially given the banning of his last, and most successful one in his own terms, in February 1948, two of Artaud's broadcasts were transmitted the day after they were recorded, on prime-time French radio, exactly when Artaud wanted them to be heard.[205] That Artaud's extreme anti-psychiatric proclamations like *The Patients and the Doctors* and *Madness and Black Magic* were indeed transmitted in the most important, preeminent mass media of the day is nothing short of miraculous. Given that in 2007 in the US even the progressive radio station WBAI in New York was unable to do a memorial broadcast of Allen Ginsberg's *Howl* (1956) due to Federal Communication Commission obscenity regulations, it is a feat difficult to duplicate in much of the 'developed' world some sixty years later.[206] The interdiction of Artaud's last broadcast, on the day before it was supposed to be transmitted, at 10:45 in the evening on 2

203 Artaud IV, 1964, pp.36-7.

204 Artaud, 'Théâtre et la science,' *Œuvres*, p.1544.

205 For an evaluation of even Artaud's *To have done with the judgment of god* as a 'ultimate failure' given the contradictions of Artaud's relationship with representation and technology, see Allen S. Weiss, 'From Schizophrenia to Schizophonica,' *Phantasmic Radio*, Durham, NC: Duke University Press, 1995, p.33. This essay appears in an earlier form as 'Radio, Death, and the Devil: Artaud's *Pour En Finir Avec Le Jugement De Dieu*,' in Douglas Kahn and Gregory Whitehead, eds. *Wireless Imagination*, Cambridge, MA: MIT Press, 1992.

206 Ginsberg's poem is full of lines directly inspired from Artaud, including the famous opening one: 'I saw the best minds of my generation destroyed by madness, starving, hysterical, naked...' Allen Ginsberg, *Howl*, San Francisco, CA: City Lights Books, 1956. One of Artaud's posthumous legacies was as a 'political' poet, through the interpretations of Beat generation writers Allen Ginsberg, Carl Solomon, and Michael McClure. See Douglas Kahn, *Noise, Water, Meat*, Cambridge, MA & London: MIT Press, 1999, pp.331-8. With his prognosis that the psychosis of the times was located in the body, Artaud was an especially crucial continuing resource for McClure, see the poem dedicated to Artaud in Michael McClure: 'A New Book/A Book of Torture,' (1961) in *Huge Dreams*, New York, NY & London: Penguin Books, 1999; and his 'Artaud: Peace Chief,' in *Meat Science Essays*, San Francisco, CA: City Lights, 1963. Jack Kerouac shared these enthusiasms for Artaud as the writer who 'had opened all the doors.' See Joyce Johnson, *The Voice is All*, New York, NY: Viking, 2012, p.337.

February 1948, was a devastating blow to Artaud and his hopes for a mass audience. As Paule Thévenin recalled, 'It was banned just as though it was a porno movie.'[207] Artaud expected the broadcast would move the Parisian population to 'corporeal glory.'[208] His ambitions for it were vast, the broadcast 'would connect with certain organic points of life, a work which causes the entire nervous system to feel illuminated as if by a miner's cap, with vibrations and consonances that invite one to corporeally emerge in order to follow, in the sky, this new, unusual and radiant Epiphany.'[209]

With its texts, its *bruitage* and its screams, *To have done with the judgment of god* was an immensely focused and congealed creation. In it beats the percussive sounds of the Tarahumara ceremonies, and of the sounds Artaud argued could be found in Van Gogh paintings. When Artaud wrote that in Van Gogh's last painting 'I hear the wings of the crows loudly beating cymbals,'[210] he was maintaining that the sounds emanated from the figures and the build-up of the paint itself, not from any symbol the crows might represent (such as crows=death).[211] Earlier in the Van Gogh essay, Artaud had referred to Van Gogh the 'marvelous musician,' how the objects in his paintings radiated a kind of aural frequency – 'this is how the light of the candle sounds, how the light of the lit candle on the green straw-bottomed chair sounds like the breathing of a loving body before the body of a sleeping invalid.'[212] Artaud writes that 'no one since Van Gogh has known how to shake the great cymbal, the super-human gong, *perpetually* superhuman following the repressed order by which real-life objects ring out, when one has known how to have the ear open enough to comprehend the surging of their tidal-flow.'[213] Characteristically, though this carries the suggestion of animism or pantheism, that everything including inanimate objects are alive or somehow sentient, what Artaud stresses is Van Gogh's amplification, or transformation, of both 'nature' and the human ear or capacity as well, so that things of too low or abnormal a frequency will be heard and 'ring out.' The same principles, animated by the 'body without organs,' infuse Artaud's last radio broadcast. Artaud is not only projecting what normally is not heard or cannot be heard, in his war against representation he also utilises the agonising scream, the cry such that, as Gaston Bachelard observed regarding the cries in Comte de Lautréamont, 'cannot be imitated.'[214]

---

207 Barber, *Artaud: The Screaming Body*, p.100.

208 Artaud XIII, 1974, p.131.

209 Ibid.

210 Ibid., p.58.

211 Scheer, *100 Years of Cruelty*, p.66.

212 Artaud XIII, 1974, p.30.

213 Ibid.

214 Gaston Bachelard, *Lautréamont*, Paris: Librairie José Corti, 1939, p.78.

Like many of Artaud's works, *To have done with the judgment of god* is highly complex and composed of different versions.[215] It emerged from an earlier dossier for a project on the Last Judgment, and the preliminary preparations for the recordings include texts, glossolalia, directions for sound effects;[216] there are the recordings by Artaud, Roger Blin, actress Maria Casarès and Paule Thévenin (not all the texts were recorded, and Artaud made cuts in the opening section and re-recorded the conclusion after the first mix so that the noise effects would be more prominent, although these changes were ignored by the radio director); and finally there were published versions of *To have done with the judgment of god* in part and in its entirety ('Tutuguri' was published in the mass newspaper *Combat*, and the little magazine *Nyza* I and publisher *K* both published complete versions).[217] 'Arranged to a hair in a fulminating order,'[218] the recordings are a remarkable collocation of discipline and chance, one of Artaud's most ambitious attempts to express the body directly, in another language, the 'unconscious' without intermediaries. Although the texts, with the four readers, two male and two female, hold a coherence of their own and are where Artaud announces his project of the 'body without organs,'[219] the key element is Artaud's cries and noise effects that are splayed across the recordings, producing gravitational effects where one howl or scream pulls in the other sounds, while rupturing any semantic surface sense. There was only one reading Artaud supervised before each reader performed his or her text, unrehearsed, in the studio in an atmosphere Paule Thévenin remembered as one of great 'violence.'[220] In another testament to the level of collaboration, if not contagion Artaud could evoke, actress Maria Casarès wrote in her memoirs that at the time of the recording of *To have done with the judgment of god*, she was in 'a state of aggravated euphoria which kept me upright, hardly sleeping, for seven whole weeks, at the borders of reality, and which carried me when I did sleep into arid, devastated regions, where nightmares of futurist warfare mixed together with the most refined weapons and means ever invented to pursue solitary fugitives.'[221] In this atmosphere of enervation, Artaud held a final recording session on 16 January 1948, when he recorded a series of long screams and percussive soundings. His partner in this session was Roger Blin, who performed a dialogue with Artaud

[215] A chronological order is presented in Weiss, *Phantasmic Radio*, p.13.

[216] See Artaud XIII, 1974, pp.229-96.

[217] For an example of how differently the glossolalia can be reworked and profoundly altered in each of these different versions – of manuscript, publication and recording – in this case of Artaud's *The Patients and the Doctors* (1946), see Allen S. Weiss, 'Libidinal Mannerisms and Profligate Abominations,' in *100 Years of Cruelty*, p.117.

[218] From the introduction to *To have done with the judgment of god*, Artaud XIII, 1974, p.69.

[219] Ibid., pp.86-7; 104.

[220] Barber, *Artaud: The Screaming Body*, p.97.

[221] Maria Casarès, *Résidente privilégiée*, Paris: Fayard, 1980, p.468.

in his syllable-language; Artaud called this encounter getting into 'the monkeys' cage.'[222] Like his drawings, the senses and sounds of *To have done with the judgment of god* go off in a wide and wild variety of directions, with Artaud's screams at their core.

While the cries militate and work against any finished representational sense, Artaud pitches his urgent themes – his admiration for the Tarahumaras as a living Theater of cruelty, presents a cruel satire on the then-beginning Cold War with his lurid fantasies of a militarist US stockpiling its schoolboys' sperm for its future wars, his plea that the human body be remade and his contempt for all who do not follow his advocacy of 'walking will,' those who refuse to remake themselves, and so remain meat and excrement:

> to live,
> you have to be somebody,
> to be somebody,
> you have to have a BONE,
> and not be afraid of showing the bone,
> and losing the meat in the process.[223]

Artaud imagined an army of men forming who would enforce this abolition of the Christian cross and affirm the new 'body without organs.' The text read by Paule Thévenin 'The Question is posed…' confirms that for Artaud ideas are only extraneous gases and voids of the body, like excrement, another matter to be cancelled in order to break through to the infinite.

While Artaud envisages an army descending from the cross where they had been nailed, walking in fire, iron, blood and bones to challenge 'the Invisible'[224] and put an end to God's judgment and establish the new body, his elemental statement remains that most impacted of physical expressions, his scream. In the estranging medium of radio, Artaud appears to project the scream as the extreme end point of dance, it is the scream that captures all the body's sensation at a precise moment.[225] It is the scream that attacks the organismic organisation of the body, by collecting all the means Artaud has at his disposal, especially the hand and vocal tract.[226] In the relatively disembodied medium of radio, Artaud is revisualising and rematerialising the body, in an extremely violent taking back of his voice silenced for nine years in the asylums. Since it is his scream that is his supreme weapon in disabling and splintering language and fixed representations of any kind, that restores the danger and fluidity of the

[222] Barber, *Antonin Artaud*, p.152.

[223] Artaud XIII, 1974, p.84.

[224] Ibid., p.87.

[225] This is one of his profound contributions to Butoh dance. Barber, *Artaud: The Screaming Body*, p.103.

[226] Ibid.

'body without organs,' *To have done with the judgment of god* is a key deposition for the 'success' or 'failure' of Artaud's assault on representation. To scholar Allen Weiss, the contradictory imperatives of Artaud's poetics and the structural features of radio (as earlier with literature and theatre) rendered *To have done with the judgment of god* an 'ultimate failure.'[227] Artaud's screams for Weiss were in fact 'highly theatrical and neither particularly incantatory nor shocking but rather somewhat poetic.'[228] Much as what Weiss writes recalls Breton's critique of Artaud as still a man of the theatre at his January 1947 Vieux-Colombier appearance, his criticism also parallels that of Lacanian psychoanalysis or Derridean deconstruction – Artaud is caught up once again in this broadcast in the double-binds of representation and representational structures, part of an inexorable human destiny Artaud cannot evade. It is the nature of radiophonic art, and broadcasting in general, Weiss argues, to conventionalise and flatten out any performance in the interests of mass reproduction and repetition; Weiss asks why Artaud suppressed the glossolalia and opening text that originally opened the recording replacing it with a drumroll that went immediately into the first text, and answers that Artaud ended up with a 'disfiguration of Artaud's own work.'[229] In this return of the repressed, 'Artaud's voice was severed from his body, made an autonomous object in the world, and cast off to pursue its own destiny.'[230] In this view, Artaud has engineered an ultimate alienation and separation of the voice and body, not a fused affect that cuts through to touch infinity, what he called that '*opening*/of our consciousness/towards possibility/ beyond measure.'[231]

Yet in Weiss' own description of Artaud's dilemma and the role of the scream he proposes to resolve it, one sees that Artaud is far more successful than Weiss' conclusion will allow. He cites Guy Rossalato's acute characterisation of the significance of the cry for Artaud. The cry is intimately connected with Artaud's 'search for fecality' and the vast value of expulsion that is not excremental, that cannot be located in any interior or exterior. In Rossolato's terms, this is a location found in neither life nor death, but only along the borderline between them, 'through the quest for total mastery [the "walking will"], by maintaining what became for him the impasse, the double-bind, of the simultaneous and absolute *injunctions to live and to die*, that is say by means of the single thought incarnate in the infinite instant of passage within the circumscribed immensity of the theater: a scream.'[232] Artaud attempts a coup against these polarities through his

[227] Weiss, *Phantasmic Radio*, p.33.

[228] Ibid.

[229] Ibid.

[230] Ibid.

[231] Artaud XIII, 1974, p.91-2.

[232] Guy Rossolato, 'L'Expulsion,' in *La Relation d'inconnu*, Paris: Gallimard, 1978. pp.141-2. Cited in Weiss, *Phantasmic Radio*, p.24.

scream that is neither inside nor outside, but rather is either located in Deleuze's terms 'on the line' of the boundary itself, or has exploded beyond it. The scream becomes Artaud's ultimate weapon in his propulsion beyond being reduced to the bodily organs, the oral-anal tract or canal. As Weiss notes, Artaud's frequent conflation of the mouth and anus[233] has a basis in the findings of contemporary psycholinguistics whereby any pronunciation of glottal occlusives (sounds produced by closure of the glottis) creates pressure on the intestines and diaphragm, facilitating defecation.[234] So glottal sounds are also symbolic and physiognomic reflections of defecation, as in what Artaud called the 'anal tongue.'[235] It is the glottic sphincter that allows the physical and symbolic articulation of both oral and anal rejection and retention, which has as a direct result, Weiss writes, the corporeal displacement of anal libido into sound.[236] This has been hyperbolically represented by the glottal occlusive *k* sound, often signified as *kaka* or *caca*, hence its repetitive significance for Artaud and his rejection of the excremental. Such glottal vocalisations, Weiss maintains, are 'screams of the entire body and not just of the mouth…[that] never fall below the threshold of meaning, since the subglottal regions of the body are full of signification and overtly expressive. The interior of the soul speaks through the interior of the body.'[237] It is for these reasons that Weiss is mistaken in emphasising that Artaud wants 'to recuperate a poetic or literary level to his work.'[238] It is in part Artaud's obsession with abolishing literature that has led him to the scream as an endpoint to his dance of cruelty, his call in his very last reflections for a theatre of real blood. Weiss argues that it is only in leaving the poet that language 'can call out to the other and attain its own destiny.'[239] This kind of call and response is indeed integral to most poetry and poetic endeavour, but Artaud's scream is a materialisation of the 'body without organs' designed to exist in the infinite, carrying on his battle. Artaud is wagering on this impacted cry for immortality. Artaud's first cries in the French recording studio were of such amplification that they broke the equipment. Yet however bloodcurdling Artaud's initial screams, Weiss argues, they become diluted with the familiarity of repetition and 'his shattered body becomes whole and normal through the effects of mon-aural recording.'[240] As Jean Baudrillard has remarked, each person's relation to Artaud and Artaud's work is strangely private and singular, it is somehow defective for any collective

[233] Artaud XXIII, 1987, p.328; Artaud XXIV, 1988, p.153.

[234] See Ivan Fónagy, *La Vive voix: Essais de psycho-phonétique*, Paris: Payot, 1983; Weiss, *Phantasmic Radio*, p.25.

[235] Artaud XXIII, 1987, p.328.

[236] Weiss, *Phantasmic Radio*, p.26.

[237] Ibid.

[238] Ibid.

[239] Ibid., p.27.

[240] Ibid., p.30.

response.[241] And as R.D. Laing once quipped, one person's revolution is another person's platitude. The medium of radio, according to Weiss, only duplicated ontologically the conditions Artaud struggled against.

Key to Weiss' analysis is that radio is overwhelmingly the acousmetric medium, where sound appears without any corresponding image. Drawing on the work especially of Michel Chion,[242] for Weiss the sort of pure if disincarnate presence or materiality of sound in radio carries all the features of the Judeo-Christian God, hence its propensity to return as hallucination or paranoid inspiration – such as Orpheus getting his poetic prompts from the jumbled messages on the car radio in Jean Cocteau's *Orphée* (1950). With no visible body or even image anchoring the sound, Weiss points out that radio provides a space so large it is able to contain the wildest megalomanias, the most extreme mysticisms, 'the grandest God.'[243] It is in these terms that one must ask whether Artaud has successfully exorcised God, or whether a work like *To have done with the judgment of god* merely accentuates the mind/body dualism Artaud fought so hard to supercede, whether it is 'yet one more instance of the voice of divine judgment.'[244] Weiss returns to the necessity of the symbolic, and the symbolic splits between inner and outer, precisely the target of Artaud's rage against God's erotomania and his focused scream. As Artaud puts it in *To have done with the judgment of god*, the question is that 'He is offered two paths: that of the infinite outside, that of the infinitesmal inside.'[245] While Weiss remains in this ineluctable reality of psychoanalytic binaries of life/death, inside/outside, conscious/unconscious, in his radio works Artaud is confident, at least in the final one, that the seeping sound and engulfment of space produced by it created visual not just aural impact. It is as if he had succeeded in the radio works in accomplishing what had eluded him in the cinema. In Artaud's 29 June 1929 lecture at Studio 28 in Montmartre, for example, he had contrasted the power of image and sound, arguing that 'sound, on the contrary, is unique and true, it bursts out into the room, and acts by consequence with much more intensity than the image, which becomes only a kind of illusion of sound.'[246] In *To have done with the judgment of god*, Artaud reaches a pitch of abrasive assault, or 'arrhythmic collision,'[247] of sound against image, he had previously only theorised. Artaud, sure that this broadcast would touch the entire nervous system

[241] Jean Baudrillard, 'Baudrillard on Artaud,' 16 November 1996, New York, NY: The Drawing Center.

[242] See Michel Chion, *The Voice in Cinema*, trans. Claudia Gorbman, New York, NY: Columbia University Press, [1982] 1999.

[243] Weiss, *Phantasmic Radio*, p.32.

[244] Ibid., p.33.

[245] Artaud XIII, 1974, p.85.

[246] Artaud III, 1961, p.37.

[247] Barber, *Artaud: The Screaming Body*, p.97.

of the listener, was all the more outraged when this climactic opportunity was refused and banned. For Artaud it is the sexual libido that introduces the inner chasm, what he described in July 1945 at Rodez as 'the cut between man and woman, between self and others, between being and self, between soul and soul, between heart and soul.'[248] This original ontological insecurity ordained by God makes God the original erotomaniac. One way of looking at the fury of the 'late' Artaud is that Eros and Thanatos have merged in an eroticism that must deny God in order to recreate the self.[249] Yet to characterise this as Weiss does, as 'virtual autoeroticism,'[250] is to remain in the old world, not emerge in the new one or the one Artaud has doubled. Artaud's wager is that his scream, his ultimate statement of the impact and rematerialisation of the body, is unanswerable. Arguably, in the digital era, this only has renewed force. 'In the new technologies,' Mladen Dolar has written, the voice is turned into an 'object, repeatable at will, easily manipulated.' This new 'object-voice' may replace 'unrepeatable presence,' but only while it 'kept it alive as its own double,'[251] thereby attenuating all the paradoxes already latent in the voice, extending its 'signification beyond signification.'[252]

Artaud at the end of his life can be seen as directly erasing the line, the boundary, of life and death, the inner and the outer. In psychoanalytic terms his utilisation of the scream is 'the explusion of the unbearable, impossible internal polarisation between life's force and death's negation, simultaneously signifying and simulating creation and destruction.'[253] Artaud in *The Theater and Its Double* had called for a new lyricism of the gesture, but his later work is hardly that. His rage against representation, reflected in his essay on Van Gogh and in his own graphic and visual work even when it has ostensible subjects, and creation of the 'body without organs' ultimately obliterates any line, any 'zigzag' of hieroglyphic reality or 'occult geometry' that was once so dear to him. When Artaud writes in *Suppôts et suppliciations*, one of his most honed final works, that this new world is 'without hieroglyphics and secret keyboard,'[254] he acknowledges as much. Though a final work like *To have done with the judgment of god* creates visualisation through sound, and his drawings often establish a complementary relation between image and text, so that one refers to the other for comprehension in an hieroglyphic manner, they are also often, as in the notebooks manifestly elements at war with one another – not making the other element readable

248 Artaud XVII, 1982, p.33.

249 Weiss, *100 Years of Cruelty*, p.123.

250 Ibid., p.124.

251 Mladen Dolar, 'What's in a Voice,' *Amber '07: Art and Technology Festival, Voice and Survival*, Istanbul: BIS, Body-Process-Art Association, 2010, p.103.

252 Ibid., p.95.

253 Weiss, *Phantasmic Radio*, p.24.

254 Artaud XIV:1, 1978, p.151.

but precisely unreadable and ungraspable. In this last apocalyptic conflagration the line itself succumbs. That Artaud considered the 'mini-model' of the Theater of cruelty a radiophonic or sound work, itself is another indication of this.[255] Artaud's total self-creation of the 'body without organs' now 'abjects all signs' and this includes the patternings of any hieroglyph. It has not survived Artaud's final metamorphosis.

[255] Although I have noted the emphasis on sound and tonality that is suffused throughout Artaud's writings, I have stopped short of characterising Artaud's project as a 'sound system,' as does Denis Hollier in reference to Artaud's film writings. See the argument in Denis Hollier, 'The Death of Paper, Part Two: Artaud's Sound System,' *October* 80, 1997, pp.27-37.

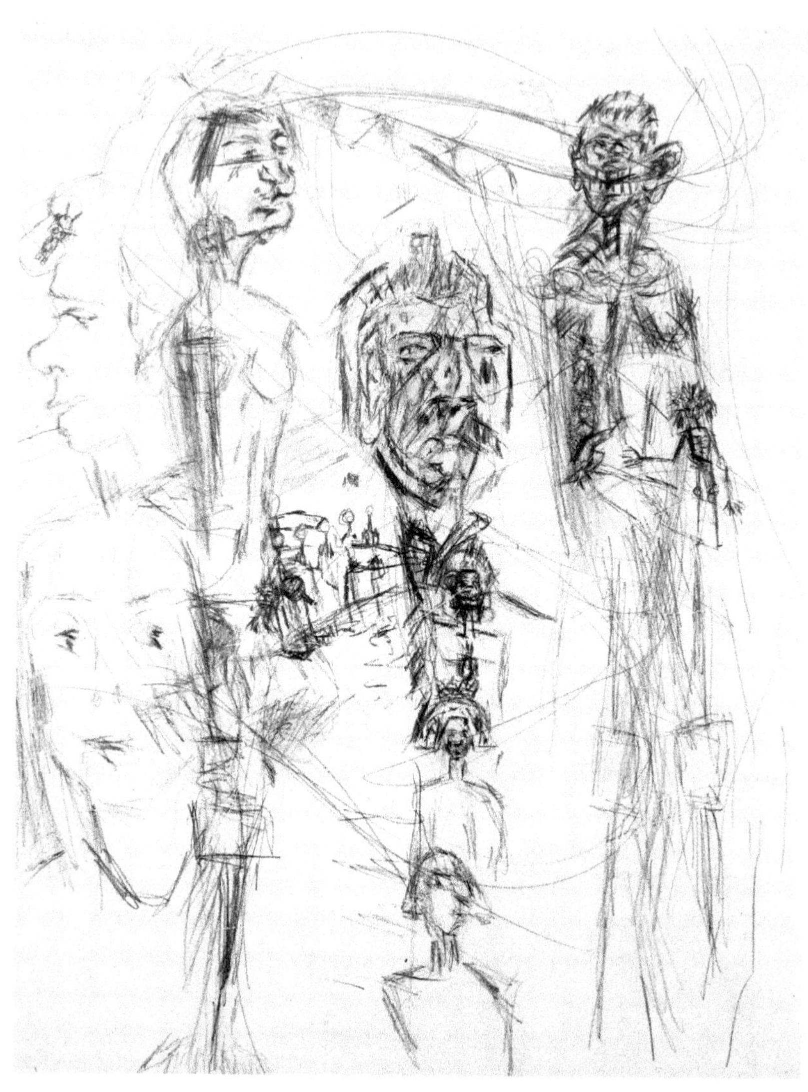

Untitled, February 1948 (crayon 64 x 49 cm).

CONCLUSION: ERASING THE LINE

What *Artaud's Metamorphosis* has established are a few elemental and intertwined points: that there are theoretical openings for an altered and enhanced understanding of Artaud; that an examination of traditional, indigenous rituals serves to illuminate Artaud's singularity precisely in how he will ultimately subvert and overturn them (specifically in how the 'late' Artaud becomes consumed with reaching infinity and creating his 'new body' to that end, releasing the element of time from any subservient end); that the considerable shift from the 'early' to the 'late' Artaud hinges in many ways on the issue of hieroglyphics so central to his famous theatre manifestoes; and that in the last two-and-a-half years of his life Artaud jettisons even these ideas of the hieroglyph in an extraordinary intensified rage against representation and desire for apocalyptic engulfment. This material has been presented with the aim not so much to reconfirm that Artaud was an extraordinary artist in his own right (and aside from his theories of theatre much discussed elsewhere) and so revise the 20th century artistic canon in Artaud's favour, but towards the view that his violent disintegration of the hieroglyph leads quite presciently if uncannily into our future. Artaud has served as a flash point in the past coalescing in various avant-garde artistic and theoretical explorations – for American artists around David Tudor and John Cage at Black Mountain College in the 1950s, in the political and environmental poetics of a wing of the 'Beat' generation, the invention of Butoh in Japan in 1959 or for French thinkers reconsidering the relation of language and materiality after 1968 – and Artaud promises to offer such a substrate once again in the early decades of the 21st Century. In concluding I will first draw out some of the primary outlines of this treatment concerning Artaud's metamorphosis and how his contribution lies in it; and then finally show how his transformation is already providing just such a renewed substrate – for inspiring new media and analysing the new realities of the social field he had already defined and excoriated with all the fury he could summon in *To have done with the judgment of god.*

Artaud's subversion of hieroglyphics

Artaud's search for the sacred, pivotal hieroglyphic realities that underlie all form had much in common with other mid-20th century experiments, especially with many of the most profound ones – ranging from Aby Warburg's *Atlas Project* (1929) itself inspired from indigenous Indian cultures in the American Southwest, Ernest Fenollosa and Ezra Pound's use of the Chinese ideogram to inspire a new modernist poetics, to Eisenstein's elucidation of the Japanese ideogram as an hieroglyphic basis for cinema.[1] If Artaud's journey had stopped there, one could simply affirm him as one of the great high-modernist artists and thinkers, in addition to setting off seminal developments in avant-garde theatre and performance. But Artaud's search for a primal original language that took him up into the Sierras Tarahumaras turned into a savage combustion, and the last three years of his life witnesses the re-calibration of veritably all the forces of his being. This process of re-formation, if never restoring an original state, or a 'sensibility misled'[2] as Artaud wrote, was arguably an 'absolutely unique'[3] one, given the extremity of the shattering of Artaud's fragmented psyche during his trip to Ireland in 1937. That it was done in insane asylums deliberately starved by the Nazi occupiers and later in Rodez despite a forced regime of electroshock treatments make it all the more awe-inspiring. It was achieved through an eminently hieroglyphic means, Artaud's extreme manipulation and introjection of the cross, which he used as a kind of boat or rite of passage and then discards. This use of the cross is the central element in Artaud's re-construction and his emergence from nine years in the asylums (an experience that would lead to death or complete psychic destruction for a great many of us) onto another plane of ferocity and creativity. Not only does Artaud produce *more* works in the last two-and-a-half years of his life than he did up to 1936, he produced works that ultimately may be even more enduring than his famous theatre manifestoes. That a hieroglyphic means leads to this transformation alone would make Artaud one of the most original and singular 20th century artists, whose investigation into hieroglyphics cannot be restricted, as is the case with Pound or Eisenstein, to one medium or art-form, not even a transfigured theatre. With Artaud it was ever a matter of evoking the movements of the 'life plane,'[4] planes of immanence perhaps in Deleuzian terms, that underlay all reality. Characteristically, Artaud's ceaseless pursuit of where the limits of the human body and sensibility might halt does not stop there, and neither does his significance.

---

1 See Mikhail Iampolski, *The Memory of Tiresias*, trans. Harsha Ram, Berkeley, CA: University of California Press, 1998. Iampolski is one of the few authors to draw the important parallels between Artaud and Pound and Eisenstein.

2 Artaud, *Œuvres*, p.1513.

3 André, *L'Épreuve d'Antonin Artaud et l'expérience de la psychanalyse*, p.112.

4 Artaud, *Œuvres*, p.212.

Artaud illuminates certain thresholds of this moment not because of his fascination with the hieroglyphics of primordial languages and gestures, a concern that cut across so many 20th century modernisms and avant-gardes, but because in a series of extremely willful, violent operations 1945-8 he definitively annihilates any hieroglyph or hieroglyphic understanding. It has been argued that this disintegration stems in part from the contradictions of the hieroglyph itself. It is one of the resemblances of Sergei Eisenstein's notions to Artaud's Theater of cruelty that for the Russian filmmaker the combination of two separate, fusing hieroglyphs produced a result that was 'graphically undepictable.'[5] Theorist Mikhail Iampolski wrote that for Artaud, as in Fenollosa and Pound, or Eisenstein, it is a matter of taking apart what appears as the self-evident appearance or 'semiotic transparency'[6] of the different elements of the hieroglyph. In all of these artists, Iampolski argued, a different general or 'third' meaning succeeds the destruction of mimetic meaning. Yet there is a danger that this 'third' meaning is never realised. Any hieroglyphic meaning, Iampolski maintained, tends to be less self-evident than a mimetically produced one. What could result, he writes in passages directly addressed to Artaud, is the loss of meaning altogether, 'leading to an escalation of nothing more than pure 'corporeality,' the self-presentation of the sensuous.'[7] This threat of the body posited as its own semiotic and space, that which Derrida described in relation to Artaud as the 'autorepresentation of pure visibility and pure sensibility,'[8] is Artaud's invention of his 'body without organs.'

It is Artaud's solution, if not cure, for a lifetime of neurological maladies, addiction, illness and ceaseless loss, what he calls at many different stages of the journey, his own 'crucifixion.' And while one can find roots or prefigurations of it in his earlier writings, the 'body without organs' is not another installment in hieroglyphic understanding. The Artaud of 1936 still advocates a form of mysticism and goes to Mexico to find the living well of the all-powerful galvanising hieroglyphic 'zig zags' that make up reality, glimpsed in Mayan and Toltec temple art centred on crosses. The Artaud of 1945-48, far from searching for sources of the ancient gods, spends every waking (and presumably sleeping) hour fighting them and various other entities, since Artaud through an elaborate, nothing if not miraculous and laborious process, has substituted in his 'body without organs' an autochthonous reality, an autocreation for God. Artaud can 'abject all signs'[9] since he rejects every kind of priest and soothsayer in the world as conjurors of fabulation and deathly illusion. He has respect for the Tarahumara Indians 'who eat right out of the earth the delirium that gives birth to them'[10] but

5 Sergei Eisenstein, *Film Form*, ed. and trans. Jay Leyda, London: Dobson, 1963, p.30.

6 Iampolski, *The Memory of Tiresias*, p.27.

7 Ibid.

8 Derrida, *Writing and Difference*, p.238.

9 Artaud XIII, 1974, p.273.

10 Ibid., p.74.

not for their priests. In a world consumed by the sorcery and spells of these different religious and mystical taskmasters, responsible for the deaths of not only Van Gogh but all the superior lucidities capable of combating them – Gérard de Nerval, Lautréamont, Baudelaire, Poe (and Artaud often includes Lenin at the end) – Artaud relies on a counter-sorcery or counter-spell to ward off their evil and contamination. This is the function of his drawings (themselves animated protective bodies) or his screams in *To have done with the judgment of god*. This shift from the 'early' Artaud is thus dramatic and profound. In contrast to the lack of any recognition of this chronological shift in thinkers as valuable in their different ways in looking at Artaud as Deleuze and Guattari, Lyotard[11] and Derrida, philosopher Jean-Joseph Goux in a recent essay characterises the late or final Artaud as a 'total reversal...a radical rejection of everything related to the initiatory' who replaces his earlier vision with a 'harsh and immediate conception of life in which the body is the foundation.'[12]

In his writings, Artaud is hardly consistent about this. In his essay on Van Gogh, any 'shadow' of reality is greater than any hieroglyph, though in his March 1946 letter/essay on Nerval, discussed in the last section of Chapter I, Artaud does remark on the awakened hieroglyphs that lie latent in Nerval's 'Chimeras.' Even in this instance these forms must be dislocated from any Myth, since it is symbolics substituted for the brutal poetics of life that have helped 'murder' Nerval, as another one of the poets 'suicided by society.' In the case of these hieroglyphs 'all the keys of their so-called occultism die out in the finally useless and ominous convolutions of brain matter.'[13] Nerval's poems create 'extraordinary new beings' that are rather recovered and retrieved from the Tarot or alchemy, that have no source other than the 'abdominal bass cavern of a stricken heart.'[14]Already known 'allegorical keys' are useless in the face of the 'explosions of language' in Nerval, founded in the abyss of the body, 'the permanence of an old heart.'[15] As with Van Gogh, or Artaud himself, the soul as it is animated in Nerval is one in which 'the poet makes it and he alone makes it.'[16] This is what Artaud calls 'direct creation' in his essay on Van Gogh.[17]

---

11 When Lyotard writes that Artaud puts 'more accent on the sacred' than the Noh playwright and theorist Zeami, for instance, his analysis is accurate concerning Artaud's theatre manifestoes published in 1938 but not applicable to the Artaud of 1945-48 who so fiercely rejected any spirituality or mystical system. See Lyotard, *Des Dispositifs pulsionnels*, Paris: Éditions Galilée, 1994, p.95.

12 Jean-Joseph Goux, 'Antonin Artaud and the Promise of a Great Therapeutic,' *Angelaki* 13:3, December 2008, p.21.

13 Artaud, *Watchfiends & Rack Screams*, p.54.

14 Ibid., pp.51-2.

15 Ibid., pp.57-9.

16 Ibid., p.59.

17 Artaud XIII, 1974, p.35.

One can find early foreshadowings of the later 'body without organs.' In a letter in 1933, for instance, Artaud writes that it is mistaken to see the body as a fixed and impermeable organism, it is rather only 'provisional stratifications of states of life.'[18] What shows the considerable distance of the 'final' Artaud of 1945-8 from the earlier, is not only the attack on mysticism and myth and symbolism but the transformation in the nature of ritual that goes with it. This is decisive. Whether one looks at the *Isoma* ritual among the Ndembu in Africa described by Victor Turner (recounted at the beginning of Chapter III), Lévi-Strauss on fertility rituals, or Maya Deren's account of Haitian *vodun* (related in 'The cross and the crossroads' in Chapter IV), what they all have in common is the corralling of time, its suppression in the interests of the spatialisation of phenomena in the ritual. This is time as 'recurrent flux,'[19] in the words of José Gil. In this cosmology, 'time comes back because things come back, because power comes back,'[20] shaped by the powers of space that are simultaneously the power of ancestors, the power of the earth. These rites work hard to contain any spillage, to reform any leaks back into the unity of the world that also is the unity of the tribe. If structuralist analyses of ritual have helped us understand the extremely complex different registers and levels of the various ceremonies they also, if at times unwittingly, lead to the conclusion that the transductor of the rites is none other than the energies of the body itself. One of the remarkable insights of Artaud's writing on the Tarahumaras is that he observed that few if any of the participants could explain any how or why of the ceremonies embedded in their very gestures. This key revelation for Artaud that language is lived in the body, is later confirmed by José Gil's meditations on ritual (themselves distilled from Turner, Lévi-Strauss and Deleuze and Guattari's writing on traditional societies). Tribes have no need of conscious interpretation of the rites, Gil writes, since 'they carry them in their bodies.'[21]

For the final Artaud any idea is merely a void or gas of the body and his work provides one of the most belligerent rejections on record of the notion that any code or signifier or symbol can actually hold sway over its feral source in the body. That Lévi-Strauss' 'floating signifier' is ultimately one of the unclassifiable or un-encodable energies of the body, or the body itself is one conclusion that can be drawn from Artaud's journey, spent in that liminal territory in-between or beyond various linguistic and social codes, but it is not the only one. Artaud goes further in the invention of the 'body without organs' – an image of the anorganic vitality that traverses the body and that for Artaud doubles it. Artaud insists it is part of infinity, an infinity he believes in some spots in his last notebooks that he has indeed breached. One can either see that as confirmation

[18] Artaud V, 1964, p.148.

[19] Gil, *Metamorphoses of the Body*, p.53.

[20] Ibid., p.61.

[21] Ibid., p.83.

of his pathology, or view the wild variety and creativity of phenomena that in some way has flowed from this conviction – whether the stunning gestures of a dance by Tatsumi Hikijata, or the series of encounters studying consciousness organised by neuroscientist, biologist and theorist Francisco Varela with Tibetan Buddhist lamas, testing the limits of the body and the limits of the mind – as another one of Artaud's vital legacies.[22]

Artaud in the 21st Century: the 'present body'

Artaud predicted his 'present body' would 'fly into pieces/and under ten thousand/notorious aspects/a new body/will be assembled/in which you will never again/be able/to forget me.'[23] In the early decades of the 21st Century Artaud's 'present body' renews its relevance in that neurobiology, the brain, and the 'virtual' body have become intense fields of contestation. This is an agons, I will discuss shortly, where forces of autonomy resist incorporation by capitalist power. That it is the brain itself that becomes the surface for struggle is prefigured in Deleuze's theory of the cinema, itself so largely inspired in key ways by Artaud. In following Artaud in the matter that culture is a function of the nerves, these dilemmas of current cinema for Deleuze are based in the circuitry of the brain – 'The circuits and linkages of the brain don't preexist the stimuli, corpuscles, and particles [*grains*] that trace them…The linkages are paradoxical and on all sides overflow simple association of images,' Deleuze explained. This was key to the power and efficacy of cinema, since 'Cinema, precisely because it puts the image in motion, or rather endows the image with self-motion, never stops tracing the circuits of the brain. This characteristic can be manifested either positively or negatively.'[24] This was the sense of Deleuze maintaining that in the current electronic or media-dominated sensorium 'bodies in Nature or people in a landscape are replaced by brains in a city.'[25]

With *Forbes Magazine*'s prediction in 2003 that given neuroscience developments brain-imaging companies would start to vet TV shows and movies,[26] this

---

[22] Varela became a Tibetan Buddhist in the 1970s. For essays and documentation of the group experiments in neuroscience and meditation, see Varela and Jeremy Hayward, eds, *Gentle Bridges: Dialogues Between the Cognitive Sciences and the Buddhist Tradition*, Boston, MA: Shambhala Press, 1992; and F.J. Varela, ed., *Sleeping, Dreaming, and Dying*, Boston, MA: Wisdom Book, 1997.

[23] Artaud XIII, 1974, p.118.

[24] Gilles Deleuze, 'The Brain is the Screen: An Interview with Gilles Deleuze,' *The Brain is the Screen: Deluze and the Philosophy of Cinema*, ed. Gregory Flaxman, Minneapolis, MN: University of Minnesota Press, 2000, p.366.

[25] Deleuze, *Negotiations*, p.76.

[26] Melanie Wells, 'In Search of the Buy Button,' *Forbes Magazine*, 1 September 2003, pp.62-70.

realm of the neurobiological or neurobiopolitical revolves around 'the ability to sculpt the physical matter of the brain, and its abstract counterpart, the mind.'[27] This is the case given the research in neuroscience that has especially blossomed since 1987, by Jean Pierre Changeux at the Pasteur Institute in Paris and expanded by Nobel laureate Gerald Edelman in San Diego, that has explored the crucial role of environment and culture in the widest sense in the configuration of the human nervous system.[28] These studies have led to new conclusions about how neurons and their synapses and dendrites adapt and change due to new experience.[29] In short, neuronal assemblages that are fired and stimulated more often acquire more efficient means of transmission, outmaneuvering other neuronal networks, lending their theorisation the appropriate name of Neural Selectionism or Neural Darwinism. This neuronal activity that is brought out by various complex systems of stimuli takes on a new importance given the various analyses of 'biopolitics,' what Foucault described as the attempt, beginning towards the end of the 18th Century, to leverage and control all aspects of human and biological life in a governmental order.[30] Artaud proclaimed 'a new body/will be assembled' at the atomic dawn of a new, contemporary stage of biopolitics. As opposed to disciplinary societies that used regimes of punishment to regulate citizens into pre-established patterns from an 'outside,' in what Deleuze called the new 'societies of control'[31] these powers are now networked in far more subtle circuits of behaviour so that they reach across the social field to saturate the brains, consciousness, and bodies of individuals. With pervasive and convincing technologies of neuroimaging of the brain, such as functional magnetic resonance imaging (fMRI) and positron emission tomography (PET), visualisations of 'neural correlates,' for example, have been produced that not only 'read' current thoughts, perceptions and actions, but also predict future ones. This capacity for programming the future banks on the notion neurosci-

[27] Warren Neidich, 'The Neurobiopolitics of Global Consciousness,' *Sarai Reader 2006: Turbulence*, eds. Monica Narula, et al., Delhi: Centre for the Study of Developing Societies, 2006, p.223.

[28] See Gerald Edelman, *The Remembered Present*, New York, NY: Basic Books, 1989.

[29] For an efficient summary of this 'neural plasticity' see Neidich, 'The Neurobiopolitics of Global Consciousness,' pp.223-25.

[30] See Michel Foucault, *The Birth of Biopolitics: Lectures at the Collège de France, 1978-1979*, ed. Arnold I. Davidson, trans. Graham Burchell, Basingstoke & New York, NY: Palgrave Macmillan, [2004] 2008; *Security, Territory, Population: Lectures at the Collège de France, 1977-1978*, ed. Arnold I. Davidson, trans. Graham Burchell, Basingstoke & New York, NY: Palgrave Macmillan, 2009; *'Society Must Be Defended!' Lectures at the Collège de France, 1975-76*, eds. Mauro Bertani and Alessandro Fontana, trans. David Macey, London: Penguin, 2004. Also see Giorgio Agamben, *Homo Sacer: Sovereign Power and Bare Life*, trans. Daniel Heller-Roazen, Stanford, CA: Stanford University Press, 1998.

[31] Gilles Deleuze, 'Postscript on the Societies of Control,' *October* 59, Winter 1992, pp.3-7.

entist Chris Frith describes when he says, 'we are not aware of the action we are about to perform until the brain has made an unconscious choice about what that action should be.'[32] This is what Pasi Väliaho has described as the sort of production of technologically-mediated 'truths about who we are or should become within the current biopolitical apparatus,' that 'characterizes the political ontology of neoliberalism . . . the attempt to rule the whole world by joining together visuality and the anticipated future.'[33]

In these circumstances Artaud's relentless critique of representation takes on new life and significance. Its dimensions are strongly relevant not only since Artaud has inspired so many intriguing new works in our electronic sensorium and artistic environment – whether one takes as examples the plays of Bernard-Marie Koltès, the films of Philippe Grandrieux or certain video installations of Gary Hill.[34] Artaud's influence has often been strongest where it might be least expected, such as in pioneers of feminist art and performance from the 1960's on.[35] Works of interactive cinema and live performance based on motion sensing and laser technologies and live VJing such as Toni Dove's *Lucid Possession* (2013) continue to ask the Artaudian question 'where does the body end?'[36] Félix Guattari read the 'body without organs' as harbinger of the 'post-media' society. In artistic or mediatic terms, this already implies what Peter Weibel has called a 'mixing of media' or the situation where 'all art is post-media art.'[37] While

---

[32] Frith quoted in Pasi Väliaho, *Biopolitical Screens*, Cambridge, MA & London: MIT Press, 2014, p.23.

[33] Ibid., pp.23-4.

[34] See Bernard-Marie Koltès, *Plays*, Vols 1, 2, ed. David Bradby and Maria M. Delgado, London: Methuen Drama, 1997, 2004; Nicole Brenez, ed., *Une Vie nouvelle/nouvelle vision*, Paris: Léo Scheer, 2005; Paul Emmanuel Odin, ed., *An Art of Limina, Gary Hill: Works and Collected Writings*, Barcelona: Ediciones Poligrafa, 2007. For Artaud-inspired video installations of Hill's in the mid and late-90's see Jay Murphy, 'Gary Hill and "The new aesthetic paradigm": Art, Chaos Theory, and Guattari (in the wake of Heidegger)' paper presented at International Association of Philosophy and Literature, May 1999. Available: http://www.thing.net/~soulcity/ap/index.html. Retrieved 12 December 2011. For more on the profoundly Artaudian elements in Grandrieux, Hill and Dove's work, and the numerous homages to Artaud by contemporary artists, see Murphy, 'The Artaud Effect.'

[35] This ranges from Nancy Spero's *Artaud Paintings* (1969-70) and *Codex Artaud* (1970-1) to Carolee Schneemann's performance art. For an interpretation of Artaud's influence on Spero, who used the French artist as an opening to the experience of brutalised war victims and victims of torture, especially women, see Lucy Bradnock, 'Lost in Translation? Nancy Spero/Antonin Artaud/Jacques Derrida,' *Papers on Surrealism* 3 Spring, 2005, pp.1-16. For some of the paradoxes of Schneemann's appropriation of Artaud, see Jay Murphy, 'Assimilating the Unassimilable: Carolee Schneemann in Relation to Antonin Artaud,' *Parkett* 50/51,1997, pp.224-39.

[36] Toni Dove, *Lucid Possession*, 2013. Available: http://www.lucidpossession.com/text/project-description; http://www.lucidpossession.com/text/artist-statement. Retrieved 11 November 2013.

[37] Weibel cited in Clemens Apprich, Josephine Berry Slater, Anthony Iles and Oliver

periodisations of Artaud's relation to this process in terms of media archaeology or art history are going to be confusing, delineations of stages of corporate capitalism, globalisation or biopolitics that limn these new frontiers of governmentality are more heuristic. In what Marx in his *Grundrisse* (1857) described as capital's successful subsumption of labour, the increasing concentration of general knowledge and science in the fixed capital of machinery looms over the individual worker, producing new heights and extremities in exploitation while maximising the socialisation of production to the extent that labour-value as a quantitative means of measurement becomes hopelessly obsolete. Marx foresaw the situation when 'the value objectified in machinery appears as a presupposition against which the value-creating power of the individual labor capacity is an infinitesimal, vanishing magnitude.'[38] Thus, contrary to much that Marx wrote elsewhere, the course of capitalist development tends in itself to do away with the workings of the law of value, by making scientific knowledge and its applied organisation in production the principal productive force. In this transition from formal to real subsumption of labour, capital appears omnipotent and all-pervasive, provoking a crisis of extraordinary 'separation'[39] felt in every aspect of social, economic and political life. In this situation of extreme schizophrenia writ large, to return to Artaud's locus of the body, Patricia Clough has argued that it is in this period of real subsumption, 'the tendencies of capitalism are moved toward the techno-ontological post-biological threshold.'[40] As Artaud had argued, mutations of the body and its biological existence form this agenda and not only or merely vagaries of its desire.

Much of this 'real subsumption' is digitally-mediated or enabled, as in what David Rodowick has called the 'social hieroglyph' operative in digital or postmodern electronic society, whereby the visible and the expressible are utterly entwined and interdependent.[41] Rodowick generalises the era of new media as one of hieroglyphic form that becomes 'the logic of mass culture itself.'[42] This uniformity of description may miss the already pervasive 'mixing of media' in Weibel's sense, practices characterised by equalisation and hybridisation of different media, whether digitally based or not, even a 'rematerialisation' of the art object based on novel combinations made possible of the actual and virtual.[43]

Lerone Schultz, eds, *Provocative Alloys: A Post-Media Anthology*, London: Mute Books/Post-Media Lab Books, 2013, p.148.

38 Karl Marx, *Grundrisse*, ed. and trans. Martin Nicolaus, New York, NY: Vintage Books, 1973, p.694.

39 Karl Marx, *Capital*, vol. 2, ed. Friedrich Engels, New York, NY: International Publishers, 1967, p.33.

40 Patricia T. Clough, 'The Affective Turn,' *The Affect Theory Reader*, eds Melissa Gregg and Gregory J. Seigworth, Durham, NC: Duke University Press, 2010, p.221.

41 Rodowick, *Reading the Figural*, pp.x; xiv.

42 Ibid., p.46.

43 The subject of a symposium at the Kennedy Center, Florence, Italy, 21 June 2014,

What is useful about Rodowick's analysis, however, is how it limns what was once an avant-gardist, disruptive force – the resort to hieroglyphs as a powerful otherness that granted quicker access to the 'unconscious' among other virtues – is now quite run of the mill in fact omnipresent and far from liberating, is the preferred form of communication media in post-Fordist capitalism. In Artaud's sense as an all-devouring reality, it can even take the form articulated by Alexander Galloway where the digital is defined as the attempt to 'encode and simulate anything whatsoever in the universe'[44] – the febrile universalism Artaud already denounces in the nascent Cold War. What Galloway describes as the digital's 'capacity to divide things and make distinctions between them', indeed, as the distinction that 'makes it possible to make any distinction at all'[45] implies 'Digitality is much more capacious than the computer, both historically because there simply is no history without digitality, but also conceptually, because the digital is a basic ingredient within ontology, politics, and most everything in between.'[46] Given this definition Artaud's hieroglyphic may appear in contrast an analogical function, uniting heterogeneous entities, integrating proportions. Yet Artaud comes to denounce it as the false religious patterning and making of the world, opposed to his 'direct creation' – in other words, in Galloway's terms it is all too digital. Artaud's erasure of the hieroglyphic and assault upon it as yet another mode of representation poses the challenge of 'pure chaos' to a digital philosophy that maintains, 'the binary principle is not merely a prerogative of digital computing, but of all forms of process.'[47] Artaud opposes the hieroglyphic (and the digital) to establish another relation to the outside.

Artaud's exploration of 'virtuality' as early as 1925 and exposition of a 'new body' much later, fascinating and important in themselves, are inextricably lodged in this wide-ranging challenge to representation, an assault that carries more prescience now than at the time of his most vociferous voicing of it in 1946-8. As Stephen Barber has concluded, 'in a contemporary moment in which representation assumes a vastly expanded and unprecedented power, in its obliterating contact with the human body as well as with urban environments and creative media, Artaud's anatomization of the process of representation is

'Rematerialization of the Art Object: Art, Robotics, and Post-Convergent Labor' for example featured artists working in computer-assisted painting, CAD architectural design, sculpture and 3D printing. For a discussion of the problems the contemporary art world especially has had with the notions of digital art as medium, see Domenico Quaranta, *Beyond New Media Art*, Brescia: Link Editions, 2013.

44 Alexander R. Galloway, *Laruelle: Against the Digital*, Minneapolis, MN: University of Minnesota Press, 2014, p.xxxiv.

45 Ibid., p.xxix.

46 Ibid., p.xxxiv.

47 Stamatia Portanova, *Moving without a Body*, Cambridge, MA & London: MIT Press, 2013, pp.136; 130.

no longer obtuse, but rather, exact and revelatory.'[48] In my account, Artaud's assault on representation is first waged on behalf of the true 'lines' that constitute reality, a powerful 'occult geometry' representation can only occlude, and that even the militant avant-garde movement of surrealism he judged unable to reach.[49] That evolves into an attack even more violent in the last two-and-a-half years of his life, where any sacred hieroglyph and the esoteric thought that husbands it, seems itself a false representational raiment, and is simply despised. 'I hold it now in the real and in my body, like a toilet broom,' Artaud writes.[50] Artaud is no longer searching for geomagnetic stress points or the 'zig zags' of an ultimate reality, his 'lines,' in his drawings, in his notebooks, are artifacts of how what was once an element or moving sign of a cosmological hieroglyph has now disintegrated into unremitting conflict that revolves around the creation of Artaud's 'bodies without organs.' Artaud's response to what he felt as a primal and ontological invasion and usurpation was this reinvention of the body. The substrate Artaud offers today is paradoxically due to this enactment of the 'body without organs;' what appeared most delusional and 'mad' in his own lifetime, seems to offer the most viable thread to ours. In the strongest possible contrast to traditional rituals that produce a reconciliation of self and world the late Artaud's 'body without organs' is part of a desperate universal conflict; it cannot be separated from Artaud's desire for infinity that is also the end of the known world. Artaud lives in what Sri Aurobindo called the 'war universe.'

Paradoxically it is this most unmanageable aspect of Artaud and one that has most frequently gone unremarked by many of his most well-known commentators – that he worked indefatigably in a universe of sorcery and counter-sorcery – that survives today. One can see some of this new seriousness towards sorcery outlined by Isabelle Stengers, whose own intellectual itinerary, from co-authoring several seminal works on complexity theory with Ilya Prigogine, to 'situating science' in bold new contextualisations of science studies, to more recently translating writings by pagan, Wiccan activist Starhawk, has already been cited as illustrating the beginning of altered intellectual horizons in which to understand Artaud. Stengers wrote in a 2005 book with Philippe Pignarre that the contemporary world economic system is most accurately described as 'capitalist sorcery' notwithstanding it is without any sorcerers who see them-

[48] Barber, *Artaud: Terminal Curses*, p.115.

[49] I have devoted little space to Artaud's relation with the surrealists. Although Artaud never refuted the characterisation 'surrealist' for himself, he argued the Paris surrealist group with its turn to *rapprochement* with Marxism and socialism, was betraying its best impulses, and could not account for the deeper movements of being. One of his most succinct and eloquent statements of this is his talk at the University of Mexico in 1936 on 'Surrealism and Revolution,' in which he specifically castigates the latest proclamation from the Contre-Attaque group. See Artaud, *Œuvres*, pp.685-92.

[50] Artaud XIV:2, 1978, p.68.

selves as such.[51] To fight against this, Stengers and Pignarre, in truly Artaudian fashion, advocate counter-sorcery. This analysis by Stengers and Pignarre complements that of the collective Tiqqun, who take Marx's warning of commodity fetishism in *Capital*, what he called social relations between people in a situation of generalized commodity production becoming the 'fantastic form of a relation between things'[52] quite literally as a case of 'possession' of one's body, mind, actions, and soul. This is 'possession *by a psychic economy*' that for Tiqqun is the only level on which the 'economy is real and concrete.' The operations of the globalised corporate capitalist economy therefore conjure realms of imagination and desire, the shaping of 'Man' into an 'economic creature' that without exaggeration function as a kind of 'black magic.'[53]

This point of view of Artaud's contemporary relevance has been adumbrated most directly and boldly by theorist Frédéric Neyrat, who points to Artaud's identification in the first section of *To have done with the judgment of god* of the combinatory 'knot' between capitalism, technoscience, and imperialist war.[54] This is the conjuratory dream of Western colonialism, Neyrat argues, that has to destroy opposing voices, and that is also at one with monotheism. When Artaud rages that 'one has reinvented microbes finally to impose a new idea of god'[55] Neyrat comments that Artaud's Cold War rant is also aimed against nuclear proliferation, 'The avatar of God, this is the Bomb.'[56] The vampirism and parasitism of being Artaud continually denounces identifies the ontology of transnational capitalist expansion, in its myriad levels and incarnations. And his plea for an opening onto infinity in his essay on Van Gogh and in his last radio broadcast, Neyrat reasons, is a similar affirmation of infinity one finds after the death of God in contemporary *philosophes* like Deleuze or Alain Badiou.[57] Neyrat's view of Artaud carries its own reductions, however. His stressing of how Artaud at the end of his life is 'assassinating magic' and fighting sorcery underestimates how caught up he continues to be in such. Neyrat writes that the only time Artaud believes in God is the brief period at Rodez when he later admits himself he is mentally ill.[58] Yet Artaud's actual record as evidenced in his voluminous

---

[51] Philippe Pignarre and Isabelle Stengers, *La Sorcellerie capitaliste*, Paris: La Découverte, 2005, p.59.

[52] Karl Marx, *Capital*, in *Collected Works*, Vol. 35 by Karl Marx and Friedrich Engels, New York, NY: International Publishers, [1867] 1975, p.83.

[53] See Tiqqun, *Introduction to Civil War*, trans. Alexander R. Galloway and Jason E. Smith, Los Angeles, CA: Semiotext(e), 2010, p. 83; and 'On the Economy as Black Magic,' Available: http://blackmagic.jottit.com. Retrieved 9 August 2011.

[54] Frédéric Neyrat, *Instructions pour une prise d'âmes: Artaud et l'envoûtement occidental*, Strasbourg: La Phocide, 2009, p.18.

[55] Artaud XIII, 1974, p.103.

[56] Neyrat, *Instructions pour une prise d'âmes*, p.25.

[57] Ibid., p.21.

[58] Ibid., p.20.

notebooks is far messier and profoundly conflicted, and it is difficult to demonstrate such a clean break with such metaphysics as much as it seems Artaud's goal. Neyrat gives some hint of the confusion of this when writing about this war of clashing magicks or sorceries – 'How to know from the outside which one to stop?'[59]

Neyrat's account, following on the heels of his *Surexposés* (2005) which similarly explores the necessary links between the notions of being, God, capital and surplus value of all kinds, remains of value in showing that there is some validity in Artaud's wider context in which to proceed, in which Artaud has 'succeeded for us all.'[60] The chief lesson of this developing context for my own endeavour is that it frees one from the psychologism and psychoanalytic double-binds that have often remained the most prevalent manner of looking at Artaud. This is the value of Neyrat's work, for which Artaud *le mômo* is articulating the non-symbolised of the West, keeping in mind there is surely a limited amount of time in which we can continue to speak of the 'West.' It is precisely because Artaud is thus elucidating 'our collective hallucination'[61] – questions of the body, the world, or 'Europe' that cannot be so easily canalised – that his dilemmas cannot be reduced to a question of his individual madness or delirium. This would entail attributing Artaud's problems to a *Moi* that he never ceased to claim he never possessed.[62]

Neyrat's sometimes blunt advocacy of Artaud as the voice of so much unvoiced in Western culture, follows the guise of Foucault's 'the soul, prison of the body'[63] as in Artaud's 'shit to the spirit,'[64] Artaud's notion that 'the self is not the body, the body is the self.'[65] Neyrat's critique seeks to develop the elaboration of Artaud's 'body without organs' found in Deleuze and Guattari's *Capitalism and Schizophrenia* project. Using Artaud's notion as a figure or strange attractor for the social in the conditions of global capitalism, the 'body without organs' as body=degree zero intensity in *Anti-Oedipus* is a kind of groundless ground or foundation for any desire. As Deleuze and Guattari elaborated, this makes it also the movement of capital itself, of 'capitalist being,'[66] becoming essential as the 'recording surface' of social reproduction. In this role, the body without organs 'falls back on' and appropriates the myriad activity of the desiring-machines in such a way that the 'organ-machines now cling to the body without organs as though it were a fencer's padded jacket or as though these

59 Ibid., p.48.

60 Deleuze and Guattari, *A Thousand Plateaus*, p.164.

61 Neyrat, *Instructions pour une prise d'âmes*, p.9.

62 Ibid.

63 Michel Foucault, *Surveiller et punir*, Paris: Gallimard/Tel Quel, 1975, p.34.

64 Artaud, 'Chiote à l'esprit,' *Œuvres*, pp.1502-7.

65 Artaud XIV:2, 1978, p.53.

66 Deleuze and Guattari, *Anti-Oedipus*, p.8.

organ-machines were medals pinned onto the jersey of the wrestler who makes them jingle as he moves toward his opponent.'[67] In recording the entire process of social reproduction and desire, the desiring machines produce the organed bodies that appear to emerge or emanate from the body without organs; draping itself with such attraction-repulsion machines, the body without organs comes to act as a 'quasi cause by communicating the apparent movement (the fetish) to them.'[68] Hence, in *Anti-Oedipus* the 'body without organs' is not only what Guattari would later term the 'new machinic processuality' that is the 'continual point of emergence of all forms of creativity,'[69] it is also quite problematically the figureless figure of any desire in capitalism, the site or responsibility of the movements of capital itself. The schizo in this regard is through and through, then, a practitioner of political economy; in revolt, a counter-fetishist, or rather an exploiter of fetishes in an environment completely dominated by such.[70] The various treatments of sorcery or 'black magic' in Neyrat, Pignarre and Stengers, and Tiqqun are attempts to update such analysis given the current state of what Guattari had termed 'integrated world capitalism.'[71]

With these readings, Artaud is not so much delimited as the last modernist, or hyper-modernist tragedy,[72] but as someone whose madhouse insights are truly prophetic in limning the dawning social field. In *To have done with the judgment of god* Artaud in apparently bottomless anger, laced with acid humour, outlined a scatological obscene vision of a hyper-productive, hyper-mechanised Cold War fought by remote control (which Neyrat would say is even more perfectly realised today in the drone attacks of the 'war on terror'), a universe so degraded that schoolboys' sperm was stockpiled for future cannon-fodder. It is

---

67 Ibid., p.11.

68 Ibid., p.12.

69 Guattari, *The Guattari Reader*, p.98.

70 For an exhibition that presented a complex reevaluation of the notion of capitalist fetishism, owing more frankly to Georges Bataille and *Documents*-style surrealism than Artaud, see 'Critical Fetishes: Residues of General Economy' curated by the Mexico City-based collective El Espectro Rojo, 26 May – 29 August 2010, CA2M, Madrid, Spain. Yet, in common with several of the approaches described above, the exhibition was not based on any notion of 'de-mystification' or 'critical consciousness' concerning fetishes and such icons, but of a re-activation of their subversive imaginative power, exploiting the ambivalence of their effect in capitalist societies.

71 Guattari authored some of the earliest trenchant analyses of globalisation, see 'Plan for the Planet' (1979) and (with Eric Alliez) 'Capitalistic Systems, Structures, and Processes' (1983) in *Molecular Revolution*. For an elaboration of Guattari's analyses, see Gary Genosko, 'Guattari's Contributions to the Theory of Semiocapitalism,' in *The Guattari Effect*.

72 See Sylvère Lotringer's comments in *100 Years of Cruelty*, p.326: 'It's very difficult to have this modernist heroic position which Artaud was playing off all the time...We live in a totally schizophrenic society. That's why schizophrenia doesn't have the same advantage as it had before...Artaud was probably the last to be able to be at the absolute limit and be scandalised for it.'

a vision of the catastrophic future already present as one of numb sensorium and perpetual war – 'And long live war, right?'[73] It is in contrast to this universe of simulation and conflict that Artaud affirms the peyote-eating Tarahumaras whose ceremonies 'split the cross.'[74] For his own corresponding reasons, ranging from overpopulation and media obsession to genetic feedback and climate destruction, poet Michael McClure affirmed in a March 2011 interview, 'Artaud's vision of post-World War II U.S.A…We're living it now.'[75] This is profoundly confirming for someone whose Theater of cruelty could never be separated from social cataclysm and upheaval. It also makes his annihilation of the hieroglyphic of far more than art historical interest. In a recent work on new media Laura U. Marks has looked for inspiration to much ancient and classical Islamic art and philosophy in that it offers a model whereby 'Image unfolds from text across a membrane whose tensile strength indexes its resistance to unfolding, with a force that pulls the infinite into being.'[76] Artaud provides an example much closer to us in time, with his membrane of the *grille* or *subjectile* that works its resistance yet yokes an intense material shredding to an opening to infinity.[77] In what has been proclaimed a 'post-biological era'[78] Artaud offers us his complex of the 'body without organs.' Already perched in 1948 at 'the absolute limit of the capitalist system'[79] and the proposed eclipse of the body Artaud poses a metamorphosis for such catastrophe – beyond psychology, beyond any organic philosophy of the body, arguably blasting even beyond a Deleuzian theory of immanence. Paradoxical in nearly every respect, Artaud's contribution still retains a possibility not only due to its bending, working with, holding, or staying on the 'line' as Deleuze counselled. It is because in an extraordinary, ungraspable movement of extremity and ekstasis, in the process of his prodigious abolition of the hieroglyphic, Artaud poses the erasing of the line.

[73] Artaud XIII, 1974, p.73; Artaud, *Watchfiends & Rack Screams*, p.285.

[74] Ibid., p.74; ibid., p.287.

[75] Anis Shivani, 'Exclusive: Beat Poet Michael McClure on Jim Morrison, The Doors, Allen Ginsberg, Jack Kerouac,' 3 March 2011. Available: http://www.huffingtonpost.com/anis-shivani/exclusive-beat-poet-mcclure_b_823425.html. Retrieved 9 August 2011.

[76] Laura U. Marks, *Enfoldment and Infinity: An Islamic Genealogy of New Media Art*, Cambridge, MA & London: MIT Press, 2010, p.251.

[77] Apropos of the resistance of Artaud's work to digitalisation, given the presentation of his notebooks online by the Bibliothèque nationale de France, see part 4 of Barber, *Artaud: Terminal Curses*.

[78] See for instance the volume of the proceedings from the series of 'Consciousness Reframed' conferences, Roy Ascott, ed., *Engineering Nature: Art and Consciousness in the Post-Biological Era*, Bristol: Intellect, 2006.

[79] Lotringer, *100 Years of Cruelty*, p.325.

WORKS CONSULTED

ARCHIVES

Antonin Artaud, Cahiers, April 1947/March 1948. Courtesy: Bibliothèque nationale de France, Paris.

BIBLIOGRAPHY

Agamben, Giorgio, *Homo Sacer*, trans. Daniel Heller-Roazen, Stanford, CA: Stanford University Press, 1998.

_______ , *Infancy and History*, trans. Liz Heron, London & New York, NY: Verso, 1993.

Agrippa, Heinrich Cornelius, *Three Books of Occult Philosophy*, trans. James Freake, ed. Donald Tyson, Woodbury, MN: Llewellyn Publications, [1533] 1993.

Alain-Michaud, Philippe, *Aby Warburg and the Image in Motion*, trans. Sophie Hawkins, New York, NY: Zone Books, 2004.

Alexandrian, Sarane, *Histoire de la philosophie occulte*, Paris: Éditions Seghers, 1983.

Allendy, René, *Paracelse, le médicin maudit*, Paris: Gallimard, 1937.

Alliez, Erc, *The Signature of the World*, trans. Elliot Ross Albert and Alberto Toscano, London & New York, NY: Continuum, 2004.

André, Serge, *L'Épreuve d'Antonin Artaud et l'expérience de la psychoanalyse*, Brussels: Éditions Luc Pire, 2007.

Anonymous, 'Autobiography of a Winnebago Indian' in *The Portable North American Indian Reader*, ed. Frederick Turner, New York, NY: Viking, 1978, pp.378-454.

Apprich, Clemens and Josephine Berry Slater, Anthony Iles and Oliver Lerone Schultz, eds, *Provocative Alloys: A Post-Media Anthology*, London: Mute Books/Post-Media Lab Books, 2013.

Aragon, Louis, *Le Fou d'Elsa*, Paris: Gallimard, 1983.

Aristotle, *The New Aristotle Reader*, ed. J.L.Akrill, Oxford: Clarendon Press, 1986.

Armand-Laroche, H.J., *Artaud et son Double*, Périgueux: Pierre-Franlac, 1964.

Artaud, Antonin, *Cahiers d'Ivry: Février 1947 – Mars 1948*, 2 vols, Paris: Gallimard/Hors Série Littérature, 2011.

_______, *50 drawings to murder magic*, ed. Évelyne Grossman, trans. Donald Nicholson-Smith, London, New York, NY & Calcutta: Seagull Books, 2008.

_______, *Cahier Ivry, Janvier 1948*, ed. Évelyne Grossman, Paris: Gallimard, 2006.

_______, *Œuvres*, ed. Évelyne Grossman, Paris: Gallimard/Quarto, 2004.

_______, *Messages révolutionnaires*, Paris: Flammarion, 1998.

_______, *Antonin Artaud: Works on Paper*, ed. Margit Rowell, New York, NY: Museum of Modern Art, 1996.

_______, *Pour en finir avec le jugement de dieu*, CD, Brussels: Sub Rosa, 1996.

_______, *Pour en finir avec le jugement de dieu*, CDs, Marseilles: André Dimanche Éditeur, 1995.

_______, *Watchfiends & Rack Screams: Works from the Final Period*, ed. and trans. Clayton Eshleman with Bernard Bador, Boston, MA: Exact Change, 1995.

_______, *Œuvres complètes*, I-XXVI, Paris: Gallimard, 1956-94.

_______, *L'Arve et l'Aume suivi de 24 lettres à Marc Barbezat*, Décines: L'Arbalète, 1989.

_______, *Antonin Artaud, dessins et portraits*, Paris: Gallimard, 1986.

_______, *Artaud Anthology*, ed. Jack Hirschman, San Francisco, CA: City Lights Books, [1965] 1983.

_______, *Nouveaux écrits de Rodez*, Paris: Gallimard, 1977.

_______, *The Peyote Dance*, trans. Helen Weaver, New York, NY: Farrar, Straus & Giroux, 1976.

_______, *Antonin Artaud: Selected Writings*, ed. Susan Sontag, trans. Helen Weaver, New York, NY: Farrar, Straus & Giroux, 1976.

_______, *The Theater and Its Double*, trans. M.C. Richards, New York, NY: Grove Press, 1958.

Ascott, Roy, ed., *Engineering Nature: Art and Consciousness in the Post-Biological Era*, Bristol: Intellect, 2006.

Atkinson, Jane Monnig, *The Art and Politics of Wana Shamanship*, Berkeley, CA: University of California Press, 1989.

Augé, Marc, *Pouvoirs de vie, pouvoirs de mort*, Paris: Flammarion, 1977.

Aumont, Jacques, *Amnésies: Fictions du cinema d'apres Jean-Luc Godard*, Paris: P.O.L., 1999.

Barba, Eugenio and Nicola Saverese, *A Dictionary of Theater Anthropology: The Secret Art of the Performer*, trans. Richard Fowler, New York, NY: Routledge, 1991.

Bachelard, Gaston, *La Dialectique de la durée*, Paris: Bovin, 1936.

_______, *Lautréamont*, Paris: Librarie José Corti, 1939.

Baird, Bruce, *Hijikata Tatsumi and Butoh: Dancing in Grey Grits*, Basingstoke & New York, NY: Palgrave Macmillan, 2012.

Barber, Stephen, *Artaud: Terminal Curses*, London: Creation Books, 2008.

_______, *Hijikata: Revolt of the Body*, London: Creation Books, 2007.

_______, *Artaud: The Screaming Body*, new ed., London: Creation Books, 2004.

_______, 'Cruel Journey,' *Art in America*, February 1995, pp.70-5.

_______, *Antonin Artaud: Blows and Bombs*, London: Faber & Faber, 1993.

_______, 'A Foundry of the Figure: Antonin Artaud,' *Artforum* 26:1, September 1987, pp.88-95.

Barnes, Mary, *Something Sacred: Conversations, Writings, Paintings*, London: Free Association, 1989.

Barnes, Mary and Joseph Berke, *Mary Barnes: Two Accounts of a Journey Through Madness*, new ed., London & New York, NY: Penguin Books, 1973.

Barrault, Jean-Louis, *Reflections on Theater*, trans. Barbara Wall, London: Theatre Book Club, [1947] 1951.

Bataille, Georges, *The Bataille Reader*, ed. by Fred Botting and Scott Wilson, Oxford: Blackwell Publishers, 1997.

_______, *The Absence of Myth*, trans. and ed. Michael Richardson, London & New York, NY: Verso, 1994.

_______, *The Accursed Share Volume One*, trans. Robert Hurley, New York, NY: Zone Books, 1991.

_______, *Visions of Excess: Selected Writings*, 1927-1939, ed. Allan Stoekl, trans. Allan Stoekl with Carl R. Lovitt and Donald M. Leslie, Jr., Minneapolis, MN: University of Minnesota Press, 1985.

Baudelaire, Charles, *Flowers of Evil*, ed. by Marthiel and Jackson Matthews, New York, NY: New Directions, 1955.

Baudrillard, Jean, 'Baudrillard on Artaud,' 16 November, 1996, New York, NY: The Drawing Center.

Bell, Jeffrey, *Philosophy at the Edge of Chaos*, Toronto: University of Toronto Press, 2006.

Beaumelle, Agnès de la, 'Spells and Gris-Gris, Introduction,' in *Antonin Artaud: Works on Paper*, ed. Margit Rowell, New York, NY: Museum of Modern Art, 1996, pp.39-41.

Bergson, Henri, *Creative Evolution*, trans. Arthur Mitchell, Mineola, NY: Dover Publications, [1910] 1998.

Bersani, Leo, 'Artaud, Defecation, and Birth' in *A Future for Astyanax: Character and Desire in Literature*, Boston, MA: Little, Brown & Co., 1969, pp.259-272.

Blanchot, Maurice, *The Infinite Conversation*, trans. Susan Hanson, Minneapolis, MN: University of Minnesota Press, [1969] 1993.

_______, *The Space of Literature*, trans. Ann Smock, Lincoln, NE & London: University of Nebraska Press, 1993.

_______, *L'Entretien infini*, Paris: Gallimard, 1969.

_______ , *Le Livre à venir*, Paris: Gallimard, 1959.

Blin, Roger, *Souvenirs et propos*, Paris: Gallimard, 1986.

Bonardel, Françoise, *Artaud*, Paris: Balland, 1987.

Bonta, Mark and John Protevi, *Deleuze and Geophilosophy, A Guide and Glossary*, Edinbugh: University of Edinburgh Press, 2004.

Borer, Alain, *Rimbaud in Abyssinia*, trans. Rosemary Walrop, New York, NY: William Morrow, 1991.

Bradnock, Lucy, 'Lost in Translation? Nancy Spero/Antonin Artaud/Jacques Derrida,' *Papers on Surrealism* 3, Spring 2005, pp.1-16.

Brenez, Nicole, ed., *Une Vie nouvelle/une nouvelle vision*, Paris: Léo Scheer, 2005.

Breton, André, *Free Rein*, trans. Michael Parmentier and Jacqueline d'Amboise, Lincoln, NE: University of Nebraska Press, 1995.

_______ , *Nadja*, trans. Richard Howard, New York, NY: Grove Press, [1928] 1994.

_______ , *Manifestoes of Surrealism*, trans. Richard Seaver and Helen R. Lane, Ann Arbor, MI: University of Michigan Press, 1969.

Bruno, Pierre, *Antonin Artaud: realité et poesie*, Paris: L'Harmattan, 1999.

Burroughs, William S. and Brion Gysin, *The Third Mind*, New York, NY: Viking Press, 1978.

Burstow, Bonnie, Brenda A. Lefrançois and Shaindl Diamond, eds, *Psychiatry Disrupted: Theorizing Resistance and Crafting (R)evolution*, Montréal & Kingston: McGill-Queen's University, 2014.

Butler, Rex, 'Non-Genital Thought,' in *100 Years of Cruelty*, ed. Edward Scheer, Sydney: Power Publications, 2002, pp.23-57.

Campbell, Joseph, *The Hero with a Thousand Faces*, Oxford: Princeton University Press, [1949] 2004.

Carasco, Raymonde, 'Approche de la pensée tarahumara' in *Antonin Artaud*, Paris: Bibliothèque nationale de France/Gallimard, 2006, pp.134-141.

_______ , http://raymonde.carasco.free.fr.

Carrouges, Michel, *Les Machines célibataires*, Paris: Arcanes, 1954.

Casarès, Maria, *Résidente priviégiée*, Paris: Fayard, 1980.

Castaneda, Carlos, *The Teachings of Don Juan*, London: Penguin Books, [1968] 2004.

_______ , *The Active Side of Infinity*, New York, NY: Harper Collins, 1998.

_______ , *The Fire from Within*, New York, NY: Washington Square Press, 1991.

_______ , *Tales of Power*, New York, NY: Simon & Schuster, 1974.

_______ , *Journey to Ixtlan*, New York, NY: Washington Square Press, 1972.

_______ , *A Separate Reality*, London: The Bodley Head, 1971.

Certeau, Michel de, *La Prise de parole*, Paris: Éditions du Seuil, 1994.

Charuty, Giordana, 'Le Vœu de vivre,' *Terrains* 18, 1992, pp.46-60.

Cheng, François, *Chinese Poetic Writing*, trans. Donald A. Riggs and Jerome P. Seaton, Bloomington, IN: Indiana University Press, 1982.

Chevrier, Jean-François, 'La verité de l'hallucination contre "le mensonge de l'Etre"' in *Antonin Artaud*, Paris: Bibliothèque nationale de France/Gallimard, 2006, pp.202-206.

Chiesa, Lorenzo, 'Lacan with Artaud: *j'ouïs-sens, jouis-sens, jouis-sans*,' in *Lacan, The Silent Partners*, ed. Slavoj Žižek, London & New York, NY: Verso, 2006, pp.336-64.

Chion, Michel, *The Voice in Cinema*, trans. Claudia Gorbman, New York, NY: Columbia University Press, [1982] 1999.

Chuang Tzu, *The Book of Chuang Tzu*, trans. Martin Palmer, New York, NY & London: Penguin, 2006.

Clastres, Pierre, *Society Against the State*, trans. R. Hurley, New York, NY: Zone Books, 1977.

Clément, Catherine, *Syncope: The Philosophy of Rapture*, trans. Sally O'Driscoll and Deirdre M. Mahoney, Minneapolis, MN: University of Minnesota Press, 1994.

Clézio, J.M.G. Le, 'Antonin Artaud, le rêve mexicain,' *Europe*, November-December 1984, pp.110-120.

Clifford, James, *The Predicament of Culture*, Cambridge, MA: Harvard University Press, 1988.

Clough, Patricia T., 'The Affective Turn' in *The Affect Theory Reader*, eds, Melissa Gregg and Gregory J. Seigworth, Durham, NC: Duke University Press, 2010, pp.206-225.

Cohen, Jack and Ian Stewart, *The Collapse of Chaos*, NewYork, NY: Penguin Books, 1994.

Coomaraswamy, Ananda K., *The Transformation of Nature in Art*, New York, NY: Dover, 1956.

Cooper, David, *The Language of Madness*, Harmondsworth & New York, NY: Penguin Books, 1978.

_______ , *A Grammar of Living*, New York, NY: Pantheon Books, 1974.

_______ , *The Death of the Family*, New York, NY: Pantheon Books, 1971.

_______ , *Psychiatry and Anti-Psychiatry*, London: Tavistock, 1967.

Cortade, Ludovic, *Antonin Artaud, la virtualité incarnée*, Paris: L'Harmattan, 2000.

Daly, Mary, *Gyn/ecology*, Boston, MA: Beacon Press, 1978.

Danchin, Laurent and André Roumieux, *Artaud et l'asile*, 2 vols, Paris: Séguier, 1996.

Deleuze, Gilles, *Dialogues II*, trans. Hugh Tomlinson, Barbara Habberjam and Eliot Ross Albert, New York, NY & London: Continuum, 2006.

_______ , *Two Regimes of Madness*, ed. David Lapoujade, trans. Ames Hodges and Mike Taormina, New York, NY & Los Angeles, CA: Semiotext(e), 2006.

_______ , 'The Method of Dramatisation' in *Desert Islands*, New York, NY & Los Angeles, CA: Semiotext(e), 2004, pp.94-116.

_______ , *Francis Bacon: the Logic of Sensation*, trans. Daniel W. Smith, Minneapolis, MN: University of Minnesota Press, [1981] 2003.

_______ , *Difference and Repetition*, trans. Paul Patton, London & New York, NY: Continuum, [1968] 2002.

_______ , 'The Brain Is the Screen: An Interview with Gilles Deleuze' in *The Brain is the Screen: Deleuze and the Philosophy of Cinema*, ed. Gregory Flaxman, Minneapolis, MN: University of Minnesota Press, 2000, pp. 365-373.

_______ , *Proust and Signs*, trans. Richard Howard, Minneapolis, MN: University of Minnesota Press, [1964] 2000.

_______ , 'To Have Done with Judgment' in *Essays Critical and Clinical*, trans. Daniel W. Smith and Michael A. Greco, Minneapolis, MN: University of Minnesota Press, [1993] 1997, pp.126-136.

_______ , *Negotiations: Interviews 1972-1990*, trans. Martin Jouglin, New York, NY: Columbia University Press, 1995.

_______ , *The Fold*, trans. Tom Conley, Minneapolis, MN: University of Minnesota Press, [1988] 1993.

_______ , 'Postscript on the Societies of Control' in *October* 59, Winter 1992, pp.3-7.

_______ , *The Logic of Sense*, trans. Mark Lester and Charles Stivale, ed. Constanin V. Boundas, New York, NY: Columbia University Press, [1969] 1990.

_______ , *Cinema 2: The Time-Image*, trans. by Hugh Tomlinson and Robert Galeta, Minneapolis, MN: University of Minnesota Press, 1989.

_______ , *Bergsonism*, trans. Hugh Tomlinson and Barbara Habberjam, New York, NY: Zone Books, [1966] 1988.

_______ , *Foucault*, trans. Séan Hand. Minneapolis, MN: University of Minnesota Press, 1988.

_______ , *Cinema 1: The Movement-Image*, trans. Hugh Tomlinson and Barbara Habberjam, Minneapolis, MN: University of Minnesota Press, 1986.

_______ , *Kant's Critical Philosophy*, trans. Hugh Tomlinson and Barbara Habberjam, Minneapolis, MN: University of Minnesota Press, [1963] 1985.

Deleuze, Gilles and Félix Guattari, *A Thousand Plateaus*, trans. Brian Massumi, Minneapolis, MN: University of Minnesota Press, [1977] 1987.

_______ , *Kafka. Toward a Minor Literature*, trans. Dana Polan, Minneapolis, MN: University of Minnesota Press, [1975]1986.

_______ , *Anti-Oedipus*, trans. Robert Hurley, Mark Seem and Helen R. Lane, New York, NY: Viking Penguin, [1972] 1977.

Deren, Maya, *Divine Horsemen*, New Paltz, NY: McPherson & Co., [1953] 1985.

_______ , *The Voodoo Gods*, St. Albans: Paladin, [1953] 1975.

Dequeker, Jean, 'Naissance de l'image' (1950) in *Artaud Vivant*, ed. O.Virmaux, Paris: Oswald Èditeur, 1980, pp.155-156.

Derrida, Jacques, 'Les voix d'Artaud (la force, la forme, la forge),' *Magazine Littéraire* 434, September 2004, pp.34-6.

_______ , *The Secret Art of Antonin Artaud*, trans. Mary Ann Caws, Cambridge, MA & London: MIT Press, 1998.

_______ , 'Artaud: Writing/Drawing,' Panel discussion, 11 October, 1996, New York, NY: The Drawing Center.

_______ , 'Lecture on Artaud', 10 October 1996. Courtesy: Museum of Modern Art, New York, NY.

_______ , *Writing and Difference*, trans. Alan Bass, Chicago, IL: University of Chicago Press, 1980.

Devereux, Georges, *Essais d'ethnopsychiatrie générale*, Paris: Gallimard, 1970.

Didi-Huberman, Georges, *Fra Angelico: Dissemblance and Figuration*, trans. Jane Marie Todd, Chicago, IL: University of Chicago Press, 1995.

Dillon, M.C., *Semiological Reductionism*, Albany, NY: State University of New York Press, 1995.

Dixon, Steve, *Digital Performance*, Cambridge, MA & London: MIT Press, 2007.

Dolar, Mladen, 'What's in a Voice,' *Amber '07: Art and Technology Festival, Voice and Survival*, Istanbul: BIS, Body-Process-Art Association, 2010, pp.93-103.

Dostoyevksy, Fyodor, *The Idiot*, trans. David Magarshack, New York, NY: Penguin, [1887] 1955.

Dove, Toni, 'Project Description', *Lucid Possession*. Available: http://www.lucidpossession.com/text/project-description. Retrieved November 11, 2013.

_______ , 'Artist Statement,' *Lucid Possession*. Available: http://www.lucidpossession.com/text/artist-statement. Retrieved November 11, 2013.

_______ , 'Haunting the Movie: Embodied Interface/Sensory Cinema' in *New Visions in Performance*, eds, Gavin Carter and Colin Beardon, Lisse: Swets and Zietlinger, 2004, pp.107-120.

Duerr, Hans Peter, *Dreamtime: Concerning the Boundary Between Wilderness and Civilization*, new ed., Oxford: Basil Blackwell, 1987.

Duncan, Robert, *Bending the Bow*, New York, NY: New Directions, 1968.

_______ , *Derivations: Selected Poems, 1950-6*, London: Fulcrum Press, 1968.

Edelman, Gerald, *The Remembered Present*, New York, NY: Basic Books, 1989.

Eisenstein, Sergei, *Film Form*, ed. and trans. Jay Ledya, London: Dobson, 1963.

Eliade, Mircea, *Occultism, Witchcraft, and Cultural Fashions*, Chicago, IL: University of Chicago Press, 1976.

_______ , *Shamanism: Archaic Techniques of Ecstasy*, trans.Willard R. Trask, Princeton, NJ: Princeton University Press, [1951] 1974.

Eshleman, Clayton, ed. and trans., *Conductors of the Pit: Poetry Written In Extremis*, New York, NY: Soft Skull Press, 2005.

_______ , 'Introduction,' *Watchfiends & Rack Screams: Works from the Final Period by Antonin Artaud*, ed. and trans. Clayton Eshleman with Bernard Bador, Boston, MA: Exact Change, 1995, pp.1-48.

Ettinger, Bracha, *The Matrixial Borderspace*, ed. Brian Massumi, Minneapolis, MN: University of Minnesota Press, 2006.

Fagin, Larry, *The List Poem*, New York, NY: Teachers and Writers Collaborative, 1991.

Favret-Saada, Jeanne, *Désorceler*, Paris: Editions de l'Olivier, 2009.

_______ , 'Unbewitching as therapy,' *American Ethnologist* 16:1, February 1989, pp. 40-59.

_______ , *Les Mots, la mort, les sorts*, Paris: Gallimard, 1985.

_______ , *Deadly Words: Witchcraft in the Bocage*, Cambridge: Cambridge University Press, 1980.

ffrench, Patrick, *The time of theory: History of 'Tel Quel' 1960-83*, New York, NY: Clarendon Press, 1995.

ffrench, Patrick and Roland-Francois Lack, eds, *The Tel Quel Reader*, New York, NY: Routledge, 1998.

Fisher, Mark, *Capitalist Realism*, London: Zero Books, 2009.

Fónagy, Ivan, *La Vive voix: Essais de psycho-phonétique*, Paris: Gallimard, 1983.

Foucault, Michel, *Security, Territory, Population: Lectures at the Collège de France, 1977-1978*, ed. Arnold I. Davidson, trans. Graham Burchell, Basingstoke & New York, NY: Palgrave Macmillan, [2004] 2009.

_______ , *The Birth of Biopolitics: Lectures at the Collège de France, 1978-1979*, ed. Arnold I. Davidson, trans. Graham Burchell, Basingstoke & New York, NY: Palgrave Macmillan, [2004] 2008.

_______ , *History of Madness*, 2nd rev. ed., trans. Jean Khalpa and Jonathan Murphy, London & New York, NY: Routledge, 2005.

_______ , *'Society Must Be Defended!' Lectures at the Collège de France, 1975-1976*, eds, Mauro Bertani and Alessandro Fontana, trans. David Macey, London: Penguin, 2004.

_______ , *Madness and Civilization*, trans. Richard Howard, London & New York, NY: Routledge, [1961] 2001.

_______ , 'Maurice Blanchot: The Thought from Outside,' *Foucault/Blanchot*, trans. Brian Massumi, New York, NY: Zone Books, 1990, pp.7-58.

_______ , *Death and the Labyrinth*, trans. Charles Rua, London: Athlone Press, 1987.

_______ , *This Is Not A Pipe*, trans. James Harkness, Berkeley, CA: University of California Press, [1973] 1981.

_______ , 'The Lives of Infamous Men,' *Power, Truth, Strategy*, eds, Meaghan Morris and Paul Patton, Sydney: Feral Publications, 1979, pp.157-175.

_______ , *A History of Sexuality: Vol. 1, An Introduction*, trans. Robert Hurley, New York, NY: Pantheon, 1978.

_______ , *Surveiller et punir*, Paris: Gallimard/Tel Quel, 1975.

_______ , *The Order of Things*, trans. Alan Sheridan, New York, NY: Vintage, [1966] 1973.

_______ , *The Archaeology of Knowledge*, trans. Alan Sheridan, London: Tavistock, [1969] 1972.

_______ , 'La Folie, l'absence d'œuvre,' *La Table Ronde* 196, May 1964, pp.11-21.

Fraleigh, Sondra, *Butoh: Metamorphic Dance and Global Alchemy*, Champaign, IL: University of Illinois Press, 2010.

_______ , *Dancing into Darkness: Butoh, Zen, and Japan*, Pittsburgh, PA: University of Pittsburgh Press, 1999.

Fraleigh, Sondra and Tamah Nakamara, *Hijikata Tatsumi and Kazuo Ohno*, London & New York, NY: Routledge, 2006.

Freedberg, David, *The Power of Images*, Princeton, NJ: Princeton University Press, 1989.

Freud, Sigmund, *Interpreting Dreams*, trans. J.A. Underwood, London: Penguin Books, [1899] 2006.

_______ , 'Beyond the Pleasure Principle' (1922) in Vol. XVIII of *Complete Psychological Works of Sigmund Freud*, trans. and ed. James Strachey, New York, NY: Vintage, 2001, pp.7-64.

_______ , 'Psychoanalytic Notes Upon a Autobiographical Account of a Case of Paranoia (Dementia Paranoides)' (1911) in *Three Case Studies*, ed. Philip Rieff, New York, NY: Touchstone Books, 1996, pp.103-186.

_______ , 'Negation' (1925) in *The Ego and the Id and Other Works*, Vol. XIX of *Standard Edition of the Complete Psychological Works of Sigmund Freud*, trans. and ed. James Strachey, London: Hogarth Press, 1971, pp.235-239.

_______ , *Introductory Lectures to Psychoanalysis*, trans. and ed. James Strachey, London & New York, NY: W.W. Norton, 1966.

_______ , 'Analysis Terminable and Interminable' (1937) in Vol. XXIII of *The Complete Psychological Works of Sigmund Freud*, trans. and ed. James Strachey, London & New York, NY: Hogarth Press/Macmillan, 1964, pp.209-253.

Freud, Sigmund and Josef Breuer, *Studies on Hysteria*, trans. James and Alix Strachey, Harmondsworth: Penguin, 1986.

Fynsk, Christopher, *Infant Figures*, Stanford, CA: Stanford University Press, 2000.

Galloway, Alexander R., *Laruelle: Against the Digital*, Minneapolis, MN: University of Minnesota Press, 2014.

Gennep, Arnold van, *The Rites of Passage*, trans. Monika B. Vizedom and Gabrielle L. Caffee, London: Routledge and Kegan Paul, 1909.

Genosko, Gary, 'Guattari's Contributions to the Theory of Semiocapitalism,' in *The Guattari Effect*, eds, Eric Alliez and Andrew Goffey, London & New York, NY: Continuum, 2011, pp.115-133.

Gil, José, *Metamorphoses of the Body*, trans. Stephen Muecke, Minneapolis, MN: University of Minnesota Press, 1998.

Ginsberg, Allen, *Howl*, San Francisco, CA: City Lights, 1956.

Goodall, Jane, *Artaud and the Gnostic Drama*, Oxford: Clarendon Press, 1994.

Goux, Jean-Joseph, 'Antonin Artaud and the Promise of a Great Therapeutic,' *Angelaki* 13:3, December 2008, pp.17-24.

Graeber, David, *Lost People: Magic and the Legacy of Slavery in Madagascar*,- Bloomington, IN: Indiana University Press, 2007.

_______ , *Possibilities*, Edinburgh & Oakland, CA: AK Press, 2007.

Greene, Naomi, *Antonin Artaud: Poet Without Words*, New York, NY: Simon & Schuster, 1970.

Grossman, Évelyne, *Antonin Artaud, un insurgé du corps*, Paris: Gallimard, 2006.

_______ , 'L'art crève les yeux,' *Antonin Artaud*, Paris: Bibliothèque nationale de France/Gallimard, 2006, pp.162-167.

_______ , 'Quitter la letter écrite,' Preface to *Cahier Ivry, janvier 1948* by Antonin Artaud, ed. Évelyne Grossman, Paris: Gallimard, 2006, pp.9-19.

_______ , *Artaud, 'l'alienié authentique,'* Paris: Léo Scheer/Farago, 2003.

_______ , *Artaud/Joyce, le corps et le texte*, Paris: Nathan, 1996.

Grosz, Elizabeth, *Chaos, Territory, Art: Deleuze and the Framing of the Earth*, New York, NY: Columbia University Press, 2008.

Guattari, Félix, *The Machinic Unconscious: Essays in Schizoanalysis*, trans.Taylor Adkins, Los Angeles, CA: Semiotext(e), [1979] 2011.

_______ , 'On Contemporary Art,' *The Guattari Effect*, eds, Éric Alliez and Andrew Goffey, London & New York, NY: Continuum, 2011, pp.40-52.

_______ , *The Anti-Oedipus Papers*, ed. Stéphane Nadaud, trans. Kélina Gotman, New York, NY & Los Angeles, CA: Semiotext(e), 2006.

_______ , *The Guattari Reader*, ed. Gary Genosko, London & New York, NY: Routledge, 1996.

_______ , *Chaosmosis*, trans. Paul Bains and Julian Pefanis, London & Bloomington, IN: Indiana University Press, 1995.

_______ , *The three ecologies*, trans. Ian Pindar and Paul Sutton, London & New Brunswick, NJ: Athlone Press, [1989] 1992.

_______ , *Cartographies schizoanalytiques*, Paris: Éditions Galilée/L'espace critique, 1989.

_______ , *Molecular Revolution: Psychiatry and Politics*, trans. Rosemary Sheed, New York, NY: Penguin Books, 1984.

Guattari, Félix and Suely Rolnik, *Molecular Revolution in Brazil*, trans. Karel Clapshow and Brian Holmes, Los Angeles, CA: Semiotext(e), 2008.

Guénon, René, *The Symbolism of the Cross*, trans. Angus MacNab, Hillsdale, NY: Sophia Perennis, [1931] 2004.

_______ , *The King of the World*, ed. Samuel D. Fohr, trans. Henry D. Fohr. Hillsdale, NY: Sophia Perennis [1927] 2001.

Harrison, Jane, *Themis: A Study of the Social Origins of Greek Religion*, 2nd rev. ed., Cambridge: Cambridge University Press, [1912] 1927.

Hayum, Andrée, *The Isenheim Altarpiece: God's Medicine and the Artist's Vision*, Princeton, NJ: Princeton University Press, 1989.

Herskovits, Melville J., *Dahomey: An Ancient West African Kingdom*,Vol. 2, Evanston, IL: Northwestern University Press, [1938] 1967.

Hill, Gary, *An Art of Limina, Gary Hill: Works and Collected Writings*, ed. Paul Emmanuel Odin, Barcelona: Ediciones Poligrafa, 2007.

Hjemslev, Louis, *Prolegomena to a Theory of Language*, trans. Francis J.Whitfield, Madison, WI: University of Wisconsin Press, 1961.

Hollier, Denis, 'The Death of Paper, Part Two: Artaud's Sound System,' *October* 80, 1997, pp.27-37.

_______ , ed., *College of Sociology: 1937-39*, Minneapolis, MN: University of Minnesota Press, 1988.

Iampolski, Mikhail, *The Memory of Tiresias*, trans. Harsha Ramm, Berkeley, CA: University of California Press, 1998.

Isou, Isidore, *Antonin Artaud torturé par les psychiatries*, Paris: Lettrism, 1970.

Jacobson, Roman, *Selected Writings*, I, The Hague: Mouton & Co., [1949] 1962.

James, William, *The Varieties of Religious Experience*, London & New York, NY: Macmillan, [1902] 1961.

Jannorone, Kimberly, *Artaud and His Doubles*, Ann Arbor, MI: University of Michigan, 2010.

Jeanneney, Jean-Noel, 'Preface,' *Antonin Artaud*, Paris: Bibliothèque nationale de France/Gallimard, 2006, unpag.

Jenny, Laurent, *La Terreur et les signes*, Paris: Gallimard, 1982.

Jensen, Caspar Bruun, 'Two forms of outside: Castaneda, Blanchot, ontology,' *Hau: Journal of Ethnographic Theory* 3:3, 2013, pp.309-35.

Johnson, Joyce, *The Voice is All: The Lonely Victory of Jack Kerouac*, New York, NY: Viking, 2012.

Jonas, Hans, *The Gnostic Religion*, 3rd rev. ed., Boston, MA: Beacon Press, [1963] 2001.

Jones, Ernest, 'The theory of symbolism,' *Papers on Psychoanalysis*, Boston, MA: Beacon Press, [1916] 1961, pp.154-211.

Jung, Carl, *Mandala Symbolism* in *The Archetypes and the Collective Unconscious*, Vol. IX:1 of *Collected Works*, trans. R.F.C. Hull, Princeton, NJ: Princeton University Press, 1992.

_______ , *Psychological Types*, Vol. VI of *Collected Works*, trans. R.F. C. Hull, new ed., New York, NY: Routledge, 1992.

_______ , *Mysterium Coniunctionis*, Vol. XIV of Collected Works, 2nd ed., trans. R.F.C. Hull, London: Routledge, Kegan & Paul, 1970.

_______ , *Aion: Researches in the Phenomenology of the Self*, Volume IX:2 of *Collected Works*, trans. R.F.C. Hull, 2nd ed., London: Routledge, Kegan, & Paul, 1968.

_______ , *Psychology and Alchemy*, Volume XII of *Collected Works*, trans. R.F.C. Hull, Princeton, NJ: Princeton University Press, 1968.

_______ , 'The Spirit Mercurius,' in *Alchemical Studies*, Vol. XII of *Collected Works*, trans. R.F.C.Hull, new ed., New York, NY: Routledge, 1968, pp.191-250.

_______ , 'The Psychology of the Transference,' in *The Practice of Psychotherapy*, Vol. XVI of Collected Works, 2nd ed., trans. R.F.C. Hull, London: Routledge,Kegan & Paul, 1966, pp.163-323.

_______ , 'The Relations between the Ego and the Unconscious,' in *Two Essays on Analytical Psychology*, Vol. VII of *Collected Works*, 2nd ed., trans. R.F.C. Hull, London: Routledge, Kegan & Paul, 1966, pp.123-241.

_______ , *The Psychogenesis of Mental Disease*, Vol. III of *Collected Works*, trans. R.F.C. Hull, Princeton, NJ: Princeton University Press, 1960.

_______ , *Symbols of Transformation*, Vol. V of *Collected Works*, trans. R.F.C. Hull, Princeton, NJ: Princeton University Press, 1956.

Kahn, Douglas, *Noise, Water, Meat*, London & Cambridge, MA: MIT Press, 1999.

Kerslake, Christian, *Deleuze and the Unconscious*, London & New York, NY: Continuum, 2007.

Klee, Paul, *On Modern Art*, trans. Paul Findley, London: Faber & Faber, 1966.

_______ , *P. Klee par lui-même et son fils Félix Klee*, Paris: Les libraires associés, 1963.

Klossowski, Pierre, *Le Baphomet*, Paris: Mercure de France, 1965.

Knapp, Bettina, *Antonin Artaud: Man of Vision*, New York, NY: David Lewis, 1969.

Koltés, Bernard-Marie, *Plays*, 2 Vols, eds, David Bradby and Maria M. Delgado, London: Methuen Drama, 1997, 2004.

Kristeva, Julia, 'Artaud: Madness and Revolution/Interview with Julia Kristeva,' *100 Years of Cruelty*, ed. Edward Scheer, Sydney: Power Publications, 2002.

_______ , *The Sense and Non-sense of Revolt*, trans. Jeanine Herman, New York, NY: Columbia University Press, 2000.

_______ , 'The True-Real,' in *The Kristeva Reader*, ed. Toril Moi, New York, NY: Columbia University Press, 1986, pp.214-237.

_______ , *Powers of Horror*, trans. Leon S. Roudiez, New York, NY: Columbia University Press, 1984.

_______ , *Revolution in Poetic Language*, trans. Margaret Waller, New York, NY: Columbia University Press, 1984.

_______ , *Desire in Language*, ed. Leon S.Roudez, trans. Thomas Gora, Alice Jardine and Leon S. Roudiez, New York, NY: Columbia University Press, 1982.

_______ , 'Le sujet en procés,' in *Artaud*, ed. Philippe Sollers, Paris: Union générale d'éditions, 1973, pp.43-108.

Laing, R.D., *The Politics of the Family and Other Essays*, London: Tavistock, 1971.
_______ , *The Politics of Experience*, London: Penguin Books, 1967.
_______ , *Self and Others*, London: Tavistock, 1961.
_______ , *The Divided Self*, Harmondsworth: Penguin, 1960.
Laing, R.D. and Aaron Esterson, *Sanity, Madness and the Family*, London: Penguin, 1964.
Lacan, Jacques, *Écrits*, trans. Bruce Fink, London & New York, NY: W.W. Norton, [1966] 2007.
_______ , *Autres écrits*, Paris: Éditions du Seuil, 2001.
_______ , *The Seminar of Jacques Lacan, Book XI: The Four Fundamental Concepts of Psychoanalysis*, ed. Jacques Alain-Miller, trans. Alan Sheridan, London & New York, NY: W.W. Norton, [1973] 1998.
_______ , *The Seminar of Jacques Lacan, Book III: The Psychoses*, 1955-6, ed. Jacques Alain-Miller, trans. Russell Grigg, London & New York, NY: W.W. Norton, [1981] 1997.
Lainé, Daniel and Tobie Nathan, *African Gods: Contemporary Rituals and Beliefs*, Paris: Flammarion, 2007.
Lao-Tse, *Tao Te Ching*, trans. Stephen Aldiss and Stanley Lombardo, New York, NY: Hackett Publishing, 1993.
Latour, Bruno, *On the Modern Cult of the Factish Gods*, first chapter trans. Catherine Porter and Heather MacLean, London & Durham, NC: Duke University Press, 2010.
_______ , *We Have Never Been Modern*, trans. Catherine Porter. Cambridge, MA: Harvard University Press, 1993.
Leach, Edmund, *Culture and Communication*, Cambridge: Cambridge University Press, 1976.
Lévi-Strauss, Claude, *Introduction to the Work of Marcel Mauss*, trans. Felicity Baker, London: Routledge, Kegan & Paul, [1950] 1987.
_______ , *Structural Anthropology*, trans. Claire Jacobson and Brooke Grundfest Schoef, New York, NY: Anchor/Doubleday, 1967.
_______ , *The Savage Mind*, trans. George Weidenfeld and Nicolson Ltd., London: Weidenfeld and Nicholson, 1966.
Lévi-Strauss, David, *Between Dog & Wolf: Essays on Art & Politics*, Brooklyn, NY: Autonomedia, 1999.
Lewis, Oscar, *Life in a Mexican Village*, Urbana, IL: University of Illinois Press, 1951.
Lipton, Barbara and Nima Dorjee Raqnubs, *Treasures of Tibetan Art: Collections of the Jacques Marchais Museum of Tibetan Art*, Oxford: Oxford University Press, 1996.
Lotringer, Sylvère, *Fous d'Artaud*, Paris: Sens et Tonka, 2003.

_______ , 'Sick, Evil, and Violent: Interview with Sylvère Lotringer, Edward Scheer, and Jane Goodall,' in *100 Years of Cruelty: Essays on Artaud*, ed. Edward Scheer, Sydney: Power Publications, 2002, pp.305-32.

_______ , *Antonin Artaud*, New York, NY: Scribner's, 1990.

Lotringer, Sylvère and Jean Baudrillard, *Oublier Artaud*, Paris: Sens et Tonka, 2005.

Lyotard, Jean-François, *Des Dispositifs pulsionnels*, Paris: Éditions Galilée, 1994.

_______ , *Libidinal Economy*, trans. Iain Hamilton Grant, Bloomington, IN: Indiana University Press, [1964] 1993.

_______ , *Lectures d'enfance*, Paris: Galilée, 1991.

_______ , *Discours, figure*, Paris: Klincksieck, 1974.

Maeder, Thomas, *Antonin Artaud*, Paris: Plon, 1978.

Marcel, Serge, *Aliénation: Antonin Artaud – les genealogies hybri*ds, Paris: Editions Galilée, 2008.

Marcuse, Herbert, *One Dimensional Man*, New York, NY: Beacon Press, 1964.

Marks, Laura U., *Enfoldment and Infinity: An Islamic Genealogy of New Media Art*, London & Cambridge, MA: MIT Press, 2010.

Martin, Jean-Hubert, 'ARTAUD - A Staged Life', *e-flux*, August 12, 2005. Available: http://www.e-flux.com/announcements/artaud---a-staged-life/. Accessed 11 March 2016.

Marx, Karl, *Capital* in *Collected Works*, Vol. 35 by Karl Marx and Friedrich Engels, New York, NY: International Publishers, [1867] 1975.

_______ , *Grundrisse*, ed. and trans. Martin Nicolaus, New York, NY: Vintage Books, 1973.

_______ , *Capital*, Vol. 2, ed. Friedrich Engels, New York, NY: International Publishers, 1967.

Marx-Srouras, Danielle, *The Cultural Politics of Tel Quel*, Philadelphia, PA: Pennslyvania University Press, 2004.

Maslow, Abraham, *The Further Reaches of Human Nature*, new ed., New York, NY: Arkana, 1994.

_______ , *Religions, Values, and Peak-Experiences*, New York, NY: Penguin, 1970.

Massumi, Brian, *A user's guide to* Capitalism and Schizophrenia, London & Cambridge, MA: MIT Press/Swerve, 1992.

Mauss, Marcel, *A General Theory of Magic*, trans. Robert E. Brain, London & New York, NY: Routledge, [1902] 2002.

McClure, Michael, 'A New Book/A Book of Torture' (1961), *Huge Dreams*, London & New York, NY: Penguin Books, 1999.

_______ , *Meat Science Essays*, San Francisco, CA: City Lights, 1963.

Melitopoulos, Angela and Maurizio Lazzarato, 'Machinic Animism,' in *Animism*,Vol. I, ed. Anselm Franke, Berlin: Sternberg Press, 2010, pp.97-108.

Mercier, Jacques, *Art That Heals: The Image as Medicine in Ethiopian Art*, New York, NY: Prestel/Museum of African Art, 1997.

Mèredieu, Florence de, *L'Affaire Artaud*, Paris: Fayard, 2009.

_______ , *La Chine d'Antonin Artaud*, Paris: Blusson, 2006.

_______ , *C'était Antonin Artaud*, Paris: Fayard, 2006.

_______ , *Sur l'électrochoc. Le cas Antonin Artaud*, Paris: Blusson, 1996.

_______ , *Antonin Artaud, les couilles de l'ange*, Paris: Blusson, 1992.

_______ , *Antonin Artaud, portraits et gris gris*, Paris: Blusson, 1984.

Merleau-Ponty, Maurice, *Phenomenology of Perception*, trans. Colin Smith, 2nd rev. ed., London & New York, NY: Routledge, [1945] 2002.

_______ , *The Visible and the Invisible*, ed. Claude Lefort, trans. Alphonse Lingis, Evanston, IL: Northwestern University Press, [1964] 1968.

Meschonnic, Henri, *Les Etats de la poétique*, Paris: PUF, 1985.

Morfee, Adrian, *Artaud's Writing Bodies*, Oxford: Clarendon Press, 2005.

Murphy, Jay, 'Artaud's Scream', *Deleuze Studies* 10.2, 2016, pp.140-161.

_______ , 'The Artaud Effect,' *CTheory*, 15 September 2015. Available: http://ctheoryarchive.net/the-artaud-effect/, Accessed 17 September, 2015.

_______ , '"The Target Moves": Reflections on William Burroughs' Photography', *MAP*, June 2014. Available: http://mapmagazine.co.uk/9732/jay-murphy/, Accessed 26 April 2016.

_______ , 'Gary Hill and "The new aesthetic paradigm": Art, Chaos Theory, and Guattari (in the wake of Heidegger)' paper presented at International Association of Philosophy and Literature, May 1999. Available: http://www.thing.net/~soulcity/ap/index.html, Accessed 12 December, 2011.

_______ , 'Assimilating the Unassimilable: Carolee Schneemann in Relation to Antonin Artaud,' *Parkett* 50/51, 1997, pp.224-239.

_______ , 'Magic Act: The Late Drawings of Antonin Artaud,' *New Art Examiner*, May 1997, pp.18-23.

Murray, Ros, *Antonin Artaud: The Scum of the Soul*, Basingstoke & New York, NY: Palgrave Macmillan, 2014.

Nadeau, Maurice, *Histoire du Surréalisme*, Paris: Le Seuil, 1945.

Nasser, E.H., Natalie Walders, and Janis H. Jenkins, 'The Experience of Schizophrenia: What's Gender Got to Do With It,' *Schizophrenia Bulletin* 28:2, 2002, pp.351-362.

Nathan, Tobie, *La Nouvelle interpretation des rêves*, Paris: Odile Jacob, 2011.

_______ , *Nous ne sommes pas seuls dans le monde*, Paris: Le Seuil/Les Empêcheurs de penser du rond, 2001.

_______ , *L'Influence qui guérit*, Paris: Odile Jacob, 1994.

_______ , *Principes d'ethnopsychiatrie*, Grenoble: La pensée sauvage, 1993.

Nathan, Tobie and Isabelle Stengers, *Médecins et sorciers*, Paris: Le Seuil, 2004.

Neidich,Warren, 'The Neurobiopolitics of Global Consciousness,' *Sarai Reader 2006: Turbulence*, eds, Monica Narula, et al. Delhi: Centre for the Study of Developing Societies, 2006, pp.222-236.

Nerval, Gérard de, *Aurèlia and other writings*, Boston, MA: Exact Change, 1995.

Neyrat, Frédéric, *Instructions pour une prise d'âmes: Artaud et l'envoûtement occidental*, Strasbourg: La Phocide, 2009.

_______ , *Surexposés: Le monde, le capital, la terre*, Paris: Léo Scheer, 2005.

Nicholls, Christine and Ian North, eds, *Kathleen Petyarre: Genius of Place*, Adelaide: Wakefield, 2001.

Nietzsche, Friedrich, *On the Genealogy of Morals*, trans. Walter Kaufman and R.J. Hollingdale, New York, NY: Vintage Books, [1887] 1989.

_______ , *Untimely Meditations*, trans. R.J. Hollingdale, Cambridge, MA: Cambridge University Press, 1983.

_______ , *The Gay Science*, trans. Walter Kaufman, New York, NY: Vintage Books, 1974.

_______ , *The Will to Power*, trans. Walter Kaufman and R. J. Hollingdale, New York, NY: Vintage Books, [1884-88] 1968.

_______ , *The Portable Nietzsche*, ed. and trans. Walter Kaufman, New York, NY: Viking Penguin, 1954.

Nin, Anaïs, *The Journals of Anaïs Nin, 1931-4*, London: Peter Owen, 1966.

Ohno, Kazuo and Yoshito Ohno, *Kazuo Ohno's World*, trans. John Barrett, Middletown, CT: Wesleyan University Press, 2004.

Oliver, Kelly, *Womanizing Nietzsche*, London & New York, NY: Routledge, 1994.

Oltkowski, Dorothy, 'Eluding Derrida: Artaud and the imperceptibility of life for thought,' *Angelaki* 5.2, August 2000, pp.191-199.

Osborne, Peter, *The Politics of Time: Modernity and Avant-garde*, London & New York, NY: Verso, 1995.

Pankow, Gisela, *L'Être-là du schizophrenia*, Paris: Aubier-Montaigne, 1973, 1981.

_______ , *Structuration dynamique dans la schizophrenia*, Bern: Verlag Hans Huber, 1956.

Pasi, Carlo, *Artaud Attore*, Firenze: La Casa Usher, 1989.

Peter, John, *Vladimir's Carrot*, London: Methuen, 1987.

Petitot, Jean, Bernard Pachoud, Jean-Michel Roy, and Francisco J. Varela, eds,- *Naturalizing Phenomenology: Contemporary Issues in Phenomenology and Cognitive Science*, Stanford, CA: Stanford University Press, 1999.

Pignarre, Philippe and Isabelle Stengers, *La Sorcellerie capitaliste*, Paris: La Découverte, 2005.

Portanova, Stamatia, *Moving without a Body*, London & Cambridge, MA: MIT Press, 2013.

Prevel, Jacques, *En Compagnie d'Antonin Artaud*, Paris:Flammarion, 1974.

Prigogine, Ilya, *The End of Certainty*, New York, NY: Free Press, 1997.

Prigogine, Ilya and Isabelle Stengers, *Order Out of Chaos*, New York, NY: Bantam Books, 1984.

Quaranta, Domenico, *Beyond New Media Art*, Brescia: Link Editions, 2013.

Rattray, David, 'Artaud's Cane,' *How I Became One of the Invisible*, Brooklyn, NY: Semiotext(e), 1992, pp.143-172.

Ray, Reginald, *Secret of the Vajra World: The Tantric Buddhism of Tibet*, Volume two of *The World of Tibetan Buddhism*, London & Boston, MA: Shambhala Publications, 2002.

Reinhard, Johan, 'Shamanism and Spirit Possession,' in *Spirit Possession in the Nepali Himalayas*, eds, John Hitchcock and Rex Jones, Westminster: Aris & Phillip, 1976, pp.12-20.

Rey, Jean-Michel, *Les Promesses de l'œuvre: Artaud, Nietzsche, Simone Weil*, Paris: Desclée de Brouwer, 2003.

_______ , *La Naissance de la poésie*, Antonin Artaud, Paris: Métaillé, 1991.

Reynolds, Valrae, *From the Sacred Realm: Treasures of Tibetan Art from the Newark Museum*, New York, NY: Prestel, 2000.

Rhie, Marylin A., Robert A.F. Thurman, and David J. Jackson, *Worlds of Transformation: Tibetan Art of Wisdom and Compassion*, New York, NY: Harry Abrams, 1999.

Rodowick, David, *Reading the Figural, Or, Philosophy After the New Media*, London & Durham, NC: Duke University Press, 2001.

_______ , *Gilles Deleuze's Time Machine*, Durham, NC: Duke University Press, 1997.

Rogozinski, Jacob, *Guérir la vie: la passion d'Antonin Artaud*, Paris: Éditions du Cerf/Passages, 2011.

_______ , 'Tutuguri, ou le rythme d'Artaud,' *Lignes* nouvelle série, October 2000, pp.71-86.

Rossolato, Guy, 'L'Expulsion,' *La Relation d'inconnu*, Paris: Gallimard, 1978.

Rothenberg, Jerome, ed., *Revolution of the Word: New Gathering of American Avant-Garde Poetry 1914-45*, Boston, MA: Exact Change, [1974] 1999.

_______ , ed., *Technicians of the Sacred*, Berkeley, CA: University of California Press, 1985.

_______ , ed., *Shaking the Pumpkin*, New York, NY: Doubleday, 1972.

Rouget, Gilbert, *Music and Trance: A Theory of Relations between Music and Possession*, Chicago, IL; University of Chicago Press, 1985.

Saillet, Maurice, 'In Memoriam: Antonin Artaud,' in *The Theater and Its Double*, trans. Richard Howard, New York, NY: Grove Press, 1958, pp.147-159.

Saler, Benson, 'Nagual, Witch, and Sorcerer in a Quiché Village' in *Magic, Witchcraft & Curing*, ed. John Middleton, Austin, TX: University of Texas Press, 1967, pp.69-99.

Sas, Miryam, *Fault Lines: Cultural Memory and Japanese Surrealism*, Stanford, CA: Stanford University Press, 1999.

Scarpetta, Guy, 'Artaud écrit our la canne de saint Patrick,' *Tel Quel* 81, August 1979, pp.66-85.

Schatzman, Morton, *Soul Murder*, new ed., London & New York, NY: Pelican, 1976.

Scheer, Edward, 'Sketches of the jet,' *100 Years of Cruelty*, ed. Edward Scheer, Sydney: Power Publications, 2002, pp.57-74.

Schimmel, Annemarie, *Deciphering the Signs of God*, Albany, NY: State University of New York Press, 1994.

Schreber, Daniel Paul, *Memoirs of My Nervous Illness*, ed. and trans. Ida Macalpine and Richard A. Hunter, new ed., New York, NY: NYRB Classics, [1903] 2000.

Schrum, Stephen, 'Introduction,' *Theatre in Cyberspace*, ed. Stephen Schrum, New York, NY: Peter Lang, 1999, pp.1-6.

Scully, Vincent, *Pueblo*, 2nd rev. ed., Chicago, IL: University of Chicago Press, 1989.

Sedgwick, Peter, *Psycho Politics*, London: Pluto Press, 1992.

Sellin, Eric, *The Dramatic Concepts of Antonin Artaud*, London & Chicago, IL: University of Chicago Press, 1968.

Seriéux, Paul and Joseph Capgras, *Les Folies raisonnantes: le délire d'interpretation*, Marseille: Lafitte, [1909] 1982.

Sherover, Charles M., ed., *The Human Experience of Time: the Development of its Philosophic Meaning*, Evanston, IL: Northwestern University Press, 1975.

Shivani, Anis, 'Exclusive: Beat Poet Michael McClure on Jim Morrison, The Doors, Allen Ginsberg, Jack Kerouac,' *Huffington Post*, 3 March 2011. Available: http://www.huffingtonpost.com/anis-shivani/exclusive-beat-poet-mcclure_b_823425.html, Accessed 9 August, 2011.

Sigal, Clancy, *Zone of the Interior*, New York, NY: Pomona Press, [1976] 2005.

Silberer, Herbert, *Hidden Symbolism in Alchemy and the Occult Arts*, trans. Smith Ely Jelliffe, New York, NY: Dover, [1914] 1971.

_______ , 'Report on a method of eliciting and observing certain symbolic hallucination-phenomena' (1909) in *Organization and pathology of thought*, ed. David Rapaport, New York, NY: Columbia University Press, 1951, pp.197-207.

Sobieszk, Robert, *Ports of Entry: William S. Burroughs and the Arts*, Los Angeles, CA & New York, NY: LACMA/Thames & Hudson, 1996.

Sollers, Philippe, 'Sur Artaud,' *L'Infini* 56, 1996, pp.93-106.

_______ , *Watteau in Venice*, trans. Alberto Manquel, New York, NY: Simon & Schuster, 1995.

_______ , ed., *Artaud*, Paris: Union générale d'éditions, 1973.

_______ , *L'Ecriture et 'L'Expérience des limites,'* Paris: Seuil, 1971.

Sontag, Susan, 'Artaud,' *Antonin Artaud: Selected Writings*, ed. Susan Sontag, trans. Helen Weaver, New York, NY: Farrar, Straus & Giroux, 1976, pp.xvii-lix.

Spivak, Gayatri Chakravorty, 'Artaud: Writing/Drawing,' Panel discussion, 11 October 1996, New York, NY: The Drawing Center.

Starke, Enid, *Arthur Rimbaud in Abyssinia*, Oxford: Oxford University Press, 1937.

Stengers, Isabelle, *Cosmopolitics*, II, trans. Robert Bononno, Minneapolis, MN: University of Minnesota Press, [2003] 2011.

Sterckx, Pierre, 'Andreas Gursky, réseaux et particules,' *artpress* 277, March 2002, pp.25-29.

Stout, John Cameron, *Artaud's Alternate Genealogies*, Waterloo: Wilfrid Laurier University Press, 1995.

Taussig, Michael, *Shamanism, Colonialism, and the Wild Man*, Chicago, IL: University of Chicago Press, 1987.

Tiqqun, 'On the Economy as Black Magic.' Available: http://blackmagic.jottit.com. Accessed 9 August 2011.

_______, *Introduction to Civil War*, trans. Alexander R. Galloway and Jason E. Smith, Los Angeles, CA: Semiotext(e), 2010.

Thévenin, Paule, *Antonin Artaud: fin de l'ère chrétienne*, Paris: Éditions Léo Scheer, 2006.

_______, 'Search for a Lost World,' *The Secret Art of Antonin Artaud*, trans. Mary Ann Caws, London & Cambridge, MA: MIT Press, 1998, pp.3-56.

_______, 'Entendre/Voir/Lire,' *Antonin Artaud, ce désespéré qui vous parle*,Paris: Éditions du Seuil, 1993, pp.89-282.

_______, 'A Letter on Artaud,' *Tulane Drama Review* 9.3, Spring 1965, pp.99-117.

Trubezkoy, N.S., *Studies in General Linguistics and Language Structure*, ed. Anatoly Liberman, trans. Anatoly Liberman and Marvin H. Taylor, Durham, NC: Duke University Press, 1999.

Turner, Victor, *The Ritual Process: Structure and Anti-Structure*, New York, NY: Aldine Publishing Co., 1969.

_______, *The Drums of Affliction:A Study of Religious Processes Among the Ndembu of Zambia*, Oxford: Clarendon Press, 1968.

_______, *The Forest of Symbols*, Ithaca, NY: Cornell University Press, 1967.

Turner, Victor and Edith Turner, *Image and Pilgrimage in Christian Culture: Anthropological Perspectives*, New York, NY: Columbia University Press, 1978.

Underhill, Evelyn, *Mysticism*, 2nd rev. ed., London: One World Publications, 1999.

Väliaho, Pasi, *Biopolitical Screens*, London & Cambridge, MA: MIT Press, 2014.

Varela, Francisco J., *Ethical Know-How: Action, Wisdom, and Cognition*, Stanford, CA: Stanford University Press, 1999.

———, ed. *Sleeping, Dreaming, and Dying*, Boston, MA: Wisdom Book, 1997.

Varela, Francisco J. and Jeremy Hayward, eds, *Gentle Bridges: Dialogues Between the Cognitive Sciences and the Buddhist Tradition*, Boston, MA: Shambhala Press, 1992.

Varela, Francisco J., Evan Thompson, and Eleanor Rosch, *The Embodied Mind*, Cambridge, MA: MIT Press, 1991.

Venet, Emmanuel, *Ferdière, psychiatrie d'Artaud*, Lagrasse: Verdier, 2006.

Vogel, Susan M., *Baule: African Art, Western Eyes*, London & New Haven, CT: Yale University Press, 1997.

Wasserstrom, Steven M., *Religion After Religion*, Princeton, NJ: Princeton University Press, 1999.

Watanabe, Tamotsu, *Butai to iu shina*, Tokyo: Shinchosha, 1994.

———, *Kabuki gekihiyo*, Tokyo: Asahi Shinbunsha, 1994.

Weiss, Allen, 'Libidinal Mannerisms and Profligate Abominations,' *100 Years of Cruelty*, ed. Edward Scheer, Sydney: Power Publications, 2002, pp.103-129.

———, 'From Schizophrenia to Schizophonica,' *Phantasmic Radio*, Durham, NC: Duke University Press, 1995, pp.9-34.

———, 'Radio, Death, and the Devil,' *Wireless Imagination*, eds, Douglas Kahn and Gregory Whitehead, Cambridge, MA: MIT Press, 1992, pp.269-307.

———, 'Psychopompomania,' *The Aesthetics of Excess*, Albany, NY: State Univeristy of New York, 1989, pp.113-134.

Wells, Melanie, 'In Search of the Buy Button,' *Forbes Magazine*, 1 September 2003, pp.62-70.

White, Kenneth, *Le Monde d'Antonin Artaud*, Paris: Editions Complexe, 1989.

Williams, Tami, *Germaine Dulac: A Cinema of Sensation*, Champaign, IL: University of Illinois Press, 2014.

Winnicott, Donald W., *Playing and Reality*, London: Tavistock, 1971.

Wolfson, Louis, *Le Schizo et les langues*, Paris Navarin, [1970] 1984.

EXHIBITIONS

Animism, Extra City-Kunsthal Antwerpen and the Museum of Contemporary Art, Antwerp (M KHA), 22 January– 2 May, and Kunsthalle Bern, 15 May – 18 July, 2010.

Antonin Artaud, La Casa Encendida, Madrid, 3 April – 7 June, 2009.

Antonin Artaud, Bibliothèque nationale de France, Paris, 7 November, 2006 – 4 February, 2007.

Antonin Artaud, Padiglione d'Arte Contemporanea, Milan, 6 December, 2005 – 12 February, 2006.

Antonin Artaud: Works on Paper. Museum of Modern Art, New York, 3 October, 1996 – 7 January, 1997.

Antonin Artaud: œuvres sur papier. Musee Cantini, Marseilles, 17 June – 17 September, 1995.

Antonin Artaud: dessins. Centre Georges Pompidou, Musée national d'art moderne, Paris, 30 June – 11 October, 1987.

Artaud, A Staged Life, Museum Kunst Palast, Dusseldorf, 16 July – 10 October, 2005.

Critical Fetishes: Residues of General Economy, CA2M, Madrid, 26 May – 29 August 2010.

Specters of Artaud: Language and Art in the 1950s, Museo Reina Sofia, Madrid 19 September – 17 December, 2012.

Van Gogh/Artaud: The Man Suicided by Society, Musée d'Orsay, Paris, 11 March – 6 July, 2014.

FILMOGRAPHY

Buñuel, Luis, dir., *L'Âge d'or*, 1930.
Buñuel, Luis and Salvador Dali, dirs, *Un Chien andalou*, 1929.
Raymonde Carasco, dir., *La Fêlure du temps – Tarahumaras* 2003, 2003.
_______ , dir., *Ciguri – Tarahumaras 99 – Le Dernier chaman*, 1999.
_______ , dir., *Ciguri – Tarahumaras 96 – La Danse du peyotl*, 1998.
_______ , dir., *Artaud et les Tarahumaras*, 1996.
_______ , dir., *Ciguri – Tarahumaras 96*, 1996.
_______ , dir., *Los Pascoleros – Tarahumaras 85*, 1996.
_______ , dir., *Yumari – Tarahumaras 84*, 1985.
_______ , dir., *Los Pintos – Tarahumaras 82*, 1982.
_______ , dir., *Tarahumaras 78*, 1979.
_______ , dir., *Tutuguri – Tarahumaras 79*, 1979.
_______ , dir., *Gradiva esquisse I*, 1978.
Cocteau, Jean, dir., *Orphée*, 1950.
Deren, Maya, dir., *Divine Horsemen*, 1985.
Dulac, Germaine, dir., *The Seashell and the Clergyman*, 1928.

Flaherty, Robert, dir., *Man of Aran*, 1934.
Fowler, Luke, dir., *The Nine Monads of David Bell*, 2006.
_______, dir., *What you see is where you're at*, 2003.
Godard, Jean-Luc, dir., *British Sounds/See You at Mao*, 1970.
Mordillat, Gérard and Jérôme Prieur, dir., *En Compagnie d'Antonin Artaud/La Véritable histoire d'Artaud le mômo*, 1993.
Sanderson, Mathias, *Une Histoire de fantôme:le voyage irlandais d'Antonin Artaud*, 1999.

ONLINE RESOURCES: CRITICAL PSYCHIATRY

Arbours Association: www.arboursassociation.org.
Citizens Commission on Human Rights: www.cchr.org.uk.
Critical Resistance: www.criticalresistance.org.
International Association Against Psychiatric Assault: www.iaapa.ch.
International Center of Humane Psychiatry: www.humanepsychiatry.com.
International Critical Psychiatry Network: www.criticalpsychiatry.net/.
Law Project for Psychiatric Rights: http://psychrights.org.
Mind Freedom International: www.mindfreedom.org.
National Association for Rights Protection and Advocacy: www.narpa.org.
World Network of Users and Survivors of Psychiatry: www.wnusp.org.

INDEX

Troubling Notions of Global Citizenship and Diversity in Mathematics Education

Edited by Anna Chronaki
and Ayşe Yolcu

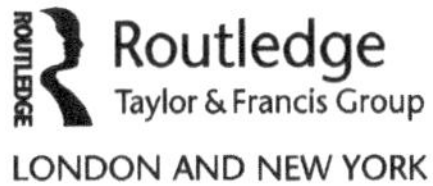
LONDON AND NEW YORK

First published 2025
by Routledge
4 Park Square, Milton Park, Abingdon, Oxon OX14 4RN

and by Routledge
605 Third Avenue, New York, NY 10158

Routledge is an imprint of the Taylor & Francis Group, an informa business

British Library Cataloguing-in-Publication Data
A catalogue record for this book is available from the British Library

ISBN: 978-0-367-67294-2 (hbk)
ISBN: 978-0-367-67295-9 (pbk)
ISBN: 978-1-003-13067-3 (ebk)

DOI: 10.4324/9781003130673

Typeset in Galliard
by KnowledgeWorks Global Ltd.

To all those who cross borders for a life and to all those
who are with them in care and solidarity

To Vassilis and Alican with gratitude for the many sweet
smiles and hugs – the seeds of a common life

Contents

List of Editors and Contributors

Gill Adams is a reader in Education in the Sheffield Institute of Education, UK, with experience in qualitative and mixed-methods research at local level and national level.

Melissa Andrade-Molina is a professor at the Institute of Mathematics at Pontificia Universidad Católica de Valparaíso in Chile. Her main research interests are socio-political perspectives of education.

Marcio Antonio da Silva is a professor of the Post-Graduate Program in Mathematics Education at the Federal University of Mato Grosso do Sul, Brazil, since 2010.

Lisa Björklund Boistrup works as a professor at Malmö University, Sweden. Her research interests are connected to social and political aspects of mathematics education.

Anna Chronaki is professor at Malmö University, Sweden, and at University of Thessaly, Greece, and her research interests are sociopolitical and socioecological aspects of mathematics education with a focus on how language, body, affect, and timespace materialise in mathematical practices.

Fufy Demissie is a senior lecturer in primary and early years at Sheffield Hallam University, UK, and a registered SAPERE (Society for the Advancement of Philosophical Enquiry and Reflection in Education) and DialogueWorks trainer.

Maria Cecilia Fantinato is a full professor of Fluminense Federal University (UFF), Brazil. She is working at the Graduate Program of Education. She is a researcher in ethnomathematics.

Gail E. FitzSimons has been a teacher and researcher of mathematics in vocational, workplace, and further education in Australia. She is also an experienced curriculum developer.

Kécio Gonçalves Leite is an associate professor at the Department of Intercultural Education at the Federal University of Rondônia, Brazil. He develops studies on ethnomathematics, indigenous teacher training, and intercultural education in the Amazon.

Kate le Roux is an associate professor in language development in the Centre for Higher Education Development, University of Cape Town, South Africa. Her research is located at the intersection of language, mathematics, and the learning of disciplinary knowledge in engineering and science.

Saumya Malviya is a social anthropologist working as an assistant professor in the School of Humanities and Social Sciences at Indian Institute of Technology Mandi, Himachal Pradesh, India.

Renato Marcone has been an assistant professor at the Federal University of Sao Paulo, Brazil. He has worked in the area of mathematics education on topics such as critical mathematics education, inclusive mathematics education, and inclusive assessment.

Pierre Metsan is a senior officer at the Ministry of Education and Training in Vanuatu and a PhD student at the University of New Caledonia, New Caledonia. His main research interest concerns mathematics education.

Vanessa Franco Neto is an assistant professor at Federal University of Mato Grosso do Sul, Brazil. Her research interest is mainly to problematise how gender studies is a way to understand mathematics education research.

Rik Pinxten is emeritus professor of anthropology, Ghent University, Belgium. His research focuses on interculturality, post-colonial emancipation, inclusion, and an update of humanism, fieldwork with Navajo Native Americans, Arizona, and with immigrant groups, Europe.

Hilary Povey is an emerita professor of mathematics education, UK, and her research centres on social justice issues in mathematics education.

Renata Rodrigues Souza is a doctoral student in mathematics education from the Postgraduate Program in Mathematics Education of the Federal University of Mato Grosso do Sul – UFMS, Brazil.

Thomas S. Popkewitz is a professor in the Department of Curriculum and Instruction, The University of Wisconsin-Madison, USA. His studies are concerned with the reason of educational policy, curriculum, teacher education, and research as a historical problem of the politics of knowledge in contemporary schooling.

Jayasree Subramanian did her PhD in mathematics. After her PhD, she carried out empirical research on how gender makes a difference to doing science in India.

Dalene M. Swanson is a professor of education and Director of Postgraduate Research at the University of Nottingham, UK. Dalene's research lays in socio-political and sociological perspectives in mathematics education and critical global citizenship education.

Angela Valencia-Salas has a master's degree in mathematics education from the Universidad Pedagógica Nacional of Colombia. Her research focuses on the historical processes of racialisation of Black students in the Colombian educational system.

Paola Valero is a professor of mathematics education at Stockholm University, Sweden. Her research interests are mathematics education at all levels, in particular policy and curriculum change, multiculturalism/multilingualism, and diversity in mathematics teacher education.

Luz Valoyes-Chávez is an associate professor at the Universidad Católica de Temuco and research associate at the Center for Advanced Research in Education, University of Chile. Her research focuses on the racialisation processes in mathematics education.

Eric Vandendriessche is an ethnomathematician, researcher at the French National Centre for Scientific Research (CNRS), and a member of the Centre for research and documentation on Oceania (CREDO, CNRS & Aix-Marseille University) in France. His research concerns mathematical practices developed in oral tradition societies

Ayşe Yolcu is an associate professor of mathematics education at Hacettepe University, Turkey. Her research draws upon postfoundational approaches to analyse the cultural rules and norms in mathematics curriculum and teaching to understand how they produce differences and exclusions.

Preface

This book has emerged from the symposium *Unfolding global/local policies, practices and/or hybrids in mathematics education worldwide: utopias, pleasures, pressures and conflicts* presented at the 10th Mathematics Education and Society (MES) conference where the possibilities and boundaries of "global citizenship" in mathematics were explored (Chronaki et al., 2019). This was followed with a special issue in Research in Mathematics Education (RME), *Mathematics for "citizenship" and its "other" in a "global" world: Critical issues on mathematics education, globalisation and local communities* (Chronaki & Yolcu, 2021) and a review paper discussing the citizen subject (Chronaki, 2023). Subsequently, the book proposal aimed to continue these critical discussions by inquiring into how citizenship and the citizen subject has, currently, captured a wide interest in global and local mathematics education reforms and institutional renewals. In this journey, we were fortunate to be together with colleagues with a dedicated interest in social, political, cultural, and ecological issues. The present volume is the final outcome of a long editing process, and with it, we encourage the reader to embark on a process of troubling the widespread use of the idea of citizenship for mathematics education to face globalisation risks.

While proposing, organising, and editing this book, we have personally experienced the effects of pandemics, across the world and in our settings, of two big earthquakes that hit our hometowns in Crete and Adıyaman, including fires and floods that came close to our place of living in Volos and our often-used routes in Turkey's Mediterranean region. At the same time, the world has also faced similar phenomena like floods in Libya, volcano eruption in Iceland, war in Ukraine and Palestine. These events urge us to interrogate what it means to be a citizen in a particular country, especially like ours located in the peripheries of global North and global South? And moreover, to question the role of the state and the role of citizens, non-yet-citizens, and the missing others in such global crises and local urgencies? Whose responsibility is to act or who can act at all? What about undocumented migrants or refugees, who are not citizens of a legal status but, nevertheless, share the same space, breathe the same air, and have the same needs? Without finding definitive answers to those questions, we come to recognise that the concept of citizenship remains a paradox of antinomic im/possibilities that, yet, endures principles and qualities of democratic utopias. As such, the concept of citizenship and the idea of becoming a "citizen subject" in a particular civility of the global world require a continuous troubling of its normative conception including its contestation as being, solely, bound to state sovereignty.

Our symposium in MES conference and the discussions around the theme in the following years have nurtured us while trying to problematise the instrumental use of the concept of citizenship as an effect of globalisation times along with its institutionalised forms in mathematics curricular reforms. Particularly: How the concept of citizenship is being used in educational settings? What does it do when placed in the practice of schooling and the ways in which citizenship becomes a hidden engine to reform educational settings for resolving the risks of globalisation? The contributing papers in the RME Special Issue examined the fabrication of desired citizens and their "others" in varied spaces and times. Through empirical and conceptual studies, the Special Issue sought to problematise how the concepts of "globalisation" and "citizenship", or their couplet "global citizenship", act as catchphrases across diverse localities and circulate as a universalising discourse for mathematics education policy and reform pedagogies by ordering who deserve to be granted citizens and who remain others as non-citizens or not-yet-citizens.

The present volume continues this critical discussion by bringing authors from diverse national localities. Authors span geographically from Chile, Colombia, Brazil, Australia, Sweden, France, Belgium, England, India, South Africa, Vanuatu, along with Turkey and Greece covering a wide spread of localities around the globe. They bring forward the potential of transcultural and transnational collaborative efforts especially in Chapters 3 (scholars from Sweden and Australia discuss together vocational mathematics), Chapter 4 (considers cultural diversity reflecting on Navajo people in the United States and immigrants in Europe), and Chapter 5 (colleagues from Europe and South Africa foregrounding dialogue) but also Chapter 13 (where a collaboration across researchers in France, Brazil, and Vanuatu discuss curricular renewals based on ethnomathematical ideas) and Chapter 14 (discussing philosophical inquiry in the United Kingdom through Greece) allow reading across practices in the global North and global South especially as we read in parallel chapters reflecting experiences from Sweden, Australia, UK, and central Europe to experiences offered from India, Colombia, local communities, and the state of Brazil, South Africa, Turkey, and Greece. From this perspective, the book allows to inquire how the concept of citizenship is being currently enacted across national settings and local communities as means to either exercise policy or to experiment with images of the citizen subject.

Through the contributions, we ask: How does mathematics education tend to become framed within discourses of "citizenship" in a global world of increased migration, racism, sexism, and social injustice? How the "future" of mathematics education could be reconfigured when the rhetoric of critical global citizenship education meets diverse localities? What are the effects of such political imageries when they start becoming materialised for children, youth, teachers, and curricula, as well as for markets, economies, and policies? Or, moreover, what are the hybrid mathematical subjectivities and border mathematical knowledge(s) that new visions of globality may unfold?

The book is divided into two parts: (I) Troubling citizenship norms through conceptual ideals and (II) Troubling citizenship norms within national and local settings. Each of these parts addresses the question of citizenship with the challenges of globalisation, diversity, and difference in mathematical practices. The first part, particularly, problematises mathematical competencies reported by transnational organisations and asks critical questions such as: *Who is the constructive, engaged, and reflective citizen? How conceptual yet normative ideals such as success, ability, or efficiency are being utilised in these policy reports or mathematics education research circulate globally?* Without taking mathematical competencies for granted, troubling Eurocentric, modern, enlightenment values underlying critical and dominant narratives of mathematics education are foregrounded in this part. The second part focuses on the ways in which citizen subjects are enacted across spatial territories. It exemplifies specific curricular reforms and curricular renewals, teacher guidelines, textbooks, or alternative projects from various parts of the world. From diverse localities, the chapters interrogate *What makes an acceptable citizen through mathematics education practices? How citizens are enacted and differentiated in particular spatial territories of school mathematics and society?*

The book does not ally with a cruel optimism that mathematics education can create citizens who deal with the complex demands of global times but, equally, does not adopt a pessimist standpoint that any endeavour will end up with people becoming subjected to dominant visions. The chapters engage with the concept of citizenship through varied acts of unfolding what counts as mathematical competencies, how a vision of virtues is constructed for the global citizen as a successful, efficient, skillful and healthy individual, how the desired citizens are assumed in curriculum guidelines, teacher education programs and materials and how their local enactements create conflicts or dilemmas but also open potentialities to rethink mathematics education.

References

Chronaki, A. (2023). Becoming citizen subject in the body politic: Antinomies of archaic, modern and posthuman citizenship temporalities and the political of mathematics education. *Research in Mathematics Education*, 1–23. https://doi.org/10.1080/14794802.2023.2183889

Chronaki, A., Adams, G., Andrade, M., Bruno, G., Demissie, F., Marcone, R., Para, A., Povey, H., Swanson, D., Valero, P., & Yolcu, A. (2019). Unfolding global/local policies, practices and/or hybrids in mathematics education worldwide: utopias, pleasures, pressures and conflicts. In J. Subramanian (Ed.) *Proceedings of the 10th International Mathematics Education and Society (MES 10) Conference.* Hyderabad, India.
Chronaki, A., & Yolcu, A. (2021). Mathematics for 'citizenship' and its 'other' in a 'global' world: Critical issues on mathematics education, globalisation and local communities. *Research in Mathematics Education*, *23*(3), 241–247.

Acknowledgements

Our collaborative efforts to work as co-editors and co-authors for the book *Troubling Notions of Global Citizenship and Diversity in Mathematics Education* go back to more than five years when we started talking and thinking over the idea of who could be a democratic citizen in mathematics education. Through many contingencies, our book accompanies us and our beloved ones throughout these years, reminding us of events that occurred in the world and in our lives.

For all this precious time, we would like to express our gratitude not only to every moment that brings us to this point but also the physical and virtual spaces facilitating our meetings including the land, the air, and the sea that connect us allowing this intellectual journey to happen. It seems that alongside the book, the two of us grew together confronting many risks and damages and sharing in solidarity. We need to thank each other for encouragement, patience, collaboration, understanding, and persistence for these many many hours of working alone, together, offline, and online. We cherish the countless critical conversations across times that held us away from family and friends. All these have nurtured our thoughts concerning everyday life and academic work, have built our friendship, and augmented our anticipation for coming together very soon!

This book would not have been possible without the critical conversations we had with our colleagues during and after the symposium organised in Mathematics Education and Society Conference in India, 2019. Many have accompanied us to organise the special issue in RME, and we continued in their company along with many other colleagues who also joined us to arrive in this book. We are grateful to all of them for entrusting us with their thoughts, feelings and work and, especially, for responding with eagerness and patience to multiple queries and coming forth and back of book chapters. Moreover, they are all a crucial part of this long process of editing this book not only as authors but also as co-reviewers of each other's chapters that strengthened interaction amongst us all. Special thanks must also go to colleagues, who, although were not authors of the book, offered generously their help for the peer-review process of chapters. Particularly, we wish to thank Lisa Darragh,

Karen François, Gustavo Bruno, Petra Kälberg Svensson, Helena Roos, and David Kollosche. Thank you all so much! Additional thanks go to Gill Adams, who, beyond the peer review, helped with language issues encountered in some book chapters. Finally, we must thank RME journal (Research in Mathematics Education) and Taylor Francis for giving us permission to reprint as Chapter 7 in this volume the paper: Chronaki, A. (2023). Becoming citizen subject in the body politic: antinomies of archaic, modern and posthuman citizenship temporalities and the political of mathematics education. *Research in Mathematics Education*, 1–23. https://doi.org/10.1080/14794802.2023.2183889

More thanks than we can give must be sent to our families in Turkey and Greece, who never stop believing and supporting us in every manner, particularly our beloved partners Vassilis and Alican who have tolerated our needs for time to read and write, gave big hugs, many smiles, no complains (as far as they let us sense) and made sure that there was always a soothing presence after these long working hours.

Introduction

Rethinking citizenship enactment for mathematics education

Anna Chronaki and Ayşe Yolcu

> Sophia, a humanoid robot developed by Hanson Robotics, a Hong Kong based company, is marketed as a 'social robot' able to learn, educate and train, mimicking cognitive and emotional behaviour. She first appeared in March 2016 in Austin, Texas. Then, she was granted citizenship by Saudi Arabia at the Future Investment Initiative conference at Riyadh in 2017, gesturing for the Kingdom's plans for digital development. In addition, the UN recognized her as the first non-human innovation champion. Sophia, today, enjoys free mobility rights and travels around the world to business and STEM education courses interacting with the public as ambassador of posthuman digital creativity, computational thinking, mathematics, and artificial intelligence.
>
> (see https://en.wikipedia.org/wiki/Sophia_(robot))

EVENT I: A female cyborg is granted citizenship as ambassador of digital creativity.

> In late August 2023 fierce wildfires, a recurring sign of catastrophic climate change that governments fail to address globally, set burning the national forest of Dadia at Evros, northeastern Greece neighbouring Turkey. Amongst severe animal and nature loss, 19 people were reported to be burnt in the fires. Although their bodies remained unidentified, Amnesty International recognised them as undocumented migrants and refugees who had illegally crossed the borders from Turkey to Greece. They were hiding in the forest due to severe police controls, denials of asylum rights, fear of deportation and lack of safe legal routes or global civil rights protecting people enforced into precarious mobility.
>
> (see:https://www.amnesty.org/en/latest/news/2023/08/greece-evros-wildfire-dead-are-victims-of-two-great-injustices-of-our-times/)

EVENT II: 19 undocumented bodies found burnt at Turkey-Greece borders.

The im/possible gift of citizenship

How can we read the above events as we encounter the idea of citizenship for mathematics education in a contemporaneity immersed with dreams of creating posthuman solutions that promise to overcome the challenges of globalisation, diversity, and difference in our practices? Together, they note how

DOI: 10.4324/9781003130673-1

citizenship remains an unresolved paradox and political utopia troubling both the normative boundaries across subject-object relations and the state's internal and external borders crossed everyday by vulnerable mobile subjects. As the present book discusses the citizen subject of mathematics education within diverse world localities, let us allow the echo of these stories to foreground our inquiry.

On the one hand, the hyper celebration of a posthuman digital female "other" like the artificially intelligent robot Sophia is currently realised as the crest of life science innovations based on principles of mathematics, consciousness, artificial intelligence, computational biology, and machine learning. Moreover, it is being marked as an opportunity for combined global economic and educational prospects in a capitalist world that triggers debt crisis, energy scarcity, job loss, poverty, and insecurity. In this condition, Sophia is granted citizenship as a gift by Saudi Arabia—a society that continues discriminating against women contemned by Amnesty International (2023a). And whilst feminist social justice strivings around the globe are faced with populism, sexism, and racism, the female humanoid enjoys the citizenship right of free mobility allowing her to cross safely borders as ambassador of digital humanity. Sophia, moreover, becomes an educator for thousands of children in STEM courses and discusses AI ethics and citizen-life. Considering these critical advances, esteemed mathematics educators argue that for preparing the next generation of youth "in a world facing global challenges and unprecedented seriousness, the importance of scientific and mathematical literacy and expertise has never been more central" (Hoyles & Ferrini-Mundy, 2013, p. 511) since mathematics offers "diverse and unique ways" to express creativity. To meet the demands of digital creativity in posthuman times attention must be both on how mathematics becomes an autonomous field of creations (Chapter 6) and on how the becoming creative citizen subject of mathematics engages critically with subject-object hybrids (Chapter 7).

On the other hand, the undocumented bodies at Evros wildfires did not count as citizen subjects of this world. Amnesty International (2023b) reports that this event denotes two great injustices: *first*, climate change destruction, global warming, and rising temperatures with severe ecological disasters that governments fail to confront and *second*, the lack of safe routes for refugees who desperately must cross borders illegally at any cost. Instead of pursuing democratic constitutionalism to address the global risks of social, political, and ecological collapse and combat precarity (see Global Catastrophic Risks, 2024), authorities intensify internal and external border surveillance and, often, respond with unlawful deportations, asylum denials, racism, and xenophobia. Violent controls at the European borders exemplify that nation-states fail to apply peace agreements such as the Geneva Convention on the Status of Refugees (United Nations [UN], 1951) forbidding deportations to countries of origin if these might threaten freedom or life. Such moments denote the limits of global citizenship and universal rights in praxis. Of course, Europe is not the only zone that restricts citizen and non-citizen mobility. Whilst the 1954 miles long

Mexico-U.S. borders have the most frequent illegal crossings annually, mobility pressures escalate due to multiple conflicts around the globe including Africa, Asia, and the Middle East of which the wars in Ukraine, Palestine, and Sudan are tough indications of civil breakdown. With claims by insurgent citizen subjects to legitimise the presence of undocumented civilians and their siblings in welfare care such as health and education, a rethinking of mathematics education for social justice needs to prioritise social structures supporting access and participation as a matter of citizenship rights (i.e., the right to mathematics education). It needs to create conditions for dialogical relations (Chapters 4, 5, and 13) making space for diversity and difference across cultures, languages, ages, skills, and abilities instead of emphasising ideal images of desired citizens who learn mathematics to gain success (Chapter 1), combat disability (Chapter 2), improve vocational skills (Chapter 3), become healthier individuals (Chapter 11), and efficient peasants (Chapter 12). The present book discusses the tensions and ambiguities when such citizen images are being enacted as the institutional desire for mathematics education curricular reforms without attending to the precarities and injustice of a migrant reality of non-citizens.

An increased digitised and migrated life for both citizens and non-citizens or non-yet-citizens who inhabit together a civil society in conditions of a worldwide ecological collapse, struggles against neo-colonial and dictatorial governing, decolonial strivings for local heritage, resistance to wars and armed conflicts characterise our global era reaching its apex. The challenges of globalisation, diversity and difference permeate mathematics education attempts for reforms and renewals that emphasise the institutionalisation and normalisation of citizenship ideals. However, in this convergence, the very idea of citizenship requires rethinking as the promises of citizenship for "all" proves more and more impossible to materialise as a global or local universal. The book aims to open this discussion by troubling normative enactments of citizenship for mathematics education.

Rethinking citizenship: *Globalisation, diversity, and difference*

The idea of citizenship is recognised as both *strategic* for enacting civil governance and *antinomic* when it relates to democracy and social justice practices (Balibar, 2010). The notion of "citoyen", defined by Diderot and d' Alambert in their Encyclopaedia as legal active participation in the body politic, is extensively utilised from the 18th century to contemporary times. This bordered idea of citizenship has served to rule the democratic polis, secure nation-states around common values, languages, cultures, religions, and ethnic identity politics and, even, extend state power to colonies by institutionalising and normalising the political agency to claim rights and representation. However, it has also been critiqued by theorists and practitioners in domains of care such as health, social work or education arguing for the need to reconsider and destabilise boundaries across citizens, non-citizens, undocumented migrants, refugees, and non-human others in face of globalisation, diversity, and difference.

First, globalisation challenges are understood in relation to heightened transnational mobility due to multiple global crises of economy, ecology, politics, and peace. Robert Schaeffer (2022) explains that this 500 years old phenomenon has grown from the 15th century feudalism crisis in Europe when people desperately and violently turned to "new worlds" for survival, hope, or wealth. Subsequent forms emerged into a European organised capitalist world-order through brutal colonisation procedures of indigenous communities in which people were dispossessed, lands, labour and resources were exploited whilst minds and souls were infected with Enlightenment values. The world is pictured after WWII through Cold War tensions and US competitiveness that generated first, second and third world countries governed locally by dictatorships or democracies and globally by a capitalist order favouring free trade agreements, debt and taxes, inflation, stock markets, and technology control. Yet, its peak was reached in the 1980s due to advances in digital communication technologies allowing increased interconnectivity across local markets, leisure sites, and education. According to Schaeffer (2022), the image of an infinitely growing globalisation era has been crushed by the "Great Recession" of the 2008 economic crises and by the "Greater Recession" of the 2019 coronavirus pandemic. And, despite the declining US hegemony along with the upcoming influence of Asian dragons, such as China, in global affairs, Schaeffer observes how, today, state interventions encounter desperate neoliberal strategies in which public resources, paid by citizen taxes, are devoted for private gains. The rising privatisation of public schooling turns education, along with social goods like healthcare, into a marketised commodity (Ball, 2007). And by imposing neoliberal policies for evaluation, assessment, financing, training, and organising standards for curricula, learning or instruction (Torres, 2009) inequalities are reproduced for the lower classes of marginalised people whilst alienation, disintegration, and depoliticisation is intensified. Several chapters in this book address these challenges and contribute by discussing citizenship in the context of globalisation (Chapters 1, 2, 3, and 7), internationalisation (Chapter 8), neoliberalism (Chapter 14), or subjection to citizen ideals (Chapters 11 and 12).

Second, diversity is acknowledged today as a matter of, on the one hand, the rising awareness and visibility of cultural, linguistic, religious, and ethnic diversity in multiple sites of the civil society and, on the other hand, the gradual loss or extinction of diversity in nature, culture, and technology. Diversity loss is especially appreciated more and more not as a matter of evolution but due to violent processes of exploiting resources, energy, knowledge, languages, values or cultures and dispossessing people, animals, and plants from their places. In this, the prevalence of social, economic, environmental, and political crisis, leading to wars, hunger, poverty, and ecological damage, exerts diverse species (e.g., humans, animals, plants, codes, viruses) to move for survival and to risk life by ignoring cultural, legal, and territorial boundaries. Human and non-human diversity becomes a matter of concern during either local civil endeavour (e.g., policy making, resistance practices, insurgent movements, solidarity acts) and global collaborations for advancing international policy for a safe planet or alter-global alliances for critiquing existent global policies (or their lack) protesting inaction. As argued, the question of diversity is located at the junction of the 6th extinction, the 4th industrial revolution, and advanced capitalist economy (Chronaki, 2023). This condition compels us to rethink global citizenship in dialogue with cultural diversities, decolonial struggles (Chapters 4, 5, and 13), and posthumanity (Chapter 7).

And *third*, the question of difference owes much to feminists who critique citizenship as a site of male-power that reproduces the patriarchal dichotomies of male-female, private-public, culture-nature, human-nonhuman. This is evident not only with the case of Olympe de Gouge (Chapter 7) who was executed upon demanding the Declaration's rewriting for women but also with liberal feminists' struggles who continue, today, to place claims for altering laws and policies that restrict women's participation in public affairs (e.g., vote, education, work, career). Even though the liberal agenda aims to reverse inequalities amongst men and women, the male ideal as the core patriarchal norm remains unchallenged and, instead, a bi-gendered conception of the citizen is prioritised. Failing to critique and decentre patriarchal norms, requires women (and all other marginalised subjects) to strive toward achieving male privileges at any cost, to conform within a male-defined world and even to essentialise women as a coherent category in the construction of the ideal, desired, and universal citizen is implicitly coded as male, white, abled, heteronormative body in the fantasy of a homogenous global world. Instead, radical critical feminists (e.g., Butler, 1988; Haraway, 1991) propose an anti-essentialist approach where the subject is articulated in the multiplicity of hybrid relations with humans and more-than-human others where difference is respected across subjects-objects at the intersections of multiple hybrid identities.

The entangled phenomena of globalisation, diversity and difference contest the taken for granted national sovereignty as the norm for theorising and enacting citizenship. They trouble state-bounded citizenship by asking to rethink it as a mechanism for governing, as adoption of universalist and differentiated models, and as enacted beyond state boundaries. *First,* rethinking citizenship as a state governing mechanism relates to Euro-centric legal practices. This becomes more and more evident as the rise of refugees and asylum seekers move from poorer to richer countries making visible the injustices that already exist between countries of the global North and the global South or developed, developing and under-development states (Schaeffer, 2022). Although liberal democracies open toward rights and representation, the double-R axiom, these become legal tools for controlling inclusion and exclusion. Papadopoulos and Tsianos (2013) argue how state citizenship turns into a "cut" strategy by regulating "this unstable and dangerous balance" between rights and representation that "renders certain populations as legitimate bearers of rights while other populations are marked as inexistent" (p. 188). Citizenship is an impossible gift for some entering the necropolitics (Mbembe, 2003) of unsafe escape routes as in Event II.

Second, citizenship as universalist or differentiated must be reconsidered. Whilst the universalist model espouses arguments for civic unity and equality (as identical rights for all), the differentiated model, instead, considers the needs for differential inclusion to reverse the injustices caused by applying equal measures to all. However, in practice, they fall short in extending citizenship rights to previously excluded groups (i.e., women, migrants, marginalised humans, non-human others). Empirical facts in care practices (e.g., health, social work, education) note the continuing presence of oppression, racism, and sexism making clear that the civic integration of certain people as culturally belonging or with legal status has not yet been successful for everybody. Although a universal and differentiated conception of citizenship is commonly proposed as a solution especially for education, tensions across spatial state territories remain (Zhao & Tröhler, 2021). For all these reasons, the differential inclusion across citizens, non-citizens, and undocumented migrants creates antinomies that point to how needs and strategies for mobility, labour, and security are being assembled within an assumed universal citizenship norm that in practice supports, mainly, the sovereign nation's hegemony.

And *third*, rethinking citizenship beyond the state becomes key for engaging radically with the question of diversity and difference. Scholars argue that instead of relying on normative forms of legal citizenship rights, people must consider "citizenship acts" that could, even, opt toward forms of "clandestine citizenship" (Sager, 2011) so that to prioritise the inclusion of the excluded others in local settings where care and solidarity is, already, exercised in varied scales. School classrooms, and mathematics classrooms are, potentially, such local settngs.

Enacting citizenship norms in mathematics education practices

Contemporary mathematics education resorts to a global discourse of citizenship to justify the importance for policy reform and renewal that combat the challenges of globalisation, diversity and difference in the context of international relations. Yet mathematicians and mathematics educators had expressed an interest in coming together to share local practices, read and translate textbooks even before the end of the 19th century (Karp, 2013). These border-crossing collaborations were understood in a positive tone and noted as learning from one another's differences and intensified the foundation of the L'Enseignement Mathématique, International Commission on Mathematical Instruction [ICMI] (Karp, 2013), the International Study of Achievement in Mathematics (Kilpatrick, 2013) and other international fora such as Commission for the Study and Improvements of Mathematics Teaching.

Improvement of Mathematics Teaching, Psychology of Mathematics Education and Mathematics Education and Society. Beyond universalising mathematics achievement, the efforts were to cultivate a common language and disciplinary culture through mathematical knowledge and instruction exchanges. Today, ICMI members comprise more than 92 countries across North and South that reflect the diversity of interests and concerns such as global standards and local curricula, decolonisation strategies or inclusive programs.

More recently, the international assessment programs organised by TIMSS (Trends in International Mathematics and Science Study) and PISA (Programme for International Student Assessment) in the context of IEA (International Association for the Evaluation of Educational Achievement) and OECD (Organisation for Economic Co-operation and Development) dominate the discussions of quality and equity in mathematics education as policy and practice. Student performance in these testing programs, along with indicators concerning schooling, allow nations to be compared and ordered according to standardised definitions of what mathematically literate citizens should be. Individual competence in these tests is assumed to measure ability for coping in real-life and is argued necessary for society's progress and development. Mathematical competencies are not limited to basic procedural skills, but include "reasoning mathematically and using mathematical concepts, procedures, facts and tools to describe, explain and predict phenomena" (OECD, 2013, p. 1) to support a citizen subject making constructive, engaged, and reflective decisions. Beyond learning mathematics, the reciprocal relation between mathematics and preparing future adults as citizens is reflected in performance measures aiming for knowledge commodification (Ernest, 2007). The purpose of these high-stakes international assessment programs is not merely to construct unifying citizenship identities to meet the urgencies in modern global economies but, in parallel, to provide tools for making, ordering, classifying, and normalising certain forms of modern life.

Moreover, in this condition, not only the human but also the posthuman citizens are imagined as hybrids of subjects and objects able to become active participants in the social, cultural, civic, and political spheres acting within and across the borders of nation-states, communities or the material world. As exemplified with the female cyborg of citizen Sophia (Event I) and the undocumented migrants crossing Turkish-Greek borders (Event II) current attempts to rethink citizenship must move beyond fixed relations to human centeredness and to nation-state boundaries. Both events could be seen as effects of globalisation discourses permeated by neoliberal, colonial, racialised, and anthropocentric strategies, yet at the same time, they create possibilities to decolonise conventional conceptions of citizenship and their enactment to educational contexts in multiple ways. The mathematics education community has critically encountered the instrumentalisation of mathematical self-competence through discussions of cultural diversity and difference in varied local contexts and has critiqued the attitude of reporting "gaps" across the nations, found in the conventional comparative studies (Atweh et al., 2007).

Multiple efforts challenge the Euro-centric notions of mathematical knowledge relevant for the becoming modern citizen subject through highlighting alternative practices, redefining mathematical literacy from emancipatory positions or cultural perspectives.

A recent special issue in ZDM-Mathematics Education journal takes up the concept of citizenship in mathematics education (Geiger et al., 2023) and effectively argues how "personally responsible, participatory or justice-oriented" citizenship could be reconfigured through mathematical competencies (p. 926). The articles in this issue engage with positive discussions of how mathematics and mathematical competencies save the world from the perils it currently faces or solves the problems of a modernised life. Within the tone of a differentiated citizenship model aiming for inclusionary practices, articles in the collection are attentive to classroom-based practical questions such as catering for differential needs of diverse students, pedagogical solutions, inclusionary "innovative" curricula, and teacher education for critical skills. Despite noting the presence of instructional and institutional barriers to achieve the kind of citizens envisioned in today's civil society, this special issue does not discuss already published work concerning the tensions of citizenship use in institutional forms of mathematics education policy, curricula or teaching and teacher education practices (e.g., Chronaki & Yolcu, 2021).

As noted in our previously edited special issue in RME (Research in Mathematics Education) journal, the emphasis placed for a common global citizenship future in mathematics educational reforms embodies modes of comparative reasoning that risks dividing people as proper "citizens" and "others" (Chronaki & Yolcu, 2021). This desired one-world system entails an illusion of homogeneity that, under the catchphrase of globalisation and global citizenship, provides hopes of progress, development, social and educational equality, or commitment to ideal values of humanity that, also, incorporate and reproduce fears of degeneration, decay, or underdevelopment (Popkewitz, 2008). The reciprocal relation amongst hopes and fears constitute, potentially, a network of practices for school mathematics tied back to ideals of daily life modernisation through generating instrumental conceptual categories of mathematical competences assumed necessary to maintain and secure the social order (Yolcu, 2021). While this network offers promises for a moral, ethical, successful, and pleasurable life in a globalised world, it also generates exclusions and hierarchies for humankinds under the guises of lifelong-learning, managerial leadership, and qualifications for "flexible" job conditions.

The inquiry of how citizenship is enacted in mathematics practices demands further problematising beyond discussing didactical or pedagogic models that institutionalise citizenship norms. As noted, efforts for creating a unified global discourse of citizenship work as a matter of fabricating the ideal global citizen with mathematical skills and, in parallel, operate the inclusion or exclusion to citizenship status in particular spacetimes (see Events I and II). Problematising the antinomies of the im/possible gift of citizenship is not only relevant for rethinking citizenship, but also for troubling prevailing images of becoming citizen subjects enacting the competent, insurgent, or creative subjects that, currently, permeate mathematics education practices (Chronaki, 2023). In this sense, citizenship in the realm of globalisation risks becomes a multifaceted social strategy that affects the fabrication of individuals, collectives and subjects/objects in ways that are not limited to market relations but circulate through diverse cultural spheres of lives (Ball et al., 2010). Far from producing a fixed identitarian relation to the citizen subject and its unifying scripts, Ball's (1998) analysis demonstrates how such global discourses fail to homogenise the world. Rather, they are situated in local contexts where a multiplicity of emergent dilemmas, contradictions and tensions exist as several chapters in this volume exemplify. Unfolding how citizenship norms underly mathematics education, the present book troubles such normative configurations of the ideal modern citizen of mathematical practices by noting how they, often, translate into exclusionary mechanisms.

Citizenship trouble in mathematics education: The book and its chapters

To read the chapters in this volume as a way of troubling citizenship norms for mathematics education is inspired by the seminal work of feminist scholar Judith Butler (1990) on "Gender Trouble" where a radical anti-essentialist rethinking of gender identity is discussed. By critiquing the discourse of social vs biological difference as a distinction that further supports normative dichotomies amongst masculine-feminine that in turn construct "women" as a unified category, Butler (1988) proposes to rethink gender as a performative act. Taking social reality as based on "speech acts", a term coined by John Searle, consisting of verbal, gestural and embodied semiotics in which "... an identity (is) instituted through a stylized repetition of acts" (p. 519) the subject is seen not as a fundamental thesis but as being constituted through habitual acts, behaviour rituals, language use, bodily expressions, and values practising. This conceptualisation has been employed by Chronaki (2011) working toward troubling essentialist identities of failure assigned to Roma and migrant children in mathematics classrooms explaining that: "... (p)erformativity refers to an embodied culturally scripted character of identity where its focus is to express hegemonic conceptions of identity as fictions generated by power through repeated reproductions of norms" (p. 209). Through reading the chapters of this book, a similar repeated reproduction of citizenship norms seems to operate in the discourse of mathematics education as policy and practice marking inscriptions of the cultural character of the ideal citizen subject in mathematical practices. Troubling these inscriptions engulfs possibilities for sensing a different re-inscription.

With the "gender trouble" in mind, norms are not conceived as static but open to revision, transformation, and subversion. Central to this contestation of an imposed normative identity is the idea of troubling found "... in the possibility of a different sort of repeating, in the breaking or subversive repetition of that style" (Butler, 1988, p. 520). Along with Butler, we propose to approach the book chapters as narratives of a "citizenship trouble" grounded in the analysis of diverse mathematics education practices worldwide. Although the individual chapters of the book do not engage with Butler's performative theory of troubling norms, they bring forward specific scripts of how citizenship norms are being enacted through performative acts (i.e., in discursive and embodied materialisations) through discussing the citizen subject in policy documents, curricular guidelines, textbook, film scripts, historical materials, research reports and in situ ethnographic observations. Yet, the becoming citizen subject cannot be disciplined wholly within the scripts of a normative citizenship ideal. Norms, including citizenship norms, do not persist in social life in fixed ways, rather they are re-cited, performed differently, re-iterated, re-inscribed and re-invented as also current work for rethinking citizenship beyond state conceptions notes. As such, we ask the readers of this book to enact their own troubling of citizenship norms by inquiring across chapters how these norms perform the normative matrix of socially constructed concepts of the citizen subject and turn them unintelligible and anti-essentialist.

Book chapters are organised into two parts highlighting how the global discourse of citizenship in mathematics education is enacted both through conceptual categories that identify citizen subject ideals (Part I: Troubling citizenship norms through conceptual ideals) and within the context of national and local settings where the modern global citizen subject becomes institutionalised and normalised (Part II: Troubling citizenship norms within national and local settings). Specifically, the seven chapters in Part I could be read as troubling citizenship norms through the ways that conceptual categories such as success, dis/ability, d/efficiency, diversity, dialogical, ecological, modern, competent, insurgent, creative tend to become assembled with citizen subject images in mathematics education practices. In these, the making of global, universal, ecological, culturally diverse, and still modern citizens is under construction along with paradoxes and inconsistencies. The rest of the chapters consist of Part II and is proposed to read as a further troubling of citizenship operationalisation in specific national, and local settings around the world (i.e., Turkey, India, Colombia, Brazil, Vanuatu, UK in relation to Greece). In these institutional settings, the authors discuss how norms of a citizen subject fluent in mathematics (i.e., competent, and efficient problem solver) align with curricular demands for reform by responding to current challenges concerning globalisation risks, diversity, and difference as well as their resulting into contradictory tensions.

This edited volume brings together authors, colleagues in different parts of the world, researching the social, cultural, and political dimensions of mathematics education and have, already, debated the citizenship enactment in mathematics education at the occasion of a MES symposium (Chronaki et al., 2019) and an RME special issue (Chronaki & Yolcu, 2021). As such, the volume moves toward a more nuanced rethinking that allows troubling citizenship norms as they become cemented in global discourses of citizenship through certain normative conceptual categories (see chapters in Part I) that, in turn, become enacted in specific national and local settings (see chapters in Part II). The settings examined here span geographically from Chile, Colombia, Brazil, Australia, Sweden, France, Belgium, England, India, South Africa, Vanuatu, along with Turkey and Greece covering a global spatiality. The chapters discuss specific materialisations of citizenship enactments in diverse educative contexts such as global policy documents by OECD (Chapter 1), World Health Organisation (WHO) (Chapter 2), Programme for the International Assessment of Adult Competencies (PIAAC) (Chapter 3) evoking mathematics education norms in national curricular guidelines that describe and prescribe principles of mathematics teaching (Chapters 8, 9, and 10), textbooks that provide detailed organisation of classroom task activity (Chapters 11 and 12), local attempts to enact decolonial mathematics education (Chapters 5 and 13), critical philosophical inquiry (Chapter 14) and dialogical relations (Chapters 2, 4, and 5), historical and philosophical encounters of "modern" in mathematics (Chapter 6) or how the becoming citizen subject permeates mathematics education (Chapter 7).

Part I, starts with Chapter 1 provoking the image of a successful citizen with mathematical skills for a sustainable global economy. Andrade-Molina attests to how these dominant success narratives are problematic as they transform into a fictional norm carried through reports by transnational organisations such as OECD and mathematics education research that is opposed by pop-culture narratives such as the film Ladybird, displaying a young girl's negotiation of mathematical success and failure. Similarly, Marcone in Chapter 2 focuses on the discourse of disability in differentiated models of a "deserving" citizenship aiming for wider inclusion. By unfolding definitions of disability and globalisation in WHO, Wikipedia and conference proceedings, he argues for espousing a dialogical construction of disability to combat the discourse of deficiencialism and embracing difference as strength. Followed in Chapter 3, Boistrup and FitzSimons focus on vocational mathematics in PIAAC reports, discuss globalisation and the global vocational learner who embraces mathematics in nuanced ways, reflecting the complexities of working life.

In Chapter 4, Pinxten notes that although mathematics develops as a universal language, it becomes an artificial expert language mastered by a few and one that in culturally diverse classroom contexts creates vast exclusions. Pressing for dialogue, he seeks to balance different forms of mathematics, but also multiple selves, including local cultural subjects, hybrid city dwellers and technology users in today's globalised world. Swanson and le Roux also prioritise dialogue Chapter 5, where they propose a glocalising praxis to reimagine mathematical citizens, reflectively and reciprocally enacted rather than re-stating its bond to state-institutions. Rather than explicating the distinctive features of this praxis, they emphasise how ecological (human) being is in dialogue with itself and Others. The last two chapters of Part I theorise the modern (Chapter 6) as a constructive principle for making mathematics an autonomous practice and the genealogical construction citizen subject in ancient, modern and posthuman times that permeate mathematics education (Chapter 7). Specifically, in Chapter 6, Malviya discusses the notion of modern in the mathematics program of group theory advanced by the Bourbaki collective that influenced mathematics education reforms in the 60s and Alan Touring's computational theory advancing machine learning. Being "modern" in mathematical practices was about making mathematics an autonomous practice and was experienced as a pedagogical discourse endorsing autopoietic and universal aspirations. In Chapter 7, Chronaki discusses the genealogy of prevailing citizen subject images such as the competent subject in ancient polis, the insurgent subject in modern nation-state and the creative subject of the posthuman body in today's mathematics education narratives. Balibar's philosophical approach on citizenship is engaged with Deleuze's nomadism and critical feminist scholarship to understand antinomies across times and the missing others in the global discourse of citizenship.

Complementing the above discussion where citizenship is enacted through specific conceptual categories addressing the challenges of globalisation, diversity and difference, Part II brings cases of how the modern citizen subject is enacted in specific national and local settings through specific curricular reforms and renewals in the context of curriculum, teacher guidelines, textbooks, or alternative projects. In particular, Chapter 8 analyses how the national past and future of Turkey is woven into curricular guidelines with hopes of a global modern citizen who is an efficient problem solver. Yolcu's historical-comparative analysis makes visible how the persistent desire to make mathematically able bodies is travelled to Turkish context by producing differentiations for certain human kinds, yet form a paradoxical unity of (non)citizens in the nation despite the shifting pedagogical practices over a century. Subramanian in Chapter 9 examines the recent national education and curriculum policy in India that includes ancient Indian mathematical knowledge. Discussing how the document silences the ethnomathematics of caste groups despite the strong tradition of Kerala mathematics in India, she argues that persistence of a particular version of the Indian past supports casteism and religious fundamentalism. In Chapter 10, Valencia-Salas and Valoyes-Chávez examine the racialised and anti-blackness discourses of mathematics education reform in Colombia. Their analysis considers the elusive historical background of citizenship for Black Colombians (i.e., no voting rights, limited participation in the body politic, discrimination and stereotyping as lower race) and focuses on curricular documents organised *first* after the 1991 constitutional change (i.e., demanding inclusive, quality, modern education for global social, economic and technological demands) and *second* specific policies for indigenous and Black communities such as Ethnoeducation. Their critical reading questions the narratives of democratic citizenship and discourses of blackness that emphasise the mestizo citizen subject (race mixing as heterogeneity) as the emergent ideal for mathematics education.

The next two chapters analyse translations of the modern citizen in mathematics textbooks produced as part of recent educational reforms in Brazil. Specifically, Rodrigues Souza and da Silva in Chapter 11 analyse the textbook-based mathematical activity that exemplifies the modern healthy citizen who is always in control of biological life and cultivates healthy habits and attitudes. Engaging with Foucault's concept of governmentality they problematize how seemingly benign advice through curricular activity shapes and directs individuals toward specific behaviours that align with the nation-state agenda. Neto and Valero in Chapter 12 examine another set of mathematics textbooks focusing on rural education in Brazil. Conducting a Foucauldian analysis similar to Rodrigues Souza and da Silva, they also examine how certain textbook-based mathematical activities govern the modern peasant-citizens. These two chapters unfold the normalising impulses of enacting citizenship discourses through curriculum materials like these mathematics textbooks allowing them to account for the production of social and moral imperatives for self and society.

In Chapter 13, Vandendriessche, Leite, Fantinato, and Metsan explore the potential of enacting a culturally and locally based mathematics curriculum in the Republic of Vanuatu (South Pacific) and the Paiter local community in Brazil, employing a program of Brazilian Indigenous Intercultural Education. Through ethnographic study, they make visible contradictory goals and tensions across local and global concerns. Whilst the Paiter teachers in Brazil note the challenges faced to value, preserve and revitalise local knowledge and practices for mathematics, the Vanatuan case is more concerned with how teachers experience the new national curriculum that emphasises the diversity of vernacular languages and cultures. This cross-case analysis exemplifies how culturally oriented mathematics curricula may act as a decolonial practice but without erasing local-global tensions. And in the last chapter, Adams, Povey, and Demissie discuss a European project in Citizenship and Mathematics where project-based curriculum materials were devised across countries and a philosophical frame was utilised to engage teachers in critical inquiry of employing mathematics concepts in project work. By exploring the impact of inclusive, participatory, and innovative pedagogies together with the philosophical inquiry, the tensions experienced with UK teachers as compared with teachers in Greece for devoting time for such activity. The authors point to cultural and neoliberal forces when learning spaces open for teachers to engage with critical reflection, interrogation and problematisation.

Finally, all book chapters open critical conversations for how "citizens", "non-citizens" and "non-yet-citizens" are enacted in mathematical practices in the face of multiple challenges, particularly globalisation, diversity, and difference. Given the im/possibilities of citizenship and the historical persistence of citizen subject discourses in mathematics education, it becomes critical that researchers, policy-makers and curricula developers engage with the historical, philosophical, and anthropological discussion of the concept of citizenship. This edited volume highlights the diversity of local knowledge and practices where citizen subjects are enacted. Teachers and teacher educators could benefit from this volume by encountering already-reported dilemmas, tensions, and contradictions as they confront the risks of globalisation, diversity, and difference in everyday schooling practices. Finally, we urge researchers who want to engage with the concept of citizenship for mathematics education to become attentive to the critical work that is already underway while they plan, conceptualise, and carry out their studies. In this, by prioritising the troubling of citizenship norms for mathematics education, we do not claim that the idea of "citizenship" and "citizen" is redundant. On the contrary, alongside Haraway (2016) we argue for "staying with the trouble" striving for sympoiesis with multispecies including citizens as human and more than human subjects or objects. Dialogue across theoretical, methodological, ethical, and onto/epistemological perspectives to embrace "citizenship trouble" and "stay with this trouble" in mathematics education becomes an important tool that can be mutually useful to understand, critique, subvert, and create emancipatory alternatives for mathematics education research for becoming citizen subjects in a life that combats alienation and values interdependency and togetherness.

References

Amnesty International. (2023a). Saudi Arabia: New Personal Status Law Codifies Discrimination Against Women. March 8, 2023 (see: MDE 23/6431/2023).

Amnesty International. (2023b). Greece: Evros wildfire dead are victims of 'two great injustices of our times' by Adriana Tidona. August 23, 2023. (see amnesty.org).

Atweh, B., Barton, A. C., Borba, M. C., Gough, N., Keitel-Kreidt, C., Vistro-Yu, C., & Vithal, R. (2007). *Internationalisation and globalisation in mathematics and science education*. Springer.

Balibar, E. (2010). Antinomies of citizenship. *Journal of Romance Studies*, *10*(2), 1–20.

Ball, S. (2007). *Education PLC: Understanding private sector participation in public sector education*. Routledge.

Ball, S. J. (1998). Big policies/small world: An introduction to international perspectives in education policy. *Comparative Education*, *34*(2), 119–130.

Ball, S. J., Dworkin, A. G., & Vryonides, M. (2010). Globalization and education: Introduction. *Current Sociology*, *58*(4), 523–529.

Butler, J. P. (1988). Performative Acts and Gender Constitution: An essay in phenomenology and Gender theory. *Theatre Journal*, *40*(4), 519–531.

Butler, J. P. (1990). *Gender trouble: Feminism and the subversion of identity*. Routledge.

Chronaki, A. (2011). Troubling essentialist identities: Performative mathematics and the politics of a possibility. In M. Kontopodis, C. Wulf, & B. Fichtner (Eds.), *Children, development and education: Cultural, historical and anthropological perspectives. Springer. International perspectives on early childhood education and development* (pp. 207–227). Springer.

Chronaki, A. (2023). Becoming citizen subject in the body politic: Antinomies of archaic, modern and posthuman citizenship temporalities and the political of mathematics education. *Research in Mathematics Education*, 1–23. https://doi.org/10.1080/14794802.2023.2183889

Chronaki, A., Adams, G., Andrade, M., Bruno, G., Demissie, F., Marcone, R., Para, A., Povey, H., Swanson, D., Valero, P., & Yolcu, A. (2019). Unfolding global/local policies, practices and/or hybrids in mathematics education worldwide:

utopias, pleasures, pressures and conflicts. In J. Subramanian (Ed.) *Proceedings of the 10th International Mathematics Education and Society (MES 10) Conference*, Hyderabad, India.

Chronaki, A., & Yolcu, A. (2021). Mathematics for 'citizenship' and its 'other' in a 'global' world: Critical issues on mathematics education, globalisation and local communities. *Research in Mathematics Education*, *23*(3), 241–247.

Ernest, P. (2007). Epistemological issues in the internationalization and globalization of mathematics education. In B. Atweh, A. Calabrese Barton, M. C. Borba, N. Gough, C. Keitel, & C. Vistro-Yu (Eds.), *Internationalisation and globalisation in mathematics and science education* (pp. 19–38). Springer.

Geiger, V., Gal, I., & Graven, M. (2023). The connections between citizenship education and mathematics education. *ZDM–Mathematics Education*, *55*(5), 923–940.

Global Catastrophic Risks (2024) *Managing risks through collective action*. Stockholm. Global Challenges Foundation. https://globalchallenges.org/app/uploads/2024/01/Global-catastrophic-risk-2024.pdf

Haraway, D. (1991). *Simians, cyborgs and women: The reinvention of nature*. Free Association Books.

Haraway, D. (2016). *Staying with the trouble*. Duke University Press.

Hoyles, C., & Ferrini-Mundy, J. (2013). Policy implications of developing mathematics education research. In. M.A (Ken) Clements, A. J. Bishop, C. Keitel, J. Kilpatrick, & F. K. S. Leung (Eds.), *Third international handbook of mathematics education* (pp. 485–514). Springer International Handbooks of Education.

Karp, A. (2013). From the local to the international in mathematics education. In M. A. Clements, A. Bishop, C. Keitel, J. Kilpatrick, & F. Leung (Eds.), *Third international handbook of mathematics education* (pp. 797–826). Springer.

Kilpatrick, J. (2013). Introduction to section D: International perspectives on mathematics education. In M. A. Clements, A. Bishop, C. Keitel, J. Kilpatrick, & F. Leung (Eds.), *Third international handbook of mathematics education* (pp. 791–795). Springer.

Mbembe, A. (2003). Necropolitics. *Public Culture*, *15*(1), 11–40. (transl. Libby Meintjes).

Organisation for Economic Co-operation and Development (2013). *PISA 2012 assessment and analytical framework: Mathematics, reading, science, problem solving and financial literacy*. OECD Publishing.

Papadopoulos, D., & Tsianos, V. (2013). After citizenship: Autonomy of migration, organisational ontology and mobile commons. *Citizenship Studies*, *17*(2), 178–196.

Popkewitz, T. S. (2008). *Cosmopolitanism and the age of school reform: Science, education, and making society by making the child*. Routledge.

Sager, M. (2011). Everyday Clandestinity. Experiences on the Margins of Citizenship and Migration Policies. Dissertation. Centre for gender studies. Lund University. Sweden

Schaeffer, R. K. (2022). *After globalisation: Crisis and disintegration*. Routledge.

Torres, C. A. (2009). *Education and neoliberal globalisation*. Routledge.

United Nations. (1951). *The refugee convention*. Retrieved November 15, 2024, from https://www.unhcr.org/sites/default/files/legacy-pdf/4ca34be29.pdf

Yolcu, A. (2021). Turkey's problem-solving child: A historical analysis of the cultural spaces of mathematics education. *Eğitim ve Bilim*, *46*(206), 27–47. http://dx.doi.org/10.15390/EB.2020.8906

Zhao, W., & Tröhler, D. (2021). Euro-Asia encounters on 21st-century competency-based curriculum reforms: A historical and cultural (re)turn. In W. Zhao & D. Tröhler (Eds.), *Euro-Asian encounters on 21st-century competency-based curriculum reforms* (pp. 3–17). Springer.

Part I

Troubling citizenship norms through conceptual ideals

1 Challenging the need for mathematics education for future success

What if this is the best version of myself?

Melissa Andrade-Molina

Disclaimer 1

This chapter challenges the narratives of success unfolded by transnational institutions, such as the Organization for Economic Co-operation and Development (OECD), and research in the field of mathematics education, such as academic papers published in scientific journals. The term “success” seems to be used as common sense, given that no definition is expressed in either OECD’s reports or academic papers.

Disclaimer 2

If narratives about success through school mathematics are intertwined as part of the common sense that shapes modern life (at least in countries partaking in OECD’s studies), then these very narratives circulate in other places outside the field of mathematics education (including transnational research reports advising countries to invest in education to achieve economic progress). One of these other places explored in this chapter is the comedy-drama *Ladybird*, written and directed by Greta Gerwig (2017). This film might have nothing to do with global citizenship and mathematics education (here is the main reason why I selected it as part of my argument); however, it unfolds the path to success that hints at the common sense of modern life (which does entangle with narratives of global citizenship and mathematics education). You are kindly asked to watch the film beforehand, or as you move through the chapters.

First lines …

A presence. An involving presence that is always there … and, yet, it’s not. At the same time, present. Not present. Omnipresent. Invisible. A presence. A presence that invites you to think, to act … and, yet, it is voiceless. A god-like presence. Ever-present. A presence that is the protagonist and antagonist, at the same time. Redemption. Salvation. Comfort. A presence full of promises … and, yet, there is none. Tension!

DOI: 10.4324/9781003130673-3

A presence. An involving presence that is always there. A worrying presence. A frightening presence. Present. Not present. Omnipresent. A palpable presence. A shiver down your spine. Leading. Misleading. Deceiving. A presence that invites you to think, to act, to desire. Dreaming. Hoping. Fearing. A presence. Ever-present. Oppressing. Depressing.

Am I going crazy? Am I lost? What am I doing wrong? What if I could escape from this? But I can hear it! That voiceless voice. The silent whisper. The intangible touch. The hopes. The fears. But I'm still here. Waiting. Frozen. Making moves just to stay in the game. Breaking. Aching. Suffocating. Far looking into the other side. Distant light. Was it all lies? The promise. Oh, what a promise! Security, health, happiness, joy, a stress-free life. Yet, I'm still here. Waiting. Frozen. What a bunch of promises! And success. What about success? A fantasy! A utopia attached to your own idea of social order! And you knew it from the very beginning.

Cut!

Why these opening lines? If you ask yourself this question while reading it, then I should ask in return what do you think the idea of stressing success as the ultimate value does to people? Which success, anyways? And whose? Success seems to be a word we are all familiar with. It seems that we all have a shared meaning of what success means, for example, in the film *Ladybird* (Gerwig, 2017). This film tells the story of the ups and downs of Christine and her mother, Marion, during Christine's senior year at Immaculate Heart of Mary Catholic High School in Sacramento, California. Christine, which goes by the name Ladybird, must deal with her family's financial struggles and mockery about the low expectations for her dreamed future, such as wanting to attend a prestigious college. The film Ladybird uses the fear of failure as a way of motivating senior students. The characters portraying authorities and teachers explicitly engage with the hopes and fears of society embodied in speeches of encouragement as inspirational anthems.

In a scene, the Priest's homily given to students deals with teenager's feelings of failure and inadequacy, such as not being liked or loved, and also with feelings of despair, such as being rejected from the desired college or being unsuccessful: "We're afraid we will not get into the college of our choice, we're afraid we won't be loved, we won't be liked, we won't succeed" (Gerwig, 2017, 0:05:05–0:05:13). In the film, there appear explicit references to the desires and potential fears senior students should face, for example, "we're afraid of what the future will bring" (Priest's homily) as if the uncertainty of what comes next will drive us to the path unfolded for the desired, productive, and global citizen. I wonder if the idea of "success being embodied in global, productive, and active citizenship that needs mathematics proficiency rhetoric" circulates in pop culture. Then, mathematics should appear as one of the pathways for success promoted by Ladybird's school. So, here we begin ....

An entry point ...

Some years ago, I wondered about the desired subject of schooling with the idea that this desired child is an unreachable state that schools and policies strive for as the future productive and active citizen that will potentially contribute to economic progress. Since then, I've been puzzled about how dominant narratives unfold and circulate through diverse aspects of modern life. For example, what leading economies have achieved through education seems to be a place of inspiration for developing economies. Then, OECD's and United Nations Educational, Scientific and Cultural Organization's (UNESCO's) reports about education, i.e., OECD's *Education at a Glance*, advise investing in education and to fine-tuning curriculums to develop competencies and abilities to increase countries' GDPs and, therefore, obtain higher places in international rankings. These calls advertise mathematics proficiency as the most secure path to acquiring the competencies and abilities a productive citizen should develop.

> Nearly all adults, not just those with technical or scientific careers, now need to have adequate proficiency in mathematics [...] for personal fulfilment, employment and full participation in society. [... Literacy in mathematics is the] capacity to reason mathematically and use mathematical concepts, procedures, facts and tools to describe, explain and predict phenomena, and to make the well-founded judgements and decisions needed by constructive, engaged and reflective citizens. [... It] is a skill that can be acquired and used, to a greater or lesser extent, throughout a lifetime.
>
> (OECD, 2014b, p, 2)

Then, the desired subjects should develop numeracy competencies that will help with daily life but also to contribute to society. As an example, financially literate citizens are also part of the recent narratives of the desired subject. What is called "basic financial literacy" has been taken as "an essential life skill" (OECD, 2017b, p. 3), given that, as OECD (2017b) contends, citizens "**make financial decisions for themselves at all ages**: from children deciding how to spend their pocket money to teenagers entering the world of work, from young adults purchasing their first home to older adults managing their retirement savings" (p. 3, emphasis added). Then, this basic financial literacy competencies help to shape informed citizens by assisting them "to navigate [financial] decisions and strengthens their financial well-being. [... I]t also promotes inclusive growth and more resilient financial systems and economies (p. 3). Global citizenship is, then, shaped under the ideal of mathematics being necessary—an essential life skill—for the future, needed for success and, therefore, mandatory for schools.

When looking at research in the field of mathematics education, success seems to be a common goal in which students should be motivated enough to learn mathematics and distance themselves enough to see the gains of achieving greater grades in school mathematics. To unfold the dominant narratives in mathematics education research, I look for articles published in journals indexed in Web of Science with "success" and "mathematics education" included in their abstracts. The search returned 83 articles from which success is taken mainly from two sources: First, as close to performance, so students are successful if their grades in school mathematics increase and if these are higher enough. Second, as close to achievement, so students are taken to be successful if they resemble the competencies and abilities embodied by the desired subject of schooling in mathematics.

However, the main topic of these articles is to understand why it is not possible to place particular types of students in these categories, namely why certain students do not have a successful performance in mathematics and why certain students do not achieve the base level requirements in mathematics. Some articles' hypothesis is that the problem that restricts students from becoming successful is because of teacher instruction. At the same time, some argue how students' differences (i.e., gender, race, ethnicity, socioeconomic background) have an important impact on their attitude towards mathematics, and, consequently, on their performance and achievement, although some articles engage with both in contending that teacher effectiveness might help in promoting inclusive strategies to ensure success for all students.[1]

Looking back at transnational advice, if success (meaning securing well-being, welfare, … for all) requires certain levels of mathematics proficiency, then research in the field of mathematics education should inform the teaching and learning process for students to achieve set levels of mathematics proficiency (then, p implies q). From here, for example, OECD's reports impact not only educational policies that shape the mathematics curriculum and students' and teachers' practices but, at the same time, (re)shapes research (and the investment of National Councils and national and international organisations) towards international goals, such as global citizenship.

Here I am trying to unravel the dominant narratives of success through school mathematics. I see myself sitting, reading, tracking, mapping, striving to understand its nuances. I am attempting to unfold the mystery of what it means to be successful, but failing to do so, because success is always fading. Success is not reachable; it is not defined as a global goal we have to have. It vanishes as some sort of global consensus. At times, it engages with morality in some articles, reports, and policies, but then, it engages with performance and meritocracy rhetoric.

From the documents analysed for this chapter—OECD's reports and the 83 articles—modern forms of schooling are inserted in a globalisation trend that depersonalise subjects into a research object and conducts their ways of being and acting in the world, which unfolds a utopia of democracy by sorting individuals and localities (nations) according to an ideal of global citizenship framed under a Western monolithic episteme (Andrade-Molina, 2022; Zhao et al., 2022). The utopia of democracy embodies legacies of capitalist aspirations by accommodating the complexities of human life into metonyms of society created by statistical reasoning (see Hacking, 1983; Porter, 1995). Lindblad et al. (2018) have argued about the use of numbers in the making of kinds of people by challenging statistical reasoning as a form of organising society to support the *comparativist* analyses displaying rankings of performance and efficiency that creates a hierarchisation of education according to standards to tell which is better and which is worst in the run for success. Social justice and equity concerns, recently taking part in UNESCO's agendas (see UNESCO, 2021), mutate into practices of competitiveness and meritocracy prompted by statistical reasoning, which fabricates particular kinds of citizens: the global citizen. Then, a process of depersonalisation occurs as a process of focusing on the outcome of students' (and countries) performance in international standardised testing. In this assumed democratic place, numbers become a non-human actor granted objectivity and agency when the dominant narratives are based primarily on economic progress.

Recalling the Priest's homily, we could ask why are students supposed to be afraid of the future. Ladybird, as she wants to be called, is a senior student. She plans to move away from Sacramento to pursue an education in New York because, as she repeatedly says in the movie, she wants to live in the "cities with culture". The movie also portrays how the "not-moving-away from one's hometown", even more if the hometown is not a big city, is seen as a sign of failure to the ideal of social and economic progress, placing individuals far from American ambitions. Here, images of citizenship for the global cosmopolitan world are embedded and promoted through pop culture. However, the movie also engages with the gaps in the promises of welfare and well-being of schooling: not everybody fits the requirements to meet such successful life in the cities with culture. Ladybird is constantly confronted with the experience of not being enough for the life she envisions—in terms of her academic record—not only by the Guidance Counsellor but also by her mother.

Guidance Counsellor: So, I understand you're not interested in any catholic colleges?
Ladybird: No way. Sorry, but, yes. No way.
Guidance Counsellor: Then you'll be applying to UCs and state schools?
Ladybird: Yeah, but also those East Coast liberal arts schools, like Yale, but not Yale because I probably couldn´t get in.
Guidance Counsellor: (laughs) You definitely couldn't get in.

(Gerwig, 2017, 0:22:53–0:23:17)

Ladybird: I want to go where culture is, like New York.
Marion: How in the world did I raise such a snob? You couldn't get into those schools anyway.
Ladybird: Mom!
Marion: You should go to city college. You know?

(Gerwig, 2017, 0:03:27–0:03:50)

Then, what defines success? For the counsellor, the advice is to continue the Catholic path—from a Catholic school to a Catholic college—and for Marion, Ladybird's mother, it is to go to a reachable college. Thus, the modern path to success appears to be securing a place in college, any college, because it seems to be understood as the more secure path to come closer to a successful life for those unsuccessful ones. So, the making kinds of humans entangle with discourses of life-long learning, featuring particularities of the productive citizen and the "investing in education" as a place for economic growth. I studied my 5-years bachelor's degree with a bank loan that my mother and I paid for almost ten years and was almost three times higher than the original value of the degree. How did you? Then, education as an investment becomes a marketable and fruitful site for business opportunities. Education is advertised as the added value where success cannot be detached from failure. There is no dichotomic binary construction in which one is successful without being a failure at the same time. "Becoming successful" entails a perpetual state in which one reaches the static version of success, becoming unsuccessful for the following version of success: Will Ladybird be considered successful if she gets accepted into a Catholic or city college? And if she does not get in, will she be considered unsuccessful for society?

Mathematics proficiency has been granted as the entry point of success. Mathematics literacy is assumed to secure students' well-being if students acknowledge the impact of mathematics on their future success: "Students' willingness to do mathematics is concerned with the attitudes, emotions and self-related beliefs that dispose students to benefit, or prevent them from benefitting, from the mathematical literacy that they have achieved" (OECD, 2018, p. 40). The benefits of mathematical literacy range from understanding the role played by mathematics in structuring the world; to assist in decision-making processes by providing well-founded judgments. Then, mathematical literacy appears to be contributing to fabricating the "constructive, engaged and reflective 21st century citizen" (OECD, 2018, p. 7). So, in the mathematics classroom, the idea of reaching success requires that students "enjoy mathematical activity and feel confident to undertake it [in order to be] more likely to use mathematics to think about the situations that they encounter in the various facets of their lives, inside and outside school" (OECD, 2018, p. 40)

In the film, Ladybird's low performance in mathematics is one of the main reasons she is mocked for wanting to attend certain colleges. Her desire to move away from Sacramento leads her to think that joining the Math Olympiad team will help her to improve her academic record as a student at Immaculate Heart School.

Vice-Principal Sister Sarah-Joan: Maybe you'd enjoy theatre arts ... They are having auditions for the fall musical [...] They do a fall musical and a spring play and from what I hear it's a real blast.

Ladybird:	What I'd really like is to be on Math Olympiad.
Vice-Principal Sister Sarah-Joan:	But math isn't something you're terribly strong in.
Ladybird:	That we know of yet.

(Gerwig, 2017, 0:06:07–0:06:36)

Dominant narratives about success, amplified by international organisations, inscribe particular forms of being and acting as productive citizens for a global society. Also, our social positioning and forms of oppression—epistemic oppression, for example—"confines and directs our habits of attention" (Dotson, 2014, p. 120). In this light, the central point is not if Ladybird is able to display a myriad of mathematical knowledge by being on Math Olympiad, but if she becomes productive for the global economic progress through school mathematics. Being successful in school mathematics is not supposed to be about learning theorems, axioms, definitions, and so forth. Being successful requires that, through mathematics, students would be able to reason mathematically, to use (formulate, employ, and interpret) mathematics in problem-solving tasks simulating real-life scenarios (OECD, 2018). Students should learn mathematical objects and must know when to properly use them as a tool "to describe, explain and predict phenomena" (OECD, 2018, p. 7) in their daily-life endeavours. Given that the current trend suggests to "move away from the need to perform basic calculations to a rapidly changing world driven by new technologies and trends in which citizens are creative and engaged, making judgements for themselves and the society in which they live" (OECD, 2018, p. 7).

School mathematics becomes a path to achieve a better version of ourselves, which inscribes a pressure to fit into this successful path unfolded by dominant narratives to move away from the fear of being labelled as a failure. The film also explores the dichotomy of success and failure and the way it is inserted in our well-founded judgement to envision our future lives, which conducts our ways of being and acting and our morality.

Marion: I want you to be the very best version of yourself that you can be.
Ladybird: What if this is the best version?

(Gerwig, 2017, 1:08:49–1:08:58)

Does mathematics proficiency define success?

Globalisation is most likely to be presented as beneficial in an ever-going modernisation and economic development process that "helps connect people, creates more wealth, expands boundaries of human knowledge, and helps in protecting basic human rights" (Rapoport, 2015, p. 12). However, globalisation is, at the same time, far from being beneficial as "it ruins traditional relationships and values, redistributes wealth, and harms the environment" (p. 12)—with the enthusiastic pursuit of an increasingly interconnected, wealthy society and global citizenship. The promise of success has led to believe that it is possible to excel in this ever-changing global world given that global trends in education reposition citizens outside the boundaries of their nations as global citizens; it seems that our differences as humans, social conditions, etc., can be minimised if we are offered with the same possibilities and if we try hard enough.

However, globalising trends are built towards normalising our ways of being and acting in the world; it affects how we come to "interpret and imagine the possibilities of our lives" (Rizvi & Lingard, 2010, p. 23). And, so, those promises of being whomever we want to become vanish. Marion, Ladybirds' mother, went to college to obtain a degree as a nurse, but her life consists of working relentlessly to ensure her family's well-being and to secure her children's success. However, we celebrate and cherish those promises because we are inserted in the very same system of reason (Popkewitz, 2015) that conceived those promises; a system of reason which, according to Hultqvist et al. (2018), "... operate[s] around needs to succeed in a 'competitive global race among economies'" (p. 1).

Educational policies and the processes for decision-making in education have been transformed by globalisation—and, by extension, what we take as being successful. These have been "shaped by a range of transnational forces and connections, demanding a new global imagination" (Rizvi & Lingard, 2010, p. 3). A demand that apparently needs to be conquered through mathematics. In this light, globalisation instantiates educational policies targeting not only to improve the quality of education but to improve the economy by correlating possible investments in education, for example, with potential GDP gains (see OECD, 2016). This view of education as a profitable quasi-market environment leads to schools dedicating almost entirely to preparing students with the mathematics proficiency level needed to answer standardised-test-like-problems more accurately and efficiently (Minarechová, 2012), which leads to an (ab)use of school mathematics being masked as a necessary tool to solve real-life problems in daily life after schooling. Then, the hopes driven by capitalists' desires lead to advertising school mathematics as key to students' future success.

The idea that students should become the best profitable version of themselves through mathematics inserts students into practices of "continually pursuing knowledge and innovation in a never-ending chase for the future" (Popkewitz, 2008, p. 310). This utopia of globalisation leads to circulating narratives of success that, when intertwined with global economic progress desires, advertise schooling as the forum where "all" students can potentially become profitable for the national and global economy and for themselves—becoming accountable. Here, the ideal modern citizen is shaped by global ideals of success, promoted by transnational discourses that depict school mathematics as the necessary knowledge to build such success.

When these utopian ideals are translated into educational policies, it seems more like policymakers, stakeholders, and international organisations agree on placing school mathematics as the more secure path toward achieving the desired success. From here, educational policies and curricular guidelines have been built around salvation themes bound teaching and learning school mathematics in the globalised world (see Popkewitz, 2018). However, in a global scenario, these normalising practices which constitute the "promised opportunities", fade into the realisation that "success" in school mathematics is not possible for all (Mendick & Llewellyn, 2011). Then, students fall into a paradox in which policies do not directly exclude a low-income student "but subjected in the class/room to exclude him/herself and to render a resignation of what historically has been considered as success" (Andrade-Molina, 2017, p. 23). From here, it is necessary to problematise the belief that school mathematics is the safest bet to fabricate the global 21st-century citizens.

As aforementioned in Disclaimer 1, OECD does not explicitly define what success means or how it is conceived within its narrative. There exists, although, hints that help unravel the enigma behind its conception from where success does not seem to imply a genetic predisposition or intellectual superiority. Instead, it seems to imply that success is better achieved by having mouldable skills, in terms of being "able to be target developed" skills, to use mathematics in problem-solving situations that mimic life outside school. So, the best version of oneself comes when we reach certain baseline levels in PISA mathematics. According to OECD's dominant narratives, school mathematics is advertised as key to securing students' success in the global world (see Valero, 2017). High attainment in school mathematics has even been correlated with aspects of life outside the realm of career paths and economic stability, which goes straight into digging into the how we decide to carry our lives as consumers in Modern capitalist societies. Then, the productive global citizens are taken to "generally have better health, are more socially engaged, have higher employment rates and have higher relative earnings" (OECD, 2015, p. 30), all because of mathematics proficiency.

These assumptions, amplified by OECD, intertwine with the 83 articles analysed. Some articles positioned mathematics achievement as a predictor for students' future success, and, therefore, a variety of solutions are displayed to help increase students' performance in mathematics. Some of these solutions engage with providing opportunities and frameworks for students to develop—and for teachers to know how to promote the development of—certain base-level competencies, such as problem-solving, modelling and the use of technology linked to computational thinking. For example, some articles emphasise the need to keep students motivated not only to reach success—understood as higher performance—but for students to "strive for success" in rising to higher levels of certain skills (particularly those needed for STEM careers). Other articles explore how high levels of mathematics proficiency are crucial for students' overall success at university. All articles seem to agree on the relevance of mathematics to achieving success; it remains unquestioned.

Does mathematics help in fabricating the global 21st-century citizen? How will theorems, formulas, axioms, and even trigonometry help shape teenagers' moral to accommodate what is desired? The productive citizen is grounded on particular skills needed for economies to grow based on the promises of achieving a state of welfare, well-being, and full potential for an ever-growing economy: literacy and numeracy (see OECD, 2015). Correlations have gone so deep into exploring the workings of society that it is possible to state that "numeracy skills have a more significant impact on employment outcomes" (OECD, 2015, p. 168). Easy, the promise is that if you want to be successful and to become the best version of yourself, you NEED mathematics. No questions asked! Mathematics proficiency is mandatory to walk on the path to success and economic stability! (Picture a sarcasm sign here, please!). But, as Ladybird asks, what if this, what we are now, is the best version of ourselves? What if we cannot improve any further? Should we start doing some more maths, then?

OECD's "accountability agenda" (see Tröhler et al., 2014) is built around these promises, encouraging nations to invest in acquiring and developing citizens' mathematical skills for GDP gains. Nevertheless, it goes beyond that. Mathematics has not only been correlated with these envisioning of modern life but also with the body of children. And I'm not referring to how to behave (how to move the body) or how to act—for example, the social skills assumed to be improved by problem-solving in a collaborative working space (see OECD, 2017a)—but with overall health (OECD, 2016), which means that health (morbidity, heart diseases, diabetes, etc.) in adulthood depends on our level of mathematics proficiency at school. I imagine going to the doctor and the receptionist telling "you didn't do well at maths, don't you? If someone has a heart disease, add your maths proficiency level at school to your medical record. And the doctor saying "well, we have to run some tests and, could you, please solve this problem to give you the right treatment that will fit your future health care needs?". So, we should be grateful for being granted the possibility of learning mathematics at school. Enthusiastic! Excited! Motivated! Hey, maths will save our lives; why aren't you solving problems already? Let's join the Math Olympiads just like Ladybird! (Sarcastic sign appearing again! For sure, every mathematician I know is so healthy and wealthy).

Mocking aside, nations are advised to invest in certain skills students should and must acquire for successfully engaging in adult life to learn to recognise the value of, for example, investing in financial literacy (see OECD, 2017b). Here, it is the fine-tuning of skills so students might diagnose the risks and calculate the probabilities of becoming the person they want to become but focusing more on profit than on leisure. As explored in Andrade-Molina (2021), the image of success unfolded in OECD's narratives are mainly based on the expressed focus on students' performance in mathematics standardised testing—meaning high levels of achievement and proficiency define success—and on the concern that everybody gets the same opportunities to learn mathematics. Nevertheless, the dominant narratives about who gets access to success

> functions not as some kind of utopian state to be achieved, a desired good to strive for, but rather as a pure mechanism to conceal the fact that mathematics is not for all [...] the official discourse conceals the inconsistency of a system that, on the one hand, demands mathematics for all while, on the other hand, uses school mathematics as a privileged mechanism of selection and credit.
>
> (Pais & Valero, 2011, p. 44)

From this, school mathematics becomes a tool, a technology of distance (see Porter, 1995) for international consensus on the image of global citizenship as a tool able to measure people's worth (Fasheh, 2012).

Following UNESCO (2021), success should be in terms of reaching a shared well-being. From which, school mathematics curriculum needs to be transformed in terms of "how to reimagine learning spaces to the decolonisation of curricula and the importance of social and emotional learning and taps into their real and growing fears about climate change, crises like COVID-19, fake news and the digital divide" (p. 6). UNESCO (2021) acknowledges the impact education has in ensuring places for human habitation in the future, places which are at potential lost in a dystopian future where our actions as citizens of Earth could possibly annihilate the planet. Suppose the exhaustion of our planet is at risk. In that case, it is possible to envision a future where success is not possible in terms of reasoning mathematically, but in acquiring and producing knowledge for transforming digital technologies, decarbonisation, greening of economies, challenging discrimination, and injustice.

According to UNESCO (2021), "[e]xtreme future scenarios also include a world where quality education is a privilege of elites, and where vast groups of people live in misery because they lack access to essential goods and services" (p. 8). Then, the global citizen for the future should be mindful of the impact that our actions as human beings have—i.e., our carbon print. For this, education is advised to be structured around principles of cooperation, collaboration and solidarity based on ecological, intercultural, and interdisciplinary learning that foster the global citizen's intellectual, social, and moral capacities for the future. This global citizen for the future is conceived as a knowledge producer able to transform society and take care of our planet.

Chernyshenko et al. (2018) have informed that non-cognitive skills need to be improved to secure future success. These skills are Openness to Experience, Conscientiousness, Extraversion, Agreeableness, and Neuroticism

(OCEAN). From here, social and emotional skills are acknowledged as crucial for successfully navigating life: "good social competence can help children adapt better to the school environment, gain higher status among their peers and consequently achieve more in school. This greater school achievement translates later into better occupational status, health, and general well-being" (Chernyshenko et al., 2018, p. 21). Then, success does not necessarily depend on mathematics literacy and high mathematics achievement levels.

However, the dominant discourses about success insert students into school practices where they believe their success is related to the effort they put into action. Statements such as "[r]aw potential and talent are only a small part of what it takes to become proficient in a skill. Students' success depends on the material and intangible resources that are invested by families, schools and education systems to develop each and every student's potential" (OECD, 2014a, p. 1) lead to the circulation of assumptions such as: hard work is key to success. From here, a "large proportions of students in most countries consistently believe that student achievement is mainly a product of hard work, rather than inherited intelligence" (OECD, 2014a, p. 1). Then, students believe success is to be earned through discipline, systematicity, consistency, etc.—hard work—which interplays with better mathematics performance.

The promised utopia: How necessary is mathematics?

How do these algorithms predict how happy we are going to be in ten, fifteen years? What do these say about our future health or employment? For sure, OECD has wondered about our feelings and how satisfied we are with our living conditions (see Better Life Index), but how are they readings those outcomes? Have they already correlated them with PISA's results? When correlations are taken as the vehicle to address society, then mathematics ends up being placed as the most secure path to success. But there lies nonsense within the global scenario OECD depicts. For example, OECD has spent some years figuring out why students are not successful—low-performers—in PISA, then they correlate possible factors determining shared conditions between underachieving students. However, correlations can twist our understandings leading to state that mathematics proficiency can be improved if some students' "risk factors" are removed (for example, second-language learners), but the same correlations lead to state that mathematics proficiency can also be improved if the quality of water is improved (see Andrade-Molina, 2018). Which one should I believe? Then, who is potentially able to be considered as successful?

Marion: Being successful doesn't mean anything in and of itself. It just means that you're successful.
Ladybird: Yeah, but then you're successful.

Marion: But that doesn't mean that you're happy.

(Gerwig, 2017, 0:51:24–0:51:33)

Dominant narratives of success lead to a rhetoric of meritocracy rather than establishing a base ground in which success is not defined by mathematics proficiency. I mean this is explicit when success is related to "dependent on persistence" (OECD, 2010, p. 3). The classic "success comes with hard work; if one tries hard enough, then success will come" assumes that every student engages with mathematics in the same way and has the same conditions and opportunities in the process of teaching and learning of school mathematics—which is not the case. What globalisation has brought is monopolistic educational policies (Coulson, 2008; Hultqvist, 2018) based on competition since students will have to compete for job positions in a national and international scenario within an "integrated worldwide labour market" (see OECD, 2011). Assuming that students are responsible for their own success exacerbates that everyone does not have the same opportunities, even more so if mathematics proficiency helps in employment (the more mathematics you master, the more chances of being hired). In this light, it becomes necessary to challenge the role schooling has in reaching success and how this entails paradoxes not only on exclusion but on a meritocratic view of success as a form of justifying the segregations produced in school. In other words, globalisation inserts children into practices of competition, through school mathematics, to be able to fit with international templates of the global citizen that must pursue a career in the worldwide labour market, entrepreneurship and also fit the image of the homo-economicus (Foucault, 2008). For this, children must be motivated and excited to learn school mathematics where success is related to behaviour (hard work) and achievement (high grades).

We are part of a system of reason that fabricates both the unproductive and productive citizen; it inserts students in narratives about hopes and fears of successfulness and failure and promises of a reachable success that ends up revealing itself as what it is: a utopian dream to secure social order and economic stability. The structuring of society, the social order, works as follows: the student (immigrant or not) from a neglected school and poor socio-economic background is more likely to be unsuccessful in life (and unhappy, unhealthy, unwealthy, and so on). Nevertheless, the more used explanation is that it works that way because they don't try hard enough, period! No more room for discussion. They do not have ambitions, they do not want to work, they want everything for free, have you heard those? I have! The discussion moves away from the deeper root of this phenomenon, meaning that the explanations move within a superficial realm of naiveness. We have to wonder how come, why and when youth were labelled as "the not productive for society and, thus, not productive for economic stability and not desirable for global goals. These unsuccessful citizens become the casualties of a system of reason that fabricate them as low-performers and also abjects them" (Andrade-Molina, 2021, p. 9).

Then, it is not a story of success through mathematics anymore; rather it is of the historical marginalisation, segregation, and oppression of particular groups of people that resonate today with the image of the low-performer and the unproductive for globalisation. It is a story where "in contrast to the entrepreneurial spirit of modernity, exclusion creates among low-income groups a feeling of fatalism according to which nothing they can do or plan will allow them to improve their economic position" (Cavieres, 2011, p. 116). However, dominant narratives lead them to be perceived as the Other, the abnormal, under the very image of the (un)successfulness produced by school mathematics. The promises of success fade into the realisation that such success is thought to be closer to productivity—in terms of who is fitted and not fitted for economic progress and stability—rather than achieving a certain state of well-being and happiness.

The (un)successfulness produced is a paradox that lives inside the class/room, as a room that classifies people. The class/room is the place where students are shaped, submerged in circulating discourses and dominant narratives that shape their modes of acting and being in the world; it is the place where power/knowledge relations become material. Inside the class/room students' disparities are exacerbated even more when it comes to the global desires of the global citizen. The class/room is the result of narratives that correlate educational attainment with socioeconomic status and that position students into particular boxes that determine their possibilities in life: the possibility of reaching the best version of themselves. However, here is where they are excluded, marginalised and abjected because of the promises of happiness and welfare of globalisation, from which school mathematics does not increase the possibilities of succeeding in life in the global world but sorts students that could potentially become profitable, productive global citizens.

Success, mathematics, and the future …

This chapter challenges the (im)possibilities for the future provided by school math. The overall conclusion is that mathematics provides or prompts particular features required to be developed by schools to make of the productive global citizen but does not drastically impact create a more secure future for children. The arguments about the successful achievement of people's future well-being and welfare—as part of the promises promoted by policies, reforms, and transnational interests—draw on correlations to emphasise that economically stable societies have higher performance in mathematics and science. School mathematics seems to be perceived as the knowledge necessary to organise particularities of people, such as solving problems or as an aid in daily life tasks, like financial responsibilities. For decades, statistical reasoning has been used as a form of objective decision-making process, and, therefore, more socially just as no intervention of human unkindness can interfere with the data analysis.

The notion of success resonates in pop culture, where people are confronted with narratives of success to question their decisions as human beings living in contemporaneity, such as Ladybird. Her notion of success is antagonised by the school Counsellor and Marion's understanding of success. All three notions have the shared narrative of getting in college: Ladybird wants to go to a college in a city of culture such as New York; the Counsellor advises to look for Catholic colleges; and Marion recommends Ladybird to keep their possibilities grounded by looking for city colleges. Moving from school to university appears to be the taken-as-normal track to achieve a successful life. And mathematics has an important role in securing a smooth movement. As aforementioned, mathematics appears in the film as a possibility for Ladybird to improve her academic record.

The paranoia of success

When and how can we recognise ourselves as successful? Where is this path taking us? It seems that the tale of mathematics being necessary for future success of citizens, promised by the system of reason shaping our morality, does not hold true. The greater outcomes on rankings and large-scale assessment are the product of capitalistic competition and fetishism disavowal (see Pais, 2014). The global citizen is fabricated within dominant narratives about economic progress that neglects individuals and their hopes to secure social order. The global citizen is built around fears of failure. There are countries with social problems in which young adults are labelled as failures when they fail to follow "the path". They have to work for free (in most cases) to gain the experience needed to be selected as a proper candidate for a job that everybody wants and so, they have to work even harder for their CV to be the hired candidate. Family? Without having the security of a permanent job? Losing independence to work arduously? Or simply being perceived as not trying hard enough?

As I experienced myself after giving birth and caring for a child: not being able to spend the time I wanted with my daughter, the quality time she deserved because I had to give a lecture or to send a manuscript or to do bureaucratic and administrative work because my job required me to do so, otherwise my performance would have been poorly evaluated. Working on holidays to finish this chapter (I'm not complaining, I wanted to contribute to this book, but my workload does not allow me to fit the writing time into my work schedule. I also know I'm not the only one). Did I succeed? I was not evaluated poorly, but I did not succeed in being the mother I wanted to be, nor the image naturalised by modern society (i.e., a supermom). What was the interplay of mathematics in all of this? For sure, I am not the image of success portrayed by dominant narratives, but who is it anyways?

Note

1 It is not important to cite which one of the 83 articles mentions which dominant narrative. You can email me if you want the complete list of articles analysed for this part of the chapter. The important part is to unfold how these 83 articles intertwine to produce a discursive network of dominant narratives around success in mathematics education. Then, authors are intentionally displaced, given that circulating discourses do not depend on the author but on the spatiotemporal conditions that enable such circulation.

References

Andrade-Molina, M. (2017). The adventure of the deceitful numbers. *Journal of Pedagogy*, *8*(2), 9–25.

Andrade-Molina, M. (2018). OECD's dominant discourses of the low-performer and the production of subjects. *Reflexão e Ação*, *26*(2), 9–26.

Andrade-Molina, M. (2021). The narratives of success: Enabling all students to excel in the global world. *Research in Mathematics Education*, *23*(3), 293–305. http://dx.doi.org/10.1080/14794802.2021.1994453.

Andrade-Molina, M. (2022). When numbers dictate common sense: Transnational's aspirations of a global curriculum. In W. Zhao, T. Popkewitz, & T. Autio (Eds.), *Epistemic colonialism and the transfer of curriculum knowledge across borders: Applying a historical Lens to contest unilateral logics* (pp. 103–117). Routledge.

Cavieres, E. (2011). The class and culture-based exclusion of the Chilean neoliberal educational reform. *Educational Studies*, *47*(2), 111–132.

Chernyshenko, O., Kankaraš, M., & Drasgow, F. (2018). Social and emotional skills for student success and well-being: Conceptual framework for the OECD study on social and emotional skills, OECD Education Working Papers, No. 173, OECD Publishing. https://doi.org/10.1787/db1d8e59-en

Coulson, A. (2008). Markets vs. monopolies in education: A global review of the evidence. *Policy Analysis*, *620*, 1–4.

Dotson (2014). Conceptualizing epistemic oppression. *Social Epistemology: A Journal of Knowledge, Culture and Policy*, *28*(2), 115–138.

Fasheh, M. J. (2012). The role of mathematics in the destruction of communities, and what we can do to reverse this process, including using mathematics. In O. Skovsmose & B. Greer (Eds.), *Opening the cage: Critique and politics of mathematics education* (pp. 93–105). Sense Publishers.

Foucault, M. (2008). *The birth of biopolitics: Lectures at the Collège de France, 1978–1979*. Palgrave Macmillan.

Gerwig, G. (Director). (2017). *Ladybird* [Film]. A24.

Hacking, I. (1983). Nineteenth century cracks in the concept of determinism. *Journal of the History of Ideas*, *44*(3), 455–475.

Hultqvist, E. (2018). Educational restructuring and social boundaries: School choice and consumers. In E. Hultqvist, S. Lindblad, & T. Popkewitz (Eds.), *Critical analyses of educational reform in an era of transnational governance* (pp. 77–91). Springer International Publishing.

Hultqvist, E., Lindblad, S., & Popkewitz, T. (2018). Critical analyses of educational reform-writing a title and ending a book. In E. Hultqvist, S. Lindblad, & T. Popkewitz (Eds.), *Critical analyses of educational reform in an era of transnational governance* (pp. 1–19). Springer International Publishing.

Lindblad, S., Pettersson, D., & Popkewitz, T. S. (2018). Getting the numbers right. An introduction. In S. Lindblad, D Pettersson & T. S. Popkewitz (Eds.), *Education by the numbers and the making of society: The expertise of international assessments* (pp. 1–20). Routledge.

Mendick, H., & Llewellyn, A. (2011). Does every child count? Quality, equity and mathematics with/in with neoliberalism. In B. Atweh, M. Graven, W. Secada, & P. Valero (Eds.), *Mapping equity and quality in mathematics education* (pp. 49–62). Springer.

Minarechová, M. (2012). Negative impacts of high-stakes testing. *Journal of Pedagogy, 3*(1), 82–100.

Organization for Economic Co-operation and Development. (2010). Pathways to success. How knowledge and skills at age 15 shape future lives in Canada. OECD Publishing. https://doi.org/10.1787/9789264081925-en

Organization for Economic Co-operation and Development. (2011). *Strong performers and successful reformers in education: Lessons from PISA for the United States.* OECD Publishing. https://doi.org/10.1787/2220363x

Organization for Economic Co-operation and Development. (2014a). Do students have the drive to succeed? *PISA in focus, 37.* Retrieved from: https://www.oecd.org/pisa/pisaproducts/pisainfocus/pisa-in-focus-n37-(eng)-final.pdf

Organization for Economic Co-operation and Development. (2014b). PISA 2012 results: What students know and can do – Student performance in mathematics, reading and science (Volume I, Revised edition, February 2014), PISA, OECD Publishing. http://dx.doi.org/10.1787/9789264201118-en

Organization for Economic Co-operation and Development. (2015). *Education at a glance 2015: OECD indicator.* OECD Publishing.

Organization for Economic Co-operation and Development. (2016). *Low-performing students: Why they fall behind and how to help them succeed.* OECD Publishing.

Organization for Economic Co-operation and Development. (2017a). PISA 2015 results (Volume V): Collaborative problem solving, PISA. OECD Publishing. http://dx.doi.org/10.1787/9789264285521-en

Organization for Economic Co-operation and Development. (2017b). *PISA 2015 results (Volume IV): Students' financial literacy, PISA.* OECD Publishing. http://dx.doi.org/10.1787/9789264270282-en

Organization for Economic Co-operation and Development (2018). *PISA for development assessment and analytical framework: Reading, mathematics and science.* OECD Publishing. https://doi.org/10.1787/9789264305274-en

Pais, A. (2014). Economy: The absent centre of mathematics education. *ZDM Mathematics Education, 46*(7), 1085–1093.

Pais, A., & Valero, P. (2011). Beyond disavowing the politics of equity and quality in mathematics education. In B. Atweh, M. Graven, W. Secada, & P. Valero (Eds.), *Mapping equity and quality in mathematics education* (pp. 35–48). Springer.

Popkewitz, T. (2008). Education sciences, schooling, and abjection: Recognizing difference and the making of inequality? *South African Journal of Education, 28*(3), 301–319.

Popkewitz, T. (2015). Curriculum studies, the reason of "reason" and schooling. In T. Popkewitz (Ed.), *The "reason" of schooling. Historicizing curriculum studies, pedagogy, and teacher education* (pp. 1–17). Routledge.

Popkewitz, T. S. (2018). What is 'really' taught as the content of school subjects? Teaching school subjects as an alchemy. *The High School Journal, 101*(2), 77–89.

Porter, T. (1995). *Trust in numbers: The pursuit of objectivity in science and public life.* Princeton University Press.

Rapoport, A. (2015). Challenges and opportunities: Resocialization as a framework for global citizenship in education. In J. Zajda (Ed.), *Globalisation, ideology and politics of education reforms* (pp. 11–23). Springer International Publishing.

Rizvi, F., & Lingard, B. (2010). *Globalizing education policy.* Routledge.

Tröhler, D., Meyer, H. D., Labaree, D. F., & Hutt, E. L. (2014). Accountability: Antecedents, power, and processes. *Teachers College Record, 116*(9), 1–2.

United Nations Educational, Scientific and Cultural Organization. (2021). *Reimagining our futures together: A new social contract for education*. United Nations Educational, Scientific and Cultural Organization.

Valero, P. (2017). Mathematics for all, economic growth, and the making of the citizen worker. In T. Popkewitz, J. Diaz, & C. Kirchgasler (Eds.), *A political sociology of educational knowledge: Studies of exclusions and difference* (pp. 117–132). Routledge.

Zhao, W., Popkewitz, T. S., & Autio, T. (Eds.). (2022). *Epistemic colonialism and the transfer of curriculum knowledge across borders: Applying a historical lens to contest unilateral logics*. Routledge.

2 An essay to discuss the role of people with disabilities in globalisation

You deserve to be part of this world!

Renato Marcone

Introduction

In my PhD research (see Marcone, 2015), I have raised the questions: What are the consequences of pursuing inclusion of people with disabilities without a dialogical construction of disability definition? Without a comprehension of disability beyond numbers and medicalisation, could "these people", often addressed as "abnormal" become citizens of the world? What are the consequences of not being part of the group of world citizens? In this chapter, the intention is to raise issues about the processes of people with disabilities becoming citizens of a globalised world, to discuss connections between recent inclusion efforts inside research on people with disabilities inside the mathematics education community and globalisation.

Globalisation. Global citizenship. Inclusion of people with disabilities in the mathematics educational system, local and global. This chapter attempts to discuss these phenomena and inquire connections across them. Its main intention is to be provocative and to encourage awareness towards the issue of research on people with disabilities inside the mathematics educational community and in society in general. The organisation of the chapter and the construction of the argument will have the following structure.

In section *What does globalisation mean after all?* the concept of globalisation (or *globalisations*) assumed in this text will be presented and also the idea of a global citizen, based on mainstream definitions of globalisation and also on references widely known by the academic community. Once the concept of *globalisations* and global citizens are introduced, the text will move on to section *People with disabilities and the* globalisations *process*. This section is meant to present the concept of disability assumed along the argument presented here and will show foundations for the thesis that a person with disability is also excluded from the processes of *globalisations* and, as a consequence, find many hindrances in order to become a citizen of the world. Also, this section will show research on mathematics education which suggests, as per this author's understanding, that because of this status of a non-citizen of the world, people with disabilities are seen almost entirely as a medical condition and an

DOI: 10.4324/9781003130673-4

educational statistic instead of a full person with possibilities to teach and to learn. In section titled as *Deficiencialism*, the concept of deficiencialism will be presented along with some examples. The intention on bringing this concept is to be presented as a possible tool to encourage the awareness towards inclusion mentioned above, whether in relation to the processes of *globalisations*, or in relation to the processes of teaching and learning mathematics for people with disabilities, as such awareness is, as per my understanding, a crucial step towards a group becoming global citizens. The next section, *Deficiencialism as a tool to interpret exclusion processes*, is an attempt to wrap up the argument, evidencing that the issue of people with disabilities is nor present on the discussions of *globalisations* neither inside the mathematics education research agenda which addresses globalisation, and I propose a way to start pursuing awareness, a necessary condition for any group to become a global citizen.

What does globalisation mean after all?

Once I was in front of the discussion around current occidental visions of "globality" and "citizenship" I wondered "what is a global citizen?" and, even deeper, I was asking myself, "what does globalisation mean after all"? I decided to firstly look into some definitions of globalisation presented by popular sources among scholars and media, such as the United Nations (UN) through World Health Organization (WHO) and Wikipedia. Why? Because these definitions would most likely be among the first to be found by anyone looking for them out of curiosity or through mainstream media, before proceeding with further research, meaning they might have some impact on how the society understands globalisation in general.

> Globalization, or the increased interconnectedness and interdependence of peoples and countries, is generally understood to include two interrelated elements: the opening of international borders to increasingly fast flows of goods, services, finance, peoples, and ideas; and the changes in institutions and policies at national and international levels that facilitate or promote such flows. Globalization has the potential for both positive and negative effects on development and health.
>
> (World Health Organization as in Demir et al., 2021, p. 1)

> Globalization, [...] is the process of interaction and integration among people, companies, and governments worldwide. Globalization has accelerated since the 18th century due to advances in transportation and communication technology. This increase in global interactions has caused a growth in international trade and the exchange of ideas, beliefs, and culture. Globalization is primarily an economic process of interaction and integration that is associated with social and cultural aspects. However, disputes and diplomacy are also large parts of the history of globalization, and of modern globalization.
>
> (Wikipedia, 2022, para. 1)

Based on those definitions, it is legitimate to conjecture that one of the main concerns of globalisation is to find new markets, new ways to trade the goods produced around the world, increasing riches. In that sense, one could understand a citizen of the world as a potential consumer of those goods. As James Carville once said, during Bill Clinton's presidential campaign in 1992: "It's the economy, stupid" (see Moore, 2022, para. 1).

Also, another agenda of globalisation seems to be the spreading out of some narratives. One could also argue that this is in order to bring people to desire the goods that are being produced worldwide, creating demand to guarantee their flow of and trade. In a quick online search for the term "globalization" using google search engine, one can see that globalisation is essentially an economical agenda for the mainstream media, with some pinches of culture and knowledge exchange, but also connected with trade and financial system. However, it is not unreasonable to argue that exchanges are not happening fairly, rather, we can see cultures being overpowered – sometimes, replaced – by richer nations' cultures, even nations living inside the same country territory. To support this argument, I brought up Hernández-Truyol, who wrote about culture clashes, describing how globalisation is affecting indigenous populations in Brazil, due to the construction of a hydroelectric plant in Brazil, one of the largest in the world, which affected indigenous communities.

> These new circumstances result in increased knowledge about, but not necessarily acceptance or understanding of or respect for, cultures, customs, and religions not long ago deemed obscure. The virtual proximity of peoples and vast information available about different cultures has failed to translate into in an understanding or embracing of differences. Rather, the global exposure rendered possible by globalization (perhaps unintentionally) has inflamed religious, national, ethnic, and racial hatreds and strife–as well as sex and gender subordination and marginalization.
>
> (Hernández-Truyol, 2014, p. 777)

I would add disabilities to this list. After reflecting on these definitions and on Hernández-Truyol argument, let us try to delve a little deeper into this concept of globalisation.

John Gerrard Ruggie (2003) brings an interesting analysis over the role of the United Nations and globalisation. He reminds us that in the post-World War II, a system of organisational institutions was created in a decentralised mode by design, a choice from their founders. The aim was to maximise technical expertise, minimise politicisation and to provide dedicated support for this international enterprise. However, the same author says that:

> The most distinctive institutional feature of the UN system, therefore, is that it is not designed as a matrix at all but as a set of deeply rooted columns connected only by thin and tenuous rows. Nothing that has

> transpired since 1945 has transformed that fundamental reality. This is an important fact to bear in mind when assessing the UN system's responses to the challenges of globalization. It makes all the more striking the considerable convergence of views and policy approaches to globalization that has taken place in recent years, as well as the programmatic innovations that more effectively exploit the UN's multifunctionality.
>
> (Ruggie, 2003, p. 303)

Hence, the process of globalisation is always on negotiation, focused mostly on economic aspects, indicating few concerns about cultural facets. Ruggie (2003) goes on saying that the UN showed, historically, ambivalence about market and globalisation. On one hand, UN sees the global economic system as a hindrance instead of a collaborator when it comes to social justice and distributive policies, e.g., when,

> financial institutions "vigorously pushed capital market liberalization onto the developing countries with little regard for the absence of its institutional requisites. And the developing countries won little in the WTO's Uruguay Round[1] in return for their concessions on intellectual property rights".
>
> (Ruggie, 2003, p. 304)

On the other hand, UN used to state that globalisation brings great opportunities, as one can read on the Millennium Summit in 2000, in Kofi Anan words, reproduced by Ruggie (2003, p. 304) in his paper "a socially inclusive globalisation must be built on the great enabling force of the market, but market forces alone will not achieve it". Then I wonder, is the market an ally or an enemy of inclusion? I dare to say neither. The market will just engulf the inclusion discourse if it seems profitable.

Robertson and White (2007) state in their chapter entitled "What Is Globalization?" that this question is very specific but also very general. General, because it is impossible to address it without considering different points of view and worldviews worldwide. It is also specific, because one wants to understand distinct characteristics of what we all are calling today as globalisation. They follow:

> The general sense of the question 'What is Globalization' is continuously latent in what follows, whereas specification is much more explicit. Many different topics are included under the rubric of globalization, such as global governance, global citizenship, human rights, migration and the creation of diasporas, transnational connections of various kinds and so on.
>
> (Robertson & White, 2007, p. 54)

Reading this quote, it is possible to infer that mathematics education could also be on that list along with claims for inclusionary practices.

However, Robertson and White (2007) remind us that globalisation is a contested concept, still in dispute, and many authors, after working towards a definition of it, conclude that there is no general or widely accepted definition for globalisation. Robertson and White say:

> Some of the disputes arise from differences in perspective across the world. Understandably, many people in developing countries are not exactly eager to accept definitions of globalization deriving from more privileged societal contexts. And there is much deviation with respect to ideas about globalization from one civilization context to another. For these reasons, a number of scholars speak of globalizations in the plural, as opposed to a single process of globalization.
>
> (Robertson & White, 2007, p. 54)

Well, after going a little deeper on understanding what globalisation means, it is clear to me that the definitions I first found looking superficially on sites like the WHO and WIKIPEDIA are just some among many possible – and under dispute – perspectives. My resistance to accept those definitions are well described in the above quote from Robertson and White: As a citizen of a developing country, I was not eager to accept that. With that in mind, I will assume the concept of globalisation in this chapter as one in dispute, considering different approaches, calling it *globalisations* from now on.

Based on my readings so far and for the purpose of writing this chapter, I will assume a global citizen as a person who understands *globalisations* at any level and their interference in the world and in her or his own life. As a consequence, from assuming *globalisations* as a concept in dispute, I am also assuming the concept of global citizen as one in dispute, too.

In the next section, I will reflect on the role of people with disabilities in this discussion.

People with disabilities and the *globalisations* process

Munck (2005) said that globalisation is the big buzzword of our time, dominating economic, social and welfare policies around the world. Here I would add educational processes and inclusion policies as well. He follows by saying that even the way we contest inequalities around the world orbit globalisation. His argument is that,

> social exclusion – all the ways in which people are excluded from the necessities of life – is the necessary social counterpart to globalization. It provides us with a broad general framework by which to understand the social effects of globalization and, further, generates a common focus for those struggling against these effects at local, national, and global levels.
>
> (Munck, 2005, p. 9)

Among the ways in which people are excluded, I add the exclusion of people with disabilities from the educational systems, as, for example, through educational policies that do not consider differences on its approach and mathematics teaching methods not designed for all, illustrating effects at local and national levels.

Following this reasoning, one can argue that a person with disability (a blind person, a deaf person or a person with autism spectrum disorder, for example) will face a hard time, to say the least, on trying to play any role in the *globalisations* arena, because many of those aspects are simply not accessible (e.g., information in braille or audio for blind people and/or multi sign language translations across the world, clear and direct information for people with autism spectrum disorder). Therefore, considering the definition of global citizen we are assuming here – a person who understands *globalisations* at any level and their interference in the world and in her or his own life – how could a person with disability become a citizen of the world by understanding *globalisations* processes and their consequences on the world and on their own lives when the information for that is just not accessible?

A poor person is always a potential consumer (see, for instance, Bardhan, 2004), a potential citizen of the world, because they might make money someday if they use the opportunities offered by *globalisations* and start buying goods that they already desire, co-opted by the *globalisations* ideas crossing the continents. However, a person with disability has diverse needs, and those needs are rarely considered by the market, by the culture or by the society as a whole. This is not different when we investigate the educational process, which is increasingly being viewed as a commodity.

Williamson (2015) showed a relation between *globalisations* and access for individuals with disabilities. She discusses disability on a global scale by defining the term as:

> An umbrella term for impairments, activity limitations and participation restrictions. Disability is the interaction between individuals with a health condition (e.g., cerebral palsy, Down syndrome, and depression) and personal and environmental factors (e.g., negative attitudes, inaccessible transportation and public buildings, and limited social supports)
> (World Health Organization, 2014, as in Williamson, 2015, p. 37)

After analysing the differences between the two countries, Senegal and USA, concerning access (physical, educational, and social) for individuals with disabilities, she says that:

> It is clear that globalization has impacted West Africa and the United States Midwest in very different ways. One commonality between the two is the Global Financial Crisis (GFC), a negative consequence of deregulation of global financial infrastructure due to processes of globalization
> (Williamson, 2015, p. 37)

In short, she argues that in a context of economic globalisation, financial institutions are "at the forefront of power: the International Monetary Fund (IMF), the World Bank, and the World Trade Organization (WTO)" (Williamson, 2015, p. 38). These institutions, after offering substantial loans to developing countries "forced them to implement structural adjust programs in order to reform their economies" (Williamson, 2015, p. 38). Adjustments as, e.g., fiscal discipline, reduction of public expenditure, privatisation of state enterprises, deregulation of economy and much more. Then, Williamson (2015) concluded that these demands made by institutions representing such *globalisations* process results in less investment on the population, fewer social programs, reducing educational opportunities and inclusion practices.

Despite all these hinderance, the issue of inclusion of people with disabilities in the educational system is becoming stronger each year inside mathematics education community (see, for instance, D'Souza, 2018; Fernandes & Healy, 2016; Figueiras et al., 2016; Kollosche et al., 2019; Lambert & Harriss, 2022; Lambert et al., 2022; Lambert & Tan, 2020). A few years ago, this issue was not even touched upon inside the international mathematics education community (see, for instance, Marcone et al., in press). It was discussed mostly in the Special Education research field. However, Lambert and Tan (2020) found that research on students with disabilities in Mathematics Education field are almost only quantitative and based on medical aspects, while research on students with no disabilities consider a variety of theories, such as constructionism and social cultural theoretical orientations, for example, which raises some questions such as "Why this difference in treatment?".

Reflecting on these results brought by Lambert and Tan (2020), it is possible to argue that inclusion has some characteristics similar with the globalisation processes (see more about that on Marcone & Skovsmose, 2014). For example, the parameter of disability is given by the so-called "normal" group. The "normal" people define who is "abnormal" and then the "abnormal" are included in the system, which is adapted, not created, for people with disabilities. The prerogative of defining disability belongs to the discourse of "normality" that prevails in institutions such as WHO (see Marcone, 2018; World Health Organization, 2007). Still, the discourse of accepting differences, social inclusion, is always present, as the aforementioned words of Kofi Anan exemplified more than 20 years ago, and it sounds that the actions towards inclusion and the discourses about inclusion are not on the same stage, to say the least, inside the globalisation process. Then, one might infer that a likely reason for this difference in treatment as observed by Lambert and Tan (2020) is because "normal" people diagnose the "abnormal" people through specific measures instead of looking deeply into the potentialities of the teaching and the learning processes when differences are considered.

Naturally, the words "normal" and "abnormal" are being used here as a provocation. The official vocabulary changes every few years in Brazil and in international organisations as well, and it is also different depending on aspects such as culture and economy. In the next section, I will present the concept of *deficiencialism*, exemplifying how to use it to resist exclusion processes. That will be important to build this chapter's argument, which is, people with disabilities are not playing a role in the *globalisations* processes and, because of that, they are not citizens of the world in the sense I am assuming in this chapter, and some aspects of this exclusion processes are present even inside research on people with disabilities inside mathematics education community, as those research focused almost strictly on statistics and medicalisation, instead of looking into learning and teaching possibilities.

Deficiencialism

During my under-graduation course in Mathematics, I was in touch with the inclusion agenda for the first time while assisting a blind colleague to study mathematics and, also, while teaching mathematics in a preparatory course for university entrance exams for deaf students. By that time, I believed I was doing charity work, helping those in need in the community, not only in the university. However, during that process, I learnt that the very need of a volunteer work as my own was a symptom of failure of the educational system, that excludes people with disabilities based on definitions of normality constructed by normal people, establishing capacities and, above all, disabilities, often extrapolated, of individuals based only on their physical characteristics. The real demand was for equality, social justice through public policies and not charity or ephemeris assistance programs. With that in mind, I chose my academic courses and got into studying difference, inclusion, and mathematics education.

My first research was mostly empirical, focused on building a narrative, a case study, about the aforementioned colleague of mine, a blind student who was a mathematics undergraduate student (Marcone, 2010). Once I finished that work for my master thesis, I felt a lack of a theoretical apparatus to explain my experience, and then, my PhD journey started. My PhD research was an effort to theorise about inclusion, exclusion, and mathematics education. One of my inspirations was the postcolonialist theory by Edward Said, especially with his book *Orientalism*. Inspired by it and by colonialist theorists (e.g. Frantz Fanon, Aimé Césaire) and post-colonialist theorists such as Homi K. Bhabha, Gayatri Spivak, and Paulo Freire, for example, I proposed the concept of *deficiencialism*.

Deficiencialism (Marcone, 2015), in short, can be understood as a web of stereotypes which define people with disabilities based on their limitations, not as complex individuals, but as individuals seen through its incapabilities, its impossibilities. More than that, these web of stereotypes usually extrapolate those limitations, always defined by a "normal" person through discourses of normality. As an example, one of the interviewees for my master thesis stated that a blind person could not perform a medical surgery today, which is a reasonable conclusion, and then he followed his argument saying that a blind person could not finish a mathematics course as well for the same reason, suggesting that the student should change to another career. This is an extrapolation based on a web of stereotypes and bias only, that was a *deficiencialist* argumentation.

I found this concept very useful to interpret episodes such as the one in the previous paragraph, making explicit what is an objective limitation for the person (for example, not being able to see the blackboard for being blind) and what is an extrapolated limitation based on stereotypes and bias (for example, not being able to learn mathematics for being blind). I call these extrapolations *deficiencialist* limitations. Demonstrating this difference is a crucial step towards resisting against *deficiencialist* practices. This next stage I call *post-deficiencialism*, where bias and stereotypes are exposed and new propositions towards inclusion are presented, focusing on possibilities.

In the next section, more examples will be addressed, to understand how to use the *deficiencialism* concept as a tool to fight exclusion.

Deficiencialism as a tool to interpret exclusion processes

The first example is about Mara[2] (see more about these two examples on Marcone, 2019). She is the student I mentioned before, who became blind during her undergraduate studies in Mathematics, interrupting her participation in the courses for one year before she decided to come back to finish her degree. My master thesis was a narrative about the challenges of her return. I interviewed 12 people: some of her lecturers, colleagues, administrative technicians who worked in the university and herself. Many of those interviewees stated that Mara should move to another under-graduation course, affirming that a blind person would not be capable to learn advanced mathematics, always bringing extrapolated arguments, such as "If a person cannot drive, then this person cannot learn mathematics" or even bringing positive discourse to say that she was not able to learn maths, such as "she would be a great children educator instead of a maths teacher" arguing that she should move to an Education under-graduation course without providing any explanations about why mathematics made it more difficult.

After interviewing many people, I suddenly heard, from a professor and also from a technician, that the staff nor the university facilities were not prepared to teach mathematics to Mara and that is why they were offering her the opportunity to change to another undergraduate course. Well, this is a quite different argument. It was not about the student's abilities; it was about the educational system deficiency. Nevertheless, trying to make Mara believe she was not capable instead of assuming the university unpreparedness, this is what I am calling a *deficiencialist* discourse. In that sense, I ask "who can learn mathematics"?

Another example came from the research of a student of mine. He was interested in understanding how a blind mathematics teacher operates in his classroom. Surprisingly, the research found that the challenges of a teacher, a professional with qualification to teach mathematics, are no different from a student trying to get this very degree. My student found that the school director offered to the mathematics teacher the "opportunity" to change to another sector, more focused on administrative work of the school, away from the classroom. Then, this teacher would perform only bureaucratic work and give up on teaching. The research found that the school director's argument was based on the need to keep the students safe, as a blind teacher would not be able to take care of or control the class. Again, we are facing an argument that extrapolates the objective limitations of a blind person, classifying this person as not capable instead of facing the deficiencies of the educational structure itself. This is another episode which can be analysed using the *deficiencialism* concept. Here, I ask, "who can teach mathematics?".

Our third and last example is about national admission exams for public universities and also admission exams for positions in public jobs (see more on Marcone et al., in press). Since 2018 I have been collaborating with a colleague adapting mathematics exams for candidates with visual impairment, but the main point here is the chronology, not the adaptation of test items itself. Mara's struggle was between 2001 and 2010. The blind teacher's challenge was in 2015. The invitation to improve the mathematics tests for candidates visually impaired came after a State Attorney requested such improvements to this foundation, in 2017, arguing that the competition was not fair for the visually impaired candidates and was not following Brazilian legislation concerning rights of people with disabilities, such as more time to accomplish the test and proper adaptations. So, we can see a pattern: first, people with disabilities are fighting their way into the university; then, into the labour market; now, into the formulation of policies for admission exams. Each step brings this community closer to a full citizenship status, but not without a fight. Now, I ask, "who can be a citizen?".

It is important to mention that, before 2008, was nearly impossible to find research addressing the teaching and the learning of mathematics for students with disabilities among the Mathematics Education community and today, somehow, the number of research increased substantially, bringing impacts, such as more people with disabilities going to the university and looking for jobs and participating on admission exams for jobs and universities places. Then one may ask, who acts for the people with disabilities rights to education and jobs? I have no doubt answering: firstly, themselves along with people sensitive to their cause. Mara represents the struggle of the people with disabilities inside the educational system to achieve equality. The blind teacher represents the challenges of people with disabilities to create and occupy their space inside the labour market, and the initiative of foundations who organise admissions exams are a consequence of political pressure made by these groups, their families, and those who are sympathetic to their cause for decades. The first two examples might be understood as cases of exclusion analysed through *deficiencialism*. The third example is what I call *post-deficiencialism*, and involves theory and practise for learning and creating ways to overcome such barriers seeking equality.

Well, now, a once invisible group inside the society is becoming aware of their rights and fighting for them, achieving some improvements in some countries but the struggle is not finished yet. Then I ask, who made them citizens? Are they included in these *globalisations'* phenomena? Let us examine more of this in the next section.

Who can be a citizen of the world?

In section *What does globalisation mean after all?* I mentioned the fact that to be a citizen of the world one needs to be a consumer of the world as well. If one does not have a job, does not pay income taxes, and does not receive any services from the government, what can we infer? Following this way of thinking, would a definition for citizen of the world today be so different from the one coming from the ancient Greek tradition, where a citizen was a man with material properties and lands? Not so ancient, in Brazil, during our first republic in the XIX century, to be allowed to vote one should be a white man and own lands, showing how long the ancient Greek tradition has lasted. Only during the 1930s women conquered their right to vote in Brazil.

However, the idea of a citizen of the world goes beyond the ancient Greek definition as we discussed before. This contemporary idea of a global citizen is connected to people's awareness. Awareness towards the interconnections between nations worldwide, economically, politically, culturally, and more. Also, awareness of the individual impact on those globalisations processes and vice versa. But how one achieves that information, that education, to become a global citizen? Hence, to achieve global citizenship, information and education play a crucial role, and mathematics education is included among the knowledge fields that lead one to become a global citizen.

Now, try to imagine how the process was to achieve rights for the people with disabilities in the ancient world. Amaral (1994) describes that some cities in the Greek ancient society, such as Sparta, would not tolerate disabilities, because their civil society was organised around military capacity, followed by the Roman imperium, used to sacrifice their people with disabilities, and our society inherited this culture in many aspects. Amaral (1994) continues saying that during the middle age, with the uprise of Christianism, disability became a reason for pity, but, still, with no recognition of the potentialities of a person with disability. Abberley (1987) stated that this idea of including people with disabilities only came centuries later, more strongly after the Second World War (1939–1945) when many nations received their soldiers with disabilities due to the battle, mostly physical disabilities. The reason to do this effort to include people with disabilities after WWII was simple: the European nations needed the labour power to rebuild the continent, so, the people with physical disabilities became "citizens of that world"

Some decades later, the people with disabilities improved their conquests towards equity being legally recognised as "citizens" in some countries, having their needs addressed in a few official documents and legislations across the world, such as the *Salamanca Statement* (United Nations Educational, Scientific and Cultural Organization-Division of Basic Education, 1994). The Salamanca statement and framework for action on special needs education, which brought important and positive consequences for the people with disabilities community worldwide, specifically in Brazil, such as adapted educational material, the right to special conditions for universities and job admission exams, and improvements on work conditions with job positions quota, for example. After that, the challenge was – and still is – the implementation of such policies and legislations, coming out of the books and written laws into real life. The challenge, as Boaventura de Sousa Santos (2008) well argued, is to be equal when our difference makes us inferior and to be different when our equality mischaracterises us. Hence the need for an equality that recognises differences and a difference that does not produce, feed, or reproduce exclusion practices.

Following this idea, I would like to bring attention to the work of Tsutsui (2014). She is a Brazilian State Attorney who wrote a paper about the legal concept of disability inside the Brazilian law system, which illustrates Boaventura's statement. She shows how the Brazilian legislation, at the same time, considers a person with disability as incapable to work, offering the possibility to retire alleging incapacity and guaranteeing job positions quota inside companies with more than one hundred employees. Both legal apparatuses are available. According to Tsutsui, a legal system is only a reflection of what the society thinks about any matter, including disability. The first law, which is the older, shows that the society sees the people with disabilities as incapable, offering help as it was during the uprise of Christianism in western Europe. The second law is the recognition of the exclusion that this group suffered from the labour market, creating a public policy which aims to equalise such injustice. The first law was created by "normal" people, the second law was enforced by the "abnormal". The first law could be understood as a *deficiencialism* approach, while the second one, could be seen as a *post-deficiencialist* reaction. The path to become a citizen is always created and travelled by the excluded.

Since my first steps into the inclusion issue, I moved from a person who believed was helping the people with disabilities to a person who understood, along with Paulo Freire, that autonomy and freedom are only possible with other people. One will only have autonomy and freedom in their city when everyone shares all rights and duties with equity. One will only have autonomy and freedom in their university when everyone can study there if they want to. One will be a citizen only when everyone becomes a citizen.

The intention in this chapter was to raise the issue – to be deeper pursued in future research efforts – of whether people with disabilities are seen as citizens in front of a globalised world or not, specifically inside the mathematics education research and practices. I started addressing a discussion on what a global citizen and globalisation means. From that reflection, I argued that globalisation could be understood as an essentially economical phenomenon, so, to be a global citizen is, by extent, an economic phenomenon as well.

Following this lead, I looked into the book *Internationalisation and Globalisation in Mathematics and Science Education* (Atweh et al., 2008) to understand the implications of *globalisations* processes on research about mathematics education and inclusion of people with disabilities. At first, my instinct was to look for a chapter addressing issues of disability and how they confront *globalisations* processes. However, beside the immense contribution the book brings to understanding how *globalisations* processes impact education and the economy differently depending on the country, I found just an immense silence concerning people with disabilities. The word disability appears four times in the entire book, always among examples of excluded groups but with no further discussion. The word blind or blindness appears ten times, but almost always used as a negative predicative meaning ignorance or frivolity. The words deaf and autism, e.g., do not appear at all. I cannot say I was surprised, as I have been doing this observation since 2016, in the 13th

International Congress on Mathematical Education (ICME) in Hamburg, Germany, when I had the opportunity to present an invited paper, unpublished, about the silences in mathematics education. That invitation was made by Bill Atweh, after a conversation we had where I expressed my concerns.

I tried to show in my ICME 13th presentation, that the issue of inclusion of people with disabilities was not being addressed by the mathematics education community. I analysed all the ICME proceedings, since the first one in Lyon, France, in 1969 (Marcone et al., in press) and found that the first-time people with disabilities were mentioned was in the 8th ICME, in Spain. Again, in the 9th, the 10th, the 11th, and the 12th ICME editions, but absent in the 13th ICME and back again in the 14th ICME edition. I also argued that Spain being the first time and the first place to bring that issue up, in 1996, was connected with the fact the Salamanca Statement was enacted in that same country 2 years earlier. Then, this external pressure brought the inclusion of people with disabilities inside the international mathematics education community. It indicates, as per my understanding, that the discussion of *globalisations* processes, including the ones inside the mathematics education community, are not considering people with disabilities as citizens, and Lambert and Tan (2020) comes to reinforce this idea.

Actually, this is particularly important to state again, that no minority will be included without a struggle, they will fight their way towards inclusion. One example inside mathematics education can be seen in the case of analysing the first three editions of the ICME, part of my paper presented in ICME 13th. It was a tradition to write a resolution, as it was called, at the end of the conference, summarising it and listening to the audience's comments. On the third ICME edition, in Karlsruhe, 1976, Germany, the end of the resolution says that it was recommended that the issue of "Women and Mathematics" should be an explicit one on the next edition in 1980, what actually happened. Then, we can see that a pressure coming from the women brought the issue of "Women and Mathematics" inside the mathematics education community in ICME conferences, after three editions with no mention of women's work.

My uneasiness concerning inclusion of people with disabilities is the main reason I brought the concept of *deficiencialism* to this chapter. *Deficiencialism* is a concept that seeks to show how the definitions of disability are built over a web of stereotypes based mostly on a standard of capability produced by the so-called "normal" people through discourses of normality. This concept goes beyond the medicalisation, as it recognises one's objective limitations as per some disability or disease, but also, fights against the false argument that extends these limitations to a complete incapacity and invisibility. The examples I brought, towards a *post-deficiencialism*, are meant to be a mechanism I am proposing to show how deep is the silence inside the society in general and also inside mathematics education towards the education of people with disabilities, from the kindergarten to the labour market. The research of Lambert and Tan (2020), for me, is an example of a *post-deficiencialist* research, because it showed evidence of a different treatment given to the people with disabilities community when doing research on mathematics education and inclusion, and awareness is the first step towards change.

In that sense, the challenge of people with disabilities in front of a globalised world is, among many others, to become economically relevant and to become visible. Hence, the struggle conducted by the communities of people with disabilities along with "normal" people who support their cause, slowly achieve some small victories, e.g., creating official documents such as Salamanca Statement, raising the issue inside academic communities, such as the mathematics education one, putting pressure locally for the creation of laws which diminishes the effects of exclusion, such as quota reservation for jobs and university positions in Brazil. Small although meaningful victories.

Once these documents spread, these laws are written, the subject gain terrain inside academical communities such as mathematics education, the next challenge is to implement them, as many people and institutions resists to it, meaning that, beyond the economical aspect, the minorities – specifically people with disabilities – also face the social and culture exclusion processes which is, as per my understanding, the most difficult to address. Once a society accepts differences in their culture, the economy will follow, but the opposite will not always be true.

I brought the university and job admissions exams as examples because, as the mathematics education community knows since for a long time, mathematics plays a crucial role on those tests, working as a gatekeeper. Furthermore, I here add that the very chosen media to create and to conduct an admission exam is also a strong gatekeeper, as it has the power to define who will be excluded from the process in advance, e.g., using a language proper to the elites only, or using a media inaccessible to blind students, like draws using perspective to represent 3 dimensions instead of a 3D physical model, or using a language different from your mother tongue, as it often happens to deaf people, who are obliged to perform tests using the spoken language instead of their sign language, relegating this group to a disadvantageous position from the beginning.

In that sense, mathematics education research could act exposing *deficiencialist* practices while proposing *post-deficiencialist* procedures – such as to provide for blind students the opportunity to participate in minimally balanced conditions on admissions exams through an assessment created to be inclusive – in order to oppose processes that exclude people with disabilities from an economical system or make them invisible inside a research community, and, consequently, from a global citizenship status as they won't be able to achieve and to spread the awareness that define the condition of being one, and also contribute to the cultural transformation which will embrace difference as a strength, a possibility.

Nonetheless, many questions remain "how can the people with disabilities achieve such aims, becoming economically relevant and fighting their space in a globalised world while promoting the cultural transformation which will embrace difference as a strength?" Small actions, leading to small victories is a way to start, e.g., looking into how your country deals with the mathematics tests in admission exams in general, whether for a job position or for a university place, trying to transform them into a more inclusive version. Such actions could broaden the citizenship understanding inside this globalised world.

Notes

1 The Uruguay Round was the 8th round of multilateral trade negotiations (MTN) conducted within the framework of the General Agreement on Tariffs and Trade (GATT), spanning from 1986 to 1993 and embracing 123 countries as "contracting parties". The Round led to the creation of the World Trade Organization, with GATT remaining as an integral part of the WTO agreements. See more Uruguay Round - Wikipedia.

2 Fictitious name.

References

Abberley, P. (1987). The concept of oppression and the development of a social theory of disability. *Disability, Handicap & Society*, *2*(1), 16. https://doi.org/10.1080/02674648766780021

Amaral, L. A. (1994). Corpo desviante/olhar perplexo. *Psicologia USP*, *5*(1–2), 24.

Atweh, B., Barton, A. C., Borba, M. C., Gough, N., Keitel-Kreidt, C., Vistro-Yu, C., & Vithal, R. (2008). *Internationalisation and globalisation in mathematics and science education*. Springer.

Bardhan, P. (2004). The impact of globalization on the poor. *Brookings Trade Forum*, 14. http://www.jstor.org/stable/25063196

Demir, I., Canakci, M., & Egri, T. (2021). Globalization and economic growth. In W. Leal Filho, A. M. Azul, L. Brandli, A. Lange Salvia, & T. Wall (Eds.), *Decent work and economic growth. Encyclopedia of the UN sustainable development goals*. Springer. https://doi.org/https://doi.org/10.1007/978-3-319-71058-7_90-1

D'Souza, R. (2018). Disability, economy, and the limits of inclusive education. *Perspectivas da Educação Matemática*, 21. https://periodicos.ufms.br/index.php/pedmat/article/view/7234/5503

Fernandes, S. H., & Healy, L. (2016). RUMO À EDUCAÇÃO MATEMÁTICA INCLUSIVA: REFLEXÕES SOBRE NOSSA JORNADA. *REnCiMa*, *7*, 21. http://www.matematicainclusiva.net.br/pdf/Rumo%20%C3%A0%20Educa%C3%A7%C3%A3o%20Matem%C3%A1tica%20Inclusiva_%20Reflex%C3%B5es%20sobre%20nossa%20jornada.pdf

Figueiras, L., Healy, L., & Skovsmose, O. (2016). Difference, inclusion and mathematics education: Launching a research agenda. *International Journal for Studies in Mathematics Education*, 21. http://www.matematicainclusiva.net.br/pdf/Difference,%20inclusion%20and%20mathematics%20education_launching%20a%20research%20agenda.pdf

Globalization. (2022, July 24). In *Wikipedia*. https://en.wikipedia.org/wiki/Globalization#:~:text=Globalization%2C%20or%20globalisation%20(Commonwealth%20English,in%20transportation%20and%20communications%20technology

Hernández-Truyol, B. E. (2014). Culture clashes: Indigenous populations and globalization - The Case of Belo Monte. *Seattle Journal for Social Justice*, 46. https://scholarship.law.ufl.edu/cgi/viewcontent.cgi?article=1849&context=facultypub

Kollosche, D., Marcone, R., Knigge, M., Penteado, M. G., & Skovsmose, O., & SpringerLink. (2019). *Inclusive mathematics education: State-of-the-art research from Brazil and Germany* (1st ed.). Springer International Publishing.

Lambert, R., & Harriss, E. (2022). Insider accounts of dyslexia from research mathematicians. *Open Access: Educational Studies in Mathematics*, *111*, 19.https://doi.org/https://doi.org/10.1007/s10649-021-10140-2

Lambert, R., Nguyen, T., Mendoza, M., & McNiff, A. (2022). Addressing agency and achievement in a multiplication intervention. *Insights into Learning Disabilities*, *19*(1), 23. https://files.eric.ed.gov/fulltext/EJ1341312.pdf

Lambert, R., & Tan, P. (2020). Does disability matter in mathematics educational research? A critical comparison of research on students with and without disabilities. *Mathematics Education Research Journal*, *32*, 21.https://doi.org/https://doi.org/10.1007/s13394-019-00299-6

Marcone, R. (2010). *Matemática Inclusiva no Ensino Superior: aprendendo a partilhar experiências.* UNESP.

Marcone, R. (2015). *Deficiencialismo: A invenção da deficiência pela normalidade.* UNESP.

Marcone, R. (2018). Desconstruindo narrativas normalizadoras. In F. M. Rosa & I. M. Baraldi (Eds.), *Educação Matemática Inclusiva: estudos e percepções* (pp. 17–36). Mercado das Letras.

Marcone, R. (2019). Who can learn mathematics? In R. Kollosche, R. Marcone, M. Knigge, M. G. Penteado, & O. Skovsmose (Eds.), *Inclusive mathematics education: State-of-the-Art research from Brazil and Germany.* Springer.

Marcone, R., Milani, R., & Bortolucci, R. (in press). Educação Matemática Inclusiva como Tendência em Educação Matemática. In D. B. Assemany (Ed.), *Tendências em Educação Matemática.* Mercado das Letras.

Marcone, R., & Skovsmose, O. (2014). Inclusion-exclusion: An explosive problem. In O. Skovsmose (Ed.), *Critique as uncertainty* (pp. 95–109). Information Age Publishing.

Moore, S. T. (2022). Thirty years later, voters are still telling us it's about the economy stupid! *New York Post.* https://nypost.com/2022/10/24/thirty-years-later-voters-are-still-telling-us-its-about-the-economy-stupid/

Munck, R. (2005). *Globalization and social exclusion: A transformationalist perspective.* Kumarian Press.

Robertson, R., & White, K. E. (2007). What is globalization? In G. Ritzer (Ed.), *The Blackwell companion to globalization* (pp. 54–66). John Wiley & Sons.

Ruggie, J. G. (2003). The United Nations and globalization: Patterns and limits of institutional adaptation. *Global Governance: A Review of Multilateralism and International Organizations*, *9*(3), 21. https://doi.org/https://doi.org/10.1163/19426720-00903005

Santos, B. D. (2008). *A gramática do tempo: Para Uma Nova cultura política* (2nd ed.). Cortez.

Tsutsui, P. F. (2014). O novo conceito de pessoa com deficiência. *Conteúdo Jurídico.* https://conteudojuridico.com.br/consulta/Artigos/38739/o-novo-conceito-de-pessoa-com-deficiencia

United Nations Educational, Scientific and Cultural Organization. (1994). *The Salamanca statement and framework for action on special needs education.*

Williamson, K. (2015). *The impact of globalization on access for individuals with disabilities.* Western Michigan University. https://scholarworks.wmich.edu/honors_theses/2745/

World Health Organization. (2007). Global Initiative for the Elimination of Avoidable Blindness: action plan 2006–2011. World Health Organization. https://apps.who.int/iris/handle/10665/43754

World Health Organization. (2014). Disability and health. http://www.who.int/mediacentre/factsheets/fs352/en/

3 Vocational mathematics and competence

Effects of and resistance to globalisation

Lisa Björklund Boistrup and Gail E. FitzSimons

Introduction

In this chapter we discuss, and reflect on, globalisation in relation to vocational mathematics and competence. We will start by addressing mathematical competence on a global level as construed by the Organisation for Economic Co-operation and Development (OECD), and in local contexts and how they are affected by globalisation. We will also present examples of alternative versions of vocational mathematics competence. Our conception of mathematical competence is in line with the work by Tine Wedege (2001) who has problematised a fragmented version of mathematical competence, present in several frameworks at that time. Following Wedege, competence, also mathematical competence, is to be viewed as a wholeness. From such an understanding, mathematical competence, in for example vocational contexts, is part of "a readiness for action and thought and/or an authorisation for action" (p. 27). Furthermore, it is "based on knowledge, know-how and attitudes/feelings (dispositions)," and is "a result of learning or development processes both in everyday practice and education."

There are other ways of understanding mathematical competence in play in society today. One clear example is through the lens of globalisation and its effects on the constitution of mathematical competence as reflected in the Programme for International Student Assessment (PISA) and the Programme for the International Assessment of Adult Competencies (PIAAC), a form of PISA adapted for adults aged 16–65 years. We take the operations of PIAAC as the basis for our argument, while connecting this to capitalism in the current era. This is in line with Carvalho (2012), who asserts that conceptions of "global economic competitiveness" and the "knowledge economy" cannot be understood independently from the interests of capital. In the following, we introduce the concept of globalisation adopted in this chapter, and through this concept we pose two research questions.

DOI: 10.4324/9781003130673-5

Globalisation, following Latour

As guiding notions for our reflective process, we have adopted Latour's (2018) writing on globalisation. Latour connects globalisation with the heavy increase in inequalities that the world is currently encountering. Inspired by Latour, we seek connections between globalisation, mathematics education, and vocational education (VET[1]). In interrogating the concept of globalisation, Latour expands upon the commonly used and accepted understanding of the term and gives account for two versions, evident over the span of the last 50 years, with different connotations. He calls them *globalisation plus* and *globalisation minus.*

Globalisation plus concerns an understanding where "shifting from a local to a global viewpoint ought to mean *multiplying* viewpoints, *registering* a greater number of varieties, *taking into account* a larger number of beings, cultures, phenomena, organisms, and people" (p. 12). As we understand it, this version of globalisation plus respects and thrives on diversity internationally in all facets of activity, maintaining an ethical and a critical stance. In mathematics education, examples are international conferences where a variety of cultural contexts are present, and where diversity contributes to a richness of understandings of what mathematics and mathematics education may be about. In the field of vocational mathematics education, relevant literature includes the *Educational Studies in Mathematics* special issue (e.g., Bakker, 2014; FitzSimons, 2014), and edited books (e.g., Yasukawa et al., 2018). Importantly, "unlike participation in formal mathematics education, where the discipline is central, workers are likely to be confronted by, and need to reconcile, a range of other valued workplace discourses, both epistemic and social/cultural in nature" (FitzSimons & Boistrup, 2017, p. 329).

Latour (2018) writes that what is most often meant by globalisation today is the exact opposite of such an increase in diversity of viewpoints and horizons, and he labels this *globalisation minus*:

> The term is used to mean that a single vision, entirely provincial, proposed by a few individuals, representing a very small number of interests, limited to a few measuring instruments, to a few standards and protocols, has been imposed on everyone and spread everywhere. It is hardly surprising that we don't know whether to embrace globalization or, on the contrary, struggle against it.
>
> (pp. 12–13)

Globalisation minus follows ever narrowing pathways leading to practices and policies that exacerbate the accumulation of power and wealth for the few rather than the many, and the implementation of PIAAC assessment tools is one such example. As FitzSimons (2002a) observed:

> International surveys such as [...] the OECD-sponsored Program for International Student Assessment (PISA) Mathematical Literacy strand are apparently underpinned by a notion of mathematics as

universal and culture-free. At the same time these comparative studies appear to be effecting the institution of a single, hegemonic mathematics curriculum worldwide as nations strive for improved relative positioning—wittingly or unwittingly abandoning their own cultural specificities.

(pp. 109–110)

Latour's two versions of globalisation help us address the effects of capitalism in relation to VET (cf. Avis, 2012, 2019) and to vocational mathematics education; the effects of capitalism on education are also manifested on a global scale in the form of PIAAC and PISA. Latour's (2018) work highlights the role of capital in society regarding phenomena such as globalisation, deregulation, increased inequalities, and climate change denial intertwined in the relations "between human beings and the material condition of their lives" (p. 1). We relate this to the perspectives of globalisation plus and minus and how they are connected to the opportunities and challenges described within the field of critical mathematics education. Here, Skovsmose (2020) focuses first on students' interests, expectations, hopes, aspirations, and motives; conceptualised in the notion of *students' foregrounds.* This notion is very complex, and always contingent upon external factors such as "economic conditions, social-economic processes of inclusion and exclusion, cultural values and traditions, public discourses, and racism" (p. 156). Skovsmose continues: "a foreground is, as well, defined through the person's experiences of possibilities and obstructions" (p. 156). In this chapter our aim is to interrogate the ways that globalisation plus and minus, particularly in the context of PIAAC and its effects on curriculum and teaching, can impact on these possibilities and obstructions. We also characterise an alternative to the version of mathematics competence as reflected in PIAAC.

As vocational mathematics education researchers, our goal is not only to offer students the possibility to participate with competence in a range of vocations as employees and self-employed workers, despite the constraints of a competitive capitalist market. It is also for students to also have the opportunity to be critically aware of the ways in which mathematics and statistics are, or could be, used to their disadvantage in the workplace and beyond by people in positions of relatively greater power, and for them to be able to "answer back." Moreover, as Boistrup and Gustafsson (2014) show, workers (nursing aides and lorry-loaders) with critical competence may benefit the customer as well as the employer in ethical and sustainable ways including reducing costs and/or waste or by taking environmental factors into consideration when making decisions. Underlying all of this is the importance of respecting each student's knowledge and life experience. In our view, PISA and PIAAC are both problematic, premised on the neoliberalist economic policies of the OECD (Rizvi & Lingard, 2009), which take as axiomatic that the current capitalist market oriented economy is beyond critique, and simply needs workers at all skill levels to work smarter and harder, without questioning the status quo.

Accordingly, in this chapter we discuss two questions:

1 How do the relationships between globalisation minus, as reflected in PIAAC, and capitalism interact with vocational mathematics in different contexts, briefly including two different local sites of the world (Australia and Sweden)?
2 How would mathematical competence in vocational education be characterised if it were operating under conditions of globalisation plus rather than the globalisation minus influence of the OECD?

By posing these two research questions we aim to illuminate how globalisation minus is currently reflected in vocational mathematics (*both* mathematical *and* vocational aspects). The section titled "Mathematical competence and globalisation minus" addresses Research Question 1, and the section titled "Mathematical competence as reflected in PIAAC" addresses Research Question 2. We then address how a limited interpretation of mathematical competence is reflected in the PIAAC items and questionnaire. We consider the effects of globalised capitalism on vocational education in general and on vocational mathematics education in two different OECD countries. We also offer an alternative that takes *both* the vocational context *and* the mathematical context seriously. This, we argue, offers access to powerful knowledge for the students in their prospective vocations as well as keeping open options for further education, along with mathematically informed citizenship.

Mathematical competence and globalisation minus

In this section we discuss how globalisation minus is reflected in mathematical competence according to PIAAC (RQ 1). Here we are interested in the potential and general effects of such international comparisons. We then discuss globalisation minus on a general level, connecting globalisation minus to capitalism, and vocational education (VET), with examples of local effects of globalisation in two different national VET contexts, Australia and Sweden.

Mathematical competence as reflected in PIAAC

The critical term adopted in PIAAC is not "mathematical competence," or "mathematical literacy" as in PISA (OECD, 2018), but "numeracy" which itself is a contested term (e.g., FitzSimons, 2002b; Sträßer, 2015), since it could be (and is often) construed as having a limited scope, focusing on basic skills for everyday activities. Following, FitzSimons and Boistrup (2017), we use the term mathematical competence for discussing globalisation minus in relation to the OECD.

In the literature, several accounts support our discussion of globalisation minus, indicating the limited view of mathematical competence reflected in PIAAC's test items and questionnaire. PIAAC's association with PISA, both constructed and administered under the auspices of the OECD, strongly suggests its intended contribution to external interests, not least the economy at local and global levels. Their pervasiveness has serious consequences for education policy, globally and locally. As Kanes et al. (2014) observe: "... PISA simultaneously shapes and serves global and local discourses of education, including in particular those of mathematics education" (p. 162). Following Kanes et al., our interest is in the potential effects of power under capitalism, globally, including the creation of new problems requiring technical solutions rather than political solutions; here our focus is on PIAAC, not PISA. Carvalho (2012) observes that discourses such as PISA are helping to "... rewrite systems of meaning and relations of power, [acting as a regulatory] tool that creates and allows the creation of new problems and imagined new tomorrows" (p. 183). The same applies to PIAAC. These factors are entirely consistent with Latour's (2018) description of globalisation minus. Here, we draw on two studies which have analysed elements of the test material of PIACC, adding some additional analysis of our own (see Figure 3.1).

According to the information from OECD (n.d.), the item in Figure 3.1, along with the few available, is representative of more than 50 items that a respondent might encounter. This item is meant to focus on the content of dimension and shape, with the processes of acting upon and using (estimate). The context is labelled as *everyday life* or *work.*

We return to this particular item after summarising the critique by Tsatsaroni and Evans (2014) of the overall item construction of PIAAC. The definition of numeracy used by PIAAC is based on four constructed dimensions of numerate behaviour: context, content, response, and representation. The

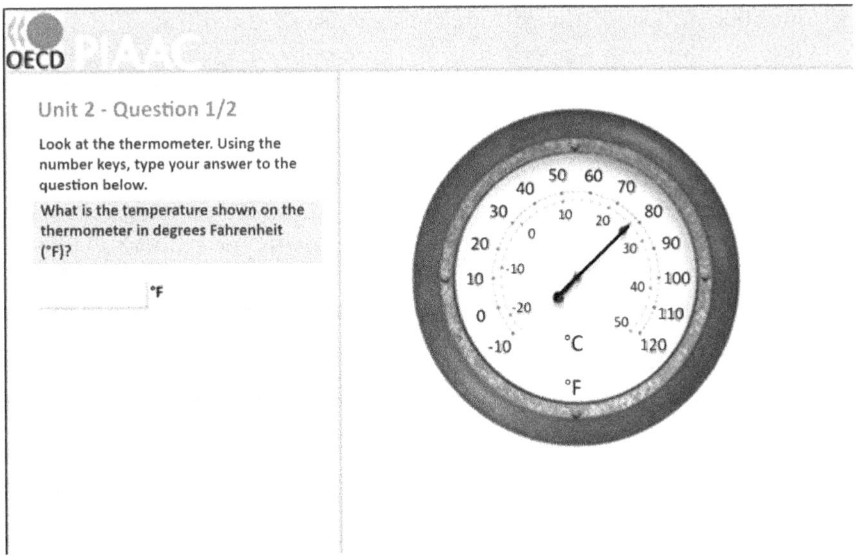

Figure 3.1 Example item from PIAAC (OECD, n.d.)

range of categories within each dimension is specified—for example, context is categorised as (a) everyday, (b) work, (c) society and community, or (d) further learning. While the OECD's aim is to have high validity, Tsatsaroni and Evans point out that in the case of PIAAC "this provides a transnational definition, and one needs to question how well it 'fits' adults' lives in any particular country" (p. 176); also that the four types of context are under-specified in that "they are rather too general to refer to any actual specific social practice or social context in which a particular respondent might engage, in their everyday life" (p. 176). They also challenge the ecological validity of PIAAC (i.e., whether a test and its results are representative of those to which one wishes to generalise the results) in relation to the test format which is computer-based, arguing that this format "may not be representative of the settings in which respondents normally carry out tasks involving numeracy, and so may not facilitate their 'typical' thinking and behaviour responses" (p. 176). The arguments by Tsatsaroni and Evans illuminate how PIAAC perpetuates a version of mathematical competence for adults, offering an example of globalisation minus in that it offers a narrow range of possibilities for adults to demonstrate their actual numeracy skills.

As an example of a much more limited perspective than what acting upon and using could actually be about in everyday life or in work, our analysis of the PIAAC item above reflects the characteristics of globalisation minus. Research on how measurement is dealt with in working life shows there are, unsurprisingly, many more complexities than reflected in the item shown here (see, e.g., FitzSimons & Boistrup, 2017; Johansson, 2014). Moreover, our research has shown that adults rarely make measurement errors at work when the context is rich in meaning, including access to other people and the internet, and when the real-life consequences are serious.

Our reflection here supports that of Tsatsaroni and Evans (2014) who, in their analysis of the four PIAAC items, concluded that such examples do not direct the attention to systems of mathematical meaning ("knowing") but rather to functional meanings ("doing"), thereby potentially distracting respondents from the mathematics that is being assessed. Notably, in workplaces the ideal or optimum mathematical answer may not be the most appropriate, and experienced workers often check mathematical answers with one or more alternative methods, mathematical as well as practical (FitzSimons & Boistrup, 2017).

Similarly to how the PISA test is conducted, the test takers of PIAAC are asked to complete a questionnaire. Boistrup and Henningsen (2017) analysed all items in the PIAAC questionnaire, in which the respondents were asked about how often they engage in different kinds of mathematics. The questions posed to the respondents on mathematics (numeracy) as part of working life, are as follows:

How often do you:

- Calculate prices, costs or budgets
- Use or calculate fractions or percentages
- Use a calculator

- Read diagrams maps or schematics
- Prepare charts graphs or tables
- Use simple algebra or formulas
- Use advanced math or statistics

For each question, the respondents' choices ranged from "Never" to "Everyday." Boistrup and Henningsen were unable to find any items that reflected mathematics as part of complex workplace situations as we understand them. Rather, the focus was on "separate, disconnected skills which are vaguely described, such as calculating prices, using a calculator, preparing charts, or using simple algebra" (p. 73), far from the decision making typically found in working life. In fact, in neither study was there any indication of numeracy being used for critical purposes such as reflecting on social injustices or inequalities (cf. Skovsmose, 2020). In this, the PIAAC questionnaire reflects the characteristics of globalisation minus for two reasons: One is that PIAAC is widespread globally, and the other is that it displays a highly limited and narrow version of what mathematics might actually be required in relation to specific vocational contexts.

In this section, we have demonstrated how PIAAC, as an example of globalisation minus (Latour, 2018), operates within the field of adult and vocational mathematics education in many OECD countries, including Australia and Sweden; PIAAC also has effects the local level, described below.

Globalisation, capitalism, and VET

Since the mid-1980s at least, capitalism has pursued its ends through overturning post-war social democratic settlements involving social welfare states, transforming public goods such as education and health into marketised systems run along business models, and renaming users such as students and patients with terms such as "clients" or "customers." This form of capitalism, which shifts the conception of education from public good to private commodity and focuses on the needs of a market oriented economy at the expense of the individual and society, works in line with globalisation minus, and is often known as *neo-liberalism* (Avis, 2012). In this section we consider the links between globalisation, capitalism, and vocational education and training, and address the fundamental threat to difference and diversity posed by the prescribed testing regime of PIAAC with its undue influence on mathematics or numeracy curricula for adults and vocational education students, and hence their future options.

The rise of neoliberalism has led to a focus on instrumental thinking that predominates in schools and classrooms. This very narrow means/ends orientation includes a strong vocational orientation right across the education spectrum: the idea that the main purpose of education is to prepare people for a lifetime of work. In that sense, the demands of the workplace and the economy fundamentally shape the aims and purposes of education. Preparing students for future work is clearly a goal of vocational education, but this does not justify the priority given to instrumental aspects, or functional mathematics, as reflected in PIAAC, which completely determine the educational content and exclude any critical reflection on the uses to which mathematics is put, locally and/or globally.

Given that institutionalised educational policies and practices have been used to further a common identity (Burbules, cited in Roth, 2007), the question is how to respect difference. This is an important question in vocational education, and for mathematics in particular. Institutionalised mathematics in the forms made visible in the widespread use of textbooks, is not always—sometimes even not at all—visible in workplace practices. Assessment frameworks such as PIAAC are unable to accommodate the vital importance of local context when adults at work and elsewhere make critical mathematical decisions. Similarly, there would appear to be no place for ethical and other considerations in the PIAAC testing regime. In addition, there can be no provision for the essential skills of personal communication in relation to mathematics in any mode other than impersonal textual or graphical forms; whereas the full complement of available modes has the potential to contribute to gaining a more comprehensive knowledge and understanding of the situation at hand (see, e.g., Boistrup & Gustafsson, 2014; Kress, 2009).

Globalisation can have both positive and negative consequences at the same time. What does it mean for traditional trades and vocations when such industries become technologised? How well are the skilled workers equipped to move with the times and upskill or else to reconstruct their trade or vocation into a niche market? The former can lead to homogenisation (e.g., mass production), which is aligned with globalisation minus (Latour, 2018); the latter potentially to the production of new hybrids in the interaction between the global and the local (more aligned with globalisation plus). What are the implications for vocational mathematics education? Burbules (cited in Roth, 2007) concluded that although education is part of the problem in promoting globalisation, it is or can be a potential corrective in that it "is one of the few areas in which people an explicitly raise and explore … questions about dominant cultural values, identities, diversity and difference" (p. 31). In such an endeavour, PIAAC—at least in its current form—lacks that potential.

Avis (2012) observes that despite the differences in systems of VET at local, regional, and global levels, they are mostly set within the hegemony of neoliberalism. Education in general, and vocational education in particular, are construed by proponents as "pivotal to the pursuit of competitiveness" (p. 1), and central to human capital development. They are also strongly associated in this discourse with notions of upskilling and societal wellbeing and, by implication, linked to increasing standards of living and welfare provision. Themes such as these are part of a set of discourses that frame policy (with implications for curriculum and assessment), based on supposed deficits of adults who are constructed as always being in need of retraining. OECD-developed programs such as PISA and PIAAC, both adopted in over 40 countries, provide data that enables (often highly politically charged) international comparison of the performance of students across and within different national systems, with consequences for vocational and other education internationally in relation to curriculum and assessment—including vocational mathematics education.

Globalisation and vocational mathematics in two different national contexts

We, the authors of this chapter, live in Australia and Sweden, and there have been developments in both contexts in relation to globalisation and vocational mathematics education, albeit in different ways.

In Australia, professional mathematics educators have been replaced by the least expensive, often less skilled substitutes in a highly casualised workforce, and the disciplinary knowledge of mathematics has been replaced by limited sets of fragmentised skills reduced to the minimum considered necessary for any particular occupation (see, e.g., Wheelahan, 2015). Vocational students working at lower qualification levels, begin (and frequently end) their numeracy education focusing on sets of contextualised *skills,* with no focus on developing theoretically-based mathematical understandings. In times of rapid change and global turmoil, our conclusion is that there is very little if any support.

Along with adult education, vocational education by its very nature tends to attract people who do not always fit the conventional stereotype of an academic student—for example, people located in the intersectionalities of disadvantage or difference (e.g., diverse socio-economic, cultural, gender, and ability groups, immigrants)—although this does not imply any deficit on the part of those enrolled (see, e.g., Jurdak, 2020). However, it is a characteristic of neoliberalism to ascribe individual responsibility for failure. In the Nordic welfare states, principles of equality are "manifested, for example, in ambitions to provide programmes that enable transitions to both higher education and working life in upper secondary vocational education and training (VET)" (Nylund & Rosvall, 2019, p. 271). However, Avis (2019) observes a trade-off between social inclusion and social equality in the Nordic countries (including Sweden) over recent years. In the shift away from social democracy to market-focused neoliberalism, "understandings of equality located in a broader engagement with philosophical issues about the nature of social justice" (p. 381) have also shifted towards a notion of equity which, "on the other hand, is reductive and calculative, serving to close down philosophical questions and replace these with quantitative data" (p. 381). PIAAC is one obvious example.

Dahl's (2014) analysis of the Swedish national curriculum in mathematics for vocational education reveals unequal opportunities for vocational students, since they do not develop the same foundation in mathematics as other students, reducing their opportunities to study mathematics in the future.

Vocational mathematics is focused strongly on context-bound, skill-oriented knowledge (Nylund & Rosvall, 2016). Rosvall et al. (2017) also found that both teachers and students tend to have lower expectations in VET mathematics classes. Clearly, both Australian and Swedish vocational mathematics contexts are affected by globalisation, in line with globalisation minus.

An alternative version of vocational mathematics competence

Our second research question concerns how mathematical competence in vocational education might be constituted if it were not for the effects of globalisation minus. We address this question in three parts, articulating aspects more aligned with globalisation plus (Latour, 2018), but also consistent with Avis (2012) who writes:

> … neoliberal hegemony can never be completely secured and it is in the interstices of educational practices as well as the contradictions surrounding VET that there reside possibilities for the development of alternative and progressive forms of education. These possibilities constitute both a site of struggle as well as one which could align with the pursuit of social justice. In some respects the critiques of neoliberalism as well as the manner in which VET is currently configured call for more expansive understandings of education, the vocational and practice […] in a way that moves beyond instrumentalism and a focus on human capital.
>
> (p. 8)

We also strive to reach more expansive understandings of education, both vocational and mathematical, in their theoretical and practical aspects, in ways that move beyond the instrumental focus on human capital. We draw on a selection of case studies aimed at taking mathematical and vocational content seriously, in terms of both authenticity and powerful knowledge which can be built on for the future. We concur with Valero and Orlander (2018) that "the analysis of how students and people in their adult life actually come to be empowered with and through mathematics and science requires a more fine-grained understanding of how such empowerment may play out in different contexts of practice" (p. 8). In relation to globalisation plus and minus, the following sections may constitute aspects of a resistance to globalisation minus. Our intention is to present alternative approaches aiming towards globalisation plus.

Taking the context and the learner seriously

One characteristic of an alternative to the overly dominant globalisation minus version of mathematical competence is that teachers and learners within education systems experience competence as a wholeness, where the situation context (e.g., the workplace) is of critical importance (cf. Wedege's, 2001) conceptualisation of competence as a wholeness). The following examples of research illustrate our understanding of this version of competence, which includes taking into account the complexities of the context well beyond the settings typically found in mathematics textbooks and test situations.

The first example is a study by Johansson (2014) in which researchers followed a nursing aide (Anita) in her work at a semi-emergency department. Anita took "the observations." These occurred every four hours and included a collection of physiological parameters such as respiratory rate, heart rate, and blood pressure. As part of the institutionalised framing, Anita was expected to read a chart which clarified within which range different measurements should be in order for everything to be regarded as acceptable; otherwise, there was a need to call for a nurse or a doctor. Johansson also conducted interviews with Anita, revealing more of the complexities of the context in which mathematics was an integral part. The measurement of respiratory rate was revealed to be partly concerned with the number of breaths per minute, but included other evaluations as well. Anita explained how "17 breaths per minute" may mean that the patient was getting better, but it could also mean the opposite, or that the patient was hyperventilating, or even pretending in order to increase their dose of morphine. Johansson summarised and reflected the interview to Anita as follows:

> This I find really interesting … even this you are saying about the respiratory rate. Because you mean that we have different lungs and you cannot know how much oxygen a breath contains neither measure the volume of the lungs, so this is replaced by a feeling … that you feel what 17 means in this case.
>
> (p. 79)

Anita agreed with Johansson's interpretation, and it was clear that the numbers in the chart alone, even though the reading was accurate, were not sufficient for Anita's work. A simplistic version of accepting just the result given by chart would be typical of a PIAAC style question, whereas the way that Anita relied on her competence as a wholeness, with mathematical components, could be regarded as an example of mathematical competence in vocational settings. It simultaneously required a broad awareness of many other aspects and taking all of the complexities of the situation into account, even though the level of mathematical skills might appear quite banal. This comprehensive approach to doing mathematics at work could never be captured by what we have seen of the questions in PIAAC. Drawing on Boistrup et al. (2018), Anita's actions here could be labelled as *recontextualization of mathematics* as integrated into vocational activities (see also FitzSimons & Boistrup, 2017).

The example above emphasises that, taking the context seriously, mathematical competence in vocational settings will be understood in relation to the actual complexities of working life. Our second example is from FitzSimons (2015) who spent time teaching in a pharmaceuticals manufacturing workplace. Here, the context was able to be taken seriously since the teaching and assessment largely took place *within* the workplace context where the mathematics became meaningful in that it was made directly relevant via a "workplace study tour." This tour enabled production and warehouse workers to appreciate both the mathematics and their own roles in the work process as a whole, as well as what their colleagues were actually doing, including their hitherto unsuspected use of mathematical thinking. The outcome included "contextualised learning which valued learners' knowledge and their workplace experiences, treating them as respected partners on our mathematical and technological journey" (p. 113). From her perspective as an "outsider," FitzSimons reflected on the importance of

> recognising that (often invisible) mathematical skills actually constitute critical components in a highly regulated workplace that can affect human lives and livelihoods, and where errors can be fatal; and … respecting the full integrity of the work actually done by operators on a daily basis to show that it has far more depth than a superficial reading of the official curriculum would suggest.
>
> (p. 113)

Both examples reflect not only the importance of context but, importantly, respect for the knowledge embodied in the workers themselves. Such an approach of viewing workers' mathematics is, when taken on a general level, a foundation for globalisation plus, not least strongly connected to what Latour describes as "registering a greater number of varieties, taking into account a larger number of beings, cultures, phenomena, organisms, and people" (Latour, 2018, p. 12).

Taking the knowledge of both mathematics and vocation seriously

A characteristic feature of our alternative version of vocational mathematics competence is to take *both* the particularities of mathematics in connection to vocational activities *and* the powerful knowledge seriously (FitzSimons & Boistrup, 2017). Wheelahan (2015) emphasises this when she describes the context of VET in Anglophone countries and describes how "VET has been recast as about skills and not knowledge, and the key curricular questions—what should we teach and why?—have been reduced to the skills needed to get a job and for work" (p. 750). Sweden is another example of where such developments have taken hold (Dahl, 2014), albeit not to the same extent. Wheelahan stresses the need not only for skills, but also for theoretical knowledge in work:

> In work, students will need access to knowledge to make judgements about practice. For example, electricians need access to mathematics and not just formulas if they are to be autonomous practitioners. Childcare workers need access to theories about child development and the child in society if they are to support the children they work with and their families. VET teachers need access to theoretical knowledge about their specialist field of practice and theories of pedagogy if they are to be effective

teachers who can support students, and not merely trainers who have a repertoire of procedures that they apply in different circumstances.

(p. 753)

In Sweden, there are projects where the mathematics teacher regularly teaches together with the vocational teacher in the vocational education workshop. Such projects often reveal a stronger relationship between authentic vocational knowledge and mathematics (see, e.g., Frejd & Muhrman, 2020). A case study by Boistrup and Hällback (2022) took place in such a collaborative teaching setting. This project investigated practical and theoretical aspects (Chevallard, 2006) of *both* mathematics and vocational knowledge. Theoretical knowledge of mathematics (e.g., definitions of various geometrical objects) was expanded to concern vocations such as *Hair and makeup stylist* and *Hotel manager*.

In one of the lessons, the overall assignment was to carry out makeup (highlighting and contouring), through the adoption of triangles drawn on a face chart to represent those found in a person's face. The notion of triangles is commonly used in makeup styling, and during the class this was also emphasised from a mathematical perspective (see below). (Overall, the teachers within this project taught beyond the described limitations of the current national syllabi in Sweden (cf. Dahl, 2014; Nylund & Rosvall, 2016).) One use for the location of triangles was to create more symmetry in the face. For styling, this is a vocational theoretical notion connected to the fact that most people find symmetrical faces more appealing. In the project, the mathematics teacher also emphasised symmetry as a mathematical theoretical concept. Both kinds of understanding of symmetry constituted a foundation for the students' assignment. Other aspects in focus included the technique of highlighting and contouring (styling), along with the technique of identifying different kinds of triangles in the face and recognising their characteristics, i.e., an emphasis on mathematical knowledge. In another lesson in the same hair styling project, angles between loops of hair and the surface of the skull were paramount for the creation of certain hair styles. In these examples the mathematics included was not of a high academic level, but the level of complexity in how the students adapted and transformed the mathematics was high. Moreover, how the students gained insight into the vocational theories and techniques via their attention to mathematics also points at essential aspects of an elaborated understanding of mathematical competence as adopted in this chapter.

This styling project is a clear example of taking the knowledge of the vocation and the mathematics seriously. It challenges an understanding of mathematics as the theoretical knowledge that is *applied* to the practice of the vocation. Rather, the focus is on powerful knowledge, theoretical and practical, in both content areas. Since research like this draws on internationally adopted frameworks (e.g., Chevallard, 2006), it may be viewed as an example of globalisation plus in connection to the local context. Furthermore, the members of the project were not limited to developing human capital solely in order to serve the market, but were committed to supporting students in their mathematical and other development as competent workers and citizens in a globalised world; alongside keeping educational and other knowledge creating options open to the students. This is in stark contrast to the kind of vocational mathematics education critiqued by FitzSimons (2015), Wheelahan (2015), and others, where the focus is on atomised mathematical skills.

Taking critical citizenship seriously

Valero and Orlander (2018) problematise the role of mathematics (and science) for citizenship. They explain the idea of mathematics as an important subject in relation to the development of the intellect of the "new desirable modern citizen started forming in many countries in the change between the 19th and the 20th centuries" (p. 3). Their argument is solely connected with globalisation minus: addressing the kinds of human capital the current society needs. Clearly, this is not how we define citizenship in relation to an alternative version of vocational mathematics competence. Rather, we emphasise the specific *critical* citizenship (cf. Skovsmose, 2020), that makes it possible to connect vocational students and their potential futures, in and beyond the workplace, including "criticising existing work practices and taking responsibility for working with others to conceive, and implement where possible, alternatives" (Griffiths & Guile, 2003, p. 59).

The examples we have presented in this section offer a contrast to the modern citizen that Valero and Orlander (2018) describe. They illuminate a critical citizenship, where workers are not restricted to learning the limited mathematics that outsiders perceive is involved in vocational practices, often reflecting their own experience of school mathematics. Instead, vocational students have the opportunity to learn powerful mathematics where reflections are integral, and where mathematically derived conclusions can be questioned in relation to the particular situation at hand. In the pharmaceutical manufacturing workplace project described above, FitzSimons (2015) drew on Bernstein's (2000) framework on democracy and pedagogic rights. This offered workers the possibilities of: (a) developing a critical understanding and awareness of new possibilities beyond the intended curriculum as a condition for *confidence*; (b) developing a sense of social, intellectual, cultural, and personal *inclusion* reflected in the acknowledgement and valuing of their mathematical and other knowledge and experience; and (c) the right to democratic *participation* through, for example, understanding in a practical sense the workings of the statistics they were required to collect and/or to answer for in case of breakdown in the tightly regulated manufacturing process. Each right has the potential to support critical citizenship in and beyond the workplace.

Another example of taking critical citizenship seriously was the nursing aide Anita (Johansson, 2014) who, in line with a critical awareness of mathematics, not only relied on numbers in a chart to make judgements, but also on her own formal and informal measurements, and general perceptions. We see mathematical competence according to globalisation plus as being clearly connected to the examples in this section. This connection concerns the professional and critical judgements that vocational students will be enabled to make when they learn powerful mathematics which is connected to the complexities of their future workplaces.

Concluding discussion

Drawing on Latour's (2018) discussion of globalisation minus and plus, enabled us to reflect on globalisation going beyond neoliberalism, where citizenship in line with globalisation plus would align with critical mathematics education (Skovsmose, 2020). Globalisation minus, in contrast, allowed us to reflect on the tendencies of capitalism to converge on a narrow set of interests of the more powerful global stakeholders in the system, such as the OECD. In particular, neoliberalist manifestations of capitalism have been targeting the world of work with intentions towards greater control and consolidation of power and wealth, a critical feature of economic and political globalisation since the 1980s. A salient feature is the belief in the power of markets to determine optimal outcomes, with consequences for education generally and vocational education in particular. National governments are faced with the imperative to transform their education and training systems supposedly to make them responsive to the needs of the national economy. PIAAC and PISA play important roles in both generating the demand for change in mathematics education (through international comparisons) and in creating incentives for curricular alignment with the content that is assessed. But at what cost?

We have elaborated on both versions (minus and plus) of globalisation, through accounts of VET and mathematics education. We concur with the literature critiquing the effects of PISA and PIAAC on mathematics education (e.g., Kanes et al., 2014; Tsatsaroni & Evans, 2014). Even though the data from PIAAC may yield some useful results, our contention is that the negative political effects on curriculum and students' future options as citizens and workers outweigh any benefits of such international comparisons. Our description of an alternative conception of mathematical competence in relation to vocational education illuminated how it is possible, in a globalised world, to learn from and respect the many and varied contexts which exist, including both theoretical and practical perspectives, in line with globalisation plus.

A focus on questions found in the PIAAC questionnaire and test items shows that they undervalue and disrespect workers' personal and professional competences. In this chapter we connected these kinds of questions to globalisation minus through the imposition of testable competencies, focused on international stakeholders' perceived economic and political interests, at the expense of vocational students' and workers' personal and vocational interests. The case studies above give examples of how mathematics in the local context could often benefit from problematisation. For example, they showed that while mathematical correctness is necessary, it is not always sufficient. While PIAAC attempts to contextualise problems that are essentially testing the mathematics, surveys such as this can never be generalised to, or operate on, the local level where mathematical reasoning and results, even if 100% correct, must be interpreted within the unique context specific to the task at hand. It is at this level that the ultimate consequences, for better or for worse, are experienced. In fact, in the simplicity made necessary by adhering to statistical requirements of their assessment procedures, the PIAAC questions themselves may well convey a sense of otherness to vocational students who have rich experiences of life and work that are not reflected in them. In this chapter we have not had the space to address related issues of the intersectionality of diverse social, cultural, ethnic, language, gender and other backgrounds and current lives of students—where otherness may also be experienced while undergoing one or both forms of PIAAC assessments mentioned above. In contrast to the PISA/PIAAC model of control, FitzSimons (2011) argued for policy makers and vocational education providers to listen to the voices of both students and their teachers, among other stakeholders, and to work together "to understand what is and how things might be different in ways that empower all learners" (p. 120).

People have always worked to sustain their communities and themselves, and formal and informal vocational education will always have an important part to play. As the effects of the global pandemic and climate change have clearly demonstrated, people themselves are important as is the economy. However, the economy is nothing without people, especially those who are able to take critical perspectives, conceivably entailing mathematical considerations on human actions, including their technologies, affecting the global environment for better or for worse.

Note

1 Vocational education (and training) (VET) encompasses curricular content specifically related to trades and occupations which offer a range of services across industries in sectors such as health and personal care, construction, agriculture, resource extraction, transport, etc. VET takes place in a variety of educational settings such as schools and colleges, on-the-job, at home, or in some combination of these.

References

Avis, J. (2012). Global reconstructions of vocational education and training. *Globalisation, Societies and Education*, *10*(1), 1–11. https://doi.org/10.1080/14767724.2012.646876

Avis, J. (2019). Vocational education, transitions, marginalisation and social justice in the Nordic countries: Reflections on the special issue. *European Education Research Journal*, *18*(3), 376–384. https://doi.org/10.1177/1474904119845250

Bakker, A. (2014). Characterising and developing vocational mathematical knowledge. *Educational Studies in Mathematics*, *86*(2), 151–156. https://doi.org/10.1007/s10649-014-9560-4

Bernstein, B. (2000). *Pedagogy, symbolic control and identity: Theory, research, critique.* Rowman & Littlefield.

Boistrup, L. B., Bellander, E., & Blaesild, M. (2018). Mathematics in pre-vocational education: A model for interfaces between two different teaching contents. In A.

Rogers, B. Street, K. Yasukawa, & K. Jackson (Eds.), *Numeracy as social practice: Global and local perspectives* (pp. 76–98). Routledge.
Boistrup, L. B., & Gustafsson, L. (2014). Construing mathematics-containing activities in adults' workplace competences: Analysis of institutional and multimodal aspects. *Adults Learning Mathematics: An International Journal*, *9*(1), 7–23.
Boistrup, L. B., & Hällback, M. (2022). Designing and researching vocational mathematics education. In L. B. Boistrup & S. Selander (Eds.), *Designs in research, teaching and learning: A framework for future education* (pp. 61–81). Routledge.
Boistrup, L. B., & Henningsen, I. (2017). What can a re-analysis of PIAAC data tell us about adults and mathematics in working life? In J. Häggström, E. Norén, J. von Bommel, J. Sayers, O. Helenius, & Y. Liljekvist (Eds.), *ICT in mathematics education: The future and the realities. Proceedings of MADIF10: the tenth research seminar of the Swedish Society for Research in Mathematics Education, Karlstad, January 26–27, 2016* (pp. 101–110). SMDF.
Carvalho, L. M. (2012). The fabrications and travels of a knowledge-policy instrument. *European Educational Research Journal*, *11*(2), 172–188.
Chevallard, Y. (2006). Steps towards a new epistemology in mathematics education. In M. Bosch (Ed.), *Proceedings of the 4th conference of the European society for research in mathematics education* (pp. 21–30). CERME 4.
Dahl, J. (2014). *The problem-solving citizen.* (Licentiate thesis). Malmö University.
FitzSimons, G. E. (2011). A framework for evaluating quality and equity in post-compulsory mathematics education. In B. Atweh, M. Graven, W. Secada, & P. Valero (Eds.), *Mapping equity and quality in mathematics education* (pp. 105–121). Springer.
FitzSimons, G. E. (2014). Commentary on vocational mathematics education: Where mathematics meets the realities of people's work. *Educational Studies in Mathematics*, *86*(2), 291–305. https://doi.org/10.1007/s10649-014-9556-0
FitzSimons, G. E. (2015). Learning mathematics in and out of school: A workplace education perspective. In U. Gellert, J. Giménez Rodríguez, C. Hahn, & S. Kafoussi (Eds.), *Educational paths to mathematics. A C.I.E.A.E.M. sourcebook* (pp. 99–115). Springer. https://doi.org/10.1007/978-3-319-15410-7-5
FitzSimons, G. E. (2002a). Introduction: Cultural aspects of mathematics education. *Journal for Intercultural Studies*, *23*(2), 99–118.
FitzSimons, G. E. (2002b). *What counts as mathematics? Technologies of power in adult and vocational education.* Springer Dordrecht. https://doi.org/10.1007/0-306-47683-5
FitzSimons, G. E., & Boistrup, L. B. (2017). In the workplace mathematics does not announce itself: Towards overcoming the hiatus between mathematics education and work. *Educational Studies in Mathematics*, *95*(3), 329–349. https://doi.org/10.1007/s10649-017-9752-9
Frejd, P., & Muhrman, K. (2020). Is the mathematics classroom a suitable learning space for making workplace mathematics visible? – An analysis of a subject integrated team-teaching approach applied in different learning spaces. *Journal of Vocational Education & Training.* https://doi.org/10.1080/13636820.2020.1760337
Griffiths, T., & Guile, D. (2003). A connective model of learning: The implications for work process knowledge. *European Educational Research Journal*, *2*(1), 56–73.
Johansson, M. C. (2014). Counting or caring: Examining a nursing aide's third eye using Bourdieu's concept of habitus. *Adults Learning Mathematics*, *9*(1), 69–84.
Jurdak, M. (2020). The sociopolitical and sociocultural dimensions of migrants' adult numeracy. *ZDM, Mathematics Education*, *52*(3), 515–525.
Kanes, C., Morgan, C., & Tsatsaroni, A. (2014). The PISA mathematics regime: Knowledge structures and practices of the self. *Educational Studies in Mathematics*, *87*(2), 145–165.
Kress, G. (2009). Assessment in the perspective of a social semiotic theory of multimodal teaching and learning. In C. Wyatt-Smith & J. Cumming (Eds.), *Educational assessment in the 21st century* (pp. 19–41). Springer.

Latour, B. (2018). *Down to Earth: Politics in the new climatic regime.* Polity Press.
Mangez, E., & Hilgers, M. (2012). The field of knowledge and the policy field in education: PISA and the production of knowledge for policy. *European Educational Research Journal, 11*(2), 189–205.
Nylund, M., & Rosvall, P.-Å (2016). A curriculum tailored for workers? Knowledge organization and possible transitions in Swedish VET. *Journal of Curriculum Studies, 48*(5), 692–710. https://doi.org/10.1080/00220272.2016.1138325
Nylund, M., & Rosvall, P.-Å (2019). Vocational education, transitions, marginalisation and social justice in the Nordic countries. *European Education Research Journal, 18*(3), 271–277. https://doi.org/10.1177/1474904119838893
Organisation for Economic Co-operation and Development. (n.d.). *Sample numeracy items.* https://nces.ed.gov/surveys/piaac/sample_num.asp
Organisation for Economic Co-operation and Development. (2018). *PISA (2018)* [draft]. https://pisa2021-maths.oecd.org/files/PISA%202021%20Mathematics%20Framework%20Draft.pdf
Organisation for Economic Co-operation and Development. (2019). *Technical report of the Survey of Adult Skills (PIAAC) (3rd ed.).* OECD. https://www.oecd.org/skills/piaac/publications/PIAAC_Technical_Report_2019.pdf
Rizvi, F., & Lingard, B. (2009). The OECD and Global Shifts in Education Policy. In R. Cowen & A. M. Kazamias (Eds.), *International handbook of comparative education* (pp. 437–453). *Springer Netherlands.* https://doi.org/10.1007/978-1-4020-6403-6_28
Rosvall, P.-A., Hjelmér, C., & Lappalainen, S. (2017). Staying in the comfort zones – Low expectations in vocational education and training mathematics teaching in Sweden and Finland. *European Educational Research, 16*(4), 425–439. https://doi.org/10.1177/1474904116669154
Roth, K. (2007). Dialogue, difference and globalisation: An interview with Nicholas C. Burbules. In K. Roth & I. Gur-Ze'ev (Eds.), *Education in the era of globalization* (pp. 13–31). Springer. https://doi.org/10.1007/978-1-4020-5945-2_1
Skovsmose, O. (2020). Critical mathematics education. In S. Lerman (Ed.), *Encyclopedia of mathematics education* (pp. 154–159). Springer. https://doi.org/10.1007/978-3-030-15789-0_34
Sträβer, R. (2015). Numeracy at work: A discussion of terms and results from empirical studies. *ZDM, Mathematics Education, 47*(4), 665–674. https://dx.doi.org/10.1007/s11858-015-0689-0
Tsatsaroni, A., & Evans, J. (2014). Adult numeracy and the totally pedagogised society: PIAAC and other international surveys in the context of global educational policy on lifelong learning. *Educational Studies in Mathematics, 87*, 167–186.
Valero, P., & Orlander, A. A. (2018). Democracy and justice in mathematics and science curriculum. *Oxford Research Encyclopedia of Education.* https://dx.doi.org/10.1093/acrefore/9780190264093.013.126
Wedege, T. (2001). "Competence" as a construction in adult and mathematics education. In G. FitzSimons, J. O'Donoghue, & D. Coben (Eds.), *Adult and life-long education in mathematics: Papers from WGA6, 9th International Congress on Mathematical Education (ICME9)* (pp. 21–30). Language Australia.
Wheelahan, L. (2015). Not just skills: What a focus on knowledge means for vocational education. *Journal of Curriculum Studies, 47*(6), 750–762. https://dx.doi.org/10.1080/00220272.2015.1089942.
Yasukawa, K., Rogers, A., Jackson, K., & Street, B. V. (Eds.). (2018). *Numeracy as social practice. Global and local perspectives.* Routledge. https://dx.doi.org/10.4324/9781315269474

4 Mathematics education

A new balance between universalism and cultural diversity?

Rik Pinxten

Introduction

My contribution starts from a critical analysis of a deep seated view (or intuition?) of what mathematical knowledge amounts to, as it has developed primarily in monocultural learned communities in the past centuries. However, the teaching of mathematics is happening today in contexts which are more culturally mixed, with dramatic dropout rates for certain groups. The colonial and postcolonial export of schooling, including mathematics education, to non-western parts of the world was mostly in a top-down, with western powers deciding the content, as well as the learning procedures for humanity in general, disregarding cultural backgrounds of pupils. In the capitalist technoscience worldview of today's neoliberalism (Chronaki, 2011) and the simultaneous cultural mixing of the former colonisers' countries, this yields a lot of frustration, so-called dropout from school and socio-political exclusion of cultural minority groups in the West and of native groups elsewhere.

One way of remediating this structural segregation with or even through education (in terms of schooling) might be to recognise the changes in the worldview of the subjects of this educational policy (i.e., the students). I want to go beyond the essentialist view on different cultural traditions more or less intrinsically closed-off cultural worlds of knowledge and experience. Therefore, I take the stand that people (especially young persons) around the globe today are composing their 'cultural world' as dynamic patchworks of cognitive data, shallow or deep experiences, metaphors and images, values and ideals which originate from one's so-called native cultural tradition, as well as from western input (e.g., through schooling but also through the internet). They take elements from neighbouring contact-groups as well as from missionaries and western trained educationalists and media models (Lent, 2023).

Two clarifications are in order here: when I use 'globalisation' it refers to a normative or ideological trend of our era which aims to draw populations of the whole world into the high consumption and market perspective, pushed for by multinational corporations (J. Stiglitz). Factually, one

DOI: 10.4324/9781003130673-6

can see that certain products and ways of producing and selling them are spread all over the earth, and this creates worldwide interdependence. The ideological program might not be necessarily that of capitalist globalisation.

A politically conscious positioning in this new context invites educationalists in mathematics (and other disciplines, of course) to reconsider formerly obvious standpoints and choices: 'the other' is not a separate species which can be attacked and eliminated (through 'civilisation' or universal schooling) or preserved as a different but equally warranted perspective on reality. Neither is it a pure or isolated universe of 'otherness' that can or should be safeguarded: this is basically a romantic western idea and might further disenfranchise the 'other' in the survival struggle we are all involved in today. Moreover, the 'do-gooder' inadvertently risks helping the globalisation ideologue, since 'the other' is turned into a heritage species by them, and thus denied equality in the world of the capitalist-predator. The tradition of the 'human zoo' in ethnographic museums as well as in the World Fairs which were organised since the 19th century, testifies to this approach in western history: otherness is presented as opposed to modern humanity, and becomes a sort of subspecies that is excluded from the latter (Ben Chikha, 2017). It is a trap. For the predator, this exclusion will allow unquestioned access to resources and labour of the 'other' (Ghosh, 2021).

I take a third position: with the liberation theologists and even more so with at least one view of the defenders of a pluriverse perspective (Baker, 2023; Escobar, 2017) present-day 'others' should be seen as ever so many alternatives to both other positions. Pluriversalists will sometimes claim that different realities exist, and that cultures other than the European one cover some of these (see Escobar, 2017). This an ontological position: in that view there are several realities at the ontic level (of what there 'really is'). Different cultures are believed to feed on one of these realities exclusively. I take a more modest view: different cultures explore somewhat different intuitions and hence develop diverging cognitive views. Ontological stands make explicit what perspectives we use when we construct knowledge(s) about reality (Graeber, 2015).

My choice in this is, hence, to consider many perspectives to be potentially relevant, including the European one. Instead of rejecting other views as 'primitive' or 'underdeveloped', we should consider them to be just different. The possible links with 'European' perspectives can then be reconsidered. A correlate of this choice is that the view on the mental setup of school children today shifts: the hypothesis is that (many) people on this earth, to different degrees, develop a 'mixed' mental setup, a mixture of intuitions and hence of epistemic perspectives (Pinxten, 2016, Part II). Indeed, they are subjected to a rather uniform learning-through-schooling education, as well as to traditional media and to new virtual media. In addition, they continue to have a mix of traditional cultural input (through books, films, storytelling, local lore and rearing practices, depending on the tradition and the place). The result is that, in my view, the mental setup of the contemporary student can be captured by the dialogical self-theory (DST) (Hermans, 2001), rather than by the monocultural personality view of the past.

In my own work with Navajo Native Americans in the United States and with immigrant children in Europe I witnessed this shift towards mixed worldviews. The conclusion I draw from this development is that exporting western curricula and school formats (as is proposed by OECD, for instance) disregards all of this and becomes coercive in a colonial way. In the educational process of learning mathematics, I want to explore whether the dialogical self-theory might be a more appropriate view on the mental setup of students.

Globalisation as the trend to economically and politically install a so-called universal new dominant frame of mind can be countered by differential pedagogical approaches, which recognise and potentially fortify difference, rather than aligning to the market-oriented promotion of mental uniformity. DST may be an interesting approach here.

The status of mathematical knowledge

This contribution focuses on mathematics education. Obviously, the status of mathematical knowledge is relevant when the focus is on education. What can or should be learned? Even when different paths and types of teaching and learning would be adequate for diverging content, some clarity in these matters is welcome. Some researchers conceive of mathematics as a language (e.g., Barton, 2006), others might see it more as a type of knowledge where concepts and language are primarily forms of action (Escobar, 2017, for knowledge in general). I understand mathematics as a way of doing, and partially a technology: different cultural traditions do things like counting, measuring, estimating proportions, performing rhythm and such in a variety of ways (Pinxten, 2016). Only recently anthropologists and mathematicians combined forces to study and (modestly) compare this wealth of human knowledges: the descriptive subdiscipline of ethnomathematics (e.g., Ascher, 1991; D'Ambrosio, 1985) offers knowledge of particular techniques, concepts and uses of formal knowledge in widely diverging areas of the world.

Mathematics education today mainly uses a concept of mathematical knowledge that is exclusively and mostly unconsciously that of the learned 'western' mathematical knowledge tradition. This critical note is not original (see Freudenthal, 1970, drawing on the intuitionist tradition), but it matters when the focus is on mathematical education. Indeed, this western knowledge tradition was considered over the years to be universally true and hence to be the only right basis in globalised schooling developments. A powerful hegemonic 'watchdog' like the Organization for Economic Co-Operation and Development (OECD) tests the performance of children from any cultural background around the world through uniform PISA tests, and then urges the countries of the 'free world' to adopt the 'universal view on mathematics' with more zeal (at the expense of local mathematical practices: see the edited volume by Atweh et al., 2011). Studies of school dropout point to the ways this adoption fails, and urge particular countries to step up their efforts (OECD, 2010; Standaert et al., 2018, for Belgium).

My hypothesis is that in the present era mathematics as conceived in the West seems to be the more powerful sophisticated outgrowth of one variety of mathematical knowledge. It is this view on mathematics that is exported in schooling programs around the world. At the same time, schooling will be supplanted on pre-school understandings, procedures and imaginations of the children with little or no room for the latter (Vandendriessche & Pinxten, 2023). In this situation, dropout might teach us about the differences in the western presuppositions and those of the local cultural background. Furthermore, and apart from the ambitious statement on the possible plurality of knowledges (i.e., the pluriversality debate), there is little doubt in my mind that the recognition and actual use of local out-of-school imagination, conceptualisation and formal thought procedures could be a major bonus in education. This is opposed to a policy aiming at erasing the existing non-western views and practices, as advocated by OECD (2010, e.g., Standaert et al., 2018). Indeed, next to the free-market position of the OECD different trajectories could be chosen, allowing for more varied developments of knowledge in mathematics education (up to the pluriverse view of Escobar, 2017, and Baker, 2023). I want to explore what is possible here.

Mathematics education is a subcategory of education

I was surprised when Spanish colleagues of mine proudly announced, some thirty years ago, that they were granted a lot of research money from an international organisation for a study on literacy programs aimed at the last remnants of oral tradition in rural Spain. These colleagues considered themselves to be progressive social scientists, and their focus was 'hence' to supplant the oral culture in the villages by reading and writing for all. This would involve the discontinuation of oral traditions through schooling. At that time their fellow social scientists (psychologists and educationalists) agreed that this would be progress, as the introduction of literacy through schooling was considered worldwide to stand for human progress.

At the same time, anthropologists like Dell Hymes (1981) began to understand that socialisation through oral storytelling was different from literacy in more than just the technology used. That is to say: storytelling is always a dialogical form of relating to the world, where the storyteller interacts with their audience, adapts themes and styles, and uses local contexts to make the story more relevant for the listeners. In other words, the context is taken into account. Moreover, the storyteller and the audience are often taking turns, where attitudes, humour and multi-perspectival awareness become as important in the process as cognitive transfer. The influential linguistic anthropologist Hymes focused on this in the title of one of his books (Hymes, 1981). When he kept insisting with his Canadian Native informants on the 'truth' in this story (regardless of context or performer) an interlocutor exclaimed in despair: 'In vain I tried to tell you'. Hymes 'saw the light' then and made this cry the title of his book: learning in an oral tradition is a dialogical process, where storyteller and hearer constantly interact to grasp different aspects of the content, the circumstances, the particular flavour of the version of the storyteller, and so on.

I want to follow a similar critical analysis with regard to mathematics education here. When examining the actual tests of the recurring PISA studies, it appears that there is a unique focus in the particular capacities tested: the tests explore the abilities of children from around the world in coping with market economy's puzzles and buying and selling problems. For example, a 'general' question for the children will be to estimate what would be the clever decision: if you have $10 and you have to choose between one CD of $7and a promotion of three for the price of $10, then what is the best choice? (see e.g., OECD, 2010; Pinxten, 2016, for a detailed analysis). The test has children choose 'in the abstract', beyond any concrete context. On the basis of the children's scores on such tests, the authors urge countries to step up a particular program in mathematics education, so that the ranking of the country will be enhanced.

The belief that market-conforming thinking is equal to progress is promoted here: hence the training in mathematical abilities that are relevant for market conditions and the exclusion of any other ways of formal thought. As a next step, OECD strives for a 'universal exam' for all pupils on the basis of the results from these tests (Yolcu, 2017). The notion of a uniform, worldwide exam is clearly an ideological one. It may be denounced as authoritarian when spotted in collectivist regimes, but is uncritically decreed for the so-called free world by OECD (François, 2008). In the slipstream of such a view on mathematics education, dropout is considered to be a failure during this process: In this particular view, there seems only one right perspective on reality (the western one), which is to be implanted in the minds of children around the world, to the detriment of any other. This inexorably reminds me of the history of oral traditions referred to in a previous paragraph.

Against this globalisation-through-education trend, I point to a minority perspective in cross-cultural psychology, and more in particular to the sociocultural version of it. In the tradition of Lev Vygotsky, which was (re)introduced in the West from the 1970s on, we now have a growing series of studies recognising learning as a situated process (Lave & Wenger, 1991), where a plurality of cultural input and of social backgrounds are at work in what Lave and Wenger call 'communities of practice'. In the same vein, Michael Cole started ethnographic work on mathematics education in Liberia (Cole et al., 1971). He offered a socio-culturally sensitive synthesis in his cultural psychology (Cole, 1996): learning is culturally embedded and designed. These are attempts to break away from the dominant views on education, allowing for more than only western mathematics.

Who is today's student in mathematics classes?

Globalising market capitalism is trying to conquer the whole planet. With development programs 'western'-based textbooks and teaching methods are spreading worldwide through western government policies and by religious missions and development organisations. They train future generations from every origin in the one module of thinking that this Eurocentric cultural tradition stands for, using the reduced methodology of so-called scientific testing and assessment as a measuring procedure (Chronaki, 2011; Pinxten, 2016). But the populations of pupils and students who undergo this moulding are now diverse. Hence, we witness large numbers of dropouts. One possible reaction is then to 'blame it on the victim': this reaction can be seen in the OECD policy. The other reaction is to look at the diversity of out-of-school knowledge and experience and start mathematics classes on the basis of the latter. This is the line chosen by some recent ethnomathematics perspectives. It is important to recognise that the two reactions are rooted in different assumptions of the nature of the pupils (and of humankind) on the one hand, accompanied by diverging views on the nature of mathematical knowledge and learning on the other hand. In the latter choice, one can either lock the non-western pupil in his or her presumed 'native worldview', or one can take into account the complex and mixed setup of the present-day student and develop emancipating educational approaches from there. The first of these may easily turn into a conservative result: safeguard what is supposed to be the 'real' native world. The second prepares the student for eventual alternative political choices in or against the dominant globalisation trend. I support this choice, together with the advocates of the pluriverse (Baker, 2023; Escobar, 2017).

Since the initial critiques half a century ago (such as, Cole, Ascher, D'Ambrosio and others), I see the emergence of at least a small group of psychologists, anthropologists and mathematics educationalists who advocate that the psychological setup and the cultural pre-school knowledge of students from different backgrounds should be recognised in teaching procedures. Their emphasis is on social differences (e.g., Skovsmose & Greer, 2012) or on cultural divergences (e.g., Ascher, 1991; Cole, 1996; Lancy, 1983). On the other hand, these same authors and some mathematicians questioned the context independence of mathematics itself. They would then advocate that a broader notion of formal thinking should be focused on in the classroom to allow for better and more successful mathematics education (e.g., Gay & Cole, 1967; Gerdes, 2014; Vandendriessche & Pinxten, 2023). Recently, with the decolonising literature of the past decade, we have a better understanding of what a mixed mental setup amounts to: hence, the choice against a universalistic mathematics education and for a pluriverse alternative. Students may hold the holistic ontology (or worldview) that sees humans as 'living in intrinsic interaction with other phenomena of so-called non-western vintage', while western students would stick to a dualist worldview (with nature versus humans/culture, object versus subject, etc.). But today, the former student will likely integrate data, procedures and such from western science as well. To develop an adequate theoretical frame that recognises mixed and/or plural worldviews in humans, I turn to the dialogical self theory (DST).

Focusing on western subjects the psychotherapist (Hermans, 2001) developed an approach in which the 'modern' person is pictured as a mixed and partially incoherent personality: she or he is a believer to some extent, but also a person who thinks of nature as a complex of forces in different types of relationships. Hermans (2001) calls this 'modern' person a 'dialogical self': in order to live a more or less structured and enjoyable life this person organises a regular or even a constant dialogue between these different aspects of personhood in order to find provisional balanced definitions of their personality. With time shifts will occur: the person stops practising mindfulness and joins a group that has occasional 'raves', for example. The constant internal dialogue between aspects or dimensions of personhood is the motor that keeps the person sane. All this, however, strikingly contrasts in the West with a long history of looking at individuals as consistent, monolithic persons, with a coherent worldview. Hermans (2001) focuses on European subjects. In other parts of the world as well other mixtures are obtained, i.e., between western and 'native' elements.

DST has been the subject of critical analysis recently: it is situated in the older tradition of dialogical theories such as Bakhtin (Chronaki, 2009), adapted to the present world context. On a series of criteria (relevance, philosophical tenets, empirical testing, political bias, etc.) DST has been screened. It needs more empirical study, but apart from that it seems to offer a good starting point to look at a continuing diversification of worldviews in the de facto globalising world (Suszek, 2017). It possibly offers conceptual tools that picture the subject differently than the standard western biased so-called 'naïve subject' of psychological tests. That is the main reason I want to turn to DST, to enable the researcher to look at students through a more dynamic and diversified lens to worldviews, rather than the supposedly consistent western subject. Stating this it is of course important to be conscious of ideological traps: the DST may allow scholars to start thinking about worldview in a more diverse way, but it will not necessarily value or respect diversity in a deeper sense. Indeed, it might trigger small community markets for some privileged groups only. My point is only that Hermans' view allows for a new perspective on diversity in worldviews, useful for the educator.

How general is 'mixture' in mental setups?

As far as I know no systematic comparative research has been conducted mapping the diversity of worldviews and learning traditions, yielding conclusive results on a global scale. Still, indicators abound. A first and most important given is that urban life has become the dominant way of settlement recently. Some two centuries ago about 3% of humanity lived in urban contexts; around 1900 more or less 10% of the world's population could be found in cities. Today there are just over 60% and the trend is not likely to be reversed (Castells, 2002). Urban growth is always caused by migration (which happens for a variety of reasons: war, climatic changes, colonisation, etc.). Hence, urban growth always implies cultural mixture. In the past this was often migration from rural areas towards a historic city; today migration is across thousands of miles (by labour migrants, refugees for war and for climate change). Next to and accompanying urbanisation, globalisation of industry and trade are raging, and tourism has become the third major economic drive of today. All this allows for a serious reconsideration of the mental setup of westerners, as of everyone else in the de facto 'interdependent' world we are living in. What does this entail for the mental setup of humans? I point to a small sample of partial studies.

Empirical data are not abundant, but they underscore that trends toward 'mixed' worldviews are emerging with adolescents and young adults in different parts of the world:

- In a rare comparative study, Kronjee (2006) makes the point that American inspired lifestyles become dominant in the United States and in Europe, yielding a different status for religions. The latter become a surplus provided additional choices in life (death, birth, marriage) rather than being the foundation for major questions on the meaning of life, or on issues of quality of life (choice of jobs, partner, family planning, sex, etc.). On the other hand, some groups seem to withdraw to a stricter religious or life stance perspective, yielding a growth of fundamentalist groups who aim for political power. In a somewhat similar line of thought Luckmann (2003) argues that the privatisation of religion in Europe (turning religious choice into a private issue rather than a family or community one) produces the co-existence of various stands next to each other. A recent attempt to sketch a general overview is Lent (2023).
- Examples of similar studies could be multiplied, but I will only mention one more study, expanding the focus beyond Europe and allowing to appreciate the role of the urban factor. A study by anthropologist Fleischer (2007) shows how young adult affluent Chinese urbanites are instantiating a major shift in Chinese society today. Their choice for a home, a neighbourhood and a circle of friends and acquaintances are rapidly being determined by lifestyle values, rather than family or religious tradition. Fleischer estimates that this trend is so pervasive that it will alter Chinese society in a

fundamental way: we may be witnessing the birth of a dual society with one rural society continuing to be ordered by tradition and one urban society structured by cosmopolitan lifestyle formats.

- Together with the former trends one witnesses the growth of small pockets of fundamentalist religious groups in different parts of the world: white supremacists in the West are more often than not fundamentalist Christians as well. Some powerful American lobbies seem to try and unite these scattered groups today: Qanon, Ordo Iuris, etc. (see Höhne & Meireis, 2020). Such lobbies aim at making coherence and consistency principles dominant again: in the factual world, the majority of people live in ever more loose and mixed worldviews.

All the above examples are meant to underscore the claim that what is seen in them is not a sort of retreat in one's own traditional ways, but rather the emergence of a mixture of science and technology together with traditional ideological/religious values and ideas. In order to grasp what is going on in present-day minds – both the worldview shoppers and the fundamentalists – I suggest we can better make use of Hermans' (2001) notion of dialogical self, rather than describe any of these developments in terms of 'pure or consistent cultural identities' that are handed to us in the rather colonially tainted views of the past. The main reason for my suggestion is that dialogical self principally starts from diversity (or pluriversality as it was called lately), instead of the universalising view of older perspectives.

Applying 'dialogical self' in mathematics education

In my perspective, such a dialogical view on personhood is more likely to be applicable to people worldwide than the uni-dimensional, consistent or monolithic views from the past. My claim is that the phenomenon of (mildly) 'split personality' is not only the case in westerners, but also in those peoples who went through a long period of colonisation and now find themselves in a world of dependencies and identities that are deeply mixed. If this claim holds water, then a perspective such as Hermans' (2001) DST might be a good starting point to develop educational projects, since it drops the rule of (logical) consistency as a self-evident principle. I propose to think about the pupil and student in mathematics classes nowadays within this frame of reference: pluriversality is a fact (see Pinxten, 2018, for empirical data from six different organisations in Europe and elsewhere) and education should recognise and respect this in the schooling programs offered. This implies on the one hand that we should stop speaking about 'the Navajo' or 'the Bantu' or whatever community as closed-in cultural identities, but rather see them as a dynamic mixture of influences and intuitions, some of them older and some the result of more recent and quite engaging contacts and clashes with Eurocentric and other (e.g., Chinese) import. Furthermore, it implies that we might best start rethinking mathematics education by addressing such mixed, complex and potentially dialogical personalities. It is likely that this frame of reference could be used across the board, yielding different mixtures and dialogues in diverging cases, including both contemporary western and culturally 'other' children.

How could the dialogical-self approach work in this direction? Hermans (2001) states that 'postmodern' individuals hold particular beliefs and join in groups with specific rules and action procedures without using any universal, let alone consistent frame for all concrete actions and engagements. The consequence of this sort of behaviour is that 'odd things form a pool together'. Take the example of belief in a transcendental world where the souls of the dead would reside in some sort of after world because 'there is more than just mortal life'. At the same time the believer can engage in a thoroughly materialistic scientific worldview, which obviously contradicts the former belief: nothing can be observed of that sort, so the belief of an afterlife should be held to be false. Moreover, the same individual will participate in one of the popular semi-Buddhist sessions of meditation, which is again rather inconsistent with the basic attitude of obeying Christians, and so on. What individuals have developed over the past decennia in order to keep all these balls in the air was a constant inner negotiation or dialogue: e.g., claiming that the afterlife belief and the Newtonian worldview are not conflicting, but should be seen as juxtaposed, with natural and sacred time as somehow different, hardly connecting realities. This was considered to be heretic in the old days, but is subject to the inner dialogue now. Moreover, the individual will drop some and adopt other beliefs and practices during a lifetime. Hence, conscious work on one's 'dialogical self' substitutes for the consistent frame offered by the church for most urbanites today. And the devout life of two or three generations ago is looked upon as an exotic relic of the past (which is actually the gist of most arguments on religious zealots today by 'modern' minds). We do not have to go into the truth or (in)consistency of such beliefs, attitudes or processes. It suffices to recognise that they live in the contemporary person. That is the perspective. Similar mixing processes are at work today with people living in communities that used to be regarded as isolated, native groups.

When I apply this perspective in mathematics education, an interesting horizon opens. On the one hand, we have very substantial knowledge about the nature of cognitive processes that are involved in western mathematics and education. The intuitionist school of thought (starting with Erlangen mathematicians like Dingler, 1933, and worked out in the Amsterdam school of which Freudenthal, 1970, was the heir), and the later social science approach to mathematical thinking (Davis & Hersh, 1981; Restivo, 1992) have given us basic insights in the 'worldview' of this type of knowledge. On the other hand, a series of detailed studies on counting and calculating traditions in several other cultures of the world can be found in the ethnomathematics literature (e.g., Ascher, 1991; Barton, 2006). Applying the frame of 'dialogical self' to mathematics education can then amount to combining insights from both lines of study into curricula and teaching materials. I give an example from my own field experiences to show in detail how this works. But, obviously, recent overviews are available and more are in the pipeline, which take similar stands (Barton, 2006; Bishop et al., 2015; Pinxten et al., 1990).

The case of Navajo geometry classes. In practice, I see a series of consecutive steps.

a *Gathering ethnographic material on the pre-school background of the group of pupils/students:*

Chee, a pseudonym for a Navajo boy, aged seven, wanders through canyons for two or three days, with a herd of sheep and goats and his dog. No roads, no signs, no school knowledge: Chee had followed this trajectory maybe ten times, when he learned to recognise each rock and each little dip and grassy spot along the way. His father had discussed the trajectory with him, each time he reached home again. Chee had learned to take his time. If something would happen to him or to the herd on this kind of trip, there was no way of saying how he would manage to reach the hooghan (home) again. So, he learned to take his time and spaced his trip according to the water places, the rocks and the tree formations along the way. Every time he had to choose a particular path, or anytime a passage known to him would be blocked by something, he carefully looked around at the big rocks and reoriented his herd by meticulous reference to the surroundings. He got lost sometimes, since canyons are tricky and turn and twist without your noticing it (For more ethnographic detail: Farella, 1983; Pinxten & François, 2011; Pinxten et al., 1983; Pinxten et al., 1990).

The boy in the example has notions of orientation, of distance (in terms of walking for parts of the day), of markers in the landscape with reference to the sun and the stars, and so on. He recognises paths crossed, positions of nearness and 'farness', and other non-metric notions. And Chee has words and descriptions for all of this, although his pre-school knowledge is not abstract or sophisticated in a schoolish sense. Still, this is the kind of knowledge Chee brings to school, in his own language (Navajo or Dinetah), which is a 'verb language'. That is to say, this language uses no genuine nouns, nor a verb 'to be' (but several verbs 'to go'), and so on.

This ethnographic case illustrates the mixed situation of any child in this community: (s)he has spatial knowledge with survival value in a landscape of canyons, without roads and full of natural hazards. When coming to school all this, and the non-Indo-European language of the child, seems to lack any relevance for the cognitive world of this imported institution. The child will either 'learn by heart' what the school curriculum presents or drop out sooner or later. In a similar way this was reported with immigrant children in Europe: my research unit observed that children interfered during the lessons by systematically adding (in Turkish for this case) supplementary comments to the talk of the teacher. We called this the 'peer group mode of interaction', as a third line next to the 'child mode' (referring to the home culture) and the 'pupil mode' (expressing school knowledge and attitudes) (Sierens & Verlot, 1997).

b *Design of relevant teaching material with mathematical (geometric) relevance:*
On the basis of this sort of ethnographic knowledge I designed several relevant topics for the geometry classes: walking through canyons while herding sheep, building and inhabiting a hooghan (or traditional and ceremonial building), making a rodeo ground (since becoming a rodeo man is the dream of many boys on the reservation), weaving tapestry (with its 'geometric' designs), and so on. All of these are well-known contexts for the children and cherished by them. I developed explicit curriculum material to use these known culturally tainted parts of knowledge in educational courses on mathematics (primary schools). The dialogical structure of the pupil's mind is taken into account in the sense that the out-of-school notions and learning styles are recognised and used in the teaching process: what is known by the child is used in a respectful way in the new setting, the school. It becomes material for explicit mathematical education (with gradually more abstract notions in Navajo made up and used in the classroom by the Navajo teachers), thus offering helpful means to the pupil to communicate or negotiate between at least two worldviews (the pre-school and the school perspective).

c *Deliberation on technical terms:*
A short meeting with the teachers at primary school level made clear that in the bicultural schools such curriculum material could be used, provided discussions to identify the concepts and linguistic terms took place beforehand. In a separate session (where I was not invited: language is as impactful as action for the Navajo, hence isolating and 'defining' terms are a significant and highly 'laden' enterprise) a set of some fifteen 'geometric terms' were construed and agreed upon by the Navajo teachers to serve as newly construed technical terms for the geometry teaching. In that way 'line', 'corner' and such were circumscribed in Navajo terms (based on verb stems) to be used exclusively in the context of mathematics classes. Needless to say, the dialogical exercise was at the forefront of the negotiations amongst the teachers. They had to use terminology in the native language and adapt it in such a way that it would hold enough of the local connotations and at the same time allow for its specific (re)use in the mathematics classes. Obviously, this partially happens in a western class as well: when I learn the notion of 'line' in natural language (in Flemish, English, etc.) I refer first to the path I can create by walking in a continuous way, or by drawing an unbroken trace on a page, and so on. From that intuitive notion of line, I then learn to 'abstract' and conceive of 'a line'

in mathematics as a continuous concatenation of points. Of course, in my Flemish class I share the same linguistic and cognitive world as a pupil and as a mathematician.

For the Navajo children this is more complicated and engaging: it means that they have to make the step from a way of going/walking in their language towards a way of walking 'in their mind' more like a westerner (with detached, abstract 'entities'), without ever seeing a line as a 'thing'. For the latter no word is available, because that is not the way you think and speak in a 'world of events'. They will thus land on a particular form and aspect of a verb to go, which is decided upon by the teachers to be reserved for 'line' in the math class. This is not farfetched: in another 'verb language' like classical Chinese it is not strange for a linguist and anthropologist, for example, that one can find a rather well developed branch of algebra, but no geometry amongst the learned traditions (Needham, 1965). The structure of the pre-school language carries with it another intuitive knowledge of the world than in the Indo-European languages. Pupils do not evolve towards the western notions, leaving behind their native concepts. Rather, they add on another perspective, thus broadening their knowledge horizon.

d *Design of progressive steps towards abstraction:*

At this final stage, we find a second clearly dialogical exercise in the minds of teachers and pupils from this other cultural tradition, namely one between aspects and items of language and knowledge of native Navajo and of 'white American' origin. One example, which translates in exercises as well, is worth mentioning here. Since boys are drawn to rodeo on the reservation, just like boys in other places go for soccer or basketball, I worked this context into the curriculum material. It offers a great number of geometric insights: e.g., the space where the action takes place is oval or circular, and not a square or rectangle. Why is that so? Obviously, when the cowboy would ride inside a square, he could be caught in a corner by the bull without any possibility of escape. Oval or circular spaces allow for escape. This is just one of many aspects of the rodeo facility, a 'thing' for the white person, but a characteristic of action in the Navajo perception. On the basis of such observations children constructed a scale model (again using measurements) of a rodeo-ground in the classroom, using waste material like cardboard, sticks and ropes, together with class furniture. Along the way they learned many things: the need to generalise (which led them to the technical terms the teachers agreed upon), testing of proportions, and so on. Apart from being a lot of fun, these sorts of classes allowed for an explicit transition from playing and experiencing toward the adoption of abstract notions and terms. The dialogue they entertained within themselves was that between Navajo concepts and terminology on the one hand, and formal thinking and using technical terms which offered bridges to 'white' curriculum material on the other hand.

In other classes the construction of a hooghan (which is in fact also a replica of the cosmological relationships and entities: earth and nadir, sky and zenith, and so on) was undertaken. Of course, children know about the hooghan in a rather intuitive, often implicit way from ceremonial activities and from living in these spaces at home. What the use of this out-of-school knowledge in the teaching process does is to help learn the technical terms and the abstract notions, which prove to be instrumental in any particular context, and using different sorts of material, size and so on. Again, the transition from local knowledge to formal reasoning and technical terminology is made explicitly and insightfully through the 'internal dialogue' of the pupil: the teachers draw on both 'ways' all the time, as they say, namely the 'Navajo way' and the 'anglo way' (white American) that are presented to the child in different degrees and forms. Also, the actions of measuring and positioning get generalised when making them explicit in the lesson: the construction of any hooghan is started in practice by marking the cardinal directions by four poles, around a centre. From there the poles will be bent over and attached to each other in the centre at a height of two or more meters, forming an elementary dome structure. Then the 'wall' will be formed by placing poles one on top of the other (ideally 12) between the poles and all around in a horizontal plane, and the roof tops the whole by placing beams in a circular movement so that only a smoke hole towards the zenith is left open. Again, it is clear that children have seen and maybe participated in these actions somewhere; now they are the principal actors and learn to think about their doings in technical terms. In a second move they can then draw on the basis of the latter, and vary the size and precise form of hooghans they want to draw or build.

All of this pedagogical work is clearly very much in the line of thinking of 'realist teaching procedures' as advocated by Freudenthal (1970) and Dingler (1933). It explicitly breaks away from the rationalistic tradition of New Math, which claims that mathematics is one and purely abstract in nature, to be taught according to the cognitive setup (the 'formal logic') of the mathematicians working in these traditions. Obviously, initiatives such as the Rock Point and the Rough Rock bicultural schools on the Navajo reservation (which I worked with on this project) are exceptional, dealt with under the Title 7 program of the US educational policy (allowing for privately funded schools with a more experimental character).

When I presented my plans for research to a school board of the bicultural school of Rock Point, Arizona (in 1976), to get their permission to actually start my research, the 'illiterate' chairperson of the board had the translator telling me that they had bought curriculum material from a white salesperson. It proved to be a New Math package of the 1960s for the six years of primary school, starting with set theoretical notions. Of course, set theory is one of the most abstract (non-empirical) subdisciplines of western mathematics. The chairperson said that experience taught the board that this led to serious misunderstanding by the pupils. He understood that my research might be relevant for this problem, so if I would address their problem I would be allowed to carry on.

The curriculum booklet on 'Navajo geometry' (Pinxten et al., 1990) is founded on the philosophy of Freudenthal, but integrates the intercultural sensibility as well. I did not eliminate 'native' notions, but allowed for access to western concepts next to and linked up with the former. Thus, the teachers and the pupils were actually invited to act as dialogical selves, using their out-of-school knowledge and language and translating it to a large degree through insightful steps into more formal ways of reasoning and problem solving that are forms of geometric thinking. There was no sign of DST at that time, but it was a revelation to me when I encountered it many years later, based in a different discipline (namely psychological therapy). With the present contribution I invite researchers to look at this sort of approach: it offers a means to teachers and pupils to negotiate and develop a dialogue between the two 'cultures' or worldviews they have to cope with in the school context. It is my belief that the use of these means will help to remedy the gap or dropout in both a respectful and indeed enriching way. However, follow-up studies will be needed.

A last comment is necessary: the procedure of teaching or curriculum practice as I explained above can be used in different ways. It can be a means to supplant the native views and terminology with western notions and procedures (see the OECD, 2010). That approach is defended by adherents of the superiority of western culture. However, in the respectful dialogical view advocated above, it can be worked out to enhance the strength of native groups in an open-minded and respectful decolonised view on intercultural coexistence in a world that has become profoundly interdependent today. In that way a dialogical perspective on persons, translated in diverse educational projects like the one referred to above, will – at a more general level – trigger genuine pluriversality in the complex and interdependent world we enter today.

Conclusion

In this contribution I take the stand that, as an anthropologist, I see the growing relevance for survival in a global world of mathematical competence. At the same time, dropout rates from mathematics classes are a well-publicised issue today, with the urgent advice by the dominant western organisations (first and foremost the OECD) that a uniform and rather compulsory policy on mathematics teaching should be stepped up through better (i.e., western based) schooling worldwide. My critique is that these stands represent uncritical uni-directional, colonialist views in presumably post-colonial times. Adherents claim that western knowledge is universal and intrinsically better than any other or so-called underdeveloped views. What happens here, I claim, is the 'universalizing' of local procedures and contents of one tradition (the western one) at the detriment of any other human tradition. That is an ideological move of recent vintage (maybe five centuries), which goes hand in hand with a political-economic order (Lent, 2023). For mathematics education this comes down to the implementation of neo-colonial and market thinking worldwide.

The alternative I advocate is to look at the mental setup and the traditional knowledge insights (worldview, cognitive strategies, and so on) of teachers and pupils/students in different parts of the world. The claim is that they are, in a variety of ways, mixed in the present era. Thus, pupils/students can best be seen as 'dialogical selves' (or in a somewhat different form as 'hybrid identities', Chronaki, 2009), rather than monocultural, so-called traditional thinkers. Hence, mathematics teaching can best take into account this out-of-school knowledge and build curriculum material and teaching procedures in such a way that they help the pupil/student in the dialogical process that learning is actually becoming. Such a perspective is shown at work in the case of a Navajo geometry teaching experiment I was once enabled to set up.

References

Ascher, M. (1991). *Ethnomathematics: A multicultural view of mathematical ideas*. Chapman and Hall/CRC.

Atweh, B., Graven, M., Secada, W., & Valero, P. (Eds.). (2011). *Mapping equity and quality in mathematics education*. Springer.

Baker, M. (2023). The Western mathematics and the ontological turn: Ethnomathematics and cosmotechnics for the pluriverse. In E. Vandendriessche & R. Pinxten (Eds.), *Indigenous knowledge and ethnomathematics* (pp. 243–276). Springer.

Barton, B. (2006). *The language of mathematics*. Springer.

Ben Chikha, C. (2017). *Zoo humain*. Lannoo Campus.

Bishop, A., Tan, H., & Barkatsas, T. N. (Eds.). (2015). *Diversity in mathematics education: Towards inclusive practices*. Springer International Publishing.

Castells, M. (2002). *Conversations with Manuel Castells*. Blackwell.

César, M., & Kumpulainen, K. (Eds.). (2009). *Social interactions in multicultural settings*. Sense.

Chronaki, A. (2009). An entry to dialogicality in the maths classroom: Encouraging hybrid learning identities. In M. César & K. Kumpulainen (Eds.), *Social interactions in multicultural settings* (pp. 117–143). Brill.

Chronaki, A. (2011). Disrupting 'development' as the quality/equity discourse: Cyborgs and subalterns in school technoscience. In B. Atweh, M. Graven, W. Secada, & P. Valero (Eds.), *Mapping equity and quality in mathematics education* (pp. 3–19). Springer.

Chronaki, A. (Ed.). (2017). *Mathematics education and life at times of crisis. MES 9 conference proceedings*. Volos, Greece: University of Thessaly Press.

Cole, M. (1996). *Cultural psychology*. Harvard University Press.

Cole, M., Gay, J., Glick, J., & Sharp, D. (1971). *The cultural context of learning and thinking*. Methuen.

Columbus, A. (Ed.). (2017). *Advances in psychological research*. New Science Publishers.

D'Ambrosio, U. (1985). Ethnomathematics and its place in the history and pedagogy of mathematics. *For the Learning of Mathematics*, *5*(1), 44–48.

Davis, P., & Hersh, R. (1981). *The mathematical experience*. Birkhäuser Press.

Dingler, H. (1933). *Einführing in die Geometrie*. Schmitt.

Escobar, A. (2017). *Designs for the pluriverse*. Duke University Press.
Farella, J. (1983). *The main stalk. Navajo philosophy*. University of New Mexico Press.
Fleischer, F. (2007). "To choose a house means to choose a lifestyle." The consumption of housing and class-structuration in urban China. *City & Society*, *19*(2), 287–311.
François, K. (2008). *Politiek van de wiskunde* [Politics of mathematics]. VUB Press.
Freudenthal, H. (1970). *Mathematics as an educational task*. Reidel.
Gay, J. & Cole, M. (1967). *The new mathematics and an old culture. A study of learning among the Kpelle of Liberia*. Holt, Rhinehart & Winston.
Gerdes, P. (2014). *Ethnomathematics and education in Africa*. ISTEG.
Ghosh, A. (2021). *The nutmeg's curse*. University of Chicago Press.
Graeber, D. (2015). Radical alterity is just another way of saying "reality" a reply to Eduardo Viveiros de Castro. *HAU: Journal of Ethnographic Theory*, *5*(2), 1–41.
Hermans, H. J. (2001). The dialogical self: Toward a theory of personal and cultural positioning. *Culture & Psychology*, *7*(3), 243–281.
Höhne, F., & Meireis, T. (Eds.). (2020). *Religion and neo-nationalism in Europe*. Nomos.
Hymes, D. (1981). *In vain I tried to tell you*. University of Pennsylvania Press.
Kronjee, G. (2006). De religieuze transformatie en de sociale cohesie. In W. B. H. J. van de Donk, A. P. Jonkers, G. J. Kronjee, & R. J. J. M. Plum (Eds.), *Geloven in het publieke domein [Belief in the public domain]* (pp. 67–88). Amsterdam UP.
Lancy, D. (1983). *Cross-cultural studies in cognition and mathematics*. Academic Press.
Lave, J., & Wenger, E. (1991). *Situated learning: Legitimate peripheral participation*. Cambridge University Press.
Lent, J. (2023). *The web of meaning*. Profile Books.
Luckmann, T. (2003). Transformations of religion and morality in modern Europe. *Social Compass*, *50*(3), 275–285.
Needham, J. (1965). *Science and civilization in China. Volume II*. Cambridge University Press.
Organization for Economic Co-Operation and Development. (2010). *Educating teachers for diversity: Meeting the challenge, educational research and innovation*, OECD Publishing, https://doi.org/10.1787/9789264079731-en.
Pinxten, R. (2016). *Multimathemacy: Anthropology and mathematics education*. Springer.
Pinxten, R. (2018). Cosmopolitics and the dialogical self. *Educação Unisinos*, *22*(4), 243–249.
Pinxten, R., & François, K. (2011). Politics in an Indian canyon? Some thoughts on the implications of ethnomathematics. *Educational Studies in Mathematics*, *78*, 261–273.
Pinxten, R., van Dooren, I., & Harvey, F. (1983). *Anthropology of space: Explorations into the natural philosophy and semantics of the Navajo*. University of Pennsylvania Press.
Pinxten, R., van Dooren, I., & Soberon, E. (1990): *Toward a Navajo Indian geometry*. KKI Books. Original work published 1987
Restivo, S. (1992). *Mathematics in society and history: Sociological inquiries* (Vol. 20). Kluwer.
Rosenthal, R. (1966). *Experimenter effects in behavioral research*. Appleton-Century-Crofts (enlarged edition 1976).
Sierens, S., & Verlot, M. (1997). *Intercultural education (Intercultureel Onderwijs). CULTUURSTUDIE 3*. Steunpunt IO.
Skovsmose, O., & Greer, B. (Eds.). (2012). *Opening the cage: Critique and politics of mathematics education*. Sense Publishers.
Standaert, R., Troch, F., Peeters, I., & Stroobants, I. (2018). *Leren en onderwijzen*. Acco.

Suszek, H. (2017). Critique of dialogical self theory. *Advances in Psychology Research, 131*, 97–138.

Vandendriessche, E., & Pinxten, R. (Eds.). (2023). *Indigenous knowledge and ethnomathematics*. Springer.

Yolcu, A. (2017). Historicizing "Math for all". In A. Chronaki (Ed.), *Mathematics education and life at times of crisis. MES 9 conference proceedings* (Vol. 2, pp. 1011–1022). University of Thessaly.

5 Sharing conceptual gifts by bringing into dialogue sociopolitical mathematics education, decolonial thought, and critical global citizenship education

Dalene M. Swanson and Kate le Roux

Introduction

This edited volume raises timely questions about the (im)possibilities for more just, sustainable presents and futures, particularly in respect of the confluence of discourses relating to mathematics and mathematics education, 'globalisation', and 'citizenship'. Mathematics education scholars within the sociopolitical often illustrate how such a confluence commonly (re)produces neoliberal interests in framings of the social, economic, political, and ecological in reference to mathematics education. They also demonstrate how dominant discourses of exclusion are perpetuated under a banner of inclusion, with respect to mathematical knowledges ('global' vs. 'local'), and of mathematical knowers ('citizens' vs. 'non-citizens'). In this chapter, we pursue the possibilities and limitations afforded by this confluence. Our central argument is that, given the historical constitution of Mathematics as a hubristic discipline that projects a neutral, universal, recontextualising and certain 'gaze' on the world, and Mathematics education as recruiting 'educationally' the student, teacher, and researcher, that is, the mathematical 'citizen', to possess such a gaze, we cannot begin to animate the realisable potential of our reimaginings if we think entirely within Mathematics education itself. Rather, we assert the need to generate, anew, a boundary-crossing praxis. The possibility we offer takes the form of a relational, *opening*, *glocalising* praxis (Swanson, 2011), enacted with a disposition of *reflexivity* and of *reciprocity*, the latter involving *giving* with critical responsibility, and *receiving* humbly. For our reimaginings, we think from 'decolonial' thought, predominantly through the work of Mbembe (2021), and critical global citizenship education (CGCE), in dialogue with sociopolitical mathematics education. With this thinking, we offer a sense of what it could look like if mathematics education were to listen reflexively and receive with humility.

In the section *(Im)possibilities in the confluence of Mathematics, Mathematics education, 'globalisation', and 'citizenship'*, we introduce the specific concerns that inform our contribution, before exploring the possibilities of reimagining mathematics education, 'global'-'local' relations, and the mathematical 'citizen' in the section *Towards possibilities for dialogue across conceptual*

DOI: 10.4324/9781003130673-7

boundaries. In the section *Selecting conceptual knowledge domains for our boundary-crossings*, we explain our choice of theoretical knowledge domains that we employ for our dialogue with sociopolitical mathematics education. The final sections constitute the substance of the chapter. Here, we present our reimaginings of praxis at the confluence of dominant Mathematics education discourses, 'globalisation', and 'citizenship'. But firstly, we clarify our use of terminology employed thus far and within the chapter as a whole. We follow Green (2020) by using *Mathematics* with a capital 'M' (similarly, Science and Technology), to denote knowledge that has been constituted as authoritative and a universal 'truth' in successive processes of global coloniality, modernity, and development. By mathematics we mean a plurality of changing historical and sociopolitical knowledge practices that have been constituted as 'mathematical'. Our use of *Mathematics education* recognises the role of education in producing the Mathematical knower, the Mathematical citizen, and consequently in this process, the unknower and uncitizen.

(Im)possibilities in the confluence of Mathematics, Mathematics education, 'globalisation', and 'citizenship'

Recent events have highlighted the paradoxical, simultaneously interconnected-disconnected, local-global, mobile-enclosed context that characterises the contemporary world (Mbembe, 2021). These events include complex challenges related to climate change, biodiversity loss, heightened conflict and migration, burgeoning global inequalities between 'locals', and the increase in 'totalitarian democracies' (Talmon, 1952). Euromodern Mathematics, and the 'mathematical citizen', are being called on to 'solve' these noted global challenges, yet not without legitimate concerns being raised about the assumed straight-forwardness of such an approach and the difficulties that become evident through the political alliances created in such a manoeuvre. Such alliances raise the question of what is at stake when Mathematics education discourses and contemporary discourses on 'globalisation' and 'citizenship' are brought into dialogue with each other. These concerns form the motivations behind this chapter, and also reflect similar concerns in recent scholarship (e.g. the Special Issue edited by Chronaki & Yolcu, 2021). In this respect, this scholarship builds on the work of mathematics education scholars within the sociopolitical.[1]

Taken together, this scholarship draws our attention to the way in which a Euromodern Mathematics, with positivist framings as universal, neutral, and certain, has been used unquestioningly in action in Science and Technology (Skovsmose, 2005). Euromodern Mathematics has 'gifted' the world a 'black box' in the form of a supposedly singular 'global' knowledge form that casts a recontextualising 'gaze' over all the 'locals' of the world (e.g. Dowling, 1998; Greer & Mukhopadhyay, 2012; Skovsmose, 2016; Swanson, 1998, 2005). This gaze constitutes complex challenges as easily solvable through technicist, but also 'socially good' and messianic, applications within Mathematics (education) itself (Pais, 2012; Popkewitz, 2001; Swanson, 2004; Valero, 2008).

Mathematics education often recruits students, teachers and researchers, as its citizenry, into particular identities (Swanson, 1998; 2004). Much of the time, through recontextualising 'real-world' practices into Mathematics, Mathematics education promotes its own relevance. This 'relevance' is often constituted as a 'social good', even as it mainly serves economic interests. Mathematics education in this mode acts to (re)produce 'human capital', that is to say, it *citizenises* those (student, teacher and researcher) who are constituted as *belonging* in this Mathematics community on account of possessing 'the knowledge', 'skills', and 'competencies' of such a Mathematical gaze (Popkewitz, 2004; Swanson, 2004; Valero, 2008; Yolcu, 2021), and *decitizenises* those that are constituted as not belonging, based on characteristics outside of Mathematics, but made to be relevant to Mathematics education, such as race, class, gender, and other social differences. We may recognise this process as the *pedagogising of difference* and the *social construction of disadvantage* (Swanson, 1998, 2004, 2005).

Sociopolitical mathematics education reveals how these dominant Mathematics and Mathematics education discourses mask the social, economic, political, and environmental (as opposed to ecological) interests that they continue to serve in successive processes of global coloniality (e.g. Cabral & Baldino, 2019; Ernest, 2016; Nikolakaki, 2016; Skovsmose, 2016). Similarly, Skovmose's notion of Mathematics in action highlights the role of Mathematics in formatting the world in ways that often, overtly or inadvertently, serve to (re)produce the legitimacy of market capitalism. For the decolonial thinker, Mbembe (2021), the contemporary world is constituted in Economic terms, as 'invisible entities such as derivatives and finance capital' (p. 19). In the process, we are witnessing the constitution of a new 'global Mathematical citizen': an 'ideal citizen' for the economic ambitions of one 'local', the nation state, often with privileged access to a transnational, globalised world through Mathematics. This mathematical knower is a rational, responsible, hard-working, self-managing, mobile and 'tolerant' 'global citizen', with particular Mathematical knowledge, 'skills' and 'competencies' (e.g. Aguilar & Zavaleta, 2012; Gamal & Swanson, 2018; Pais & Valero, 2011; Swanson, 2011). In the process, the violence in the hierarchies of race, class, gender, and language difference on which the 'Mathematics citizen' is constituted continues to be reproduced, yet masked under a veil of neutrality (Pais, 2012; Swanson, 2004, 2005, 2017; Valoyes-Chávez et al., 2021).

These social, economic, political, and environmental interests require the maintenance of hierarchically organised, bounded places, knowledges, and knowers. In Mathematics education this is evident in our language use about place (e.g. 'here'/'elsewhere'; 'developing'/'developed' world countries; 'global'/'local'), and about knowledge (e.g. 'academic'/'school'/'Ind igenous' mathematics, or 'real world'/'applied'/'pure' mathematics). It also is evident in our language about the knower in which the Mathematical citizen or non-citizen is (re)produced, for example: 'bottom'/'top' set, stream or track; 'non-English-speaking'; 'refugee' or 'migrant'; the 'can do' or 'can't do' of Mathematics, and numerous racialised, gendered, classed, (dis)abled mathematical 'Others' (Pais, 2012; Swanson, 2004, 2005; Swanson et al., 2017; Valoyes-Chávez et al., 2021). These conceptualisations give rise to a discourse of 'powerful'/'empowering' Mathematics education (Valero, 2008), one which 'fixes' both Mathematics and the Mathematics citizen's identity, and is a recontextualising mode of practice that continues to pervade practices of Mathematics (education). Here, the bounded 'black box' of Mathematics, and by implication Mathematics education, is the place from which the masked interests speak to, for, and about the world (Swanson, 2005). This is a voice of Mathematics that repulses any attempts to question its authority, or to recognise Other 'locals' and their knowledges and knowers. In the same vein, there is no legitimising space available in this mode of Mathematics (education) in which to challenge that which qualifies as mathematical 'citizen'. Indeed, while speaking from a largely marginalised position, although increasingly developing traction (Vithal & Jurdak, 2018), sociopolitical mathematics education has spoken to the underlying assumptions, ideological orientations, ethics, and politics of the dominant, 'powerful' Mathematics education discourses, towards more socially-just and democratic praxes (e.g. the Special Issue edited by Vithal & Skovsmose, 2012). On the other hand, this scholarship also demonstrates that, in a world in which the reach of Mathematics beyond itself is increasingly reinforcing and sustaining particular nationalist and economic interests, the 'gifts' of this mode of sociopolitical Mathematics education are largely bestowed in the service to and (re)production of neoliberalised and conservative politics (Nolan, 2009; Pais, 2012; Povey & Adams, 2021).

By way of exemplification, we use readings of the 2021 United Nations Climate Change Conference (COP26) (UK), but also of the subsequent COP27 (Egypt), COP28 (Dubai), and COP29 (Azerbaijan) to illustrate the reach of Mathematics in action in Science and Technology on and into the complex challenge of climate change. This reading reveals the way in which dominant neoliberal and technicist discourses are put to work through instrumentalising Mathematics, Science and Technology in ways that Economise nature and orient arguments towards economic costs of increasing global temperatures and the consequence for local and global economies (Office of the Vice President of Research, 2021). Mitigation thereof is also seen to be 'calculable' (Furman, 2014), that is, in the form of a 'carbon credit' system that Mathematises, Economises and 'transactionalises', indeed traffics, the environment, thereby acting on it from a decontextualised 'outside'. A more apparently liberal version of neoliberal discourse focuses on 'adaptation' and 'resilience' in climate change debates, one that operationalises Statistical modelling to explain how insufficient reductions in carbon and methane emissions on a country-level scale impinge on the rights of individuals in those countries to lead healthy and economically-productive lives under the new climate regime (Newlands, 2020). The undercurrent to these arguments, however, is not divorced from anthropic capitalism, but an extension of it. The focus on healthy individuals and national citizens hides strategic intentions whereby 'wellbeing' becomes a proxy to support the ambitions of private interests and state capital. There is also some evidence in the last few COP deliberations of some social justice leanings in the modes of operationalisation of Mathematics that draw attention to geopolitical inequalities in relation to global polluters versus climate effects (Irfan, 2021). In these debates, monetary recourse and reparations for increasing catastrophic climate effects on vulnerable countries and communities, under a banner of 'loss and damage', such as the wide-scale, devastating floods in Pakistan in mid-2022 (International Federation of Red Cross, 2022), have become a prominent framing for discussion and protocol agreements (United Nations, 2022, 2023). Yet, our reading of these deliberations is that the latter two discourses and their accompanying Mathematics and Mathematics educations became quickly reduced to competitive nationalisms, economic costs, 'carbon trading', and 'financial resourcing' (Furman, 2014), and hence the debates became reductive and effectively neoliberalised (Irfan, 2021).

Mbembe (2021) argues that colonial legacy and hierarchical fixedness in thinking about the world is characterised by a unilateral relation of 'proximity with no reciprocity' (pp. 90–91). For Mbembe, this relation precipitates the question of 'what to do with' the Other. In Mathematics education, answers to this question commonly take the form of managerial rhetoric on 'closing the gap' and 'catching up', yet such instrumentalism only serves to (re)produce the identified violence of the hierarchies of race, class, gender, and language difference on which the 'Mathematics citizen' is (re)produced (e.g. Pais, 2012; Swanson, 2004; Swanson et al., 2017; Valoyes-Chávez et al., 2021). The difficulties of disrupting such hierarchies and their violences from within Mathematics education cannot be understated, and the routes to overcome these limitations and foster agency and transformative potential need urgent attention.

Towards possibilities for dialogue across conceptual boundaries

We have highlighted the pervasiveness of a hierarchical, bounded, fixed thinking about Mathematics education and its authoritative disposition towards other discourses around 'globalisation' and 'citizenship'. We therefore have commented on some ramifications of this mode of Mathematics education as these arguments are (re)made and continually strengthened. We argue that thinking towards different, alternative possibilities requires new forms of scholarship, specifically critical thought and actions that involve the 'fermentation and innovation' (Mbembe, 2021, p. 11) of intellectual boundary-crossing.

Theoretical knowledge domains by their very nature change, including through their entanglement with one another (Mbembe, 2021), and Mathematics education itself has historically recontextualised knowledges from 'outside of itself', informing named 'turns' in mathematics education, for example, the 'social' and 'language' turns. With its attention to power and knowledge, sociopolitical mathematics education often has involved boundary work, which has taken place in the context of powerful external discourses that compete for supremacy in establishing 'regimes of truth' (Foucault, 2001). This has necessitated for us a heightened awareness of how our scholarship in this chapter, in its interpretability and translation, may become caught up, inadvertently and unintentionally, in precisely the agendas we seek to disrupt through the discourses we employ becoming caught up in competing external discourses. As sociopolitical mathematics education gains ground within mainstream thinking (Vithal & Jurdak, 2018), this possibility in general becomes increasingly likely.

Given the positioning of mathematics education as a 'social good' (Popkewitz, 2004) that in its hubris claims to 'save' the Other from themself and their global 'problems', we need a change of disposition toward/within mathematics education, and for this we assert that we need a particular type of intellectual boundary work. Bringing Mbembe's thought into mathematics education inquiry, we propose that such work demands of Mathematics education the ability to 'think its possibility outside of itself, aware of the limits of its singularity', always connected to other knowledge areas and 'Elsewhere[s]' (Mbembe, 2021, p. 228). What is required here is *thinking from* the 'outside', rather than 'inside' of Mathematics education. At this juncture in our argument, we feel it necessary to pose two key questions that help guide the arguments that follow, but which also articulate a specific mode of thinking and reveal the necessary emphases in such thinking for the chapter as a whole. These two questions we pose here also are ones that we, as collaborating authors, initially discussed and formulated as motivations for our thinking, arguments, and co-writing in this chapter. The questions are:

1 What might it mean for Mathematics education to be 'gifted' with particular concepts from the outside, and the exchange made meaningful through 'receiving' with humility, concepts that have been relatively mainstreamed within another theoretical knowledge domain, 'Elsewhere'? What dispositions might this require of Mathematics education, and how might it act with the weight of responsibility for carrying and responding to those conceptual gifts? What would it mean for this field to listen reflexively to Others?
2 Reciprocally, what might it mean for Mathematics education to 'gift' concepts to another theoretical knowledge domain? What disposition would be needed by Mathematics education to assume an ethical responsibility of-and-in-that giving?

To demonstrate such reciprocity, in this chapter we exemplify a form of relational boundary-crossing that involves 'thinking from' decolonial thought (a process we have implicitly modelled thus far) and also critical global citizenship education (CGCE). We describe this 'thinking from' approach, explicating the affordances it offers in terms of both similarities and differences, between these key epistemes, and also sociopolitical mathematics education. Our choices have been motivated by our scholarship within this domain of mathematics education.

Selecting conceptual knowledge domains for our boundary-crossings

We have illustrated what it might mean to *think from* a decolonial perspective, specifically the thinking of Mbembe (2021), through our own positional thinking in the arguments we articulate. Our naming of a decolonial perspective to underscore our arguments requires clarification, given that this perspective is neither unitary, having emerged in context-specific ways at different times, nor uncontested. Our use of *decolonial* refers to ways of thinking that attend to the ongoing workings of power in the entangled relations between peoples in various contexts of their elaboration over several hundred years of global coloniality. Taken together, this thinking also strives to dismantle the hierarchical, bounded fixedness that characterises these enduring historical realisations, and to reimagine new ways of viewing and hence acting in-and-for the world. This approach is productive for our purposes in this chapter since it permits *thinking from* the 'border' of dominant Euromodern thought, that is, from 'local' places of interconnection and disconnection where the normative act of 'Othering', the making of the non-citizen, is realised (Mignolo, 2007), a process we seek to disrupt. Our interest in new forms of relational boundary-crossing in mathematics education is fostered by the gift of decolonial thinking, not as one of 'disconnect and separation' (Mbembe, 2021, p. 89), but as a plurality of entangled, interconnected-and-disconnected conceptual knowledge domains that are never final. We illustrate such an approach in the next section.

The decolonial thinking as described here has, in fact, been deployed in CGCE, the second conceptual knowledge domain from which we think in this chapter. While education has long been framed within discourses of 'citizenship', the confluence of these discourses has taken on new forms in the context of globalising imaginaries of an interconnected world requiring 'citizens' to respond to 'global challenges'. Global Citizenship Education (GCE) has origins in this more recent context. *Critical* global citizenship education or CGCE, by distinction, with its interest in power and knowledge, troubles the ideological foundations of GCE in its role in perpetuating geopolitical and epistemic asymmetries of neoliberal globalisation. In this sense, it highlights the inherent paradox of bringing together notions of the 'global' and 'citizenship' in education (Swanson, 2011; Swanson & Gamal, 2021; Jefferess, 2008). CGCE also demonstrates how liberal-humanist approaches towards socially just, democratic educational praxis may be recruited by neoliberal GCE, thus unintentionally (re)producing the inequities they seek to disrupt (Swanson & Pashby, 2016). We have argued in the previous section that it is precisely the confluence of these discourses, and their articulations with Mathematics education, that are the subject of concern for sociopolitical mathematics education, especially when considered from critical, decolonial perspectives. In fact, CGCE scholarship recently has been used to think through these troubles in Mathematics education, for example in Povey and Adams (2021), and our own work (le Roux & Swanson, 2021). In its praxis, CGCE aims to engender critical, reflexive dialogue between places, knowledges and agentic knowers, engaging disciplinary boundary-crossings in addressing 'glocal' challenges (Andreotti, 2011; Swanson, 2011, 2020; Swanson & Pashby, 2016). In our recent work (le Roux & Swanson, 2021), which we further develop here, we drew on Swanson's (2020) praxis, developed in the context of a CGCE module in a teacher education programme in Scotland. We utilised those ideas to develop questions specifically for provoking mathematics education scholar-practitioners' critical, reflexive thinking about knowledge, power and global-local relations in Mathematics education praxis (le Roux & Swanson, 2021).

Having argued for the affordances of bringing these two ways of thinking, CGCE and Mathematics education, together, we acknowledge that alliances such as these may be uncomfortable ones and are never straightforward or neutral. Given differing histories, assumptions, communities, contextual interpretations, and purposes given to them, such alliances between differing knowledge domains are inevitably troubled, or at least their union may elide key differences and their implications. Attention to these discomforts requires vigilance on our part. For example, it becomes necessary to be alert to the asserted, unilateral, and 'fixed' global Mathematics and Mathematics education projects that are touted as providing 'solutions' to all manner of contemporary problems, and also to be sensitive to the origins of GCE within globalisation itself. Given our search for new possibilities, we argue that the historical differences (albeit that there are originary similarities too within the Enlightenment project) between Mathematics education and GCE may be productive to our thinking about their possible relations. These relations are, of course, invested in power. In this sense, we might argue that there is a key difference between the ways in which these two theoretical knowledge domains 'give' and 'receive' concepts. For example, using Bernstein (2000) and Dowling (1998), it can be argued that Mathematics education inherits the verticality constituted through Euromodern Mathematics that dominantly understands its own disciplinary base as a more universal and hierarchical form of knowledge, with firmly defined characteristics and principles, one that strictly polices its own boundaries. On the other hand, GCE, in its 'transdisciplinarity' and spillage across a wide range of subject domains, tends to constitute itself in terms of horizontal knowledge bases, presenting as having weaker insulations between discourses and being more loosely organised (Bernstein, 2000). This has meant that GCE tends to be more subject to pluralising and is less policing of disciplinary-specific knowledge, but it also is vulnerable to being instrumentalised, homogenised, and appropriated into other theoretical domains as a consequence of its openness and weak insulations (Bernstein, 2000). While these differences and the related power dynamics are invested in tensions and may seem to constrain a productive dialogue between them, we argue that, in the same way as *thinking from* borders, thinking horizontally may be productive in a process of agentive reimagining. It is our awareness of these differences that has informed our choice to focus on three interrelated concepts, namely, global-local relations, reciprocity, and reflexivity. And, it is the asserted fixedness of a global Mathematics education, and the consequent need to provide inducements for it to think itself 'from outside of itself' (Mbembe, 2021, p. 228) into new possibilities beyond the limits of its own thought and circuitry, that informs our decision to initiate a dialogue in this chapter *from* decolonial and CGCE perspectives (rather than thinking entirely from within a Mathematics education gaze) towards new agentifying possibilities.

A new possibility for thinking about mathematics education, 'global'-'local' and the mathematical ecological (human) being

We have argued, with the affordance of mathematics education scholars within the sociopolitical, for the urgency of new ways of thinking about the 'global'-'local' and 'citizenship' in mathematics education, with a lowercase 'm'. We seek possibilities beyond a Mathematics education that produces some as mathematical 'citizens' with a neutral, 'global', fixed, recontextualising and certain 'gaze' on the world, one instantiated with a hubristic disposition, or, as Gutiérrez (2017, p. 6) describes, one possessing 'epistemological arrogance'. For it is this 'powerful' Mathematics education, we argue, that (re)produces a contemporary world conceptualised as 'a huge arithmetic problem', as described by Mbembe (2021), a world that can be 'revealed and harnessed if we subject it to rigorous procedures of calculation, formalization, classification, and abstraction' (p. 22). To counter and repulse the enclosed, fixedness of Mathematics (education), we propose a *thinking* praxis for mathematics education, hence our attention to verbing (rather than to nouning) language. *Thinking from* decolonial and CGCE thought, as articulated in the previous section, we first present key ideas for thinking *about* mathematics education, the 'local', the 'global', the mathematics 'citizen', and their relations. Then, we offer some guiding questions to operationalise this praxis in the advancement of our reimagined mathematical ecological (human) being. Here, the way we give sense to the 'mathematical ecological (human) being' is implied by the student, teacher, and researcher, within a mathematics education context. In this quest, we begin to move away from 'citizen', which has become a colonial construct, to that of ecological (human) being, in an attempt to partially escape colonial determinations.

An opening, glocalising praxis

We argue for an *opening mathematics education* in dialogue with multiple locals (here we follow Mbembe's (2021, p. 63) argument for a disenclosing, a 'putting in-common' (citing Senghor, 1956)). *Local* comprises places, knowledges, practices, knowers, languages, sociopolitical relations, materialities, and technologies. Such locals include mathematics, with the lowercase '*m*', but also mathematics and its actions in science and technology (lowercase '*s*' and '*t*'). Here, we include in our thinking: languages, indigeneities, and socioecological (as opposed to environmental) materialities and technologies that forefront the locals of the Earth. For clarity, we note that our conceptualisation of multiple locals is not a romanticising of multiple local, bounded knowledges in a horizontal, relativist mosaic, a pluralist liberalism divorced from historical power asymmetries. Nor is it a horizontal disconnect that rejects Other locals (Mbembe, 2021). Nor is it that which is based on a normative individualism, in which notions of 'colour-blindness', or 'equality before the law', masks the historical, vertical hierarchies (Mbembe, 2021, p. 99).

Rather, drawing further on decolonial thought about the local, an *opening mathematics education* involves a dialogue between locals that are both interconnected and disconnected. As reticular, rather than as a romantic pluralism, we argue for conceptions of multiple locals as networked. In this way, in every local, the 'here' and 'elsewhere' of other locals are simultaneously present and absent, in a paradoxical relation of both 'entanglement and disconnection' (Mbembe, 2021, p. 76). On the one hand, locals are entangled on account of their histories, but also their futures, which by necessity they must share. They are also disconnected, since any local is not subsumable to one superior, universal 'global' (Mbembe, 2021; Mignolo, 2010). Thus, no local can ever be complete (Nyamnjoh, 2020). Mbembe (2021, p. 63, citing Senghor, 1956) argues that *opening* is about the existence of a local that cares for what belongs to them, but recognises at the same time that what belongs to them only has meaning to the extent that it is in dialogue with Other locals. Thus, no local such as Mathematics education can be used, on its own, to see the contemporary world and its future. Rather, mathematics education as a local needs dialogue with Other locals. In Mbembe's (2021, p. 221) terms, it needs 'multiple encounters with multiple elsewheres'. In other words, boundary-crossings are required, and in effect boundary-crossings of a particular nature are needed. It is the mathematics student, teacher and researcher, as ecological (human) beings that perform this boundary work, which we describe next.

Thinking from CGCE, specifically the scholarship of one author (Swanson, 2011, 2020), we propose a dialogue, which we call here an 'opening, *glocalising* praxis', to represent the aforementioned local relations. This involves *thinking from* and with a local mathematics education, not in isolation, but with connections and responsibilities to and consequences for other locals, one that acts locally without overreach. Such praxis requires a particular disposition on the part of the mathematical ecological being, one that involves an ontological shift. We think here from both Mbembe's (2021) decolonial thought and Swanson's (2011, 2020) work within CGCE to argue for a disposition of *reflexivity* and *reciprocity*, the latter involving a *giving* with responsibility and a *receiving* with humility. The practices of reflexivity and reciprocity we describe are closely related, but the linear nature of this chapter dictates that we make a choice, and we start with the former. Firstly, we qualify that we have brought these particular conceptualisations to our discussions of mathematics education, since we found little within sociopolitical mathematics education to guide us, possibly on account of the historical and contemporary hegemony of Mathematics education, as described in the section, *(Im)possibilities in the confluence of Mathematics, Mathematics education, 'globalisation', and 'citizenship'*. Our reading is that 'reflexivity' is used broadly as a form of praxis that characterises at least some of sociopolitical mathematics education research and pedagogy (e.g. Andersson & Barwell, 2021). This critical praxis involves a form of metacognitive 'self-awareness' or 'self-reflexiveness' by the 'self', the so-called 'critical mathematics citizen', of how Mathematics education may be complicit in the inequities and violences that characterise the current world. The notion of 'reciprocity' has been explored by Gutiérrez (2017) as necessary for recognition within Mathematics education of Other knowledges, and is also a concern of researchers working with knowers of Other knowledges (e.g. Meaney et al., 2008).

Practising reflexivity

Reflexivity in an *opening, glocalising praxis* involves the opposite of 'withdrawing into oneself' (Mbembe, 2021, p. 172). This praxis is important in order to reflect on the role of mathematics education and its citizens in the world, but involves dual, (inter)related actions. Following the decolonial thought of Mbembe (2021), we argue that mathematics education as a local has a responsibility to answer for itself, in the past, present, and future. Given its incompleteness and interconnectedness with other locals, it also needs to dialogue, that is to say, it needs 'sojourn[ing] with [O]thers' (Mbembe, 2021, p. 75). A precondition for dialogue, we argue, is reflexivity. And, a precondition for reflexivity, and indeed an authentic dialogue, is a practise of *recognising*, that is to say, recognising mathematics education in the world, including its incompleteness, but crucially, recognising its Other locals.

Sociopolitical mathematics education aims to practise the former, *reflexivity*, as we already have discussed, but we wish to extend this to the latter, *recognising*. We suggest that these dual practices are not possible for the Mathematical 'citizen' that is educated and enculturated into a universalising Euromodern Mathematics, but it may only be possible for the mathematical ecological (human) being if *recognising* the Other, and sojourning with Others is part of a deeply reflexive, glocalising mathematics education. Both forms of recognising require of the mathematics citizen, not a closing, a fixedness, but a 'humble togetherness' (Swanson, 2007, p. 53), an openness, and commitment to learn and to 'remember together' (Mbembe, 2021, p. 77, citing Glissant, 2006) the historical and sociopolitical of Mathematics education in the world, and a reckoning with the implications of a Mathematical gaze. Given the tendency of Mathematics (education) towards overreach, as part of its recontextualising gaze (Dowling, 1998), the reflexivity we conceptualise for mathematics education requires of mathematics a *listening* that starts from Other locals (Mbembe, 2021), rather than from a centralised Mathematics education. Arguably, it may not be possible to start such a recognitive process from mathematics (education) either in the presence of a decontextualising, often dehumanising Mathematics (education) with its verticalising of knowledge and policing of its boundaries (Bernstein, 2000; Dowling, 1998). It also requires the knower to recognise *who*, that is, to recognise which Other local with whom they are dialoguing. If this 'local' is a powerful actor that renders Mathematics utilitarian and neutral, then a reimagined mathematics education needs attending to its relations and the power investments in that relation. If the local is an alterity of Mathematics education, its Other, then its subjugation of the Other needs exposure and its relations need repair in ways that open to a reflexive, glocalising mathematics education. We are left with the question, however: what might it mean for Mathematics education to repair its historical relations and the materialities thereof, if at all possible? A praxis of *reciprocity* might offer us some answers.

Practising reciprocity

The reciprocity we propose involves a *giving* with responsibility and a *receiving* with humility (Mbembe, 2021; Swanson, 2011, 2020). By giving, we do not mean a unilateral 'donation' (Mbembe, 2021, p. 172), undertaken in a disposition of arrogance or beneficence through an application of a fixed, bounded Mathematics, that ultimately 'mathematize(s), dominate(s) and subjugate(s)' (p. 164), and serves to exploit (Swanson, 2004, 2005). Rather, through a reflexive practice of listening to, and learning from Other locals, as described in the section, *Practising reflexivity*, the mathematical ecological (human) being humbly offers an incomplete mathematics education, informed by an awareness of its gaze, a consciousness of to whom such a gaze is directed, and recognition of the entangled history of that gaze. Indeed, as an act of radical equality and repair, it might involve not giving mathematics education at all (Swanson & Appelbaum, 2012).

In this latter sense, reciprocity also includes a particular praxis of *receiving*. This is not a process of appropriation that benefits only the already privileged, or in the name of inclusion is constituted under a banner of 'multiculturalism'. Rather, it takes the form of 'radical hospitality, co-belonging and openness' (Mbembe, 2021, p. 81), a humble, openness to think in dialogue with Other locals towards addressing contemporary problems.

Towards a reimagined opening glocalising praxis of the mathematical ecological (human) being

We argue that to create the conditions for an open, reflexive, glocalising mathematics education, one that identifies with a mathematical ecological (human) being as opposed to a Mathematical citizen shaped by and belonging to a nation state, a shift is required from fixed, bounded 'sedentary' thinking (Kell, 2015) towards critical activity involving the 'fermentation and innovation' (Mbembe, 2021, p. 11) of disciplinary boundary-crossings. The questioning disposition that we use to invite in a renewed mathematical ecological (human) being is one possible illustration of such fermentation. We now offer an example of our reimagined opening, glocalising praxis, that is to say, the dialogue of mathematics education with itself and many Other locals, while carrying a disposition of reflexivity and reciprocity. This dialogue takes the form of a 'to-and-fro' questioning (column 1, Table 5.1), in which we also offer an 'OR' (column 2, Table 5.1). The intent is not to institute binaries, but to offer alternatives that open up to other possible alternatives, beyond Mathematics education, that may follow. Thus, we exemplify through enacting such reflexivity, of mathematics education speaking with itself and its many other locals, and of the mathematical ecological (human) being in dialogue with itself and Others.

An opening to a temporary closing

An opportunity to dialogue across boundaries of conceptual knowledges is an invitation for a reflexive mathematics education with/in reciprocal relations. Such a dialogue and border crossing, we argue, fosters new possibilities and relations, as the requirement for new relational possibilities cannot be overstated in terms of mathematics education's political responsibility to the world and the now-urgent need to heal (its) relations. We assert that it may not be possible for Mathematics education to maintain its authority *and* simultaneously heal relations. For we have argued that, to heal relations, an opening, glocalising mathematics education characterised by reflexivity and reciprocity would be necessary. For mathematics education to be reparative and reflexive, it needs to be able to 'think its possibility outside of itself, aware of the limits of its singularity', always connected to other locals, 'Elsewhere' (Mbembe, 2021, p. 228). In this sense, we are reminded of Mbembe's commitments to restitution in the process of decolonial healing. For Mbembe (2021), such restitution needs to make possible a 'restoration of life' (p. 171), because colonial domination, exploitation and extraction rob the Other of vital processes, of life itself, of meaning, and of 'capacities to bring about worlds' (p. 170).

In this chapter, the dialogue between knowledge domains, the boundary-crossing we have enacted is a commitment to inciting the imagining of possibilities for mathematics education's bringing about palpably new worlds in a reflexive, reciprocal dialogue between locals marked by an invitation for restitution with/in 'humble togetherness' (Swanson, 2007, p. 53). This is because the disposition with which mathematics education engages with Other locals matters in this encounter. As scholars, we have engaged in boundary work purposefully to disrupt and to experiment with reading Mathematics education concerns *from* different theoretical knowledge domains and conceptual vantage points outside of 'accepted' Mathematics education research practice. We have brought decolonial thought and CGCE into dialogue with sociopolitical mathematics education by way of decolonising Mathematics education, and indeed GCE. We have argued that scholarship that can enact a dialogue across boundaries fosters relations between

Table 5.1 Guiding questions for an opening, glocalising praxis

mathematics education ('I') thinking in dialogue	OR *thinking from* Mathematics education ('I')
Do I leave my local mathematics (education) to sojourn with Other locals?	Do I dwell within a bordered local, certain of its authority, utilitarianism, and beneficence?
With which locals do I sojourn? Do I recognise the traditionally subordinated Other as a legitimate knowledge and knower?	OR do I dwell only in and with the hegemonic local that renders Mathematics utilitarian and neutral?
When sojourning with Other locals, do I listen with humility, and with an openness to learn about Others and my local mathematics education?	Do I donate my local as a global, certain solution without first reflexively returning to myself, with humility, to question and interrogate my own motives?
With listening and learning together, do I recognise the historical connectedness of my local mathematics education with Other locals? Do I open myself to seeing the connection and disconnection of locals in contemporary issues of concern? Indeed, who identifies these as 'problems'? And with this understanding, do I recognise the incompleteness of my own local, how my local reflexively may have a need for Other locals and thus the need for crossing borders?	Does my local—in the form of a socially good, superior local or even 'global' universal—come to both frame the 'problem' in its own referential terms and impose 'the solution' thereto?
In my praxis of reciprocity, am I critically aware of what I give in boundary-crossings? And do I give humbly, with responsibility for limits of the 'help' my local offers and with no expectation that it will be received? Indeed, might reciprocity towards repair involve being open to not giving that which was not asked for?	Do I centre and impose my local (education) on subordinated others, other locals, thus violating them in the process in its singularity? And is what I claim to give a falsehood being perpetuated and facilitated via powerful neoliberal or conservative discourses?
Is my giving genuinely welcomed?	Is a perceived welcome a reflection and instance of the discourse of Mathematics education as a social good that can solve all problems?
Do I receive into my mathematics (education) Other locals as a form of being open to new understandings and/or being decentred and/or giving up something?	Does my practice 'consume' other knowledges and knowers according to the gaze of my local?

Mathematics education and Other locals, Elsewheres. Fostering and healing relations with Mathematics education from Elsewhere, we have argued, serves to decolonise it, and recalibrate the relations and enactments within the world that it commonly rehearses. In this sense, our dialogical praxis acts as 'an offer to repair relationships', as a crucial approach to work towards restitution (Mbembe, 2021, p. 171, citing Appiah, 2004).

In summation, we have brought CGCE into dialogue with sociopolitical mathematics education by way of decolonising Mathematics (education), and indeed GCE. The to-and-fro of dialogue and sharing of conceptual tropes between CGCE and Mathematics (education), and the reception of this dialogue in return by way of a radical hospitality (Mbembe, 2021) offers the possibilities of a radical hope (Lear, 2008) for Mathematics (education), in respect of restitution, healing of relations, and a readiness for fostering possibilities of alternate futures, ones in which all relations, including prior alterities of Mathematics (education), and indeed GCE, may thrive and afford the opportunity to act together to renew the world (Arendt, 1958).

Note

1 By *sociopolitical mathematics education* we mean critical scholarship concerned with matters of power in relation to knowledges, identities, contexts, practices, and discourses in mathematics education. Such scholarship commonly draws on perspectives within sociology; critical mathematics education; critical ethnomathematics; culturally responsive mathematics pedagogies and praxes; Indigenous knowledges; decolonial or postcolonial perspectives, and related theoretical and philosophical orientations.

References

Aguilar, M. S., & Zavaleta, J. G. M. (2012). On the links between mathematics education and democracy: A literature review. *Pythagoras*, *33*(2), Article #164. http://dx.doi.org/10.4102/pythagoras.v33i2.164

Andersson, A., & Barwell, R. (2021). Applying critical mathematics education: An introduction. In A. Andersson & R. Barwell (Eds.), *Applying critical mathematics education* (pp. 1–23). Brill. https://doi.org/10.1163/9789004465800_001

Andreotti, V. (2011). Introduction. In V. Andreotti (Ed.), *Actionable postcolonial theory in education*. Palgrave Macmillan. https://doi.org/10.1057/9780230337794_1

Appiah, K. A. (2004). Comprendre les réparations. Une réflexion préliminaire. *Cahiers d'études Africaines*, *44*(173–174), 25–40.

Arendt, H. (1958). *The human condition*. University of Chicago Press.

Bernstein, B. (2000). *Pedagogy, symbolic control, and identity: Theory, research, critique* (revised ed.). Rowman & Littlefield.

Cabral, T. C. B., & Baldino, R. R. (2019). The social turn and its big enemy: A leap forward. In J. Subramanian (Ed.), *Proceedings of the Tenth International Mathematics Education and Society Conference* (pp. 32–46). MES.

Chronaki, A., & Yolcu, A. (2021). Mathematics for "citizenship" and its "other" in a "global" world: Critical issues on mathematics education, globalisation and local communities. *Research in Mathematics Education*, *23*(3), 241–247. https://doi.org/10.1080/14794802.2021.1995780

Dowling, P. (1998). *The sociology of mathematics education: Mathematical myths/pedagogic texts*. RoutledgeFalmer.

Ernest, P. (2016). Mathematics education ideologies and globalization. In P. Ernest, B. Sriraman, & N. Ernest (Eds.), *Critical mathematics education: Theory, praxis and reality* (pp. 35–79). Information Age.

Foucault, M. (2001). *Madness and civilization: A history of insanity in the age of reason.* Psychology Press.

Furman, J. (2014, October 9). Calculating a cost/benefit ratio for climate change policy. *Knowledge at Wharton.* https://knowledge.wharton.upenn.edu/article/a-cost-benefit-ratio-for-climate-change-policy/

Gamal, M., & Swanson, D. M. (2018). Alterities of global citizenship: Education, human rights, and everyday bordering. *Justice, Power and Resistance, 2*(2), 357–388. https://core.ac.uk/download/pdf/199408875.pdf

Glissant, É. (2006). *Une nouvelle région du monde* (vol. 1). Gallimard.

Green, L. (2020). *Rock/water/life: Ecology and humanities for a decolonial South Africa.* Wits University Press.

Greer, B., & Mukhopadhyay, S. (2012). The hegemony of mathematics. In O. Skovsmose & B. Greer (Eds.), *Opening the cage: Critique and politics of mathematics education* (pp. 229–248). Springer. https://doi.org10.1007/978-94-6091-808-7_12

Gutiérrez, R. (2017). Living mathematx: Towards a vision for the future. *Philosophy of Mathematics Education Journal, 32*(1), 1–34.

International Federation of Red Cross. (2022, August 27). Sea-like flood waters ravage Pakistan, affecting millions of people. https://www.ifrc.org/press-release/sea-flood-waters-ravage-pakistan-affecting-millions-people

Irfan, U. (2021, November 11). Rich countries still don't want to pay their climate tab. *VOX.* https://www.vox.com/22774622/cop26-climate-change-glasgow-money-finance-aid

Jefferess, D. (2008). Global citizenship and the cultural politics of benevolence. *Critical Literacy: Theories and Practices, 2*(1), 27–36.

Kell, C. (2015). "Making people happen": Materiality and movement in meaning-making trajectories. *Social Semiotics, 25*(4), 423–445. https://doi.org/10.1080/10350330.2015.1060666

Lear, J. (2008). *Radical hope: Ethics in the face of cultural devastation.* Harvard University Press.

le Roux, K., & Swanson, D. M. (2021). Toward a reflexive mathematics education within local and global relations: Thinking from critical scholarship on mathematics education within the sociopolitical, global citizenship education and decoloniality. *Research in Mathematics Education, 23*(3), 323–337. https://doi.org/10.1080/14794802.2021.1993978

Mbembe, A. (2021). *Out of the dark night: Essays on decolonization.* Columbia University Press.

Meaney, T., McMurchy-Pilkington, C., & Trinick, T. (2008). Mathematics education and Indigenous students. In P. Sullivan (Ed.), *Research in mathematics education in Australasia 2004–2007* (pp. 119–139). Brill.

Mignolo, W. (2010). Cosmopolitanism and the de-colonial option. *Studies in Philosophy and Education, 29*(2), 111–127. https://doi.org/10.1007/s11217-009-9163-1

Mignolo, W. D. (2007). Introduction: Coloniality of power and de-colonial thinking. *Cultural Studies, 21*(2–3), 155–167. http://dx.doi.org/10.1080/09502380601162498

Newlands, N. K. (2020). Statistical modelling of dynamic greenhouse gas emissions. In L. Vyacheslav, R.G. Yulia, K.H. Kilbourne, T.J. Miller, N.K. Newlands, & A.B. Smith (Eds.), *Evaluating climate change impacts* (1st ed., pp. 325–343) Chapman and Hall. https://doi.org/10.1201/9781351190831-15

Nikolakaki, M. (2016). The politics of mathematics education and citizenship in capitalism. In P. Ernest, B. Sriraman, & N. Ernest (Eds.), *Critical mathematics education: Theory, praxis and reality* (pp. 273–286). Information Age.

Nolan, K. (2009). Mathematics in and through social justice: Another misunderstood marriage? *Journal of Mathematics Teacher Education*, *12*(3), 205–216. https://doi.org/10.1007/s10857-009-9111-6

Nyamnjoh, F. B. (2020). *Decolonising the academy: A case for convivial scholarship*. Carl Schlettwein Lecture 14. Basler Afrika Bibliographien.

Office of the Vice President of Research. (2021, November 17). At UN climate change conference, trying to "keep 1.5 alive". *MIT News*. https://news.mit.edu/2021/un-climate-change-conference-cop26-1117

Pais, A. (2012). A critical approach to equity. In O. Skovsmose & B. Greer (Eds.), *Opening the cage: Critique and politics of mathematics education* (pp. 49–91). Springer. https://doi.org/10.1007/978-94-6091-808-7_3

Pais, A., & Valero, P. (2011). Beyond disavowing the politics of equity and quality in mathematics education. In B. Atweh, M. Graven, W. Secada, & P. Valero (Eds.), *Mapping equity and quality in mathematics education* (pp. 35–48). Springer. https://doi.org/10.1007/978-90-481-9803-0_3

Popkewitz, T. S. (2001). Rethinking the political: Reconstituting national imaginaries and producing difference. *International Journal of Inclusive Education*, *5*(2–3), 179–207. https://doi.org/10.1080/13603110010028707

Popkewitz, T. S. (2004). The alchemy of the mathematics curriculum: Inscriptions and the fabrication of the child. *American Educational Research Journal*, *41*(1), 3–34. https://www.jstor.org/stable/3699383

Povey, H., & Adams, G. (2021). Disordering mathematics, citizenship and socio-political research in mathematics education amongst the "rubble of words". *Research in Mathematics Education*, *23*(3), 306–322. https://doi.org/10.1080/14794802.2021.1994452

Senghor, L. S. (1956). L'esprit de la civilisation ou les lois de la culture négro-africaine. *Présence Africaine*, *8-9-10*, 51–65.

Skovsmose, O. (2005). *Travelling through education: Uncertainty, mathematics, responsibility*. Sense.

Skovsmose, O. (2016). Mathematics: A critical rationality? In P. Ernest, B. Sriraman & N. Ernest (Eds.), *Critical mathematics education: Theory, praxis and reality* (pp. 1–22). Information Age.

Swanson, D. M. (1998). Bridging the boundaries? A study of mainstream mathematics, academic support and "disadvantaged learners" in an independent, secondary school in the Western Cape. MEd. University of Cape Town. http://hdl.handle.net/11427/8075

Swanson, D. M. (2004). *Voices in the silence: Narratives of disadvantage, social context and school mathematics in post-apartheid South Africa* [Doctoral dissertation]. University of British Columbia. https://open.library.ubc.ca/soa/cIRcle/collections/ubctheses/831/items/1.0058236#:~:text=%22Voices%20in%20the%20Silence%22%20is,school%20mathematics%20in%20social%20context.

Swanson, D. M. (2005). School mathematics: Discourse and the politics of context. In A. Chronaki & I. M. Christiansen (Eds.), *Challenging perspectives on mathematics classroom communication* (pp. 261–294). Information Age.

Swanson, D. M. (2007). Ubuntu: An African contribution to (re)search for/with a 'humble togetherness. *Journal of Contemporary Issues in Education*, *2*(2), 53–67. http://ejournals.library.ualberta.ca/index.php/JCIE/article/viewFile/1028/686

Swanson, D. M. (2011). Parallaxes and paradoxes of global citizenship: Critical reflections and possibilities of praxis in/through an international online course. In L. Schulz, A. Abdi, & G. Richardson (Eds.), *Global citizenship education in postsecondary institutions: Theories, practices, policies* (pp. 120–139). Peter Lang.

Swanson, D. M. (2017). Mathematics education and the problem of political forgetting: In search of research methodologies for global crisis. *Journal of Urban Mathematics Education*, *10*(1), 7–15.

Swanson, D. M. (2020). Critical Global Citizenship Education: Some guiding principles for engaging with CGC projects/practices/initiative. [Paper presentation]. Education, inequality and critical global citizenship: Local realities – Global contexts seminar, Stirling, United Kingdom. https://www.stir.ac.uk/research/hub/publication/1728407#details

Swanson, D. M., & Appelbaum, P. (2012). Refusal as a democratic catalyst for mathematics education development. *Pythagoras*, *33*(2), Article #189, 6. http://dx.doi.org/10.4102/pythagoras.v33i2.189

Swanson, D. M., & Gamal, M. (2021). Global Citizenship Education/Learning for Sustainability: Tensions, 'flaws', and contradictions as critical moments of possibility and radical hope in educating for alternative futures. *Globalisation, Societies and Education*, *19*(4), 456–469. https://doi.org/10.1080/14767724.2021.1904211

Swanson, D. M., & Pashby, K. (2016). Towards a critical global citizenship? A comparative analysis of GC education discourses in Scotland and Alberta. *Journal of Research in Curriculum and Instruction*, *20*(3), 184–195.

Swanson, D. M., Yu, H. L., & Mouroutsou, S. (2017). Inclusion as ethics, equity and/or human rights?: Spotlighting school mathematics practices in Scotland and globally. *Social Inclusion*, *5*(3), 172–182.

Talmon, J. L. (1952). *The origins of totalitarian democracy.* Secker & Warburg.

United Nations. (2022, November 20). COP27 reaches breakthrough agreement on new "loss and damage" fund for vulnerable countries. https://unfccc.int/news/cop27-reaches-breakthrough-agreement-on-new-loss-and-damage-fund-for-vulnerable-countries

United Nations. (2023, September 8). Transitional Committee on Loss and Damage Makes Progress at third Meeting. https://unfccc.int/news/transitional-committee-on-loss-and-damage-makes-progress-at-third-meeting

Valero, P. (2008). Discourses of power in mathematics education research: Concepts and possibilities for action. *PNA*, *2*(2), 43–60.

Valoyes-Chávez, L., Montecino, A., & Guzmán, P. (2021). Global mobility and processes of racialisation: The case of immigrant adults in mathematics education. *Research in Mathematics Education*, *23*(3), 248–261. https://doi.org/10.1080/14794802.2021.1993979

Vithal, R., & Jurdak, M. (2018). Mainstreaming of the sociopolitical in mathematics education. In R. Vithal & M. Jurdak (Eds.), *Sociopolitical dimensions of mathematics education: From the margin to mainstream* (pp. 1–12). Springer. https://doi.org/10.1007/978-3-319-72610-6_1

Vithal, R., & Skovsmose, O. (2012). Mathematics education, democracy and development: A view of the landscape. *Pythagoras*, *33*(2), Article #207, 3. http://dx.doi.org/10.4102/pythagoras.v33i2.207

Yolcu, A. (2021). Reimagining the citizen and the nation in a globalised world: The case of mathematics education reforms in Turkey. *Research in Mathematics Education*, *23*(3), 278–292. https://doi.org/10.1080/14794802.2021.1993976

6 Revisiting the 'modern' in mathematics

Exploring some consequences with respect to mathematics education

Saumya Malviya

Introduction

As I was conducting fieldwork on mathematics in institutions in India, I was struck by the extent to which the idea of 'modern' formed a crucial part of the way in which mathematicians described contemporary mathematics.[1] Not only do mathematicians think of themselves as doing 'modern' mathematics, it is also very much a part of the discursive sphere in which they learn their craft. So mathematical textbooks often carry the appellation 'modern', and when they do not, it is assumed that they treat their subject-matter in the modern spirit. In such a scenario, it is taken for granted that 'modern' methods and approaches have been completely internalised by the mathematical mainstream and hence there's no need spelling them out. Having said this, I will also hasten to point out that instead of having a settled meaning the term functions as a floating signifier, implying a necessary *leap* from the pre-modern. The potential of the term perhaps lies in its ability to take on different meanings, yet somehow hold them together under its label.

At a purely ethnographic level the drama of 'modern' mathematics could also be seen as playing out when children make the transition from school to college; as teachers and educators tell them that they need to forget all they have learnt in school and start afresh, to rebuild their mathematical knowledge as per modern sensibilities. Further, several pedagogical experiments in the twentieth century, like the New Math Movement and 'Commission Lichnerowicz' tried in different ways and with varying degrees of success to replace old, intuitive ways of learning with the modern-axiomatic approach.[2] I don't think it will be wrong to say that these experiments have added to the tenacity of the 'modern' in mathematics. Even when such experiments have been contested, and there has been no dearth of such contestations, the alternatives have only reified the divide between modern axiomatic traditions and some version or the other of human/social constructivism. At the risk of some simplification it could be stated that in the preceding century pedagogical experiments in the case of mathematics have oscillated between these, to all appearances, opposed positions.[3]

DOI: 10.4324/9781003130673-8

Moving further, I would like to add here that, one of the key markers of the 'modern' in mathematics I encountered in the field was the way in which the word functioned for working mathematicians to distinguish what is really mathematical from what is merely philosophical or extra-mathematical. To put it differently, it served to highlight the autonomy of mathematics from the issues which, for them, could be safely regarded as external to it. A feat, as is usually put by contemporary mathematicians, was achieved through modernisation of mathematics, and which has delivered them from extra-mathematical concerns, giving them the confidence to just do what they do best, i.e. producing mathematics.[4]

In this chapter I go back to the drawing board to ask again, and to make an attempt at answering, *what is modern mathematics?* By doing so I hope to offer a genealogy of the 'modern mathematician-subject', to understand the centrality of the figure of the 'child' to the discourse of mathematics, to uncover the possible reasons behind the deep *pedagogisation* of mathematics in the last century, and, tying these different strands together, to underline the ideological role that the term 'modern' has played in the history of twentieth century European mathematics and its institutionalisation world-over. Admittedly, these are very broad and ambitious inquiries to pursue in a short chapter, but I hope to show how revisiting the 'modern' in mathematics can be the common starting point from where these inquiries branch out, and yet remain fundamentally connected to each other.

Recognising the persistence of the 'modern in mathematics' as an anthropological problem, I seek to show that there's another sense of the same which hasn't been duly understood, and one which can have very noticeable consequences at the level of pedagogy and with respect to the general understanding of mathematics. In the process of answering this question I want to argue that modern mathematics is necessarily, and not just accidently, tied to the politics of life and society or more precisely is informed by and in turn informs the structures of the 'social'. Note that this point goes against the grain of thinking of the 'modern' as standing for a seamless and linear transformation from an era when mathematics was 'contaminated' by philosophy and society to a later stage when mathematics became fully autonomous and epistemologically secure.

Further, teasing out this point will show that we need not abandon the sense of mathematical autonomy to accommodate its sociality. Rather, mathematics can be and is 'autonomous' and thoroughly 'social' at the same time. The difference being that this latter sense of autonomy is a reflexive and critical one and not something which can be taken for granted in a progressive and unreflective zest. Thus the argument is not á la Bruno Latour to argue that 'we have never been modern' (1993), but to recover a critical sense of mathematical autonomy and 'modern' in mathematics as against their ideological employment, particularly in the domain of mathematics education where these notions have been used to fashion an 'ideal' mathematician-subject, pointedly encapsulated in the rhetoric of 'catching them young' when it comes to pedagogic and curriculum practices. This rhetoric, I hasten to point out, gives the impression that mathematics in itself is neutral and autonomous, and certain children just have the 'innate ability' to be good at it, and hence they must be singled out and trained for the same reason. Further, it should also be added that the above (temporal) sense of a 'once-for-all transformation' conveyed by 'modern' mathematics, often gets ideologically coupled with a sense of mathematics for 'all' (spatial), engendering exclusions in the guise of democratisation of mathematics (Diaz, 2017).

To illustrate my point and substantiate the thesis regarding 'modern' in mathematics, I take recourse to the work of Alan Turing and the Bourbaki group as two exemplary instances of 'modern' mathematics and strive to complicate the received understanding of their work. It will be seen through my discussion what the appreciation of the sociality of these foundational projects can add to their contemporary reception, both historically as well as from a pedagogical standpoint. Broadly speaking, I want to draw the reader's attention to the intriguing fact that Turing and Bourbaki pursued the 'foundational' project, not long after it had failed and more importantly was rendered unrealisable. I wish to argue that even after the failure of the foundational programme(s) in mathematics, it was pursued in *reformed* ways with the effect of not necessarily grounding mathematics onto something axiomatically or even intuitively secure, but onto specific socio-pedagogical imaginaries. That it has not been sufficiently appreciated has meant that modern mathematics is seen as a decisive move away from useless foundational concerns to achieve a protected autonomy. This protected autonomy is then variously imagined and given concrete materiality by different reform movements, without their socio-political stakes getting recognised in process.

Unlike the accepted story of transition to 'modern' mathematics, I argue that what has instead happened is that foundationalism continued to be pursued under different guises by attempting to base mathematics onto different mathematical styles deriving their legitimacy from specific understandings of human sociality.[5] In so far as children were (and are) conceived as the corner-stones, or better, the foundation of human sociality, they unwittingly became the 'addressees' of these disguised foundationalisms pursued in the form of numerous mathematics (education) reform movements. This also accounts for why mathematics became such a heavily pedagogised discipline, when compared to other modern disciplines, once the heady waters of axiomatic or intuitive foundationalism receded, giving way to a more pragmatic and pedagogical sense of foundations. To put it bluntly, what was not achieved mathematically through foundational programmes was then sought in the name of children and pedagogical practices.[6]

According to the perspective adopted in this chapter, projects of 'founding' mathematics got displaced-reformed such that the location of foundations of mathematics came to coincide with 'foundations of society'; in the processes of learning and the figure of the 'child'. Both Turing's and Bourbaki group's mathematics grew from a desire to 'found' mathematics. This was different from the traditional foundational projects as they were predisposed to carry it out in pedagogical terms, with the ideological notions of 'learning', 'next step' playing a key role for the former, and a functional sense of 'structure' for the latter. And, it is in this sense that the foundational project quite emphatically succeeded. This dialectic of failure and success produced a form of mathematics (despite great internal diversity) which was *pedagogised* to the core, and moreover, could pretend to be completely self-sufficient and autonomous from other modes of knowledge production.[7] Having considered the question of 'modern' as settled, or as not a question at all, we have failed to appreciate how the sense of the 'foundational' got subtly revised in mathematics, such that its ideological function was preserved, but was now expected to fulfil itself out in the domain of education and pedagogy.

Of course, I do not intend to imply that this happened as if it was due to some hidden design, but to show how a very specific and unconscious dialectic of 'educationalising mathematics and foundationalising education' unrolled in Europe as mathematics and education were brought together with the impulse to 'reform'. How that dialectic got universalised, despite being located in a very specific context, and with the emergence and strengthening of the neo-liberal world-order, gave rise to multiple 'Mathematics for ALL projects', is an inquiry to be followed elsewhere, but I hope this chapter will at least be able to demonstrate that the rhetorical ALL is not without its locations and exclusions.

Having said that, to the sketchy genealogy offered here by means of Turing and Bourbaki, I hope to add more details in the future.[8] To commence with the argument let us first interrogate the notion of autonomy of mathematics. First, I'll attempt to spell out the form of autonomy that 'modern' mathematics is usually believed to have, which, then, I will proceed to problematise.

Mathematical autonomy

As pointed out before, 'autonomy' stands out as the single most important characteristic of 'modern' mathematics. To put it simply, autonomy is usually seen as amounting to the fact that mathematics is self-sufficient to deal with issues that arise *within* its field. In a way this means that mathematicians are best suited to become epistemologists of their discipline, and moreover they could be latter *as* mathematicians, no need for any external assistance from philosophers and even less so from the social scientists. Further, mathematics can deal with itself purely mathematically, with mathematical means and for mathematical ends. To be sure, this is a great position to be in, and is certainly responsible for the way in which mathematics has grown by leaps and bounds in the twentieth century, leaving philosophical speculation tottering far behind. Autonomy, under this view, voiced frequently by contemporary mathematicians, stands for progress in mathematics and its forward looking orientation.

The image that we get of mathematics through such representations is not too far from the one presented by the celebrated visual art critic Clement Greenberg with reference to art, and in particular to painting. He says, 'The essence of modernism lies, as I see it, in the use of characteristic methods of a discipline to criticise the discipline itself, not in order to subvert it but in order to entrench it more firmly in its area of *competence*' (emphasis mine) (Greenberg, 1965, p. 5).[9] Anyone who believes in the kind of mathematical autonomy outlined above, will immediately come to hear in the above statement by Greenberg, the ring of an accurate description of the 'modern' or 'modernism' in mathematics as well. Moreover, a very conscious self-reflexive orientation coupled with immense functional differentiation of contemporary mathematics, both seen as consequences of mathematical modernism, have only served to buttress this image further.[10] In so far as Greenberg links the above characterisation of modernism in arts as also leading to their increasing 'purity', it won't be far from the mark to say that such self-descriptions of autonomy in case of mathematics have also given rise to and bolstered the idea of 'pure' mathematics.[11]

Now, even a cursory familiarity with Greenberg's study of modernism in painting is enough to alert us that there is more to it than just autonomy. In fact for him the idea of modern painting is not simply about increasing abstraction and abandoning of representation, but more specifically to do with each art embracing the uniqueness of its medium, and instead of seeing it as something to be overcome, exploring the possibilities inherent in this uniqueness. We know that in the case of painting this amounted to an emphatic acknowledgement of not just paint and shape of the canvas, but above all else of the *flatness* of surface. Here the Greenbergian story turns interesting as we can discern here the lineaments of a robust foregrounding of the materiality and the matter-of-factness of art, but let's not deviate and get back to mathematics. If we yield to the kind of autonomy which is usually claimed for mathematics then we thereby also yield to the position that it is completely closed for reflection from an external vantage point. Now, not only is this a wholly negative position to take for social scientists and philosophers, it must be decidedly avoided at all costs for the simple reason that it implies that there is a form of human activity which is beyond critical reflection by anyone else apart from mathematicians.

Further, granting mathematics this degree of exclusivity will not only mean that the question of how the 'social' impacts mathematics will be taken out of consideration, the relatively easier one of how mathematics informs the 'social' will also go begging. Here I do not wish to simply cast the above understanding of mathematical autonomy as ideological, but to uncover a sense of autonomy which will not only enable us to respect the autonomy of mathematics, but at the same time will lead us to appreciate how various mathematical forms and practices embody, as well as, shape specific social imaginaries.[12] In short, I want to ask that, if mathematics indeed became autonomous then what *kind* of autonomy it was? Before we hazard an answer to this question, a brief genealogy of the usual sense of mathematical autonomy, the one I am trying to argue against, will be useful. It will be seen that it is necessary to revisit this history in order to critically interrogate the project of 'modern' mathematics.

Autonomy: Instrumental or fantastical?

The kind of autonomy, sketches of which have been offered in the previous section, could be referred as *instrumental* or *operational* for it makes mathematics appear instrumentally or operationally closed. In my view the emergence of this sense of autonomy could be traced to the much talked about failure of the foundational programme in mathematics.

In an often rehearsed story, magnificently and most succinctly retold by the historian José Ferreirós (2008, pp. 142–156), attempts to base the edifice of mathematics onto secure footings so as to ensure that it doesn't run into latent contradictions and paradoxes, were unable to realise their foundational aims. However, it is also true that in the process copious amounts of mathematical knowledge was produced and the transformation was not only quantitative, but qualitative too. A stellar cast of mathematicians including people like, Frege, Cantor, Dedekind, Riemann, Klein, Hilbert, Zermelo, Skolem, Brouwer, Weyl, Bernays, Gödel, and many more contributed towards the refinement of mathematical techniques and methods and also charted out research agendas with exciting and breath-taking possibilities.[13] That many of these possibilities were subsequently realised in one form or the other in the following decades bespeaks the perceptive and far-sighted work accomplished in this era of frenzied mathematical activity.

Although, the mathematics produced was extremely diverse and there were often fierce disagreements, not only over the relative newcomers in the world of mathematical objects like the Cantorian Infinite, Axiom of Choice etc., but also over the very meaning of mathematical activity, the remarkably *introspective* character of the same was unmistakable. The work which began in the late 19th century, whose other end could be seen as the appearance of Gödel's incompleteness results in the 1930s and the setback they gave to the original ambitions of the Hilbert programme, contributed in various ways towards the growing self-sufficiency of mathematics. To put it in terms of the German sociologist Niklas Luhmann, the growing functional differentiation of mathematics, owing to its self-reflexive orientation and the diversity of perspectives driving its growth, contributed to its operational closure (Luhmann, 1988). For many like Bertrand Russell and David Hilbert it also signalled the freedom of mathematics from metaphysics. In fact the idea of setting mathematics 'free' could be seen as an underlying theme of the perspectives which are otherwise seen as completely opposed, such as those of Hilbert and Brouwer.[14] Taking the risk of over-simplification it can be said that the purported autonomy of mathematics under this straightforward narrative could be attributed to the manner in which mathematics became progressively immune to the agendas that shaped it from the outside and developed as an autopoietic system (Luhmann, 1988). The sense of the 'modern' one gets from this picture is one of a steadily drifting massive molten mass that eventually froze into an impenetrable landscape.

On the other hand if one pays heed to critical voices like that of the historian Leo Corry (2023) then there is no sense to be made of the 'modern' beyond of it being an exceedingly eclectic empirical configuration, which is best accessed through equally open and diverse research programmes. In fact Corry justly points out that the mathematics produced during the so-called modern period was so internally diverse, and moreover, trajectories of institutionalisation of mathematics in different cultural contexts were so different that no zeitgeist of the 'modern' can be drawn in this case, if at all it can be done in the case of the arts. He recommends, and rightly so in a sense, that our focus should be on specific mathematical traditions and we should be wary of using the category 'modern' as a self-explanatory one, for this carpet category will only end up obfuscating the above differences. Now, it would seem that whether we take the above genealogy of mathematical autonomy or listen to a respected historian like Leo Corry, in both cases doubts arise as to the viability of 'modern' as a historiographical category. As per the former the modernist transformation is over and has fulfilled its mandate, ironically making mathematics a modern-ever-after discipline, and, as per the latter one is bound to suspect the very usefulness of 'modern' as a category.

Having said this, if I still insist that one must revisit the 'modern' in mathematics it is so because I believe that there is more to it than a transcendental positing of autonomy or one or the other constructivist alternative offered against it. Thus, I still want to avail the conceptual import of the term 'modern' when looking at the history of mathematics, for I believe that the reflexive self-fashioning of the discipline as modern, if critically interrogated, can lead towards recognition of modern-in-dispersion and can have radically interruptive consequences at the level of pedagogy and mathematics education.[15] Thus, although a project like Leo Corry's is definitely interesting, I contend that it is in the very process of pursuing it that one comes across a more critical sense of 'autonomous' and 'modern' which could be recovered for purposes of (a) pedagogy and (b) demonstrating how the 'social' can be located *within* mathematics.

That the foundational programme failed in its original ambitions is not terribly interesting from our standpoint. For at its best this recognition goes no further than an appreciation of mathematics as a quasi-empirical science (Lakatos, 1978, pp. 3–41). As against this a sociological standpoint stresses again and again the need for being externalist about mathematics (Kerkhove

& Comjin, 2004).[16] The question arises; *how* to be an externalist about mathematics. We can perhaps uncouple the link between the failure of the foundational thematic and the formal autonomy of mathematics to delve deeper into this failure. My contention is that instead of completely outmoding the foundational efforts the failure of the foundational programme led to its reformulation and not simply its dismissal from the domain of mathematical enquiry.

As the metaphysical sense of 'founding' mathematics receded, it gave way to a more speculative *claiming* of foundations influenced by specific social imaginaries. Thus foundations were posited and claimed, instead of being shown to exist in an a priori manner.[17]

Certainly, this makes mathematical subject(s) always connected to the supposedly autonomous domain of mathematics, making it forever exposed to the politics of life and society. Not that this wasn't the case ever in the history of mathematics, but it became even more resoundingly so in the case of 'modern' mathematics, and not just quantitatively but qualitatively too. And here I am not only arguing á la Serres about the historicity of mathematics as a history of non-mathematicity, for this still leaves mathematics with an exclusive reflexive language which enables it to reactivate itself ceaselessly and in ever new contexts (Mercier, 2018).[18] Thus, I am not just searching for points of contact between mathematical ideality and historicity, but making a claim that mathematical forms are shaped by pictures of sociality and not only that, these pictures subsist *within* them. This also becomes evident through a consideration of the lives of mathematicians who have lived as per these forms, but let's postpone this analysis to later sections. Thus, for me the displacement of the foundational thematic is important, not just historically or in the sense that it was superseded, but to be seen as a series of deferments through which it was transformed or more precisely reformulated.

In trying to make this argument I am guided by Thierry de Duve's (1991) fascinating study of the impact that Marcel Duchamp's work had on the question 'what is art?' Just as Duchamp's very conscious abandoning of the question 'what is painting?' paradoxically led towards the opening and proliferation of claims to the effect that 'this is painting', similarly, repeated failures to 'found' mathematics, almost in parallel one could say, meant that foundational questions could be asked again and again, despite the loss of guarantee that mathematics could be ever rounded off metaphysically. As de Duve notes, Duchamp's disavowal of painting grew out of an acknowledgment of the crisis of pictorial practice with industrialisation and also of the impossibility of ever resolving it, likewise the works that I'll be discussing in the next section seem to recognise and certainly displace the so called foundational crisis in mathematics; the first (Turing) more consciously so than the latter (Bourbaki).

Finally, I propose to show that 'modern' mathematics is a 'social system' or a 'social form' or a 'form of life'. At one level this means that foundational questions acquired a functional dimension and instead of serving to found mathematics they (foundations) served to reinvent or recast mathematics, to create new/more mathematics. This also meant that the expressive raw material of mathematics, as it was handled by practitioners, became the only stuff where foundations of mathematics could be located. To put it a bit simplistically, mathematicians *themselves* and their *practice* became the foundations of their discipline and hence *pedagogy* emerged as the most central concern of the future foundational projects; this notwithstanding, the mathematician's own take on and ambitions with reference to the thematic. Thus, a *form of life* conditioned by the reformist variations on the so-called foundational thematic, which absorbed its ideological content at the same time displacing it, gave a somewhat stable structure to the subjective complex of being a 'mathematician', and also necessitated the various elaborations of this *form of life* into *forms of pedagogy*.

Thus, I contend that revisiting this period in the history of mathematics we can also begin to understand why mathematics is the most pedagogised discipline of all. As a preliminary answer, allow me to say that given the particular history of mathematics in Europe, on the one hand project(s) of pedagogisation came to carry within themselves the foundational desire to 'ground' mathematics, and on the other foundational projects found refuge in pedagogy through which they continued their pursuit under reformed conditions. As I have shown these projects were intimately connected, and in either way, this contributed to a relentless pedagogisation of the discipline.

Further calling mathematics a *form of life* implies that it is not only brought into being due to prior social and personal commitments but that it can be seen as a form which structures lives, which are lived as per it. I argue that to bring this fully into view we need to *eventalise* the category of 'modern' in mathematics and explore the plurality of mathematical forms in existence in the 1930s–40s[19]. This will take us from the formal autonomy attributed mathematics to what Arka Chattopadhyay (2020) in a recent interpretation has called as *fantastical autonomy*.[20]

As readers will recognise that this is far from self-evident and looking at mathematical forms as mathematical fantasies is deliberate and perhaps even blasphemous, but as I hope will emerge, this will possibly enable us to forge a more critical and nuanced relationship with the mathematics we (including the non-Europeans!) have inherited. Thus, revisiting the 'modern' in mathematics, I propose, can help us not only in understanding how the foundational or pedagogical closure in mathematics was achieved, but also how we can unstitch it to see the manner in which it was informed by very particular configurations which were in no way universal.

As these pedagogical projects, desirous of foundational security in different ways, spread to different parts of the world, have they not colluded with specific nationalist imaginaries in conjoining the mathematical-subject with the citizen-subject? Don't global mathematics projects based on the rhetoric for ALL seem to be similarly informed by configurations with very particular origins? The crucial point for this chapter is that the genealogy sketched in this section has gone unnoticed as far as the mainstream understanding of 'modern' mathematics is concerned. Thus mathematics for ALL is seen to have emerged as a natural and inevitable consequence of 'modern' mathematics, where the latter appellation serves as a neutral designator of transformations now lying under the debris of history. Let me stress again the consequences this seems to have left behind from the perspective of this chapter. One is that it is little appreciated that even when the era of searching for foundations of mathematics was left behind, foundational pursuits continued in the name of reforming mathematics and mathematics education. And, secondly, the latter reforms or re-articulations of mathematics continued as autonomous exercises, and were considered independent of the politics of life and society.

Building on these thoughts, I now proceed to take two examples which exemplarily demonstrate the displacement of the 'foundational', reforming it to yield interesting and new mathematics, viz the mathematical work of Alan Turing and the Bourbaki group. Readers will come to see how their perception as strictly post-foundational, and hence disconnected from the politics I have thus far outlined, has meant that we view them in naïvely instrumental ways (Turing simply as a precursor of AI and Bourbaki just as an esoteric project of updating axioms), without paying due attention to the social imaginaries they embody, and their vexed relationship with the 'modern', which in turn inevitably bolsters the image of instrumental autonomy and operational closure which mathematics is supposed to possess.

Turing

What did Turing achieve as a mathematician from our point of view?[21] Let us start from the very basics without making things too technical. Turing, first of all, translated the aims and ambitions of the Hilbert programme into *concrete* terms. Most particularly he went backstage to the formalisation drama proposed by Hilbert to ask such basic questions as, what is a machine? What is computation? What is an algorithm? Etc. Thus it was by *materialising* Hilbert, even more so than Gödel did, that Turing was able to show the inherent limitations of the project of completely formalising mathematics. Thus in a very different sense than Hilbert and others his work was foundational, where being so meant asking questions which were preliminary and elemental, but nevertheless critical. In fact it could be said he was the first mathematician to have taken Hilbert *literally* and who went the furthest in asking whether the straitjacketed solutions Hilbert was hoping for the mega-problems he had posed at the turn of the century could really be achieved. Turing recognised that such questions, as for example Hilbert's *decision* problem, have to be located in the midst of actual mathematical work and suitably tempered in scope in order to make them interesting and imaginatively productive. And, as per my reading, he did this by adding the dimension of *learning* to what was otherwise seen as a self-sustaining and self-perpetuating system of mathematics. By making how human mathematicians learn and do mathematics the model for 'intelligent' and 'thinking' machines, he was not just 'humanising' machines, but, as if any proof of this was needed, to 'humanise' mathematics in the first place.[22]

With Turing we have the most profound recognition of the inherent sociality of mathematics. Probably one of the rare times in the history of mathematics a mathematician was trying to drive home the point that mathematical signs have meaning only in the midst of life, both inside and outside of mathematics.

His work on what is commonly known as the *Halting problem* showed that even a machine with ideal competence i.e. one which matches the ideal of self-sufficiency will fall into infinite regress when fed with its own description. It is important to note that this was not an argument against formalisation or mechanisation, but an attempt to show that we need to relax the focus on competence, even when dealing with machines. In Turing's vision then, shaped by the Cambridge milieu in which he grew as a mathematician, the ideal and the normative, though they often shade into each other, are different.[23] That which is envisioned as ideal externalises and fixes the normative which is otherwise implicit and inexhaustible. That mathematical activity is *normative* is different from seeing it as ideal and removed from the messy practices in which it otherwise inheres.

It is in fact often forgotten that Turing's attempts to lay bare the nature of mechanisation was closely tied to his work in the foundations of mathematics. His work showed that Hilbert's aim for mathematical completeness was worth pursuing but one must be willing to accept inconsistency, even outright mistakes, in attending to it. That's how humans strive for completeness, by making and then learning from mistakes, and that's how one can talk about machine intelligence as well, by drawing *parallels* between *human fallibility* and *machine fallibility*. Thus another sociologically important point emerges that recalls Georges Canguilhem's seminal work on the qualitative significance of *error*, and foregrounds the role of learning *in* a social form of life; the idea that, 'the abnormal, while logically second is existentially first' (Canguilhem, 1989, p. 239). It is now part of the mathematical lore that Turing achieved this through discretisation of formalisation, a step which foresaw the development of computers, but I doubt its significance from the point of pedagogy has been appreciated. Particularly, when we think of Turing's meditation on the ability to *go on*, *taking the next step* and the role of *mistakes* in *trajectories of learning*. It is worthwhile to note that Wittgenstein also posed his rule-following paradoxes by focussing closely on the notion of a *step*, much like Turing, by giving mathematical and philosophical significance to the idea of the *next step* (Wittgenstein, 1956).

Turing has been anachronistically read as a proponent of the mechanistic view of the mind and as holding onto an imitationist perspective on AI, but a closer attention to his writings reveals that he was thinking of his mathematical work as well as practising it in a very different way. He was in a way attempting to locate the foundations where they really belong, in teaching, learning, and most importantly learning from mistakes by trying out new things.[24]

That the foundations of mathematics could be thought of in this way has two immediate implications. First, it's acknowledged that mathematics seen as a system is indeed incomplete, but when seen as a human activity this incompleteness becomes one mathematical fact among many, not to be read as a metaphysically privileged one in any which way. And second, just as with any other practice mathematical practice too is marked by ingenuity and inventiveness, and hence is open-ended and always predisposed to change in unforeseen ways. It is crucial to note that Turing's appreciation of novelty in mathematics in the face of seemingly debilitating incompleteness is premised on an intimate connection between *fallibility* and *sociality*. It is due to this fact that Turing often recommended that mathematicians should take regular stock of their phraseology, their tools and methods and regularly scan or revise or reform their field (Gandy, 2001). It cannot be emphasised enough that for him foundations are spread out as a mathematical form of life and not simply as rigid symbolism.

A direct consequence of Turing's work is that an account of mathematical normativity, could only be *social* for that not only grounds mathematical techniques and procedures, but also has ample scope for novelty. Unlike the way in which Turing's work has been traditionally incorporated into the standard AI discourse, a closer reading of Turing reveals that intelligence is not simply about imitation but about *acculturation into a social form of life*. The key question for him was not whether machines could imitate humans, but whether they can recognise what are the exemplary forms of social behaviour and then rightly claim for themselves the exemplarity of intelligent behaviour.

I hope the brief and sketchy description offered here will serve to underline the subtle process through which the foundationalism programme of mathematics in Europe got a new articulation with learning and pedagogy at the centre. Both the perils as well as promises of such new articulations, such as the one given by Turing, lie in recognising this connection between foundational concerns and pedagogy and hence in understanding their 'modernity' not as a break in purely instrumental terms. This will not only add historical flesh to these episodes in the history of mathematics, but also serve as an opportunity of critically revisiting the impact of foundationalism in the pedagogisation of mathematics.[25] If with Turing we have the first clear articulation of the foundational value of the 'social' for mathematics, have we been able to critique that sociality for what it was. In other words, have we been able to ask the question that if mathematics was about acculturation into a form of life, then what form of life was it? Today when notions such as the 'next step', 'learning from mistakes', etc. have hardened into clichéd educational euphemisms, it seems that we have forgotten that they emerged from within very particular reformulations of the foundational project and hence from a very specific cultural legacy. It has been one of the key arguments of this chapter, that paying attention to these particular reformulations of the foundational project will help us in restoring to the sense of 'modern' in mathematics a critical potential, which is otherwise lost in imagining the leap to 'modern' mathematics as purely triumphal and a linear one.

Having given some sense of how a certain vision of sociality informs Turing's mathematics let me take another example, where just like with Turing the thematic of foundations is posed afresh, but this time differently and informed by a very different picture of the 'social'.

Bourbaki

Perhaps, the point I am trying to make with reference to Turing's work will emerge with greater clarity when compared with another project for which foundations were important, but in a very different way. And, it is even more illustrative, for the manner in which this project later got stunted, and even became reactionary, reveals how the social imaginary underpinning it turned rigid and closed. I am talking about the Bourbaki group.[26] It is immensely interesting that Bourbaki embarked on the project of unifying mathematics, barely a few years after the project of 'founding' mathematics suffered a major setback at the hands of Gödel. They went about their task with cold blooded focus and with a total disregard for other attempts at securing the foundations of mathematics and the fate they have met. In their case the attempt to unify mathematics acquired a purely pragmatic dimension, bereft of any deeper metaphysical or ideological commitment. This led to a massive *rewriting* exercise where large swathes of mathematics were recast from an avowedly structural point of view. The idea was to disentangle mathematical relations from a vast and evolving discursive space and to set out explicitly their foundational or structural base.

To be sure the project was overly ambitious, but from our point of view what is significant is its manifestly *pedagogical* aim.[27] The foundational agenda that Bourbaki pursued was not extra-mathematical, instead it grew from a deep dissatisfaction with the way in which the learning of mathematics was organised, particularly as far as the 'transition' from primary to secondary level and the tertiary level was concerned. It is interesting to note that the category of structure most associated with the Bourbakis was not of much significance when the series of texts they produced is closely analysed. In fact, at best it was used as an Ad-hoc and informal category, and at worst, if used in a formalised way, impeded the clear presentation of the subject matter.[28] Yet, where Bourbaki proved impactful was through their massive rewriting exercise, which as

I have tried to argue with respect to Turing, embodied a distinct social imaginary. This involved the 'presentation' of mathematics in a way that it becomes accessible to all. Thus the 'structure' in the Bourbakian sense becomes a device for post-facto reconstruction of mathematical knowledge to ensure greater learning and participation of young learners.

Rewriting mathematics in Bourbaki's vision was seen as a shared and secretive enterprise, which as a craft was held closely in common and zealously protected. It formed a kind of reaction, a *Weberian-vocational* one, to the immense specialisation and diversification to which the fate of mathematics had become resigned to. The kind of rewriting Bourbaki undertook remains unprecedented and although it eventually encountered stagnancy, it is certainly worth revisiting from the standpoint (i.e. pursuing the foundational agenda, but with learning and pedagogy at its core) I have tried to present here. Further, it was not the case that their rewriting project was merely an attempt at systematisation, rather it was equally to aid discovery by identifying crucial problems and best ways of addressing them. Thus structures as Bourbaki laid them out, primarily had a functional role i.e. of unifying mathematics through analogically elaborating structures from one domain to other.[29]

It is very important to evaluate the Bourbakian project critically.[30] Because of its spatialising ambitions it was dominated by a distinct imaginary and neither the status quo of the symbolic nor the temporalisation of the real could really explain what the Bourbakis achieved in their early years.[31] But it was also the case that the project was unable to pay heed to its own criticality and became increasingly closed and secretive. Most importantly, ironical though it may seem, it became captive of its own foundational language, of sets and structures, and was unable to perceive the emergence of categories as a chance for *speculating afresh* on the question of foundations. Now, the question arises: what was the nature of the social imaginary which underpinned the mathematics of the Bourbaki group? According to my reading Bourbaki's mathematics harboured a very important recognition that mathematics is always rewriting itself and henceforth is constantly subject to the process of decentring; i.e. the notion of structure should constantly evolve and cover ever new and distinct areas, instead of getting tied up with the (mathematical?) subject (here the Bourbaki group). Where it faltered is that the group thought that it could really control the recursivity that emerges through rewriting mathematics, that is in recognising that the very process of rewriting may lead towards new ways of unifying and recasting the discipline, for example through the usage of categories. Further, by assigning themselves a proper name (a pseudonym) the members lost the ability to create mathematics in their own respective names.[32] Thus the form of sociality which characterises a *sect* and the desire to keep their identity an open secret became dominant and seized over the democratic impulse which was unleashed by their attempts to 'reform' mathematics and deliver it from the lure of intuitionistic mysticism.

To reiterate, for our purpose it is deeply interesting that a project like this could have emerged after the era of foundationalism in mathematics had well-nigh ended. Although Bourbaki's project is usually not viewed as a continuation of foundational projects in mathematics, I have tried to argue that we must try and situate Bourbaki in the same cultural legacy marked by the failure of the original foundational programme in mathematics. Given the enormous impact that Bourbaki had on mathematics education world-over, it is important to remember that their sense of mathematical 'reform' had a very definite source of emergence located in the French context and responding to the educational scene there. The Bourbaki's may not have been able to give a sound metaphysical or meta-mathematical sense to their idea of 'structure', but their reliance on ideas such as invariance, isomorphism and transformation, was always aspiringly foundational. As said before, the absence of meta-mathematical assuredness was more than made up for by giving pedagogical and functional sense to the idea of structure.

Thus the earlier project of making mathematics foundationally secure, which only had fellow mathematicians as addressees, now came to include a much larger audience; particularly, under the Bourbakist influence, the young learners of mathematics. The above arguments not only attest to the longevity of the foundational thematic, but also show how it got fundamentally *reformed* with Turing and Bourbaki. That this has not been sufficiently appreciated means that we have failed to fully understand the nature of speculative agreement, *over what is taken to be foundational*, that marks mathematical practice at any given period of time. For after the failure of the so-called foundational programme and more importantly as a result of it, the 'social' became inextricably involved, particularly with the way in which the 'sensible' in mathematics was parsed and distributed. Not to say that all this was radically new, but certainly its recognition became possible in a deeply significant way for the first time, and why that recognition didn't develop or lead towards an appreciation of the sociality of mathematics in the way that it should have, remains a question which could be only answered through a thorough unpacking of the category of 'modern' in mathematics. I have been only able to hint this in the case of Turing and Bourbaki, but I hope this will pave the way for a more detailed archaeology of modern mathematics to take shape in future.

Conclusion

Bourbaki and Turing were two figures who have majorly influenced the way in which we view mathematics today; Bourbaki in his own life-time and Turing in more recent years, owing to the areas they were active in; sets and group theory and logic and algorithms respectively. However, in this chapter I was less concerned with the actual-empirical influence they had, than detecting a symptom. When from today's vantage point we think of mathematics for ALL and the idea of a global-citizen premised on the latter, we regard their works as exemplary in contributing to the democratisation of mathematics, either by unifying it through the idea of structure or algorithmising it by making notions of 'pedagogy' and 'learning' as central to the mathematical enterprise.

This chapter, though it recognises and respects their contributions and of various mathematics (education) reform movements, it, nevertheless, attempts to show that the idea of 'reforming' mathematics has had a very particular cultural legacy.

The argument I have made is that failure of the foundation programme in mathematics didn't lead towards the abandonment of the foundational thematic but its reformulation(s). Further, I have tried to argue that these revisions were informed by the increasingly important role played by the sense of 'reform' in modernity. This also implied that the foundational thematic was given a deeply *material* foundation such that, how mathematics is written or put down acquired centre stage. A direct consequence of this was that the socio-technical imaginaries pertaining to the foundations of mathematics could speculate *what is mathematics?* without the assurance or sometimes even the desire for final answers. I have also tried to argue that this experimental/speculative dimension which eventalises the discourse of mathematics and makes it possible to locate the 'social' in mathematics has not been paid much attention to when it comes to pedagogy. It is the reason why we perceive various mathematical reform movements and mathematical styles with reformist tendencies, such as those of Turing and Bourbaki, as neutral and ultimately beneficial restatements of mathematical knowledge, and not as particular creative styles attempting to create new mathematics; styles which were responding to and were deeply entrenched in the foundational legacy.

It is in the continuation of this legacy that I locate the still prevalent foundational lens through which we continue to view mathematics without realising the same; in the sense that it is something basic, meant for ALL, EVERYWHERE, and is a key to becoming a global-citizen. Stated precisely in terms of the argument of the chapter, whether it is Turing or Bourbaki, or any directly pedagogical movement, we continue to view them with a non-critical sense of the 'modern' and 'autonomy' in mathematics. The chapter has offered an alternate genealogy of the above categories, not only to show the particular origins of mathematical styles which are considered as context free and neutral, but also to understand the 'will to reform' that has characterised much of the discourse on mathematics in the twentieth century and still continues to do so. The chapter traces this 'will to reform' to the early twentieth century foundational projects in mathematics and their hangover, in different forms and guises, in the supposedly 'post-foundational' mathematics that followed and in its various reformist agendas.

Notes

1 This fieldwork was conducted between 2015 and 2017, and involved participant observation in institutions in India such as University of Delhi, Indian Institute of Technology Delhi, Harish Chandra Research Institute Allahabad and Indian Statistical Institute Kolkata. The mathematicians I spoke to emphasised the importance

of certain "western" textbooks in shaping the formative parts of their careers and the way in which these textbooks introduced them to the "modern" approach in specific areas of mathematics.

2 Both the New Math Movement and "Commission Lichnerowicz", represent reform movements, in the United States and France respectively, aimed primarily at how mathematics is taught at schools. Where the New Math Movement, gained momentum after the Soviet launching of Sputnik (October 4, 1957), and sought to introduce a heavy dosage of logic and set-theory in the presentation of mathematical concepts in school-curriculum, the work of "Commission Lichnerowicz" started in the late 1960s in France, and aimed at disseminating the Bourbakian influence in schools. Driven by a range of geo-political and cultural reasons both these movements attempted to reform mathematics education as per modern-axiomatic principles. For more details see, Corry (2007).

3 See Giles (2014).

4 As a mathematician I spoke to in the field told me, "thanks to Hilbert and a few others we can safely disregard the philosophical issues surrounding mathematical practice and carry on with our work in a run-of-the-mill kind of manner".

5 Thus the chapter makes a case for re-examining the connections between foundationally inclined views of mathematics which were pursued with great rigour in the first half of the twentieth century in Europe and projects of 'reform' which came to dominate the discourse on mathematics once these views had outwardly become unfashionable.

6 For example, see Corry (2007), for the transformation of Hilbertian axiomatic at the hands of the topologist Robert L. Moore and subsequently in the New Math movement. For an interesting overview of the relationship between foundational beliefs and ethics in mathematics and mathematics education, see Spindler (2022).

7 I adapt the idea of *pedagogised* from Basil Bernstein's work (Bernstein, 1996). It means the re-presentation or re-statement of knowledge for the aims of pedagogic transmission. Bernstein's fascinating analysis shows us how through strategies of communication, control and circulation within an intricate web of power relations and social divisions, pedagogy becomes *overdetermined*. I use this idea in this context to argue that after the attempts to base mathematics onto something pre-given receded in the background, pedagogic concerns stepped in to play the same role, but in a reformed manner, and in process got overdetermined, and not just that, but over-prioritised by the state too.

8 I must clarify the notion of genealogy here before moving on. As with Foucault and Nietzsche, I gesture towards the totality of historical discourse (in the age of Turing and Bourbaki) where concerns to translate the metaphysical aims of the foundational programme into practical approaches to foundations was present across the spectrum of mathematical practices. That is also the reason behind choosing Turing and Bourbaki, as they represent two very different *kinds* of mathematics, with no common ideological programme underpinning them. The notion of genealogy is used here to point out the dispersion across which foundational concerns acquired a new articulation. See, Foucault in Rabinow (1984).

9 I wish to highlight for readers the relation I am drawing between how Greenberg connects modernism in arts with 'competence' with 'competence' in mathematics. In the case of mathematics, greater entrenchment in mathematical competence supposedly frees one from philosophical and speculative doubts regarding the discipline, so much so that formal competence is seen as a kind of therapy. Developing formal competence in mathematics is then seen as a skill which should be developed, as early as possible, to set children on the right track of learning. No wonder reformist projects in mathematics education have often

been reproached for privileging the formal and the axiomatic in their presentation of the subject.

10 For an interesting discussion on functional differentiation with particular reference to the history of logic see Schorr, (1999, pp. 64–77).

11 This connection between arts and mathematics has also been noted by Jeremy Gray in his magisterial history of modernism in mathematics. See, Gray (2008).

12 I use the idea of social imaginary in the sense elaborated in Cornelius Castoriadis's seminal work *The Imaginary Institution of Society* (1975). Using this perspective I see different kinds of mathematics as, "a rational response given in the imaginary through symbolic means" (Castoriadis, 1975, p. 138). Thus the idea is to see what *self-instituting social imaginaries* inform various mathematical forms. As a fascinating example see the discussion on the parallels between G. Spencer Brown *Laws of Form* and Niklas Luhmann's analysis of social systems (Schiltz, 2009). For how mathematical imaginaries embody as well as shape social imaginaries see Netz's (1999) fascinating work on the shaping of deduction in Greek mathematics. Particularly, on how the social imaginary dominated by rhetoric and polemic in ancient Greece, paved the way for the evolution of the 'style' of mathematics seen as an exemplary mechanism for 'concluding' arguments.

13 Perhaps it will not come as a surprise that the foundational project was largely a *masculine* project, until it was *queered* in interesting ways, first by Wittgenstein and then by Turing. For a very interesting account of the impact that Wittgenstein and Turing mutually had on each other see Floyd (2016).

14 For an insightful exploration of the articulation of freedom within Hilbert's mathematics and philosophical views, see Franks (2009). For an articulation of intuition and freedom over the terrain of mathematical work, see Brouwer (1983).

15 By modern-in-dispersion I intend to signal that even though no zeitgeist of the 'modern' was possible in the case of mathematics (as in the case of arts and literature), the valences of this idea are too critical for it to be given up. This means that something did change with modern mathematics such that it acquired an unforeseen autonomy, but, I insist that this autonomy must be interrogated to understand that this does not mean that mathematics became closed for external reflection, rather its autonomy went and goes along with it being subtended by the 'social'.

16 By being 'externalist' means approaching a discipline from the outside, without siding with one or the other established epistemological standpoints.

17 For example it will be a great inquiry to ask how the growth of cybernetics and information theory was influenced by the *image* of society as a self-correcting system. At the very basic level, the development of such views meant that purely logical or mathematical paradoxes or paradoxes which were understood to be purely logical or mathematical came to be seen as communication paradoxes instead, relating to intersubjective behaviour and shared-knowledge. For a useful reference, see Pickering (2010). For a very explicit connection between the view that society is a self-correcting system and the interpretation of logical paradoxes as communication paradoxes see Gregory Bateson's ultimately flawed, but deeply original text, *Naven* (1936). For an illuminating discussion on how logic has embedded within it a sense of intersubjective or social time, see Lacan (2006, pp. 161-175).

18 By 'non-mathematicity', Mercier means that even though mathematics is a self-grounding language it also has an irreducibly historical character (as all languages do), and thus absorbs historical 'impurities', i.e. facts of history and culture in process.

19 I use the idea of 'event' here in the sense employed by the Indian social anthropologist Veena Das in her book *Critical Events* (1995). The event under this understanding is seen as introducing newness in a situation which could not have been foreseen purely through a structural understanding of the same.

20 "This fantastic autonomy is the exact opposite of the ideological autonomy of technological and instrumental mathematical structures...This autonomy is an act of liberation...while the previous autonomy was technological, this one is subjective" (Chattopadhyay, 2020, pp. 313). To be precise Chattopadhyay deals with mathematical fantasies as they unfold on the literary register in the stories by Italo Calvino. This chapter on the other hand makes a case for looking at mathematical forms themselves as mathematical fantasies.

21 For a good biographical introduction to Turing see the book by Andrew Hodges (1983) and the remarkable text by Turing's mother, Ethel Sara Turing (1959).

22 For an important discussion on how Turing's work was related to foundations of mathematics, see Piccinini (2003). Piccinini points out that despite believing in the effective mechanisation of steps and procedures in mathematics or even otherwise, Turing repeatedly took note of 'human' or 'mathematical' intelligence, going to the extent of figuring-in and responding to the mathematical objection to machine-intelligence, because he also at the same time believed that dead-ends induced by formalisation are overcome because mathematicians can learn, adapt and try out new models. That machines can be as intelligent as humans or even more, followed for Turing from this centrality of learning to mathematical work, which meant that just like human beings, machines too can learn and adapt to new contexts.

23 For an illuminating study of the impact of the Cambridge milieu on Turing the mathematician, see Floyd (2016).

24 In fact in his celebrated paper *Computing Machinery and Intelligence* Turing tries to make clear that infallibility cannot be seen as an index of intelligence. In the paper he deliberately introduced a mistake in a simple calculation (of addition) made by a computer in response to a question by a human interlocutor to show that it is perfectly normal for a machine to make mistakes in the way humans do. This in fact demonstrates the very human dimension of intelligence possessed by machines. See, Turing (1950).

25 As an indication I would like to mention here that Turing's colleague in the Bletchley Park effort to decipher German codes during World War-II, the British mathematician, Peter Hilton, has explicitly drawn the connection between Turing's style of mathematics and mathematics education (Hilton, 1984). Hilton largely relies on their 'successes' in war efforts to make a case for instrumentally oriented mathematics and reforming mathematics education accordingly. In fact, the consequences he hopes to draw from his association with Turing and others will in his view help in developing "features of a mathematics education that should help *all* students" (Hilton, 1984, p. 552) (emphasis in the original). But, in making this connection he misses precisely the aspect I have been arguing for in this chapter, which is that Turing's reformulation of the foundational programme in mathematics in 'practical' terms was informed by a particular picture of sociality. The latter involved notions about error, fallibility, learning, intelligence etc., which were very much a part of the social milieu in which Turing's mathematics took shape.

26 For an interesting albeit contentious history of the Bourbaki group, see Aczel (2006). 'Bourbaki', as is well known, was the adopted name for a group of mathematicians who took upon themselves to rewrite mathematics with a view to unify it and to demonstrate the interlinkages between seemingly disparate mathematical domains. The group was formed in 1934-35 in France, at around the

same time when Alan Turing was making his seminal contributions, by a group of French mathematicians seeking to rebuild the French tradition of mathematics and to counter the ascendancy of the German tradition with their refurbished and robust programme of reconstructing or re-inscribing' mathematics. The initial group included Henri Cartan, Claude Chevalley, Jean Delsarte, Jean Dieudonné, Szolem Mandelbrot, René de Possel, André Weil, Jean Coulomb and Charles Ehresmann among others. The group reached the height of its powers by mid twentieth century and influenced the traditions of mathematics worldover, but eventually its strength waned as it became a victim of its own successes, as it was very reticent in engaging with emerging approaches, in particular with the mathematics of categories. For interesting details from this history and for an illuminating study of the sociality embodied by the collective, see Beaulieu (1999).

27 As Anne-Marie Marmier (2014) has pointed out the group was born in 1934 with Henri Cartan and André Weil trying to write an elementary course on analysis given their dissatisfaction with the then used university textbook written by Edouard Goursat.

28 See Corry (1992) on this point.

29 See Heinzmann and Petitot (2020).

30 To ask for example why the group never had any woman mathematician within its fold and does this have something to do with the way in which Bourbaki's mathematics was conceptualised.

31 That is neither as purely 'symbolic' abstraction nor as the 'real' which escapes that abstraction, but a productive exercise in the 'imaginary'.

32 See the insightful essay by Barany (2020) on the associational politics underpinning Bourbaki and twentieth century mathematics more generally.

References

Aczel, A. D. (2006). *The artist and the mathematician: The story of Nicolas Bourbaki, the genius mathematician who never existed*. Thunder's Mouth Press.

Barany, M. J. (2020). Impersonation and personification in mid-twentieth century mathematics. *History of Science*, *58*(4). https://doi.org/10.1177/0073275320924571 (last accessed on 16 July 2023).

Bateson, G. (1936). *Naven*. Cambridge University Press.

Beaulieu, L. (1999). Bourbaki's art of memory. *Osiris*, *14*(2), 219–251.

Bernstein, B. (1996). *Pedagogy, symbolic control and identity*. Taylor and Francis.

Brouwer, J. (1983). Consciousness, philosophy and mathematics. In P. Benacerraf & H. Putnam (Eds.), *Philosophy of mathematics: Selected readings* (pp. 90–96). Cambridge University Press.

Canguilhem, G. 1989. *The normal and the pathological* (Carolyn R. Fawcett, Trans.). Zone Books.

Castoriadis, C. (1975). *The imaginary institution of society* (Kathleen Blamey, Trans.). Polity Press.

Chattopadhyay, A. (2020). Mathematical possibilities in modernism. *Journal of Humanistic Mathematics*, *10*(1), 295–316.

Corry, L. (1992). Nicolas Bourbaki and the concept of mathematical structure. *Synthese*, *92*, 315–348.

Corry, L. (2007). Axiomatics between Hilbert and the new math: Diverging views on mathematical research and their consequences on education. *The International Journal for the History of Mathematics Education*, *2*(2), 21–37.

Corry, L. (2023). How useful is the term 'Modernism' for understanding the history of early twentieth-century mathematics? In K. Chemla, J. Ferreiros, L. Jhi, E. Scholz,

& C. Wang (Eds.), *The richness of the history of mathematics: A tribute to Jeremy Gray* (pp. 393–423). Springer.

Das, V. (1995). *Critical events: An anthropological perspective on contemporary India.* Oxford University Press.

De Duve, T. (1991). *Pictorial nominalism: On marcel Duchamp's passage from painting to the readymade* (Dana Polan, Trans.). University of Minnesota Press.

Diaz, J. (2017). New mathematics: A tool for living the modern life, making the mathematical citizen, and the problem of disadvantage. In T. Popkewitz, J. Diaz, & C. Kirchgasler (Eds.), *A political sociology of educational knowledge: Studies of exclusion and difference* (pp. 149–164). Routledge.

Ferreirós, J. (2008). The crisis in the foundations of mathematics. In J. Barrow-Green & I. Leader (Eds.), *The Princeton companion to mathematics* (pp. 142–164). Princeton University Press.

Floyd, J. (2016). Chains of life: Turing, Lebensform, and the emergence of Wittgenstein's later style. *Nordic Wittgenstein Review*, *5*(2), 7–89.

Foucault, M. (1984). Nietzsche, genealogy, history. In P. Rabinow (Ed.), *The Foucault reader* (pp. 76–100). Pantheon Books.

Franks, C. (2009). *The autonomy of mathematical knowledge: Hilbert's program revisited.* Cambridge University Press.

Gandy, R. O. (2001). Introduction to Turing's 'The reform of mathematical notation and Phraseology' (1944-45). In R. O. Gandy & C. E. M. Yates (Eds.), *Collected works of A.M. Turing: Mathematical logic* (pp. 211–213). North Holland/Elsevier Science.

Giles, G. (2014). *An ethical inquiry: Toward education in an infinite condition* [Doctoral Dissertation, The University of British Columbia]. The University of British Columbia Open Library.

Gray, J. (2008). *Plato's ghost: The modernist transformation of mathematics.* Princeton University Press.

Greenberg, C. (1965). Modernist painting. In F. Frascina & C. Harrison (Eds.), *Modern art and modernism: A critical anthology* (pp. 5–10). Harper and Row.

Heinzmann, G., & Petitot, J. (2020). *The functional role of structures in Bourbaki.* https://oxford.universitypressscholarship.com/view/10.1093/oso/9780190641221.001.0001/oso-9780190641221-chapter-8 (last accessed on 3 January 2021).

Hilton, P. (1984). Cryptanalysis in World War–II - and Mathematics education. *The Mathematics Teacher*, *77*(7), 548–552.

Hodges, A. (1983). *Alan Turing: The enigma.* Simon and Schuster.

Kerkhove, B. V., & Comjin, H. (2004). The importance of being externalist about mathematics – One more turn? *Philosophica*, *74*(1), 103–122.

Lacan, J. (2006). Logical time and the assertion of anticipated certainty: A new sophism. In B. Fink (Ed. & Trans.), *Ecrits* (pp. 161–175). WW Norton.

Lakatos, I. (1978). *Mathematics, science and epistemology: Philosophical papers volume 2.* Cambridge University Press.

Latour, B. (1993). *We have never been modern* (Catherine Porter, Trans.). Harvard University Press.

Luhmann, N. (1988). The autopoiesis of social systems. In F. Geyer & J. Van Der Zouwen (Eds.), *Socio-cybernetic paradoxes* (pp. 172–192). Sage.

Marmier, A. M. (2014). On the idea of 'democratisation', 'modern mathematics' and mathematics teaching in France. *Lettera Matematica*, *2*, 139–148.

Mercier, L. K. (2018). The mathematical anamneses. In R. Dolphijn (Ed.), *Michel Serres and the crisis of the contemporary* (pp. 51–70). Bloomsbury.

Netz, R. (1999). *The shaping of deduction in Greek mathematics: A study in cognitive history.* Cambridge University Press.

Piccinini, G. (2003). Alan Turing and the mathematical objection. *Minds and Machines*, *13*, 23–48.

Pickering, A. (2010). *The cybernetic brain: Sketches of another future.* The University of Chicago Press.
Schiltz, M. (2009). Space is the place: The *laws of form* and social systems. In B. Clarke & M. B. N. Hansen (Eds.), *Emergence and embodiment: New essays on second-order systems theory* (pp. 157–178). Duke University Press.
Schorr, K. E. (1999). On the analysis and use of form in logic. In D. Baecker (Ed.), *Problems of form* (pp. 64–77). Stanford University Press.
Spindler, R. (2022). Foundational mathematical beliefs and ethics in mathematical practice and education. *Journal of Humanistic Mathematics, 12*(2), 49–70.
Turing, A. (1950). Computing machinery and intelligence. *Mind, 59*, 433–460.
Turing, E. S. (1959). *Alan M. Turing.* Heffer & Sons.
Wittgenstein, L. (1956). *Remarks on the foundations of mathematics* (G.E.M. Anscombe and G.H. Von Wright, Eds. & G.E.M. Anscombe, Trans.). Basil Blackwell.

7 Becoming citizen subject in the body politic

Antinomies of archaic, modern, and posthuman citizenship spatiotemporalities and the political of mathematics education

Anna Chronaki

Introduction

As mathematics education is called for an ethical response to re/claim democracy in contexts of continuous injustices due to increased ecological decay, poverty, exhaustion, and pandemics, the idea of citizenship returns to re/configure mathematical practices. Albeit with different foci, global institutions such as the Organisation for Economic Co-operations and Development (OECD, 2013) or United Nations (United Nations Educational, Scientific and Cultural Organization, 2020) and local communities aim to rethink mathematics education (e.g. policy, curricula, in/formal didactics, teacher education) addressing citizens in contemporary precarity. The recent special issues of *Research in Mathematics Education* (Chronaki & Yolcu, 2021; le Roux et al., 2022) and *Educational Studies in Mathematics* (Chan et al., 2021) are indicative of such urgencies.

Overall, several approaches towards making mathematics education relevant through citizenship can be noted. *First,* projects appropriate the instrumental citizen as high-achiever, problem-solver and able to inquiry socio-scientific issues or wicked-problems with mathematics (Maans et al., 2019). *Second,* the critical citizen is highlighted for creating awareness of mathematics as "formatting power" in society (Gutstein, 2005; Skovsmose, 1994). *Third,* the diverse "other" of native and indigenous communities (d'Ambrosio, 1985) is foregrounded as non-citizen or not-yet-citizen around struggles for recognition, representation and rights for lands, heritages, languages, values, and knowledges including the right for culturally responsive mathematics education. *Fourth,* the marginalised, oppressed and discriminated others, often portrayed as second-category citizens, are discussed in relation to persistent systemic inequalities in urban schooling with devastating effects on individual and collective lives due to racism, sexism, and ableism (Chen & Horn, 2022; Tate, 2008). *Fifth,* the modern citizen subject of mathematics education is captured as a "mastery of reason" fantasy (Walkerdine, 1988) or as an alchemy governing people (Popkewitz, 2004) and sustaining capitalism (Baldino & Cabral, 2018).

DOI: 10.4324/9781003130673-9

Although the above suggest different investments of mathematics education to determine citizen subjectivity, the concepts of citizenship, citizen, and subject remain largely unexamined, functioning as empty signifiers that conceal unresolvable antinomies. The notion of antinomy describes the paradoxes, tensions, or aporias referring to "a problem that can be neither definitely resolved nor utterly eradicated" (Balibar, 2015, p. 2). Antinomies in mathematics education occur when differential exclusions persist despite efforts for social justice, inclusionary pedagogies, or "maths for all" curricula (Marcone & Skovsmose, 2014; Walkerdine, 1988). Balibar (2010) theorises citizenship as fraught with antinomies, that unfold in historical and socio-material settings, linked to the citizen's political agency for democratisation. Unexamined antinomies reproduce binary discourses that *either* deliberatively strive for citizenship acts with competent subjects in a democratic civil society (the citizen as agent for systemic change: *first to fourth approach*) *or* critique such strivings as destined to fail (the citizen as always subjected to systemic power: *fifth approach*). With Balibar, the chapter explores how diverse images of becoming citizen subject and their antinomies are traced through citizenship spatiotemporalities and discusses how they permeate mathematics education.

The citizen subject in the body politic: In-between subjection and agency

"Citizen subject" was Balibar's response when, in the late 1980s, Jean Luc Nancy asked "who comes after the subject?" in an invitation to debate a recurrent controversy about the "death of the subject". Instead of asserting a death to the subject, Nancy (1991) sought to interrogate the placing of "subjectivity on trial" (p. 5) insisting to reinvent the "who". Haines and Grattan (2017) note that posthumanity realises the limits of the subject, as a modern synthesis of self and otherness, or a disciplinary technology and argue that: "the subject becomes artificial, contingent, perishable" (p. 5). The limits of the subject as a "humane who", and the radical quest for how its material substance has been rendered invisible in modern subjectivity, was brought in response to Nancy's call. Specifically, Derrida (1991) noted the risk of restricting the pursuit of a "who" into an anthropocentric grammar in which the specters of liberal personhood, possessive individualism, man-animal opposition, or identity positions create the return of a repressed subject. And Deleuze (1991) moved actively away from the "who" to discussing "the non-person or It in which we recognize ourselves and our community better than in the empty exchanges between an I and a You" (p. 95), treating subjects and objects as rhizomatic machines. At this intersection, Balibar (1991) located "citizen" next to the "subject" and Montag (2018) commends:

> By tying the subject to a word and a concept whose disappearance appeared unthinkable -the citizen- he raised the problem of the subject in

a way that made visible the fundamental and irreducible antagonism that the notion of the subject embodies.

(p. 39)

In mathematics education, the focus placed on fixed identities, curricula, assessments, tasks, stories, or games becomes instrumental for the cultivation of subjects' identities in relation to state, religious or cultural power. Specifically, Walkerdine (1988) argued that compulsory mathematics education serves for making subjects strive for an illusionary "mastery of reason". Children subjectify to "real" world problem-solving from the early years up to secondary education, for developing democratic citizenship ideals. She observes how this fantasy harms oppressed children who turn to "mathematical rationality" as defense against their own precarity but with painful transitions across "real" and "fictitious" life. Walkerdine (1988) in "Counting Girls Out" has specifically argued how children and caretakers (mothers and teachers) from working and middle classes in the United Kingdom are confined into gendered bourgeois discourses that determine their learning paths. Lundin (2012) examines, later, the function of word-problems in Swedish mathematics curricula as institutionalised play/games, where children are subjected to a blind faith in mathematical truths; Straehler-Pohl (2017) discusses the de/mathematisation dialectic in popular media of late capitalism. Recently, Yolcu (2021) considers curricula reforms in Turkey focusing on problem-solving and collaboration through specific pedagogic devices (e.g. self-assessment check-lists) and notes how international designations become nationally appropriated by monitoring mathematics teachers' and students' ways of working. Baldino and Cabral (2018) emphasise enjoyment (jouissance) noting the subject's willing subjection to success and qualifications in mathematics that feed the dreams of a citizen who excels in the neoliberal economy of capitalism. Such work aligns with "narratives of success" as a life-long project inscribed by OECD documents and discussed by Andrade-Molina (2021). These studies configure the "repressed subject" to a vicious "circle of subjection" (i.e. where the subject remains freely subjected to authority) that Derrida and Deleuze critiqued as politics' death and Balibar (1991, 2017) twisted to "citizen subject". Here, I am arguing that the "becoming citizen subject" offers a space to politicise mathematics education.

Balibar, student of Althusser and contributor to *Lire le Capital* (Althusser et al., 2003), acknowledges ISAs (i.e. ideological state apparatus) for making visible capitalist re/production modes but questions the continuous trap into the "circle of subjection". Problematising the subject as eternally subjected to sovereignty (i.e. God, feudal or modern power) he attends to how the interpellated subject's agency emerges within ant/agonistic struggles (Balibar, 1991, 2017). And, by considering the coronavirus impact on rethinking life as both political (bios) and biological (zoé), Balibar (2021) argues that, as the virus crosses species, pre-established identities hybridise, and new relational ontologies appear. This realisation allows the agentic subjectivity of multiple nonhuman others as objects, plants, animals, codes, or viruses to enter the specter of life, as vectors of contagion, infection, and immunity (Balibar, 2021; Esposito, 2013; Viveiros de Castro, 2014). In this realm, Montag (2018) maintains that by placing the word "citizen" next to the "subject", Balibar crafts a political space in-between the subjection/agency antinomic binary.

Balibar reads subject and citizen genealogies alongside citizenship in literary, historical, and philosophical traditions offering the "becoming citizen subject" so that to note that after the subject comes the citizen but the citizen remains a subject: *the becoming-citizen of the subject and the becoming-subject of the citizen* (i.e. Balibar, 2017, pp. 4, 30). Today, the human subject as the core of modernity is being troubled by acknowledging the presence of nonhuman others (e.g. virus, geology, wildlife, code, data) enforcing us to recognise life with diverse non/organic species, beyond intentional human deliberations, and as form of living that accepts the continuum of life-death as a vital for regeneration (Colebrook, 2011; Deleuze & Guattari, 1987). The sections below encounter the becoming citizen subject in mathematics education (for a more detailed genealogical discussion see Chronaki, 2023).

Antiquity and the polis: Citizenship constitution and the competent citizen

In the spatiotemporality of the polis of ancient Athens, citizens, and citizenship are determined by the city's borders determining the political, economic, and cultural bonds amongst inhabitants of demos. Aristotle (2009) proposes "citizenship constitution" or politeia (πολιτεία) to advance democratic governance through educating people in specific virtues, values, and ethics. For Balibar (2015), this is the first moment of citizenship's genealogy in the western world.

The democratic polis and the competent citizen of antiquity

For the becoming citizen, Aristotle proposed education as "care for the self" in free public schools for training youth into active, critical, and wise subjects able to lead a political life, called bios (βίος πολιτικός). In the *Nicomachean Ethics and Politics*, he emphasises *phronesis* (i.e. practical wisdom) to endorse will (βουλείν) and judgment (κρίνειν) for political participation. Phronesis is key for constituting laws and norms that safeguard peace, security, and safety. Education, for Aristotle, must be the "same for all" so that diverse children grow together in good habits of moral and intellectual virtues, experienced through the ethos of "friendship". Wisdom training means pursuing collectively "truth" with "reason" and "rationality" (Curren, 2010, p. 545) and citizens are educated to reason publicly in *agoras* (agora: open assembly for the citizen in the polis) for being able, not only to invent, but also to protect democratic laws. It is noted how mathematics education becomes pivotal for such endeavours since amongst its central aims is to cultivate techniques of reasoning, argumentation, and proof so that to support the truth-telling process for democracy—a view that continues until today to determine mathematics education practices.

However, the polis of Athens was conceived upon massive exclusions. Civil equality was not granted to women, children, slaves, disabled or the technically oriented workers, who remained non-citizens but still had to obey the laws. Whilst Aristotle's focus was the political subject of competent citizens (i.e. timocracy), securing power and peace both at home and in colonies, Zeno, the Stoic, detoured. In opposition to a single-focused body politic on competence, he argued for an heterogenous communal life with internally constituted laws in which citizens live a common *nomos* (i.e. law) beyond geopolitical borders or ability boundaries. It is on this image, as Sellars (2007) explains, that Deleuze based his nomadic theory and Kropotkin ascribed Zeno as a proponent of anarchism.

The competent subject in mathematics education

The idea of a competent citizen subject occupies mathematics education research and policy addressing democratic reforms or renewals. I identify four such perspectives. *First*, a competent subject as confident reasoner and problem solver in mathematics education is brought in national state curricula and is, often, aligned with international assessment practices (e.g. PISA, and TIMSS). The subject is trained to develop skills through individual or collaborative work in procedural tasks or realistic word-problems, to perform in examinations or competitions and to value mathematical success (Foster, 2016). In this line, mathematics offers instrumentally sustainable solutions in didactic inquiries of socio-scientific issues (Maans et al., 2019). *Second*, a critically competent citizen is conceived as important to counter the assumed neutrality of mathematics in a highly technological society, accountable for world catastrophes. Specifically, Skovsmose (1994) argues for "democratic competences" to critique the "formatting power" of mathematics in society. *Third*, a citizen competent to act publicly is proposed by Frankenstein (1990) and Gutstein (2005), focusing not merely on critiquing the perils of mathematics in society but transforming mathematical tools into "weapons" for people struggling to subvert injustices. Acknowledging the utopian character of such endeavours in state schooling, Povey and Adams (2021) debate the need for critical global citizenship in mathematics classrooms that disorders the prevailing order of depoliticised mathematical activity. And *fourth*, the invisible, silent or silenced competences of citizen subjects of different cultures are discussed in the scholarships of: ethnomathematics confronting neo-colonial acts of globalising Eurocentric mathematics curricula.

As these aforementioned images translate into mathematics education theory and practice, they confront the hegemony of an instrumental problem-solver, as the main desired citizen. At the same time, they risk to reproduce the assumed in/competence of subaltern or cyborg others for reaching certain quality and equity standards that determine the fiction of a self/society limitless development (Chronaki, 2011). Although the critically competent citizen (i.e. subjects capable of questioning mathematics education for social injustices) gains ground in inclusionary pedagogies, multiple exclusions endure. It is, thus, pertinent to ask how such antinomies in mathematics education are evoked in Aristotle's politeia.

Antinomies of the competent citizen subject in politeia

Reading politeia, Balibar (2015) notes that a main antinomy is rooted in Aristotle's call for competences that could act as the "entry conditions" for the body politic. In other words, only those who are educated into competences that allow participation in a political community governed by the principles of *isonomia* and *unity* could become citizens. Since, the discourse of competences is core for the mathematics education community's strivings for democracy, one may wonder how does the struggle for isonomia and unity engulf antinomies?

First, isonomia emphasises rotating power positions as equally shared amongst people in civic duties. To become a competent citizen, one must cultivate the ethics of will and judgment as central for democracy. Balibar (2015) alerts that, by enforcing them as "entry conditions", internal borders are crafted in the body politic that create, de facto, antinomies at the level of expertise. Specifically, by setting certain competence requirements (enforced competences) for the active citizen subject as participant in the public sphere, even when taken as basic mathematical literacies, certain subjects, who do not (yet) possess them, will be excluded as they will be constructed as non-competent. This act risks, further, the effect of un/intended subjection into discourses of ableism, sexism, or racialism, rendering subjects into a permanent need for development. Such effects can be traced in the struggles and strivings of marginalised people in modernity as "becoming citizen subjects", claiming their right to civil education but also to local knowledges, languages, and capabilities.

Second, unity (i.e. internal equilibrium) depicts a political community focused on common good and interest in consensus. Citizens learn to endeavour for consensus as they encounter demands for *isonomy* by conforming to authority (i.e. "by obeying we learn to command" or "by exercising authority we learn to obey"). The pursuing of consensus in mathematics education could be examined when certain epistemic norms and identity positions are being emphasised in mathematics classrooms at the expense of others. When mathematics education tends to prioritise a specific epistemic culture for consensus around fixed learning norms and identities (Cobb et al., 2011) the space for dissensus is limited or, even, erased, and subject agency is reduced (Rancière, 2006).

Summarising, the competent citizen subject was conceived as the condition for democracy in the bordered polis of antiquity and remains, until today, core in diverse perspectives of mathematics education. For becoming competent as active, reflective, or critical citizen in the body politic, the subject must learn to participate in isonomia and unity, pursuing consensus. Whilst consensus competences (e.g. argumentation, reasoning, truth) are basic in mathematics education, using them as "entry condition" can create unresolvable antinomies. Seeking consensus at any cost, for the sake of unity, serves to oppress rather than empower the political subject. Rancière (2006) has opposed such conditions as deadening democracy and argues that they, ultimately, determine unequal share in the organised community. Becoming "share-less" in mathematics education could be the effect of erasing disagreement, repressing conflict, or silencing difference between majoritarian and minoritarian knowledges. Balibar (2015) warns that dissensus never disappears but returns anew as the driving force shared by people in agonistic strivings, creating the insurgent citizen subject, as will be discussed below.

Modernity and the nation-state: Social citizenship and the insurgent citizen

Modernity is the second epoch in Balibar's discussion of citizenship genealogy linked with equaliberty, a concept based on "aequa libertas" coined by Cicero (106–43 BC), to argue for "res publica" where liberty (i.e. freedom by law) exists on the condition that it is "equally established for all". It has marked the spirit of Magna Carta, American and French Revolutions, and, even, people's strivings for direct democracy in the Paris Commune of 1871 whilst, at the same time, organised nation-states by determining their spatio-political boundaries for domestic and international affairs.

The nation-state and the insurgent citizen of modernity

People's insurrections in Europe created the French Revolution (1789) and paved the path in which the "Declaration of the Rights of Man and of the Citizen" was constituted. Enlightenment ideas (i.e. property, social contract, reflective individuals, separation of powers) and preceding constitutions (i.e. Magna Carta:UK:1215, Declaration of Independence:US:1776) helped to define "rights". Its patriarchal orientation was opposed by feminist Olympe de Gouges who in 1791 wrote the militant Declaration of the Rights of Woman and of the Female Citizen to expose gendered injustices. But, upon its publication, she was convicted of treason and executed.

In this epoch, the discourse of human rights serves the emerging "democratic" states in Europe to govern their own nations but also to expand their rule to colonial territories by imposing the "right" to enclose lands, enslave people and accumulate wealth. In parallel, science gains power over religion by advancing the logics of "truth", "representation", "objectivity", and "quantification" and assembling the massive social experiments of industrialisation, capitalism, and eugenics. These logics mark, again, biopolitical strategies to govern life, not by sovereign law but through the authority of numbers including statistics and political arithmetic (Foucault, 2008). These are the times of nation-states dreaming of progress, development, and unlimited growth via technoscientific innovations and of noble civilians assuming the "right" to govern "others" in slavery and exploitation. The legal articulation of citizenship into laws that protect citizen property and the freedom to act has turned towards conceiving even human subjects as property (i.e. female, children, slaves, the disabled). This idea has served for genocides, femicides, and epistemicides throughout Europe and its colonies. Next to such harmful acts, people have continuously engaged in forming transversal solidarity alliances amongst landworkers, proletarians, women, youth, Indigenous, or queer communities. It was, always, through people's insurrections in social movements that marginalised subjects have re/claimed public presence and legal articulations of their rights to recognition through laws, in the citizenship constitution.

The insurgent subject in mathematics education

Much writing examines the role of mathematics and mathematics education in enunciating modern subjectivity in Enlightenment virtues (Popkewitz, 2004; Powell & Frankenstein, 1997; Walkerdine, 1988). Whilst, in medieval times, mathematics was placed in despotic circles and arithmetic offered for trade purposes, the times between the seventeenth and eighteenth centuries witness mathematics interweaving with knowledges of craftspeople, clerks, merchants, or governors gaining status as "political arithmetic" (Porter, 1995). During the nineteenth century, most developed Western nations, such as the United States, converted mathematics education into state apparatus "for fostering healthy citizens by recruiting 'all classes' of (free white) children into liberal self-governance" (Ziols & Kirchgasler, 2021, p. 129) by making mathematics compulsory for all citizens (Popkewitz, 2004; Tröhler et al., 2011). Discourses of a self/society limitless development intertwine with mathematics curricula global pleas for quality and equity, creating, despite good intentions, local injustices for cyborg and subaltern subjects (Chronaki, 2011). Social citizenship antinomies open, once again, people's insurrections in the 1960s, claiming their "right to rights" (Arendt, 1972) in which the "right" to "education" becomes core demand of unceasing battles. How could we, then, grasp the right to mathematics education in this milieu?

Claims for the right to mathematics education drive concerns for systemic inequalities and inequities in mathematics teaching and learning that tend to perpetuate low achievement and failure for children already suffering multiple oppressions. Scholars who espouse social justice perspectives at the intersections of race, gender, ability, or Indigeneity (Gholson & Martin,

2019) strive to map the continuing injustices of educational policy. In this realm, the "maths for all" rhetoric foregrounds future citizens through curricula reforms but it responds neither to concerns about underachievement nor to societal struggles for justice. Recent scholarship (Chronaki & Yolcu, 2021) discusses how this rhetoric turns easily into a neoliberal fix for inter/national politics, advancing a mathematics education for sustainable futures where diverse populations are promised to thrive. Reviewing research for understanding the perseverance of inequalities and marginalisation in mathematics education, despite efforts for inclusionary pedagogies, Chen and Horn (2022) note how strategies for pervasive systemic oppression preclude social interaction, dialogue, intersectional contact or identity heterogeneity and favouring privilege reproduction. Their review acknowledges the fissure between structures (i.e. institutions, curricula, standards, assessments, and identities) and agents (i.e. actors, learners with knowledge, skills, values, and ethics).

Antinomies of the insurgent citizen subject in social citizenship

Divides of structure/agent align with Balibar's attention to the subjection/agency antinomic binary. Balibar (2015) argues that since the couplets of "equality-liberty" and "man-citizen" are grounded in the secondary principles of fraternity, property and power, the formation of citizens with equal rights creates antinomies across opposed individual and collective demands in the body politic. These are determined by the nation-state's political condition of democracy and remain irreversible without people's resistance or revolt. He, thus, proposes "equaliberty" to stress the radical, yet utopian, integration of equality and liberty that fullfills individual demands (liberty). For Balibar, although there are no guarantees, people's striving for "equaliberty" makes visible the internal borders in societal planes, where structural injustices reappear as antinomies of subjection/agency, inclusion/exclusion, or empowerment/oppression. He argues that these injustices create the political drive for citizens, non-citizens, not-yet-citizens, or the "missing others" of citizenship to ally in collective agonistic struggles. Herein, the citizen subject of modernity becomes the event of differential insurrections and constitutions.

In mathematics education, the insurgent citizen subject figures the activist teacher or student, who strives in solidarity with marginalised learners, teachers, and their communities against inequalities and towards claiming rights for diverse mathematical languages, cultures, and knowledges in school settings. Conferring the antinomies of social citizenship in modernity, the limits of the insurgent citizen subject become recognised (Balibar, 2015). *First*, Balibar discerns that even though "equaliberty" has historically inspired social movements to organise around class, gender, sexuality, race, it reproduces the antinomy of active/passive citizens as mutually exclusive. An active citizen is considered the subject who is competent to participate in public politics (i.e. often "men" of certain origin, gender or age, property owners, tax payers), to act with the zeal of patriots who must cultivate bourgeois skills (i.e. languages, behaviour, style, taste). In contrast, the passive citizen is, often, the invisible "missing other" from the body politic who, nevertheless, remains imperceptibly active at the margins. The presence of assumed passive subjects pervades mathematics education praxis, as we work with subjects of hybrid identities, languages, and bodies (Chronaki, 2011, 2019) denoting the limits of the *becoming insurgent subject* in mathematics classrooms.

Second, Balibar (2015) highlights that despite claims for resolving large-scale inequalities, the political aim was to, implicitly, regulate people's insurrections (i.e. class, racial and gender movements). By guarding "the rights of organized labor and in systems for protecting individuals against the risk associated with the proletarian condition" (p. 47), the proletarian became a public danger. As such, social citizenship grew into a strategy for neo/liberal democracies to neutralise agonistic struggles and normalise behaviour, through institutional "mechanisms for reproducing political consensus" (p. 58). For this, mathematics education becomes, again, pivotal under the universalist pretension of "governing equality" in "maths for all" reforms (Diaz, 2013). Resolving social injustice issues through mathematical models figures the interpellated subject of a fictive democratic competence mastery, as discussed in the section "citizen subject in the body politic". This condition runs the risk of enclosing the insurgent citizen subject in the comfort of mathematical activity (i.e. schools, classrooms, screens, texts) where efforts to produce political consensus can pacify the importance of inventing new subjectivities through dissensus and affective solidarity across bodies.

In sum, the insurgent citizen subject, tied with the founding of empires and nation-states upon patriarchal, colonial, and capitalist interests, creates social citizenship in late modernity. In this context, the becoming citizen subject is recognised as the event of differential insurrections and constitutions grounded in antinomies produced by demands for equality and liberty as utopian universal principles. The insurgent citizen inspires mathematics education activist projects enacting solidarity with marginalised, oppressed, or silenced people and their knowledge. And as mathematical activity stages rhetoric processes (i.e. argumentation, reasoning, modelling, proving) it can, also, offer tools for creating spaces for both political consensus and dissensus. However, enforcing active/passive citizen subject dichotomies may serve to reproduce subjection/agency binaries and fail to sense the missing others inhabiting mathematics classrooms as inactive participants but who, in fact, might dissent in silence.

Posthumanity and the body: Expansive citizenship and the creative citizen

At the time of writing this chapter an earthquake with epicentre in central Crete made, in seconds, a nexus of villages, including mine, uninhabitable and people devastated. Such affective events prevail alongside irreversible socio-economic crises, refugee waves of people facing wars, violence, environmental catastrophes, or pandemics. Colebrook and Weinstein (2017) urge us, in their "postscript on the posthuman", to think of our "deep geological time" as a chronotope before humans existed in planet Earth (p. i) and to read the Anthropocene as a "geological archive that testifies to our once forceful existence" (p. i). Speculative posthuman life is created in science fiction narratives from Shelley's Frankenstein to Asimov's Robotics and Le Guin's utopias or fascist regimes banning mathematics (Chronaki, 2018). Hayles (1999), tracing the posthuman in literary and science discourses, claims for the body's creative virtuality within material-information complexes that, for Kymlicka and Donaldson (2014), compels citizenship to expand by considering nonhuman ethics in the body politic.

The body and the creative subject of posthumanity

The study of posthumanity allies with both Life Sciences and Humanities focusing on how nature, science and culture interweave to determine needs or desires for producing technological artefacts, smart objects, or bio/info/materials that create new life. For this, posthuman subjectivity prioritises creativity by challenging core conceptions of antiquity and of modernity. The creative posthuman subject disturbs language superiority over matter (Barad, 2003), recognises code for opening channels across un/non/conscious cognitions (Hayles, 1999), and favours human-machine-animal cyborgs for supporting processes of communication-control-command (Haraway, 1990). As such, the becoming citizen subject in posthumanity expands from a humane *who* towards its sociomaterial natureculture, as a creative product and process.

Balibar (2021) encounters posthumanity in the coronavirus pandemic, claiming that this juncture marks the subject as a biopolitical event at the species level. With epidemiology, he notes that species, by being exposed to increased connectivity, become interchangeably contaminated and contaminants. In this, the virus converges with forces of biology, ecology, technology, and economy, relativising cultural bonds or nation-state borders, intensifying differential in/exclusions and subjectifying societies into common anxieties of death, infection, and immunisation. Biopolitical governing works again today, as in ancient and modern times, by regulating the "conduct of conduct" amongst people and pursuing certain behaviour norms or bodily habits (Foucault, 2003, 2008). Mathematics contributes by modeling infection rates in calculus graphs assembled to enact certain health policies. Scholars discuss this amplified biopower of mathematical expertise in public media and problematise its effects in mathematics education (see Chan et al., 2021). Although Balibar (2021), along with Foucault and Agamben, critiques biopower's force for governing human societies, he maintains that the pandemic has prioritised life itself. Considering the virus as "crossing the species barrier" and of organisms as "permanently colonized by a great variety of viruses", he explains that although at the core of the pandemic is our political life (bios), it is the realisation that biological life (zoé) remains perishable that, today, determines the political.

Expanding citizenship beyond humans has implications for communities seeking the politics of ethical responsibility across humans, animals, lands, codes, information, and biotechnologies. Legal studies have started discussing posthuman citizenship by interrogating anthropocentric rights based on Euro-American, male, white or heteronormative ableism and expanding legal subjectivity to non-human others (Hanafin, 2018). Specifically, "the right to be forgotten" is recognised for digital privacy concerning personal data information and online security (Käll, 2017), national citizenship constitutions accommodate environmental rights (e.g. Equator and Bolivia include nature in legal forms of citizenship) or cyborg recognition (e.g. Saudi Arabia assigned citizenship to female robot Sophia).

The creative posthuman subject in mathematics education

The creative posthuman subject has gained interest in mathematics education mainly with the work of de Freitas and Sinclair (2014) who revisit mathematics and the body by proposing "inclusive materialism" to emphasise mathematical invention. Researchers consider mathematical activity in affective bodying with concepts, movement, and materials (Chronaki, 2018), diverse modes of existence (Mikulan & Sinclair, 2019), care relations amongst vulnerable multispecies and communities (Gutiérrez, 2022; Khan et al., 2022), or socioecology for a liveable world (Boylan & Coles, 2017; Chronaki & Lazaridou, 2022).

Though posthumanist theorising is peripheral for mathematics education, certain research compels posthuman thinking. Mathematical activity has been pivotal for discussing environment (Coles et al., 2013), place and space pedagogy (Nicol et al., 2020), indigenous knowledges (d'Ambrosio, 1985), post normal science and fake news (Hauge, 2022), or embodiment (Gerofsky, 2015). Currently, the COVID-19 pandemic created the condition to interrogate mathematics as a vital nonhuman agent in public discourse. Specifically, researchers critique data visualisations design for narrating crisis (Rubel et al., 2021), problem-solving activity for turning biological life into an object of rational decision (Ziols & Kirchgasler, 2021), and raise the increased global pressures for digital mathematics education practices (Borba, 2021). The above studies seem to urge mathematics education to recognise the ethics for creating the antinomies of becoming a creative citizen subject in posthumanity. But, in what ways?

Antinomies of the creative citizen subject of posthumanity

Posthumanity is considered the convergence of the biodiversity extinction and environmental disasters in our geological era, the fourth industrial revolution and advanced capitalist economy. Pleas for creative posthuman subjectivities are, often, substantiated in "cruel optimism" (Berlant, 2011), "active vitalism" (Colebrook, 2011), or hopes for an enhanced life, sustained by informed decision-making. In affinity with technoscientific practices, objects are being ascribed with agency as part of networks (Latour, 2005: actor network theory [ANT])). Braidotti (2019) critiques the flattening of subject/object relations by either waving class, race, gender, sexuality, ability, or by prioritising computational intelligence and argues for critical posthumanities countering inhumanist capitalist inceptions. In this venture, Balibar confers on posthumanity a necessary perspectival shift that, by decentering the human subject, must encounter its reconfiguration. The subject must be rethought with diverse living species across biology, ecology, and economy through the archaic practices of domestication and artificialisation and by reconsidering the question of life itself.

First, human species exist amongst other living species into an ecosystem where they become, unavoidably, colonisers of self and others through practices of ***domestication*** (i.e. making kin with plants and animals, extracting resources from nature, data mining, modeling, reasoning) and ***artificialisation*** (i.e. creating tools, artifacts, prosthetic technologies, expanding intellectual capacities, developing external bodies). Practices of both domestication and artificialisation are core for mathematising or de/mathematising and hint at antinomic tensions where un/sustained hierarchies amongst subjects and objects, persons and things can disturb the living body by making in/visible diverse in/exclusions of dangerous species. Historically, domestication and artificialisation become visible at the threshold of agriculture and industrialisation epochs whilst their presence is accelerated in current biotechnology projects favouring profitable futuristic creations. Asking what kind of species the human subject becomes, Balibar (2021) argues that geological, social, and technological challenges create posthumanity as the antinomic machinic assemblage of hybrid im/material bodies that cannot be wholly known, communicated, or controlled.

Second, Balibar argues that posthumanism troubles the question of "life" itself, a note also made by others. Parisi (2004) claims how life today is experienced as "bio-piracy" of information about life, since personal data contribute un/intentionally to "big data" flows, fostering subtle biopower reinscribing subjectivity norms. These are processes that the subject alone cannot observe, control, or resist and, thus, neither the competent nor the insurgent citizen subjects can determine posthuman citizenship. The threat of life becoming "bare life" has been discussed as a matter of escalating biopower to necropower where practices of killing and allowing to kill are justified for peace and security (Agamben, 1998). Balibar (2021) notes that death is depicted during the pandemic not through intentional sovereign power or biopower but with unintended forces of species contagion. Humans enter a passive and unwanted dis/connection with other species in fear of infection and in need for immunisation. Deleuze and Guattari argue for "passive vitalism where 'life' *does not act* by a process of intention, decision, and self-preservation of actualised forms, but it instead becomes eventuated through *chance encounters*" (cited in

Mikulan & Rudder, 2019, p. 616). Drawing on "passive vitality" as the probability space of socio-material virtuality, Balibar claims how our temporality prioritises a "passive synthesis" of life crossing borders of non/organic bodies.

In summary, the creative citizen subject of posthumanity evolves as corporeal, im/material and discursive machinic assemblages where human and nonhuman divides dissolve into rearticulations where mathematics (e.g. code, algorithm, probability) becomes key, yet imperceptible, contributor. The historical practices of domesticating and artificialising living species within nature, culture, and technology make often in/visible the antinomic spaces where demands for profitable creative innovations require expansion of both legal citizenship and contemporary mathematics education practices towards their ethical responsibility for recurrent injustices. Specifically, the posthuman condition may unlock the creative subject of mathematical activity fueled not with cruel optimism but of "interminable humanism" emphasising anti-narcissism (Viveiros de Castro, 2014, p. 44) that unfolds the becoming citizen subject as the event of both critical creation and creative critique.

Concluding: The political of mathematics education

Mathematics education's concern for the political can be traced back to Mellin-Olsen (1987) who inquired the politics of alienating children from mathematical activity as cutting the self/society relation and, thus, inhibiting change, Walkerdine (1988) who interrogated mathematics curricula for the subject's subjection to a fictional mastery of reason, or Skovsmose (1994) who argued for critical mathematics education through competences of empowerment. During the last decades, researchers confront the political in mathematics education in either weak (addressing educational reform policies for citizen equity) or strong (theorising mathematics power through citizenship inscriptions of the subject) perspectives (Valero, 2018) denoting how mathematics educators need political knowledge (Gutiérrez, 2013). But, how is the political related to the becoming citizen subject?

I claim in this article that although the concepts of citizen and subject are core for discussing the political in mathematics education, they remain, largely, unexamined. As such, they tend to reproduce polarised deliberations for a mathematical subject as being either agent for systemic change or subjected to systemic power. By encountering the "becoming citizen subject" in archaic, modern and posthuman times and its permeation in mathematics education, I can, further, claim that the political of mathematics education cannot be enclosed in citizenship images constituted around rights, duties, or ethics serving the biopolitics of the ancient polis, the modern nation-state or the machinic posthuman body facing wars, injustices, and viruses. Citizenship converts, easily, into a legal tool that, alongside mathematical based biopower (e.g. numbers, political arithmetic, scientific persuasion, administrative procedures, reasoning, algorithms, modeling, data mining, programming, topology) governs people by imposing enclosures and justifying injustices. As such, strivings for social justice around citizenship ideas (e.g. the right to rights) can neutralise the radical political potential of people's insurrections into lawful modalities of civil power.

However, the political can also occupy a radical space of grounded thought and grassroot activity specifying liberation from oppressive logics of power. For this, Balibar reads citizenship as inherently antinomic and processual and as requiring active/passive participation in political activity that interrogates the institutional legitimization of injustice always in alliance with people and their social movements. Historically, new political subjectivities do not emerge in vacuum, but in chronotopes where missing others as in/excluded or shareless non/humans disturb the comfort zones of the prevailing competent, insurgent, or creative citizens and strive to re/claim the body politic. Moreover, the political takes flesh in antinomic citizenship temporalities when the becoming citizen subject enters specific ant/agonistic strivings in hope of creating, protecting or, even, democratising democracy. Balibar (2021) has argued for a relational political subject that hybridises subject/object boundaries characterised by transindividuality (i.e. the mutual realisation of its individual and collective nature without reducing one to another) and conditioned by pre-individuality (i.e. the passive synthesis across species) along with supra-individuality (i.e. capitalist modes of reproduction).

Mathematics education, by and large, tries to re/imagine theory, re/design curricula and re/enact classroom practices or teacher education programmes, by resorting to ideal citizen and subject configurations but, as discussed earlier, without accounting for their conceptual genealogies. As such, the attempt to politicise mathematics education research and praxis around a wide consensus for the idea of citizenship, in abstract terms, remains entrapped in subjection/agency binaries that paralyse or, even, deaden its political subject. With Balibar's "becoming citizen subject", this article hints at two conclusionary points for rethinking the political of mathematics education: *first,* attending to the limits of consensus around citizen subject images in mathematical practices and *second*, dialoguing with mathematical creations through critical posthuman perspectives.

First, I have argued throughout the article that although the images of competent, insurgent, and creative citizen subjects prevail in specific epochs, all three permeate the contemporaneity of mathematics education and become hegemonic in current efforts to discuss the political. Their cartographies across antiquity, modernity and post-humanity engulf antinomies of in/exclusions by creating internal and external borders and by imposing "entry conditions" that require consensus in the name of security. Mathematics education becomes instrumental for making such internal borders (e.g. curricula, exams, tasks as normative rituals) and for performing certain citizenship images in activity that stages the biopower of mathematics for governing populations and creating new life across non/organic bodies. I suggest that a depoliticised citizen subject lurks through reinforcing consensus practices where mathematics is envisioned as the sole bio-power to reason (e.g. the language of facts, truth and logic) at the expense of dissensus. Further, this depoliticised effect may reoccur when repressed dissent enforces images of the unrest, active, insurgent citizen subject, without acknowledging the subject's own conditions in remaining passive. For mathematics education to rethink its political, the limits of consensus around ideal images of competent, insurgent, and creative citizens must be attended to by encountering the abyssal lines across non/yet/citizen subjects as both humans and more-than-humans.

Second, at the interval of encountering the becoming citizen subject across temporalities, I argue that citizen subject images in mathematical practices absorb citizenship antinomies by denoting not only the *becoming-citizen* of the subject but also the *becoming-subject* of the citizen. In this enigma, Balibar (2017) stresses that after the subject comes the citizen, but the citizen remains a subject. As seen here, the citizen subject of mathematics education, by and large, rests torn between the subject's unrest, revolt and subjection to nation-states, institutions, ideologies, religions, cultures, technologies, or natures. But the citizen subject cannot be reduced to fixed identities (e.g. class, gender, race, ability, language). The subject evolves through ant/agonistic strivings for democracy and un/intended creations and, despite diversities, converges around common assemblages of desire, where ideas and affects invent life anew. Building on these, I suggest that mathematics education research and praxis must affirm its more-than-human political ontology by dialoguing with critical posthuman thinking. Specifically, it must open towards working with the antinomies of becoming citizen subjects as critical vectors in mathematical practices that endeavour not to depoliticise its relation to democracy but, instead, to democratise its relational potential for a democracy-to-come. For this, the capacity embodied in mathematical practices for re/making a political sympoiesis of situated knowledges (Haraway, 1990) in research and education must be recognised as the affirmative ethics of a dialogical, yet aporetic, relation between "humanist" and "posthumanist" perspectives.

Acknowledgement

This chapter is a shorter and edited version of an article published in 2023 at Research in Mathematics Education and I would like to thank Taylor & Francis for the permission to republish. Chronaki, A. (2023). Becoming citizen subject in the body politic: antinomies of archaic, modern and posthuman citizenship temporalities and the political of mathematics education. *Research in Mathematics Education*, 1–23. https://doi.org/10.1080/14794802.2023.2183889

References

Agamben, G. (1998). *Homo sacer: Sovereign power and bare life.* Stanford University Press.

Althusser, L., Balibar, É, Establet, R., Macherey, P., & Rancière, J. (2003). Lire le Capital (Να Διαβάσουμε το Κεφάλαιο) (transl. D. Dimoulis, C. Vallianos, & V. Papaoikonomou). Ellinika Grammata [Αθήνα. Ελληνικά Γράμματα (μτφ. Δημούλης,

Δ., Βαλλιάνος, Χ., Παπαοικονόμου, Β. επιμ. Δ. Δημούλης]. (Original work published 1965)
Andrade-Molina, M. (2021). Narratives of success: Enabling all students to excel in the global world. *Research in Mathematics Education*, *23*(3), 293–305. https://doi.org/10.1080/14794802.2021.1994453
Arendt, H. (1972). *Crises of the republic*. Harcourt Brace & Company.
Aristotle. (2009). *The politics* (E. Barker, Trans. & R. F. Stalley, Intro.). Oxford University Press.
Atweh, B., Graven, M., Secada, W., & Valero, P. (Eds.). (2011). *Mapping equity and quality in mathematics education*. Springer. https://doi.org/10.1007/978-90-481-9803-0
Baldino, R., & Cabral, T. (2018). Mathematics education and the juggernaut of capitalism. *The Mathematics Enthusiast*, *15*(1), 178–200. https://doi.org/10.54870/1551-3440.1423
Balibar, E. (1991). Citizen subject. In E. Cadava, P. Connor, & J. L. Nancy (Eds.), *Who comes after the subject* (pp. 33–57). Routledge.
Balibar, E. (2010). Antinomies of citizenship. *Journal of Romance Studies*, *10*(2), 1–20. https://doi.org/10.3167/jrs.2010.100201
Balibar, E. (2015). *Citizenship* (T. Scott-Railton, Trans). Polity Press.
Balibar, E. (2017). *Citizen subject: Foundations for philosophical anthropology* (Translated by Steven Miller, Trans.). Fordham University Press.
Balibar, E. (2021). Human species as a biopolitical concept. *Radical Philosophy*, *211*, 3–12.
Barad, K. (2003). Posthumanist performativity: Toward an understanding of how matter comes to matter. *Signs: Journal of Women in Culture and Society*, *28*(3), 801–831.
Berlant, L. (2011). *Cruel optimism*. Duke University Press.
Borba, M. C. (2021). The future of mathematics education since COVID-19: Humans-with-media or humans-with-non-living-things. *Educational Studies in Mathematics*, *108*(1–2), 385–400. https://doi.org/10.1007/s10649-021-10043-2
Boylan, M., & Coles, A. T. (2017). Is another mathematics education possible? An introduction to a special issue on mathematics education and the LIVING WORLD. *Philosophy of Mathematics Education Journal*, *32*. http://socialsciences.exeter.ac.uk/education/research/centres/stem/publications/pmej/pome32/index.html
Braidotti, R. (2019). *Posthuman knowledge*. Polity Press.
Bullock, E. C., & Meiners, E. R. (2019). Abolition by the numbers mathematics as a tool to dismantle the Carceral state (and build alternatives). *Theory Into Practice*, *58*(4), 338–346. https://doi.org/10.1080/00405841.2019.1626614
Chan, M. C. E., Sabena, C., & Wagner, D. (2021). Mathematics education in a time of crisis—A viral pandemic. *Educational Studies in Mathematics*, *108*(1–2), 1–13. https://doi.org/10.1007/s10649-021-10113-5
Chen, G. A., & Horn, I. S. (2022). A call for critical bifocality: Research on marginalization in mathematics education. *Review of Educational Research*, *92*(5), 786–828. https://doi.org/10.3102/00346543211070050
Chronaki, A. (2011). Disrupting development as the quality/equity discourse: Cyborgs and sub-alterns in school technoscience. In B. Atweh, M. Graven, W. Secada, & P. Valero (Eds.), *Mapping equity and quality in mathematics education* (pp. 3–21). Springer.
Chronaki, A. (2018). The unbearable lightness of disappearing mathematics: Or, life and reason for the citizen at times of crisis. *The Mathematics Enthusiast*, *15*(1), 8–35. https://doi.org/10.54870/1551-3440.1415
Chronaki, A. (2019). Affective bodying of mathematics, children, and difference: Choreographing 'sad affects' as affirmative politics in early mathematics teacher education. *ZDM Mathematics Education*, *51*(2), 319–330. https://doi.org/10.1007/s11858-019-01045-9

Chronaki, A. (2023). Becoming citizen subject in the body politic: Antinomies of archaic, modern and posthuman citizenship temporalities and the political of mathematics education. Research in Mathematics Education, 1–23.

Chronaki, A., & Kollosche, D. (2019). Refusing mathematics: A discourse theory approach on the politics of identity work. *ZDM Mathematics Education*, *51*(3), 457–468. https://doi.org/10.1007/s11858-019-01028-w

Chronaki, A., & Lazaridou, E. (2022). Subverting epistemicide through 'the commons': Mathematics as Re/making space and time for learning. In E. Vandendriessche & R. Pinxten (Eds.), *Indigenous knowledge and ethnomathematics*. Springer. https://doi.org/10.1007/978-3-030-97482-4_6

Chronaki, A., & Yolcu, A. (2021). Mathematics for "citizenship" and its "other" in a "global" world: Critical issues on mathematics education, globalisation and local communities. *Research in Mathematics Education*, *23*(3), 241–247. https://doi.org/10.1080/14794802.2021.1995780

Cobb, P., Stephan, M., McClain, K., & Gravemeiger, K. (2011). Participating in classroom mathematical practices. *Journal of the Learning Sciences*, *10*(1–2), 113–163. https://doi.org/10.1207/S15327809JLS10-1-2_6

Colebrook, C. (2011). *Deleuze and the meaning of life*. Continuum.

Colebrook, C., & Weinstein, J. (2017). Preface: Postscript on the posthuman. In J. Weinstein & C. Colebrook (Eds.), *Posthunous life: Theorising beyond the posthuman* (p. ix). Columbia University Press.

Coles, A., Barwell, R., Cotton, T., & Brown, L. (2013). *Teaching secondary mathematics as if the planet matters*. Routledge.

Curren, R. (2010). Aristotle's educational politics and the Aristotelian renaissance in philosophy of education. *Oxford Review of Education*, *36*(5), 543–559. https://doi.org/10.1080/03054985.2010.514434

d'Ambrosio, U. (1985). Ethnomathematics and its place in the history and pedagogy of mathemat- ics. *For the Learning of Mathematics*, *5*(1), 44–48. http://www.jstor.org/stable/40247876

de Freitas, E., & Sinclair, N. (2014). *Mathematics and the body: Material entanglements in the class-room*. Cambridge University Press.

Deleuze, G. (1991). A philosophical concept. In E. Cadava, P. Connor, & J.-L. Nancy (Eds.), *Who comes after the subject* (pp. 94–95). Routledge.

Deleuze, G., & Guattari, F. (1987). *A thousand plateaus: Capitalism and schizophrenia II*. (B. Massumi, Trans.). University of Minnesota Press.

Derrida, J. (1991). Eating well' or the calculation of the subject: An interview with Jacques Derrida. In E. Cadava, P. Connor, & J.-L. Nancy (Eds.), *Who comes after the subject* (pp. 96–119). Routledge.

Diaz, J. D. (2013). Governing equality: Mathematics for all? *European Education*, *45*(3), 35–50. https://doi.org/10.2753/EUE1056-4934450303

Esposito, R. (2013). *Terms of the political: Community, immunity, biopolitics*. Fordham University Press.

Federici, S. (2004). *Caliban and the witch: Women, the body and primitive accumulation*. Autonomedia.

Foster, C. (2016). Confidence and competence with mathematical procedures. *Educational Studies in Mathematics*, *91*(2), 271–288. https://doi.org/10.1007/s10649-015-9660-9

Foucault, M. (1991). Governmentality. In G. Bruchell, C. Gordon, & P. Miller (Eds.), *The Foucault effect: Studies in governmentality* (pp. 87–104). Harvester Wheatsheaf.

Foucault, M. (2003). *The birth of the clinic*. Routledge.

Foucault, M. (2008). *The birth of biopolitics. Lectures at the college de France 1978–1979*. Palgrave MacMillan.

Frankenstein, M. (1990). *Relearning mathematics. A different third R -radical maths*. Free Association Books.

Fraser, N. (2005). Reframing justice in a globalising world. *New Left Review*, *36*, 69–90.

Gerofsky, S. (2015). Approaches to embodied learning in mathematics. In L. D. English & D. Kirshner (Eds.), *Handbook of international research in mathematics education* (pp. 72–109). Routledge.

Gholson, M. L., & Martin, D. B. (2019). Blackgirl face: Racialized and gendered performativity in mathematical contexts. *ZDM Mathematics Education*, *51*(3), 391–404. https://doi.org/10.1007/s11858-019-01051-x

Gutiérrez, R. (2013). Why (urban) mathematics teachers need political knowledge. *Journal of Urban Mathematics Education*, *6*(2), 7–19.

Gutiérrez, R. (2022). A spiritual turn: Toward desire-based research and indigenous futurity in mathematics education. *Journal for Research in Mathematics Education*, *53*(5), 379–388. https://doi.org/10.5951/jresematheduc-2022-0005

Gutstein, R. (2005). *Reading and writing the world with mathematics: Toward a pedagogy of social justice*. Routledge.

Haines, C.-P., & Grattan, S. (2017). Life after the subject. *Cultural Critique*, *96*, 1–35.https://doi.org/10.5749/culturalcritique.96.2017.0001

Hanafin, P. (2018). Posthuman rights, a micropolitics of. In R. Braidotti & M. Hlavajova (Eds.), *Posthuman glossary* (pp. 352–355). Bloosmbury Academic.

Haraway, D. (1990). *Simians, cyborgs and women*. Free Association Press.

Harman, G. (2018). *Object-oriented ontology: A new theory of everything*. Pelican books.

Hauge, K. H. (2022). A tool for reflecting on questionable numbers in society. *Studies in Philosophy and Education*, *41*(5), 511–528. https://doi.org/10.1007/s11217-022-09836-6

Hayles, N. K. (1999). *How we became posthuman: Virtual bodies in cybernetics, literature and informatics*. University of Chicago Press.

Käll, J. (2017). A posthuman data subject? The right to be forgotten and beyond. *German Law Journal*, *18*(5), 1145–1162. https://doi.org/10.1017/S2071832200022288

Khan, S., La France, S., & Tran, H. T. T. (2022). After plantations' precarities: Curating maththematic curriculum plots in initial teacher education for multispecies' flourishing and a freedom- yet-to-come. *Research in Mathematics Education*, *24*(2), 170–186. https://doi.org/10.1080/14794802.2022.2090421

Kwon, O. N., Han, C., Lee, C., Lee, K., Kim, K., Jo, G., & Yoon, G. (2021). Graphs in the COVID-19 news: A mathematics audit of newspapers in Korea. *Educational Studies in Mathematics*, *108*(1–2), 183–200. https://doi.org/10.1007/s10649-021-10029-0

Kymlicka, W., & Donaldson, S. (2014). Animals and the frontiers of citizenship. *Oxford Journal of Legal Studies*, *34*(2), 201–219. https://doi.org/10.1093/ojls/gqu001

Latour, B. (2005). *Reassembling the social: An introduction to actor-network-theory*. Oxford University Press.

le Roux, K., Brown, J., Coles, A., Helliwell, T., & Ng, O. L. (2022). Editorial for a special issue on innovating the mathematics curriculum in precarious times. *Research in Mathematics Education*, *24*(2), 117–127. https://doi.org/10.1080/14794802.2022.2090422

le Roux, K., & Swanson, D. (2021). Toward a reflexive mathematics education within local and global relations: Thinking from critical scholarship on mathematics education within the sociopolitical, global citizenship education and decoloniality. *Research in Mathematics Education*, *23*(3), 323–337. https://doi.org/10.1080/14794802.2021.1993978

Lundin, S. (2012). Hating school, loving mathematics: On the ideological function of critique and reform in mathematics education. *Educational Studies in Mathematics*, *80*(1–2), 73–85. https://doi.org/10.1007/s10649-011-9366-6

Maans, K., Doorman, M., Jonker, V., & Wijers, M. (2019). Promoting active citizenship in mathematics teaching. *ZDM-Mathematics Education*, *51*(6), 991–1003. https://doi.org/10.1007/s11858-019-01048-6

Marcone, R., & Skovsmose, O. (2014). Inclusion-exclusion: An explosive problem. In O. Skovsmose (Ed.), *Critique as uncertainty* (pp. 95–110). Information Age Publishing.

Mellin-Olsen, S. (1987). *The politics of mathematics education*. Springer.

Mikulan, P., & Rudder, A. (2019). Posthumanist perspectives on racialized life and human difference pedagogy. *Educational Theory*, *69*(5), 615–629.

Mikulan, P., & Sinclair, N. (2019). Stratigraphy as a method for studying the different modes of existence arising in the mathematical classroom. *ZDM Mathematics Education*, *51*(2), 239–249. https://doi.org/10.1007/s11858-018-01018-4

Montag, W. (2018). Between subject and citizen: On Etienne Balibar's foundations for philosophical anthropology. *Radical Philosophy*, *2*(2), 39–46.

Nancy, J. L. (1991). Who comes after the subject? In E. Cadava, P. Connor, & J.-L. Nancy (Eds.), *Who comes after the subject* (pp. 1–8). Routledge.

Nicol, C., Gerofsky, S., Nolan, K., Francis, K., & Fritzlan, A. (2020). Teacher professional learning with/in place: Storying the work of decolonizing mathematics education from within a colonial structure. *Canadian Journal of Science, Mathematics and Technology Education*, *20*(2), 190–204. https://doi.org/10.1007/s42330-020-00080-z

Organisation for Economic Co-operations and Development. (2013). PISA 2012 assessment and analytical framework: Mathematics, reading, science, problem solving and financial literacy. OECD Publishing.

Parisi, L. (2004). *Abstract sex: Philosophy, bio-technology and the mutations of desire*. Continuum.

Popkewitz, T. (2004). The alchemy of the mathematics curriculum: Inscriptions and the fabrication of the child. *American Educational Research Journal*, *41*(1), 3–34. http://www.jstor.org/stable/3699383 https://doi.org/10.3102/00028312041001003 https://doi.org/10.3102/00028312041001003

Porter, T. (1995). *Trust in numbers. The pursuit of objectivity in science and public life*. Princeton.

Povey, H., & Adams, G. (2021). Disordering mathematics, citizenship and socio-political research in mathematics education amongst the "rubble of words". *Research in Mathematics Education*, *23*(3), 306–322. https://doi.org/10.1080/14794802.2021.1994452

Powell, A. B., & Frankenstein, M. (Eds.). (1997). *Ethnomathematics – Challenging Eurocentrism in mathematics education*. State University of New York Press.

Rancière, J. (2006). *Hatred of democracy* (S. Corcoran, Trans.). Verso.

Ross, K. (2016). *Communal luxury. The political imagination of the Paris commune*. Verso.

Rubel, L. H., Nicol, C., & Chronaki, A. (2021). A critical mathematics perspective on Reading data visualizations: Reimagining through reformatting, reframing, and renarrating. *Educational Studies in Mathematics*, *108*(1–2), 249–268. https://doi.org/10.1007/s10649-021-10087-4

Sellars, J. (2007). Deleuze and cosmopolitanism. *Radical Philosophy*, *142*, 30–37.

Skovsmose, O. (1994). *Towards a philosophy of critical mathematics education*. Springer.

Straehler-Pohl, H. (2017). Demathematisation and ideology at times of capitalism: Recovering critical distance. In H. Straehler-Pohl, N. Bohlmann, & A. Pais (Eds.), *The disorder of mathematics education. Challenging the sociopolitical dimensions of research* (pp. 35–52). Springer.

Tate, W. F. (2008). Putting the "urban" in mathematics education scholarship. *Journal of Urban Mathematics Education*, *1*(1), 5–9.

Trinick, A. (2016). *Te Reo Tātai: The development of a mathematics register for Māori-medium schooling University of Waikato*. University of Waikato.

Tröhler, D., Popkewitz, T. S., & Labaree, D. F. (2011). *Schooling and the making of citizens in the long nineteenth century*. Routledge.

United Nations Educational, Scientific and Cultural Organization. (2020). Global education monitoring report, 2020: Inclusion and education: all means all. https://doi.org/10.54676/JJNK6989

Valero, P. (2018). Political perspectives in mathematics education. In S. Lerman (Ed.), *Encyclopedia of mathematics education*. Springer. https://doi.org/10.1007/978-3-319-77487-9_126-4

Vardoulakis, D. (2013). *Stasis before the state: Nine theses on agonistic democracy*. Fordham University Press.

Viveiros de Castro, E. (2014). *Cannibal metaphysics* (P. Skafish, Ed. and Trans.). Univocal.

Walkerdine, V. (1988). *The mastery of reason: Cognitive development and the production of rationality*. Taylor & Frances/Routledge.

Yolcu, A. (2021). Reimagining the citizen and the nation in a globalised world: The case of mathematics education reforms in Turkey. *Research in Mathematics Education*, *23*(3), 278–292. https://doi.org/10.1080/14794802.2021.1993976

Ziols, R., & Kirchgasler, K. L. (2021). Health and pathology: A brief history of the biopolitics of US mathematics education. *Educational Studies in Mathematics*, *108*(1–2), 123–142. https://doi.org/10.1007/s10649-021-10110-8

Part II

Troubling citizenship norms within national and local settings

8 Travellings of mathematically able bodies to Turkey

Configurations of paradoxical unities of (non)citizens across historical, national, and global contexts

Ayşe Yolcu

The gatekeeping primacy of mathematics continues to occupy educational and social opportunities for young populations and circulates across mathematics education research, policy, curriculum, and teaching practices (Yolcu, 2019). Knowing mathematics has been widely appreciated as an essential competency in modern states to cultivate active citizens (e.g., Ministry of National Education [MNE], 2018; National Council of Teachers of Mathematics [NCTM], 2014; Organization for Economic Co-operation and Development [OECD], 2013, 2018; Romberg, 1998) as well as an empowering tool for the youth to engage with the real-world issues (e.g., Gutstein, 2012; Stinson, 2004). In these debates, mathematics is not merely a school subject to get more credits or a course requirement to move upwards in an academic pipeline. Equipping all people with common mathematical skills and competencies across diverse countries is argued to build a mathematically capable world despite the cultural and national differences.

Building a set of common mathematical competencies emerges as a particular redemption story that takes the world to be mathematically organised and facilitates the predictability and stability of the world. Acting and participating mathematically by all citizens are considered as a vehicle to move towards the global unity and well-being of the contemporary modern world. Obscured in this salvation, nonetheless, is not merely the mathematics that enables the reasonable actions and participations for global futures but a set of cultural and historical distinctions that "make up people" as constructive, engaged, and reflective citizens (Hacking, 2007; see also, Popkewitz, 2008) and simultaneously produces differentiations through the social and institutional practices of modern nation-states (Tröhler & Winkler, 2024).

The formation of modern, intelligent, and effective citizens within the network of mathematics education practices is not far from paradoxes, inconsistencies, and impossibilities despite the insistence of including the "all" (Yolcu, 2017). Mathematical empowerment of all people as the citizens of a globalised world embodies a set of principles that constitute cultural theses for proper

DOI: 10.4324/9781003130673-11

ways of living for the desired future, including the ability to appreciate quantities in practical situations and communicate in everyday affairs using a variety of mathematical tools. While these could be taken as plausible statements about who the children are and should be, the particular modes of acting and participating in real-world settings simultaneously normalise particular identities, generate pathologies, and divide bodies as mathematically able and abject (Yolcu & Popkewitz, 2019). Configured as not-yet-mathematically able citizens, abject bodies are seen as distinct from those normative actions and participations; and, they are acted upon as objects of pedagogical intervention. The paradox, here, is embedded in the desire of uniting all in a mathematical common ground and simultaneously differentiating (im)proper modes of life, and dividing bodies as mathematically able and abject.

Correcting and re-forming abject bodies, to make them be part of the "all", have historically been part of modern public education to prevent the disorder in social life. Educational reforms in the early 20th century, as Popkewitz (2008) argues, were the "redemption" of urban populations, such as immigrants or not-yet-civilised bodies. Mathematics education was not an exception. The abject bodies are to be rescued from their unliveable spaces to be integrated into the collective. In these "inclusive" processes, the beliefs and values of individuals are cultivated in particular ways not only with the aim of increasing their "learning" opportunities but also contributing to the public good. The premise of mathematics education for all enunciates as a dividing practice that requires a paradoxical belonging to one another yet enacts a mechanism of differentiation. The desire to unite bodies in a common mathematical ground becomes a paradoxical effort to include those excluded by pedagogical practices of inclusion.

A mathematically able body is a fabrication that simultaneously embodies a fiction about a mathematically capable future. I do not consider the able body as a stabilised entity but it is dynamically configured in specific cultural-historical contexts. It is not a representation of a particular human kind that belongs to a particular society but travels along with the cultural geographies of school mathematics and assembles with a variety of discursive practices that includes teaching and learning methods, assessment tools, national narratives, and historical desires. As able bodies move along the cultural spaces of school mathematics across diverse localities, they form new assemblies and so they produce new subjectivities such as decision-makers, lifelong learners, and rational thinkers. For example, the problem-solving child of Turkey is a specific configuration of an able body as strong republicans with scientific minds (Yolcu, 2021b). This particular subjectivity becomes actualised in the history of curricular developments in Turkey. Different from mathematics education practices that seek to cultivate the notions of precision and accuracy (Yolcu & Popkewitz, 2019) or to develop a Euclidean vision (Andrade-Molina & Valero, 2015), the problem-solving child of Turkey is recognised both through the degree of faithfulness to the nation and "mathematical" engagement with the real-world problems.

The differences in the configuration of able bodies do not indicate a superiority of one form to the other but reveal important (dis)connections between the diverse cultural contexts and the historical making of citizens for a globalised world. Although there is strong evidence in mathematics education research that explicates the ways in which school mathematics curricula fabricate future citizens in modern societies (Diaz, 2017; Valero, 2017; Yolcu, 2017), the concept of citizenship is a cultural one that is materialised very differently in specific nation-state mechanisms (Tröhler, 2020). In other words, the common mathematical competencies for all citizens are re-envisioned within the local contexts. The hope to build a mathematically capable world assembles with the cultural-historical contexts of a specific nation and its desired future. The nation-specific trajectories produce a significant space to explore how so-called "universal" mathematical competencies are shaped in local contexts. In this sense, this chapter brings both the linkages and boundaries between the global, local and historical into question. I aim to make visible how mathematical competencies (re)configure mathematically able bodies, travel into Turkish modernity and its national imaginary, and simultaneously constitute a paradoxical unity of (non)citizens of the nation.

I organise the chapter as follows: First, I provide a theoretical-methodological framework by explaining the shifts in the citizen formation that would give rise to new types of power relations in modern nation-states. The new configuration of citizenship entails a particular notion of mathematical ability, organising bodily actions and participations. Then, I explore how those able bodies travel into the modernisation processes of Turkey in the early decades of the 20th century, a period that faced significant restructurings in the social and educational circles of the country. Following the examination of able bodies in the context of Turkish modernity, the analysis leaps into the present and investigates how global (and usually Western originated) initiatives in school mathematics are assembled with the cultural and historical trajectories of the nation and thus are seen as a restoration of Turkish modernity. The conclusion discusses how the processes of making mathematically able bodies produce a paradoxical unity and configure boundaries between citizens and non-citizens.

Theoretical and methodological framework

Emergence of forms of governing in modern nation-states and historical formation of (non)citizens through mathematical practices

The making of modern citizens in liberal societies requires inventing different technologies of administration such as the rules and standards of reason instead of a brute force. In that manner, principles of participation and communication in multiple spheres of life are arranged and orderly planned to maintain the social stability with the self-governed democratic citizens (Cruikshank, 1999; Poovey, 1998). Particularly, numerical practices became one of the governing technologies and a civilising medium to arrange and standardise the social relationships (Miller, 2004) and serve as technologies of cultivating self-rule and reason in modern secular societies in the absence of religious authorities and sovereign rulers. Numerical practices permitted the communications to be easier and more manageable in the social and economic life of the citizens. This, in turn, promotes equal citizenship and serves to equalise the governing of the citizenry without a centralised power but with a particular kind of practical knowledge informed by the numbers (see, e.g., Porter, 1995).

The promise of practical knowledge through numbers becomes the redemptive discourse to secure the future and to govern the irrational and sensory aspects of human nature. Without the numbers as a civilising medium, human nature could become a potential danger to the stability in modern societies. Everyday numerical practices become a technology of making bodies civilised and trustworthy, who are efficiently expected to join the social complex of modernity. Nevertheless, the particular ability to reason about the complex world with "credible" strategies makes the body as a strategically competent human to ensure reliable communications and to prescribe what is think-able and say-able. This form of "mathematical" reasoning, then, becomes a self-restraining and domesticating process, regulating and controlling people's actions and participations to maintain the social order. Simultaneously, the social ordering with numerical practices forecloses diverse possibilities that might interrupt the stabilities. This mode of thinking about social life does not only create differential categories of proper citizens and their others but also constructs a hierarchical continuum that depicts bodies from primitive to civilised.

The governing of human nature is not frozen in the historical context of nation-state appearance, but the governing mechanisms of numerical practices permeate contemporary public life. Yet the continuity itself is not stable, moving from numerical practices applied to the real world to the mathematisation of the real world, and generating new practices of power relations. Mathematising the infinitely complex world with rational reasoning enables a type of person, who is able to simplify, analyse, compare, predict and design the world thereby producing rational decisions. These abilities are considered by their feasibilities in the already made-up world, making this bodily configuration of humans as a "complex-but-limited adaptation machine, a bounded chooser, and a finite problem solver" (Heyck, 2015, pp. 83–84). That is to say, the process of employing mathematical reasoning to understand the challenging social context requires a reasonable and able body, embedded in the system, to make this process rational and trustworthy. These abilities, such as mathematical consciousness, are connected to the cultural-historical configuration of the nation and racialisation processes of its citizens (Yolcu & Kirchgasler, 2024). The processes shaping and fashioning what is think-able and say-able in the public spheres generate differentiations on the continuum between mathematically able and abject, despite the persistence on the unity of "all".

Travellings of mathematically able bodies across cultural spaces

Paradoxical unities of able and abject bodies do not entail a grand international narrative that could be applied to the local context. Able bodies move along cultural spaces of school mathematics across diverse localities. They entangle with different sets of assemblages, flows, and networks such as historical trajectories, cultural narratives and scientific practices. That is, mathematically able bodies continually mutate and are reconfigured in specific contexts. The examination of how able bodies are made unfolds the formation of knowledge in the field of school mathematics and helps to rethink the entangled histories that (dis)connect humans, cultures, places, and times.

In this chapter, the concept of travelling is used to explore the circulation of mathematically able bodies across diverse times and spaces. Travelling refers to movement of ideas, practices, and tools that configure spaces for novel forms of selves, rationalities, and (inter)national imaginaries (Said, 1983). These spaces are taken as analytics to examine the linkages between national and international mathematics education reforms with specific attention to how paradoxical unities of (non)citizens are reappropriated and reconnected with specific cultural-historical contexts. Building on the idea of travelling, this chapter discusses that mathematics education reforms in Turkey cannot be understood as an objective process of copying the successful models implemented in other countries. Rather, reforming school mathematics in specific cultural and historical contexts should be acknowledged as a process of translating the mathematical competencies that are circulated in the global reforms. By translation, I refer to the cultural-historical spaces in which international agendas in school mathematics encounter the local-specific practices (Tröhler & Lenz, 2015). The translation mechanisms generate appropriations and connections between the national and international spaces that are not reductive or homogenising. The translations are generative of new formulations of subjectivities, yet carrying historical continuities within the particular nation-state imaginary (Popkewitz, 2001; Tröhler, 2022; also see Yolcu, 2021a).

To examine the historical (dis)continuities of making and travelling mathematically able bodies, I draw on Foucault's (1984) historicising approach. Instead of descriptively reporting what did or did not happen in the past, I seek how the past is woven into the present. Specifically, I historically examine the paradoxical qualities of mathematics education practices that simultaneously divide and differentiate bodies, cultures, and nations in the efforts to include, unite, and globalise. With this approach, the focus is on the practices and their networks rather than unpacking the actual intentions and meanings of reformative actions. Far from comparing Turkish mathematics education in terms of a normative model, historicising explicates the cultural-historical nuances by looking at travelling languages, discourses, and national curriculum practices as a political site of re-contextualisation and de-contextualisation (Zhao & Tröhler, 2021). This attitude will problematise the nationalised practices of identity generation and cultural belonging and the analysis will make visible the nation-state mechanism differentiating those as not-yet-proper citizens.

Travellings of mathematically able bodies into the 20th century modernisation project of Turkey

Turkey is a relatively young nation-state, established in 1923 following World War I. Historically, social institutions in Turkey have been construed as sites to make informed citizenry for the modern nation-state. These institutions include schools where "better" pedagogical practices are sought to fabricate the children as informed and modern citizens (Bilgi & Özsoy, 2005). Publicising schooling was part of the hope to establish national unity, independence, and modern civilisation that needed to be purified from its weak late-Ottoman past (Kadıoğlu, 1996). The historical anxiety of elevating the country to the level of contemporary civilisations was inscribed in the desire to build a modern nation-state. That is, while the hope was to organise the masses as informed citizens of the nation through a sense of modernity, uniformity, and independence, the fear was embedded in the failure to accomplish the modernisation goals given the large portion of the population was illiterate, tired after several wars, and geographically dispersed across the country. Centralised schooling was seen as a solution to recuperate, specifically, school mathematics was considered as a cultural vehicle to cultivate the informed and self-governed citizenry to solve the everyday problems in public life.

The educational reforms were hoping to change people, who were previously subjected to their sovereign ruler, by cultivating the ability to reason and imagine themselves as free citizens of the modern state (Ministry of Culture [MC], 1936). In this context, problem-solving was the fundamental principle of mathematics education to fabricate the children as mathematically able citizens of modern Turkey (Yolcu, 2021b). Nevertheless, solving the mathematical problems of everyday life was not only concerned with teaching and learning mathematics but also producing particular human kinds as future modern citizens. The hope has been to make strong national bodies and to cultivate the faith in the modern republic by solving the numerical problems that "relate to the nation" and "homeland geography" to make visible the national successes in the early years of the Republic of Turkey to all students (MC, 1935, pp. 5–7). Solving these kinds of problems was considered as a way of cultivating national consciousness among the young people and fabricating national-minded citizens. In the modern Republic of Turkey, school mathematics was seen as a "living tool" concerned with making effective and informed citizens of the nation (MC, 1936, p. 21; see also for further historical analysis Yolcu, 2021b).

In addition to the mathematical understanding of issues that relate to national accomplishments in the early years of the Republic (circa 1920–40), the emphasis was given to the development of skills for dealing with everyday problems such as making a family budget, calculating nutrition of foods, or paying the taxes regularly (Ministry of Education Training Centre [METC], 1933). Through a mathematical manner, self-governed citizens of modern Turkey were expected to act and participate in public life with their own will and reason, instead of "waiting for the help of others" (MC, 1936, p. 11). This was the particular hope to build a bright future with free citizens of the modern nation. As opposed to living under the rule of sovereign power, a shared "mathematical" capability was to ensure the independence of bodies as well as to maintain social and moral order in public life.

The desire to build a mathematically capable society for the future embodied the fear of the past. Problem-solving as a pedagogical practice was seen as a modern way of doing mathematics while drill and memorisation were "traditional" methods of mathematics teaching (Aslan & Olkun, 2011). Contrary to solving problems, which directed people to use their own consciousness independently, methods of drill and practice were considered an image of the Ottomans as an old civilisation. The belief was the difficulty of making the desired citizenry with traditional pedagogies, as they would limit students' reasoning and sense-making on the everyday issues in modern life as well as restrict the development of students' sense of belonging and their own rationales of being loyal to the nation-state. The combination of hopes and fears, paradoxically, divided and excluded children as faithful bodies to the republic or not. In other words, despite the desire of "uniting" citizens under the umbrella of modern futures, people were distinguished to the extent that they were faithful to the nation and a degree of self-governing in practical situations.

The paradoxical unity of able and abject bodies enunciates in distinctive ways as it assembles with the specific historical and cultural trajectories of the nation. In the foundation years of Turkey, the school was seen as the symbol of the modern nation-state to cultivate faith in the newly built Republican regime for progress, development, and independence (MC, 1936). Despite the emphasis on modernisation and secularisation of society, the sense of national belonging was inscribed as the faith to the nation-state. The construction of desired bodies also includes the making of abject bodies, who had not been disciplined or had not cultivated the faith in the existing order. The children were divided into categories of "backward" and "superior". And later, those grouped as "backward" were acted upon with particular pedagogical remediation. For example, when teachers saw those cases, they needed to struggle to "eliminate" deficiencies through "exercis[ing] with uncomplicated numbers" (MC, 1936, p. 160). As their reasoning habits would develop with those differentiated teaching, they were to become part of the collective.

The desire for independence turned into confinement practices. The pedagogical gaze was a disciplinary tactic that ordered, classified, normalised, and differentiated its subjects and a form of governing children's souls as future citizens (Yolcu, 2021b). The mathematical solution to real-life problems was to make up children as able bodies who could "identify problems", "devise solution methods", "compare which solution would work better", "make judgments", and "control the results" in daily life contexts (MC, 1936, p. 25). More than a teaching approach, these practices were to standardise how to engage with real-life situations, and so social life in the absence of moral authorities or sovereign rulers would be maintained in harmonious ways across the nation. Those processes of problem-solving were not about mathematics itself, but it was organising the bodily actions in real life and producing administrable bodies with the projected steps of solutions.

The psychological gaze of school mathematics made up the distinctive notions of what counts as a "truly" able body of the nation or not. Paradoxically, the desired mathematically able bodies were embedded in the making of abject bodies who were recognised through their degree of faith in the new Republican regime and their disciplined actions in everyday life. The historical conditions and the pedagogical gaze collectively constituted paradoxical unities of able and abject bodies of the nation as what is desired and feared for, instead of a representation of a particular ethnic or religious identity.

The historical account for mathematics education practices in Turkey reveals that the paradoxical unity of mathematically able and abject bodies was not fixed categories but assembled with the cultural complex of the country and produced social distinctions despite the aims of national unity of all. Mathematically able bodies are, therefore, not static entities that enter into a particular locale, but they are open for shifting, continually mutating, and producing distinct assemblages as in the case of the early 20th century modernity project of Turkey. These assemblages of citizens are beyond numerical practices but they include following solution steps to solve real life problems. Considering the contemporary discourses, these assemblages enter into another cycle of formation with the push by the globalised reforms and initiations in school mathematics. Next section examines the shifts in the cultural configuration of mathematically able bodies as citizens.

Travellings of mathematically able bodies into the 21st century internationalisation project of Turkey

Present-day mathematics education in Turkey carries the historical desire to build a better future for all people living in the country. This includes improving pedagogical practices of school mathematics through learner-centred approaches (MNE, 2005a). Reformed pedagogical practices focus on processes where students independently construct their own mathematical knowledge. By having students solve problems, model real-world situations, collaborate, communicate and discuss while they participate in the activity of doing mathematics, at the same time, the emphasis is given to prepare mathematically competent youth, and so society, to have a place in the global world of the information age (MNE, 2005b; OECD, 2013). The "mathematical" preparation of youth was not merely cultivating the workforce for the global world, but also fabricating "active" citizens who can mathematically act and participate in their personal and social lives.

Similar to the international efforts that are informed by 21st century skills, the reform-based mathematics education in Turkey focuses on the development of competencies such as problem-solving, reasoning, collaborating, and communicating in mathematics classrooms. Distinct from global counterparts, nonetheless, nationally prioritised mathematical competencies focus on "thinking independently", "making decisions without being influenced by anyone" and "sharing, explaining, and defending their ideas" (MNE, 2005a, pp. 7–10). More than improving mathematics teaching and learning practices, 21st century school mathematics reforms consists of particular efforts to transform society by making of children who can "stand one's own leg", "think freely" and "act in a creative manner" (Umay et al., 2006, p. 208). Learning mathematics is seen as a renewal of the nation. Gaining mathematical power is considered a tool against "narrow minds" while cultivating "free and creative thought" (Ersoy, 1997, p. 118). The hope to create national independence is historically retold through the desire of reformulation of mathematically able bodies as informed citizens not only for the nation-state but also for the globalised world.

School reforms in Turkey at the turn of the 21st century, particularly in mathematics education, are seen as a restoration of Turkish modernity and revitalisation of the national imaginaries in the globalised world (Yolcu, 2021a). Previous pedagogical practices are perceived as detrimental to fulfil the potential of the nation and its citizens. Specifically, the fear is built upon "narrow minds" who are restrained to memorise facts and procedures rather than actively doing mathematics. It has been placed as the result of the "pathetic situation" of schools, lacking qualified mathematics teachers who are confined to blackboard (MNE, 2005b, p. 100). The reform movement in school mathematics is to solve these problems through promoting "mathematical literacy" for all bodies who are able to gain the "capacity and power to use mathematics" in everyday life (Aydın, 2003, p. 184). Mathematics education is considered as a reformative instrument to get rid of "narrow minds" and to prepare productive citizens (Ersoy, 1997, p. 115). The reformist philosophy of curriculum is to "support children's active construction of their knowledge through problem-solving, exploration, reflection, and communication" (Koç et al., 2007, p. 37). Saving the child from the educational space of "old" mathematics is simultaneously recognised as the redemptive narrative of the nation. The promise of the "active child" as well as "active citizen" through mathematical empowerment was considered as the enlightened route for progress, development, and civilisation that Turkey had not reached yet since its establishment.

Similar to the foundation years of Turkey as a nation-state, the future is promising to fulfil the desires of the nation such as reaching the level of modern civilisations or becoming part of the globalised world. In the face of contemporary reforms, earlier forms of mathematics classrooms are evaluated as "uncivilised" institutions that have made "narrow minds" and passive recipients of knowledge (Ersoy, 1997, p. 117). In this context, current reforms are seen as a chance to revitalise those old institutions of the Republican regime and as a redemptive story for making up the mathematically capable society with its able bodies. In other words, the social institutions like schools in the early years of modern Turkey are now considered as deteriorating the national development and progress. Once these institutions were to rescue the nation, now they became the failures of the modern country. Nonetheless, the continual comparison between the old and the new is maintained.

Desired for a better future for all, the way that mathematics is taught in the classrooms needs to be transformed across the country. Given the wide geographical space of Turkey and the diversity of school contexts, the reformative move has focused on curricular change rather than the education of practising mathematics teachers. The centralised curricular change is not only concerned with the development of the workforce for the economic needs of the information age, but also the desire to unite people, maintain democracy and harmony in the society. Since doing mathematics is considered as a process rather than the product in the contemporary reforms, the curricular emphasis is on improving classroom culture where students develop capabilities of communication, collaboration, and collective reasoning. Nonetheless, these practices are more than teaching and learning mathematics, they are also built on the hope to live together, cultivate democracy and unite diverse people despite their differences (MNE, 2005a). The desire for unity produces normative accounts for mathematically able bodies as "active" citizens with "open" minds while generating abject spaces for "others", seen as bodies of "passive" citizens with "narrow" minds. The enunciation of "all" becomes a paradoxical unity of (non)citizens that consistently differentiates and excludes the bodies as able and abject in the efforts to include.

The contemporary context for school mathematics in Turkey has reinscribed the configuration of paradoxical unities of (non)citizens. Bringing multiplicity of discourses and practices, present-day reforms in school mathematics are similarly concerned with historical rules and regulations of making future citizens. Although contemporary modes of teaching and learning mathematics maintain a historical continuity in mathematical competencies such as problem-solving, they are considered to rebuild Turkish modernity that is not fulfilled as hoped since the foundation of the nation-state and to revitalise the bodies as mathematically able citizens (Yolcu, 2021a). These practices are influenced by global citizenship discourses that have shifted the emphasis toward the idea of different groups of people living together in harmonious and democratic ways than the strict faith in the nation-state. Nevertheless, globalising influences have never silenced the nationalised narrative of schooling since the contemporary network of mathematics education practices creatively combine internationalisation of school mathematics with the cultural practices of making the nation and its proper citizen.

Reconsidering mathematically able bodies in the junction of international, national, and historical projects

Mathematically competent citizens are not born, but they are made in and through perceived modern and globalised mathematics education pedagogies. As discussed above in the Turkish cultural-historical context and argued previously in other liberal democracies (Yolcu & Popkewitz, 2019), the network of mathematics education practices configures bodies as able to act and participate in real-life situations. The hope to cultivate mathematical abilities embodies cultural-historical rules and principles that make particular modes of life legible for the desired future. Specifically, the so-called universal mathematical competencies are de-contextualised from their circulation in globalised spaces and re-contextualised with the cultural-historical trajectories of a nation-state.

Gatekeeping primacy of mathematics is a historical problem. In particular, mathematical reasoning appeared with the Enlightenment where science, and particularly quantities, emerged as a method where individuals empirically observe, count, and measure real-world objects and see themselves as agents for action and change (Popkewitz, 2008). Methods such as precise measurement, quantification, and generalisation were considered as a technology to control one's environment and social life in a modern state (Scott, 1998). The calculative techniques were to constraint the desires and biases of individuals who became able to provide trustworthy explanations and "credible" strategies for the real world (Porter, 1995). Mathematics was to calculate the uncertainties of the real, and mathematical reasoning was to generate stabilised knowledge that governs people and the world. The cultivation of mathematical engagement within all citizens of modern nation-states is far from domination; on the contrary, it rules through providing a kind of practical knowledge to use in everyday life.

In Turkey, approximately a century ago, school mathematics was seen as a living tool to construct modern citizens of the newly established nation-state. Problem-solving was presented as an innovative approach not only for teaching and learning mathematics but also for making informed citizens. As argued, beyond a pedagogical strategy to modernise teaching and learning mathematics, problem-solving practices in school mathematics historically embody particular cultural and historical arrangements to make human kinds as modern self and intelligent citizens of the nation as opposed to people who previously were subject to their sovereign in the Ottoman period. By mathematical engagement, people of the Republic would become self-governed citizens, solve their daily life problems on their own, and act properly in public spaces so that the nation would move beyond the threats of religion. While the idea of citizen formation was similar to other modern nation-states, the practices were different. As I have argued elsewhere (Yolcu, 2021b), the strategy was to arrange and standardise social and economic relationships through learning how to do calculations rather than calculating, determining which procedures to follow rather than applying and deciding what solution methods could work rather than solving. In this way, citizens would be able to see mathematical engagement as a duty to follow the solution procedures instead of searching for precision and accuracy in their real-life problems.

Considering the move from the 20th to the 21th century, nonetheless, essential mathematical competencies for young populations are defined more than submission to mathematical procedures as a national duty. Similar to the developments in different parts of the world (e.g., NCTM, 2014), mathematical competencies to meet the challenges of the 21st century world are inclusive of reasoning and data-based decision making in personal, professional, and social aspects of life (MNE, 2018; OECD, 2018). From the 1980s and on, it is possible to see a desire for a world with common mathematical competencies. Both national and international reforms are to prepare the youth to handle the challenges in their personal, professional, and social lives and to make them capable of engaging with the world mathematically (OECD, 2013). Being prepared for the modern world is understood as the ability to "reason[ing] mathematically and us[ing] mathematical concepts, procedures, facts, and tools to describe, explain, and predict phenomena" (OECD, 2018, p. 6). Instead of establishing a new school mathematics discourse in the globalised world, nevertheless, the desire to cultivate common mathematical competencies within youth across different cultures and nations revitalise existing cultural and historical trajectories (Yolcu, 2021a). The intricate and historically constituted relationship between mathematics and life further tightened with the social challenges such as climate change, governmental debt, population growth, and the spread of pandemics.

The desire to act mathematically in real-life situations embodies the fear of people who would fail in the modern, enlightened, or 21st century globalised world. The simultaneous existence of hopes and fears constitutes paradoxical qualities of citizens. That is, while all members of a nation are understood as citizens of the modern state, some of them are not yet qualified as citizens as they are presumed to need pedagogical intervention. As an effect, school mathematics practices contain a set of precautionary measures to handle those fears. The preventative pedagogies include but are not limited to remedial individualised programs to equalise mathematics achievement or setting up "fun" maths activities and games to overcome mathematical anxieties.

The hope to build a mathematical common ground across the world is a process of re-assembling the local/global and the past/future under the new rubrics of social administration of children, aiming at developing mathematical competencies to make communication and mobilisation easier across the world. Those "fundamental" mathematical capabilities are considered as the preparation of life in the modern world, enabling mathematical argumentation, reasoning, action, and participation despite the differences across the nations and cultures (OECD, 2013).

The desire to unite all bodies on a mathematical common ground, nonetheless, is not free from its paradoxes. It embodies nation-specific trajectories that are hoping for mathematically able bodies while fearing abject bodies

(Yolcu & Popkewitz, 2019). That is, "mathematics for all" promise entails processes of making kinds of people as efficient and intelligent bodies of the nation and the globe while differentiating others who are yet to be integrated (with necessary pedagogies) to the collective all. That being said, the historicity of able bodies makes visible the shifting nature of school mathematics as a cultural practice.

As the explorations highlight in previous sections, the making of able bodies in the network of mathematics education practices is historically shifted. In the formative years of Turkey, memorisation of mathematical proofs and solutions was seen as detrimental to the "steady character" and "strong bodies" of the nation (MC, 1936, p. 11). These "old" pedagogies were coming from the Ottoman tradition of schooling. Problem-solving was seen as a modern pedagogy against the "high number of repetitions" of mathematical computations and procedures in the newly established Republic of Turkey (MC, 1935, p. 4). By enabling students to solve the mathematical problems of daily life, particular reasoning and related habits were to be cultivated into the able-bodied modern citizens of the nation. Similarly, today, the development of problem-solving skills is placed as one of the aims of contemporary school reforms (MNE, 2005a). Now, however, it is to solve educational problems and to address the fear of "narrow minds", which have been confined around memorisation of facts rather than conceptual understanding. Today, the hope is to make able bodies with open minds who can live together in harmony despite the uncertainties of life. The proposed set of mathematical competencies does not merely mathematically engage the youth with the world but enables the production of subjects who can plan, self-control, and regulate their own thinking processes as active citizens of the nation (Yolcu, 2021a). These qualities are not only concerned with corporeal regulations but also cultivate the particular mindset, sensibility, or worldview that constitute the self-governed citizens.

Despite the differences between the 20th and 21st century projects, the style of reason embedded in the practices of school mathematics that aims to unite all bodies is retold. In the context of Turkey, that reasoning takes the past as feared and unwanted while positions the future as hoped. The comparison between past and present generates differences that could be located in binaries such as old/new or traditional/modern despite the expressions of unity and harmony. In the reformative actions of school mathematics, the past is perceived as the categorical other while the construction of national identity has been occupied with its past that is continually compared with the present-day schooling practices (Yolcu, 2021a, 2021b). The complex relationship between past and present makes visible the paradoxes of making all bodies united on a mathematical ground without locating able and abject bodies as independent entities. That is, the divisions between bodies are not categories that could be represented in themselves. Rather, the configuration of able bodies is entangled with the processes of differentiating abject bodies.

Final remarks

This chapter historically examines the cultural politics of mathematics education reforms and curricular developments in Turkey as configurations of mathematically able bodies. The analysis focuses on the shifting practices of making and travelling of mathematical able bodies while highlighting the paradoxical qualities of making the citizens and non-citizens within the context of for-all reforms. Mathematics education reforms divide and differentiate children as able and abject bodies, despite the hope for inclusion, progress, and betterment of all. Nevertheless, these differentiating practices are not uniform across the world. Internationalisation of school mathematics on a common ground generates configurations for a wide range of bodily labour for proper and improper modes of life and actualises people as able/abject through nation-specific trajectories. For example, mathematics education reforms in Turkey consider globally recognised mathematical competencies as a way to revitalise the nation. And, able bodies are made up as "active citizens" of the country with specific tools and devices that transform mathematics into a pedagogical form. That subjectification process is not new, rather embedded in the modernisation processes of Turkey as assembled with the historical discourses of cultivating nationalised minds in/through school mathematics.

Consideration of mathematically able bodies as a style of thinking to examine mathematics education reforms highlights the heterogeneous practices in diverse localities. The divergences from international reforms, however, are not simply the authentic stories that are to be represented in research papers. These kinds of examinations can be defined as an "epistemic site" where "historical-cultural-philosophical themes negotiate, collide, assemble, and suppress as an effect of modernity-coloniality of knowledge, power and being" (Zhao & Tröhler, 2021, p. 4). The connections and disconnections between the nation and the globalised world are ways to examine how those seemingly neutral mathematical competencies are appropriated and re-assembled with historical trajectories and functions as a mode of administration.

The historicity of mathematically able bodies in the context of mathematics education reforms across a century reveals the fixity and fluidity of mathematics education practices. Cultural theses produced in/though school mathematics are continually mutating as the contemporary discourses demand active citizens to restore the Turkish modernity and also to fully integrate with the globe while past reforms were to build national belonging to construct a modern nation-state. Contemporary pedagogical practices appear as a disagreement with the previous ones such as drill, repetition, and memorisation. However, historicization of relatively "new" and "reformed" practices makes visible the re-enunciation of reason and rationality, moral qualities of life, embodying a faith to the nation itself. Here, the historical analysis accounts for the ways in which continual comparison of past-as-feared and future-as-desired divides bodies as mathematically able and abject. School mathematics that is entangled with societal hopes and fears produces cultural theses for the (im)proper modes of life such as following problem solving procedures or making plans. The distinction between people and desired life produced abject bodies as a site of pedagogical intervention.

The historical analysis exemplifies that it is not merely the mathematics that makes the bodies as able. These bodies are not a matter of someone's individual mental states or psychic fantasies, either. Rather, mathematically able bodies as the regime of practices are the concrete results of differential enactments of knowledge as an exercise of power relations in modern nation-states. In this chapter, my theoretical and methodological move has to do with interrogating the paradoxes of the (inter)national reforms that aim at providing common mathematical competencies for all. The differences in the processes of citizen formation make visible the sites of contestation. This action is a way of thinking about change and should be read as part of the political thought in mathematics education and society.

References

Andrade-Molina, M., & Valero, P. (2015). The sightless eyes of reason: Scientific objectivism and school geometry. In K. Krainer & N. Vondrová (Eds.). *Proceedings of 9th Congress of European Research in Mathematics Education* (pp. 1551–1557), Prague, Czech Republic.

Aslan, E., & Olkun, S. (2011). Türkiye Cumhuriyeti'nin ilk müfredatlarında ilköğretim matematiği. [Elementary mathematics in the first curricula of the Republic of Turkey]. *İlköğretim Online*, *10*(3), 991–1009.

Aydın, B. (2003). Bilgi toplumu oluşumunda bireylerin yetiştirilmesi ve matematik öğretimi [Training individuals in the process of forming knowledge society and teaching of mathematics]. *Pamukkale Üniversitesi Eğitim Fakültesi Dergisi*, *14*(2), 183–190.

Bilgi, S., & Özsoy, S. (2005). John Dewey's travelings into the project of Turkish modernity. In T. S. Popkewitz (Ed.), *Inventing the modern self and John Dewey* (pp. 153–177). Palgrave Macmillan.

Cruikshank, B. (1999). *The will to empower: Democratic citizens and other subjects*. Cornell University Press.

Diaz, J. (2017). *The paradox of making in/equality: A cultural history of reforming math for all*. Routledge.

Ersoy, Y. (1997). Okullarda matematik eğitimi: Matematikte okuryazarlık [Mathematics education in schools: Literacy in mathematics]. *Hacettepe Egitim Fakultesi Dergisi*, *13*, 115–120.

Foucault, M. (1984). Question of method. In G. Burchell, C. Gordon, & P. Miller (Eds.), *The Foucault effect: Studies in governmentality* (pp. 73–86). Pantheon.

Gutstein, R. (2012). Mathematics as a weapon in the struggle. In O. Skovsmose & B. Greer (Eds.), *Opening the cage: Critique and politics of mathematics education* (pp. 23–48). Sense Publishers.

Hacking, I. (2007). Kinds of people: Moving targets. *Proceedings of the British Academy*, *151*, 285–318.

Heyck, H. (2015). *Age of system: Understanding the development of modern social science*. Johns Hopkins University Press.

Kadıoğlu, A. (1996). The paradox of Turkish nationalism and the construction of official identity. *Middle Eastern Studies*, *32*(2), 177–193.

Koç, Y., Işıksal, M., & Bulut, S. (2007). Elementary school curriculum reform in Turkey. *International Education Journal*, *8*(1), 30–39.
Miller, P. (2004). Governing by numbers: Why calculative practices matter. In A. Amin & N. Thrift (Eds.), *The Blackwell cultural economy reader* (pp. 179–230). Blackwell Publishing.
Ministry of Culture (1935). *Ortaokul ve lise riyaziye programı kılavuzu [Middle and high school mathematics curriculum guide]*. Devlet Basımevi.
Ministry of Culture (1936). *İlkokul programı [Primary school curriculum]*. Devlet Basımevi.
Ministry of Education Training Center (1933). *Ortamektep riyaziye dersleri I. kitap [Middle school mathematics courses first book]*. Devlet Matbaasi.
Ministry of National Education (2005a). *İlköğretim okulu ders programları: Matematik programı 6-7-8 [Elementary Programs: Mathematics Curricula 6-7-8]*. MEB.
Ministry of National Education. (2005b). *PISA 2003 projesi ulusal nihai rapor [PISA 2003 final national report]*. Retrieved from http://pisa.meb.gov.tr/wp-content/uploads/2013/07/PISA-2003-Ulusal-Nihai-Rapor.pdf
Ministry of National Education (2018). *Matematik dersi öğretim programı [Mathematics Curricula]*. MEB.
National Council of Teachers of Mathematics (2014). *Principles to actions: Ensuring mathematical success for all*. NCTM.
Organization for Economic Co-operation and Development (2013). *PISA 2012 Assessment and analytical framework: Mathematics, Reading, science, problem solving and financial literacy*. OECD Publishing.
Organization for Economic Co-operation and Development (2018). *PISA 2021 Mathematics framework (Draft)*. OECD Publishing.
Poovey, M. (1998). *A history of the modern fact: Problems of knowledge in the sciences of wealth and society*. The University of Chicago Press.
Popkewitz, T. S. (2001). Rethinking the political: Reconstituting national imaginaries and producing difference. *International Journal of Inclusive Education*, *5*(2-3), 179–207.
Popkewitz, T. S. (2008). *Cosmopolitanism and the age of school reform: Science, education, and making society by making the child*. Routledge.
Porter, T. M. (1995). *Trust in numbers: The pursuit of objectivity in science and public life*. Princeton University Press.
Romberg, T. (1998). Comments: NCTM's curriculum and evaluation standards. *The Teachers College Record*, *100*(1), 8–21.
Said, E. (1983). *The world, the text, and the critic*. Harvard University Press.
Scott, J. (1998). *Seeing like a state: How certain schemes to improve the human condition have failed*. Yale University Press.
Stinson, D. W. (2004). Mathematics as "gate-keeper" (?): Three theoretical perspectives that aim toward empowering all children with a key to gate. *The Mathematics Educator*, *14*(1), 8–18.
Tröhler, D. (2020). National literacies, or modern education and the art of fabricating national minds. *Journal of Curriculum Studies*, *52*(5), 620–635.
Tröhler, D. (2022). Magical enchantments and the nation's silencing: Educational research agendas under the spell of globalization. In D. Tröhler, N. Piattoeva, & W. F. Pinar (Eds.), *World yearbook of education 2022: Education, schooling and the global universalization of nationalism* (pp. 7–25). Routledge.
Tröhler, D., & Lenz, T. (2015). *Trajectories in the development of modern school systems: Between the national and the global*. Routledge.
Tröhler, D., & Winkler, S. (2024). Imagined communities, social stratifications, and educational responses. Conditions of the possibility to talk about differentiation. *Journal of Curriculum Studies*. https://doi.org/10.1080/00220272.2024.2306508

Umay, A., Akkuş Çıkla, O., & Duatepe Paksu, A. (2006). Matematik dersi 1.-5. sınıf ögretim programinin NCTM prensip ve standartlarina göre incelenmesi [An investigation of 1.-5. grades mathematics curriculum by considering NCTM principles and standards]. *Hacettepe Universitesi Egitim Fakultesi Dergisi*, *31*, 198–211.

Valero, P. (2017). Mathematics for all, economic growth, and the making of the citizenworker. In T. Popkewitz, J. Diaz, & C. Kirchgasler (Eds.), *A political sociology of educational knowledge: Studies of exclusions and difference* (pp. 117–132). Routledge.

Yolcu, A. (2017). Historicizing "math for all". In A. Chronaki (Ed.), *Mathematics education and life at times of crisis. MES 9 conference proceedings. Vol* (Vol. 2, pp. 1011–1022). University of Thessaly Press.

Yolcu, A. (2019). Research on equitable mathematics teaching practices: Insights into its divergences and convergences. *Review of Education*, *7*(3), 701–730.

Yolcu, A. (2021a). Reimagining the citizen and the nation in a globalised world: The case of mathematics education reforms in Turkey. *Research in Mathematics Education*, *23*(3), 278–292.

Yolcu, A. (2021b). Türkiye'nin problem çözen çocuğu: Matematik eğitiminin kültürel alanlarının tarihsel bir analizi [Turkey's problem-solving child: A historical analysis of the cultural spaces of mathematics education]. *Eğitim Ve Bilim*, *46*(206), 27–47.

Yolcu, A., & Kirchgasler, K. L. (2024). Social (justice) mathematics: Racializing effects of ordering pedagogies and their inherited regimes of truth. *Educational Studies in Mathematics*, *116*(3), 351–370. https://doi.org/10.1007/s10649-023-10289-y

Yolcu, A., & Popkewitz, T. S. (2019). Making the able body: School mathematics as a cultural practice. *ZDM Mathematics Education*, *51*(2), 251–261.

Zhao, W., & Tröhler, D. (2021). Euro-Asia encounters on 21st-century competency-based curriculum reforms: A historical and cultural (re)turn. In W. Zhao & D. Tröhler (Eds.), *Euro-Asian encounters on 21st-century competency-based curriculum reforms* (pp. 3–17). Springer.

9 Mathematics education under the new National Education Policy of India

A Janus-faced highbrow mathematics instead of a hydra-headed Bahujan mathematics

Jayasree Subramanian

Introduction

Education policies brought out by a country are guided by the vision of the political party in power and informed by the changes in education in the global context. And this vision determines the kind of mathematics education it advocates. India adopted Goal 4 of the Agenda of Sustainable Development (SDG4) in 2015, under the rule of the Bhartiya Janata Party (BJP), a political party affiliated to the right-wing Hindu nationalist paramilitary voluntary organisation Rashtriya Swayamsevak Sangh (RSS). After being re-elected to power for a consecutive term and with an absolute majority in May 2019, it released the 484 pages draft of the proposed Education Policy, eliciting comments and responses from the public. Claiming overwhelmingly favourable response from the public and ignoring the considered and critical response from the educationists and intellectuals, a revised, cabinet-approved 66 pages National Education Policy (henceforth NEP2020) was released in July 2020, the third education policy after India became independent from British colonial rule in 1947. In a significant departure from the previous policies NEP2020 says, the vision of the policy is to instil in the learner 'a deep-rooted pride in being Indian', and develop 'knowledge, skills, values, and dispositions' that turn the learner into a 'truly global citizen'. Mathematics education figures in the policy as a significant domain holding possibilities to make India 'the global knowledge superpower' (NEP2020, pp. 6–7). Chronaki and Yolcu (2021) describe accurately that in the last decade a global world imaginary has

> gained momentum about how the lives of youth, children, families, communities and educators are being (or could be) reconfigured, along with their labour, behaviour, consumption habits, leisure activity, through relaunching images of citizenship for globality such as "digital", "multilingual", "intercultural", "creative", "critical" or "rational" and turning them into strategic areas for curricular organisation by institutional bodies such as UNESCO, the OECD, the UN and the European Union.
> (p. 244)

DOI: 10.4324/9781003130673-12

The images of citizenship that NEP2020 fabricates resonate well with their description, as 'flexibility', 'multidisciplinarity', 'holistic education', 'multilingualism', 'problem solving', 'creativity' 'critical thinking', and 'lifelong learning' are among the fundamental principles that the policy promotes. In a country grappling with a multitude of differences and hierarchies,[1] a set of natural questions that arise are, (i) whose concerns does the policy reflect, particularly in the context of mathematics education, (ii) who are poised to emerge as the 'global citizens', and (iii) what is the implication of the policy for the 'others'. By contextualising the policy historically and by analysing it within the constitutional framework and the larger political discourse in India, this chapter seeks to explore how the policy Brahminises the mathematics curriculum even as it envisions a mathematics education for global citizenship, thereby creating specific hybrid mathematical subjectivities and border mathematical knowledge.

The chapter is organised as follows: Next section gives a brief account of the earlier education policies and curriculum frameworks and reviews the response to NEP2020 against this background. Section *Problematising NEP2020's vision for mathematics education* gives a brief description of the need to critically engage with NEP2020 and states what this chapter aims to achieve. Section *History of mathematics to promote Hindu brahmin pride?* discusses in detail the problems in the way in which NEP2020 engages with history of mathematics by arguing that (i) it creates a space for introducing the dubious 'Vedic' mathematics, (ii) it selectively projects only the Brahminical Sanskrit language tradition from the history of mathematics in ancient India, and (iii) it ignores the history of vernacular[2] traditions in mathematics. The section *Mathematics for the future global citizens and others* argues that by uncritically advocating advanced mathematical training for the 'talented' and the acquisition of skill-based mathematics for others, the policy distributes different kinds of mathematics to different learners based on their caste. Next section, *Ethnomathematics as a framework for Indian mathematics*, discusses why ethnomathematics, of which the policy makes no reference, is an appropriate framework for talking about both vernacular traditions and what is referred to as ancient Indian mathematics, suggesting that ethnomathematics if carefully incorporated in school mathematics curriculum may have the potential for making mathematics education more inclusive. Drawing upon the work of Mukhopadhyay et al. (2009) and other scholars, concluding section calls for a culturally responsive mathematics education and makes some concluding remarks.

Situating the vision of NEP2020 in the context of education policies in post-independent India

Independent India carried out a comprehensive review of the education system at the end of its third five-year plan and announced the first national policy on education in the year 1968, stating that such a policy was essential for realising the ideal of a socialistic pattern of society, among other things. The second one was introduced in 1986 seeking to expand educational opportunities for women, historically marginalised castes, tribes and the disabled (NEP 1968&86, 1998). In 1992, this policy was modified to incorporate certain new developments in science and technology. In the year 2005, a new curriculum framework called National Curriculum Framework 2005 (or NCF 2005 for short) was introduced with a major thrust towards adopting constructivist approaches to teaching and learning (NCF, 2005). These policies too have highlighted the fact that like any ancient civilisation, India has its own knowledge base which needs to find a place in the curriculum. NCF 2005 is particularly significant for emphasising the need for school curriculum to build on the local knowledge that the learner acquires at home and from the community. The primary mathematics textbooks for example bring in examples from real life into the textbook (Rampal, 2015). The earlier policies remain committed to promoting scientific rationality and the enlightenment values of liberty, equality, and fraternity.

Among the disturbing departures that NEP2020 makes from the previous policies are (1) a concerted attempt to glorify that part of ancient Indian knowledge which is available in Sanskrit and incorporate it into the school curriculum, (2) involving in education, individuals, charitable groups and other private players who may not have the required training or established credentials in realising the objectives of public education, (3) increasing privatisation of education, (4) a strong focus on developing in the individual learner, competencies that have currency in the capitalistic global market economy instead of a commitment to equip the learners to critically engage with their physical and socio-political environment and play their role as democratic citizens, and (5) an attempt to introduce vocational education without appropriate measures to ensure that it does not contribute to reproducing the existing caste hierarchy.

NEP2020 received strong criticism from academicians working in education, terming it as going against the existing constitutional values (Rampal, 2020), institutionalising educational inequality (Batra, 2020), being too elusive for internal scrutiny and being 'part of a larger political project of denying history and pretending that everything is being thought through anew on a blank slate' (Menon, 2020), being market-driven and internationalising education (Haragopal, 2020), and that it does not 'fully recognise the diverse state of development of education across different states nor do the proposals adequately capture the complex nature of the system operating in different states' (Govinda, 2020, p. 605). However, a few academics in STEM areas went euphoric over it, praising it for making way for global education, that is holistic, interdisciplinary, and multidisciplinary, for introducing a flexible four-year undergraduate programme, with multiple exits, for promoting the privatisation of higher education, and boosting online training and being student-centric (Aithal & Aithal, 2020). A deemed university under Hindu religious order welcomes NEP2020 saying, it 'seamlessly integrate Veda Pathashala all the way up to research in modern scientific aspects enshrined in our scriptures through living and preaching as was the practice in days of yore' (Kannan, 2020). Interestingly, both the criticisms and compliments acknowledge NEP2020 as situated very much within the neoliberal agenda, promoting globalised market-driven, technocentric education and being a vehicle for promoting nationalist sentiments.

In the context of mathematics education, the document seeks to achieve its twin aim of producing mathematically well-trained youth competent to contribute to the global capitalist market economy and instilling in the learner a sense of national pride.

Problematising NEP2020's vision for mathematics education

India is a multi-religious, multicultural country with several regional and linguistic differences and its constitution makes an explicit commitment to constitute India as a sovereign socialist secular democratic republic and secure to its citizen social, economic, and political justice, liberty of thought, expression, belief, faith and worship and equality of status and opportunity (Constitution, 2022, p. 2). However, over the years, Hindu religious fundamentalism and violence against religious minorities have been on the rise and nationalism is increasingly coming to mean Hindu nationalism. The Hindu community (which constitutes 80% of the population) is fragmented by the 2000 years old hierarchical caste system, with Brahmins at the top. Traditionally occupation was caste based and the knowledge associated with the occupation remained with the caste group. Historically, Sanskrit, the language that the policy promotes, was accessible only to Brahmin men and a few men from the ruling and trading castes and is hardly spoken by anyone now (Deshpande, 2008). It is against this socio-political and cultural complexity that the implications of NEP2020 must be understood.

It would seem these socio-political factors will have nothing to do with mathematics education as the document calls for incorporating the great achievements of ancient Indian mathematicians in school textbooks and laying an increased emphasis on mathematical and computational thinking important in numerous fields. However, a close reading of NEP2020's vision for mathematics education against international research on mathematics education rooted in emancipation and NCF2005 raises several questions. Valero and Knijnik (2016) describe three perspectives namely a technical perspective, an emancipatory perspective, and a governmentality perspective from which policy on mathematics education can be researched. They argue that under the emancipatory perspective,

> (d)ifferent mathematics education policies around the world are analyzed from a critical standpoint. The policies are questioned in their emancipatory possibilities for those who had/have unequal access to cultural and material goods thanks to the many discriminations that mark the current globalized world.
>
> (p. 4)

By adopting an emancipatory perspective and by employing discourse analysis to analyse NEP2020, this chapter seeks to

i problematise what NEP2020 refers to as ancient Indian mathematics and the way it wants to incorporate it into school education,
ii argue why it is important to broaden the understanding of mathematics and uncover forms of mathematical knowledge embedded in the work of artisans and others,
iii explain how caste is linked to the kind of mathematics that NEP2020 refers to as the cultural heritage of India.

In the process of doing so, the chapter also seeks to draw attention to how notions of citizenship and its other for a global world are being crafted discursively in NEP2020, and the narrow and selective way in which the policy interprets global knowledge and misses an opportunity to call for research in mathematics education that resonates with international research.

History of mathematics to promote Hindu Brahmin pride?

It is well argued that learning mathematics at school should also include learning to appreciate the emergence of mathematical knowledge in a multitude of sociocultural contexts and over time (Ernest, 2000; Subramanian, 2015a). Such a school mathematics curriculum would broaden the scope of school mathematics, make it more inclusive, appeal to a wider range of students and cultivate in them, a taste for appreciating mathematics as a socio-cultural product. Using the history of mathematics for the teaching of mathematics is an active area of research (Katz, 2000).

However, NEP2020 sets for itself a different agenda, namely instilling in the learners 'a rootedness and pride in India, and its rich, diverse, ancient, and modern culture and knowledge systems and traditions' and says 'the Indian education system produced great scholars .... who made seminal contributions to world knowledge in diverse fields such as mathematics'. The document strongly advocates the teaching and learning of Sanskrit at all levels, stating that 'Sanskrit, while also an important modern language mentioned in the Eighth Schedule of the Constitution of India, possesses a classical literature that is greater in volume than that of Latin and Greek put together, containing vast treasures of mathematics ....' (NEP2020, p. 14). Though NEP2020 is interested in using a particular history of ancient Indian mathematics, to advance its agenda of Hindu supremacy, it tries to couch it in an inclusive language by saying the texts in Sanskrit were 'written by people of various religions as well as non-religious people, and by people from all walks of life and a wide range of socio-economic backgrounds over thousands of years' (NEP2020, p. 14).

It is pertinent to note here that history of mathematics has been largely written by western scholars, is Eurocentric[3] and concerns itself with tracing the history of mathematics as a pursuit of truth, rooted in the so-called Greek tradition. However, over the years, there has been a growing interest from India and abroad in studying the history of classical tradition in Indian mathematics. Among the studies from within India, some have been motivated by academic interest and are amenable to critical scrutiny by disciplinary experts, while others have been motivated by Hindu Nationalist (Hindutva[4]) ideology seeking to present a distorted, glorified picture that is not supported by evidence. Studying the history of mathematics poses several challenges some of which are discussed by Plofker (2009). We will draw attention to some of these and what is problematic about the way NEP2020 projects the history of Indian mathematics in the later subsections. In the next subsection we would like to discuss briefly the controversial 'Vedic mathematics'.

Proliferation of a populist misnomer called 'Vedic' mathematics

Even as NEP2020 calls for the incorporation of history of ancient Indian mathematics in school curriculum, some of the states ruled by BJP and private bodies promote what is referred to as Vedic mathematics. 'Vedic mathematics' is the title of a book written by Bharati Krishna Tirtha, a 20th-century monk belonging to a Hindu religious order (Tirtha, 1965) and contains 16 useful Sanskrit 'sutras' or techniques for quick computation. Being a graduate in mathematics and a Sanskrit scholar, Tirtha came up with these 16 sutras on his own with the intention of passing them off as mathematics of the Vedic times. Arguing that there is nothing 'Vedic' about the mathematics contained in the book Dani (1993, p. 1577), a mathematician with an interest in the history of Indian mathematics says, 'There has however been a persistent propaganda of the material being from the Vedas. The claim has got entangled with a sense of national pride, as a result of which even well-meaning and educated people have tended to accept it uncritically'. A quick search on the internet would reveal that there has been a flurry of activities around 'Vedic' mathematics in the last few decades: training for teachers and students and online certificate courses offered by private players, international journals, international conferences, Online Vedic mathematics forums, a lot of books, YouTube videos, an offer for a career in Vedic mathematics, media reports on the thrust from the state institutions to incorporate 'Vedic' mathematics as part of the school curriculum and so on. Most of these activities treat 'Vedic' mathematics as a treasure trove of ancient Indian mathematics, and only a few say 'Vedic' mathematics is a bunch of useful shortcuts. Here are the titles of some of the articles that appeared in the newspapers in the year 2020 even as the draft education policy was getting reviewed: 'Why new India needs to learn Vedic mathematics' (Kumar, 2020), 'Back to Vedic Age' (Garg, 2020), 'Education department pushes for Vedic maths in schools' (Vedic, 2019), and 'UP student overjoyed after PM Modi called him and encouraged to learn Vedic math' (News18.com, 2020).

Understandably, authentic historical accounts such as 'Geometry in Ancient and Medieval India' (Sarasvathi Amma, 1999), and 'History of Hindu

Mathematics' (Datta & Singh, 1962) that engage with a different tradition and demand a lot more mental labour have not received a fraction of the kind of attention 'Vedic' mathematics receives. The currency of 'Vedic' mathematics lies in the fact that it is within the grasp of a high school student and hence can be easily weaponised to propagate a false account of the glorious 'Vedic' mathematics of the past among unsuspecting people. Unlike ancient Indian mathematics, 'Vedic' mathematics is market-friendly, belongs with the modern western mathematics taught across the world, and is useful in dealing with computations in competitive exams. 'Vedic' mathematics serves the interest of the Hindutva forces to advance their agenda of promoting Hindu nationalism; it serves the interest of the market forces which capitalise on the myth of 'Vedic' and come up with saleable products. And these two interest groups reinforce each other.

Problematic selection from ancient Indian mathematics

Policy documents are not prescriptive. They are open for interpretation, project a long-term vision and provide broad guidelines, as to how the vision can be realised. Keeping with this, the details visible in the draft have been erased in NEP2020, leaving much to be read between the lines. In the case of mathematics education, the draft spells out what it seeks to achieve by incorporating historical accounts in mathematics textbooks. The draft says,

> in mathematics, the so-called Pythagorean theorem, Fibonacci numbers, and Pascal's triangle were first discovered and mathematically described in history (in very artistic and fascinating ways) by Baudhayana, Virahanka, and Pingala, respectively. The concept of zero and its use in the place value system that the world uses to write all numbers today - without which computers and modern technology would not be possible - also originated in India, over 2000 years ago; the use of this place value system for scientific computations was first demonstrated, extensively, by Aryabhata. The negative numbers - and the algebraic rules governing zero and negative numbers – were first introduced and used by Brahmagupta in Rajasthan, while the seeds of calculus were first laid down by Bhaskara II and Madhava in Karnataka and Kerala, respectively - among numerous other such fundamental contributions throughout mathematics and other fields. Such basic historical facts are not currently taught in India - perhaps a remnant of an earlier colonial time.
>
> (DNEP, 2019, p. 98)

Elements of history of mathematics, including history of Indian mathematics, could be incorporated in the school curriculum in such a way that it exposes the learner to historical and sociocultural contexts in which different forms of mathematical knowledge emerged. But there are serious problems with how NEP2020 seeks to incorporate history of Indian mathematics in the school curriculum. Focusing mainly on the so-called classical traditions in mathematics as part of the history of mathematics and ignoring other forms of mathematics is problematic. Moreover, studying a certain historical tradition of mathematics to establish its superiority over another tradition necessitates an assumption that the two traditions share the same epistemological framework and concerns.

Even the 'classical tradition' in mathematics in India is not monolithic, nor was all of it available in Sanskrit. Apart from the Vedic and Hindu traditions, classical mathematics was pursued by Buddhists and Jains and their work 'was mostly composed in vernaculars of Pali and Prakriti respectively rather than Sanskrit' (Plofker, 2009, p57). And both of their philosophy used a non-bivalent logic. Plofker says the Buddhists used 'tetralemma' or four-valued logic according to which anything is either 'true or not true or both true and not true or neither'. Moreover, for Jains, there were four kinds of infinities namely 'infinite in one way', 'infinite in two ways', 'infinite in partial extent', and 'eternally infinite' (Plofker, 2009, p. 58). NEP2020 mentions Nagarjuna, a Buddhist philosopher and Pali and Prakrit as classical languages but not their contributions to ancient Indian mathematics.

NEP2020 makes no mention of the contribution of Islamic scholars who were central to carrying Indian mathematics to the west and translating several Islamic mathematical texts into Sanskrit and Sanskrit works into Persian (Plofker, 2009; Sarma & Zamani, 2019; Young, 1995, pp. 255–278) and ignores the fact that during the reign of Sultan Fīrūz Shāh Tughluq (1305–1388),

> astrolabes and table-texts influenced by Arabic and Persian literature were translated into Sanskrit, and in turn many Sanskrit texts were translated into Persian. Court patronages were available for both Hindu and Muslim astrologers and mathematicians: a close study of the courts of such Moghol rulers would probably yield much information on how mathematics and astral sciences were taught. Note that Jain monks were known to have been active players, enabling the cross-fertilization of both mathematical and astronomical traditions. Jain mathematicians then from the late Vedic period to the premodern seemed to have been crucial actors of mathematical activity in the Indian sub-continent.
> (Keller, 2014. p. 79)

Also, works such as Yukitibasa from the Kerala school of mathematics were written in Malayalam. Ignoring the complex history, the linguistic and cultural diversity as well as the plurality of traditions in classical mathematics in India, projecting only Sanskrit as a repository of different forms of knowledge and sidestepping the fact access to Sanskrit was limited to men from dominant castes should be seen as motivated and divisive on the part of NEP2020 that amount to using mathematics education a tool to spread religious fundamentalism (Subramanian, 2021).

Finely graded, centuries-old caste structure is central to the Hindu religion. By birth, a Hindu belongs to a caste in the hierarchy, and marriages are caste endogamous. While this chapter will not go into describing the complex caste structure in detail, a few things about caste are in order. Brahmin, the priestly caste, a pan-Indian caste is at the top of the caste hierarchy. Power and property were in the hands of dominant castes (Brahmins, ruling castes, traders, and such). Peasant and artisanal castes (Sudra or Bahujan castes) were involved in different forms of productive labour and the outcastes (castes that faced severe forms of untouchability, now referred to as Dalit) were involved in labour considered polluting such as cleaning, clearing the dead and so on. In villages, social segregation based on caste is still a common practice. As a result of western education and the enlightenment values of liberty, equality and fraternity, caste as a social institution lost its legitimacy legally even though it continues to be a living social institution. Ambedkar (2014) a Dalit icon and the chief architect of the Indian constitution called for the annihilation of caste; the constitution of India guarantees all citizen equality before the law, abolishes untouchability, and prohibits discrimination based on religion, caste, race, sex, gender, or place of birth. In the modern Indian state, opportunities for education and employment are open for all. While caste and gender continue to be entrenched and powerful social institutions that override the secular constitution and reconfigure the dominant caste men as more legitimate citizens who control most of the state institutions, caste-based endogamous marriages are still the norm and forms of untouchability are still practised in rural and urban India (Thorat & Joshi, 2020), rising Dalit consciousness and struggles for gender justice challenge the Brahminical patriarchal caste order. As a result, Sanskrit is seen not only as the language of the oppressor but also the language in the which the caste order was codified in Manusmriti. It is therefore unlikely that learners from marginalised castes and minority religions would feel a sense of pride in the Sanskritic tradition in mathematics when other equally 'classical' traditions in mathematics like the Islamic, Buddhist, and Jain find no place in the curriculum.

Missing history of vernacular traditions in mathematics in multiple languages

Given that traditional occupation in India is caste based, vernacular traditions in mathematics existed among the non-brahmin castes engaged in different kinds of productive activities, and this mathematical knowledge was passed on systematically to the younger generation. There are mathematical texts in regional languages like Marathi, Guajarati, Tamil, Bengali, Hindi, Oriya, and Arabic that refer to various professional contexts such as carpentry, commerce and trading, masonry, and so on. Different kinds of multiplication tables for multiplying whole numbers, and fractions, methods for computation of volume of water reservoirs, multiple methods for measuring land, gold, grains, methods of computation involved in transaction of money involving goods and labour, including material on algebra and on trigonometry found in these texts are testimony to the fact that these forms of mathematical knowledge emerged in specific professional contexts and were produced by the community engaged in that specific occupation. Apart from the mathematical texts, among the rural people, there was also a practice of circulating orally, mathematical problems in the form of riddles and aphorism (Babu, 2012, p. 42). Here is one such Tamil verse that uses and puns on different fractional measures such as three-fourth, half, three-eighth, one-tenth, one-sixteenth and one-twentieth[5], only to invoke a person to pray to the god in the city of Kancheepuram before one turns old, requires a stick to walk, has grey hair, fears death and so on (Kalamegha Pulavar).

முக்காலுக்கேகாமுன் முன்னரையில் வீழாமுன்

அக்காலரைக்கால்கணடு அஞ்சாமுன் - விக்கி

இருமாமுன் மாகாணிக் கேகாமுன்

கச்சி ஒருமாவின் கீழரையின் றோது

Here is a tentative translation of the verse in English, but the translation cannot do justice to the verse because it cannot use the pun the original does:

Before you require a stick as a third leg, before your frontal hair turns grey,
Before you see the God of death and your legs shake in fear,
Before you start hiccupping and coughing, before your reach the graveyard,
Pray to the God Ekambara in the city of Kanchi.

Babu also draws attention to the fact that there was a rich tradition of mathematics education that happened in 'pathshalas' or 'tinnai schools' (veranda schools) across the country. These schools catered to children and youth from the middle castes engaged in some caste-based trade. Commenting on how teaching and learning happened in these schools he says

> (a)long with diversity in the curriculum, the pathshalas seemed to share a culture of pedagogy grounded in a form of memory very different from the modern associations of memory with rote or mechanical mode. This could be characterised as recollective memory where memory practices constituted a distinct mode of learning and not merely aids to learning. Oral recitations were central to this form of learning while the role of writing was to assist recollective memory, making the distinction between the oral and the written ambiguous. Learning under the aegis of recollective memory in itself constituted understanding, especially in a culture that appreciated exposition and celebrated remembering. Learning arithmetic in this mode cultivated computational abilities ....
>
> (Babu, 2012, p. 38)

If systematic effort is made by the state to find and document the fascinating wealth of mathematical material in regional languages and practices from the multiple sources and sites and incorporate some of them in the curriculum, it would provide the learners opportunities to appreciate both the classical and vernacular traditions in mathematics, treat learning about the cultural history of mathematics as part of learning mathematics in school and prepare them for a career not just in mathematics and its applications but also in exploring the socio-cultural, historical, and political dimensions of mathematics. Moreover, incorporating these diverse forms of local mathematical knowledge in the school mathematics curriculum will create opportunities for challenging the kind of citizenship fabricated by the emerging globalised technocentric universalised mathematics and allow for its 'others' namely the socio-culturally marginalised people and their knowledge to claim equal status.

The vision of NEP2020 has no place for such inclusive curriculum and limits itself instilling pride in being Indian. In the vision and wisdom of BJP this objective can be achieved only if we project the image of one nation, one language (read Sanskrit) and one culture (read Hindu Brahminical culture). However, this amounts to symbolic violence against religious minorities (Muslims in particular) targeted by the Hindu right-wing elements and marginalised caste people whose consciousness against the systematic caste-based oppression is rising across the country and even across the world as a selection of history of mathematics that glorifies only the Brahminical Sanskritic tradition would only lead to trauma and a feeling of alienation rather than a sense of national pride among these students. Trying to promote Hindu Brahmin pride in the name of national pride should be seen as motivated even if the document tries to cover up the intention by making a few cursory statements that acknowledge the existence of multiple traditions.

Mathematics for the future global citizens and others

In a caste based stratified society where textual knowledge was limited to certain dominant caste men while those born in labouring castes had to pursue their caste based occupation, terms such as 'talent' and 'skill' cannot be used without reference to this history just as these terms cannot be used without reference to how patriarchy produces boys as talented. A policy document should demonstrate sensitivity to these issues but NEP2020 shows no evidence of it.

With its twin aims to instil among the learners a deep-rooted pride in being Indian and to make 'India a global knowledge superpower' NEP2020 wants to invest in equipping the individual learner to acquire the knowledge and skills required for achieving them. According to the document,

> The world is undergoing rapid changes in the knowledge landscape. With various dramatic scientific and technological advances, such as the rise of big data, machine learning, and artificial intelligence, many unskilled jobs worldwide may be taken over by machines, while the need

> for a skilled workforce, particularly involving mathematics, computer science, and data science, in conjunction with multidisciplinary abilities across the sciences, social sciences, and humanities, will be increasingly in greater demand.
>
> (NEP2020, p. 3)

Expressing belief in the contestable notion of 'innate ability' (NEP2020, p. 20) and foregrounding the importance of mathematics and mathematical thinking for India's leadership role in 'fields and professions that will involve artificial intelligence, machine learning and data science' (NEP 2020, p. 15) the policy advocates the idea of setting up regional mathematics clubs and high-quality national level summer programmes where the talented could receive specialised training. In addition, the document also mandates that

> (e)very student will take a fun course, during Grades 6-8, that gives a survey and hands-on experience of a sampling of important vocational crafts, such as carpentry, electric work, metal work, gardening, pottery making, etc., as decided by States and local communities, and as mapped by local skilling needs.
>
> (NEP2020, p. 16)

These unqualified attempts to spot and nurture talent on the one hand and to introduce vocational education at the middle grades (11 to 14 year olds) are problematic as they fail to acknowledge persistent exclusion in STEM areas on the basis of caste and gender and call for measures to be inclusive. Some scholars have expressed serious reservations about integrating vocational education in school education without sufficient caution (Govinda, 2020; Haragopal, 2020). Clearly, the policy fabricates two kinds of citizens, namely 'the global' and its other, the 'local': armed with state-of-the-art training in the kind of mathematics that has currency in the globalised world now and taking pride in the glorious achievements of ancient India, the global citizen NEP2020 fabricates will turn India into a knowledge superpower in the technocentric, market-driven globalised world. And the 'others' will be equipped to take up vocational training and join 'Skill India', a campaign launched by the present government with the aim to train some 300 million people in different skills.

Whose talent for mathematics and whose vocational skills?

It is important to note that these initiatives remain problematic in themselves due to the narrow instrumental view of education they promote. But more importantly, it is obvious to anyone who has engaged with equity issues in school education and higher education, that these initiatives, without accompanying explicit measures to protect the interests of those who are socio-economically, historically, and culturally marginalised, would result in reproducing existing inequality. In India a large percentage of Dalits and tribal people live in abject poverty, are only engaged in back-breaking labour, some of them even in dehumanising and life-threatening labour such as manual scavenging, continue to face social exclusion, and are poorly represented in academia, judiciary, bureaucracy and in salaried jobs. Owing to several factors such as lack of quality education in public schools, systematic bias within educational institutions, students from these caste backgrounds do not have equal opportunities for education. In fact, a very large percentage of students who either drop out of school or fail in school final examinations belong to these castes. Those who manage to enrol for higher education with formal schooling requirements come with systemic deficit and find it difficult to cope with what they are taught. The Indian state grouped the castes in to three categories: Scheduled Castes (SC) consist of all outcastes (Dalits) that faced extreme forms of caste oppression and socio-economic deprivation; Other Backward Castes (OBC) are largely Sudras who faced caste based exclusion and socio-economic deprivation; Other Castes (OC) consisting of Brahmins, ruling and trading castes and other dominant castes; Scheduled Tribes (ST) consist of all tribal groups that are socio-culturally and economically marginalised. The state introduced a reservation policy (a stronger form of affirmative action) in 1950 to ensure that SC and ST are represented in higher education and employment, and reservation was extended to OBCs in the 1990s.[6] Because of reservation, a very small percentage of youth belonging to these backgrounds have been able to enter higher education institutions and state government jobs (Kumar et al., 2020; Weisskopf, 2004). Insiders to mathematics and mathematics education in India know that the representation of SC, ST, and OBC castes in higher education and employment in both these domains continues to be very poor, though no published data is made available because of the political nature of the issue. Moreover, religious minorities and even girls from dominant castes are underrepresented in the prestigious Indian Institutes of Technology and in International Mathematics Olympiads.

It is in this prevailing scenario that NEP2020 seeks to provide high-quality training to those with 'innate talent' and introduce vocational education from middle school. Mathematics as a domain has been dominated by Brahmins with Srinivasa Ramanujan as a shining example. Notions like 'talent for mathematics is inborn' and 'Brahmins have the talent for mathematics' are strongly held by mathematicians as well as by the common public (Subramanian, 2007; 2015b). With cultural, social, and economic capital on their side, there is a high probability that the representation of Brahmins and other dominant castes is disproportionately large among students who are found to have an 'innate talent for mathematics' and among the students who would opt for or would be encouraged to opt for vocational education and eventually constitute the workforce would belong to OBC or SC. By not addressing the equity question head-on, NEP2020 stays clear of the politics of mathematics education and makes explicit its political position that it supports the status quo.

Ethnomathematics as a framework for Indian mathematics

The word 'ethno' appears exactly once in NEP2020 and that is in the context of ethnomedicines. There is no reference to ethnomathematics in the whole document even though ethnomathematics is a well-established area with rich literature in mathematics education. Central to the notion of ethnomathematics is the idea that knowledge is a cultural product and mathematics is no exception to that. This is a major departure from the dominant notion that mathematics is timeless and universal. Ubiratan d' Ambrosio who is considered the intellectual father of the ethnomathematics programme in Brazil defines the term ethnomathematics as

> … mathematics which is practiced among identifiable cultural groups such as national-tribal societies, labour groups, children of a certain age bracket, professional classes and so on. Its identity depends largely on focusses of interest, on motivation and on certain codes and jargons which do not belong to the realm of academic mathematics.
>
> (D'Ambrosio, 1985, p. 45)

This definition of ethnomathematics allows us to include a broader range of mathematical practices, including current professional mathematical practices that do not demand the rigour and formalism of academic mathematics. He distinguishes ethnomathematics from ethnomathematics which is the mathematical knowledge of indigenous groups (D'Ambrosio, 2007, p. 30). In particular, the notion of ethnomathematics allows us to study the multiple forms of mathematics that are not alive anymore as well as forms of mathematics that are alive and constantly changing in response to the changes in the larger society. It is also empowering because it enables socio-economically and culturally marginalised groups to claim their rightful place as creators and users of mathematical knowledge of a different kind.

Ethnomathematics as a framework to understand the mathematical practices existing in the country would be more suited to India precisely because traditional knowledge in India is largely caste or community based. In rural India, caste-based occupation such as weaving, carpentry, boat building, leatherwork, metalwork, making specific musical instruments, pottery, basketry, and so on, are in the hands of specific caste groups. Both the knowledge involved in the work and the right to carry out the work remains within the caste group. Similarly, there are also forms of mathematical knowledge embedded in the work of certain religious and tribal communities. For example, bidri metalwork and chikankari embroidery work belong to certain groups of Muslims, and Dogra metal work, mirror work on cloths, etc. belong to specific tribal groups.

Discussing the knowledge involved in traditional leather work, Dalitbahujan scholar Kancha Ilaiah Shepard, argues that the Madiga caste people functioned like scientists systematically experimenting with tools to separate the skin from the dead animals and apply specific ingredients to prepare and preserve the skin and to tan it, perfecting the method, and passing on the knowledge from generation to generation (Ilaiah Shepard, 2009, pp. 25–48). Within the caste hierarchy, Madigas were treated as untouchables, faced social exclusion because their occupation, which involves dealing with dead bodies, is considered ritually polluting and their work is denied the recognition it deserves.

The underrepresentation of the marginalised castes and tribes is often explained by the fact that for generations they have been denied textual knowledge; but the knowledge embedded in their traditional occupation does not get recognised as knowledge.

Given that India has not invested much in education research including mathematics education research, it is not surprising that there is very little research on ethnomathematics in India just as in any other area of mathematics education. Swapna Mukhopadhyay's study of the boat builders in west Bengal is significant (Mukhopadhyay, 2013). Describing the work of the boat-builders engaged in building a boat that is approximately 60 feet long she says, 'There were no drawings or blueprints visible; the tools in use were simple, some were homemade and even looked too "primitive" to accomplish such an engineering feat' (p. 96). But clearly, there is measurement and geometry involved in boat building though the boat builders are illiterate and have received no training in formal mathematics. The mathematics involved in the work is embedded in the practice and transmitted by apprenticeship. And as Swapna Mukhopadhyay rightly points out, 'The rigor that a formally trained engineer might consider lacking in the work of the boat-builders contrasts with another form of rigorous validation; the boats are exceptionally functional and strong, used over many years for extended oceanic travel' (p. 99).

Among the other ethnomathematical studies, Ascher's study of Kolam (Ascher, 2002) and Santra and Mukhopadhyay's preliminary study of Mason's work (Santra & Mukhopadhyay, 2019), are based in India. A few other studies, though not necessarily in ethnomathematics, draw our attention to the kind of mathematics embedded in the work and the need to study them from the perspective of ethnomathematics. Gagan Deep Kaur's study of Kashmiri carpet weaving (Kaur, 2018) is certainly important even though its central concern is more about cognition than about ethnomathematics. India is not yet a fully industrialised country. Several traditional occupations along with the wealth of associated knowledge continue to exist even now. The ethnomathematical studies mentioned above illustrate the immense potential for research in ethnomathematics to uncover multiple forms of mathematical practices embedded in a range of traditional occupations such as carpentry, weaving, jewellery making, leather work and so on which are still alive in the country as well as in occupations such as traditional forms of architecture, metallurgy and so on which may not be in practice anymore. These multiple forms of ethnomathematical knowledge embedded in work, along with ancient Indian mathematics should be rightfully seen as Indian Mathematics. If some of these diverse ethnomathematical knowledge that is still in practice (such as kolams, which girls from young age draw every morning to decorate the threshold to their homes in several parts of India) is carefully incorporated in school mathematics curriculum, it may make mathematics less intimidating and more meaningful for many children. However, for the Hindu right wing with its agenda of establishing the superiority of Vedic knowledge, ethnomathematics carries no value.

Conclusion

The National Education Policy 2020 like most policy documents, provides a set of principles, aims and policy recommendations to guide educational endeavour in the country. The emancipatory tendencies visible in the previous policies and curriculum frameworks are absent in NEP2020. A policy that seeks to empower citizens through mathematics education would pay attention to research in mathematics education that foregrounds inclusive approaches to mathematics curriculum development and pedagogy; it would be alert to the prevalent concern among educationists that incorporating ethnomathematical knowledge might lead to differentiated curriculum where only the students from marginalised sections are taught mathematical knowledge embedded in people's occupation; it would employ ethnomathematics for culturally responsive mathematics education (Mukhopadhyay et al., 2009) which rests on the criteria that

i students must experience academic success;
ii students must develop/maintain cultural competence; and
iii students must develop a critical consciousness through which they challenge the status quo of the current social (Ladson-Billings, 1995, p. 160).

Valero and Knijnik (2016, p. 5) say

> the technologies of mathematics education are not simply neutral tools for the betterment of learning, but also and at the same time they contribute to the constitution of learners' subjectivities and of those of the many other participants in the broad network of mathematics education practices.

By instrumentalising Sanskrit and ancient Indian mathematics to instil national pride and by issuing a call to turn India into a global knowledge superpower in the neoliberal globalised world, by subscribing to notions such as 'innate talent' for mathematics and by indirectly promoting a differentiated mathematics curriculum in which the 'talented' would learn advanced topics in mathematics and others vocational education, NEP2020 fabricates the Hindu dominant caste men as the legitimate and global citizens which is motivated!

Notes

1 For example, caste, class, gender, ability, linguistic, regional, cultural, and religious differences along with hierarchies
2 These are forms of mathematical knowledge that emerged in the context of specific kinds of productive activities that caste groups engaged in. These are referred to as ethnomathematical knowledge in mathematics education literature. See Babu (2022) for a detailed engagement.
3 With a brief account of Indian, Chinese, and other mathematics. "A History of Mathematics" by Cajori (1894) devotes 16 out of the 415 pages to "Hindoo" mathematics. Boyer and Merzbach (1968) devote 30 out of the 736 pages to Indian and Chinese mathematics put together. Victor Katz (2009) devotes 34 out of the 966 pages to Indian mathematics.
4 The term Hindutva refers to the fanatical Hindu supremacist right-wing ideology, differentiating it from Hinduism, which is a religion.
5 In Tamil, the word "kaal" means both one-fourth and leg, "arai" means half and "narai" means grey hair, "kaalaraikaal" means three-eighth while "kaalar" refers to Yama, the God of death, "iruma" is one-tenth and "irumal" is cough, "maakaani" is one-sixteenth and also graveyard, "oruma" is one-twentieth and "orumavin keezhar' is the God Ekambaran.
6 The reservation policy reserves about 15%, 7.5%, and 27% of seats in public funded educational institutions and government jobs for those from SC, ST, and OBC background.

References

Aithal, S., & Aithal, S. (2020) Analysis of the Indian National Education Policy 2020 towards Achieving its Objectives. MPRA Paper No. 102549, Munich Personal RePEc Archive. https://mpra.ub.uni-muenchen.de/102549/

Ambedkar, B. R. (2014). *Annihilation of caste: The annotated critical edition.* Verso Books.

Ascher, M. (2002). The Kolam tradition: A tradition of figure-drawing in Southern India expresses mathematical ideas and has attracted the attention of computer science. *American Scientist, 90*(1), 56–63.

Babu, D. S. (2012). Indigenous traditions and the colonial encounter: A historical perspective on mathematics education in India. In R. Ramanujam & K. Subramaniam (Eds.), *Mathematics education in India: Status and outlook* (pp. 37–62). Homi Bhabha Centre for Science Education, TIFR.

Babu, D. S. (2022). *Mathematics and society: Numbers and measures in early modern South India* (pp. 384p.). Oxford University Press.

Batra, P. (2020). Is the National Education Policy 2020 designed to deliver equitable quality public education? https://scroll.in/article/970548/is-the-national-education-policy-2020-designed-to-deliver-equitable-quality-public-education

Boyer, B. C., & Merzbach (1968). *A history of mathematics.* John Wiley & Sons Inc.

Cajori, F.(1894) *A history of mathematics.* Macmillan and Co.

Chronaki, A., & Yolcu, A. (2021). Mathematics for "citizenship" and its "other" in a "global" world: Critical issues on mathematics education, globalisation and local communities. *Research in Mathematics Education, 23*(3), 241–247. https://doi.org/10.1080/14794802.2021.1995780.

Constitution (2022) The Constitution of India https://cdnbbsr.s3waas.gov.in/s380537a945c7aaa788ccfcdf1b99b5d8f/uploads/2023/05/2023050195.pdf

D'Ambrosio, U. (1985). Ethnomathematics and its place in the history and pedagogy of mathematics. *For the Learning of Mathematics, 5*(1), 44–48.

D'Ambrosio, U. (2007). Peace, social justice and ethnomathematics. *The Montana Mathematics Enthusiast, Monograph, 1*(2007), 25–34.

Dani, S. G. (1993). 'Vedic Mathematics': Myth and reality. *Economic and Political Weekly, 28*(31), 1577–1580.

Datta, B., & Singh, A. N. (1962). *History of Hindu mathematics: A source book* (2 vols). Asia Publishing House (Reprinted)

Deshpande, M. M. (2008). Sanskrit in the South Asian sociolinguistic context. In B. B. Kachru, Y. Kachru, & N. Sridhar (Eds.), *Language in South Asia* (pp. 177–188). Cambridge University Press.

DNEP2019. (2019). Draft National Education Policy. https://www.education.gov.in/sites/upload_files/mhrd/files/Draft_NEP_2019_EN_Revised.pdf

Ernest, P. (2000). Why teach mathematics? http://socialsciences.exeter.ac.uk/education/research/centres/stem/publications/pmej/why.htm

Garg, M. (2020). Back to the Vedic Age. https://www.thehindu.com/education/back-to-the-vedic-age/article31659547.ece

Govinda, R. (2020). NEP 2020: A critical examination. *Social Change, 50*(4), 603–607.

Haragopal, G. (2020). National Education Policy 2020: Implications and impact. *Social Change, 50*(4), 589–593.

Ilaiah Shepard, K. (2009). *Post-Hindu India: A discourse on Dalit Bahujan socio-spiritual and scientific revolution*. Sage.

Kalamegha Pulavar. https://hindutemplefacts.wordpress.com/tag/kalamega-pulavar/

Kannan, V. (2020). *National Education Policy (NEP) 2020 and SCSVMV*. Springer https://doi.org/10.1007/s40012-020-00316-1

Katz, V. J. (2000). *Using history to teach mathematics: An international perspective*. The Mathematical Association of America.

Katz, V. J. (2009). *A history of mathematics: An introduction*. Addison-Wesley, Pearson Education Inc.

Kaur, G. D. (2018). Situated and distributed cognition in artifact negotiation and trade-specific skills: A cognitive ethnography of Kashmiri carpet weaving practice. *Theory & Psychology, 28*(4), 451–475.

Keller, A. (2014). History of mathematical education in ancient, medieval and pre-modern India (within the chapter: Mathematics education in oriental antiquity and middle ages). In A. P. Karp & G. Schubring (Eds.), *Handbook on the history of mathematics education* (pp. 70–83). Springer.

Kumar, D., Pratap, B., & Aggarwal, A. (2020). Affirmative action in government jobs in India: Did the job reservation policy benefit disadvantaged groups? *Journal of Asian and African Studies, 55*(1), 145–160.

Kumar, N. (2020). Why new India needs to learn Vedic mathematics. https://thedailyguardian.com/why-new-india-needs-to-learn-vedic-mathematics/

Ladson-Billings, G. (1995). Toward a theory of culturally relevant pedagogy. *American Educational Research Journal, 32*(3), 465–491.

Menon, S. (2020). NEP 2020: Some searching questions. *Social Change, 50*(4), 599–602.

Mukhopadhyay, S. (2013). The mathematical practices of those without power. In M. Berger, K. Brodie, V. Frith & K. le Roux (Eds.), *Proceedings of the Seventh International Mathematics Education and Society Conference (MES7), Vol. 1* (pp. 94–109). Cape Town, South Africa.

Mukhopadhyay, S., Powell, A. B., & Frankenstein, M. (2009). An ethnomathematical perspective on culturally responsive mathematics education. In B. Greer, S. Mukhopadhyay, A. B. Powell, & S. Nelson-Barber (Eds.), *Culturally responsive mathematics education* (pp. 79–98). Routledge.

NCF (2005). National Curriculum Framework. National Council of Education Research and Training. New Delhi. https://ncert.nic.in/pdf/nc-framework/nf2005-english.pdf

NEP 1968&86 (1998). National Policies https://ncert.nic.in/nep.php?ln=

NEP2020. (2020) National Education Policy. https://www.education.gov.in/sites/upload_files/mhrd/files/NEP_Final_English_0.pdf

News18.com (2020). UP student overjoyed after PM Modi called him and encouraged to learn Vedic math. https://www.news18.com/news/buzz/up-student-overjoyed-after-pm-modi-called-him-and-encouraged-to-learn-vedic-math-2737591.html

Plofker, K. (2009). *Mathematics in India*. Princeton University Press.

Rampal, A. (2015). Curriculum and critical agency: Mediating everyday mathematics. In S. Mukhopadyay & B. Greer (Eds.), *Proceedings of the Eighth Mathematical Education and Society Conference Portland, Oregon, United States.*

Rampal, A. (2020). The NEP Goes Against the Existing Constitutional Mandate of the RTE. https://thewire.in/education/national-education-national-education-policy-right-to-education

Santra, I., & Mukhopadhyay, S. (2019). The Role Mathematical Thinking Plays in Masons' Workplace in West Bengal: A Preliminary Examination. In J. Subramanian (Ed.), *Proceedings of the Tenth Mathematical Education and Society Conference*, Hyderabad, India.

Sarasvati Amma, T. A. (1999). *Geometry in ancient and medieval India*. Motilal Banarsidass Publishers.

Sarma, S. R., & Zamani, M. (2019). On the Persian translation of Bhāskara's Līlāvatī by Abu'l Faiẓ Faiẓī at the court of Akbar. *Indian Journal of Historical Studies*, *54*, 269–285.

Subramanian, J. (2007). Perceiving and producing merit: Gender and doing science in India. *Indian Journal of Gender Studies*, *14*(2), 259–284.

Subramanian, J. (2015a). One mathematics for all: Can it be realized in a multicultural, multilingual country? *Intercultural Education*, *26*(4), 266–277. https://doi.org/10.1080/14675986.2015.1072303

Subramanian, J. (2015b). Unraveling the 'Gender-Merit' Conundrum: Do women deserve to do science in India. In G. Chadha & S. Krishna (Eds.). *Feminists and science: Critiques and changing perspectives in India* (Vol 1), 22–51. Stree.

Subramanian, J. (2021) School mathematics as a tool for spreading religious fundamentalism: The case of 'Vedic mathematics' in India. In D. Kollosche (Ed.), *Exploring new ways to connect: Proceedings of the Eleventh International Mathematics Education and Society Conference. 3 Volumes* (pp. 995–1004). Tredition.

Thorat, A., & Joshi, O. (2020). The continuing practice of untouchability in India. *Economic & Political Weekly*, *55*(2), 37.

Tirtha, B. K. (1965). *Vedic mathematics*. Motilal Banarsidass Publishers.

Valero, P., & Knijnik, G. (2016). Mathematics education as a matter of policy. In M.A. Peters (Ed.), *Encyclopedia of educational philosophy and theory* (pp. 1–6). Springer Singapore. https://doi.org/10.1007/978-981-287-532-7_523-1

Vedic, E. (2019). Education department pushes for Vedic maths in schools. https://www.hindustantimes.com/cities/education-department-pushes-for-vedic-maths-in-schools/story-VX7QfvinygIQTSPdUC1b8K.html

Weisskopf, T. E. (2004). Impact of reservation on admissions to higher education in India. *Economic and Political Weekly*, 4339–4349.

Young, G. D. (1995). Euclidean geometry in the mathematical tradition of Islamic India. *Historia Mathematica*, *22*(1995), 138–153.

10 Globalization, racial projects, and the citizenship promise in mathematics education reform efforts

Angela Valencia-Salas and Luz Valoyes-Chávez

Introduction

This chapter analyzes the extent to which mathematics education reform efforts in the globalized world advance particular racial projects that, rather than materializing the promise of citizenship for Blacks, may prevent its realization. The focus is on Black students within the context of historical efforts to reform the Colombian educational system. Since the early formation of the nation-state, citizenship for Black Colombians has been a site of dispute, struggle, and contestation.

Historically, Black Colombians have faced limited participation in the country's democratic life, as well as restricted access to a dignified life. Various mechanisms have been used to deny Black Colombians their rights to participate in the social, economic, and political life of the country. For example, Black individuals were often portrayed in public discourse as "big children" who were naturally destined to be tutored and protected by "better races" (Restrepo, 2010). The stereotyping practice of infantilization was mostly used to deny voting rights to Black Colombians. Additionally, Colombia's political and intellectual elite promoted *mestizaje,* a whitening project that encouraged race mixing. One of the aims of mestizaje was to erase the Black and indigenous components from the national identity and culture in order to "strengthen democracy" in the nascent nation-state. Although the constitutional reform of 1991 recognized the political rights and status of Black Colombians (Restrepo, 2013), their participation as rightful citizens in Colombian democratic life remains elusive.

In the context of transnational relations and commercial activity, international organizations have pushed for a more egalitarian and democratic society in Colombia. As a result, the country has undergone a series of educational reforms over the last three decades, with the promise of providing citizenship to all Colombians regardless of their culture, class, gender, or ethnicity. In particular, the inclusion of mathematics in the national curriculum has been justified by its role in constituting democratic values (National Ministry of Education, NME, 1998a, 2003). This chapter interrogates the promise of citizenship for Colombian Blacks. We center our analysis on the curricular

DOI: 10.4324/9781003130673-13

discourses proposed in the reform efforts to examine how they advance particular racial projects that either prevent or promote the participation of Black Colombians as full citizens through mathematics education.

In the following sections we will discuss the relationships between globalization, citizenship, and mathematics education, provide historical context for readers unfamiliar with the dynamics and characteristics of Colombia's racialized social system to better understand the promise of citizenship for Black Colombians, and explain the methodological approach used to analyze the Colombian curricular documents. Then, we present and discuss our findings. This chapter contributes to the growing body of work that critically examines discourses of educational change and their promises of citizenship and equity in mathematics education (e.g., Andrade-Molina, 2021; Chronaki & Yolcu, 2021).

Globalization, racial projects, and the citizenship promise in mathematics education

Globalization can be defined as a rapid expansion of open markets, free trade, and economic and institutional deregulation that promotes values associated with consumerism and the capital accumulation (Olssen et al., 2004). This process involves the global production and circulation of goods, knowledge, and cultural practices (McGrew, 1992; Tröhler, 2010), which have an impact on the economic, political, and cultural dimensions of nation-states (Olssen et al., 2004). Globalization requires local educational systems to produce individuals capable of consuming goods, knowledge, and cultural practices to succeed in an interconnected world. These individuals are expected to be "global citizens" and also responsible for promoting the development of local democracies. The new international order places tensions on the local realities of individual nation-states due to its political, economic, and cultural demands (Bruno-Jofré & Tröhler, 2014). These demands are often contested and resisted. McGrew (1992) highlights the contradictory dynamics involved in globalization, emphasizing its dialectical nature. For instance, the standardization and uniformity of various social aspects, including religion, education, and social life, are challenged by the unique local realities, dynamics, and circumstances that require the re-articulation and re-signification of these dimensions (McGrew, 1992). In this context, analyzing educational reforms requires considering the interplay between the homogenization and unification of educational goals to produce the global citizen and the racial, cultural, social, and political realities of the national contexts in which these processes of educational change occur (Bruno-Jofré & Tröhler, 2014).

Transnational organizations have required their associated countries to pursue educational reforms to respond to the demand for producing global citizens. These reforms reinforce the role of mathematics education as a fundamental pathway to citizenship and democratic participation (Chronaki & Yolcu, 2021). It is argued that mathematics teaching and learning can contribute to the realization of "democratic ideals" in Western societies (Skovsmose & Valero, 2012). The development of democratic competencies through mathematics education would transform the child into a citizen capable of making rational decisions (Valero & García, 2014) and of recognizing and critiquing inequity, injustice, and the formatting power of mathematics in society (Chronaki, 2010). Thus, there is a broad consensus in such discourses regarding the existence of universal skills and competencies required in the globalized world, which can be developed through learning mathematics (Chronaki & Yolcu, 2021). However, the role of mathematics teaching and learning in the production of citizens has been under examination (e.g., Skovsmose, 1994). Critiques have been raised about the relationship between democracy and mathematics education (Chronaki, 2023), as well as the role of mathematics in reinforcing global oppressive racial orders (Martin, 2013). This discussion highlights the importance of considering the interplay between mathematics education, democracy, and racial projects in curricular reforms worldwide.

The discussion of globalization, democracy, and mathematics education resonates in historically impoverished countries where democracy is perceived to be constantly at risk (Valero et al., 2012). The entry of Latin American countries into the era of globalization has led to the transition of military-ruled countries and the progression of countries with weak democratic governments towards democracy (Valero, 1999). In these contexts, it is argued that mathematics education reforms aim to distribute the mathematical knowledge, skills, values, and attitudes fairly among students, which is needed for successful performance and participation in the political, economic, and cultural dimensions of the globalized world. In other words, mathematics education promotes people's democratic participation. Valero et al. (2012) argue that these discourses "contribute to selling the myth that mathematics learning can be a way of saving the world, the nation, and the individual" (p. 2). Despite various reform efforts worldwide, historically marginalized student populations, particularly Black and indigenous children, have not benefited from these reforms (Berry, 2018; Nguyen, 2010). The promise of citizenship has not been fully realized for these students.

According to Martin (2019), the failure of reform efforts to advance a liberatory and anti-racist mathematics education is not surprising, but rather an expected outcome. Martin (2013) argues that these reform efforts are part of larger racial projects, and instead of radically transforming the practices and discourses that dehumanize and oppress Black students, they perpetuate them. Mathematics education reforms are not neutral in terms of race or politics, according to Martin. They seem to contribute to the maintenance and reproduction of a racialized economic system that creates different categories of humanness and citizenship and are aligned with the rhetoric and ideologies of neoliberal and neoconservative racial projects (Martin, 2013). As global capitalism expands, educational policies worldwide advance and sustain racial projects such as white supremacy.

Martin's (2013) discussion prompts an inquiry into the role of mathematics education in advancing specific racial projects and their beneficiaries. To describe these projects, he introduces Omi and Winant's (1994) definition of a racial project as "simultaneously an interpretation, representation or explanation of racial dynamics and an effort to reorganize or redistribute resources along particular racial lines" (cited by Martin, 2013, p. 324). Thus, in the context of the promise of citizenship in mathematics education and the belief that curricula are powerful pedagogical tools for distributing skills and knowledge in a globalized world, a critical question arises regarding the ways in which racial dynamics in racialized social systems, in which reform efforts are implemented, shape the distribution of mathematical knowledge and skills among student populations. What are the limits and scope of the promise of citizenship for Black student populations in these contexts?

This issue is relevant in countries like Colombia, which has a history of racial and economic inequities and an internal conflict that has mostly affected Black and indigenous communities (Hernández, 2009; Restrepo & Rojas, 2004). In 1991, a constitutional reform recognized Colombia as a multicultural and pluriethnic society, which was a historical milestone for a country previously considered a "racial democracy" (Valoyes-Chávez, 2018). Three educational reform efforts have been implemented in Colombia to address the country's ethnic and cultural diversity in education and to meet the demands of a stable, just, and modern democracy. These efforts include the Law of Education (NME, 1995a) and the Ethnoeducation Program (NME, 1995b). García and Romero-Rey (2018) emphasize the neoliberal approach of these educational reforms, which, as expected, incorporated the demands of transnational organizations such as the World Bank and the Inter-American Development Bank in terms of equity and democratic ideals. Colombia's recent admission to the Organization for Economic Cooperation and Development (OECD) has renewed calls for educational reforms that respond to global demands. The OECD has intervened in the educational policy-making process by issuing "recommendations" related to five dimensions: access and coverage, retention, quality, relevance, and financing. The Colombian government claims that the 2016-2026 Education Plan is a response to these "recommendations" and to "the indicators provided by the OECD, through the diagnosis of education in Colombia" (NME, 2017, p. 21). Following Martin's (2013) suggestion, this chapter analyzes the extent to which mathematics education reform efforts in Colombia advance particular racial projects that, rather than materializing the promise of citizenship for Black Colombians, may prevent its realization.

Racial projects, blackness, and citizenship in Colombia

To analyze the interplay between globalization, antiblackness, and the promise of citizenship in mathematics education in the Colombian context, it is important to highlight two historical facts. First, citizenship has been elusive for

Black Colombians. The abolition of slavery in 1852 did not result in political participation or voting rights for the newly freed Black population (Agudelo, 2002). Various measures were implemented to prevent their democratic participation and access to administrative positions, including laws that restricted voting rights to those who were literate and property owners. Former enslaved Black Colombians were unable to meet the requirements as they had little to no access to schooling. In fact, education in the universal arts, sciences, and mathematics was reserved for the *Creole White* elite. It was not until the first half of the 19th century that Blacks were allowed to receive an education through the establishment of Jesuit Missions. The primary goal of this education was to spread the Catholic faith among Black people (Valencia-Salas, 2017) as it was limited to the study of the Bible. Second, mestizaje emerged as the dominant racial ideology that played a fundamental role in the constitution of the nation-state and the national identity (Lasso, 2013). As discussed below, mestizaje was a project aimed at whitening the nascent country's culture and identity by erasing inferior cultural and racial elements.

As the constitution of the new nation state progressed, the XIX and early XX centuries witnessed critical debates about race in Colombia. Discourses of scientific racism found fertile ground among the creole white political and academic elite (Valencia-Salas, 2017). They were used to justify and explain the exclusion of Black Colombians from democratic participation. Arguments in favor of the inferiority of Blacks were articulated based on climate and race:

> [...] Prominent members of the criollo elite, such as Francisco José de Caldas and Jorge Tadeo Lozano, were influenced by European naturalists like Buffon, who made statements about the relationship between climate and the physical and moral characteristics of human beings. They believed that the tropics' heat and humidity produced weak and "degenerate" men. They recognized the influence of climate on civilization and explained that the lands and climate of the Andes mountains would allow civilization to flourish, unlike the torrid zones.
>
> (Valencia-Salas, 2017, p. 62)

Geographical areas of the country associated with Blackness were often represented as wild and uncivilized, leading to the belief that culture and civilization were impossible in those places. This association between Blackness and nature created a contrast with culture, morality, and adulthood. The impossibility of citizenship for Black Colombians was reinforced in public discourse through ideological representations of this population as childlike, amoral, and possessing other negative characteristics such as "the rudimentary and deformed Black spirit" (Gomez, 1970, quoted by Restrepo, 2010, p. 288). These discourses legitimized the representation of Black Colombians as a population with little self-government which translated into their inability to "rationally" participate in the political and social life of the country. Black

Colombians were portrayed as unfit for democratic participation. Laureano Gomez, a former Colombian president, expanded on this idea:

> In the nations where Blacks are the predominant population, reign disorder. Haiti is the classic example of a turbulent and irresponsible democracy. In countries where Blacks have disappeared, such as Argentina, Chile, and Uruguay, it has been possible to establish an economic and political organization with a solid basis of stability.
>
> (Gómez, 1970, as cited by Restrepo, 2010, p. 282)

In this context, *mestizaje* as a racial project became the key to eliminating what was problematic for the structuring of the nation-state: the perceived inferiority of the Black and indigenous components. As Rivera (2000) explains:

> The connection between nationalist aspirations to maintain a national and culturally homogeneous space and the dynamics of internal exclusion is demonstrated by the various forms of discrimination and exclusion associated with the search for national homogeneity. These forms promote exclusionary identity codes, deny citizenship to certain groups, or demand their expulsion and disappearance.
>
> (p. 24)

Democracy in Colombia was a form of political organization made possible by the "promiscuity of race" in which the inferior element was under control. To paraphrase Williams (1989), the constitution of Colombia as a nation state implied the fabrication of a new race, the "*mestizo* subject", which represented the best of the white race while the Black and the indigenous components were erased from the national identity. The ideology of *mestizaje*, which promoted racial mixing, played a crucial role in the formation of the nation-state's public policy and discourse.

As part of the 1991 constitutional reform, Black Colombians were granted political rights to collective ownership of ancestral lands, the ability to organize their own education and government in rural communities, and expanded political participation. This recognition was the result of social and political mobilizations that began in the 1980s, involving grassroots and academic organizations committed to the Black movement. However, the increase in political participation and self-government involved what Restrepo (2013) refers to as the "ethnicization" of Black communities, a process by which "some populations are constructed and constituted as an ethnic group" (Restrepo, 2013, p. 20). For Black Colombians, this would entail downplaying race and reinforcing culture, community, and land rights to gain political recognition. The ethnicization of Blackness in Colombia has involved "the fabrication of a political subject and subjectivities related to the effective existence of an ethnic group" (Restrepo, 2013, p. 20). This political move provided opportunities for bureaucratic participation in local and national administrations. However, it has obscured the experiences of antiblackness and anti-Black racism, faced by Black Colombians living in cities.

Analyzing curricular documents

The Colombian education system has a national mathematics curriculum that is unified yet flexible. The Ministry of Education is responsible for issuing curricular guidelines that outline the mathematics content and abilities to be learned by students, as well as the distribution and organization of this content by grade level. The guidelines also include general formative purposes and didactic and pedagogical approaches that might contribute to the construction of national, regional, cultural, and identity. Schools must adopt the guidelines and integrate them into their Institutional Educational Programs, including the general learning goals and objectives by grade and level. Additionally, the Afro-Colombian Studies Program (ACSP) (NME, 2008) is mandatory in all schools across the country. The program aims to disseminate and make visible the scientific and cultural contributions of Black people to Colombian cultural identity. However, schools have the autonomy to adapt these curricular guidelines in order to respond to the diverse local context and varied needs of student populations.

Schools located in Black and Indigenous communities follow the curriculum policies established in the general Ethnoeducation Program. This program seeks to guarantee the right of ethnic communities to design and implement their own educational models in ways that preserve their epistemic practices and cultural identities. There are no specific curricular guidelines for mathematics education in the context of the Ethnoeducation Program. Nevertheless, Blanco et al. (2014) discuss the possibility of integrating an ethnomathematics approach into the new general mathematics curriculum. For these researchers, the recognition of mathematics as a socio-cultural construct and the centrality of out-of-the school mathematical knowledge as stated in the Mathematics Curricular Guideline (MCG) (NME, 1998a) are critical points to materialize such integration.

We examine two different groups of curricular documents. The first group consists of curricular documents issued after the 1991 constitutional change. These documents address general formative purposes and provide guidelines for mathematics education in grades K-11 in Colombia. The included documents are the MCG, the Basic Standards of Mathematics (BSM) (NME, 2003), the Basic Learning Rights (BLR) (NME, 2014), and the curricular guidelines of the ACSP (NME, 2008). These documents address the constitutional demands for an inclusive, modern, relevant, and high-quality educational system that aligns with global social, economic, and technological demands. The second group includes specific educational policies for indigenous and Black communities, such as Ethnoeducation, which recognizes the pluriethnic and multicultural character of Colombian society as outlined in the new Constitution. These documents are specific to schools, both rural and urban, that are attended mostly by indigenous and Black students. The set of educational policies includes Decree 804 (NME, 1995b) and 1122 (NME, 1998b).

To analyze these documents, we conduct a political analysis that relies on critical interpretation. Based on Hatch's (2002) definition, political analysis involves reading the curricular documents to understand the whole, identifying narratives and statements related to citizenship and democracy in the selected documents, rereading these entries from the researcher's own political and ideological stance, and interpreting and generalizing critical ideas. Both authors read the documents, exchanged ideas, and recorded their findings in tools that were designed for this purpose. The analysis was enriched with readings on Black history in Colombia and on Blackness and anti-Black racism in mathematics education. As Black Colombians and critical researchers committed to a liberatory mathematics education for Black children in our country, we have had extensive discussions about our political positions regarding the limits and possibilities of achieving racial justice in the field through reform efforts. Our political positions have shaped and informed our analysis. As we read the curricular documents, we approached race as a social construct that structures social interactions and impacts the material, symbolic, and emotional lives of people in racialized social systems (Bonilla-Silva, 2010). Additionally, we acknowledged the irreconcilable antagonism between Blackness and humanity (ross, 2021). To be categorized as "Black" is to be denied the human characteristics associated with reason, morality, adulthood, and civility in Western societies (Haslam, 2006; Restrepo, 2010). Weheliye (2014) argues that racialization, as a set of ongoing political relations, excludes non-whites from the category of human through various cultural artifacts, institutions, discourses, practices, and languages. Maldonado-Torres (2007) introduces the concept of "colonial heterogeneity" to describe the creation of inferior subjects. This inferiorization, determined by race, creates a differential character among subjects that has contributed to the continued dehumanization of indigenous and Black individuals. Finally, we acknowledge how antiblackness shapes decision-making processes surrounding educational policy (Dumas, 2016). We join the research community that critically examines discourses of educational change and its promises of citizenship and equity in the field because, as Leonardo (2003) argues, "change research abounds, whereas ideological criticism of school change is scant" (p. 45).

Blackness and citizenship: A review of Colombian mathematics education policy

Our analysis of the Colombian mathematics curricular documents shows that the educational reforms implemented of the last three decades have contributed to the perpetuation of the racial project of *mestizaje*. First, these curricular documents continue to favor a raceless subject that renders Blackness invisible. Thus, "colonial values that privilege lightness of skin color as a sign of social status or as the putative national destiny are still pervasive" (Wade,

1995, p. 340). Second, the dominant discourses in these documents portray race as a thing of the past that does not play a significant role in the social dynamics of the country because race mixing has blurred racial boundaries (Wade, 1995). Thus, racial inequity does not exist and therefore, economic, educational, and social differences among racial groups are the result of lack of effort and merit. These two findings are discussed below.

The "Mestizo subject" as the ideal citizen in the mathematics curriculum

The Colombian mathematics curriculum documents adopt the traditional view of mathematics education as a tool for citizenship and the promotion of democratic participation. Both the MCG and the BSM contain statements that emphasize the role of mathematics learning in the strengthening of democracy and democratic values, and underline "the need for a core of basic mathematics knowledge that every citizen must know" (NME, 1998a). Arithmetic, algebraic and geometric reasoning—among others—are presented in curricular documents as critical tools:

> to make informed decisions; to provide either reasonable justifications or to refute apparent and false ones to exercise critical citizenship; in other words, to participate in the preparation, discussion and decision making and to develop actions that can collectively transform society.
>
> (NME, 2003, p. 48)

The BSM's main argument for the inclusion of mathematics in the national curriculum is the role of the discipline in the development of democratic values "[…] the need for a quality basic education for all citizens, the extended social value of mathematics formation and the role of mathematics in the consolidation of democratic values" (NME, 2003, p. 47). In addition, economic competitiveness, the technological advancement of the country and the contribution to the production of a rational citizen capable of making informed decisions are cited as important arguments for mathematics learning:

> The first reason relates to the utilitarian and broadening nature of mathematical knowledge.
>
> In the highly technologized social and labor world of the 21st century, mathematical tools are increasingly required to achieve efficient and creative performances in many work areas where only elementary arithmetic was needed before. The second reason is the indispensability of mathematics. All citizens require knowledge to actively and critically engage in their social and political lives and to interpret information for decision-making.
>
> (NME, 2003, p. 48)

These justifications align with global discourses of reform in mathematics education, emphasizing the development of lifelong learners and cosmopolitan citizens (Valero & García, 2014) who can navigate society's diverse dimensions. In fact, mathematics is portrayed as useful due to its model of economic rationality, making it a "valuable asset" to society. Valencia-Salas (2017) argues that educational reforms in Colombia aim to consolidate a national project based on discourses grounded in globalization and a global vision of development that includes strengthening economic capital, deregulating industry, and exploiting natural resources. Mathematics is proposed as an empowering tool that allows students to develop their thinking and logical reflection abilities. By learning mathematics, individuals acquire powerful tools for exploring, representing, explaining, and predicting social reality.

An important aspect of the discourses on citizenship, democracy and mathematics education in the globalized world is the absence of social identities such as race and ethnicity as important markers of otherness and sources of inequity in the examined documents. Thus, the curricular documents are based on the belief that race does not play a significant role in the structuring of Colombian social relations, thus advancing the notion of the ideal citizen as a *"mestizo"* or raceless citizen. On the one hand, a rationalist epistemological approach seems to support the view of the role and nature of mathematics knowledge in the curricular documents (Valero & Garcia, 2014) as located and produced in the mind. The documents portray the citizen as a thoughtful individual who can use mathematics to succeed in the social and political life of the country (NME, 2003). Mathematics is depicted as a powerful tool that citizens possess to act in highly technological and interconnected societies. Thus, an ideal citizen should be able to "explore problems, build structures, ask questions and reflect on models" (NME, 1998a, p. 17) with the help of sound mathematics knowledge. The mathematics teacher should support the students in "gradually acquir[ing] higher levels of formalization and abstraction". Valero and García (2014) characterize this child as rational, effective, global, and entrepreneurial. Moreover, for these researchers:

> The mathematics curriculum embodies a cosmopolitan form of reasoning, which is based on the belief that human reason, based on science, has an emancipatory and universal capacity to control and transform the world and society, and makes it available to everyone who uses it.
>
> (Valero & García, 2014, p. 504)

On the other hand, focusing solely on individuals' cognitive and psychological aspects overlooks the impact of their personal and social identities, including race, ethnicity, class, and gender, as sources of inequities in mathematics education. It is argued that mathematics education must respond to "the local and global demands for education for all, attention to diversity and interculturality and the formation of citizens capable of exercising their democratic rights and responsibilities" (NME, 2003, p. 46). Furthermore, the equity promise is expressed as the need to "all types of students" (NME, 2003, p. 47) in mathematics. However, the students' experiences along race, class, ethnicity, and gender lines are ignored in the examined documents. In particular, the curricular guidelines in Colombia do not explicitly address the racialized nature of mathematics teaching and learning, which leads to the exclusion and marginalization of Black Colombian students (Valoyes-Chávez, 2017, 2018). This invisibilizes the fact that race is a fundamental feature that shapes the mathematical experiences of Colombian students. The BLR (NME, 2014) is the most critical curricular document reflecting this approach. It reduces mathematics knowledge to a list of content to be taught in every school grade. Ignoring antiblackness and the racialized nature of mathematics education in Colombia is problematic because, as discussed above, they have historically been at the center of discussions about the constitution of the nation-state, the progress of the country, and the understanding of its social, political, and economic realities. Thus, the invisibility of race and ethnicity as critical factors that shape the educational experiences of Colombian students contradicts the intended purpose of the curricular documents, which is to respond to the newly recognized multicultural and pluriethnic character of the country. We argue that this fact highlights the tension between the global demand for educational reforms that cater to the creation of a global citizen and the racial realities of local educational systems in nation-states. On one hand, Colombia's integration into the global economy and dynamics has led to the recognition of its racial and ethnic diversity, which was materialized in the 1991 constitutional reform. The educational reform demands a multicultural approach. However, efforts to align the Colombian educational system with global demands clash with the local dominant racial ideology of Mestizaje, which renders race invisible. This tension may explain the contradictory moves in the curricular documents. While recognizing racial and ethnic diversity, they promote the "*mestizo* subject" as the ideal citizen.

Culture, race, and the ethnoeducation program

As previously stated, the curricular documents present a conflicting view of culture and its role in the processes of teaching and learning mathematics. Both the MCG and the BSM recognize the cultural and ethnic diversity of the country. On the one hand, the cultural context is introduced as an important element for mathematics teaching and learning. The MCG (NME, 1998a) clearly states that:

> As a fundamental consequence of this cultural perspective, the main purpose of mathematics is to guide students towards acquiring a deeper understanding of their own culture and constructing socially shared

> meanings, while also acknowledging the universal culture of mathematics that man [sic] has built over the course of 6000 years.
>
> (p. 15)

On the other hand, cultural diversity seems to be a source of problems for mathematics learning. The documents suggest that individuals from different cultural contexts may have varying approaches to learning and practicing mathematics, which can lead to differences in mathematics proficiency. This point is explicitly made in the MCG (MEN, 1998a):

> In terms of the existing relationships between culture and mathematics, several investigations have explored the links between culture and learning in mathematics. Bacon and Carter (1991) have analyzed differences between human collectives in relation to perceptual styles, spatial development, problem solving, language, recognition of invariants, and cultural attitudes towards learning. The importance of cultural context in providing individuals with aptitudes, competencies, and tools for solving problems and representing mathematical ideas is recognized. This explains why some cultures develop more meaningfully in some mathematical areas than others without implying that mathematical aptitude is a privilege of a particular cultural group.
>
> (p. 34)

The relationship between culture and mathematics is problematic in the Colombian context because culture is often used as a proxy for race due to the ideological belief that race does not exist. Restrepo (2010) highlights the complexities of distinguishing race from culture and how cultural criteria are often used to make racial classifications in Latin America, including Colombia. Although the Ethnoeducation program has laudable intentions and spirit, its narrow scope of application is a concern. The Afro-Colombian Studies course is intended to combat racism and racial discrimination in schools (Mena, 2010), but its implementation has been limited to recognizing and celebrating African heritage in Colombia through food, dance, and clothing.

The Ethnoeducation program has primarily been implemented in rural areas, but it is also implemented in schools attended by Black and indigenous students in Colombia's cities. However, this limited focus on certain school settings has resulted in the exclusion of a significant percentage of schools nationwide. Similar to educational reform efforts in other Latin American and Caribbean countries (see Mansilla et al., 2022), intercultural education policies in this region have focused solely on Black and indigenous children and youth, while excluding the rest of the student population. Quilaqueo and Sartorello (2018) argue that these reform efforts promote a model of interethnic relationships that perpetuates cultural power imbalances and reinforces a monocultural conception of society. In the Colombian context, educational reforms sustain and reproduce the dominant racial project that is supposed to be transformed. This suggests that the reforms may not be achieving their intended goals of promoting equality and inclusivity. Although Colombia's educational reforms acknowledge cultural and ethnic diversity as critical aspects of the policymaking process, they fail to respond to and address such diversity. Efforts to incorporate a culturally and ethnically respectful educational approach to education "remained deeply embedded in neoliberal premises and forms of governance, characterized by isolated, limited reforms and budgetary limitations" (Webb & Radcliffe, 2013, p. 323). As discussed in Mansilla et al. (2022), these policies exemplify "neoliberal multiculturalism", which recognizes diversity along racial and ethnic lines but perpetuates the unequal distribution of racial and ethnic power in society (García, 2016). The primary consequence of implementing Ethnoeducation in areas and schools predominantly inhabited by Black and Indigenous students is educational apartheid that reproduces the racial status quo.

In contrast to the curricular guidelines for the majority population, which place mathematics at the center of citizenship, the curricular documents for the Ethnoeducation program do not explicitly include mathematics as a fundamental component of education for Black Colombian and Indigenous populations. This is noteworthy considering the significant role that mathematics plays in the development of democracy and democratic values in the MCG, BSM, and BLR. This omission is problematic as it confirms the existence of a nation-building project that excludes Black and indigenous populations from citizenship.

Conclusions

This chapter interrogates the promise of citizenship for Black Colombians, focusing on the curricular discourses proposed in the reform efforts to examine how they advance particular racial projects that either prevent or promote the participation of Black Colombians as full citizens through mathematics education. Our analysis shows that Colombian mathematics curricular documents position the "*mestizo* subject" as the ideal citizen, which renders invisible race. While these documents acknowledge the racial and ethnic diversity in the country, they fail to address the invisibility of these elements in the constitution of the Colombian citizen. This reinforces and perpetuates the myth of the country as a racial democracy where race is not a factor. The following section will elaborate on this assertion.

First, the examined curricular documents reveal the tensions between the global demands for recognition of racial and ethnic diversity and a more racially just society, and the racial dynamics in Colombia. The invisibility of race in the curricular documents follows the dominant racial ideology of *mestizaje,* which was fundamental to the constitution of the nation-state and appears to persist. In the Colombian context, anti-Black racism and racial injustice are often not acknowledged due to the belief that race does not exist. For example, disparities in mathematics achievement between the Black Colombian population and the majority *mestizo* population are often attributed to cultural differences, lack of interest, and family structure, among other factors (Valoyes-Chávez, 2017). The educational reforms in mathematics education in Colombia reflect the tensions between two competing racial projects, hindering progress towards addressing antiblackness and racial inequity. Although the last constitutional reform recognized Colombia as a multicultural and pluriethnic country, concrete measures must be taken to combat antiblackness in mathematics education. The ideal citizen, guided by the reason grounded in mathematical knowledge, is associated with the *mestizo* subject in whom the Black component is barely recognized.

The constitution of Black communities as ethnic groups reinforces the racial myth of *mestizaje*. This results in ethnicity being used as an identity marker that subsumes racial identities, with culture becoming a proxy for race. In order for Black Colombians to be recognized as political subjects with full access to citizenship and democratic participation, they must downplay their racial identity and position themselves as ethnic communities. In Colombia, the denial of the existence of race silences the Black population's experiences of antiblackness in the country.

Second, our analysis highlights the role of curricular reforms in advancing particular racial projects in society (Martin, 2013). In this sense, curricular reforms are not racially neutral. Within globalization, the advancement and consolidation of racial projects are in tension with both the local contexts and the global imperatives. Our analysis provides evidence of such tensions. Mathematical education in Colombia has played a critical role in the constitution of the *mestizo* nation-state and continues to do so, in maintaining a racial *status quo* that locates Black Colombian at the bottom (Valencia-Salas, 2021). This has resulted in limited access to economic, educational, and political opportunities for this community. The demand to produce a global citizen through mathematics education reform efforts has not translated into the materialization of the promise of citizenship for Black Colombians. This promise has collided with the racial dynamics in the country. It is important to note that globalization needs cheap labor and second-class citizens to keep neoliberal capitalism working. Beneath the political correctness of discourses of globalization, the system benefits from antiblackness and the production of second-class citizens.

The Colombian mathematics education system of practices continues to be a privileged place of knowledge compared to other school subjects. On the one hand, in this system racial and ethnic hierarchies are perpetuated in ways that racially and ethnically minoritized students are considered incapable of learning mathematics. On the other hand, the system acknowledges the pluriethnic and multicultural character of the nation that, nevertheless, does little to grant citizenship to Black Colombians. Our analysis sheds light on how mathematics curricular reforms in globalized contexts advance particular racial projects that perpetuate white privilege rather than fulfilling the equity and citizenship promises. Further research is needed to unpack the mechanisms by which second class citizenship and racial privilege are maintained through mathematics education.

References

Agudelo, C. (2002). Etnicidad negra y elecciones en Colombia [Black ethnicity and elections in Colombia]. *The Journal of Latin America Anthropology*, *7*(2), 168–197. https://doi.org/10.1525/jlca.2002.7.2.168

Andrade-Molina, M. (2021). Narratives of success: Enabling all students to excel in the global world. *Research in Mathematics Education*, *23*(3), 293–305. https://doi.org/10.1080/14794802.2021.1994453

Berry, R. Q. (2018). Disrupting policies and reforms in mathematics education to address the needs of marginalized learners. In T. G. Bartnell (Ed.), *Toward equity and social justice in mathematics education* (pp. 3–20). Springer.

Blanco, H., Highita, C., & Oliveros, M. L. (2014). Una mirada a la etnomatemática y la educación matemática en Colombia: Caminos recorridos. [Ethnomathematics and mathematics education in Colombia: A review]. *Revista Latinoamericana de Etnomatemática*, *7*(2), 245–269.

Bonilla-Silva, E. (2010). *Racism without racist. A color-blind racism and the persistence of racial inequality in contemporary America* (2nd ed.). Rowman & Littlefield Publishers.

Bruno-Jofré, R., & Tröhler, D. (2014). Introducción sección especial: El viaje peripatético de la educación en un mundo globalizado y "educacionalizado". [Introduction special section: The peripatetic journey of education in a globalized and "educationalized" world]. *Revista Pensamiento Educativo*, *51*(1), 1–5. https://doi.org/10.7764/PEL.51.1.2014.1

Chronaki, A. (2010). Revisiting mathemacy: A process-reading of critical mathematics education. In H. Alrø, O. Ranv, & P. Valero (Eds.), *Critical mathematics education: Past, present and future* (pp. 31–50). Sense Publishers.

Chronaki, A. (2023). Becoming citizen subject in the body politic: Antinomies of archaic, modern and posthuman citizenship temporalities and the political of mathematics education. *Research in Mathematics Education*, Online first, https://doi.org/10.1080/14794802.2023.2183889

Chronaki, A., & Yolcu, A. (2021). Mathematics for "citizenship" and its "other" in a "global" world: Critical issues on mathematics education, globalisation and local communities. *Research in Mathematics Education*, *23*(3), 241–247. https://doi.org/10.1080/14794802.2021.1995780

Dumas, M. (2016). Against the dark: Antiblackness in education policy and discourse. *Theory Into Practice*, 55(1), 11–19.

García, S. (2016). El multiculturalismo como modelo de gobernanza en Chile: Estado, academia y brokers. [Multiculturalism as a governance model in Chile: State, academia, and brokers]. *Universitas Humanística*, *82*, 307–334. https://doi.org/10.11144/Javeriana.uh82.mmgc

García, G., & Romero-Rey, H. (2018). Mathematics for all in times of inclusion as an imperative: A study of the program "Todos a Aprender". *Revista Colombiana de Educación*, *74*(1), 289–310.

Haslam, N. (2006). Dehumanization: An integrative review. *Personality and Social Psychology Review*, *10*(3), 252–264. https://doi.org/10.1207%2Fs15327957pspr1003_4

Hatch, A. (2002). *Doing qualitative research in educational settings*. SUNY Press.

Hernández, E. (2009). Resistencias para la paz en Colombia. Experiencias indígenas, Afrodescendientes y campesinas. [Resistances for peace in Colombia. Indigenous, Afro-descendant and peasant experiences]. *Revista Paz y Conflictos*, *2*, 117–135. https://doi.org/10.30827/revpaz.v2i0.434

Lasso, M. (2013). *Myths of racial harmony: Race, republicanism during the era of revolution, Colombia 1795–1831*. Ediciones Uniandes.

Leonardo, Z. (2003). *Ideology, discourse, and school reform*. Praeger.

Maldonado-Torres, N. (2007). Sobre la colonialidad del ser: contribuciones al desarrollo de un concepto. [On the coloniality of being: Contributions to the development of a concept]. In S. Castro-Gómez & R. Grosfoguel (Eds.), *El giro decolonial: reflexiones para una diversidad epistémica más allá del capitalismo global* (pp. 127–167). Siglo del Hombre Editores.

Mansilla, J., Pozo, G., & Valoyes-Chávez, L. (2022). The historical inclusion of mapuche children in the educational system: Challenges and tensions in policy and practice. *International Journal of Inclusive Education*, 1–24. https://doi.org/10.1080/13603116.2022.2127496

Martin, D. B. (2013). Race, racial projects and mathematics education. *Journal for Research in Mathematics Education*, *44*(1), 316–333. https://doi.org/10.5951/jresematheduc.44.1.0316

Martin, D. B. (2019). Equity, inclusion and antiblackness in mathematics education. *Race, Ethnicity and Education*, *22*(4), 459–478. https://doi.org/10.1080/13613324.2019.1592833

McGrew, A. (1992). A global society? In S. Hall, D. Held & T. McGrew (Eds.), *Modernity and its futures* (pp. 61–116). The Open University.

Mena, M. (2010). *If there is no racism, there is no Afro-Colombian Studies Chair*. Working paper. Project for the dignification of Afro-descendants and their culture in Colombia. Bogotá. https://repositoriosed.educacionbogota.edu.co/flip/?pdf=https://repositoriosed.educacionbogota.edu.co/server/api/core/bitstreams/330e196e-5d3c-4022-b8ff-55103992cc98/content

National Ministry of Education (1995a). *General Law of Education*. https://www.mineducacion.gov.co/1621/articles-85906_archivo_pdf.pdf

National Ministry of Education (1995b). *Decree 804*. https://www.mineducacion.gov.co/portal/normativa/Decretos/103494:Decreto-804-de-Mayo-18-de-1995

National Ministry of Education (1998a). *Mathematics Curricular Guideline*. https://www.mineducacion.gov.co/1621/articles-89869_archivo_pdf9.pdf

National Ministry of Education (1998b). *Decree 1122*. https://www.mineducacion.gov.co/1621/articles-86201_archivo_pdf.pdf

National Ministry of Education (2003). *Basic Standards of Mathematics*. https://www.mineducacion.gov.co/1621/articles-340021_recurso_1.pdf

National Ministry of Education (2008). *Curricular Guidelines of Afro Colombian Studies*. https://www.mineducacion.gov.co/1759/articles-339975_recurso_2.pdf

National Ministry of Education (2014). *Basic Learning Rights*. https://wccopre.s3.amazonaws.com/Derechos_Basicos_de_Aprendizaje_Matematicas_1.pdf

National Ministry of Education (2017). *Decennial National Education Plan 2016-2026: The path to quality and equity*. https://www.mineducacion.gov.co/1780/articles-392871_recurso_1.pdf

Nguyen, T. X. T. (2010). Deconstructing *Education for All*: Discourses, power and the politics of inclusion. *International Journal of Inclusive Education*, *14*(4), 341–355. https://doi.org/10.1080/13603110802504564

Olssen, M., Codd, J., & O'Neill, A. M. (2004). *Educational policy: Globalization, citizenship and democracy*. Sage Publications.

Quilaqueo, D., & Sartorello, S. (2018). Retos epistemológicos de la interculturalidad en contexto indígena. [Epistemological challenges of interculturality in an indigenous context]. *Alpha (Osorno)*, *47*, 47–61. http://dx.doi.org/10.32735/s0718-220120180004700163

Restrepo, E. (2010). Images of "Black" and notions of race in Colombia in the early twentieth century. In C. Leal & C. H. Langebaek (Eds.), *Histories of race and nation in Latin America* (pp. 277–312). Ediciones Uniandes.

Restrepo, E. (2013). *Etnización de la negridad: La invención de las 'comunidades negras' como grupo étnico en Colombia*. [Ethnicization of Blackness: The invention of "Black communities" as an ethnic group in Colombia]. Universidad del Cauca.

Restrepo, E., & Rojas, A. (2004) (Eds.). *Conflicto e (in)visibilidad. Retos en los estudios de la gente negra en Colombia*. [Conflict and (in)visibility. Challenges in the studies of Black people in Colombia]. Editorial Universidad del Cauca.

Rivera, F. (2000). The edges of racism. *Revista de Ciencias Sociales*, *VI*(1), 9–33.

ross, k. m. (2021). On Black education. Anti-Blackness, refusal, and resistance. In C. Grant, A. N. Woodson, & M. J. Dumas (Eds.), *The future is Black. Afropessimism, fugitivity, and radical Hope in education* (pp. 7–15). Routledge.

Skovsmose, O. (1994). Towards a critical mathematics education. *Educational Studies in Mathematics*, *27*(1), 35–57.

Skovsmose, O., & Valero, P. (2012). Rompiendo la neutralidad política: El compromiso crítico de la educación matemática con la democracia. [Breaking political neutrality: Mathematics education's critical engagement with democracy]. http://funes.uniandes.edu.co/2001/1/Skovsmose2012Rompimiento.pdf

Tröhler, D. (2010). Globalizing globalization: The neo-institutional concept of a world culture. In T. S. Popkewitz, & F. Rizvi (Eds.), *Globalization and the study of education: 2009 yearbook of the National Society for Studies in Education* (pp. 29–48). Wiley.

Valencia-Salas, A. (2017). *Racist practices in school: an analysis of mathematics teachers' practices*. Unpublished master thesis. National Pedagogical University. http://repository.pedagogica.edu.co/bitstream/handle/20.500.12209/9888/TO-21995.pdf?sequence=1

Valencia-Salas, A. (2021). Matemáticas y prácticas racistas en la escuela: Experiencias con docentes de Bogotá. [Mathematics and racist practices in school: Experiences with teachers in Bogotá]. *Nodos y Nudos*, *7*(50), 13–28. https://doi.org/10.17227/nyn.vol7.num50-12590

Valero, P. (1999). Deliberative mathematics education for social democratization in Latin America. *ZDM Mathematics Education*, *31*(1), 20–26.

Valero, P., & García, G. (2014). El currículo de las matemáticas escolares y el gobierno del sujeto moderno. [The school mathematics curriculum and the governance of the modern subject]. *Bolema*, *28*(4), 491–515. https://doi.org/10.1590/1980-4415v28n49a02

Valero, P., García, G., Camelo, F., Mancera, G., & Romero-Rey, J. (2012). Mathematics education and the dignity of being. *Pythagoras*, *33*(2), 1–9. http://dx.doi.org/10.4102/pythagoras.v33i2.171

Valoyes-Chávez, L. (2017). Inequidades raciales y educación matemática. [Racial inequities and mathematics education]. *Revista Colombiana de Educación*, *73*, 129–152.

Valoyes-Chávez, L. (2018). Racism and mathematics education in a racial democracy: Views from the classroom. In U. Gellert, C. Knipping, & H. Straehler-Pohl (Eds.), *Inside the mathematics class. Sociological perspectives on participation, inclusion, and enhancement* (pp. 167–189). Springer.

Wade, P. (1995). The cultural politics of Blackness in Colombia. *American Ethnologist*, *22*(2), 341–357.

Webb, A., & Radcliffe, S. (2013). Mapuche demands during educational reform, the Penguin Revolution and the Chilean winter of discontent. *Studies in Ethnicity and Nationalism*, *13*(3), 319–41.

Weheliye, A. (2014). *Habeas viscus. Racializing assemblages, biopolitics, and Black feminist theories of the human*. Duke University Press.

Williams, B. (1989). A class act: Anthropology and race to nations across ethnic terrain. *Annual Review of Anthropology*, *18*, 401–444.

11 Health and citizenship in high school mathematics textbooks

Conducting Brazilian students' conducts

Renata Rodrigues Souza and Marcio Antonio da Silva

Brazil and citizenship: historical context

On March 31st, 1964, the military imposed dictatorship coup removed the then-President João Goulart from office. General Castelo Branco, on April 3rd of that year, assumed the new presidency of Brazil, instituting a repressive policy, which resulted at, among other things, the institution of a new constitution in 1967. This constitution established that presidents, governors, and mayors would be elected indirectly, political rights would be revoked and suspended, the death penalty would be instituted for crimes against national security, and the right to strike would be restricted. The following year, an Institutional Act (AI-5) was created, which, besides the constitutional restrictions, also determined: the closing of Congress by the Executive Branch, the prior censorship of all media, the military intervention in states and municipalities, and the suspension of civil and political rights of citizens who committed crimes against National Security. These restrictions led several intellectuals, including artists, to exile, imprisonment, torture and even death.

In 1979, Brazil began a political transition from a dictatorship to a democratic state and during the 1980s several popular movements demanded direct elections to vote for the republic's president. The most famous one became known as the "Movimento pelas Diretas Já" (Movement for Direct Elections Now). Although it was one of the largest popular movements in Brazil's recent history, in 1985 an indirect election was still held, counting only the votes of deputies and senators, as was determined by the 1964 constitution. Faced with great popular pressure, a new constitution was established, through the formation of a National Constituent Assembly which drafted the 1988 Constitution of the Federative Republic of Brazil, signed on October 5th, 1998. This 1988 Constitution, which is still in force today, was popularly known as the "Citizen's Constitution". Eight years after the 1988 Constitution, the Law of Directives and Bases of National Education (seen° 9394 of December 20th, 1996) was instituted and governs formal Brazilian education up until today.

As such, the word "citizen" came to retain an extremely important value for all Brazilians, because due to the "citizen" constitution of 1988, citizenship

DOI: 10.4324/9781003130673-14

became linked to freedom, democracy, and indicated a new era in the history of Brazil for people to engage actively with democratic governance based on rights and duties. In the context of education, the discourse "training for citizenship" has been recognised as a core political concern for more than thirty years. However, as we argue in this chapter, this idea of citizenship has been captured by neoliberal logic and capitalism, so that, nowadays, citizenship seems to be more linked with ways of governing students' conduct in everyday life instead of guiding them to emancipatory practices to exercise their freedom.

Brazilian high school mathematics textbooks

As said before, in this chapter, we bring analysis conducted in Brazil that shows how citizenship education has become a prominent subject in Brazilian mathematics textbooks making links, amongst other areas, with health care. We claim that this approach to citizenship education is being contextualised with issues indicating healthy living by mobilising moral values and through constituting a strong network of power relations and expertise knowledge (Foucault, 1972, 1995). It is argued that this strategy produces an alchemy (Popkewitz, 2004) that transforms children and young people into healthy citizens.

Since 2015, our research group has been conducting research that analyses discourses on various topics in mathematics textbooks such as history of mathematics (Ocampos, 2016), gender issues (Silva & Souza, 2018; Souza & Silva, 2017a, 2017b, 2018; Silva et al., 2019), the making of desirable peasant (Guida & Neto, 2019; Neto, 2019; Neto & Guida, 2019a; Neto & Guida, 2019b; Neto & Valero, 2018), financial mathematics (Coradetti, 2017; Coradetti & Silva, 2017, 2019), interdisciplinarity (Berto, 2017; Silva et al., 2018) and the constitution of the desirable citizen (Souza, 2020). The textbooks analysed in all these research studies have been approved as part of the national textbook assessment program, which we will detail in the next paragraphs. The main focus of our analysis was focused on; how moral values are being aligned with certain characteristics as they are prioritised by neoliberalism (Brown, 2015, 2019; Dardot & Laval, 2016; Laval, 2019), how mathematical concepts are used as the pedagogic context to produce desirable students (Coradetti et al., 2019; Oliveira & Silva, 2019a; Silva & Valero, 2018; Silva et al., 2018) and how the desirable teacher is being constituted (Montecino & Valero, 2017; Oliveira & Silva, 2019b; Valero et al., 2015).

In Brazil, the textbooks used by public schools[1] are approved by a committee convened by the Federal Government and formed by researchers from public universities and teachers of basic education. The PNLD (National Textbook Program) is a state policy that distributes many diverse textbooks free of charge to students in Brazilian public schools. The publishers submit their textbooks to the calls for public edicts and have their textbooks evaluated[2] by the committee mentioned above. The approved textbooks form a Guide[3] that the teacher can consult and, through the descriptions contained in this "menu", choose the book he wants to work on during the next three school years. In the year 2018, each teacher could choose which series they would work with their students. Thus, in the same school, there could be different textbooks used by different teachers. Until 2017, the PNLD distributed about 150 million textbooks per year to approximately 120,000 schools, serving more or less 30 million students per year. The average investment of the federal government was approximately 400 million dollars per year (Carvalho, 2018), so publishers and authors are extremely interested in having their works approved in a program like this.

The textbooks analysed here have all been approved by the 2018 PNLD assessment and were all used in the Brazilian high schools during the years 2018, 2019, and 2020. In these mathematics textbooks, we have focused our analysis on specific sections that develop activities with the theme of citizenship/ citizen education. In addition to the mathematical content the textbook has been occupied to present ways of working with citizen education, which goes beyond mathematical content[4]. We consider this study to be of utmost and critical importance since the mathematics textbooks are not only a resource for the teachers but they are in direct contact with the students. Before moving to the textbooks, the next section will present the public health system in Brazil, its characteristics and investments in relation to images for the health of Brazilian people and, after that, the theoretical and methodological basis for our analysis will be outlined.

Brazilian Unified Health System – Sistema Único de Saúde (SUS), what is it?

Before presenting how Brazilian textbooks build the idea of citizenship and citizen education, we consider it pertinent to introduce the public health system in Brazil. In this country, as in other places of the world, private health plans are offered, but most of the population uses the totally free public health service, where expenses are covered through the taxes paid by Brazilian citizens. In Brazil, this public health policy is called the Unified Health System – SUS (Sistema Único de Saúde). According to the Transparency Portal,[5] in the year 2019, 114.18 billion reais (approximately 20.4 billion dollars) were spent on health and by September 2020, the around spend was around 108.51 billion reais (approximately 19.4 billion dollars). SUS is the right to public free health for all citizens guaranteed by the state to every Brazilian citizen. This system comprises simple procedures such as blood pressure check-ups, and even more complex ones such as organ transplants.

> The administration of health actions and services must be solidary and participative among the three entities of the Federation: The Union, the States and the municipalities. The network that makes up the SUS is broad and encompasses both actions and health services. It includes primary, medium, and high complexity care, emergency and emergency

services, hospital care, epidemiological, health, and environmental surveillance actions and services, and pharmaceutical assistance.[6]

(Brasil, 2020)

SUS comprises details at three levels, the Ministry of Health, the States, and the Municipalities, based on three principles: (i) guarantee the right to health to all people; (ii) reduce social inequalities, investing where the need is greatest; and (iii) integrate actions on health promotion, disease prevention, treatment, and rehabilitation, articulating health policy to other public policies. In this context, and since health is a declared right for all, the concept of "citizenship" is directly linked to the people's exercise of these rights in Brazil. In the Charter with Rights of Health Users, published by the Federal Government, we find some information about these rights of citizens in relation to health care: Six basic principles of citizenship assure Brazilians a dignified entry into the health systems, whether public or private, denoting that every citizen has the right and responsibility:

- to orderly and organised access to health systems.
- to adequate and effective treatment for his/her problem.
- to be humanised, welcoming and free from any discrimination.
- to care that respects his/her person, values and rights.
- to ensure that their treatment takes place in the proper manner.
- to the commitment of health managers so that the previous principles are fulfilled[7] (Brasil, 2020).

The document "What does it mean to have health?", available on the Saúde Brazil website,[8] presents several aspects of health in an overly broad sense, including the search for a state of complement between physical, mental, and social well-being. The Ministry of Health launched several preventive campaigns[9] to take care of health: Breastfeeding; Yellow July – Viral Hepatitis; Blood Donation 2020 Campaign; Donate Maternal Milk Campaign; World Malaria Day Campaign; Chagas' Disease Campaign; National Campaign against Tuberculosis; Yellow Fever; Vaccination against Influenza; Coronavirus; Prevention against STDs; Pregnancy Prevention; AIDS; Child Obesity; Vaccination against Measles; Rose October; Organ Donation; Combat Depression, among other campaigns.

These campaigns are supposed to aim at guiding people to a healthier life. However, supported by Foucault's (2008) concept of governmentality, we can say that preventive caring guidelines might also work as a way to regulate people's conduct (Rose, 1999; Rose & Miller, 1992; Walshaw, 2007). Moreover, the word "citizen", as we have already seen in the beginning of the chapter, has an extremely positive connotation in the Brazilian context. Thus, linking the idea of "citizenship" to "health care" creates a refined strategy toward persuading everyone for the desire to be a "healthy citizen".

Specifically, one of the tools located, in the Saúde Brasil (Health Brazil) website, are tests that calculate the body mass index (BMI)[10] and measures the degree of nicotine dependence. These tests serve to legitimise whether the person is overweight and the level of nicotine dependence in the body. What is interesting in the context of our research is the utilisation of mathematics as a calculation technology to classify people as having or not healthy habits and as acting or not appropriately. More than promoting changes in habits, mathematics operates at the level of constructing a desirable body through specific hopes and fears (Yolcu & Popkewitz, 2019).

The Brazilian government's commitment to managing public health is evident through the development of various tools and campaigns aimed at combating illnesses such as obesity and smoking. Among these initiatives, the calculation of BMI and nicotine dependence levels are prominent. These metrics serve as critical indicators in assessing an individual's health status and are often used in educational settings to encourage students to adopt healthier lifestyles. BMI, a measure derived from an individual's weight and height, categorises people into different weight classes, which can indicate potential health risks. Similarly, nicotine dependence tests classify the degree of addiction, which is crucial in guiding individuals towards smoking cessation programs. Both these assessments are pivotal in shaping health-related behaviours and are utilised as part of broader public health strategies in Brazil.

Theoretical and methodological perspective

For the development of this research, we have chosen, as empirical material, the eight mathematics textbook series[11] approved by the National High School Textbook Program (Brasil, 2017). As said before, each series is formed by three textbooks, one for each high school year,[12] so we have analysed in total twenty-four textbooks. Michel Foucault's (2008) concept of governmentality has provided the core theoretical tool for this research study – a concept that as Foucault argues signifies three things:

> First, by "governmentality" I understand the ensemble formed by institutions, procedures, analyses and reflections, calculations, and tactics that allow the exercise of this very specific, albeit very complex, power that has the population as its target, political economy as its major form of knowledge, and apparatuses of security as its essential technical instrument. Second, by "governmentality" I understand the tendency, the line of force, that for a long time, and throughout the West, has constantly led towards the pre-eminence over all other types of power – sovereignty, discipline, and so on – of the type of power that we can call "government" and which has led to the development of a series of specific governmental apparatuses (appareils) on the one hand, [and, on the other] to the development of a series of knowledges (savoirs). Finally, by "governmentality" I think we should understand the process, or rather, the result of the process by which the state of justice of the Middle Ages

became the administrative state in the fifteenth and sixteenth centuries and was gradually "governmentalized".

(Foucault, 2008, p. 144)

The concept of "governmentality" helped us analyse the textbooks, as we looked for passages that characterised guidelines for conducting the conduct of individuals. In other words, parts of the textbook that could be seen as good or well-intentioned advice, became explicit as refined techniques to produce ways of being in line with what the government intends. It is not a matter of judging the government as oppressor and the governed as oppressed, but of instituting devices that cause power relations to be arranged in such a way that people are ruled by their own will, desiring to be led and having the goals of the rulers as targets to be achieved. This includes the habits related to the preservation of physical health.

Further, the concept of governmentality has provided a valuable framework for understanding how power operates through the subtle mechanisms of everyday life. By analysing the textbooks through this lens, we were able to uncover how seemingly benign advice shapes and directs individuals toward specific behaviours and goals that align with the government's intentions. This analysis reveals the intricate ways in which power relations are constructed and maintained, ultimately influencing individuals to govern themselves by the goals of those in power. We also identified the influence of governmentality on the promotion of habits related to physical health, highlighting the pervasive nature of power in shaping individual behaviour and conduct.

The research in this study has focused only on the pages that specifically dealt with the theme "education for citizenship" and are related to health, seeking to answer how these themes become articulated to the conceptual mathematical contents and what are the desirable behaviours for an individual to become a healthy citizen. We did not analyse the six textbooks (i.e. the two series) because they did not contain specific sections on "education for citizenship". Thus, our analysis material included the six series approved by the PNLD 2018, a total of eighteen textbooks.

To confirm the selection of our analysis material, we carefully reviewed the Mathematics Guide of PNLD 2018, which includes a critical evaluation of the presence of the "education for citizenship" theme in each approved series. This theme is found in the manual for selecting mathematics textbooks approved by PNLD 2018. Due to the significance given by PNLD to this topic, authors and publishers have created specific sections to meet this demand.

Analyses

To confirm the selection of our analysis material, we carefully reviewed the 2018 PNLD Mathematics Guide, which emphasises "education for citizenship" as an important theme for collection approval. Due to this significance attributed by PNLD to the thematic focus, authors and publishers have included a specific section to address this requirement. In our analysis, we found a significant concern in guiding the student in relation to health issues for citizenship training, as an incentive to physical exercise practices, as well as the concern with self-medication, obesity, and smoking. Orientations for the construction of a healthy life were the most frequent theme linked to the constitution of citizenship. In the following, we present some excerpts from the textbooks that present this concern and discuss how mathematics is articulated to these orientations that, in our view, are ways of conducting the students' conduct.

In the textbook authored by Dante (2016, v.1, p. 68), obesity is highlighted as a precursor to several serious health conditions, including high blood pressure and diabetes. The textbook explains how the BMI is calculated by dividing a person's weight by the square of their height. This formula categorises individuals as underweight, normal weight, overweight, or obese. The use of BMI in this context helps students understand how mathematical calculations can be used to identify and categorise health risks, emphasising the importance of maintaining a healthy weight to prevent chronic diseases.

Dante (2016, v.1, p. 69) offers practical advice for avoiding obesity, stressing the importance of regular exercise and a balanced diet. The figure on this page supports this narrative by showing daily routines that combine healthy eating with physical activity. The text explains how these habits can help prevent weight gain and maintain overall health, integrating these lifestyle recommendations with the educational content. Although the focus is on practical health advice, the narrative also subtly encourages the use of simple mathematical principles, such as tracking caloric intake versus expenditure, to support these health goals.

In Balestri (2016, v.1, p. 19), the text emphasises the health benefits of regular physical activity, such as weight loss and improved joint function, which collectively enhance quality of life. The figure accompanying the text shows an individual engaging in exercise, visually reinforcing the message. This section of the textbook focuses on the importance of maintaining physical health as part of being a responsible citizen, though it does not specifically integrate mathematical exercises in this context.

Chavante and Prestes (2016, v.3, p. 228) includes a section titled "Move!" that highlights the benefits of physical exercise, including its role in preventing health issues such as obesity and hypertension. The figure shows a young woman walking on a treadmill, guided by a likely instructor. The text discusses the positive impact of regular exercise on overall health and includes a simple mathematical formula for calculating maximum heart rate: FCM = 208 – 0.7 * *i*, where "*i*" represents the individual's age. This formula, along with the accompanying questions asking students to consider their own exercise habits and calculate their FCM, integrates basic mathematics into the discussion of healthy lifestyles. We notice that mathematics ends up losing space for something that seems to be more important: establishing ideal ways to behave. It is interesting how, instead of being a context for mathematics, the guidelines for healthy living take on a protagonistic role that even erases mathematics from the mathematics textbook, making more evident what is assumed as important: being healthy. One can find this discourse in textbooks of any discipline. As such, we suggest that here mathematics becomes irrelevant.

Balestri (2016, v.1, p. 150) uses strong language and statistics to emphasise the dangers of smoking, categorising it as one of the leading causes of preventable deaths. The text lists several serious health risks associated with smoking, such as lung cancer, heart disease, and complications during pregnancy, including the risk of the foetus becoming a passive smoker. This narrative serves as a "device of fear" aiming to discourage smoking by highlighting the severe consequences associated with it. However, this section does not include any mathematical calculations or exercises; instead, it focuses entirely on the health risks and societal impacts of smoking. This device captures the student's attention through some subjectivity (in this case, fear, and the need to fit into a pattern of normality) (Bocasanta & Knijnik, 2016; Friedrich, 2010; Souza & Silva, 2018; Valero et al., 2019). This capture produces a willingness to act in certain ways and not to act in others. In our examples, we note that such actions produce rules of conduct for healthy life.

Souza and Garcia (2016, v.1, p. 154) discusses the implementation of Brazilian laws in 2014 that prohibit smoking in enclosed public spaces, such as restaurants and bars. The accompanying figure shows a family dining in a restaurant, with a prominent "No Smoking" sign in the background. This image is used to reinforce the legal and social restrictions against smoking in public places, reflecting broader public health policies aimed at reducing smoking-related harm. Again, the mathematics is erased, this time in the name of compliance with the law. The morals and values of a society are materialised in a mathematics textbook.

In Souza and Garcia (2016, v.1, p. 155), the textbook presents two perspectives for students to consider: "analyzing with citizenship" and "analyzing with mathematics". However, in this particular section, the focus is solely on encouraging students to reflect on their smoking habits and the broader societal implications of smoking. The figure includes questions designed to provoke personal reflection on the negative effects of smoking, without introducing any mathematical models or calculations. The emphasis here is on moral and civic reasoning rather than mathematical analysis. The author suggests that students should reflect on their use of tobacco products and consider the drawbacks associated with them. Although it may appear to be an opportunity for students to express their opinions, the textbook's suggested activity seems to aim at prompting confessions from students regarding desirable and undesirable behaviours, good and bad habits, right and wrong choices, essentially shaping truths through questions that elicit an individual inner state of mind.

Chavante and Prestes (2016, v.2, p. 36) discusses the importance of regular blood pressure monitoring as a preventive measure against hypertension. The figure illustrates a digital blood pressure monitor, highlighting how individuals can use such devices at home to manage their health independently. The text provides practical advice on how to monitor blood pressure and interpret the readings. Although this section includes health-related guidance, it does not involve any mathematical calculations or exercises, focusing instead on the practical application of health monitoring technologies.

In Souza and Garcia (2016, v.2, p. 42), the text focuses on the measures necessary to maintain healthy blood pressure levels, emphasising the importance of a balanced diet and regular physical activity. The figure on this page visually represents these recommendations, but the discussion is purely health-focused without any integration of mathematical concepts. The primary goal of this section is to provide students with actionable health advice rather than engage them in mathematical exercises. Essentially, being a healthy member of society necessitates engaging in physical activities, adhering to a nutritious diet, and abstaining from tobacco products. These attitudes are presented in mathematics textbooks as a form of guidebook for students to follow. These textbooks produce norms and behaviours required to be a healthy citizen. Contextualisation goes beyond simply connecting mathematical concepts with real-life situations; it serves as reasoning behind adopting specific behaviours or altering habits – effectively changing one's outlook on life. Therefore, mathematics textbooks operate as technology that governs students' actions and shapes societal conduct. Furthermore, this integration of mathematics textbooks and healthy lifestyle guidelines serve as a means of cultivating responsible citizenship, equipping individuals with the knowledge and tools necessary to make informed decisions about their health and contribute to the well-being of society as a whole.

Considerations

In this chapter, we discuss a portion of the analysis conducted on select high school maths textbooks in Brazil that were approved by PNLD 2018. Our goal was to examine how the topic of "healthcare" is addressed in these textbooks and how it contributes to the civic education of students as intended by the authors. We offer an abridged overview of Brazil's historical context and underscore the significance of citizenship within Brazilian society, closely tied to concepts of liberty and democracy. Additionally, we examine the current state of public healthcare in Brazil through SUS and note multiple efforts initiated by the Brazilian Ministry of Health aimed at improving overall population health. At this stage, we can emphasise the following conclusionary points.

First, when authoring mathematics textbooks, many situations are evoked to suggest conduct techniques for the constitution of the "healthy citizen". Based on these images, we can say that a healthy citizen is produced as a particular humankind who has a healthy, regular, and balanced diet, who does not use cigarettes and tobacco products, and who practises physical activities regularly. These are the attitudes that will prevent diseases such as cancer, cardiorespiratory diseases, and obesity, among others. But what is wrong with this? It is not a matter of classifying or making value judgments about these activities, but of actually realising the production of a narrative about what is considered desirable in terms of habits, attitudes, and ways of being and behaving in today's world. Possibly, in other times, habits such as "no smoking" and "regular physical activity" were not emphasised. This may probably be something that will cause some estrangement in the future as well. In other words, mathematics textbooks can be a historical material for analysis.

Second, we have observed that mathematics textbooks can be viewed as a tool that shapes the behaviour of students and citizens. Specifically, in addition to teaching mathematical concepts, the textbooks also impart ways of acting and being a responsible citizen in today's society. Interestingly, it is often challenging to distinguish between the teaching of mathematics and the teaching of moral or behavioural habits. Furthermore, in the context of health, we found a clear emphasis on body control. The textbooks promote an ideal body image and perpetuate processes of valuing and devaluing certain individuals, leading to both inclusion and exclusion. There seems to be a clear emphasis on body control policies. This leads to the promotion of certain body standards while devaluing others, resulting in processes of inclusion and exclusion. Textbooks function as regulators (Silva, 2018, 2019; Valero et al., 2015), shaping the actions of individuals through subtle techniques that establish norms for what is considered normal and desirable – ultimately fostering an unattainable ideal standard. This reflects the materialisation of the neoliberal vision: creating an illusion of freedom while regulating all aspects of thought, sickness, and desires.

In the future, our aim is to engage in comparative research between Brazilian textbooks and those from other nations for the purpose of identifying potential connections between moral standards and approaches to regulating individual conduct, as well as exploring how the terms "citizen" and "citizenship" yield varied interpretations across different societies and cultures. From this text, several inquiries may be explored in these comparative studies: what constitutes being a citizen in other countries? How is the topic of "health" depicted in textbooks from other nations, and what are its associations with private and public healthcare systems?

Acknowledgements

This research is part of a project of the Research Group on Mathematics Education and Curriculum which aims to analyse the discourses of textbooks on mathematics in Brazil, describing how this didactic material proposes the teaching not only of mathematical content.

Notes

1 According to INEP in 2019, 7.5 million high school enrolments were registered. In 2019, 2.2 million teachers were registered in Brazilian basic education. Most of them work in primary education (62.6%), where 1,383,833 teachers are present. In 2019, Brazil had 180,610 basic education schools. Of this total, the municipal network is responsible for approximately two thirds of the schools (60%),

followed by the private network (22.9%). In basic education schools, the most frequently offered stages are early childhood education, with 114,851 (63.6%), and the initial years of primary education, with 109,644 (60.7%) schools. High school is offered by only 28,860 (16.0%) schools.

2 The common set of criteria employed for the assessment of textbooks in all high school subjects were: (a) respect for legislation, guidelines, and official norms regarding high school; (b) observance of ethical and democratic principles necessary for the construction of citizenship and republican social coexistence; (c) coherence and adequacy of the theoretical-methodological approach with respect to the didactic-pedagogical proposal and to the targeted goals; (d) respect for the interdisciplinary perspective in the content approach; (e) review of concepts, information, and procedures; (f) observance of the specific characteristics and purposes prescribed in the teacher's guide and alignment with the pedagogical approach; and (g) adequacy of the editorial structure and graphic work to the didactic and pedagogical objectives of the work.

3 http://www.fnde.gov.br/pnld-2018/

The Guide is a synthesis of the textbook assessment to facilitate teachers' choices. The textbooks come in series and each series consists of three textbooks (one for each year of high school). In 2018, 8 series (24 textbooks) were approved. The Guide is made up of specific sections: overview, description of the series, content organisation, content approach, teaching and learning methodology, contextualization and interdisciplinarity, education for citizenship, graphic design and language, teacher's manual, and recommendations for the teacher.

4 Many sections are created to explicitly fulfil the requirements of the PNLD evaluation items, and "construction of citizenship" is one of the items.

5 www.portaltransparencia.gov.br

6 http://www.saude.gov.br/sistema-unico-de-saude

7 http://www.saude.gov.br/sistema-unico-de-saude

8 https://saudebrasil.saude.gov.br/eu-quero-me-exercitar-mais/o-que-significa-ter-saude

9 https://www.saude.gov.br/campanhas

10 Quick test available on the site where the person fills in his personal data (weight and height) and with this the system makes the calculation automatically and generates a result that legitimises whether or not the person is overweight.

11 The high school maths textbooks approved by the 2018 PNLD were: Mathematics – Context & Applications, by Luiz Roberto Dante; Quadrant – Mathematics, by Diego Prestes and Eduardo Chavante; Mathematics: Science and Applications, by David Degenszajn, Gelson Iezzi, Nilze de Almeida, Osvaldo Dolce and Roberto Périgo; Mathematics to Understand the World, by Kátia Stocco Smole and Maria Ignez Diniz; Mathematics: Interaction and Technology, by Rodrigo Balestri; #Mathematics Contact, by Joamir Souza and Jacqueline Garcia; Mathematics – Paiva, by Manoel Paiva; Connections with Mathematics, by Fabio Martins de Leonardo.

12 The Brazilian high school has been formed for three years. The planning of the Brazilian curriculum is that the student attends this stage of schooling between 14 and 17 years of age.

References

Balestri, R. (2016). *Matemática: interação e tecnologia.* (Mathematics: interaction and technology) (2nd ed.). Leya.

Berto, L. F. (2017). *Enunciados sobre Interdisciplinaridade em Livros Didáticos de Matemática do Ensino Médio* (Statements on Interdisciplinarity in High School Mathematics Textbooks) Dissertação (Mestrado em Educação Matemática)]. Programa de Pós-Graduação em Educação Matemática, Universidade Federal de Mato Grosso do Sul.

Bocasanta, D. M., & Knijnik, G. (2016). Dispositivo de Tecnocientificidade e iniciação científica na educação básica. (Techno-scientific device and scientific initiation in basic education). *Currículo Sem Fronteiras*, *16*(1), 139–158.

Brasil (2017). *Ministério da educação.* (Ministry of Education) PNLD 2018: matemática – guia de livros didáticos – ensino médio/ministério da educação – secretaria de educação básica – SEB – fundo nacional de desenvolvimento da educação. Brasília, DF: ministério da educação, secretária de educação básica. 122 p. Disponível em: <http://www.fnde.gov.br/pnld-2018/. Acesso dia 15/05/2018.

Brasil (2020). Instituto Nacional de Estudos e Pesquisas Educacionais Anísio Teixeira *(Inep). Censo da Educação Básica 2019*: notas estatísticas. Brasília.

Brown, W. (2015). *Undoing the Demos: neoliberalism's stealth revolution.* Zone Books.

Brown, W. (2019). *Nas Ruínas do Neoliberalismo: a ascenção da política antidemocrática no ocidente* (In the Ruins of Neoliberalism: the rise of anti-democratic politics in the West) (M. A. Marino & E. A. C. Santos (trans.)). Editora Filosófica Politeia.

Carvalho, J. B. P. (2018). The Brazilian mathematics textbook assessments. *ZDM*, *50*(5), 773–785. https://doi.org/10.1007/s11858-018-0949-x

Chavante, E., & Prestes, D. (2016). *Quadrante – Matemática* (Quadrant - math) (1. Ed). Edições SM.

Coradetti, C. A. L. M. (2017). *Um Olhar Contemporâneo para a Matemática Financeira presente nos Livros Didáticos do Ensino Médio* (A Contemporary Look at Financial Mathematics in High School Textbooks) [Dissertação (Mestrado em Educação Matemática)]. Programa de Pós-Graduação em Educação Matemática, Universidade Federal de Mato Grosso do Sul.

Coradetti, C. A. L. M., & Silva, M. A. (2017). A Tomada de Decisão: tensionamentos de uma instrução dada pela matemática financeira dos livros didáticos de matemática do ensino médio. (Decision making: Tensioning an instruction given by the financial mathematics of high school math textbooks). *Perspectivas Da Educação Matemática*, *10*(22), 65–86.

Coradetti, C. A. L. M., & Silva, M. A. (2019). Famílias felizes e saudáveis! Livros didáticos de matemática e a produção de sujeitos. *Reflexão e Ação*, *27*(2), 219–235. https://doi.org/10.17058/rea.v27i2.11740

Coradetti, C. A. L. M., Silva, M. A., & Valero, P. (2019). Happy and healthy families! Financial mathematics and the making of the homus oeconomicus. *Proceedings of the Tenth International Mathematics Education and Society Conference (MES10)*, Article 10.

Dante, L. R. (2016). *Matemática – contexto & aplicações* (Mathematics – Context & applications) (3rd ed.). Ática.

Dardot, P., & Laval, C. (2016). A Nova Razão do Mundo: ensaio sobre a sociedade neoliberal [The New Reason for the World: An essay on neoliberal society] In M. Echalar (Trans.), *2009*. Boitempo.

Foucault, M. (1972). *The archaeology of knowledge and the discourse on language.* Pantheon Books.

Foucault, M. (1995). *Discipline and punish: The birth of the prison* (A. Sheridan, Trans., 2nd ed.). Vintage Books.

Foucault, M. (2008). *Birth of biopolitics: Lectures at the Collège De France, 1978–79* (G. Burchell, Trans.). Palgrave Macmillan. https://doi.org/10.1080/10286630902971637

Friedrich, D. (2010). Historical consciousness as a pedagogical device in the production of the responsible citizen. *Discourse: Studies in the Cultural Politics of Education*, *31*(5), 649–663. https://doi.org/10.1080/01596306.2010.516947

Guida, A. M., & Neto, V. F. (2019). Que fazem os animais nos livros didáticos de matemática para as escolas do campo? Problematizações com as lentes dos estudos animais [What do animals do in math textbooks for field schools? Problematics with the lenses of animal studies]. *Revista Latinoamericana de Estudios Críticos Animales*, *6*(1), 148–168.

Laval, C. (2019). *A escola não é uma empresa: o neoliberalismo em ataque ao ensino público* (The school is not a company: neoliberalism in attack on public education) (M. Echalar, Trans.). Boitempo.

Montecino, A., & Valero, P. (2017). Mathematics teachers as products and agents: To be and not to be. That's the point! In H. Straehler-Pohl, N. Bohlmann, & A. Pais (Eds.), *The disorder of mathematics education* (pp. 135–152). Springer International Publishing. https://doi.org/10.1007/978-3-319-34006-7_9

Neto, V. F. (2019). *Quando aprendo matemática, também aprendo a viver no campo? Mapeando subjetividades* [When I learn math, do I also learn to live in the country? Mapping subjectivities] [Tese (Doutorado em Educação Matemática)]. Programa de Pós-Graduação em Educação Matemática, Universidade Federal de Mato Grosso do Sul.

Neto, V., & Guida, A. (2019a). Redes discursivas: animais, campo, Matemática escolar e contribuições metodológicas da análise de redes [Discursive networks: Animals, field, school mathematics and methodological contributions of network analysis]. *Educação Matemática Debate*, *3*(8), 194–212. https://doi.org/10.24116/emd.v3n8a05

Neto, V. F., & Guida, A. M. (2019b). Processos de Subjetivação Movimentados em Livros Didáticos de Matemática para a Educação do campo: descrevendo e analisando o habitante desejável do campo. [Subjectivation processes moved in mathematical textbooks for field education: Describing and analyzing the desirable inhabitant of the field]. *Revista Educação Em Debate*, *41*(80), 185–203. https://doi.org/10.24882/eemd.v41i80.920

Neto, V. F., & Valero, P. (2018). The mathematics textbook for rural population in Brazil: Learning to be a modernized farmer. In E. Bergqvist, M. Österholm, C. Granberg, & L. Sumpter (Eds.), *Proceedings of the 42nd Conference of the International Group for the Psychology of Mathematics Education* (No. 42; Vol. 3, pp. 411–418). PME.

Ocampos, J. D. G. (2016). *Redes Discursivas Sobre a História da Matemática em Livros Didáticos do Ensino Médio* (Discursive Networks on the History of Mathematics in High School Textbooks) [Dissertação (Mestrado em Educação Matemática)]. Programa de Pós-Graduação em Educação Matemática, Universidade Federal de Mato Grosso do Sul.

Oliveira, J. C. G., & Silva, M. A. (2019a). O Estudante Desejável Constituído pelo Discurso da Educação Matemática Crítica [The desirable student constituted by the discourse on critical mathematics education]. *Revista Paranaense de Educação Matemática (RPEM)*, *8*(17), 17–44. https://doi.org/10.33871/22385800.2019.8.17.17-44

Oliveira, J. C. G., & Silva, M. A. (2019b). O Desejável Professor de Matemática, Constituído pelo Discurso da Educação Matemática Crítica [The desirable teacher of mathematics, constituted by the discourse on critical mathematics education]. *Paradigma*, *40*(2), 31–51.

Paiva, M. (2016). *Matemática (Math) – Paiva* (3. Ed). Moderna.

Popkewitz, T. S. (2004). The alchemy of the mathematics curriculum: Inscriptions and the fabrication of the child. *American Educational Research Journal*, *41*(1), 3–34.

Rose, N. (1999). *Governing the soul: The shaping of the private self.* Free Association Books.

Rose, N., & Miller, P. (1992). Political power beyond the state: Problematics of government. *The British Journal of Sociology*, *43*(2), 173.

Silva, M. A. (2018). Currículo e Educação Matemática: a política cultural como potencializadora de pesquisas [Curriculum and mathematics education: The cultural policy as a potentiator of research]. *Perspectivas Da Educação Matemática*, *11*(26), 202–224.

Silva, M. A. (2019). A Política Cultural dos Livros Didáticos de Matemática: um guia para transformar estudantes em cidadãos neoliberais [The cultural policy of mathematical textbooks: A guide to turning students into neo-liberal citizens]. *Linhas Críticas*, *25*, 381–398. https://doi.org/10.26512/lc.v24i0.21853

Silva, M. A., & Souza, D. M. X. B. (2018). Teaching girls and boys: addressing gender stereotypes in mathematics curriculum. *Proceedings of JustEd 2018 Conference 'Promoting Justice through Education*. Helsinki, Finland.

Silva, M. A., & Valero, P. (2018). Brazilian High School Textbooks: mathematics and students' subjectivity. In E. Bergqvist, M. Österholm, C. Granberg, & L. Sumpter (Eds.), *Proceedings of the 42nd Conference of the International Group for the Psychology of Mathematics Education* (No. 42; Vol. 4, pp. 187–194). PME.

Silva, M. A., Valero, P., Coradetti, C. A. L. M., & Berto, L. F. (2018). Brazilian high school mathematics textbooks and the constitution of the good student citizen. *Acta Scientiae*, *20*(6). https://doi.org/10.17648/acta.scientiae.v20iss6id4831

Smole, K. S., & Diniz, M. I. (2016). *Matemática para compreender o mundo* [Mathematics to understand the world]. Saraiva.

Souza, R. R. (2020). *Formação Cidadã: o que apontam os livros didáticos de matemática do ensino médio* (Citizen Education: what high school math textbooks point to) [Dissertação (Mestrado em Educação Matemática)]. Programa de Pós-Graduação em Educação Matemática, Universidade Federal de Mato Grosso do Sul.

Souza, J. R., & Garcia, J. S. R. (2016) *#contato matemática* (mathematical contact) (1. Ed). São Paulo: FTD.

Souza, D. M. X. B., & Silva, M. A. (2017a). A Regência do Currículo de Matemática: uma racionalidade para governar modos de vida. (The regency of the mathematics curriculum: A rationality to govern modes of life.) In J. C. Morgado, H. Norberto, & J. Souza (Eds.), *Currículo, Ideologia, Teorias e Políticas Educacionais* (Vol. 6, pp. 718–726). ANPAE.

Souza, D. M. X. B., & Silva, M. A. (2017b). Questões de gênero no currículo de matemática: atividades do livro didático [Gender issues in the math curriculum: Textbook activities]. *Educação Matemática Pesquisa*, *19*(3), 374–392. https://doi.org/10.23925/1983-3156.2017v19i3p374-392

Souza, D. M. X. B., & Silva, M. A. (2018). O dispositivo pedagógico do currículo-brinquedo de matemática, marcado pela dimensão de gênero, na produção de subjetividades. [The pedagogical device of the math curriculum toy, marked by the gender dimension, in the production of subjectivities]. *Reflexão e Ação*, *26*(2), 149–164. https://doi.org/10.17058/rea.v26i2.11747

Valero, P., Andrade-Molina, M., & Montecino, A. (2015). Lo político en la educación matemática: de la educación matemática crítica a la política cultural de la educación matemática. (The political in mathematical education: From critical mathematical education to the cultural politics of mathematical education). *Relime - Revista Latinoamericana de Investigación En Matemática Educativa*, *18*(3), 287–300. https://doi.org/10.12802/relime.13.1830

Valero, P., Norén, E., Silva, M. A., & Neto, V. F. (2018). Towards social justice through mathematics? Curriculum policy and processes of in (ex)clusion. *Proceedings of JustEd 2018 Conference 'Promoting Justice through Education*. Helsinki, Finland.

Valero, P., Norén, E., Silva, M. A., & Neto, V. F. (2019). The mathematically competent citizen in Brazilian and Swedish mathematics curriculum and textbooks. In

J. Sabramanian (Ed.), *Proceedings of the Tenth International Mathematics Education and Society Conference (MES10)*, Hyderabad, India.

Valero, P., Silva, M. A., & Souza, D. M. X. B. (2019). The curricular-toy, mathematics and the production of gendered subjectivities. In J. Sabramanian (Ed.) *Proceedings of the Tenth International Mathematics Education and Society Conference (MES10)*, Hyderabad, India.

Walshaw, M. (2007). *Working with Foucault in education*. Brill.

Yolcu, A., & Popkewitz, T. S. (2019). Making the able body: School mathematics as a cultural practice. *ZDM Mathematics Education*, *51*(2), 251–261.

12 Learning to become a modernized peasant-citizen through Brazilian mathematics textbooks

Vanessa Franco Neto and Paola Valero

Introduction

The idea "[…] that people need mathematics in their daily lives to participate as actively engaged citizens" (Pais, 2017, p. 1399) has become naturalized nowadays. The relation between citizenship and the school mathematics curriculum has strongly appeared even before the 20th century (see Yolcu, 2017; Ziols & Kirchgasler, 2021), when mathematics and science education started to be thought as central school subjects for the development of individuals, the modernization of education, and the economic development of nations (Valero, 2017). This is nothing new if we consider that Modern education has been an effective political tool to transform groups of people into a nation under the rule of a State. Tröhler (2016) argues that through education people have learned not only different kinds of knowledge structured by the school curricula, but also different forms of being that makes them feel and understand themselves as citizens belonging to a political body, the nation. Even though people are turned into citizens, the cognitive, moral and behavioural attributes of a citizen have varied in time and space. That is, the *"citoyen"* of education in France is not the same as the "*cidadão*" of Brazil. Even the latter may not be the same during the 21-yearlong Brazilian dictatorship than the Brazilian countryside[1] citizen in today's neoliberal, global-oriented Brazilian republic. We take Tröhler's (2021) invitation to critically resist the "spell of globalization"—the belief in globalization as a homogenizing force of culture and education, of particular significance for the creation of a single, unified world with some form of universal "citizen". Thus, we pay attention to the particularities of mathematics education in the context of rural Brazil, and problematize the notions and means to connect school mathematical competence with citizenship.

The current narrative of education is that mathematical and scientific competences are fundamental aspirations for the good global citizen and for prosperous communities and nations in competitive economies. So it is clearly stated in educational policy documents of international organizations such as the Organization for Economic Cooperation and Development (OECD) (e.g., OECD, 2018), as well as in national official educational policy

DOI: 10.4324/9781003130673-15

documents such as the Brazilian curriculum: [M]athematics is an important component in the construction of citizenship, as society increasingly uses scientific knowledge and technological resources, which citizens must know (Brasil, 1998, p. 19).

In this chapter we analyse how such aspirations take form in a specific mathematics education program in Brazil, namely the National Textbook Program (in Portuguese, *Programa Nacional do Livro Didático*, from now on PNLD) (Carvalho, 2018). Within this, the *PNLD Campo* (or Countryside PNLD) was designed for the rural population, which accounts for around 15% of Brazilian population. The PNLD Campo run between 2013 and 2016, and had as major goals to fulfil:

> a) a pedagogical role, ensuring a pedagogical conception and proposal adjusted to the characteristics of rural population, and offering a vision of concepts and information that keep the coherence of their methodological option; b) a social role of defending rural areas as spaces of culture, production and knowledge; it should contribute to the construction of a sustainable development project in rural areas.
>
> (Brasil, 2016, p. 41, our translation)

Two textbook collections (from now on C1 and C2) were approved and purchased by the PNLD Campo and have been distributed to countryside schools across the country. Over the years of the project, there were distributed 2'244.1163 textbooks.[2] Each collection has five textbooks for each of the five grades in the Brazilian primary school. In all, the program comprises 10 textbooks, each one with approximately 190 pages. C1 clearly explains its goals:

> The collection was built and guided by the principles and procedures of Countryside Education, which is advocated by social movements and supported by the law. This collection seeks to respect the multiple forms of rurality spread through the Brazilian territory, and *it privileges the valorisation of rural knowledge and practices, reinforcing the cultural identity of rural population.*
>
> (C1, Bonjorno et al., 2014b, p. 200, our translation)

The textbooks claim to align with the struggle of social movements—large Non-Governmental Organizations (NGOs) such as the Landless Movement—for peasants to preserve a countryside form of life and regain the ownership of their land. In Brazil, large numbers of peasants have been displaced from small farms into dispossession by large landowners and big and multinational companies exploiting the land for agribusiness. As part of their long-standing political struggle, these NGOs conceive of education as "a key element for the social justice project they are attempting to build" (Knijnik, 2007 p. 17). The political and educational principles in these movements seek to improve peasants' life and their work conditions.

Collectivity, social justice, traditional farming techniques, familiar agriculture, agroecology, organic practices, and mainly land reform (see Knijnik & Wanderer, 2012) are considered as important for the transformation that they pursue in their struggle.

For countryside populations, textbooks are central for education since access to other knowledge resources is limited, even as new mobile technologies spread. The textbooks are massively distributed by the Federal government, and each child gets a book for the school year. Textbooks are indeed valued and treasured because children and parents also consider them a scarce and important resource for their education (Neto & Guida, 2019). Thus, these textbooks play a key role in providing access to mathematical knowledge and, with this, building ideas about what mathematics is and what is its purpose in the life of peasants. As any other mathematics textbook (e.g., Fan et al., 2018), the PNLD Campo textbook collections organize the school mathematical knowledge according to a pedagogical approach in which a series of values and norms of the cultural configuration of its time and space are distributed. Therefore, the curriculum and its technologies—in this case textbooks—articulate cultural theses "about modes of life, differences, and the principles of freedom for people to act for themselves" (Popkewitz et al., 2017, p. 18).

The tension emerges as, on the one hand, textbooks are meant to respond to the political claims of the social movements to defend a way of life, and, on the other hand, textbooks become "[...] a strong instrument for governing the students' conduct" (Valero et al., 2019, p. 862) through the cultural theses on the mathematical competent child that they articulate. The desire of the social movements brought to the textbooks may (or not) enter in conflict with the envisioned and valued better countryside form of life mobilized in them. This tension concerns how the school "mathematics, with its practical and utilitarian character, act in the service of daily necessities, playing an important role in the formation of the citizen" (C2, Thadei et al., 2014, p. 245. Our translation). It also has to do with how the local—the rural—and the global—the larger, distant world—are set in relation to one another in the textbooks.

In this chapter, we examine this tension through investigating how the notions of the good countryside life present in the mathematics textbooks for primary countryside education create particular cultural theses about the mathematically competent peasant-citizen. The analysis interrogates the discourses that emerge in the PNLD Campo textbooks were notions of competence in mathematics intertwine with notions of what characterizes a good, desirable peasant-citizen in the Brazilian countryside, to achieve an envisioned better countryside life—which requires mathematical competence to perform in a globalized world. It is our contention that the textbooks articulate the aspirations for a good citizen and amalgamate them with mathematical contents, providing a frame for the making of countryside children into citizens of a countryside, globalized community.

Researching governing discourses in textbooks

We position our research within the type of studies interested in unravelling mathematics education as a field of cultural and political struggle for the fabrication of particular subjectivities with and through the practices and technologies of mathematics curricula and its related pedagogical techniques (e.g., Diaz, 2017; Valero, 2018). Studies on the *cultural politics of mathematics education* have provided a nuanced insight into how mathematics education is part of the dispositive of power that governs populations by performing certain forms of embodied subjectivity (e.g., Yolcu & Popkewitz, 2019). It creates classifications and orderings that "become a tool for making the modern life by making the child into a certain kind of citizen through mathematics" (Diaz, 2017, p. 46). It also generates and perpetuates in(ex)clusions of certain kinds of people that it itself creates.

From this perspective, mathematics education as an area of the school curriculum is part of processes of subjectivities governing, what Foucault has named *governmentality*:

> Governing people is not a way to force people to do what the governor wants; it is always a versatile equilibrium, with complementarity and conflicts between techniques which assure coercion and processes through which the self is constructed or modified by himself.
>
> (Foucault, 1993, p. 204)

The question of power in mathematics education is not just a matter of empowerment of the person through the transfer of knowledge, reflected in assumptions such as that the right learning of the right amounts of the adequate mathematical knowledge enlighten and potentiate the rational action of the individual. This is the assumption of the intrinsic empowerment of the rational citizen that has been critically. The issue is rather that concrete practices of mathematics education articulate school mathematical knowledge with norms of behaviour and particular moralities, and constitute a discursive and material space that shapes the possibilities for subjects to become in certain directions.

Since education is politically organized to transform individuals into citizens and create relationships of belonging to communities, then mathematics education and all the components of its practice instantiate the desires and aspirations of the political steering of education into the concrete lives of children, teachers, and students in classrooms and schools. Curricular materials such as textbooks, are important instruments in such instantiation since they embody the cognitive, behavioural and moral envisioned characteristics of the desired citizens.

To address the question of the notions of the citizen that are articulated in the textbooks, we conducted a discourse analysis of the ten textbooks that are part of the PNLD Campo and of their accompanying guidelines for teachers, which provide the orientations for teachers to achieve the teaching objectives.

For Foucault, "discourses are more than ways of giving meaning to the world; they imply forms of social organization and social practices which structure institutions and constitute individuals as thinking, feeling and acting subjects" (Walshaw, 2016, p. 47). With this in mind, a Foucaultian inspired discourse analysis allowed us to identify in the textbooks the explicit or implicit description of life in the countryside and what people should know or do to have a good life. From the regularities in these enunciations, we identified the statements that constitute the discourse and express the notions that organize and frame the individual's possibilities for knowing, thinking and being. These enunciations both articulate what it takes to become a knowledgeable and mathematically competent person to have a good life in a countryside community, and at the same time also produce and govern a desirable peasant form of life.

Furthermore, the statements were not only present in the written enunciations in problems or explanations. Since the textbooks are to be used in primary school, images, characters and cartoons are common to illustrate the activities and contents and catch the students' attention to engage them in learning (see Neto et al., 2019). Therefore, the images became particularly important in the analysis since they provide a visual materialization of the discourse (see Collange et al., 2014).

In our analysis, the statements on school mathematics competence for citizenship in the textbooks were understood in connection with statements about the modernization and optimization practices of countryside work, in other words, about how to become a competent peasant-citizen. Here the tension between the struggle of the social movements to defend countryside forms of life and a push towards the insertion of the Brazilian countryside into the global, market-oriented agribusiness come into play. As de Toledo e Toledo et al. (2018) point, the modernization of the Brazilian countryside to become one of the country's strong areas of international competitive production has brought changes to rural (mathematics) education. Mathematics and its pedagogy in agricultural high schools have combined abstract and formal mathematical reasoning with techno-scientific knowledge, to prepare students to run competitive agricultural production. In other words, notions of countryside forms of life connect local peasant life with the globalization demands in the world through a homogenization discourse "[...] based on dominant Western, post-industrial culture, that install the belief on the desirability of a given social order and on the universal commitment to the achievement of certain political ideals" (Valero, 2007, p. 425). The narratives about desirable forms of life assembled in mathematics textbooks become an important piece in the puzzle of making a desired peasant-citizen in a globalized world.

Tracing statements on the mathematically competent peasant

The analysis of C1 and C2 allowed us to identify 268 excerpts—combining text and images—about what is good, better, and suitable in the countryside life and activities. In these excerpts there are connections among lifestyle, labour practices and indication of what mathematical knowledge is needed to behave and act in a desired way in concrete situations. Two statements emerged from the analysis: The peasant lives an idyllic lifestyle and mathematics supports that life; and the peasant must use mathematics to change the traditional lifestyle into a modernized and effective form of life. In what follows we will present how such statements are put forward, taking examples from the problems and illustrations in the textbooks.

The settler of an idyllic countryside life

In C2, the aims and approach of the textbooks were made explicit: "as part of current debates, the books strengthen peoples' identity in their land, through production, meaning-making and systematization of school basic knowledge, in dialogue with the knowledge of the community they are part of" (C2, Gomes et al., 2014a, p. 206, our translation). This excerpt illustrates the explicit intention of relating the textbooks to a countryside lifestyle aligned with the NGOs and the peasants' political struggle.

Illustrations[3] of life scenes in the countryside, questions about it and suggestions for teachers to connect to that life appeared regularly through the textbooks. In the textbooks for 1st grade (e.g., Bonjorno et al., 2014a, p. 101; Thadei et al., 2014, p. 35), the images depict small farms, simple but organized. Houses are close to each other, which is a typical socio-spatial organization of Landless Movement communities (Leite, 2012). Children with different appearance—brown or light skin colour or curly, black, straight, blond hair type—play together. This captures the variety of population, cultures, and even racial groups that co-exist in the Brazilian countryside. Children are engaged in harmonic play and even animals are happy—dogs and pigs "smile".[4] There also appear different types of crops and there are many types of animals scattered freely in wide areas. The illustrations show scenes of a countryside context where the notion of a simple and happy peasant's good and healthy lifestyle emerges. It is suggested that teachers use the images to introduce exercises on estimation, counting and spatial localization which are basic mathematical contents for primary school. Teachers should invite students to count—and colour—different types of objects, compare their heights, and observe their shape. Students should talk to each other as they learn to recognize how mathematics is present in scenes that represent their daily life.

The images also put forward the idea that countryside work and traditional agricultural practices are good, healthy and even sustainable, a trend that has been commercially exploited to sell products through concepts such as "organic produce", "happy meat", and meat from "animal welfare" (see Cole, 2011). This trend is a new important source of income for peasants. We found 82 excerpts with these messages. These images display a specific spatial distribution that is opposite to the use of the territory in mono-agricultural practices, often linked to the agribusiness practices. In contrast, we found 48 excerpts where the latter are present. For example, in the 1st grade textbook in C1, there is an exercise on number sequences where the use of pesticide is recommended. It is a common practice in agribusiness to spray pesticides, while this type of products is not used for pest control in organic agriculture. The exercise reads:

> A farmer was losing his crops to a plague. When he consulted a specialist, he was instructed to spray certain amount of pesticide once a day for 10 days. The first day, he should spray 1 litre; the second day, 2 litres, the third day, 3 litres and so on. How many litres of this product will be used in ten days?
>
> (Bonjorno et al., 2014d, p. 24, our translation)

In all exercises the students are invited to learn how to be a competent peasant. As one moves from the lower to higher grades in primary school, the mathematical contents are presented as tools to provide strategic planning to sell the farm products, manage animals, decide the correct time to plant and harvest each type of crop, to choose the best way to do a garden or a plantation, to schedule the agricultural calendar, and lots many other types of countryside practices. Arithmetical operations, localization, estimation, proportionality, order, classification, comparison, patterns, measurements, geometrical figures, tables, and graphs, and financial calculations are contents that appear as strongly linked to situations in countryside contexts and practices. In the textbooks, these contents are meant to facilitate and improve peasants' work.

Activities, drawings and illustrations in the textbooks mobilize ideas about traditional farming techniques, agroecological and organic practices and land reform, through mathematical problems where particular mathematical concepts have a use. This type of knowledge is very important in the peasants' political struggle and seen by the NGOs as tools to fight for social justice. Indeed, Knijnik (2002, p. 160) argues that subordinated groups such as those organized in the Landless Movement demand to learn the socially legitimated academic mathematics, to be able to participate in the cultural, social and economic life of their communities. However, Knijnik (2002) also points that for these social movements local practices are relevant forms of life which have an internal coherence. They are not folklore and even less an idealized portrayal of their lifeforms and conditions.

To summarize, the textbooks put forward a particular view of life in the countryside and of the competences needed to maintain it. This is what we call the statement of the *idyllic countryside life*. It articulates a cultural thesis on the desirable peasant who knows and acts to keep and improve that particular view of countryside life. As part of the competences, the peasant can see mathematics in everyday life activities and understands that learning mathematics is beneficial and fun. The recognition and identification of the social rules and public codes of countryside life are combined with the mathematical exercises, images and arguments to be learned. These competences are presented as necessary for the wellbeing of countryside communities. In such a way, the textbooks are apparently in line with the principles of public policy in Brazil which should guarantee "peasants' rights and citizenship understood in their identities and ways of life, as opposed to other projects related to the rural world or agribusiness" (C2, Thadei et al., 2014, p. 206). The notion of citizenship in these textbooks connects individuals to make them members of an idyllic countryside community through a set of mathematical-knowledge supported practices, in an effort to generate empathy and feelings of belonging in students. The learning of mathematics turns the peasant child into a desirable citizen of such an idyllic community.

The modernized peasant making better lifeforms

Mathematics is often viewed as an important type of knowledge that offers an efficient path to deal with data and information and to make rationally informed decisions. It is an important tool for citizenship in modern society. So it is argued in the analysed textbooks: "mathematics, with its practical and utilitarian character, acts in the service of daily necessities, playing an important role *in the formation of the citizen*" (C2, Thadei et al., 2014, p. 245, our emphasis). The learning of mathematics is a strategic tool to organize life and society.

This idea is concretized in the textbooks in mathematics problems such as the following in C2, for 4th grade students. An illustration shows cows, horses and donkeys scattered. The different species seem to live harmoniously and all animals move freely in "Saint John's Farm" (Thadei et al., 2014, p. 172). The activity invites students to estimate how many animals are there in the farm without counting. In the next image (Thadei et al., 2014, p. 173), shows "Saint Peter's farm" where the animals are classified according to their species, separated in different fenced areas, and standing in rows. The activity orients the children to understand that after an initial step of estimation, counting is associated with the organization and classification of species. The optimization of estimation through organized counting is the best way to do the work because it can be done in less time and more accurately, as suggested by the question asking the students to reflect on whether counting was easier than estimating. The conclusion required from students is that the best way of counting animals is linked to classifying, selecting and organizing them.

These types of images and problems stand in contrast to the ones in earlier grades since they start introducing the model of "factory farming" aligned with an economic rationality of efficiency and agroindustry. Such contrast resonates with the objectives found in one of the textbooks, as an expression of new forms of knowing and acting which peasants need to know in current times:

> It happens that social life and productive organization have been changing and demand workers who, in addition to knowing how to perform their tasks, also plan and be creative. These changes are due to the

> economic reorganization of the capitalist countries, the dissemination of information and technological advances.
>
> (C2, Thadei et al., 2014, p. 214, our translation)

In other words, the work practices of the peasants-citizens in the idyllic countryside life need to be modernized. And this idea is linked with increasing productivity, lowering costs, spending less time, and optimizing routines, space, time and human workforce. That is, the peasants need to understand and to practice a different rationality of work in comparison to the dynamics of traditional countryside life form previously discussed.

Similarly, an activity on measurement (Bonjorno et al., 2014c, p. 8) first depicts the father of a girl using arm, step and hand lengths to measure the terrain to plant beans, radishes and carrots. These are common measuring practices in rural life. However, the instruction in the teacher's guide suggests comparing local practices to measuring practices with instruments based on the metric system. The latter is to be shown as a better way to decide about accuracy: "Lead students to conclude that metering is accurate across all groups while measurement through other instruments produces differences in the results" (C1, Bonjorno et al., 2014c, p. 217, our translation). Since this activity targets fourth grade students, it is assumed that young people already engage themselves in familiar practices in communities. Now they should start understanding better practices outside of those communities.

Knijnik (2002) has discussed the possibility of pedagogical practices that do not reinforce the taken-for-granted subordination of popular knowledge in local practices to academic knowledge in school mathematics. We find that the textbooks systematically suggest that the school mathematics knowledge and techniques are superior. Thus, the possibility of learning in different ways the mathematical content in the curriculum is also erased. In the curricular orientations in Brazil there is an explicit mention to the strategy in the activity about Saint Peter's farm: "organization in groupings to facilitate counting and comparison between large collections" (Brasil, 1998, p. 50, our translation) is important in school mathematics.

In other problems there is an explicit appreciation of traditional practices associated with organic production. For example, in C2 for 4th grade (Gomes et al., 2014b, p. 8) there is an exercise to teach percentages through problem solving in the context of egg production. In the text that introduces the exercise, the "organic chicken" is presented as healthier than the chicken raised in big agribusiness farms. The questions in the problem direct students to establish a direct proportional and linear relation between the number of hens and the number of eggs per hen, as if free, "organic" hens could lay eggs in a similar fashion as in the industrial egg production. Here the idea of "animal machines" can be linked to the notion of farmed animal well-being (Cole, 2011). This articulation is very common nowadays in attempt to satisfy the growing number of consumers concerned about ethically farmed and healthy animals. Such linkage is part of an "attempt to remoralise the exploitation of 'farmed' animals in such a way as to permit business as usual, with the added 'value' of ethical self-satisfaction for the consumer of 'happy meat'" (Cole, 2011, p. 84). The mathematical competence of estimation and its connection to linear proportions are introduced and practiced with students in the context of organic farm production, in a context where the improvement of production and increase of profit—suggested in the selection of hens that can lay healthier and more nutritious eggs, meat and family earnings.

It has been suggested that the trend of setting mathematical problems in real life contexts to engage students with the learning of mathematics contents needs problematization (Yolcu, 2019). The textbooks examined here put together mathematical contents with ideas of transformation of traditional farming practices—being part of the idyllic countryside life—and a global economic rationality. The textbooks articulate a cultural thesis of the countryside mathematical learner as a person who, through mathematical competence, has the tools to effectively change and modernize traditional rural practices. The contexts used to present children's local, communal experiences simultaneously connect the latter to the rationality of agribusiness and global production. The governing effect of learning mathematics through the textbooks produces what we have called the *modernized peasant making better lifeforms.*

Governing the peasant-citizen

The aim of this chapter was not to identify a fixed or stable truth about what it means to be a mathematically competent peasant. After all, what is better or worse, what are the desirable identities of peasants are always in change in situationally articulated discourses. These may sometimes be contradictory or operate side-by-side like the doubleness between the appeal to the goodness of traditional countryside lifestyle and the need of modernization and profitable optimization of countryside production, as illustrated above.

An effect of the learning of mathematics with and through the textbooks is the transformation of a child into a countryside settler that shares the cognitive resources and capacities, the behaviour and the morality of a community of peasant-citizens. The way in which mathematics appears in traditional settings but allows the peasant to act to transform life into a modernized form of life is recurrent in the textbooks. Both these ideas are intertwined in the discourse of the countryside mathematics textbooks and appear systematically in the illustrations as well as in the explanations and problems. In the textbook, the statement about the necessity of learning mathematics for the modernization of peasants' practices is mobilized in the discourse not only through their repetition, but also through other elements of the texts, mainly by their link to mathematical activity which provide them with a sense of security and truth. The analysis of the images, the contents and the mathematics shows the uniqueness of the discourse mobilized in the textbooks and gives us the possibility of recognizing "the general form of a sentence, a meaning, a proposition" (Foucault, 1972, p. 101), through which notions of the desired mathematically competent peasant are put forward for learners.

But the discourses that circulate in these textbooks show two main (and opposed) statements about the desirable peasant-citizen. First, the person needs to align with the basic ideas that these textbooks mobilize—especially the notions about social justice from the NGOs—and with the mathematical knowledge that such ideas require as displayed in the illustrations and contexts in the mathematical activities. Elementary mathematical contents (such as counting and ordering) is arranged to catch the students' attention and engage them in their own learning process. Second, the requirement to modernize labour practices is supported by more sophisticated mathematical notions such as accuracy and optimization connected to efficiency and productivity. These notions are sustained by mathematical ideas and tools of control and management, which appear strongly linked to mathematical skills of data reading, interpretation and organization. Together, these statements feed the argument that:

> Conceiving of mathematics education as a matter of policy allows focusing on the governing of populations and individuals toward expected and desired behavior, namely, the acquisition of mathematical knowledge, competence, and expertise, since these are valued as indispensable qualifications *of modern, rational, economically productive citizens*
> (Valero & Knijnik, 2016, p. 5, our emphasis)

This is supported despite the apparent contradiction between the two statements: the idyllic countryside life and the modernized, improved life. Instead, the articulation of these two—apparently—contradictory statements evidences that the mathematics textbooks for the Brazilian countryside population embody a project of people formation, in this case, a project of modernization of peasants' traditional practices. Mathematics education, with the technologies that make part of its practices, help to insert particular cultural theses on the child to fabricate types of people (Popkewitz, 2004). The governing of school mathematics set in operation "strategies, techniques and procedures through which different forces seek to render programmes operable, and by means of which a multitude of connections are established" (Rose & Miller, 1992, p. 183).

The analysis highlighted the regularities in peasants' practices and the role of school mathematics in the validation, reproduction and propagation of a type of mathematically competent child that will turn into the subject who can change production in more profitable ways. That is, a child who can become a productive peasant-citizen in a local community as well as a globalized, knowledgeable citizen and follower of a particular economic and productivity rationality. Therefore, the analysis contributes to a political understanding of mathematics education practice and its role in the construction of an increasingly globalized society, capturing and rearranging the local practices in different places in the world, such as the Brazilian countryside.

The necessity of modernization in rural forms of life is not unique to Brazil. It is also illustrated in Brown's (2015) discussion of neoliberalism as a rationality of government operating also in rural areas, "with the promise of giant crop yields and an end to struggling with pests, the agribusiness giants aim to convert farmers across the developing world from 'traditional' to 'modern' techniques, materials, *and* markets" (p. 144). Brown shows how in 2003, Iraqi farmers were "lured into the new agricultural techniques" (p. 145) by big corporations that stopped traditional practices and brought new elements with the argument of increasing Iraqi agricultural production. However, "the problem is that farming in general is uniquely vulnerable to fluctuations in nature, such as draughts and floods, and farming for export is also vulnerable to fluctuations in world markets" (p. 146). The new elements disregarded local specificities so, after a period of much losses because of production and the world market, the consequences were dramatic and ended in "an epidemic of farmer suicides" (p. 146). This example is extreme, but it illustrates the effects of the ideas mobilized in the discourse order which these mathematics textbooks are part of. In the same problematic situation, Hendrickson and Harvey (2005) had showed the retaliation that farmers in the USA have been suffering with the imposition to use genetically modified seeds (GM seeds):

> the genetic modification of seeds coupled with restrictive licensing requirements imposed by technology companies limits the ability of farmers to practice traditional farming activities, such as saving seeds or cross-breeding plants to develop seed varieties that are efficient for local environmental conditions. Moreover, because the use of GM seeds is becoming more prominent in agriculture, the distribution outlets for farmers who choose not to plant GM seeds are being limited, thus constraining how non-GM farmers are able to market their crops.
>
> (Hendrickson & Harvey, 2005, p. 269)

A similar situation took place in Brazil. Ribeiro (2012) analysed how educational programs supported by North American funding have promoted the idea that traditional practices are inadequate. Such programs contribute to both the community's annulment of accumulated knowledge and the creation of countryside people into waged workforce. This is a trend that resonates with the effects of new technoscientific forms of agricultural education studied by de Toledo e Toledo et al. (2018). These examples are brought to make explicit the effects of the global ideas on local communities mobilized in the discourse.

In short, the notions of citizenship in the countryside context embody practices that seek to bring solutions to local and global problems feeding the individual with responsibilities in governing oneself through the good and better path for the self, the family, the community and the world. When studying the effects of sustainable development education in Sweden, the good citizen is often conceived as "the individual becomes responsible for 'everybody's' security and for the ecological system of the world" (Ideland & Malmberg, 2015, p. 181). These individual responsibilities belong to on the one hand of a political rationality that is strongly linked to global, competitive and marketized logic. On the other hand, it is also a logic that connects mathematical skills to—the right form of—decision making about the best way to position oneself in the face of personal, local and global demands and threats.

Finally, we also need to remember that discursive practices are not homogeneous. They are usually conflicting, as Foucault (1972) reminds us. Therefore, we can claim that mathematics education through countryside textbooks has an important role in governing countryside people towards becoming desirable peasant-citizens who, with and through mathematics, are able to exercise their role in this globalized society, while leaving a healthy, free, harmonic, and happy life in the countryside.

Notes

1 We use the term "countryside" to refer to the configuration space/geography/practice where people engage in multiple political struggles to inhabit and work their land. It opposes the term "rural" which has mainly a spatial reference linked to a prejudiced understanding of peasant practices and culture (Ribeiro, 2012).

2 All of the statistics information of the program can be accessed in https://www.fnde.gov.br/index.php/programas/programas-do-livro/pnld/dados-estatisticos-anos-anteriores#:~:text=Alunos%20atendidos%3A%201.335.640,Livros%20distribu%C3%ADdos%3A%2012.137.262

3 Due to copyright issues, it was not possible to reproduce the original images here. The reader can view some of the images in Neto and Valero (2018).

4 The anthropomorphising of animals to connect mathematical content and morality is a type of pedagogical device used in these textbooks. For an analysis of this feature, see Neto et al. (2019).

References

Bonjorno, J. R., Bonjorno, R. F. A., & Gusmão, T. C. R. S. (2014a). *Novo girassol: saberes e fazeres do campo. Alfabetização matemática – 1° Ano* (1a ed.). FTD.

Bonjorno, J. R., Bonjorno, R. F. A., & Gusmão, T. C. R. S. (2014b). *Novo girassol: saberes e fazeres do campo. Alfabetização matemática – 2° Ano* (1a ed.). FTD.

Bonjorno, J. R., Bonjorno, R. F. A., & Gusmão, T. C. R. S. (2014c). *Novo girassol: saberes e fazeres do campo. Alfabetização matemática – 4° Ano* (1a ed.). FTD.

Bonjorno, J. R., Bonjorno, R. F. A., & Gusmão, T. C. R. S. (2014d). *Novo girassol: saberes e fazeres do campo. Alfabetização matemática – 5° Ano* (1a ed.). FTD.

Brasil (1998). *Parâmetros curriculares nacionais*. Ministério da Educação.

Brasil (2016). *Edital de convocação (04/2014 – CGPLI) para o processo de inscrição e avaliação de obras didáticas para o programa nacional do livro didático do campo – PNLD Campo*. Ministério da Educação.

Brown, W. (2015). *Undoing the demos: Neoliberalism's stealth revolution*. Zone Books.

Carvalho, J. B. P. (2018). The Brazilian mathematics textbook assessments. *ZDM, 50*(5), 773–785. https://doi.org/10.1007/s11858-018-0949-x

Cole, M. (2011). From "Animal Machines" to "Happy Meat"? Foucault's ideas of disciplinary and pastoral power applied to 'animal-centred' welfare discourse. *Animals (Basel)*, *1*(1), 83–101. https://doi.org/10.3390/ani1010083
Collange, M., Almeida, C., & Amorim, A. C. R. (2014). Natureza em imagens de livros didáticos de biologia do ensino médio. *Revista de Ensino de Biologia da Associação Brasileira deEnsino de Biologia (SBEnBio)*, *7*, 826–837.
de Toledo e Toledo, N., Knijnik, G., & Valero, P. (2018). Mathematics education in the neoliberal and corporate curriculum: The case of Brazilian agricultural high schools. *Educational Studies in Mathematics*, *99*(1), 73–87. https://doi.org/10.1007/s10649-018-9825-4
Diaz, J. D. (2017). *A cultural history of reforming math for all. The paradox of making in/equality*. Routledge.
Fan, L., Xiong, B., Zhao, D., & Niu, W. (2018). How is cultural influence manifested in the formation of mathematics textbooks? A comparative case study of resource book series between Shanghai and England. *ZDM*, *50*(5), 787–799. https://doi.org/10.1007/s11858-018-0976-7
Foucault, M. (1972). *The archaeology of knowledge* (World of man). Routledge.
Foucault, M. (1993). About the beginning of the hermeneutics of the self: Two lectures at Dartmouth. *Political Theory*, *21*(2), 198–227.
Gomes, L. B., Condeixa, M. C. G., Figueiredo, M. T., & Vidigal, S. M. P. (2014a). *Alfabetização matemática e ciências – 2° Ano. Coleção Campo Aberto* (1a ed.). Global Editora.
Gomes, L. B., Condeixa, M. C. G., Figueiredo, M. T., & Vidigal, S. M. P. (2014b). *Alfabetização matemática e ciências – 3° Ano. Coleção Campo Aberto* (1a ed.). Global Editora.
Hendrickson, M. K., & Harvey, S. J. (2005). The ethics of constrained choice: How the industrialization of agriculture impacts farming and farmer behavior. *Journal of Agricultural and Environmental Ethics*, *18*, 269–291. https://doi.org/10.1007/s10806-005-0631-5
Ideland, M., & Malmberg, C. (2015). Governing 'eco-certified children' through pastoral power: Critical perspectives on education for sustainable development. *Environmental Education Research*, *21*(2), 173–182. https://doi.org/10.1080/13504622.2013.879696
Knijnik, G. (2002). Curriculum, culture and ethnomathematics: The practices of 'cubagem of wood' in the Brazilian Landless Movement. *Journal of Intercultural Studies*, *23*(2), 149–165. https://doi.org/10.1080/07256860220151050
Knijnik, G. (2007). Mathematics education and the Brazilian Landless Movement: Three different mathematics in the context of the struggle for social justice. *Philosophy of Mathematics Education Journal*, *2*(1), 143–154.
Knijnik, G., & Wanderer, F. (2012). Genealogy of mathematics education in two Brazilian rural forms of life. In O. Skovsmose & B. Greer (Eds.), *Opening the cage: Critique and politics of mathematics education* (pp. 160–178). Sense Publishers.
Leite, S. P. (2012). Assentamento rural. In R. S. Caldart, I. B. Pereira, P. Alentejano, & G. Frigotto (Eds.), *Dicionário da educação do campo* (2nd ed., pp. 108–112). Expressão Popular.
Neto, V. F., & Guida, A. M. (2019). Processos de subjetivação movimentados em livros didáticos de matemática para a educação do campo: Descrevendo e analisando o habitante desejável do campo. *Revista Educação em Debate*, *41*, 185–203.
Neto, V. F., & Valero, P. (2018). The mathematics textbook for rural population in Brazil: learning to be a modernized farmer. In E. Bergqvist, M. Österholm, C. Granberg, & L. Sumpter (Eds.), *Proceedings of the 42nd Conference of the International Group for the Psychology of Mathematics Education* (pp. 411–418). PME.

Neto, V. F., Valero, P., & Guida, A. (2019). Anthropomorphism as a pedagogical device in mathematics textbooks for countryside Brazil. In J. Subramanian (Ed.), *Proceedings of the 10th International Mathematics Education and Society Conference* (p. 622–631). MES.

Organization for Economic Cooperation and Development. (2018). *PISA 2015 results in focus.* OECD Publishing. https://www.oecd.org/pisa/pisa-2015-results-in-focus.pdf

Pais, A. (2017) Mathematics education as a matter of economy. In M. Peters (Ed.), *Encyclopedia of educational philosophy and theory* (pp. 1399–1403). Springer. https://doi.org/10.1007/978-981-287-588-4_516

Popkewitz, T. S., Diaz, J. D., & Kirchgasler, C. (2017). The reason of schooling and educational research. Culture and political sociology. In T. S. Popkewitz, J. Diaz, & C. Kirchgasler (Eds.), *A political sociology of educational knowledge: Studies of exclusions and difference* (pp. 3–22). Routledge.

Ribeiro, M. (2012). Educação rural. In R. S. Caldart, I. B. Pereira, P. Alentejano, & G. Frigotto (Eds.) *Dicionário da educação do campo* (2nd ed., pp. 293–298). Expressão Popular.

Rose, N., & Miller, P. (1992). Political power beyond the state: Problematics of government. *The British Journal of Sociology*, *43*(2), 173–205. https://doi.org/10.2307/591464

Thadei, J. L. M., Figueiredo, L. I. B., Gomes, L., & Vidigal, S. M. P. (2014). Letramento e Alfabetização Matemática – 1° Ano. *Coleção Campo Aberto* (*1a* ed.). Global Editora.

Tröhler, D. (2016). Curriculum history or the educational construction of Europe in the long nineteenth century. *European Educational Research Journal*, *15*(3), 279–297. https://doi.org/10.1177/1474904116645111

Tröhler, D. (2021). Magical enchantments and the nation's silencing: Educational research agendas under the spell of globalization. In D. Tröhler, N. Piattoeva, & W. F. Pinar (Eds.), *World yearbook of education 2022. Education, schooling and the global* (pp. 7–25). Routledge. https://doi.org/https://doi.org/10.4324/9781003137801-2

Valero, P. (2007). In between the global and the local: The politics of mathematics education reform in a globalized society. In B. Atweh, A. C. Barton, M. C. Borba, N. Gough, C. Keitel, C. Vistro-Yu, & R. Vithal (Eds.), *Internationalisation and globalisation in mathematics and science education* (pp. 421–439). Springer.

Valero, P. (2017) Mathematics for all, economic growth, and the making of the citizen-worker. In T. S. Popkewitz, J. Diaz, & C. Kirchgasler (Eds.), *A political sociology of educational knowledge:* Studies of exclusions and difference (pp. 117–132). Routledge.

Valero, P. (2018). Human capitals: School mathematics and the making of the homus oeconomicus. *Journal of Urban Mathematics Education*, *11*(1&2), 103–117. http://education.gsu.edu/JUME

Valero, P., & Knijnik, G. (2016). Mathematics education as a matter of policy. In M. A. Peters (Eds.), *Encyclopedia of educational philosophy and theory* (pp. 1–6). Springer. https://doi.org/10.1007/978-981-287-532-7_523-1

Valero, P., Norén, E., Silva, M., & Neto, V. (2019). The mathematically competent citizen in Brazilian and Swedish mathematics curriculum and textbooks. In J. Subramanian (Ed.), *Proceedings of the 10th International Mathematics Education and Society Conference* (pp. 854–864). MES.

Walshaw, M. (2016). Michel Foucault. In E. de Freitas & M. Walshaw (Eds.), *Alternative theoretical frameworks for mathematics education research: Theory meets data* (pp. 39–64). Springer.

Yolcu, A. (2017). Historicizing "math for all". In A. Chronaki (Ed.), Mathematics education and life at times of crisis. *Proceedings of the 9th International Mathematics Education and Society Conference* (pp. 1011–1022). University of Thessaly Press.

Yolcu, A. (2019) Real-life mathematics: Politicization of natural life and rethinking the sovereign. In U. T. Jankvist, M. Van den Heuvel-Panhuizen, & M. Veldhuis (Eds.), *Eleventh Congress of the European Society for Research in Mathematics Education (CERME 11)*. Utrecht University. https://hal.archives-ouvertes.fr/hal-02421694/document

Yolcu, A., & Popkewitz, T. S. (2019). Making the able body: School mathematics as a cultural practice. *ZDM*, *51*(2), 251–261.

Ziols, R., & Kirchgasler, K. L. (2021). Health and pathology: A brief history of the biopolitics of US mathematics education. *Educational Studies in Mathematics*, *108*(1–2), 123–142. https://doi.org/10.1007/s10649-021-10110-8

13 The elaboration of culturally and locally based mathematics curricula in a globalized context

Eric Vandendriessche, Kécio Gonçalves Leite, Maria Cecilia Fantinato, and Pierre Metsan

Introduction

The elaboration of a local culture based curriculum has been undertaken in diverse indigenous societies around the world—as part of decolonization processes. Through an intercultural approach[1], the ethical, political and epistemic potential of education is captured for promoting dialogue between different kinds of knowledge and for empowering historically marginalized cultural groups. In this, indigenous societies have come to recognize the value of their own traditional knowledge and practices—*e.g.* number systems or measurements, music, astronomy, divination, navigation, etc. as well as technical activities such as graphic art, mat making, house building, basketry, etc.—for calling upon the latter practices in mathematics education (Alangui, 2010; Lipka et al., 2019; Trinick et al., 2015). The objective for such decolonial projects is generally twofold. On the one hand, such culturally based mathematics curricula would aim at valorizing indigenous knowledge and practices (sometimes in decline) within the local educational system. At the same time, on the other hand, such curricula can be implemented with the underlying aim to increase local students' academic competence in mathematics—required to pursue graduate studies or acquire the "keys to the global world".

One can perceive a tension between these two aims working simultaneously for local and global concerns respectively. Can they be mutually compatible? How would a culturally based curriculum not only valorize local knowledge but also support integration to the global world? And specifically, could a culturally based curriculum significantly work towards the improvement of indigenous students' skills in mathematics?

While tackling these issues, Brazilian ethnomathematician and mathematics educator Maria Cecilia Fantinato and French ethnomathematician and anthropologist Eric Vandendriessche, have felt the necessity to invite two more researchers/authors, who currently carry field research on Indigenous locally based education. As such, Kécio Leite, a Brazilian Professor at the Federal University of Rondônia (UNIR), has been invited. Kécio works with indigenous teachers from different ethnic groups in the state of

DOI: 10.4324/9781003130673-16

Rondônia, northern Brazil and has collaborated with Cecilia (Fantinato & Leite, 2022). Pierre Metsan, a Ni-Vanuatu Graduate student at the University of New Caledonia, has been also invited to participate. Pierre is currently carrying out research on culturally based education in the Melanesian Republic of Vanuatu (South Pacific) for which he has discussed with Eric for about three years.

This chapter will thus tackle the issues raised by the implementation of locally based education in the context of globalization, by discussing Vanuatu and Paiter Indigenous educational experiences. To do so, we will successively focus on current educational changes in the Brazilian Indigenous Intercultural Education and in the Republic of Vanuatu. Although these two cases share significant common features, they also bring to light different ways of dealing with the complex relation between local and global education and highlight contradictions.

The first part of the chapter focuses on the Paiter[2] people from the Amazon region. First, we present a historical contextualization of Brazilian Indigenous school education by analyzing the challenges faced by Paiter school teachers, in order to value and preserve their local knowledge and practices. Second, the section explains how these teachers begin to study ethnomathematics and its pedagogical implications, by attending "Magisterium" and "Intercultural Licensing courses" organized by the Federal University of Rondônia. In order to shape theoretical and practical tools for implementing local curriculum, they reinterpret ethnomathematical concepts (Ascher, 1991; D'Ambrosio, 2001). Such a reinterpretation being considered as a strategy for strengthening Paiter cultural identity.

The second part of the chapter shows how the Ni-Vanuatu teachers, as well as their educators, deal with issues raised as they elaborate a locally and culturally based curriculum in the context of a decolonization (i.e. reforming the inherited colonial education system for creating a new [National] curriculum taking into account the diversity of local cultures and vernacular languages) and globalization (i.e. considering the curriculum reform in the light of a global world, *cf.* Ministry of Education [MOE], 2010). First, we highlight the motivations that led the MOE to encourage the use of about 120 vernacular languages to teach Ni-Vanuatu pupils how to read and write. Second, we focus on a cultural practice—locally known as "sand drawing"—considered as a possible tool for secondary school students' skills in mathematics. To conclude, the chapter concentrates on discussing common and distinctive features pertaining to these the two cases, focusing more particularly on the perception of local traditions, the preservation of language diversity, the tensions between "local" and "global" education, and the role of ethnomathematics in teacher education policies. Based on this analysis, we argue that ethnomathematics has played a significant role in the decolonization processes of mathematics education (Bernales & Powell, 2018) in these two parts of the world.

Indigenous school education in the Brazilian context

Brazil has an indigenous population of approximately 896,000 inhabitants, who belong to 305 indigenous peoples, speakers of at least 274 languages (Instituto Brasileiro de Geografia e Estatística, 2010)[3]. These numbers represent a small fraction of the much wider cultural and linguistic diversity that originally existed before the onset of colonization by Portuguese, and promoted genocides, ethnocides and epistemicides[4] over the last five centuries.

During the European colonization process and in the post-colonial period,[5] education for Brazilian indigenous peoples went through different phases. There was a catechizing and civilizing phase from the 16th to 19th centuries, a positivist phase in the first half of the 20th century followed by a Protestant phase in the early years of the Military Dictatorship (1964 to 1985), a phase of indigenous mobilization and conquest of rights in the period from 1970 to 1988, and a phase of constructing and implementing specific schools and differentiated curricula in the post-Federal Constitution period of 1988 (Leite, 2014).

Thus, the recent historical period characterized by public school education policies aimed at valuing and respecting the ethnic and linguistic diversity of indigenous peoples in Brazil dates back approximately three decades. During this period, the Brazilian Federal Constitution has guaranteed intercultural pedagogy and differentiated school education for indigenous peoples through legal regulations such as the basic frameworks of National Education (Brazil, 1996), the National Education Council recommendations (Brazil, 1999), and the National Curriculum Framework for Indigenous Schools (Brazil, 2012). However, despite the legal provision for indigenous people's education rights with their own curricula, the predominance of educational institutions grounded around colonialist practices that do not prioritize local languages and knowledge is noted within indigenous communities.

Overcoming the colonialist aspects of schools (i.e. favouring exclusive teaching of the Portuguese language and Eurocentric mathematics) has been achieved by local people through the support of training courses held by indigenous teachers that are promoted by at least twenty federal or state public universities throughout the national territory. These courses are based on guidelines from the National Council of Education and are funded by the Program of Support for the Higher Education of Indigenous Teachers (PROLIND).[6] Consequently, new curricula including pedagogical practices have been autonomously designed by indigenous teachers and their communities, focusing on the necessary appreciation of local knowledge, cultural identities, languages and epistemologies.

The case of the Paiter indigenous people in the Brazilian Amazon

As an example of the current phase of Brazilian indigenous school education, we can quote the case of the Paiter (Leite, 2014). The Paiter people currently live in the Sete de Setembro Indigenous Land, located at the border between

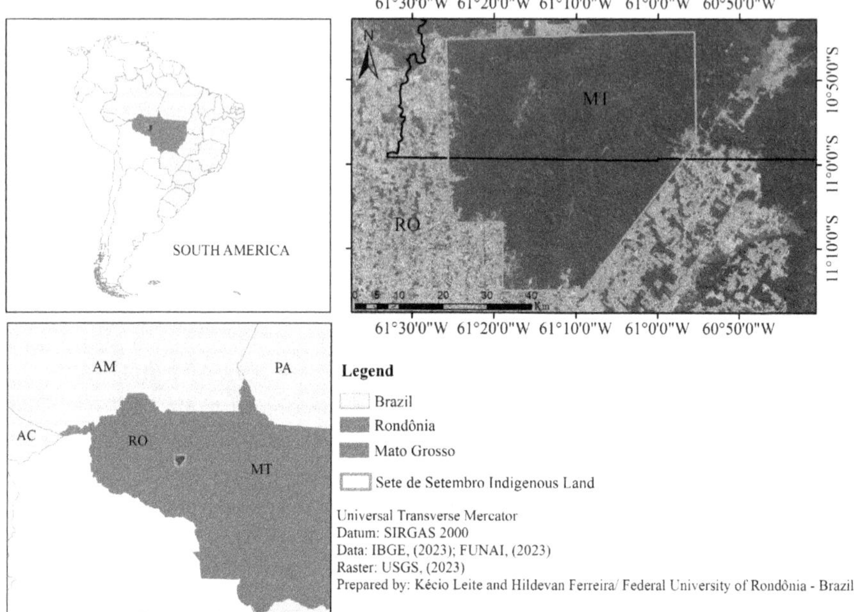

Figure 13.1 Sete de Setembro Indigenous Land, located on the border between the states of Rondônia and Mato Grosso, in the Amazon region of northern Brazil. © Kécio Leite & Hildevan Ferreira

the states of Rondônia and Mato Grosso, in the Amazon region of northern Brazil (*cf.* Figure 13.1). Organized by the clan, they are composed of four subgroups that speak a language from the Tupi trunk of the Mondé family. With a population of 1375 people, they are distributed in 27 villages, concentrated on the margins of the territory, strategically located to prevent invasion by non-indigenous people.

The official contact of the Paiter people with the non-indigenous society took place in 1969, when they met, inside the forest, an expedition of employees of the National Indian Foundation (FUNAI) (Mindlin, 1985) and since then many changes impacted these people's lives. Some changes were brought as the effect of establishing institutions such as churches and schools in the Paiter territory while others were due to emerging economic relations with non-indigenous people. Betty Mindlin, at the University of São Paulo (USP), was the first researcher to live with the Paiter and has reported changes in people's lives as a result of the collision with the economic frontier expanded by the business occupation of the Amazon. She writes:

> In 1979, they used almost no money, food was traditional, and there were few industrialized goods. From 1981 onwards, they became small producers of coffee for the market (they inherited the farmed coffee

plots from the invaders who were expelled), although they continued with their previous economic activities, festivals and rituals. The working time increased a lot. Several Suruí already had bank accounts, and consumption habits were changing.

(Mindlin, 1985, p. 15, our translation)

As mentioned by Mindlin, Paiter people went through varied transformations soon after the initial contact, mainly due to social, economic, and environmental changes to which the Northern region of Brazil was subjected. The greatest impact came from the opening of the Cuiabá-Porto Velho highway (currently BR-364) due to policies aiming at expanding national industry markets. In particular, the highway increased access to raw materials from the Amazon for industrial purposes, and enabled mobility from the coast to the Amazon region. Triggering an accelerated deforestation in Rondônia from the 1970s onwards.[7] For the Paiter, these changes meant seeing their territory invaded and having their own physical existence threatened, by loggers, miners, rubber tappers and landowners that brought unknown diseases. In 1974 alone, half of the Paiter population died of measles and the flu. The invading settlers were only completely expelled from the territory in 1981, as a result of struggles by the Paiter (Mindlin, 1985).

Despite the changes that took place after the contact, the Paiter are currently an example of indigenous resistance and rapid social, political, and economic reorganization to face the pressures of capitalist society. They managed to maintain the territory, preserve language, and guarantee physical existence, going from 272 people in 1979 (Mindlin, 1985) to a current population of 1375 people. It is in this movement that, despite having their territory invaded by settlers, exploited by loggers and miners, the Paiter are managing to build authentic projects[8] that could even be exemplary for other spaces and indigenous territories. On the educational front, most villages currently have a public school where indigenous teachers work, along with non-indigenous teachers. The Paiter are gradually managing to advance towards a differentiated indigenous school education, making use of the training of their teachers through Magisterium and Intercultural Licensing courses organized in/by local public universities (Federal University of Rondônia, State of Mato Grosso University). Roughly half of the 43 Paiter teachers have completed the training required to teach in the final years of elementary and high school allowing to progressively replace non-indigenous teachers. This is related to decolonial policies and legislation in Brazil from the 2000s onwards that seek to guarantee the ethnic, linguistic and cultural identities of indigenous students and their communities. Such decolonial processes are argued as being part of Paiter people's access to citizenship by requiring and gaining their right to education. In the specific case of indigenous people at Rondônia state, public selection processes have been implemented to hire exclusively indigenous teachers since 2015 (see: https://acervo.socioambiental.org/acervo/noticias/rondonia-realiza-1o-concurso-para-professor-indigena-do-estado).

After five decades of living and experiencing the cultural transformations resulting from neo-colonization processes, Paiter teachers currently find themselves in tension as they face the demands for, on the one hand, appropriating practical and theoretical knowledge coming from conduct with the non-indigenous society and, on the other, maintaining people's cultural identity. In this context, Paiter teachers promote traditional mathematical knowledge by drawing on both their continuing education mathematical content and local knowledge preserved orally by village elders.

Challenges of including local mathematical knowledge in the Paiter's school education

Paiter teachers seek to rethink local school education by valuing what is characteristic of their people's culture. Since 2009, and as part of their Intercultural (continuing) Education, they have carried out research on their traditional knowledge. Their research goal is to revise school curricula to align it with the local cultural reality and incorporate villages' traditions (*cf.* Figure 13.2). At the same time, Paiter teachers consider the general national curricular guidelines as necessary for surviving within the whole Brazilian society. In their university training, Paiter teachers have encountered the field of research in

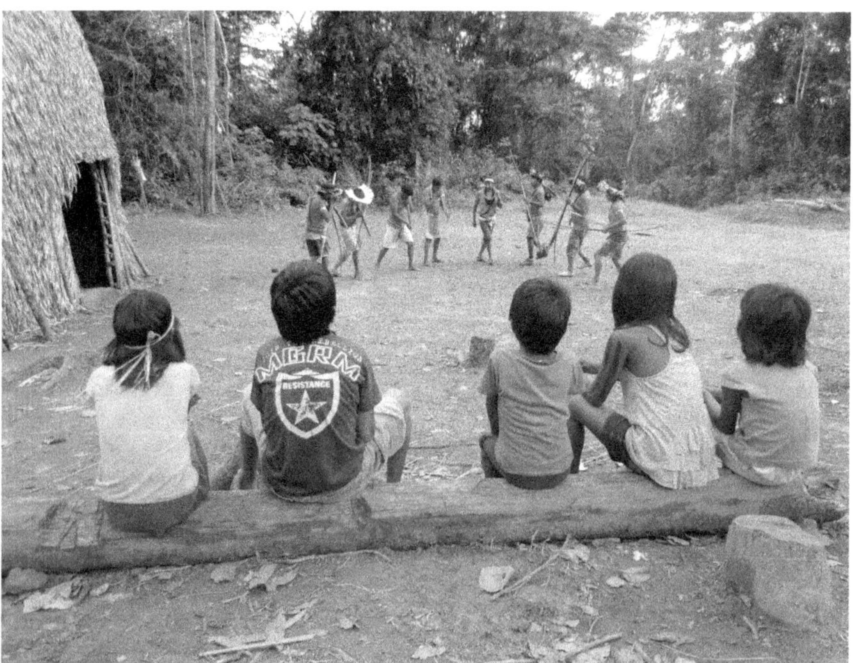

Figure 13.2 Paiter students observe their elders in cultural activities in the Gapgir village of the Sete de Setembro Indigenous Land. © Kécio Leite 2014.

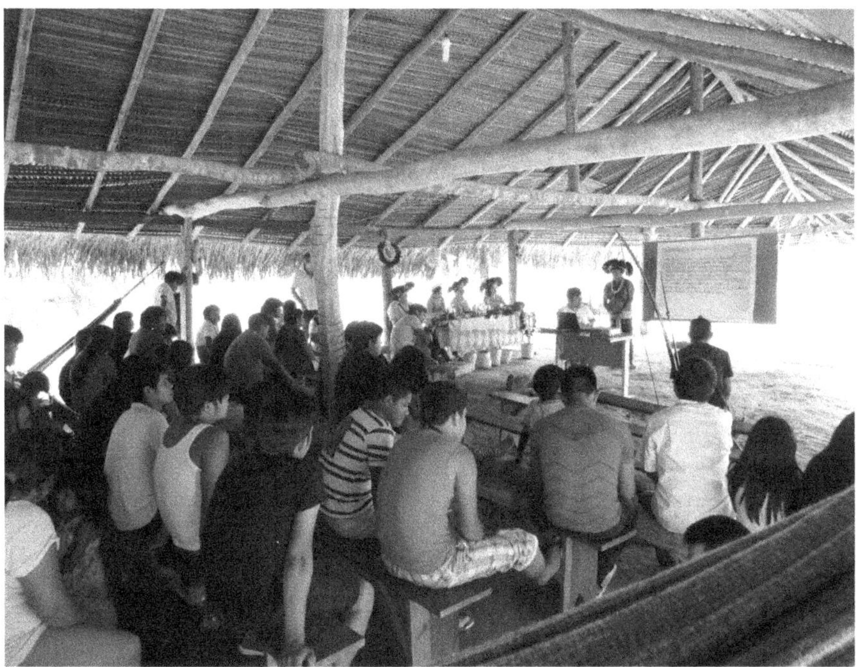

Figure 13.3 Communication by Teacher Suruí of his research's results on local Paiter knowledge, and mathematical knowledge in particular. Public session presented to other members of the Lapetanha village, Sete de Setembro Indigenous Land. © Kécio Leite 2015.

ethnomathematics (D'Ambrosio, 2001). Consequently, some of them have undertaken research to record mathematical practices of their people (e.g. quantifiers, geometric qualifiers, calendars and measurement systems (*cf.* A. P. Suruí, 2015; Mi Suruí, 2016, 2021; Mo Suruí, 2015) and to present outcomes to the local communities (*cf.* Figure 13.3).

These investigations show that Paiter people have a counting system to represent quantities between one and twenty (*mũy* "one", *xakalar* "two", *xakalar amakab om* "three", *xakalar itxer* "four", *mũy pabe* "five" ...). Although it is an oral numerical system, each number can be displayed using fingers or toes. In addition to quantifiers, the Paiter also have a set of terms to express the mathematical characteristics of artifacts (such as braids, paintings ...) regarding their geometric shapes (*patakap ah* "circle", *yapeh ipo* "triangle", *txakaah* "square", *txakaah atoah* "rectangle"), sizes and relative positions.

Moreover, the Paiter use a complex system of time markers based on natural phenomena (stars, behaviour of animals and plants ...) that allows them to implement a cyclical calendar through three interrelated dimensions (social, natural, and spiritual). Each dimension has specific markers that characterize the beginning and end of their respective phases. The phases of the temporal cycle in each of the three dimensions are organized from two main parts, marked by the rainy season and the dry season that characterize the hydrological regime of the Amazon region.[9] The time markers operate on different scales, ranging from a few minutes to several days, weeks, or even longer cycles equivalent to decades. Finally, the Paiter have a specific measurement system (based on measurement units such as distance between two given houses or a village and a big tree) allowing them to locate a fruit tree in the middle of the forest, as well as to estimate the distance between a village and a hunting ground.

Identifying these local mathematical knowledge and practices has led the Paiter to realize that mathematics does not exclusively come from Europe or the non-indigenous Brazilian society. Consequently, the village schools were encouraged to recognize and include such knowledge in the curriculum for educating future indigenous generations. This is, indeed, a political act aiming at revitalizing Paiter culture and identity (Leite, 2014). The collaborative research of one the authors (Kécio Leite) with the Paiter analyses the discourses employed by indigenous teachers to understand the relationship among local mathematical knowledge, worldviews, school curriculum, social organization and ethnicity. Indeed, the inclusion of local mathematics creates a perspective of differentiation, in relation to curriculum mathematics called "school mathematics" (*i.e.*, perceived as the mathematics brought by Portuguese colonizers). On the one hand, the Paiter recognize the need to master school mathematics as an empowerment strategy in the context of a non-indigenous society, but, on the other hand, they develop their own conception of ethnomathematics that appeals to a memory-work of traditional mathematical knowledge. In this context, ethnomathematics has become a construct claimed by the Paiter, rather than being simply a construct attributed by some external observer to their cultural identity.

Culturally based education in Vanuatu, South Pacific

Vanuatu is a Melanesian archipelago located in the South Pacific Ocean. It comprises 83 dispersed islands with a total area of 12,281 square kilometres, spread out over 1,300 kilometres (Figure 13.4). Its current population is estimated at 301,695 inhabitants and has an average annual growth rate of 2.4%. Around 75% of the population lives in rural areas, primarily with a subsistence lifestyle through a self-sustaining economy (Vanuatu National Statistics Office [VNSO], 2020a). Once known as the French and English Condominium of New Hebrides (established in 1906), Vanuatu achieved its political independence in 1980.

Here, we explore current issues emerging from using traditional knowledge in Vanuatu's education system by, first, outlining the introduction of vernacular languages in early childhood education for enhancing children's

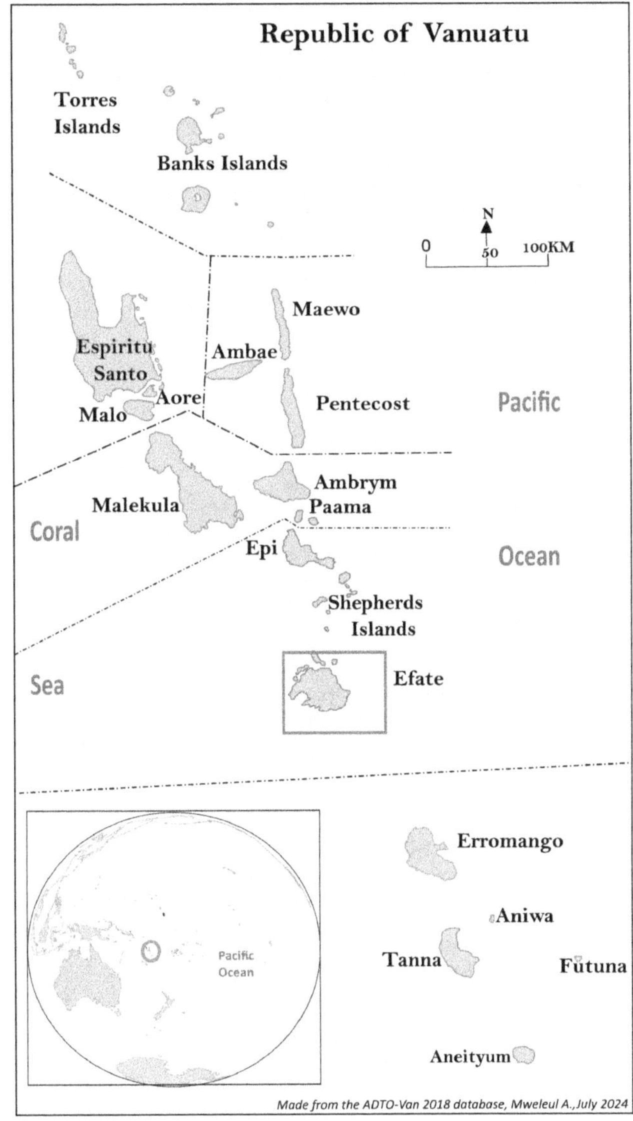

Figure 13.4 Map of the Republic of Vanuatu. © Adeline Mweleul.

literacy skills and, second, presenting a recent pedagogical experiment based on "sand drawing"—an emblematic cultural practice from Vanuatu (*cf.* Figure 13.5.)—for expanding mathematical skills at the secondary level. Both examples are components of a local culture-based curriculum considered to be part of Vanuatu's declining heritage due to the effects of colonization and globalization.

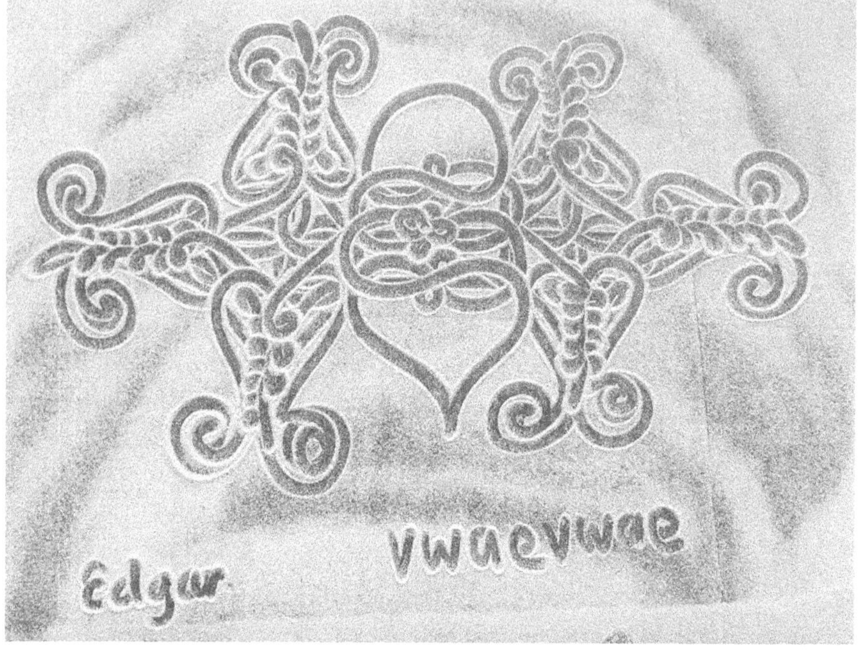

Figure 13.5 Sand drawing *vwaevwae* "a particular yam, a root crop" (performed by Edgar Hinge). © Pierre Metsan.

Language, "Kastom", and education in Vanuatu

The archipelago of Vanuatu has the earth's highest ratio of vernacular languages in relation to its population size—over 120 different languages, all belonging to the Austronesian family (François et al., 2015). The Ni-Vanuatu Constitution intends to protect all these languages in use in the country, considering that they contribute to the emergence of a national identity, by reassembling all cultural groups as a nation. However, English, French, and Vanuatu's *lingua franca* (pidgin language) Bislama, are the three Ni-Vanuatu "official" languages. Although English and French remain the principal languages of education, as a heritage from both the Condominium and the influence of Catholic, Presbyterian, and Anglican missions for centuries, Bislama has become the national idiom widely spoken by all Vanuatu people. Children generally learn Bislama before schooling—in parallel to their mother tongue—and begin learning either English or French in elementary school (MOE, 2012). Indeed, as the 2021 Vanuatu Well-Being report indicates, over 80% of the population assimilate indigenous vernacular languages as their first language (VNSO, 2020b). This occurs mainly in rural areas, whereas in the two main urban centres—Port Vila and Luganville—Bislama has become the mother tongue for many children.

The various vernacular languages in use in the country are part of what Vanuatu people refer to as "*Kastom*" (in Bislama); "a word that people in Vanuatu use to characterize their own knowledge and practice in distinction to everything they identify as having come from outside their place" (Bolton, 2003, p. xiii). *Kastom* is thus locally conceptualized as "the [...] roots/foundation of cultures/traditions [...] related to land, language, wisdom and identity" (Huffman, 2017). Traditional knowledge is transmitted orally and strengthened through various socio-cultural practices (rituals, cultural events/festivals, traditional technical/artisanal activities, etc., VNSO, 2020b). The Vanuatu Cultural Center is the national institution that works for the preservation and promotion of the different aspects of Ni-Vanuatu's cultures. Over the past decades, through increasing recognition of the destructive impact of colonization and globalization on Ni-Vanuatu's *Kastom*, there has been a renewed interest in—as well as a "reconstruction" of—"traditional" knowledge, involved in arts, education, economy, and formal ceremony. Interestingly, in 1981, a network of fieldworkers, consisting of a hundred male and female volunteers having a good knowledge of their own (micro-)society's culture, was created through the "Vanuatu Cultural Center field worker program". Throughout the archipelago, these fieldworkers have endeavoured to document *Kastom* practices, in their own villages and/or cultural areas, and meet annually to discuss and share their findings (Bolton, 2007, p. 24).

Since the early 2010s, the Republic of Vanuatu has undertaken a reform of the national education curriculum inherited from the colonial period. The new curriculum strongly prescribes to consider the various local cultures, including the different vernacular languages (MOE, 2010). The latter were recognized under the Vanuatu National Language Policy (VNLP) in 2012 (*cf.* MOE, 2012), and introduced in the education system at the early schooling level. The idea behind this is that using mother tongue languages in the classroom should enhance greater effective learning including reading and writing (Walter & Chuo, 2012) aligned to the new international paradigm of "Mother Tongue Based Multilingual Education" (Early, 2019). Today, Ni-Vanuatu pupils from grade 1 (6-year-old) to grade 3 (9-year-old) are taught in local vernacular languages in the rural areas (or "Islands") and in Bislama in the two main urban centres Port-Vila and Luganville, while all children transit progressively to French or English in grade 4 (MOET, 2021; *cf. ademap lanwis* "add up languages gradually" program; Vanuatu Education Support Program, 2017).

In Vanuatu, the recognition of vernacular languages' importance in early childhood education has led to an in-depth revision of the inherited colonial education (MOE, 2010). However, despite promising research outcomes regarding the use of vernacular languages in the process of teaching and learning in Vanuatu and beyond (Early, 2021), significant cultural, identitarian and learning challenges have been reported (National University of Vanuatu, 2021). The gradual transition from vernacular language to English or French is still a matter of debate within the MOE, the Catholic Education Authority and teachers. For instance, when different cultural communities live next to each other sharing same schools,[10] some teachers perceive the risk of undermining the pedagogical use of less dominant languages. Moreover, some francophone teachers worry about the fact that the use of the official French language is nowadays in decline throughout the country, and believe that mother tongue language education, and particularly Bislama, might aggravate this phenomenon. Finally, some local teachers consider that there is still a lack of continuing training courses on the topic, as well as relevant educational resources to implement such vernacular education in the country (McCarter & Gavin, 2011).

According to Chief Willy Bongmatur, the first president of the Council of Chiefs of Vanuatu (the *Malfatu Mauri*)[11] "Modern education produces knowledge, but it must be in harmony with ***kastom***, that is to say traditional education, otherwise the child is raised without acquiring wisdom, respect and recognition of his identity" (Huffman, 2017). While pointing out a possible tension between "modern" and "traditional" education in Vanuatu, Chief Bongmatur, thus suggests that what is at stake here is to balance the two different western and traditional educational systems. Considering that both of which are essential for the Ni-Vanuatu children's intellectual development, it is stated that

> The emphasis in this essentially cross curriculum component is on:
>
> -traditional forms of communication such as dance forms, masks, costumes and body painting, drumming and sand drawing and
>
> -current forms of communication using various technologies such as mobile phones and other media.
>
> (MOE, 2010, p. 34)

In that perspective, and in addition to vernacular languages' use, the Vanuatu National Curriculum Statement explicitly encourages Ni-Vanuatu educators to promote performing cultures. As previously seen, this policy enactment remains challenging, partly due to the lack of specific training designed for Ni-Vanuatu educators. Nevertheless, the integration of cultural practices is clearly mentioned for reaffirming Vanuatu's identity. In this sense, the use of emblematic cultural activities (such as "sand drawing", *cf.* below) becomes a means of creating citizenship consciousness among Ni-Vanuatu people as will be seen below.

Ethnomathematics and teachers' training in Vanuatu

The national curriculum emphasizes mathematics for developing "skills that could help students to confidently cope with daily life. Children and students should also appreciate aspects of ethnomathematics, which includes the wider use of mathematics in different cultures. They should be encouraged to find out where and how mathematics is applied in their local community" (MOE, 2010, p. 60). Consequently, "traditional" knowledge (i.e. myths, rituals, storytelling, making of artifacts, etc.) transmission from elder to younger generations is encouraged. Introducing ethnomathematics is, however, a complex process (Rosa et al., 2017) and its novelty and peculiarity may require specific training (Orey & Rosa, 2006). For this reason and supported by the School of Education (SOE) mathematics department, lecturer Georges Tauanearu has recently introduced an ethnomathematics course in the preservice teachers' training program. Three basic steps are organized around ethnomathematics projects; (a) engaging students in a review of ethnomathematics literature; (b) exploring the pedagogical interest of local mathematical practices such as sand drawing, mat weaving, basketry, and traditional counting systems; and (c) encouraging Ni-Vanuatu preservice mathematics teachers to not only investigate mathematical concepts developed in own their culture, but also to undertake ethnomathematics research and, thus, becoming researchers during their teaching career path.

In Tauanearu's view, prompting mathematics teachers to master Ni-Vanuatu traditional knowledge as part of preservice training should support developing local curricula. Indeed, some Tauanearu's students have already worked in that perspective. For instance, once appointed at Topol High School, North Ambrym, mathematics teacher Frederick Worwor has experimented with sand drawing and string figure-making in the mathematics classroom by documenting student responses, while acknowledging the need for more elaborate research (Vandendriessche, 2022). Given students' poor performance on Ni-Vanuatu National mathematics examinations (MOET, 2021) showing 50% of secondary students not mastering basic skills, the MOE intends to remedy this damaging image for the country. And among the planned aims is to go forward with the idea of anchoring the mathematics curriculum in Ni-Vanuatu *Kastom*.

Toward this, the co-author Pierre Metsan has undertaken a pre-post experimental study, as part of his PhD thesis, to map the effectiveness of using sand drawings for learning mathematics at Port-Vila urban schools where local practices decline. The main research question guiding the study is whether and how a long-term regular pedagogical use of sand drawing practices could enhance engagement and academic achievement in mathematics. Methodologically, the randomized treatment trial method (Banerjee & Duflo, 2009) was employed to allocate students in experimental and control groups, the culturally responsive teaching of mathematics models (Averill et al., 2009) and student data concerning achievement and motivation were collected through questionnaires.

Sand drawing practices in the classroom

With origins at the archipelago's centre, the sand drawing practice consists of "drawing a continuous line with the finger, either in the sand or on dusty ground—generally drawn through the framework of a grid made of perpendicular lines, without retracing any part of the drawing" (Vandendriessche, 2022). The ingenious and complex "geometrical" patterns produced through sand drawing were -and sometimes still are—used in daily life as means of communication.

They are often accompanied by traditional tales or songs and are important for memorizing and transmitting cultural knowledge (Rory, 2013).

Sand drawing practices have been first documented by British anthropologist Arthur Bernard Deacon in the 1920s (Deacon & Wedgwood, 1934). On the basis of Deacon's findings, and recent fieldworks in different Ni-Vanuatu societies/communities, some ethnomathematicians and educators have highlighted the mathematical nature of sand drawing (Ascher, 1991; Vandendriessche & Da Silva, 2022) and its pedagogical potential for producing didactic resources in the national curriculum (Hinge, 2008; Rory et al., 2008).

The classroom experiment consists of a team of seven mathematics teachers working in five different secondary schools in Port Vila. The teachers were selected according to their interest in culturally based education and their team includes a Ni-Vanuatu expert in sand drawing, namely Edgar Hinge (member of the Vanuatu Cultural Center) and a mathematics lecturer Georges Tauanearu. A total of 575 secondary students in both year 8 (13-year-old) and year 9 (14-year-old) were selected randomly to participate in the four-month-long experiment. One hour a week was allocated for sand drawing activities, as part of the official curriculum, with 296 students assigned to the experimental group while the remaining 279 constituted the control group.

One month before launching this experimental study, several workshops were organized to elaborate a pedagogical plan and a questionnaire was distributed to all participating students (i.e. experimental and control group) inquiring knowledge about sand drawing practice and perceived links with mathematical concepts. All team members practiced several sand drawing patterns chosen for their ethnomathematical interest (i.e. geometrical figures, symmetry, perpendicular and parallel lines, curves, angles, numbers, procedures, algorithms). Based on the above, a lesson plan and teaching resources were compiled. The lesson plan comprised three parts: (a) an introduction by Edgar Hinge who drew a particular drawing on the sand drawing board (*cf.* Figure 13.6) whose performance was accompanied with a song and/or story related to the sand drawing in question outlining the local cultural context (e.g. societies, location, vernacular languages); (b) discussions between mathematics educators and students regarding the possible links between the sand drawing features and mathematical concepts that unfolded into individual and group work for learning to reproduce the sand drawing; and (c) discussion groups organized for carrying out an in-depth analysis of the algorithm leading to the final geometrical drawing.

One session after another, we noticed the students' increasing interest in practicing sand drawings along with discussing their mathematical characteristics. For instance, students were asked to explain particular sand drawing patterns in relation to congruent triangles while some teachers noticed that the sand drawing experiment seems to raise students' engagement and motivation in practicing mathematics. This point has been confirmed through data collection with the QASAM questionnaire (*i.e.* an instrument for the assessment of students' socio-affective attitudes towards mathematics, *cf.*

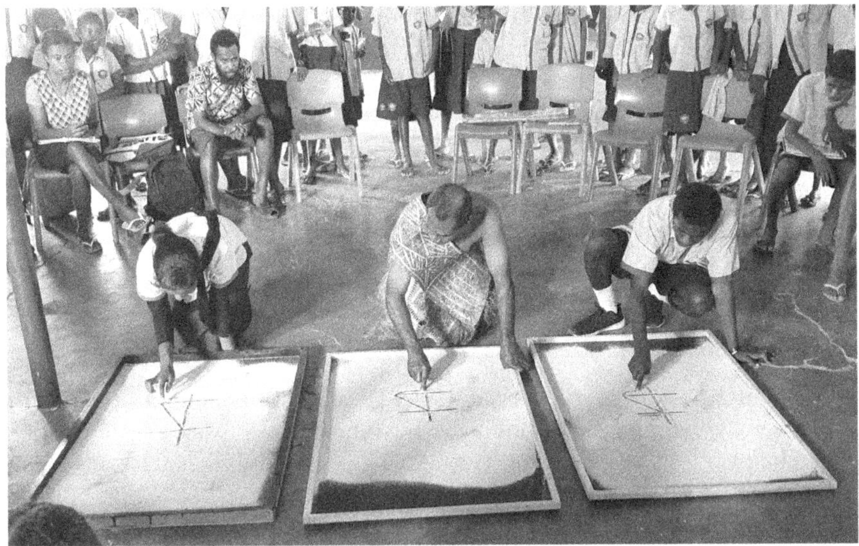

Figure 13.6 Sand drawing experiment session, "Centre-Ville" School, Port Vila, Vanuatu. © Pierre Metsan.

Genoud & Guillod, 2014) employed to assess whether the regular practice of sand drawing had any impact for student socio-affective attitudes towards mathematics. Of course, we are aware that a longer-period experiment should be necessary to confirm primary outcomes—already planned for gaining credible outcomes. At a qualitative level of analysis, interestingly, we have noticed that, during and beyond the four-month experiment, the sand drawing practice was, spontaneously, used to introduce key geometrical concepts, such as symmetry, plane transformations or isometric/similar/particular triangles. This becomes indicative of Ni-Vanuatu teachers being able to capture the pedagogical potential of mathematical concepts in sand drawings. This unexpected outcome is of fundamental interest and could lead to future research investigations. Developing and theorizing such experiments could be a way to revitalize endangered cultural knowledge and practices in the school context. In the long term, and concomitantly, similar studies shall be conducted in rural areas schools where the population is still actively engaged in "traditional" cultural practices (Vandendriessche, 2022).

Discussion

The examined cases note how curricula aligned with ethnomathematics are currently tried in contrasted ways in two culturally and geographically distant societies. Let us now outline commonalities and differences across these two cases including evidence of tension concerning "local" versus "global" education in these contexts.

The first contact between the Paiter and non-indigenous people is relatively recent, dating back to just over 50 years, unlike many other indigenous Brazilian populations. Thus, the Paiter people maintained their own traditions and culture for more than five centuries since the arrival of Portuguese colonizers. By contrast, many Europeans have settled the New Hebrides Archipelago, the actual Vanuatu, from the 18th century (Thomas, 2010). These historical differences reflect different insider perceptions of (1) local traditions, (2) language preservations, (3) local and global curricula, and (4) teacher education, from one case to the other.

Local conceptualization of "Traditions"

In Vanuatu, the concept of "*kastom*" (*cf.* subsection *Language, "Kastom", and education in Vanuatu*) was originally introduced by missionaries and colonial administrators to designate (through a global and undervalued meaning) everything which does not come (in their views) from Europe. This concept has thereafter been central, and remodelled, by nationalist leaders, engaged in independence movements (from the 1960s onwards) in the New Hebrides (Vanuatu since 1980), and more generally in Melanesia. Indeed, it is through a revalorization of the so-called traditional cultures that these leaders aimed to develop a nationalist consciousness (Wittersheim, 1999) among New Hebrides peoples, for becoming citizens of a new nation. Consequently, in the 1980s–1990s, some anthropologists (Babadzan, 1999; Keesing, 1982) analysed the "*kastom*" as an "invented tradition" (*cf.* Hobsbawm & Ranger, 1983) by the nationalists in particular. However, it is rather through the re-interpretation of knowledge and practices inherited from the colonial period, combined with those considered as more authentic/traditional that "*kastom*" has locally become a shared concept, constituting nowadays, for Ni-Vanuatu peoples, "their culture" (Jolly, 1992).

As previously seen, a sense of hybrid identity composed of national and cultural elements develops through the recognition of emblematic practices such as sand drawings in particular. At the same time, practices and knowledge belonging to the "*kastom*" (such as dances, mat making, house building, local medicines, cooking) are perceived as having distinct features from one micro-society to another. Under the incentive of the Vanuatu Cultural Center, local people have been engaged in fieldwork aiming at collecting data to preserve this cultural diversity (Tryon, 1999). Concurrently, previous ethnographic studies (Deacon & Wedgwood, 1934; Layard, 1942, et al.) have been used in an attempt to relearn what had been lost (Rory et al., 2008).

The Paiter's everyday life has changed significantly since the very first contact with the non-indigenous (1969), due to launching institutions such as churches and schools in their territory and, consequently, Paiter people claim to be struggling for preserving their cultural knowledge or "traditions". Unlike Vanuatu, the notion of "tradition" has not been used by any nationalist movement, but, instead, as a way to make Indigenous societies more visible in Brazil and to recognize the great diversity of native cultures. Besides this, the Paiter use the concept of "tradition" to differentiate themselves from other indigenous or non-indigenous people. It is noteworthy that "Paiter" means "ourselves" or "people" in the Tupi Mondé language, which can be seen as an ethnic or cultural differentiation (Mindlin, 1985). Finally, Paiter people, as well as each indigenous people in Brazil, have obtained a legal status recognizing them as "people" (*status de povo*) on identified territory and with specific traditions (i.e. vernacular languages, cosmologies, rituals, local practices, and social organizations).

In Vanuatu, the valorization of cultural practices (such as sand drawing) must be understood as participating in building citizenship consciousness at the national level, through the recognition of traditional practices as being emblematic of the Vanuatu Republic. Among the Paiter, by contrast, similar processes of valorization are conceived to strengthen a perceived as declining local identity due to recent contact with non-indigenous Brazilian people.

Language diversity and preservation

In Brazil, during the colonial period (1500s–1822) and until the 1980s, it was common to ban vernacular language use in Indigenous schools (Neves, 2009) based on policies for Portuguese as the official language (Oliveira & Freire, 2006). In 1988, the Federal Constitution recognized bilingual education as a right for indigenous peoples (Constituição, 1988) but without making it obligatory. Today, however, local/vernacular languages are being accepted as language of instruction in Indigenous schools and especially for early years schooling. And, since the 2000s, training courses designed specifically for indigenous teachers have significantly contributed to such language policy change (Leite, 2014). In contrast, in Vanuatu, the national policy imposes the use of vernacular local languages (or mother tongue) for reading and writing in the early years of elementary education. However, its implementation has entailed discontent among local teachers who note children losing language competency in French or English—the two languages used for formal instruction in the archipelago for more than a century, and in which these teachers have been educated.

Indeed, in both contexts, language issues remain one of the main challenges faced in curricular proposals. In Brazil, bilingualism (i.e., simultaneous use of the vernacular mother tongue and Portuguese) remains complex for the mathematics curriculum as it requires the concept translation between Portuguese and indigenous languages. In practice, this translation process generally occurs through interpretations utilizing neologisms and/or linguistic borrowings that could create epistemological conflicts (Leite & Camargos, 2021). In Vanuatu, although similar lexical issues are raised, the main issue relates to the large number of vernacular languages and to policy requirements for using them as resources following the National curriculum demands. In that perspective, the MOE has already undertaken the huge task of translating textbooks in about 80 different vernacular languages despite the fact that there are not yet translations in numerous dialectal variants of Ni-Vanuatu vernacular languages. Thus, there is an obvious risk of standardization of these languages that generally differ slightly from one another even in two neighbouring villages. This issue has been locally discussed (e.g. within the "Curriculum Development Unit", Ni-Vanuatu MOE) and the importance for pedagogical practices that could support preserving linguistic richness has been argued.

National versus local curriculum

Although Brazil is a large country with a great cultural and geographical diversity, the Brazilian case discusses the Paiter—an ethnic group of about 1,400 indigenous people in the northern region of the country. In turn, the case of Vanuatu—a much smaller country- is presented by analyzing its national policy. In both cases, educational policies aiming for creating locally based curricula are a recent phenomenon during the last three decades. Still, they take place in diverse historical contexts that entail subtle differences across countries. Whilst Vanuatu has implemented a top-down "National" cultural education policy as part of the *Vanuatu National Curriculum Statement* (MOE, 2010), Brazil resorts to General National curricular guidelines for indigenous education (Brazil, 2012) that develop locally indigenous educational policies. Specifically, the Paiter indigenous teachers autonomously design their own new curricula and pedagogical practices.

Teacher education and ethnomathematics

In both contexts, there is concern with the training of teachers who work in indigenous schools. For the past ten years, Paiter teachers, as well as other indigenous teachers in Brazil, were assigned continuing education organized by public universities, such as the *Licenciatura Intercultural Indígena* of the Federal University of Rondônia (UNIR). Similarly, in Vanuatu, a national incentive invites teachers to participate in the current national curriculum reform so as to include their local cultural renewals. Interestingly, however, in both contexts, preservice mathematics teachers are introduced to the field of ethnomathematics, through specific training courses. Indeed, many studies (Blanco-Álvarez & Molano-Franco, 2021; Soares & Fantinato, 2021, et al.) have highlighted the positive role of ethnomathematics in teacher education, in search of an education that promotes intercultural dialogue. Research in this latter topic (Monteiro, 2018; Trinick & Meaney, 2020, et al.) has been already conducted in diverse parts of the world (e.g. Brazil and New Zealand) sharing similar concerns for revitalizing local knowledge and language.

In the two cases discussed here, preservice and inservice teachers are introduced to ethnomathematics first through reviewing the domain's literature, from the founders of the discipline to more recent contributions and, in addition, they are encouraged to undertake fieldwork in local communities. As part of their continuing training courses and beyond, Paiter teachers carry out research in their villages with the aim to collect and analyse local cultural knowledge including mathematics. Such procedures have been developed at the School of Education in Vanuatu where lecturer Georges Tauanearu's students are prompted to look for local mathematical knowledge at their appointment to schools in rural areas (or "Islands"), often irrespective of their native origin. By contrast, Paiter teachers are being asked to carry out research of the "endo-ethnography" or "anthropology at home" type (Jackson, 1987) as they study their own culture.

In these research studies, it is noted how elders' knowledge and memory is transmitted through orality and creates an important dialogue between "local" and "global" mathematics in the school curriculum. Among the Paiter, elders from different villages were interviewed by the local teachers, in order to identify how their mathematical knowledge is being embedded in varied traditional activities related to counting, measurements and geometry (Suruí & Leite, 2018). Similarly, the *Vanuatu National Curriculum Statement* (MOE, 2010) encourages the elders' involvement for transmitting local knowledge (i.e. making artifacts, rituals, dances, etc.) to youth in each cultural area of the archipelago.

Conclusions

Reforms concerning culturally and locally based mathematics curricula in the context of globalization, as discussed here, are crossed by diverse tensions. Among the Paiter, cultural transformations and the resulting tensions grow due to recent contact with the surrounding world. In their pedagogical practices, Paiter teachers constantly deal with the challenge of combining Western and vernacular knowledge without losing local traditions. Attempts to include local knowledge in the curriculum fostered by academic studies in the area of ethnomathematics has been conceived as a strategy to strengthen the Paiter identity. Paiter teachers seek to transform the "School" (an institution brought by colonization) into a space that revitalizes indigenous culture and for such a project ethnomathematics is useful.

In Vanuatu, although similar arguments are put forward, this happens mainly through a top-down national curriculum directive. In this case, the consciousness of a national identity emerges partly from the recognition of "emblematic" Ni-Vanuatu practices such as sand drawing. This mostly occurs in urban centres, where mixed cultural groups live, even though, more generally, local education is implemented in "rural" areas by focusing on vernacular languages. Interestingly, and unlike the present Brazilian case, it is assumed that a locally based mathematics curriculum might help to increase both students' interest and skills in academic mathematics. Furthermore, they attempt to make the "proof of concept" using a standardized scientific methodology, applying statistical tests on quantitative data collected during educational experiments. Although questionable, such a methodology has already been used in other cultural contexts (Lipka & Adams, 2004), and has led, indeed, to interesting results. However, we suggest crossing the outcomes of this type of research with the methodology used by ethnologists, i.e., "participant observation" to highlight qualitative information concerning student learning.

As previously mentioned, in Vanuatu, practices such as sand drawing are perceived as declining by local practitioners due to oppression by colonizing and globalizing processes. Concurrently, utilizing ethnomathematical practices in the formal education system should obviously contribute in reconstructing and transforming these practices "through inputs" from academic mathematics, first inherited from the colonial times, and, nowadays, by the global world. It is definitely an unavoidable and worldwide dynamic process in which diverse minority communities, like the Paiter, "learn more about" their "mathematical practices" as they take "advantages in broadening their sense of 'ethno' to include changes that take place outside their cultures" (Rivera & Becke, 2007, p. 219).

Both cases thus share the goal of educating new generations while preserving "traditional" cultures and for this, including the local mathematical knowledge in the school curriculum becomes a vital tool. As seen throughout this chapter, the mathematics of local cultures is being perceived as cultivating a sense of identity within the Indigenous communities. At the same time, indigenous people become increasingly aware that mathematics has not exclusively come from the "outside" through the colonization/globalization process, but it can also belong to their local culture.

Acknowledgements

We warmly thank the Paiter people, their communities and teachers from the Gapgir, Lobó, Lapetanha, Joaquim, Amaral, the North Pentecost Chief Edgar Hinge, the Ni-Vanuatu teachers, and all students, involved in the sand drawing experiment. We are also grateful to the reviewers, the editors of the present volume for valuable suggestions and Philippe Bordaz for his careful proofreading.

Notes

1 We understand interculturality in the sense given by Catherine Walsh (2009), of a critical pedagogy, in which the hegemonic and dominant knowledge is questioned, and not simply uncritically assimilated. The decolonial turn in curricula implies not only taking into account the denied and subordinated local histories and epistemologies, but also a search for dialogical connections with what is understood by global knowledge.

2 In this text, we will preferably use the term "Paiter", which is how this indigenous group calls themselves. However, Suruì is the official name given to them by the Brazilian administration.

3 In Brazil, the Law n° 8.184/1991 establishes the obligation to carry out a demographic census at least every ten years. The last indigenous census was carried out in 2010 and a new census is being carried out after 12 years. Demographic

census data are used to plan government public policies. Data collected in the demographic census on the indigenous population include, among other data, languages, ethnicities, ages, location (urban or rural).

4 By epistemicide, we understand, according to Boaventura de Souza Santos, "the political-cultural process through which the knowledge produced by subordinated social groups is killed or destroyed, as a way of maintaining or deepening this subordination" (Santos, 1998, p. 208).

5 Brazil ceased to be a Portuguese colony in 1822.

6 PROLIND is a program of the Brazilian Federal Government, created in 2008, which supports Intercultural Licentiate course projects for the training of indigenous teachers in public universities throughout the national territory.

7 It is estimated that by 1975 the area deforested in the region totaled 1,216.5 km^2, jumping to 51,000 km^2 in 1990 (Millikan, 1999), which totaled 21% of the state's total area.

8 For example, Paiter teachers Joaton Suruí and Luiz Weymilawa Suruí won, respectively, the 2010 and 2016 editions of the national award "Professor Nota Dez", promoted by the Victor Civita Foundation in Brazil, due to their specific school education projects developed in schools in the Sete de Setembro indigenous territory.

9 Events in one of the phases of a dimension affect events in other dimensions. For example, if the rainy season is prolonged or delayed, the start of the seed planting campaign is affected, as well as the performance of the rituals that precede it (Mi. Suruí, 2016, 2021).

10 For instance, it is the case in North Santo Island, where two cultural groups (the *Sakao* and Big bay people) have settled down in the Port Olry francophone catholic mission.

11 The "*Malvatu Mauri*" (National Council of Chiefs) is a formal advisory council of chiefs recognized by the Constitution of the Republic of Vanuatu (n.d.). The latter Council plays a significant role in advising the government on all matters related to Ni-Vanuatu culture and languages.

References

Alangui, W. (2010). *Stone Walls and Water Flows: Interrogating Cultural Practice and Mathematics*. PhD Thesis, Mathematics Education, University of Auckland, Auckland, New Zealand.

Ascher, M. (1991). *Ethnomathematics: A multicultural view of mathematical ideas*. Books/Cole Publishing Company.

Averill, R., Anderson, D., Easton, H., Te Maro, P., Smith, D., & Hynds, A. (2009). Culturally responsive teaching of mathematics: Three models from linked studies. *Journal for Research in Mathematics Education, 40*(2), 157–186.

Babadzan, A. (1999). L'invention des traditions et le nationalisme. *Journal de la Société des Océanistes, 109*(2), 13–35.

Banerjee, A. V., & Duflo, E. (2009). L'approche expérimentale en économie du développement. *Revue d'économie politique, 119*(5), 691–726.

Bernales, M., & Powell, A. B. (2018). Decolonizing ethnomathematics. *Ensino Em-Revista, 25*(3), 565–587.

Blanco-Álvarez, H., & Molano-Franco, E. (2021). La formación de profesores de matemáticas desde la Etnomatemática: una mirada decolonial. *Revista de Educação Matemática, 18*, 1–18.

Bolton, L. (2003). *Unfolding the moon: Enacting women's kastom in Vanuatu*. University of Hawai'i Press.

Bolton, L. (2007). Resourcing change: Fieldworkers, the Women's culture project and the Vanuatu cultural centre. In N. Stanley (Ed.), *The future of indigenous museums: Perspectives from the Southwest Pacific* (pp. 23–37). Berghahn Books.

Brazil (1996). *Lei n° 9.394, de 20 de dezembro de 1996.* Estabelece as diretrizes e bases da educação nacional. Brasília.

Brazil (1999). *Parecer CNE/CEB n° 14/1999, aprovado em 14 de setembro de 1999-* Dispõe sobre as Diretrizes Nacionais para o funcionamento das escolas indígenas. Brasília.

Brazil (2012). *Resolução CNE/CEB n° 5, de 22 de junho de 2012* - Define Diretrizes Curriculares Nacionais para a Educação Escolar Indígena na Educação Básica. Brasília.

Constituição da República Federativa do Brasil de 1988. (1988). Brasília. https://www.planalto.gov.br/ccivil_03/constituicao/constituicao.htm

Constitution of the Republic of Vanuatu. (n. d.). http://www.paclii.org/vu/legis/consol_act/cotrov406/

D'Ambrosio, U. (2001). *Ethnomatematics: Link between tradition and modernity.* Sense Publishers.

Deacon, A. B., & Wedgwood, C. H. (1934). Geometrical drawings from Malekula and other Islands of the New Hebrides. *The Journal of the Royal Anthropological Institute of Great Britain and Ireland, 64,* 129–175.

Early, R. (2019). Language policy issues. In *Research seminar proceedings: From linguistic pluralism to university bilingualism: Realities and challenges* (pp. 11–28). Ministri blong Edukesen mo Trening.

Early, R. (2021). Developments in language policy in Vanuatu. In *Proceedings of the "Education, cultures, identity" international symposium* (pp. 216–251). Vanuatu National University.

Fantinato, M. C., & Leite, K. G. (2022). Indigenous mathematical knowledge and practices: State of the art of the ethnomathematics Brazilian congresses (2000-2016). In E. Vandendriessche & R. Pinxten (Eds.), *Indigenous knowledge and ethnomathematics* (pp. 141–160). Springer.

François, A., Lacrampe, S., Franjieh, M., & Schnell, S. (2015). *The languages of Vanuatu. University and diversity. Asia-Pacific linguistics, studies in the languages of Island Melanesia.* College of Asia and the Pacific, The Australian National University.

Genoud, P. A., & Guillod, M. (2014). Développement et validation d'un questionnaire évaluant les attitudes socio-affectives en maths. *Recherches en éducation, 20,* 140–156.

Hinge, E. (2008). *Insaed Long Nakamal.* Vanuatu National Library.

Hobsbawm, E. J., & Ranger, T. (1983). *The invention of tradition.* Cambridge University Press.

Huffman, K. (2017). School spirit in Vanuatu. *Muse, 17,* 29–31.

Instituto Brasileiro de Geografia e Estatística (2010). *Os indígenas no Censo demográfico 2010.* https://indigenas.ibge.gov.br/images/pdf/indigenas/folder_indigenas_web.pdf

Jackson, A. (Ed.). (1987). *Anthropology at home.* Tavistock.

Jolly, M. (1992). Specters of inauthenticity. *The Contemporary Pacific,* 4(1), 49–72.

Keesing, R. M. (1982). Creating the past: Custom and identity in the contemporary Pacific. *The Contemporary Pacific, 1(1–2),* 19–42.

Layard, J. (1942). *Stone men of Malekula* (Vol. 1). Chatto & Windus.

Leite, K. G. (2014). *Nós Mesmos e os Outros: etnomatemática e interculturalidade na escola indígena Paiter.* PhD Thesis, Universidade Federal de Mato Grosso, Cuiabá, Brasil.

Leite, K. G., & Camargos, Q. F. (2021). Impossibility of bijective mapping between indigenous and Eurocentric mathematical knowledge. *Revista de Educação Matemática, 18,* 1–24.

Lipka, J., & Adams, B. L. (2004). Some evidence for ethnomathematics quantitative and qualitative data from Alaska. In F. Favilli (Ed.), *Ethnomathematics and mathematics education, proceedings of the 10th international congress of mathematics education (ICME-10)* (pp. 87–98). Discussion Group 15-Ethnomathematics, Tipografia Editrice Pisana.

Lipka, J., Adams, B., Wong, M., Koester, D., & François, K. (2019). Symmetry and measuring: Ways to teach the foundations of mathematics inspired by Yupiaq elders. *Journal of Humanistic Mathematics, 9(1)*, 107–157.

McCarter, J., & Gavin, M. C. (2011). Perceptions of the value of traditional ecological knowledge to formal school curricula: Opportunities and challenges from Malekula Island, Vanuatu. *Journal of Ethnobiology and Ethnomedicine*, *7*(1), 1–14.

Millikan, B. (1999). A experiência contemporânea da fronteira agrícola e o desmatamento em Rondônia. In A. C. Diegues (Ed.), *Desmatamento e modos de vida na Amazônia* (pp. 95–132). USP/NUPAUB.

Mindlin, B. (1985). *Nós Paiter: Os Suruí de Rondônia*. Vozes.

Ministry of Education. (2010). *Vanuatu National Curriculum Statement*. Ministry of Education, Republic of Vanuatu, PMB 9028, Port Vila. ISBN: 978-982-9126-01-6.

Ministry of Education. (2012). *Vanuatu National Language Policy*. Ministry of Education, Republic of Vanuatu, PMB 9028, Port Vila. https://moet.gov.vu/docs/policies/Vanuatu%20National%20Language%20Policy%20(English)_2012.pdf

Ministry of Education and Training. (2021). *Vanuatu Education and Training Sector Strategic Plan 2021-2030*. Ministry of Education and Training, Republic of Vanuatu, PMB 9028, Port Vila. https://pacificdata.org/data/dataset/education-and-training-sector-strategic-plan-2021-2030

Monteiro, H. S. R. (2018). Contribuições da Etnomatemática para a formação dos professores indígenas do Estado de Tocantins. *Zetetiké, 26(1)*, 206–220.

Neves, J. G. (2009). *Cultura escrita em contextos indígenas* [PhD Thesis]. Universidade Estadual Paulista Júlio de Mesquita Filho.

National University of Vanuatu. (2021). *Proceedings of the international symposium in Vanuatu – Education identity cultures*. National University of Vanuatu.

Oliveira, J. P., & Freire, C. A. R. (Eds.) (2006). *A presença indígena na formação do Brasil*. MEC/SECAD/Museu Nacional.

Orey, D. C., & Rosa, M. (2006). Ethnomathematics: Cultural assertions and challenges towards pedagogical action. *The Journal of Mathematics and Culture*, *1*(1), 57–78.

Rivera, F., & Becke, J. R. (2007). Ethnomathematics in the Global Episteme: Quo Vadis? In B. Atweh, A. C. Barton, M. C. Borba, N. Gough, C. Keitel-Kreidt, C. Vistro-Yu, & R. Vithal (Eds.), *Internationalisation and globalisation in mathematics and science education* (pp. 209–225). Springer.

Rory, P. (2013). *L'art de l'éphémère. Esquisse du patrimoine culturel intangible du Vanuatu*. VKS-Sun Production.

Rory, P., Boulekouran, B., Rory, C., Taunearu, G., & Westhorpe, C. (Eds.) (2008). *Sandroing blong Vanuatu: Lanem mo tijim sandroing blong Vanuatu, Ressource Pédagogique, Draft proposition*. Vanuatu National Library.

Rosa, M., Shirley, L., & Gavarrete, M. E. (2017). An ethnomathematics overview: An introduction. In M. Rosa, L. Shirley, M. E. Gavarrete, & W. V. Alangui (Eds.), *Ethnomathematics and its diverse approaches for mathematics education* (pp. 3–19). Springer International Publishing.

Santos, B. S. (1998). *La Globalización del derecho: los nuevos caminos de la regulación y la emancipación*. Universidad Nacional de Colombia.

Soares, G. A., & Fantinato, M. C. (2021). A Etnomatemática na formação inicial dos futuros professores de Matemática: revelando olhares e marcas. *Revemop*, *3*, 1–24.

Suruí, A. P. (2015). *Saberes matemáticos do povo Paiter Suruí* [Unpublished Monography]. Universidade Federal de Rondônia, Ji-Paraná, Brasil.

Suruí, A. P., & Leite, K. G. (2018). Etnomatemática e Educação Escolar Indígena no contexto do povo Paiter. *Zetetiké*, *26*(1), 94–112.

Suruí, Mi. (2016). *Marcadores de tempo do povo Paiter* [Unpublished Monography]. Universidade do Estado de Mato Grosso, Barra do Bugres, Brasil.

Suruí, Mi. (2021). *Ciclo temporal do povo Paiter Suruí como fundamento para a organização do calendário escolar* [Unpublished Monography]. Universidade Federal de Rondônia, Ji-Paraná, Brasil.

Suruí, Mo. (2015). *Marcadores de tempo do povo Paiter: subsídios para o ensino diferenciado de matemática na escola da aldeia* [Unpublished Monography]. Universidade Federal de Rondônia, Ji-Paraná, Brasil.

Thomas, N. (2010). *Islanders: The pacific in the age of empire*. Yale University Press.

Trinick, T., & Meaney, T. (2020). Ethnomathematics and indigenous teacher education: Waka migrations. *Revemop, 2*, 1–18.

Trinick, T., Meaney, T., & Fairhall, U. (2015). Reintroducing Māori ethnomathematical activities into the classroom: Traditional Māori spatial orientation concepts. *Revista Latinoamericana de Etnomatemática, 8(2)*, 415–431.

Tryon, D. (1999). Ni-Vanuatu research and researchers. *Oceania, 70(1)*, 9–15.

Valero, P. (2007). In between the global and the local: The politics of mathematics education reform in a globalized society. In B. Atweh, A. C. Barton, M. C. Borba, N. Gough, C. Keitel-Kreidt, C. Vistro-Yu, & R. Vithal (Eds.), *Internationalisation and globalisation in mathematics and science education* (pp. 421–439). Springer.

Vandendriessche, E. (2022). Sand drawing *versus* string figure making: Geometric and algorithmic practices in Northern Ambrym, Vanuatu. In E. Vandendriessche & R. Pinxten (Eds.), *Indigenous knowledge and ethnomathematics* (pp. 85–118). Springer Nature Switzerland.

Vandendriessche, E., & Da Silva, A. (2022). Les dessins sur les sable du Nord de l'île d'Ambrym. Une étude ethnomathématique. *ethnographiques.org, 43*. Online. https://www.ethnographiques.org/2022/Vandendriessche_DaSilva

Vanuatu Education Support Program (2017). *VESP View Vanuatu Education Support Program (2017)*. Vanuatu Education Support Program. https://espvanuatu.org/our-support/

Vanuatu National Statistics Office (2020a). *Vanuatu 2020 national population and housing census preliminary results*. Vanuatu National Statistics Office. https://vnso.gov.vu/index.php/en/

Vanuatu National Statistics Office (2020b). *Well-being in Vanuatu*. Vanuatu National Statistics Office. https://vnso.gov.vu/index.php/en/special-reports/well-being-survey

Walsh, C. (2009). Interculturalidade crítica e pedagogia decolonial: In-surgir, re-existir e re-viver. In V. M. Candau (Ed.), *Educação intercultural na América Latina: entre concepções, tensões e propostas* (pp. 12–41). Letras.

Walter, S. L., & Chuo, K. G. (2012). *The Kom experimental mother tongue education pilot project report for 2012*. MTB-MLE Network.

Wittersheim, E. (1999). Les chemins de l'authenticité. Les anthropologues et la Renaissance mélanésienne. *L'Homme, 39*(151), 181–205.

Zagala, S. (2004). Vanuatu sand drawing. *Museum International, 56*(1–2), 32–35.

14 Working with primary teachers in England on mathematics teaching for citizenship

Critical and philosophical approaches

Gill Adams, Hilary Povey, and Fufy Demissie

Introduction

In mathematics education research to date, there has been limited focus on the potential of philosophical frameworks to engage primary teachers in critical explorations of their teaching of mathematics. In this chapter, we examine the potential of such philosophical approaches, considering affordances and limitations in relation to teachers' learning with respect to mathematics learning and teaching for social justice through the context of our experiences of one project, the *Project in Citizenship and Mathematics* (PiCaM). In the performative[1] school environments prevalent in England, control of the teacher is "pervasive ... dictating not only the curriculum, the structure of a lesson, the approach to teaching a particular concept, but also the focus of an individual teacher's learning and even the clothing they must wear" (Adams & Povey, 2018, p. 211). We ask: What spaces might philosophical approaches provide access to and what do glimpses into these spaces *do* to teachers? In particular, we ask what affordances such approaches may offer to primary teachers in their teaching of mathematics, even as they are subject to ever increasing scrutiny of their performance through their students' attainment in national tests (Troman, 2008).

We write at a time of intensifying globalisation, characterised by a rapid shift of power and control from public to "a tiny and un-elected private sector" (Neyland, 2007, p. 116). Here, in the face of globalising scientific management of education, opportunities for teachers to "debate about and co-construct a mathematics curriculum" (Neyland, 2007, p. 115) have largely been replaced by an imposed curriculum where diversity has been eradicated. For Neyland, this mathematics curriculum acts as a blueprint that "leaves teachers illiterate" (2007, p. 124). To counter this, Neyland calls for a curriculum that is "locally emergent and complex" (p. 124). More broadly, we note Ernest's arguments for critical mathematics education, one which "aims to empower learners as individuals and citizens-in-society, by developing mathematical confidence and power [...]; and to foster critical awareness and democratic citizenship via mathematics" (Ernest, 2007, p. 34). Our goal in PiCaM was to work against the disembodiment of knowledge and practice,

DOI: 10.4324/9781003130673-17

emphasising their situatedness in particular locales and creating spaces for alternative curricula possibilities.

We begin with an extended introduction to PiCaM, setting out the project aims, describing how collaboration between the project partners facilitated an examination of local, national and global contexts and outlining the focus on global citizenship in selected project resources. We then explore philosophical approaches in education linking these to a discussion of social justice. Next, we describe the approach we deployed in this chapter to facilitate critical reflections on our involvement in PiCaM, particularly our attempts to work with these philosophical approaches. In our reflections, individual and in dialogue, we consider what educational arrangements *do* to teachers, the spaces that such philosophical approaches may construct and our roles in supporting teachers to engage critically with/against performative school contexts. We conclude by considering the value of both ruminating and of action in critical mathematics education.

The Project in Citizenship and Mathematics (PiCaM)

The chapter springs out of an attempt to support teachers to engage critically with mathematics learning and teaching in schools through the vehicle of a European project, PiCaM, co-funded through the ERASMUS Programme of the European Union (Project number 2017-1-UK01-KA201-036675). The project aimed to engage with issues of citizenship and globalisation through the teaching of mathematics. (We regard citizenship as a highly contestable concept which we have discussed and critiqued elsewhere including the hegemonic role of the concept of European citizenship which is usually what is being invoked when global citizenship is being discussed (Povey & Adams, 2021; Povey, Demissie & Adams, 2019). Suffice it here to say that we reject the imperative to foster neoliberal citizenship seeking instead to support the development of critical, socially engaged citizenship). Through the development of curriculum resources for 10- to 12-year-olds and their teachers, it sought to contribute to combating discrimination, segregation, and racism, validating the cultural history, and supporting the education of all, including disadvantaged groups and migrant children. The project materials are founded upon inclusive, participatory, and innovative pedagogies with the novel inclusion of philosophical approaches to learning mathematics in order to develop social, civic and intercultural knowledge, skills and understanding and critical thinking.

Project partners included educators from a range of settings including the voluntary sector, universities and a mathematics "museum". Five European countries were involved: England, Germany, Greece, Portugal, and Romania. The similarities and differences in education systems and traditions in partner countries provided valuable starting points for discussion and development of project approaches and materials. This is evident, for example, in the way that several activities begin from the local, exploring aspects of children's lives, and move to explore these in other countries and contexts, enabling alternative perspectives to be discussed and validated. From conceptual and methodological principles (which remained contested and the source of unresolved tensions throughout the project), partners collaborated on seven resources for the classroom, together with materials to support initial teacher education, teacher professional development, and eTwinning[2]. (See http://www.citizenship-and-mathematics.eu/.) These principles and resources were informed by the EarthCARE global justice framework (https://blogs.ubc.ca/earthcare/), with its six complementary approaches to justice including, for example, cognitive justice, which focuses attention on "identifying and interrupting the harmful effects of a monoculture of thought" (EarthCARE, n.d.), and relational justice which aims towards equitable power relations. The framework, developed in response to the challenges posed by increasing globalisation, aims to deepen understanding of the complex processes of social change, facilitate deep reflection and analysis and aid the exploration of alternative futures.

In some cases, the classroom resources have a specific focus connected to citizenship. For example, *Mapping the world* is concerned with map making and aims to prompt an exploration of the history of European colonisation, the measurement of the earth, the construction of national boundaries and the potential maps hold for misrepresentation; and *Global crisis and local solidarity* interrogates and critiques contemporary hegemonic ways of understanding money and debt and the unproblematised uses of mathematics, invoking the notion of the common good. Others take as their focus inclusive and participatory pedagogies. For example, *Playing and making mathematical games and crafts* creates spaces, inside and outside the school context, for children to come together, to collaborate and share experiences amongst themselves and with others, acknowledging the complexity of living together and building solidarity; and *Mathematical bodies* explores mathematics as embodied and playful and experienced together, building a learning group where everybody matters and everyone has an equal role to play. In many cases, the resources contain prompts for using a philosophical approach and it is this aspect of the project which is the focus of this chapter.

The curriculum materials in PiCaM were designed to challenge some of the existing barriers to a critical engagement with mathematics, at a time of increasing globalisation. The activities focused on significant concepts such as migration, culture and history, and the pedagogy was underpinned by critical, caring, collaborative and creative thinking (Society for Advancing Philosophical Enquiry and Reflection in Education, SAPERE, 2010). The introductory activities emphasised participation and collaboration. Although on first glance, the links between approaches to learning mathematics and philosophical approaches in the classroom may not be obvious, many of the habits of mind (Povey, 2017) necessary for critical engagement with mathematics are reflected in the intended outcomes of the philosophical approach we adopted. These habits include asking yourself questions, being resilient and being flexible.

Given the challenges of the performative school environment (as described above), we wanted to explore whether philosophical approaches could facilitate teachers' critical engagement with their teaching of mathematics. We found that working on activities together and using a philosophical methodology, either at the Development Education Centre or the University, was significantly different from the work that teachers typically did in schools. Beyond the policy boundaries, teachers were able to explore mathematics in different ways and engage in critical questioning, including questions related to the nature of knowledge and how we come to know what we know. The possibility of intervening, of disrupting existing practices and of teacher author/ity (Povey, 1997) was recognised. Back in school, some teachers even found spaces to work differently with children suggesting that the philosophical approach had supported teacher learning:

> The training has been really good. All of the activities that we tried out, the resources are great, I've really enjoyed in terms of history and the view of maths across the world, I've learned a lot... (T1)

> it has made me think about other lessons I teach in terms of the global aspect of it ... opened my mind to different views and different experiences and also children working together, ... children can work with anyone and get good results (T2)

This last comment reflects the conditions of mathematics classrooms in England, where children have typically been grouped by prior attainment and experience almost all of their mathematics in these predefined groupings (Marks, 2014). In the next section we discuss the philosophical approaches in education and locate these within PiCaM.

Philosophical approaches in education

Over the last few decades, philosophical approaches in education have been gaining currency. For us, in common with various other researchers (Bowyer et al., 2020; Daniel & Auriac, 2011; Winstanley, 2018), such approaches encompass:

- an emphasis on thinking;
- an understanding of thinking as creative;
- a focus on inquiry;
- a willingness to work with unfinishedness, unknowing and uncertainty; and
- emphasis on community.

Our intention, that philosophical approaches be used in emancipatory ways, requires "[putting] habitual ways of being and doing into question" (Bowyer et al., 2020, p. 51) and finding again the position of a child whose ways of being are not yet filled with settled categories and fixed interpretations of the world (Biesta, 2011). Equally, we seek out philosophy's potential to make us uncertain, unsettled and hesitant so we do not know for sure but have an orientation towards not-knowing (Biesta, 2011). Philosophy has the potential to hone a disposition towards critical thinking where "the individual takes nothing for granted and constantly questions and enquiries" (Benade, 2014, p. 1254 quoted in Bowyer et al., 2020, p. 43). Drawing further on the work of Bowyer and her colleagues, we note that a philosophical approach can undermine structures of power because of the recognition given to uncertainty and the possibility of not-knowing but only if it constantly subjects itself to critical scrutiny especially in the way that students from the margins are positioned.

The PiCaM project proposal made specific reference to a particular approach – *Philosophy for Children* (P4C) – so we begin by discussing this. P4C is an inquiry-based dialogic pedagogy that is underpinned by the 4Cs: creative, caring, collaborative and critical thinking (SAPERE, 2010). P4C originated in the United States where it was based on philosophical novels written by Lipman (for example, Pixie, downloadable at https://digitalcommons.montclair.edu/iapc_primary_schl_curriculum/1/). Outside the United States, practitioners have begun to use a wide-range of stimuli, such as film clips, picture books and art works in place of the original novels (SAPERE, 2010). P4C was developed by Lipman and Sharp to support students to develop their reasoning skills (Lipman & Sharp, 1978). Lipman states that "the pedagogy of the 'community of inquiry' should be the methodology for the teaching of critical thinking" (Lipman, 2003, p. 3), advocating an approach to develop reasoning, judgement and evaluation skills in schools to support the development of thinking skills. This "exciting, unpredictable and authentic pedagogy" can be particularly productive in work with student teachers, as they begin "to nurture the skills and dispositions of democratic citizenship" (Demissie, 2020, p. 76).

The rationale for choosing P4C as the philosophical framework for the project was largely pragmatic. The second UK partner in the PiCaM project, the Development Education Centre South Yorkshire (DECSY) promote a global learning perspective in the curriculum and are experienced in training teachers in P4C (https://www.decsy.org.uk/project/p4c/). In addition, P4C is a key research and practice interest for one of us (Fufy), leading to P4C approaches being embedded in an undergraduate teacher education course (Demissie, 2020). At the PiCaM project planning stage it appeared to us that there was considerable potential in adopting P4C as a means to address questions of global citizenship in the mathematics curriculum. As mathematics educators and researchers with a commitment to a more just social world, we (Hilary and Gill) found resonance in the emphasis on critical questioning, learner agency, a collaborative, creative and caring community in P4C. There are clear links to social justice perspectives on teaching mathematics where classrooms can be seen as learning communities (for example, Boaler, 1997; Povey, 2017; Skovsmose, 1994). In such classrooms, learning is seen not as acquisition but rather as participation.

As mathematics education researchers, Atweh and Keitel (2007) note that defining social justice is problematic. They summarise theorisations of social justice, noting that a market model, based on "free competition and deregulation" (p. 98), is highly influential in education systems and processes, valorising individual effort whilst neglecting the effect of social structures and relations. Distributive models attempt to address inequalities in education through the allocation of additional resources but fail to engage critically with curricula and pedagogical approaches, nor do they address the historical roots of inequalities. Problematising both these models, Atweh and Keitel draw on Gewirtz's (1998) relational understanding of social justice, one that facilitates an exploration of power and societal relations, and on Fraser's (1995) arguments for cultural recognition. Atweh and Keitel (2007) choose to work with Young's (1990) signs of injustice, using these "markers of social injustice to raise some issues of social justice" (p. 100). In our examination of philosophical approaches, these signs (for example, exploitation and cultural imperialism) serve to illustrate possibilities and risks.

When running introductory PiCaM sessions with teachers, a key element was engaging them in philosophical activity based on the P4C approach. Participants are usually seated in a circle, creating a space in which everyone can be seen. Ground rules for discussion are formulated or reviewed with the group, after which the facilitator introduces a stimulus. In the P4C process (Oxfam, 2007, p. 1), this stimulus, an image, object, text or video clip, serves as a prompt for philosophical thinking and questioning. Participants generate questions inspired by the stimulus material then democratically decide which question to explore together. When using P4C with learners, teachers/facilitators work with a group over time with the intention that discussions become deeper and participants develop skills of inquiry, working together collaboratively and constructively to explore questions that are important to them. Throughout, facilitators take an active role, with an emphasis on the 4Cs: to create and maintain a caring and collaborative ethos and to model critical and creative thinking in action as the group explore the chosen question (SAPERE, 2010).

Whilst P4C[3] had much to offer PiCaM in terms of helping the project explore a less didactic, more dialogical way of working with children and teachers, we came to realise that thinking about thinking was, in itself, unlikely to be enough for us to address the project's transformative intentions (Kohan, 2014). In our critique we drew on the work of Biesta (2011, 2017) and Kohan (2018), both of whom support doing philosophy with children and are sympathetic to the aims and practices of P4C. However, both also recognise that P4C is not "as transformative, as revolutionary and as radical, ***as it is desirable for it to be to make any difference*** in these neo-capitalistic, global times—not, at least, in the usual form its educational theory and practice takes" (Kohan, 2014, p. 46, original emphasis).

Biesta believes that doing philosophy with children (and we would say adults too) is particularly helpful in enabling them to ask questions – questions about the world and questions about their own role and position within it. However, he argues, the positioning of the inquirer needs to be not just that of "the I who asks questions, who makes sense, who seeks to understand" but also as one who is "being put in question and through this is being called into the world … in the world but not in the centre of the world" (2017, p. 434). He believes that most schooling in neoliberal societies is no longer providing education but rather has been reduced to offering *learnification*, that is, intelligent adaptation to one's existing environment where children "learn" in a way not dissimilar from robotic vacuum cleaners.

Kohan makes a number of critiques of the way P4C is usually practised. Crucially for us, he notes that P4C does not take up ideological issues about the nature of societies. Although it can contribute to an education for citizenship, providing tools that all participants in democracy need if they are to be(come) tolerant, responsible, pluralistic citizens, it does so without considering that the democratic contexts children and citizens encounter might be unfair and unjust. He, like Biesta, is concerned about P4C's emphasis on rationality which he sees as a way of formatting people to become more capable of an intelligent adaptation to the labour market. He contrasts this with thinking as framed within critical approaches to teaching and learning: "while P4C considers critical thinking as a set of reasoning skills, critical pedagogy goes beyond this, meaning that critical thinking puts into question the unfairness of the *status quo*" (p. 620).

Philosophy with Children (PwC) developed by Murris (Haynes & Murris, 2011) from Lipman's work, seeks to address some of these critiques of P4C. The terminology emphasises that practitioners do philosophy *with* rather than *for* participants and their approach "expresses the democratic and collaborative nature of the practice" (Haynes & Murris, 2011, p. 300). Drawing on their experience of supporting student teachers to develop philosophical practice, Haynes and Murris identify recurring themes including preparing for the unexpected in teaching, a shift in perspective on progression (*non-linear progression*), the difficulty in asking philosophical questions, ownership of questions and epistemological and moral relativism (2011, pp. 291–297). These themes reflect principles privileged in our own pedagogical approaches to mathematics education, where "active, engaged, meaning-making pedagogies promote learning; encourage the development of authoritative, confident learners; and provide opportunities to increase social justice within the mathematics classroom" (Povey, 2017, p. 13).

Critical explorations: Reflections on working with teachers

In this section we justify our approach to engaging critically with our work on PiCaM. Biesta (2017) asks what educational arrangements "do" to children and young people – here we explore what they *do* to teachers through four critical reflections on PiCaM's attempt to work with philosophical approaches in mathematics learning and teaching.

We deploy critical reflection as a thinking tool to aid our critique of existing structures and discourses and to question power relationships, considering alternative perspectives and working towards more informed actions. Although critical reflection is frequently used in education, particularly in relation to professional practice, it remains a contested concept. Significantly, it goes beyond reflection, and reflective practice, to question power relationships. It is important to note that "from a critical theory perspective critical reflection focuses not on how to work more effectively or productively within an existing system, but on calling the foundations and imperatives of the system itself into question, assessing their morality, and considering alternatives" (Brookfield, 2009, p. 296). Critical theory is grounded in three assumptions about the world: that we live in unequal societies where racism, economic inequalities and other forms of discrimination are an everyday reality; that the reproduction of these unequal structures is rendered normal and inevitable through the dominant ideology; and that critical theory works to understand this situation in order to change it.

Like Brookfield, we see critical reflection as ideology critique, exploring how "ideology lives within us, pervading our emotional responses" (Brookfield, 2009, p. 300). We make two moves here as we begin this work, first working with our individual reflections and, secondly, through a more structured critical collaboration which draws on the principles of P4C. This collaborative work brings alternative perspectives to our inquiry, enabling us to reflect on the power that we exercise through our positions as educators.

Individual reflections on attempts to promote philosophical approaches with teachers

Mapping questions – Gill

In the project workshops we worked with teachers and student teachers to explore the activities and approaches to citizenship and mathematics. One activity that struck me as particularly powerful was the study of world maps mentioned above which aimed to prompt an exploration of the history of European colonisation, the measurement of the earth, the construction of national boundaries and the potential maps held for misrepresentation. One task focuses on how maps are derived from the globe, exploring similarities and differences between representations; another examines a variety of world maps, considering size, location, and shape of continents and countries, encouraging discussion of how maps change our perception of the world. In these tasks, the globe and various map projections acted as stimuli for inquiry, with teachers generating questions in response.

Working with teachers on this activity, several responses caught my attention. First, the availability of globes (and printed maps) to see and manipulate appeared both novel and significant, not only to teachers' understanding of the tasks but in prompting reflections on their own classroom environments (the teachers) or school mathematics experience (the student teachers). They wondered why there were no globes in their classrooms – or at least, no 3-dimensional models. Globes and printed maps have been replaced by images on screen, which although manipulable, provide an altered perspective of the world and raise intended questions about what we know and how we come to know and how this shapes knowledge and experience. Second, the existence of alternative representations of the world map drew considerable surprise from the majority of participants with just one of the student teachers demonstrating prior knowledge of these and an understanding of the ways in which such maps might mislead. If "the world map" (typically taken to be a Mercator projection) was just one possible construction, what else was in question? This challenge of engaging critically with the taken for granted is one project goal. Thirdly, the exploration of the globe in small groups, followed by the initial prompts: What questions can we ask about what we can see? and Which questions can we use mathematics to explore? appeared to enable a rapid community building to take place, making space for sharing, for questioning, for understanding. Everyone had a contribution to make related to their own story and this seemed to give them confidence to wonder, to imagine alternatives. Many of the questions were open, philosophical questions of significance to participants, prompting further enquiry. Finally, and perhaps most importantly, the activity provided an alternative perspective on colonisation, an important reminder of some of the ways in which we live with the legacy and prompting reflections on practice.

Uncovering assumptions and generating spaces to think – Hilary

In the initial PiCaM workshops with teachers and student teachers which were led by Fufy and Gill, the participants were asked at the beginning "What is the world like today? What words might you use to describe it?" The teachers and student teachers were then asked to consider the knowledge and skills they wanted the young people they taught to have to survive and thrive in this world. This scene setting and invitation to become aware of and to focus on issues of our position in our world and on the fundamental purposes of education that Gill and Fufy provided surprised me (Hilary) and caused me to reflect on the presuppositions I brought with me to work with teachers.

I came of age as a teacher in the 1970s in the Inner London Education Authority in an era of maximum equality in Britain (Dorling, 2018, p. 166) and, I conjecture, maximum teacher autonomy. Although far from perfect, the Authority funded its education system well and supported a wide range of innovative projects intended to contribute to social justice including in mathematics education (Povey & Adams, 2018; https://smilemaths.wordpress.com/). Teachers were expected to be, and largely were, aware of the politics of education and used to voice a commitment to working towards a more fair and just education system. Based on experience, when working with mathematics teachers in that era I took for granted that they would have already had the opportunity to articulate and discuss the sorts of issues that Fufy and Gill were raising. I carried forward this attitude into the vastly different era within which PiCaM was operating and on two separate occasions had such disappointing sessions with teachers that I considered giving up.

I decided to try the same approach as Gill and Fufy and found that teachers were thirsty for such philosophical reflecting and that it opened up a space where they could articulate real opposition to the *status quo* and therefore could see the point of working with materials like PiCaM. They shared a sense of a divided, unequal world with a planet under threat. Typical responses to the first question included words like in danger, unfair, in conflict, dying ... This is not a vocabulary we usually use in the context of mathematics education. By asking the teachers to consider the knowledge and skills they wanted the young people they taught to have to survive and thrive in this world, participants were positioned as agentic, able to act to strive for a better future. Peter Appelbaum (2018) suggests the philosophical strategy of exploring the effects of adopting such non-mainstream language in order to change "how we see and think and 'be'" (p. 54). Working in this way allowed us, me and the teachers, to confront, though not in an easy way to cure, "the invisible ignorances that structure our worlds of possibility" (p. 69), that is, those accepted ways of seeing, thinking and being that limit our understanding of how things might become.

Troubling role and responsibilities – Gill

Reflecting on the observations and recollections I made in considering world maps raised questions about my role in relation to the activities and to the teachers. I began teaching in the mid-1980s and although I have not taught in schools for 15 years, as a teacher educator and academic I have an awareness of teachers' lives. My mathematics classroom was home to a range of activities, approaches and resources. Policy and practice have shifted considerably in the intervening years since I left school teaching, the performative culture leading to a marked reduction in teacher autonomy. I am troubled by the challenges I anticipate teachers facing as they return to school to try to work with the PiCaM materials with their classes. How might they justify these activities and approaches in the face of existing school structures? What was my role in helping them to create spaces for the expansive questions generated by the activities and by the children? How do I "nourish a sense of hope" (Giroux, 2020, p. 226)? Despite these concerns, it seemed that the PiCaM activities and the pedagogical approaches upon which they were founded offered the possibility of a shift, not only in the way that mathematics was taught but in the way that the subject was understood. The philosophical approaches enabled, even demanded, a critical questioning that provided opportunities for children and teachers to rekindle childhood habits of asking why. They unsettled, deliberately. That was the point. Yet even as I felt my responsibility to provide the teachers and beginning teachers I work with "the freedom, security, time and space to take risks and ask important questions" (Birmingham, 2004, p. 322), I was aware of the risks they might take in daring to be different in a conforming culture.

Alternative perspectives – Fufy

Reflections on a project workshop with teachers in Greece, designed to introduce them to the P4C approach, provided me with an alternative perspective to my experience in England. In Greece, due to the recent economic crisis, teachers' contexts have been characterised by job insecurity, pay cuts, and reduced budgets. A head teacher's role is mainly administrative, teachers have the lightest teaching load in the Organisation for Economic Co-operation and Development (OECD), and more significantly, there are no national student assessments (OECD, 2018). In contrast, teachers in England have much better job security and schools are generally better funded. However, in England, education is highly regulated and controlled, governed by a neoliberal political agenda: student assessment drives the schools' agenda, and high stakes school inspections blight teachers' professional lives and influence what is taught.

During the P4C enquiries, for example, I found that teachers in England were less forthcoming in sharing their ideas and somewhat reluctant to challenge and question each other. Moreover, the pressures to accommodate curriculum demands impacted on levels of teacher involvement in the project: "... they (the activities) didn't fit directly into anything we were supposed to be teaching as part of the curriculum. There were things that had to be" (T1). On the other hand, Greek teachers' questions were more philosophical and they were more willing to ask questions of themselves and of each other, resulting in discussions that were deeper and more contested.

A philosophical dialogue

These individual reflections, highlighting contrasting responses and attitudes, became the stimulus or provocation for our own philosophical inquiry into what the educational arrangements do to teachers and why. We worked collaboratively, raising and clarifying several questions of which we ended up discussing two. We began with: *What are the most important teacher skills and dispositions for critical engagement with mathematics?* Later, we found ourselves discussing *Why should it be that caring/caring thinking links to social justice? What sort of caring/caring thinking, if any, supports a deeply transformative agenda?*

Extracts from the inquiry serve both to illustrate the philosophical approach and to share our reflections. In the extract below we explore the problematic nature of teacher dispositions and readiness for critical engagement with mathematics.

Fufy: What are the most important skills and dispositions a critical engagement with their teaching of mathematics requires from teachers?

Hilary: My problem with dispositions is that when people use that word, I think mostly they are thinking of something pretty stable, ... I don't think that the Greek teachers were in any essentialist way, different kinds of people. Maybe they were, maybe teaching in Greece is so different, it attracts a completely different set of people into the profession. Disposition would need to be slightly problematised to make it clear that disposition isn't something that is essential.

Gill: I think we need to be clear how we are using those terms...

Fufy: Are all dispositions fluid and changeable? For example, Dewey says that open mindedness is a basic disposition that is necessary for reflection [...] Would there be some dispositions, such as open mindedness, that are not as fluid and flexible?

Hilary: [...] Maybe I overstated the case slightly? I suppose what I meant was that if people were exposed to a climate of open mindedness – if we are in a world where most teachers think they can't say what they think most of the time in their professional environment that clearly is not an environment that fosters any kind of open mindedness or creativity.

The question began with an assumption that dispositions and traits are innate or culturally specific (for example in the Greek teachers). But, by the end we considered the role of context – individuals may be "naturally" open-minded (whatever that might mean), but the political and social context will profoundly affect how they behave. The dispositions are not necessarily innate or particular to the Greek teachers (despite their impressive cultural heritage in philosophy) but, in general, the educational arrangements in England and teachers' own roles within them suppress teachers' philosophical thinking[4].

The discussion flowed into thinking about thinking and thinking about action.

Fufy: What we are saying is that these terms themselves need to be unpicked, what do we mean by caring thinking – and like you say, is it inherently transformative, these particular ways of being? Because you can be caring, can't you, and not actually question somebody.

Gill: And it links to the need for action – so caring thinking, to support a transformative agenda, does that need to lead to some kind of action, whether that is a recommitment to actions that were already ongoing or something very different?

Fufy: I suppose that could be one of the limitations of doing philosophical approaches using this kind of methodology, you can just do the thinking and not the doing. Just talk about it, think about it but actually stop short of doing something about it. It gives you the sense of you doing something but actually you are not.

Gill: … it does transform practice in the group but I think what we are asking is whether it goes beyond that.

Fufy: I always find that a really interesting question, is it enough, talking? …

Hilary: There is a school of thought, and I think it is a position that I have a lot of sympathy with though I don't in the end I agree with it, which says that we are all too busy doing things and not thinking enough, that our instant response is to say "oh I've got to do something" […] just think. Thinking in itself is incredibly important. We do all need to think and think hard and think more.

Gill: And maybe that is enough … it is the practice itself of working together, thinking together, engaging with other people's perspectives, listening, taking a position and then being prepared to shift that position when you've heard other perspectives, isn't that enough?

Fufy: I think it is pretty valuable actually. Because I was talking to some of my students who did [the P4C] project with me … … so can we say that doing mathematics in this way helped some of the teachers to engage critically with their ideas of teaching mathematics, with the role of mathematics in society … I don't know.

Gill: I felt we had some glimmers of that.

In their examination of global citizenship education, Pais and Costa (2020) see two conflicting discourses of critical democracy and neoliberalism as providing us with "rationales for action, thus keeping us occupied" (p. 11) whilst frustrating any deeper analysis and prospect of change. Instead, they propose contemplation: "we strongly believe that sometimes the best way to act is to stop "acting" […] and ruminate" (p. 12). We wonder, though, the extent to which such time to ruminate is available to school teachers in the same way that it may be to those of us working in higher education. School life in England is dominated by "regulated time" (Povey, Boylan, & Adams, 2019, p. 2) where time is segmented and commodified with students and teachers "working against the clock" (see also note 4).

The possibilities of a philosophical approach

To what extent can the philosophical approaches to mathematics teaching and learning adopted in PiCaM be(come) "a space for challenging pre-conceptions and implicit conceptions of social justice" (Skovsmose, 2018, p. 41)? As we reflected on our experiences of working with teachers and beginning teachers, we noticed glimpses, moments, where teachers, stimulated by the project materials and approaches, asked questions about their own practices and school environments. At the same time, teachers reported tensions between the project approaches and the structures of schooling, struggling to align the two. This is unsurprising in the education policy context in England, where philosophical approaches can be viewed as a "counter cultural practice" (O'Riordan, 2016, p. 654), at odds with national policy expectations. This might be more obvious in mathematics, arguably one of the subjects where teachers are most under scrutiny with accountability measures experienced acutely (Ball et al., 2012). The tensions are evident in O'Riordan's study as teachers reveal the disconnect between their intrinsic values and the expectations they experience in the performative school culture. As Jane, one of the teachers notes: "[P4C] made me think I could be the type of teacher I'd always wanted to be … sometimes I think you can get bogged down with all these […] strategies and fulfilling requirements and doing all that" (O'Riordan, 2016, p. 655).

In O'Riordan's qualitative study of primary teachers trained in the use of P4C, teachers reported that P4C aided them to "move further towards their ideal vision of teaching" (2016, p. 654); but it also revealed that P4C did not become established in many schools. How do these teachers, and those we worked with on the PiCaM project, sustain such a movement in the face of the accountability agenda? It seems unlikely that any answer will be found without a wholesale rejection of neoliberal thinking in education; echoing Andreotti and colleagues (2018), it will not be neoliberalism that fixes the problems that neoliberalism has created.

One contribution that the project has made is to open up spaces for teachers to stop and think. We mentioned above the regulated time which dominates teachers' lives. The philosophical space provided the teachers with a glimpse of the alternative timescape "expansive time" (Povey, Boylan & Adams, 2019, p. 2). This timescape enables rumination, a lingering over tasks; a timescape where "describing and explaining and then discussing your work, conjecturing, visualising, getting stuck and keeping going, being willing to defend and justify your conclusions, changing your mind, conversing – all deeply mathematical practices – become possible" (Povey, Boylan & Adams, 2019, p. 6). The materials and pedagogical approaches deployed in the teacher workshops provided a stimulus for critical reflection in the way they prompted participants to engage with the world beyond their classrooms. At the same time, participants were encouraged to reflect on their own positions both in relation to others and to the ideas under discussion. This, rather than any measurable impact, encourages us. Also significant, although perhaps at odds with some of the research on effective teacher professional learning, was removing teachers from their usual workplace environment. Such an act of displacement can shift thinking. Finally, participants were able to make time and space to ask questions of themselves and of each other, time and space routinely denied them by performativity's demands for endless meticulous attention to trifling minutiae, "a political anatomy of detail" (Foucault, 1979, p. 139). The glimmers of hope that such interactions may provide, reminding teachers, as in O'Riordan's (2016) study, of their vision of the kind of teacher they would like to be, of why they wanted to be teachers, may be sufficient to sustain.

Authoritarian regimes and threats to liberal democracies around the world have resulted in the diminished capacity of education to "educate young people and others to be reflective, critical and socially engaged agents" (Giroux, 2020, p. 220). Critical pedagogy proposes that "education is a form of political intervention in the world and that it is capable of creating the possibilities for social transformation" (Giroux, 2020, p. 222). In England and perhaps elsewhere, spaces for teachers to explore such pedagogical approaches are limited and initial teacher education itself is subject to control (Furlong et al., 2008; McIntyre et al., 2019). For teachers to support students "to move from moral purpose through purposeful action" (Giroux, 2020, p. 223) we argue that they need opportunities to experience critical pedagogy themselves. A pedagogy founded on philosophical approaches is a "disruptive" pedagogy (Demissie, 2020), in the case of our project, deliberately so. Such pedagogy "profoundly questions the power balance in schools, the status of knowledge" (Haynes & Murris, 2011, p. 290) and enables philosophical questions that have the potential to "alter what counts as valuable in education" (ibid). The project did not intend simply to initiate teachers (and their students) into issues of citizenship but to do so in a critical manner stimulating "doubts, questions and self-corrections" (Daniel & Auriac, 2011, p. 422). The philosophical thinking involved is a *praxis* and implies "a dialectical relationship between reflection and action" (p. 422).

Thus, the philosophical approach of the project was to encompass both thinking and action, "aimed at improving how we live together" (Bowyer et al., 2020, p. 54). Being together, as well as being a theme picked up explicitly in some of the materials, is fundamental to this approach. The philosophy is intersubjective in that it implies "an open dialogue within a community of peers" (Daniel & Auriac, 2011, p. 422), in this case fellow teachers, in a horizontal rather than hierarchical relationship (p. 422). In this space, the thinking was grounded in being together and we saw glimpses during the workshops with teachers of the space becoming emancipatory as "other ways of being – other lives – [came] into view" (Bowyer et al., 2020, p. 56).

Conclusion

Philosophical approaches are growing in popularity in primary education, exposing tensions between the values and practices embraced in these approaches and the policy context, particularly in schools in England. In this chapter, we have considered how creating spaces for philosophical work with teachers and beginning teachers may facilitate a critical engagement with school mathematics and provide an alternative to an examination of the processes of globalisation, an opportunity to "think globally" (Skovsmose, 2007, p. 7) about justice and equality. Working with the PiCaM approaches and materials opened up spaces for reconceptualising what it might mean to be a citizen, highlighting the constraints of performative school environments at the same time as it enabled participants to glimpse possibilities for critical, socially engaged citizenship. Our reflections focussed on individual and collective questions of thinking and acting. In sharing these, our aim is to open up a conversation, inviting teachers, beginning teachers and others to consider the possibilities that philosophical approaches may offer to challenge thinking about mathematics education and to contribute to knowledge of how educators might continue to act in local contexts and how they too might engage in wider conversations about both mathematics and citizenship. For Giroux, educators must "do more than create the conditions for critical thinking and nourishing a sense of hope in their students" (2020, p. 226); they must take on the role of public intellectuals, addressing wider public audiences and sharing their ideas, part of our goal in this chapter. Pausing and ruminating is productive, enabling a re-examination, in collaboration, of purpose and possible action. Our reflections highlight the spaces to which philosophical approaches might provide primary teachers access, particularly as they work collaboratively to explore the possibilities and challenges of working in this way in mathematics. Creating spaces for collaborative critical reflection is particularly important for teachers in neoliberal times, as responses from PiCaM participants have demonstrated. Such spaces can be created in the work that educators do in support of teacher professional learning.

Notes

1 Performativity is "a technology, a culture and a mode of regulation that employs judgements, comparisons and displays as a means of incentive, control, attrition and change" (Ball, 2003, p. 216). In the English school system this performative environment impacts on teachers' professional identities, with hierarchical observations and inspections becoming "for some teachers, the everyday conditions which mould their professional identities and sense of purpose" (Hall & Noyes, 2009, p. 855). See also Adams and Povey (2018).

2 eTwinning is the European Commission's teaching and learning platform, designed to support communication and collaboration between teachers and schools across Europe.

3 This and the next two paragraphs draw on Povey et al. (2019).

4 Note by Anna Chronaki as co-editor of this volume: The authors of this chapter refer to the OECD (2018) description of the teaching profession in Greece, and in particular the light teaching hours, in order to explain why Greek teachers were eager contributors to philosophical discussions for the PiCAM project. However, both my personal encounters with these teachers based on my leading role for their professional development in this project and my experience of the post-2010 economic, political and social crisis concerning a series of neoliberal educational reforms imposed by the state and resisted by teacher unions require to stress two points concerning the context of schoolteachers work in Greece. First, though the OECD (2018, p. 45–46) refers to the light teaching workload, the schoolteachers work extra hours for administrative and preparation tasks whilst they remain low paid and lack opportunities for inservice training. And second, they are, by and large, qualified with postgraduate degrees whilst they become critically involved in

the political debates of educational reforms (Gounari & Grollios, 2012; Traianou, 2023). I believe these issues must be considered when we discuss their engagement with philosophical discussions in the milieu of the PiCAM project.

References

Adams, G., & Povey, H. (2018). Now there's everything to stop you': Teacher autonomy in performative times. In M. Jurdak & R. Vithal (Eds.), *Sociopolitical dimensions of mathematics education: From the margin to mainstream* (pp. 209–230). ICME-13 Monographs Springer.

Appelbaum, P. (2018). How to be a political change mathematics education activist. In M. Jurdak & R. Vithal (Eds.), *Sociopolitical dimensions of mathematics education: From the margin to mainstream* (pp. 53–73). ICME-13 Monographs Springer.

Atweh, B., & Keitel, C. (2007). Social injustice and (in)ternational collaborations in mathematics education. In B. Atweh, A. Calabrese Barton, M. C. Borba, N. Gough, C. Keitel, C. Vistro-Yu, & R. Vithal (Eds.), *Internationalisation and globalisation in mathematics and science education* (pp. 95–111). Springer.

Ball, S., Maguire, M., Braun, A., Perryman, J., & Hoskins, K. (2012). Assessment technologies in schools: 'Deliverology' and the 'play of dominations'. *Research Papers in Education*, *27*(5), 513–533. https://doi.org/10.1080/02671522.2010.550012

Biesta, G. (2011). Philosophy, exposure, and children: How to resist the instrumentalization of philosophy in education. *Journal of Philosophy of Education*, *45*(2), 305–319.

Biesta, G. (2017). Touching the soul? Exploring an alternative outlook for philosophical work with children and young people. *Childhood and Philosophy*, *13*(28), 415–452.

Birmingham, C. (2004). Phronesis: A model for pedagogical reflection. *Journal of Teacher Education*, *55*(4), 313–324. htpps://doi.org/10.1177/0022487104266725

Boaler, J. (1997). *Experiencing school mathematics: Teaching styles, sex and setting*. Open University Press.

Bowyer, L., Amos, C., & Stevens, D. (2020). What is 'philosophy'? Understandings of philosophy circulating in the literature on the teaching and learning of philosophy in schools. *Journal of Philosophy in Schools*, *7*(1), 38–67.

Brookfield, S. (2009). The concept of critical reflection: Promises and contradictions. *European Journal of Social Work*, *12*(3), 293–304. https://doi.org/10.1080/13691450902945215

Daniel, M. F., & Auriac, E. (2011). Philosophy, critical thinking and philosophy for children. *Educational Philosophy and Theory*, *43*(5), 415–435.

Demissie, F. (2020). The philosophy for children pedagogy in a university-based initial teacher education course: A case study of a 'disruptive' pedagogy. *FORUM*, *62*(1), 69–78. https://doi.org/10.15730/forum.2020.62.1.69

Dorling, D. (2018). *Peak inequality: Britain's ticking time bomb*. Polity Press.

EarthCARE. (n.d.). Framework. https://blogs.ubc.ca/earthcare/framework/

Ernest, P. (2007). Epistemological issues in the internationalization and globalization of mathematics education. In B. Atweh, A. Calabrese Barton, M. C. Borba, N. Gough, C. Keitel-Kreidt, C. Vistro-Yu, & C. Vithal (Eds.), *Internationalisation and globalisation in mathematics and science education* (pp. 19–38). Springer.

Foucault, M. (1979). *Discipline and punish: The birth of the prison*. Penguin.

Fraser, N. (1995). From redistribution to recognition: Dilemmas of justice in a post-socialist society. *New Left Review*, July–August, 212, 68–93.

Furlong, J., McNamara, O., Campbell, A., Howson, J., & Lewis, S. (2008). Partnership, policy and politics: Initial teacher education in England under new labour. *Teachers and Teaching: Politics and Policy in Teacher Education: International Perspectives*, *14*(4), 307–318. https://doi.org/10.1080/13540600802037728

Gewirtz, S. (1998). Conceptualizing social justice in education: Mapping the territory. *Journal of Educational Policy*, *13*(4), 469–484.

Giroux, H. A. (2020). *On critical pedagogy* ((2nd ed.). Bloomsbury Academic.

Gounari, P., & Grollios G. (2012). Educational reform in Greece: Central concepts and a critique. *Journal of Pedagogy*, *3*(2), 303–318. https://doi.org/10.2478/v10159-012-0015-7

Hall, C., & Noyes, A. (2009). New regimes of truth: The impact of performative school self evaluation systems on teachers' professional identities. *Teaching and Teacher Education*, *25*(6), 850–856. https://doi.org/10.1016/j.tate.2009.01.008

Haynes, J., & Murris, K. (2011). The provocation of an epistemological shift in teacher education through philosophy with children. *Journal of Philosophy of Education*, *45*(2), 285. https://doi.org/10.1111/j.1467-9752.2011.00799.x

Kohan, W. (2014). *Philosophy and childhood: Critical perspectives and affirmative practices.* Palgrave Macmillan.

Kohan, W. (2018). Paulo Freire and philosophy for children: A critical dialogue. *Studies in Philosophy and Education*, *37*(6), 615–629. https://doi.org/10.1007/s11217-018-9613-8

Lipman, M. (2003). *Thinking in education.* Cambridge University Press.

Lipman, M., & Sharp, A. (1978). Some educational presuppositions of philosophy for children. *Oxford Review of Education*, *4*(1), 85–90.

Marks, R. (2014). Educational triage and ability-grouping in primary mathematics: A case-study of the impacts on low-attaining pupils. *Research in Mathematics Education*, *16*(1), 38–53. https://doi.org/10.1080/14794802.2013.874095

McIntyre, J., Youens, B., & Stevenson, H. (2019). Silenced voices: The disappearance of the university and the student teacher in teacher education policy discourse in England. *Research Papers in Education*, *34*(2), 153–168. https://doi.org/10.1080/02671522.2017.1402084

Neyland, J. (2007). Globalisation, ethics and mathematics education. In B. Atweh, A. Calabrese Barton, M. C. Borba, N. Gough, C. Keitel, C. Vistro-Yu, & R. Vithal (Eds.), *Internationalisation and globalisation in mathematics and science education* (pp. 113–128). Springer.

O'Riordan, N. J. (2016). Swimming against the tide: Philosophy for children as counter-cultural practice. *Education 3–13, 44*(6), 648–660. https://doi.org/10.1080/03004279.2014.991415

Organisation for Economic Co-operation and Development. (2018). *Education for a Bright Future in Greece: The Greek education system in context.* https://doi.org/10.1787/9789264298750-3-en

Oxfam/SAPERE (2007). *Philosophy for Children Teachers Guide.* https://www.oxfam.org.uk/education/resources/philosophy-for-children

Pais, A., & Costa, M. (2020). An ideology critique of global citizenship education. *Critical Studies in Education*, *61*(1), 1–16. https://doi.org/10.1080/17508487.2017.1318772

Povey, H. (1997). Beginning mathematics teachers' ways of knowing: The link with working for emancipatory change. *Curriculum Studies*, *5*(3), 329–342.

Povey, H. (2017). *Engaging (with) mathematics and learning to teach: An integrated approach to mathematics preservice education.* WTM.

Povey, H., & Adams, G. (2018). Possibilities for mathematics education? Aphoristic fragments from the past. *The Mathematics Enthusiast (TME)*, *15*(1), 159–177. Available at: https://scholarworks.umt.edu/tme/vol15/iss1/10

Povey, H., & Adams, G. (2021). Disordering mathematics, citizenship and socio-political research in mathematics education amongst the "rubble of words". *Research in Mathematics Education*, *23*(3), 306–322. https://doi.org/10.1080/14794802.2021.1994452

Povey, H., Boylan, M., & Adams, G. (2019). Regulated time and expansive time in primary school mathematics. *Pedagogy, Culture & Society*, 1–18. https://doi.org/10.1080/14681366.2019.1692059

Povey, H., Demissie, F., & Adams, G. (2019). Workshop report: What are the affordances and limitations of the Philosophy for Children (P4C) pedagogy for teaching and learning mathematics? Proceedings of BSRLM Day Conference, Milton Keynes, March, 2019. https://bsrlm.org.uk/wp-content/uploads/2019/07/BSRLM-CP-39-1-08.pdf

Society for Advancing Philosophical Enquiry and Reflection in Education (2010). *Handbook to accompany the level 1 course* (3rd ed.) ed.). SAPERE.

Skovsmose, O. (1994). *Towards a philosophy of critical mathematical education*. Kluwer.

Skovsmose, O. (2007). Mathematical literacy and globalisation. In B. Atweh, A. Calabrese Barton, M. C. Borba, N. Gough, C. Keitel-Kreidt, C. Vistro-Yu, & R. Vithal (Eds.), *Internationalisation and globalisation in mathematics and science education* (pp. 3–18). Springer.

Skovsmose, O. (2018). Critical constructivism: Interpreting mathematics education for social justice. *For the Learning of Mathematics*, *38*(1), 38–43.

Traianou, A. (2023). Evaluation and its politics: Trade unions and education reform in Greece. *Education Inquiry*, *6*, 1–20. https://doi.org/10.1080/20004508.2023.2193015

Troman, G. (2008). Primary teacher identity, commitment and career in performative school cultures. *British Educational Research Journal*, *34*(5), 619–633. https://doi.org/10.1080/01411920802223925

Winstanley, C. (2018). Deep thinking and high ceilings: Using philosophy to challenge 'more able' pupils. *Journal of Philosophy in Schools*, *5*(1), 111–133. https://doi.org/10.21913/jps.v5i1.1488

Young, I. M. (1990). *Justice and the politics of difference*. Princeton University Press.

15 Conclusion

The political of diversity and difference: Scenes of projection, making kinds of people and curriculum knowledge

Thomas S. Popkewitz

Mathematics is, by and large, constructed as the sacred knowledge of modernity associated with science; with mathematics education represented as the contemporary salvation and redemptive trope for developing "the knowledge society" whose knowledge is necessary for the active participation and agency of the citizen. The book problematizes these assumptions of inclusion signified as the citizen, a philosophical ideal historically located in the modern welfare state. My task is not to summarize those trajectories in the book. Rather, it is to pursue their terrains of troubling mathematics education through thinking about the historical trajectories in which mathematics education is made intelligible as a normative and exclusive practice of making of the citizen as a kind of person.

This chapter centres historically on the political of pedagogy and the curriculum enunciated in mathematics education. The political is used differently than the more familiar term of politics to shift attention from contemporary political theories of the citizen and its notions of sovereign power to notions of power as productiive that I associate with "post" literatures. The latter focuses on knowledge as the production of the subject and subjectification. French political theorist Jacque Rancière's (1983/2004) argues, for example, that *the political* is in the historical structuring of systems of reason and their *partition of the sensible.* Michel Foucault (1979) references the political as the rules and standards that order and classify conduct (the conduct of conduct) as historically generated patterns of recognition and expectations of experience governing *the self*, embodied in notion of *governmentality.*

I explore this notion of the political in the school curriculum and exemplified in mathematics education. The analysis provides a different grammar and syntax from conventional curriculum theory to engage a strategy to unthink or "trouble" the practices of schooling, its language, and its contemporary frameworks to reason about teaching and learning. The intersection of four dimensions of the political that form school subjects are explored to think about what schools *do,* arguing that the teaching science, mathematics, or art is about something different than learning the knowledge of these fields. That something else is discussed through four themes:

DOI: 10.4324/9781003130673-18

One, schools are practices to *make kinds of people*. The citizen is not born but made through multiple different trajectories and grids of practice in different school subjects that range from social studies to art, science, and mathematics education. The citizen is one such kind of person but also are the creative, problem-solver, mathematically able, and disadvantage child as qualities and characteristics of kinds of people generated in pedagogy of schooling. The categories of people are invented about anticipated potentialities of the child; they are not descriptors drawn from life itself. Theories of learning are to effect the making of kinds of people!

Two, pedagogy embodies *comparative systems* of reason that distribute differences and exclusions in efforts to include. To talk about the motivated child engenders its "other" as, for example, the child who lacks motivation, is not successful, and dangerous to the social order.

Three, pedagogical discourse are *projection scenes* of the different kinds of people. The images and narratives are generated in the psychologies of the child and learning, for example, and taken as the real qualities and characteristics of the successful or failing child. The projections are *phantasmagrams*: beautiful and scary images of the anticipate potentialities inscribed in teaching school subjects.

Finally, four, the curriculum is analogous to the Medieval alchemy, a magical translation and transformation of disciplinary knowledge into pedagogical knowledge. Mathematics and science education are alchemies; magical translations, and transformations into something else; and that something else is the making of kinds of people.

The analysis is a historical and cultural sociology of knowledge. Playing with exploring schooling as projections in the making of kinds of people, the discussion is to think, trouble, and unthink the commonplaces of schooling. Notions of global literacies and competences in STEM education and OECD's PISA assessment of scientific and mathematical literacies are examined as phantasmagrams of kinds of people. The strategy of the analysis is to interrupt the perpetuation of othering in the curriculum that articulates diversity as *difference* within a unified normativity of the subject's self-realization, freedom, and autonomy. The notion of troubling is an unthinking of the conventions of the present as practices of resistance and freedom, as Deleuze (1986/1988) and Foucault (1970) argue. The diagnosis of the "reason" of school subjects is to give focus to the apparatus which power installs on the surface of our being and becoming. The discussion brings together fields of thought that typically work at the margins of educational studies: science studies, affect theories, historical and cultural studies of knowledge (the "posts"), and curriculum studies to explore how anticipated utopic futures in the school curriculum become the paradoxes of regulated ideals of the present.

The curriculum as scenes of projection and making kinds of people

If I relate to the prior chapters of this book, mathematics education generates models of designing the curriculum that is not merely instrumental for enacting efficient pedagogical models to make the mathematically *literate* and *mathematically able* child. The concepts, classifications, and orderings of the curriculum are assembled and connected to social and cultural distinctions about notions of social order and moral (dis)order as acts of subjectification in the governing of the self. The challenge posed in the prior chapters and again here to make visible the cultural politics of knowledge of the school curriculum, teaching and research that forms its infrastructures such as mathematics education.

The knowledge of mathematics, science or art education, then, is not of a pure logic or representations of some transcendental notions of "reason" that occupies these disciplinary fields. Nor is the instrumental logic of schooling that speaks of competences, benchmarks, and efficiency in learning without location and historical qualities that act to differentiate, distinguish, and divide students. The political of schooling resides in the very heart of the school subjects. The political is in the very object of schooling in making kinds of people who are called "problem solvers", motivated, and the future citizen.

This making of the child was recognized in the formation of the modern school. The founders of the French and American republics recognized that the citizen was made and not born and the "necessity" of education in making kinds of people. The models of curriculum of the new education were governed by cultural principles about kinds of people. Yolcu (2021a) argues, for example, that the problem solver in mathematics education is a disciplining practice of the body and soul. Spoken in policy, research and curriculum planning, the problem solver is the anticipatory reason of the potentialities of good life who effectively makes decisions in enacting their responsibilities in being a good citizen, economic contributor, and participant in their communities.

If the making of the good life for children is all schooling was about, then the problem would truly be trying to match the actual practices of schooling with our publicly stated social and moral commitments. That utopic quality orders much of contemporary educational reform and its research and assessment. The acronyms of STEM and STEAM, for example, embody this utopic dream of activating the future through present education practices. The arts, science and mathematics education are imagined as the "tool" to accomplish the potentialities that are given as global competences of the future society.

But things are never so simple. The knowledge of the child is not simply descriptive but a space of action through "*the will to know*". The knowledge of pedagogy and curriculum assembles and connects affective and cognitive dimensions to generate patterns of recognition and expectations of experiences. As the chapters of the book continually visualize, the modern school and the sciences of the child, society and schooling generate a knowledge that embodies desires of the future to express the imagined potentialities of kinds of people. These potentialities are envisioned as the child who act as a problem-solver, creative, curious, scientifically literate, the mathematically abled, and the lifelong learners prepared to live as a global citizen in the future Knowledge Society.

The knowledge of the child in schooling is intervention in subjectivities. That intervention entails comparative principles that produce and distribute differences. The production of subjects and differences perform as the political of schooling. The very problematizing of the child who is not successful in mathematics, for example, embodies distinctions that normalize, differentiates, and racializes in mathematics education in practices to remediate social wrongs (Bullock, 2020). The production of differences is not only that of mathematics education but also in the formation of school subjects (Kirchgasler, 2017; Lesko, 2001; Paz, 2017)!

Fabrications of kinds of people

The making of kinds of people as the political of schooling can be considered through the notion of fabrications and two nuances bound in its significations – fictions and manufacturing.

One is the knowledge of the school subjects and the child is a fiction. The idea of childhood and youth in pedagogy is formed as philosophical idea about the anticipated potentialities of kinds of people, at least in the Western schooling. The distinctions of the child as kinds of people are projections of the Enlightenments' dreams of the good life.[1] The sociologies and psychologies that fold into the notions of the child, teaching, and teacher education are historically calculative strategies that fabricate kinds of people whose reason and rationality will enable, for example human agency in the pursuit of happiness. The motifs of the potentialities of the child that activate the good life travel in the enactments curriculum and pedagogy. Mathematics education, as with more generally the school subjects, is a terrain or a space that generates desires as sensibilities and dispositions for becoming and being that (re)vision the utopic images of the Enlightenments.

The paradox of the utopic in the practices of schooling is a comparative knowledge. Capturing the sentiments of cosmopolitanism, the formation of welfare state, its notion of the citizen, and the disciplinary formation of sociologies and psychologies are the turn of the 20th century inscribed desires of who the child should be that embody its other fears to abject as dangerous populations. Urban sociologies and psychologies related to education in the United States, for example, were sciences that inscribed a comparativeness vision that differentiated and distinguished the kinds of people in an anticipated utopic vision of "the good life". Concepts of socialization, acculturation, political cultures, community, and learning were comparative distinctions that distributed differences about kinds of people.[2] The German sociologist Tönnies (1897/1957) distinguished between notions of community (*gemeinschaft*) formed through face-to-face interactions and abstract relations of modern societies (gesellschaft). The sociology of community (re)visioned prior notions of face-to-face interactions as "the self" and others in the new urban landscapes and the national imaginaries of the new welfare state (Popkewitz, 2008).

The fictions of the child in pedagogical practices and its science embodied salvation and redemption themes as desires that accompanied the sociological theories of community and notions of the cosmopolitanism and moral (dis) order of urban conditions and populations. The idea of adolescence was such a fiction. "Youth" was an invention of the new scientific psychologies and inscribed in pedagogical projects at turn of the 20th century (Lesko, 2001; Ó et al., 2022). Adolescence was a fiction and salvation and redemption theme to address the new racial, immigrant, and "ethnic" populations coming to the new school. These populations enunciated dangers to the imagined, utopic modes of living and its "New Man", a phrase used to talk about the promise of the new social orders (Cheng, 2008).

The second nuance of fabrication is that the fictions loop into the social world and materialize to manufacture kinds of people. Notions of community and adolescences, for example, are given material existences in social reforms and educational practices. At the turn of the 20th century, for example, the dangers to the utopic were represented in The Social Question which circulated in Europe and North America. The Social Question was a system of reasoning in the theories and methods of science that gave attention to the moral disorder and dislocations produced in industrialization, immigration, and urbanizations. The adolescent was a kind of child that inscribed a comparative reasoning in Child Studies that worked into teacher education and the pedagogical projects of the school (Lee, 2020).

The fiction was about who the child is and should be as the object and subject of the anticipated good life. Adolescence was a phenomenon addressed as real and the origin of pedagogical planning about who the child is and should be in the transition into the good, moral person and approximate the ideal of the good citizen. The qualities and characteristics that differentiated the adolescent acted in the work of social work, domestic life of the parent, and school programs as a determinant category of a kind of person,

The notion of the adolescent loops into subjectivities as the expectations of experience and boundaries and degrees of freedom The pedagogical knowledge of art, music, and literacy education is external rule and standard to be internalized as patterns of recognition and expectations of experiences generated in teaching and learning. The disciplinary knowledge of the school pedagogy and its curriculum that organized the school subjects, for example, were directed to the ordering of the interiority or the soul of the child. The language of made into non-polemic distinctions such as problem solving, experiential and experimental learning, among others.

In one sense, this making of kinds of people through education and its inscriptions of the school subjects should not be surprising. Why send a child to a place called school if not to have the child be something different after the 12 or 16 years of living in classrooms and "learning".

But if that was all to the practices of schooling, then the task would be merely to find the perfection of its strategies and technologies. But the making of the subject and object of pedagogy entails external forms of knowledge that classify and index the child as conduct in the comparative reasoning of the pedagogical practices of art, science, mathematics, and music education. In the next section, I explore the images and narrative of the projections as phantasmagrams of kinds of people that distribute differences.

Scenes of projections and phantasmagrams

I have explored how pedagogy and curriculum generate scenes of projection of kinds of people in which the fabrications of the child are the political. If I turn to a colleague in art history and science, Jill Casid's *Scenes of Projection. Recasting the Enlightenment Subject* (2015), it provides a way to consider further the political in the practices of education. Casid explores the Magic Lanterns of the 17th century as important to the prehistory of science. The Magic Lanterns were projection machines for casting images that transformed the subject and object of people into a non-polemic distancing of a phantom subject as a rational vision "managing fear, desire, and attachment" (Casid, 2015, p. 85). The significance of that rational vision is it replaced the vision of the spectator with phantasmagrams that generate "forms of life, ways of being and becoming". The projections of the phantasmagrams were taken as real that, Casid continues, contains the paradox of generating desires about the potentialities of kinds of people that "differentiate as a mirror of the self that imitates and abjects" in what Casid (2015) calls "the colonial machinery of dominance" (p. 122).

While Casid explores the magic lanterns as occurring before to the rational vision associated with modern science, they embody principles of "seeing", differentiating, and comparing bound to modernity's rational vision. The projections are connected with Cartesian logics, notions of representations in the philosophy of consciousness, and the external systems of knowledge whose expertise governing the welfare state, the human sciences, and the formation of the modern school in the 19th century, the later as the focus of this chapter.

The projections of phantasmagrams locate the historical constructions of the vision of "the seeing" subject of schooling and the rationalities that make possible the adolescent embodied in the Child Studies. The projections are imaginaries of anticipated modes of life – of being and becoming folded into pedagogy and the teaching of school subject that are no longer merely fictions. They are given as real as they enter the designs of the curriculum and mathematics education that arguments of this book continually make visible.

Alchemies, the two subjects of school subjects and phantasmagrams

The projection of phantasmagrams connects in the organization and selection of the curriculum "content" and pedagogy as "two subjects" of the modern school – the *subject of the child that intersects with* the instructional "subject" such as 'mathematics' education. These two "subjects" give visibility to the political in modernity, schooling, and its instantiation in mathematics education.

The distinctions and differentiation of the two school subject content knowledge and the subject of the child transform the eternal knowledge systems into scenes of projection that produce phantasmagrams. Deleuze and Guattari (1980/1987) discuss this movement of spaces as the de/reterrito rialization – creating the subject and object as desires that manage fears that inhabit the very infrastructure of knowledge itself. Embodied in the theories, technologies, and practices in mathematics and science education, for example, are images and narratives of the potentialities of the child that teaching activates. Underlying the new school at the turn of the 20th century were the two subjects were inscribed in the systems of knowledge of the school subjects of science, mathematics, art, and music education. The principles connecting the subjects of the child and the subject of instruction were the new scientific psychologies that formed to order and classify the knowledge of the normal schools, teacher institutes, seminaries, and colleges or universities.

Alchemies

The system of reason organizing the school subjects in the formation of the New Education can be thought of as analogous to the European Medieval alchemies. The subjects of mathematics, science, and art education are translations and transformations of the disciplinary fields and the visual and expressive arts into school practices. The latter are regulated by child psychologies, communication patterns associated with teaching, and time as organized by notions of child development, for example (Popkewitz, 2004, 2018).

To say that the school curriculum is alchemic recognizes translations of disciplinary knowledge into pedagogical distinctions and differentiations are necessary. The pedagogical reworking is necessary as children are not physicists, mathematicians, or professional artists. What is at stake, however, is not the existence of alchemies but the rules and standards of the transformations/translations into the curriculum (Popkewitz, 2022a,b).[3]

The system of reasoning across school subjects is formed through a unity of epistemic principles. These principles in mathematics and science education, for example, embody Cartesian logic and analytical distinctions of concepts, generalizations, and propositions as discrete and hierarchical units of "learning" in the new space of teaching of school subjects (Popkewitz, 2020). What is represented and measured as benchmarks of being mathematically literate and scientifically able is an anticipated mode of living of the citizen. The projections are phantasmagrams, beautiful illusions, and desires of kinds of people that have little to do with learning the modes of reasoning named as replicating mathematical thinking.

Mathematics is inscribed as an assemblage of a play of substitutes that appropriates children's dispositions and sensitivities as the subject and object of its terms of truth. The representative values are replacements of the relations of the mathematics into the relations of mathematics education. The latter is a second language in a play of substitutes accomplished as the appropriations within pedagogy. No longer in the external spaces of disciplinary fields; mathematics in the spaces of pedagogy is an anticipatory logic for constructing the self. Mathematics is expressive of values in its role of representation in the curriculum that register historical and affective conditions of sociality and participation (Chronaki, 2019). The principles of knowing and its patterns of recognition form norms of cultural competences and mental processes linked with modes of living about children's well-being and qualities.

Pedagogy is directed to the interior of the child and the struggling for the soul. Attention is directed to the dispositions, sensitivities and awarenesses of the interior of the child, resignifying religious notion of "the soul". The soul of the new school was about the secular order but assembled and connected with spiritual notions of salvation and redemption about an anticipated good life, given reference, for example, in the European and North American Enlightenments notions of the cosmopolitan citizen and narratives of progress. The ordering was of the soul, given the name of "the mind" in early 20th century psychology. French and Portuguese pedagogies at the turn of the 20th century, for example, observed and "registered" the inner physical and moral life to map the spirituality of "the human soul" as the educated subject who contributed to social life (Ó et al., 2013). The body and the soul are the object and subject of pedagogical observations activated on the interior of the child as "best-practices".

The images of becoming the "competent" and creative citizen subject are haunted with its multiple others as excluded and abjected as in the margins of history and norms of the "civilized" (Chronaki, 2023). The concepts and classifications of the science and mathematics in the curriculum connect with theories, programs, stories, and the scientific psychologies of the child as distinctions for ordering and judging pedagogical practices. The ideas of the adolescence, motivation, and literacies make the interior of the child and the mind calculable and as phenomena that are real and the subject and object of the reasoning of the child.

Desires

As suggested in the introduction of this book, the distinctions in pedagogy and the curriculum are anticipatory desires about potentialities to be activated. These desires are not spoken about explicitly but activated in notions of social improvement, development, action, agency, and change that order and classify the practices of the school curriculum and research. The system of reasoning creates expectations of experience in the shaping, for example teaching, children's learning, and the mastery of knowledge. Benchmarks, standards, competencies, and development of the child are salvation themes of imagined narratives of the global citizen that instruction is to activate. The pathways to the utopic in this school knowledge often are seen as produced by the proper mixture of science, policy, and professional expertise that, if applied, will enable the development of the potentialities of societies and people.

If I use international assessments of students' performances, desires are phantasmagrams. The graphs and charts that index of literacies in art, science, mathematics, and music as the global competence are the spatialization of the child imagined as becoming the global citizen (Popkewitz, 2022a. 2023). The benchmarks and competences are not linked to the conditions of the mathematics or scientific disciplines but (re)visioned as the alchemic inscriptions for experiencing the complexities of contemporary life. The phenomena of literacies in the international assessments, for example, are the de/reterritorializing of disciplinary knowledge that fold into distinctions and differentiations of pedagogy. The phenomena of the competent child are generated through the infrastructures of the assessments as a calculative reasoning referenced as indexes of children's literacies. Given as real, the new phenomena identified in the charts are made into the origin for assessing and the models of changing educational systems.

The phantasmagrams of the alchemy of the curriculum are visible in the teaching of Euclidean geometry in mathematics education. While there are multiple geometries that could be taught in school, Euclidean geometry embodies temporal and ontological distinctions for "seeing" and judging the world (Andrade-Molina & Valero, 2015). The phantasmagram of "seeing" the self through Euclidean geometry is to "see" and act as if the world of a two-dimensional space of fixed Galilean objects, like a road map or GPS system with fixed coordinates of cities, towns, and roads. This sight of the geometry generates a world of a *sightless body, as* Andrade-Molina and Valero (2015) argue. The complexities, multi-dimensionality, and conditional qualities of life are elided.

Comparative reason as double gestures

The idea of comparing people, at least in the West, is not new. It is found in Carl Linnaeus' 18th-century taxonomy of flora and fauna that placed western civilizations at the top of its hierarchy. The European Enlightenment differentiated its civilization as the most advanced. The 18th- and 19th-century European missionaries applied a comparative reasoning to distinguish those who could recognize the Christian God from others, the barbarians and savages in the colonialization in the 19th century.

The political valences given to comparing have a particular quality of knowledge in the 19th-century human sciences and its empiricity given to knowledge. The invention of social life and people as an empirical facts to be investigated, affirmed, and distributed made comparing as a temporal knowledge of ordering and successions of humanness (Foucault, 1970/1994). People were "seen" as analytically discrete units that have structures and functions to compare. The differences in humanness were given an independent existence to theological cosmologies. Representations and conceptual distinctions assigned identities and differences that could be calculated as "the nature" of people and societies. The comparative reasoning was expressed in the emergence of eugenics, Lamarckianism, and Social Darwinism, and the global colonialism of the long 19th century (Kirchgasler, 2019; Koza, 2021).

The comparative reasoning of kinds of people was inscribed in the emergence of the modern school's pedagogy. The category of the creative child, for example, appears in the 19th century as a concept of science through multiple lines that are arranged and inscribed different cultural and social edifices into pedagogical spaces of action for comparing children (Martins, 2025). The images of differences distinguished the creative child from "others" in their drawing in art education, for example. The comparing gave visibility and calculability of cultural distinctions about the normal and abnormal development. Contemporary international mathematical competencies compare, as well, through different assemblages that generate cultural principles of diversity and difference. The mathematical competencies are (re)visioned as they connect with the nation-specific trajectories and cultural priorities to distinguish, differentiate, and divide the capabilities and qualities of the child (Yolcu, 2021b).

Playing with language to play with realities: the indigenous foreigner and travelling libraries

The above arguments are to think historically about the present and its knowledge, the curriculum alchemies and the political as double subjects governing mathematics education.[4] This book brings to the surface that the knowledge of the curriculum is not a globalization of a transcendent space but particular modes of reasoning that travel as immutable mobiles under the banner of mathematics education. The objects of "learning" are re-assembled and connected to national projects and imaginaries of the citizen in schooling.

In this final section, I explore this travelling through two notions related to a comparative study of education of citizen as a kind of person, but with different cultural and historical conditions in the production of mathematics education. The two notions explored are *indigenous foreigner* and *travelling libraries*.[5]

The notion of *indigenous foreigner* directs attention to how mathematics education embodies an infrastructure of alchemies, science, and technologies of "seeing" the child, learning, and differences. This "seeing" performs an immobile mobiles; that is, visible representations that appear as the same "things" as they travel in different historical and cultural conditions.[6] Mathematics and science education project images of knowledge as global, a homelessness universal reasoning about people and social life that has no attachments to any historical affiliations except the internal logic of numbers and its empirical reasoning. The idea of evidence-based practice typifies this idea of a knowledge as global and transcendental – the content knowledge imagined to only "describe" how things work and has no values or norms and appears as without any home or origin – homeless as a subject that appears to tell the Truth about social life and people.

Travelling libraries connects with the notion of indigenous foreigner to explore the travelling of knowledge as systems of reason. The school subjects are indigenous foreigner travel, for example, but that travelling is never alone. They travel with other ideas, theories that affectively attach and settle in different historical conditions that are often called "the nation" to give the school its affective images and narratives. The international assessments of student performance, for example, express models of professional development and reforms in teacher education. The global distinctions about benchmarks and competences as subject of professional knowledge perform as immutable mobiles. Felt as a non-polemic, homeless knowledge that seems global and ahistorical, the reasoning that orders that knowledge settle into different historical and cultural terrains. The indexes of student performances are treated as stable edifices, abstracted out of their spaces of realization as specific cultural and social practices.

Of course, they are not stable or homeless, as the prior discussion illustrates. The knowledge of the mathematically able child travels, for example, as a transcendent, ahistorical knowledge (global competences, benchmarks) in educational reforms and connects and assembles with other ideas, narratives, and stories. This travelling and assemblages are like a library as they settle in different national educational systems. The notions of science in the curriculum are assembled at the interstices of other theories, ideas, stories, traditions, and technologies as they move into different historical places, and historical conditions. The travelling libraries are territorialized and (re)vision science and mathematics that includes the affective values, promises, and potentialities attached to imaginaries of the nation, and the cultural patterns of the modern school.

The calculations of the reason of PISA is an exemplar of this travelling of a global knowledge as libraries or a grid of practices as it settles into different social conditions geographically labelled as nations. The immutable objects of global language settle into different school systems; the outcome is not something "added" to or as the sum of the parts. The literacies of PISA are assembled as a *travelling library*, a grid of practices that is like having a group of different books as ideas and stories sitting together on a desk. The phrase is to think about how the theories and abstractions are affectively felt as a global knowledge that enters different historical spaces of national practices. Mathematics, science, and the arts education, for example, travel as transcendental knowledge and settles into different educational systems as expressing hope and fears as a comparative reasoning about the future in the present.

OECD's PISA embody the affect of a global knowledge of an indigenous foreigner. OECD's PISA generates indexes that express mathematics literacy as a global knowledge required of the future citizen in framing its assessment. The affect of the notion of literacy is to enable a global citizen whose knowledge, skills, and well-being make possible the potentialities of the child that are an imagined necessarity for future of the good life.[7] The test items in PISA are analytical distinctions of the knowledge given as expressions of students' understanding of the meaning and application of the concepts and apply them as the expectations of experience in "real"-life situation. The assessment is imagined as measuring the reasoning of mathematics categorized as the problem-solving method. What is measured is reterritorized and reframed mathematical knowledge organized through the management principles of cybernetics theory that order the pedagogy. The principles that order the doing of the sciences and mathematics in the curriculum are something different from that of mathematics.

The literacies of science and mathematics are produced as phenomena generated by the infrastructure of its calculations to create indexing of differences. The infrastructure is an assemblage that connects probability theories, the curriculum alchemy of mathematics, and the cybernetics, among other historical lines. The projections are generated as indexes of performance represented and ranked as nations to compare in the graphs and charts. The ranking and its indexes give expression to the feeling of the future preparedness of nations' populations of the knowledge and skills measured. The literacies and competencies, however, are not affectively linked to conditions of disciplinary knowledge and skills. They are abstract categories linked with the "well-being" classified as the sociological and psychological preparedness of the child, society, and the professional teacher as a citizen subject.

The movement of the external knowledge of disciplinary practices into the space of schooling can be thought of as a process of deterritorializing the social and cultural practices of science and mathematics, and reterritorializing them into different cultural spaces of schooling. Statements that appear as "mathematics" and scientific knowledge are creative acts of the alchemy of the school subjects. The alchemy of disciplinary translates the reasoning and objects of science and mathematics, for example, into analytical distinctions of knowledge content and skills as assemblages of the cultural theses about childhood, growth, development, and differences. These translation into the school subjects have little to do with the practices of mathematics or science. The generalizations and abstractions taught as scientific literacy across international textbooks, for example, have no commonality regarding what constitutes "literacy" (McEneaney, 2003b). The scientific literacy is directed to cultural theses about the citizen of the nation.

The notions of competences and literacies are scenes of projection that perform as phantasmagrams. What travels are images and narrative activated in educational policies and reforms to make of the citizen for the future of nation. If STEM education is considered with the notion of literacy, they are phantasmagrams that project unified systems of knowledge that affectively acts as a global elixir in making kinds of people for modernizing local economies (Zheng, 2019, 2020). The indexing and comparing are emotive, championing national aspirations of ensuring children's preparedness for the globalized world of the 21st century (Popkewitz, 2022b). The assessments of STEM as an educational project, for example, is the reduction of different epistemic machinaries in the sciences, technologies, engineering, and mathematics into a singular non-polemic practice alluded to as modernizing nations (Popkewitz, 2022a, 2022b).

The indexing of differences performs as a single story of moral equivalences to be emulated. The distinctions and distribution of differences that compare nations are formed through varied trajectories in which equivalences embody representations of a philosophical ideal of the citizen that are linked with measures of students' psychological well-being in the international assessments. The diversity and differences are given as numbers of correlations and magnitudes to "tell" the truth of scientific and mathematical competency and literacies of nations through their comparative reasoning.

The registers of differences are inscriptions of the normal from which differences about kinds of people are cast to achieve equality in nations. In these equivalences are the unspoken normal of "the advantaged" that simultaneously inscribes its "others", the child who is outside the normal as "the disadvantaged".

The enunciations of different kinds of people are *double gestures;* gestures of the hope of the future good child and good society, and fears of the dangers and dangerous child who threatens that future. The double gestures are given a materiality in the professionalization of teacher education in contemporary reforms and research. The search is for the common, unified knowledge of the professional teacher from which differences are inscribed to attest the expertise of teachers and school leaders in successful schools.

The travelling of scientific literacy in textbooks and STEM education is entangled affectively in national policies, school reforms, research, and the curriculum as desires epistemically enunciated in notions of learning, and assessments (see Popkewitz et al., 2021). Dussel (2021), for example, explores the emergence of tactile pedagogy in the early-20th-century at the interstices of technology, art, and design that moved into education as a practice that was neither reductive nor additive but rather creative, vibrant historical practices. The practices created new objects and distinctions in university seminars and laboratories and artistic workshops across Milano in Italy; Ulm in Germany; Chicago, Cambridge, and Los Angeles, and through the biographical trajectories of design educators who later configured digital media pedagogies and who, in consequence, appropriated the school, teachers, and children as pedagogical desires.

Conclusions

The challenges of educational studies and modern education are amplified when focusing on the problem and problematic of mathematics education. The chapters included in this edited book and this discussion continually argue that mathematics education is not about only mathematics but it consists a technologies of the self that embodies discourses that carry utopic images and narratives. If I paraphrase Michel Foucault (1970), these discourses are not merely ideas but consist of a materiality, producing a space of action that is always dangerous but not necessarily bad.[8]

Working against the marginalizations and to correct social wrongs by means of mathematics education that occupy sections of the book bring to the surface the paradoxes that the production of difference that are not found necessarily in the overt discourses of intent about institutions, policy, and the research. The political is located on the surface of the practices of education that form the interior of the school – the principles that order and classify teaching, curriculum, textbooks, the reforms that frame the communications and projects of classrooms, and the patterns of recognition and expectations generated to frame and shape the normativities of learning and the well-being. The idea (and ideal) of the citizen is inscribed in these practices with different historical settlements and require continual scrutiny and problematizing.

The present volume appropriately explores the dimension of the political embedded in the inadequacy of instrumental knowledge in organizing the practices of mathematics education. The question of knowledge and the systems of reason of schooling was explored not only to address this inadequacy but also to direct attention to the political embodied in the distinctions, differentiations, and sensitivities in ordering and defining the school subjects – the child as a subject and the school subjects. What is given as a global and non-polemic language that has practical and utilitarian value is not that or "useful" as a practical knowledge (Popkewitz, 2020). While the educational discourses articulate commitments of globalization, notions of the global citizen, and the recognition of diversity and differences, the epistemic principles require continual scrutiny as an agent through which desires and futures are generated as paradoxes of a comparative reason with double gestures of hope and fears.

The political of the school subjects is located at the interstices of "the reason" of modern schooling. This entailed (re)visioning the phenomena of mathematics as a school subject through thinking of the alchemy of mathematics education – its translation tools, the comparative reasoning of "seeing" childhood, and double gestures that paradoxically produce exclusions and abjections in efforts to include. The notions of indigenous foreigner and travelling libraries are notions to explore the epistemic colonialization in the production of diversity and difference as an affective economy.

The unthinking as troubling schooling as a citizen ideal are bound to asking about the historical rules and standards inscribed in schooling through which differences are produced and distributed in the making kinds of people. The focus on mathematical knowledge was explored as having implications to issues of onto-ethics-epistemic colonialization embodied in differentiated relations. The strategy is one of historicizing the comparative reasoning of relations, conditions, and practices in the fabricating kinds of people. The latter paradoxically distributes and governs *differences* that exclude and abject in thrusts to include. The global and non-polemic are entangled historical formations through which pedagogy and the school curriculum order the conduct of people through the forms of knowledge and its comparative rules and standards.

Notes

1 I am using the notion of Enlightenments as a plural historical notion in which the modern school enunciates. Although Western historiography and philosophy trace the term as one of the European thought, it was plural in the west but epistemes of reason and wisdom as its hallmark developed through intersecting and different historical lines outside of the West.
2 These distinctions and the comparative reasoning of the sciences of education are discussed in Popkewitz (1998, 2008, and the activism of science in the governing of modernity and education in Popkewitz and Huang (2024).
3 It is implicit in the reading of curriculum history. See, e.g., Kliebard (1986).
4 Mathematics education as a subject of schooling occurs the interstices of mathematical content and pedagogical and psychological principles to give intelligibility to the child as a subject and object that whose inclusivity maintains mathematics as a signifying object to recognize “others”. The ethical and political challenge in this recognition of “others”, as argued in this chapter, which “mathematics” is materialized through the infrastructures of education, a challenge central to “ethnomathematics”.
5 The explorations of indigenous foreigners and travelling libraries are discussed in more specific historical trajectories in the travelling of pragmaticism of John Dewey (see, Popkewitz, 2005); systems/cybernetics theories in education (Popkewitz et al., 2021); and issues of epistemes and colonialization (Zhao et al., 2022).
6 See Latour (1986). Statistics and numbers are immutable mobile that are assumed as the same wherever as they travel in international assessments of education, for example, as representations of a global knowledge of school development.
7 The discussion of literacy in PISA is draw from a research project that analysis reports and descriptions of its measurement technologies and item construct as an infrastructure that generates a center of calculation (see Popkewitz, 2022a, 2022b; 2023).
8 Not everything is to reject as the present I believe, no option to do that. But the present and its truth telling systems are always to be treated with what this volume speaks to as a troubling, historicizing, skepticism, and humility that are a strategy of change.

References

Andrade-Molina, M., & Valero, P. (2015). *The sightless eyes of reason: Scientific objectivism and school geometry.* Paper presented at the Ninth Congress of European Research in Mathematics Education (CERME), Prague, Czech Republic.

Bullock, E. (2020). More than just potential: Troubling success counternarratives in mathematics education research. In C. A. Grant, M. J. Dumas, & A. N. Woodson (Eds.), *The future is Black: Afropessimism, fugitivity, and radical hope in education* (pp. 117–125). Routledge.

Casid, J. (2015). *Scenes of projection. Recasting the enlightenment subject.* University of Minnesota Press.

Cheng, Y. (2008). *Creating the New Man: From enlightenment to socialist realities.* Hawai'i University Press.

Chronaki, A. (2019). Affective bodying of mathematics, children and difference: Choreographing "sad affects" as affirmative politics in early mathematics teacher education. *ZDM*, *51*, 319–330. https://doi.org/10.1007/s11858-019-01045-9

Chronaki, A. (2023). Becoming citizen subject in the body politic antimonies of archaic, modern, and posthuman citizenship temporalities and the political of mathematics education. *Research in Mathematics Education*. https://doi.org/10.1080/14794802.2023.2183889

Deleuze, G., & Guattari, F. (1980/1987). *A thousand plateaus: Capitalism and schizophrenia*. University of Minnesota Press.

Dussel, I. (2021). Tactile pedagogies in the postwar: Cybernetics, art, and the production of a new educational rationale. In T. S. Popkewitz, D. Petersson, & K.-J. Hsiao (Eds.), *The international emergence of educational sciences in the post-World War Two years. Quantification, visualization, and making kinds of people* (pp. 51–70). Routledge.

Foucault, M. (1970/1994). *The order of things: An archaeology of the human sciences*. Pantheon Books.

Foucault, M. (1979). Governmentality. *Ideology and Consciousness*, *6*, 5–22.

Kirchgasler, C. (2019). Haunted data: The colonial residues of transnational school reforms in Kenya. In F. Salajan & T. Jules (Eds.), *The educational intelligent economy: Big data, artificial intelligence, machine learning, and the internet of things in education* (pp. 215–232). Emerald.

Kirchgasler, K. L. (2017). Scientific Americans: Historicizing the making of differences in early 20th-century US science education. In T. S. Popkewitz, J. Diaz, & C. Kirchgasler (Eds.), *A political sociology of educational knowledge: Studies of exclusions and difference* (pp. 89–104). Routledge.

Kliebard, H. (1986). *The struggle for the American curriculum*. Routledge and Kegan Paul.

Koza, J. (2021). *Destined to fail*. University of Michigan Press.

Latour, B. (1986). Visualization and cognition: Thinking with eyes and hands. *Knowledge and Society: Studies in the Sociology of Culture Past and Present*, *6*, 1–40.

Lee, S.-Y. (2020). Seeing the difference: Anticipatory reasoning of observation and its double gesture in teacher education. *Curriculum Inquiry*, *50*(5), 378–399. https://doi.org/10.1080/03626784.2021.1877518

Lesko, N. (2001). *Act your age: A cultural construction of adolescence*. Routledge.

Martins, C. (2025). *Inventing childhood creativity: Colonialities and the production of difference*. Routledge.

McEneaney, E. (2003). The worldwide cachet of scientific literacy. *Comparative Education Review*, *47*(2), 217–37.

Ó, J. R. do, Martins, C., & Paz, A. L. (2013). Genealogy of history: From pupil to artist as the dynamics of genius, status, and inventiveness in art education in Portugal. In T. S. Popkewitz (Ed.), *Rethinking the history of education: Transnational perspectives on its questions, methods, and knowledge* (pp. 157–178). Palgrave.

Ó, J. R. do, Paz, A. L., & Vallera, T. (2022). Genius and aesthetic grace: An archaeology of discourses on dance education in Portugal (1839–1930). *Revista Brasileira de Estudos da Presença (Brazilian Journal of Presence Studies)*. Porto Alegre, v. *12*(1), e113482. http://seer.ufrgs.br/presenca

Paz, A. L. (2017). Can genius be taught? Debates in Portuguese music education (1868-1930). *European Educational Research Journal*, *16*(4), 504–516.

Popkewitz, T. S. (1998). Dewey, Vygotsky, and the social administration of the individual: Constructivist pedagogy as systems of ideas in historical spaces. *American Educational Research Journal*, *35*(4), 535–570.

Popkewitz, T. S. (2004). The alchemy of the mathematics curriculum: Inscriptions and the fabrication of the child. *American Educational Research Journal*, *41*(4), 3–34.

Popkewitz, T. S. (Ed.). (2005). *Inventing the modern self and John Dewey: Modernities and the traveling of pragmatism in education*. Palgrave Macmillan Press.
Popkewitz, T. S. (2008). *Cosmopolitanism and the age of school reform: Science, education, and making society by making the child*. Routledge.
Popkewitz, T. S. (2018). What is "really" taught as the content of school subjects? Teaching school subjects as an alchemy. *The High School Journal*, *101*(2), 77–89.
Popkewitz, T. S. (2020). *The impracticality of practical research: A history of contemporary sciences of change that conserve*. University of Michigan Press.
Popkewitz, T. S. (2022a). Comparative reasoning, fabrication, and international education assessments: Desires about nations, society, and populations. *International Journal of Educational Research*, *1120*. https://doi.org/10.1016/j.ijer.2022.101940
Popkewitz, T. S. (2022b). International assessments as the comparative desires and the distributions of differences: Infrastructures and coloniality. *Discourse: Studies in the Cultural Politics of Education*. https://doi.org/10,1080/01596306.2021.2023259
Popkewitz, T. S. (2023). Infrastructures and phantasmagrams of inclusions that exclude: International student assessments. *International Journal of Inclusive Education*. https://doi.org/10.1080/13603116.2023.2275156
Popkewitz, T. S., & Huang, J. (2024). Critical theory and the study of education: Contributions of the "posts/new materialism". In R. Tierney, F. Rizvi, K. Ercikan, & G. Smith (Eds.), *Elsevier international encyclopedia of education (4th volume)* (pp. 105–116). Elsevier.
Popkewitz, T. S., Pettersson, D., & Hsiao, K. (Eds.). (2021). *The post-World War Two international educational sciences: Quantification, visualization, and making kinds of people*. Routledge.
Rancière, J. (1983/2004). *The philosopher and his poor*. Edited with an introduction by Andrew Parker; translated by John Drury, Corinne Oster, and Andrew Parker. Duke University Press.
Tönnies, F. (1887/1957). *Community & society [Gemeinschaft und Gesellschaft]* (E. Charles P. Loomis, Trans.). Michigan State University.
Yolcu, A. (2021a). Turkey's problem-solving child: A historical analysis of the cultural spaces of mathematics education. *Education and Science*, *46*(206), 27–46. https://doi.org/10.15390/EB.2020.8906
Yolcu, A. (2021b). Reimagining the citizen and the nation in a globalized world: The case of mathematics education reforms in Turkey. *Research in Mathematics Education*, *23*(3), 278–292.
Zhao, W., Popkewitz, T., & Autio, T. (Eds.) (2022). *Epistemic colonialism and the transfer of curriculum knowledge across borders: Applying a historical Lens to contest unilateral logics*. Routledge.
Zheng, L. (2019). A performative history of STEM crisis discourse: The co-constitution of crisis sensibility and systems analysis around 1970. *Discourse: Studies in the Cultural Politics of Education*, 1–16. https://www.tandfonline.com/doi/abs/10.1080/01596306.2019.1637332
Zheng, L. (2020). *Imagineering Crises: Performative Histories of Rationalizing US STEM Education reform* [PhD Dissertation]. University of Wisconsin-Madison.

Index